The Pilot's Manual

2

Private
& Commercial

The Pilot's Manual

2

Private & Commercial

Second Edition

Covers all aeronautical knowledge
required to pass the FAA Knowledge
Exams and operate as a Private and
Commercial pilot.

Trevor Thom

Foreword by Barry Schiff

Aviation Supplies & Academics, Inc.
Newcastle, Washington

The Pilot's Manual 2: Private & Commercial

Aviation Supplies & Academics, Inc.
7005 132nd Place SE
Newcastle, Washington 98059-3153

Originally published by Center for Aviation Theory
© 1990–1998

Printed in the United States of America

99 98   9 8 7 6 5 4 3 2 1

ISBN 1-56027-304-6

ASA-PM-2

Acknowledgements

The Federal Aviation Administration (FAA),
The National Ocean Service (NOS),
The National Weather Service (NWS),
Allied Signal Aerospace, Bendix/King
(a division of Allied Signal Aerospace),
Cessna Aircraft Company, Department of the
Air Force, Environment Protection Authority
(Vic. Australia), Flight Data Center,
Wilkes-Barre PA, General Aviation
Manufacturers' Association (GAMA),
Jeppesen Sanderson, Inc. *(Jeppesen charts
have been reproduced with permission, and are
copyrighted by Jeppesen Sanderson, Inc.)*,
Narco Avionics, Piper Aircraft Corporation,
II Morrow, Inc.

Dora Muir (ASA—design), Bookworks Ltd
(origination), Rob Fox (main cover picture).

Bill Bennett, Fred Boyns, Robert G. Carter,
Bill Constable, Elizabeth Copping,
Mindy Desens, Jeffrey Hanson, Tony Harper,
Brian Hill, Robyn Hind, Richard James,
Detlef Kracht, Ron Labby, Bruce Landsberg
(Executive Director, AOPA Air Safety
Foundation), Robert Lawson,
Dr. Michael Leahy, Richard Logan,
Robert Loriente, Debbie Miles,
Graeme Molineux, Jim Prendergast,
Ola Rustenberg, Daniel Thom, Marc Vogel,
Dr. Jacqueline Waide, Lynley Walters,
Tony Wilkinson (AOPA, Australia).

Also, to the many students, instructors and
FAA personnel whose comments have helped
in developing and refining the material in this
manual.

Contents

This book is dedicated to my father, Bill Thom.

Foreword

When it was time to take my private pilot written examination in 1955, my flight instructor handed me a pocket-size booklet. It was published by the Civil Aeronautics Administration (FAA's predecessor) and contained 200 true/false questions (including answers).

"Study these well," he cautioned with a wink, "because the test consists of 50 of these."

As I flipped through the dozen or so pages, my anxiety about the pending examination dissolved into relief. Nothing could be easier, I thought. One question, for example, stated "True or False: It is dangerous to fly through a thunderstorm." Really. (I passed the test with flying colors—but so did everyone else in those days.)

The modern pilot, however, must know a great deal more to hurdle today's more-challenging examinations. This has resulted in a crop of books developed specifically to help pilots pass tests. Unfortunately, some do little else, and the student's education remains incomplete.

An exciting exception is "The Pilot's Manual"—a series of outstanding books written by Trevor Thom, a former flight and ground instructor and former airline captain. These voluminous manuals provide far in excess of that needed to pass examinations. They are also chock-full of practical advice and techniques that are as useful to experienced pilots as they are to students.

"The Pilot's Manual" is a refreshingly creative and clever approach that simplifies and adds spice to what often are regarded as academically dry subjects. Thom's extensive teaching background is reflected by the careful manner in which he explains complex subjects and concepts. Reading these books is like sitting with an experienced flight instructor who senses when you might be having difficulty with a subject and patiently continues teaching until confident that you understand.

Barry Schiff
Los Angeles

Barry Schiff has over 25,000 hours in more than 250 types of aircraft. A thirty year veteran with Trans World Airlines, he flew the Lockheed L-1011, and has received numerous honors for his contributions to aviation. He is well known to flying audiences for his many articles published in some 80 aviation periodicals, notably *AOPA Pilot*.

About the Author

Trevor Thom. A former Boeing 757/767 training captain, Trevor has also flown the Airbus A320, Boeing 727, DC-9, Fokker F-27 and the DC-4. He has represented pilots on many international technical committees, including the International Federation of Airline Pilots' (IFALPA) Aircraft Design and Operations Group (London), SAE S7 Flight Deck Design Committee (USA), the Australian Air Pilots' Technical Council, and the International Civil Aviation Organization (ICAO) in Montreal. Trevor holds B.Sc. and B.A. degrees, and a Diploma of Education. He has been a lecturer in physics and mathematics, and a ground and flight instructor.

Trevor is also the author of several series of popular pilot-training manuals in the United Kingdom and Australia, for which he received the inaugural Bicentennial Award for Aviation from the Guild of Air Pilots and Air Naviagators (London, 1988).

Editorial Team

Amy Laboda. Freelance writer, editor, active flight instructor, executive board member, Women in Aviation, International; columnist for *Flight Training* magazine; contributor to numerous other aviation magazines; former editor at *Flying* magazine; has rotorcraft category, gyroplane rating, glider rating and multiengine ATP rating; holds a B.A. in Liberal Arts from Sarah Lawrence College.

Martin E. Weaver. An experienced flight and ground instructor in airplanes, helicopters and gliders; a former chief flight instructor and designated pilot examiner; has been closely involved with standardization procedures for the past 14 years; holds a B.S. from the University of Southern Mississippi; also currently a pilot in the Oklahoma Army National Guard.

David Robson. David Robson is a career pilot with over 35 years of aviation experience in military and civil operations. He holds an Airline Transport Pilot license, instrument rating and Grade One instructor's rating. He served in the Australian Air Force for 21 years as a fighter pilot and test pilot. During his military career, he completed a tour in Vietnam as a Forward Air Controller with the United States Air Force. He holds flight safety awards from the Flight Safety Foundation and the Ausralian Aviation Safety Foundation.

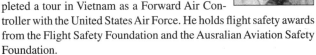

Ian Suren. Former chief, Personnel Licensing and Training with ICAO in Montreal for 10 years; senior examiner in charge of Flight Crew License Examinations with the Australian Department of Civil Aviation; certificated pilot.

Editorial Team

Michael T. Demchak. Assistant Professor, Aviation Studies, The School of Aeronautics, Florida Institute of Technology; previously at Embry-Riddle Aeronautical University; 24 years in the US Air Force, with experience in Europe and Far East; over 7,600 hours as pilot; BS and MA degrees; ATP (MEL) plus Commercial; wide range of general aviation and instructional experience; formerly instructor in the military; presently certificated as a Gold Seal Flight Instructor (CFIA/CFII/MEI), Ground Instructor (AGI/IGI) and Aircraft Dispatcher.

Kent H. Eckhart. Retired USAF Lt. Colonel; former corporate pilot, chief pilot and chief flight instructor; 12,000 hour ATP pilot, 6,400 hours flight instruction given, including 1,200 hours mountain-flying instruction; AOPA ASF Aviation Safety lecturer and flight instructor, ASEL, AMEL, INST, FAA-designated Accident Prevention Counselor; Director of Operations and Training with a Colorado aviation organization.

Tom W. Emanuel. Formerly Ground School Supervisor at the University of Illinois Institute of Aviation, then Assistant Director of Academic Affairs; presently a pilot examiner at the university; has taught over 250 Flight Instructor Refresher Courses for the AOPA Air Safety Foundation; active flight instructor for the past 27 years; FAA-designated Accident Prevention Counselor.

Gerald L. Lawhon. Former Executive Vice President of the AOPA Air Safety Foundation; Master of Science degree in Aerospace Engineering; retired colonel in the U.S. Air Force having flown amphibians, all-weather interceptors and fighter-bombers; corporate pilot, chief pilot, chief instructor, and airport manager; 9,000 hour Airline Transport Pilot with over 3,300 hours of flight instruction given.

John E. McLain. Self-employed flight instructor and a designated pilot examiner; staff instructor and lecturer with the AOPA Air Safety Foundation for over 25 years; over 13,000 hours flight time with 8,000 dual given; former chief instructor for several Part 141 flight schools; chief pilot; regular contributor to The Southern Aviator magazine; articles published in other aviation journals; selected 1991 Flight Instructor of the Year for the FAA Southern Region; initial recipient of State of North Carolina Captain of First Flight award.

Ken Medley. Aviation consultant; AOPA Air Safety Foundation Instructor/Lecturer; FAA-designated pilot/instructor examiner; former AOPA Mid-Atlantic Regional Representative; holds flight and instrument instructor certificates, all ground instructor certificates, and is single and multi-engine rated in land and seaplanes.

Steve Raichelson. Assistant Professor and Director of Flight Standards and Teaching, Aviation Division, Daniel Webster College, New Hampshire, where he developed the current meteorology course; since 1987 has lectured for the AOPA ASF in aviation safety, instructional techniques and human factors of flight; holds ATP (single-engine), Commercial (multi-engine), and flight instructor certificates (FAA Gold Seal), with over 6,500 hours as pilot, 5,000 as instructor.

Andrew Serrell. Licensed aviator for 50 years, including 32 years as a US Naval Aviator; 14,500 hours with over 5,000 hours flight instruction given; associated with the AOPA Air Safety Foundation since 1964, teaching at Flight Training Clinics, Refresher Courses, Standardization programs and Flight Instructor Refresher Courses; airplane owner; Commercial Pilot Certificate with CFI and CFII instructor ratings.

John W. Steuernagle. Director of Program Development, AOPA Air Safety Foundation; ATP, and single and multi-engine flight instructor certificates; over 7,000 hours flight time; FAA-designated Pilot Examiner, Accident Prevention Counselor; member of the Central Pennsylvania Flight Safety Committee.

Jack C. Williams. Editor of USA TODAY's weather page; instrument-rated private pilot and aviation ground instructor; extensive experience in "weather journalism;" has flown into two hurricanes and one tropical storm aboard research aircraft, and chased tornados and severe thunderstorms with researchers in Oklahoma and Colorado.

Introduction

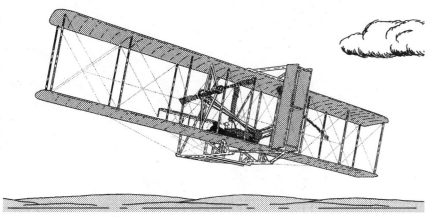

The Wright brothers understood basic aerodynamics

You are about to become a flyer, and join the worldwide family of pilots. To do this safely, you need some knowledge, and the aim of *The Pilot's Manual* is to introduce you to this knowledge in an easy-to-follow manner that is both practical and thorough, so that you will fly the airplane confidently and pass the FAA Knowledge Exams with flying colors.

You will learn to be a safe pilot, to take off and fly in the vicinity of your home airport, and to navigate around the country without getting lost or tangled up with thunderstorms and airliners.

The Pilot's Manual has been written not only to help you to pass the FAA Knowledge Exams, but also for you to keep on your bookshelves as a ready reference containing items of practical importance to a pilot. The team involved in producing *The Pilot's Manual* includes many very experienced pilots from a wide range of backgrounds — flight instructors, ground instructors, mountain-flying experts, professors of aviation, meteorologists, FAA inspectors, examiners, air force pilots, naval aviators, airline pilots and others. The accumulated knowledge between these covers is yours for the taking!

Private & Commercial is divided into five sections and introduces you to:

- **Aerodynamics**—the basic principles of flight and airplane design;
- **The Airplane**—the piston engine, airplane systems and flight instruments;
- **Airplane & Pilot Performance**—the factors which affect takeoff and landing performance, climbing and the cruise, how to safely load your airplane and basic physiology so that you can maximize your personal performance;
- **Weather**—the main processes of weather and how to interpret charts and forecasts; and
- **Flight Operations**—the Federal Aviation Regulations (to keep everyone safe), the basic principles of navigation, charts, airspace and airports, flight planning and radio navigation.

This manual is designed for both the Private and Commercial Pilot. The main body of each chapter contains the knowledge required for the Private Pilot Certificate, with review questions. The questions highlight important points and give you practice at typical Knowledge Exam questions.

When required, a small section at the end of some chapters covers the additional Commercial Pilot Certificate knowledge, with review questions. It is not necessary for the prospective Private Pilot to read these small additions, but we hope, when you see how straightforward they are, you will be encouraged to further your aviation knowledge at some stage and take the Commercial Pilot Knowledge Exam. If you plan to go straight to Commercial, this book is ideal for you.

A Few Points on Studying

Keep your study periods short and intense. Quietness, good lighting, and a clear and fresh mind are important to efficient study. Leisure is important too. Occasional walks and breaks for relaxation are beneficial to study, as is a day a week away from it all.

Make your own notes and summaries as you read through our text. The summary that you prepare is a most important aid to your learning. We suggest you work your way through the manual chapter-by-chapter, making your own notes and completing each set of review questions as you go. The reviews are not difficult because the knowledge required is in the text. The review questions are designed to give you confidence in your own knowledge and ability while giving you practice for the Private or Commercial Knowledge Exams.

The FAA Knowledge Exams consist of multiple-choice questions which are quick and easy to process. However, multiple-choice questions are not a good learning aid as they present you with a choice of answers, some of which are wrong. To continually read incorrect statements is confusing, so in our reviews we question you in a more positive manner, while retaining some multiple-choice questions in the examination style for your practice.

Our advice when working multiple-choice questions is, prior to reading through the selection of possible answers, think in your own mind what the answer might be. Then read through the choices and quite often you will find the answer you already have in mind is among them. If not, then proceed to eliminate the incorrect statements.

Please note that if you are preparing for the Commercial Knowledge Exam you should complete both the private and commercial reviews.

Conclusion

The Private & Commercial is designed to develop an in-depth understanding of the main facets of aviation. Not only will it help you pass the Knowledge Exams easily, it will also provide an excellent basis for becoming a competent and safe pilot, irrespective of whether you plan to use your skills for personal recreation and travel, or in a full-fledged career as a flight instructor or with the airlines.

Best wishes for success in your Knowledge Exams and practical flying.

Trevor Thom

An Invitation

You are invited to write to me personally at the address on page iv with any suggestions for improvements to our manuals. Please do.

Aerodynamics Section One

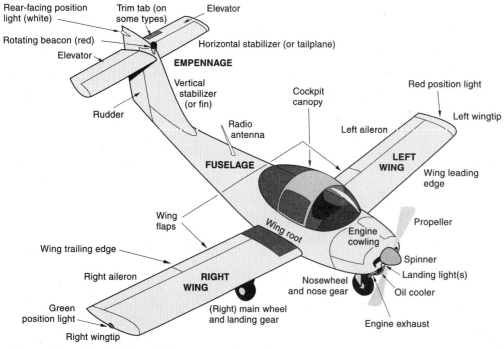

Rear-facing position
light (white)

Trim tab (on
some types)

Elevator

Rotating beacon (red)

Horizontal stabilizer (or tailplane)

Elevator

EMPENNAGE

Red position light

Rudder

Vertical
stabilizer
(or fin)

Cockpit
canopy

Left wingtip

Radio
antenna

Left aileron

LEFT
WING

FUSELAGE

Wing leading
edge

Wing
flaps

Wing root

Engine
cowling

Propeller

Wing trailing edge

Spinner

Right aileron

RIGHT
WING

Landing light(s)

Nosewheel
and nose gear

Oil cooler

Green
position light

(Right) main wheel
and landing gear

Engine exhaust

Right wingtip

Features of a modern training airplane

The Forces Acting on an Airplane 1

Introduction

Like all things, an airplane has **weight,** the force of gravity that acts through the center of the airplane in a vertical direction toward the center of the earth.

While the airplane is on the ground, its **weight** is supported by the force of the ground on the airplane, which acts upward through the wheels.

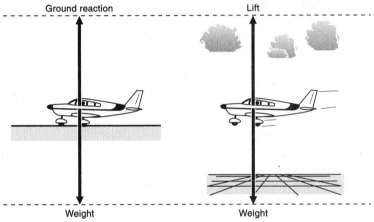

Figure 1-1. The airplane is supported by the ground, and in the air by lift

During the takeoff roll, the task of supporting the weight of the airplane is transferred from the ground to the wings (and vice versa during the landing).

While in level flight, the weight of the airplane is supported by the **lift** force, which is generated aerodynamically by the flow of air around the wings. In addition, as the airplane moves through the air it will experience a retarding force known as **drag,** which, unless counteracted, will cause the airplane to decelerate and lose speed.

In steady (unaccelerated) straight-and-level flight, the drag (or retarding force) is neutralized by the **thrust** (Figure 1-2). In most smaller airplanes, thrust is produced by the engine–propeller combination; in pure-jet airplanes, the thrust is produced by turbine engines, without the need for a propeller.

Figure 1-2. Drag counteracted by thrust

In Figure 1-3, the forces are equal and opposite, canceling each other out, so that the resultant force acting on the airplane is zero, and it will neither accelerate nor decelerate. In this situation the airplane is in a state of **equilibrium:**

- **weight** is equal to **lift,** and acts in the opposite direction; and
- **drag** is equal to **thrust,** and acts in the opposite direction.

During steady (unaccelerated) flight the four main forces are in equilibrium and the airplane will continue flying at the same speed and in the same direction.

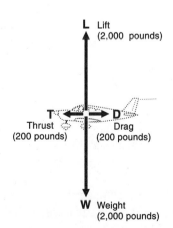

Figure 1-3. The four main forces are in equilibrium during unaccelerated flight

For the type of airplane that you are likely to be flying during your training, the magnitude (size) of the lift (and therefore the weight) during cruise flight will be approximately 10 times greater than the drag (and thrust). This relationship of lift to drag is very important and is referred to as the **lift/drag ratio.** The L/D ratio in this case is 10 to 1.

If the airplane is to accelerate in level flight, the thrust must exceed the drag; if the airplane is to be slowed down in level flight, the thrust must be less than the drag. During acceleration or deceleration, a state of equilibrium does not exist.

Weight

Gravity is the downward force attracting all bodies vertically toward the center of the earth. The name given to the gravitational force is **weight,** and for our purposes it is the total weight of the loaded airplane. This weight may be considered to act as a single force through the **center of gravity (CG).**

The CG is the point of balance. Its position depends on the weight and position of the various parts of the airplane and the load that it is carrying. If the airplane was supported at its center of gravity, the airplane would balance.

The weight of an airplane varies depending on the load it has to carry, the number of passengers, and the amount of fuel on board. Airplane gross weight will gradually decrease as the flight progresses and fuel is burned off.

The magnitude of the weight is important and there are certain limitations placed on it—for instance, a maximum takeoff weight will be specified for the airplane. Weight limitations depend on the structural strength of the components making up the airplane and the operational requirements that the airplane is designed to meet.

The balance point (center of gravity) is very important during flight because of its effect on the stability and performance of the airplane. It must remain within carefully defined limits at all stages of the flight.

The location of the CG depends on the weight and the location of the load placed in the airplane. The CG will move if the distribution of the load changes, for instance by transferring load from one position to another by passengers moving about or by transferring fuel from one tank to another. The CG may shift forward or aft as the aircraft weight reduces in flight, such as when fuel burns off or parachutists jump out.

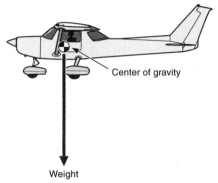

Figure 1-4. Weight acts downward through the center of gravity (CG)

✍ Review Questions and Answers

Work the questions by first covering the answer with a sheet of paper at the appropriate arrowhead, uncovering the answer when you have decided on your answer. Now complete **Review 1, Part (a)** on page 32.

Airfoil Lift

An airfoil is a surface designed to help in lifting, controlling or propelling an airplane. Some well-known airfoils are the wing, the horizontal stabilizer (or tailplane), the vertical stabilizer (or fin), and the propeller blades.

A wing is shaped so that as the air flows over and under it the wing creates a pressure difference—a low pressure above the wing and a higher pressure below the wing—resulting in the upward aerodynamic force known as lift. The wing also bends the free stream of air that meets it, creating downwash.

The airplane's control surfaces—ailerons, elevator and rudder—form part of the various airfoils. You can move these to vary the shape of each airfoil and the forces generated by the air flow over it. This enables you to maneuver the airplane and control it in flight. These control surfaces also operate based on Newton's Third Law of Motion, by deflecting the remote free stream of air that flows over them, causing the airplane to roll, yaw or pitch as the reaction.

The wing shape can also be changed by lowering the flaps to provide better low-speed airfoil characteristics for takeoff and landing.

Air Flow Around An Airplane

The pattern of the air flow around an airplane depends on the shape of the airplane and its attitude to the relative air flow. There are two air flow types: streamline flow and turbulent flow.

Streamline Flow

If successive parcels of air follow the same steady path in a flow, then this path can be represented by a streamline. There will be no flow across the streamlines, only along them.

At any fixed point on the streamline, each parcel of air will experience the same velocity and pressure as the preceding parcels of air when they passed that particular point. These values of velocity and pressure may change from point to point along the streamline.

A reduction in the velocity of streamline flow is indicated by wider spacing on the streamlines, while increased velocity is indicated by decreased spacing of the streamlines.

The existence of streamline flow is very desirable around an airplane.

Turbulent Flow

In turbulent flow, the air flow does not follow a streamlined flow pattern. Succeeding parcels of air may travel a path quite different to the preceding parcels of air. This turbulent flow is also known as unsteady flow, or eddying, and is an undesirable feature in most phases of flight.

The point where the air flow separates from the surface of an airfoil and becomes turbulent is known as the **separation point.** *See* Figure 1-6.

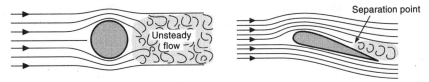

Figure 1-6. Turbulent flow

Bernoulli's Principle

The production of the lift force by an airfoil is explained by **Bernoulli's principle**—also known as the *venturi effect*. Daniel Bernoulli (1700–82) was a Swiss scientist who discovered this effect.

A fluid in steady motion has energy:

- static pressure energy; and
- dynamic pressure energy (kinetic energy caused by motion).

Air is a fluid, and if we assume it to be incompressible, it behaves as a so-called "ideal" fluid. Bernoulli's principle states that for an ideal fluid the total energy in steady streamline flow remains constant. Therefore:

Pressure energy	+	kinetic energy	=	constant total energy
(static)		(dynamic)		

Newton's Third Law of Motion *(for every action there is an equal and opposite reaction)* **explains how the wing, generating the upward lifting force, must also generate an equal and opposite downward force (downwash).**

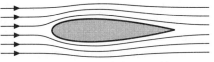

Figure 1-5. Streamline flow

Total energy in a steady streamline flow remains constant.

Within any steady streamline flow the total energy content will always remain constant, but the relative proportions of pressure energy and kinetic energy can vary. If kinetic energy increases because of a greater speed of flow, then static pressure energy will decrease accordingly.

Dynamic Pressure

Kinetic energy is the energy of motion, and may be expressed as:

Kinetic energy = $\frac{1}{2}$ mass × Velocity-squared.

The kinetic energy of a parcel of air in motion relative to an object allows it to exert a force on the object. This force, when calculated per unit surface area, is called **dynamic pressure.** If you hold your hand up in a strong wind or out of the window of a moving automobile, then wind pressure or moving pressure is felt because of the air striking your hand and flowing around it. This pressure is dynamic pressure—pressure caused by the relative movement between your hand and the air.

Dynamic pressure involves **air density** (mass per unit volume) which is denoted by the Greek letter *rho* (ρ). When discussing aerodynamics, dynamic pressure is a more useful quantity than kinetic energy, and is expressed as:

Dynamic pressure = $\frac{1}{2}$ *rho* × Velocity-squared,   or $DP = \frac{1}{2}\rho V^2$

The strength of dynamic pressure therefore depends on:

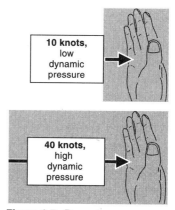

Figure 1-7. Dynamic pressure increases with airspeed

- The **velocity** (speed in a particular direction) of the body relative to the air—the faster the automobile drives or the stronger the wind blows, then the stronger the dynamic pressure that you feel on your hand. This is because of the greater number of air molecules that impact per second. Note that it is the **relative velocity** of the airplane and the air flow that matters, not whether it is the airplane moving through the air or the air flowing past the airplane. Either approach gives us the same answers.

- The **density** of the air—at the same speed, the denser the air, the more molecules per second that will strike your hand and so the greater the dynamic pressure.

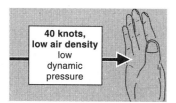 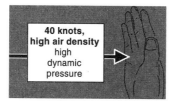

Figure 1-8. Dynamic pressure is greater in dense air

Static Pressure

The air is made up of many molecules, all of which are moving at high speed and in random directions, even though the parcel of air as a whole might be stationary. The molecules act like small tennis balls, and bounce off any surface with which they come in contact and exert a force on the surface. The size of the force is greatest when the collision is head-on, and becomes less when the collisions are more glancing blows. All of these small forces, when added up over an area, exert a pressure on the surface. This is known as **static pressure.**

Figure 1-9. Static pressure exerted by the molecules in a stationary parcel of air

If the parcel of air is moving relative to the surface, the collisions are more likely to be glancing blows rather than head-on, and so the pressure exerted on the surface will be less.

Figure 1-10. Static pressure decreases with the speed of air flow

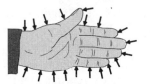

Figure 1-11. Static pressure acts in all directions

The static pressure at any point in a fluid acts equally in all directions. Static pressure of the atmosphere is being exerted at all points on your hand right now.

Bernoulli's Principle in Terms of Pressure

Pressure is itself a form of energy. Therefore Bernoulli's principle can also be applied to pressure, and the energy equation (page 7) can be rewritten.

Static pressure + dynamic pressure = constant total pressure
(p)   ($\frac{1}{2}\rho V^2$)

From this equation, we can see that if the speed (V) of the air flow increases, the dynamic pressure increases and the static pressure must decrease. Conversely, if the velocity (and therefore the dynamic pressure) decreases, the static pressure must increase. Decreased velocity means increased static pressure.

As the speed of an air flow increases dynamic pressure increases and static pressure decreases.

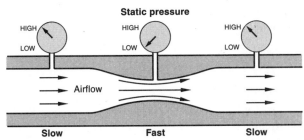

Figure 1-12. The venturi tube—high flow velocity and low static pressure in the narrow central section

Notes:

1. Dynamic pressure is also called *impact pressure.*
2. Bernoulli's principle may be used to satisfactorily explain many aspects of aerodynamics, but only if it is assumed that air is incompressible. At the Private and Commercial Pilot level such an assumption is valid because we are mainly concerned with airplanes that operate at relatively slow speeds, and at altitudes below 10,000 feet. At higher speeds and altitudes, compressibility of air must be accounted for, but this is only applicable when you are studying at the Airline Transport Pilot (ATP) level.

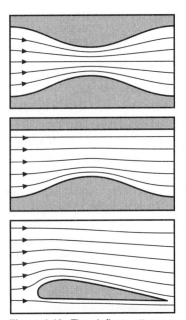

Figure 1-13. The air flow pattern around an airfoil resembles that occurring in a venturi

Airspeed

Dynamic pressure and the term $\frac{1}{2}\rho V^2$ are very important in aviation; you will meet them in a number of topics. Most importantly, for an airplane to fly there must be dynamic pressure. The airspeed indicator in an airplane shows **indicated airspeed (IAS)** which in fact is not a real speed, but dynamic pressure. Since dynamic pressure ($\frac{1}{2}\rho V^2$) is related to an actual speed, the real speed of the airplane relative to the air flow can be determined and is known as the **true airspeed (TAS or V).** Although indicated airspeed is of most concern to you when flying, you will need to find true airspeed when navigating.

The Airfoil and Bernoulli's Principle

All parts of the airplane contribute to both lift and drag, but it is the **airfoil,** or wing, that is specifically designed to provide the lift force needed to support the weight of the airplane in flight.

If a thin, flat metal plate is oriented parallel to a streamline air flow, it causes virtually no alteration to that air flow, and consequently experiences no reaction (aerodynamic force). If, however, the plate is inclined with respect to the air flow, it will experience a reaction that tends to both lift it up and drag it back. This is the same effect that you feel if you hold your hand out the window of a moving vehicle. The amount of reaction depends on the relative speed and the angle between the flat plate (or your hand) and the airstream.

Because of the angle of the plate to the air flow, the straight-line streamline flow of the air is disturbed. A slight **upwash** is created in front of the plate, causing the air to flow through a more constricted area, almost as if there was an invisible venturi above the plate. As it passes through this constricted area, the air speeds up. The velocity increase produces a decrease in static pressure (Bernoulli's principle).

The static pressure above the plate is now lower than the static pressure beneath the plate, causing a net upward reaction. After passing the plate there is a **downwash** of the airstream. Note that if the angle of the flat plate to the air flow becomes too large, the streamline air flow breaks down resulting in less lift and more drag. *See* Figure 1-14.

The reaction, or aerodynamic force, on the plate caused by its disturbance of the air flow has two components: one at right angles to the relative air flow, known as **lift;** and one parallel to the relative air flow, opposing the relative motion, known as **drag.**

Airfoil Shape

The wing is the largest generator of lift for most airplanes, and is often referred to as "the airfoil" on an airplane. Most airplanes do not have flat plates for wings. A flat plate is not the ideal airfoil shape because it breaks up the streamline flow, causing eddying (turbulence), with a loss of lift and a great increase in drag. In addition, it is difficult to construct a thin, flat wing.

A curved airfoil surface not only generates more lift and less drag compared to a flat plate, it is also easier to construct in terms of structural strength. Note that as the air flows through the narrow part of the venturi, or over a wing, the speed increases, the dynamic pressure increases, and static pressure reduces.

Airfoils can have many cross-sectional shapes. Airplane designers choose that shape which has the best aerodynamic characteristics to suit their purposes. Our discussion will be only in broad terms that can be generally applied to most airfoils.

Bernoulli's principle is the easiest non-mathematical way to understand the production of lift (and drag) by an airfoil.

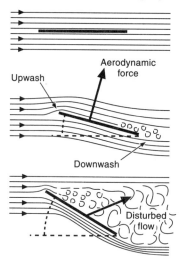

Figure 1-14. Air flow can lift a flat plate

Figure 1-15. Examples of various airfoil shapes

Definitions

- **Camber** is curvature. Wings with a large camber have a good lifting ability, making them suitable for low-speed flight and carrying heavy loads. The position of greatest camber is usually about 30 percent back from the wing leading edge. As camber increases, the air flow path lengthens, resulting in the air flow speeding up, static pressure reducing and lift increasing.

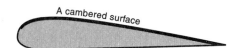

Figure 1-16. A cambered surface

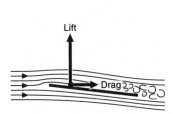

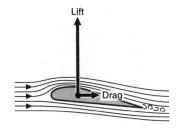

Figure 1-17. More camber, more lift

- The **mean camber line** is the line drawn halfway between the upper and lower surfaces of the airfoil cross-section. This line gives a picture of the average curvature of the airfoil.
- The **chord line** is the straight line joining the leading edge and the trailing edge of the airfoil or, in other words, the straight line joining the ends of the (curved) mean camber line.
- The length of the chord line is called the **chord.**
- The **camber** is the distance between the mean camber line and the chord line.

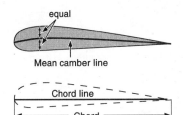

Figure 1-18. Mean camber line and chord line

The Aerodynamic Force

In normal flight, the static pressure over most of the upper surface of the airfoil is slightly reduced when compared with the normal static pressure of the air flow well away from the airfoil. The static pressure beneath much of the lower surface of the airfoil is greater than that on the upper surface, because a greater number of air molecules are impacting the airfoil's lower surface and the air flow is being slowed down. This pressure difference is the origin of the **total aerodynamic force** exerted on the airfoil, with the greater contribution coming from the upper surface.

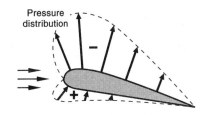

Figure 1-19. The production of lift and drag

In the same way that the total weight of an airplane can be considered to act through a single point—the center of gravity—the aerodynamic forces on an airfoil can be considered to act through a single point known as the **center of pressure (CP)** or center of lift.

It is convenient for us to consider the aerodynamic force (sometimes referred to as *total reaction*) in its two components: lift and drag.

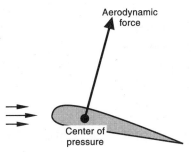

Figure 1-20. The aerodynamic force acts through a point on the wing called the center of pressure

- **Lift** is the component of the aerodynamic force at right angles, or perpendicular, to the relative air flow.
- **Drag** is the component of the aerodynamic force parallel to the relative air flow and opposing motion.

The **relative air flow,** or *relative wind,* refers to the relative motion between a body and the remote air flow—that is, the air flow far enough away from the body not to be disturbed by it. The relative air flow is the direction opposite to the flight path of the airplane.

The **angle-of-attack** is the angle between the chord line of an airfoil or wing and the remote relative air flow.

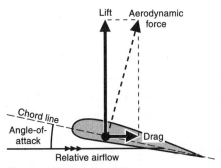

Figure 1-21. Relative air flow

Notes:

1. Do not confuse the *pitch attitude* of the airplane (relative to the horizontal) with the angle-of-attack of the airfoil (relative to the remote air flow). *See* Figure 1-22 and Figure 1-23 below.

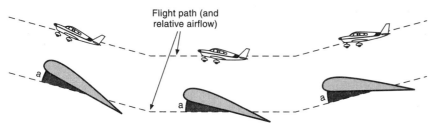

Figure 1-22. Same angle-of-attack, but different pitch attitudes

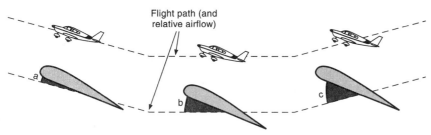

Figure 1-23. Same pitch attitude, but different angles-of-attack

2. Do not confuse angle-of-attack with *angle-of-incidence*—the angle at which the wing is mounted onto the fuselage, relative to the longitudinal axis. The angle-of-incidence is fixed at construction (Figure 1-24), while the angle-of-attack changes in flight.

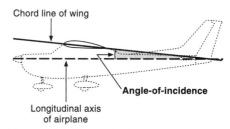

Figure 1-24. The angle-of-incidence is fixed during design and construction

Lift from a Typical Wing

The amount of lift that a wing can produce depends on:

- the lifting ability of the wing (angle-of-attack and camber);
- the airspeed;
- the wing area.

> **Lift = lifting ability of the wing × airspeed squared × wing area**

The equation shows that for constant lift, a reduction in airspeed must be countered by an increased lifting ability of the wing (increase in angle-of-attack). Conversely as airspeed is increased, to maintain level flight the pilot will need to lower the airplane's nose to reduce the angle-of-attack and decrease the wing's lifting ability. Also notice that if the lifting ability and area of the wings remain constant, and the airspeed doubles, the lift will increase four times (two squared).

Pressure Distribution and CP Movement

Bernoulli's principle links a decrease in static pressure with an increase in velocity, which means a decreasing static pressure goes hand-in-hand with an accelerating air flow. The shape of the airfoil and its angle-of-attack determine:

- the acceleration of the air flow above and below the wing; and
- the distribution of the static pressures over the surface and the lifting ability of the airfoil.

If we reduce speed while flying straight-and-level, and we progressively increase the angle-of-attack, two important things occur:

1. The lifting ability of the wing increases, allowing the wing to produce the same amount of lift (required to counteract the weight) at a lower airspeed.

2. The center of pressure (CP) moves forward—the furthest forward is about $\frac{1}{5}$ of the chord (20 percent) back from the wing leading edge.

At normal cruise speeds (about 4° angle-of-attack), the CP is located approximately $\frac{1}{3}$ of the chord back from the wing's leading edge. As the angle-of-attack increases with the reduction in airspeed, the CP moves forward until a point is eventually reached where the air flow over the wing upper surface cannot follow the curved surface, but separates and becomes turbulent, and produces significantly less lift. This is known as the *critical* or *stall* angle-of-attack.

At the critical angle-of-attack—about 16° (where the streamline air flow over the wing upper surface breaks down)—the CP moves rearward.

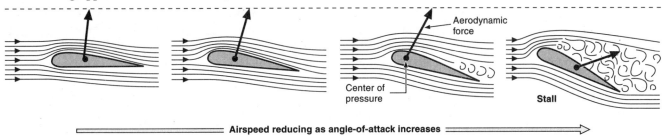

Figure 1-25. The size of the aerodynamic force and the CP position change at various angles-of-attack

Changes in the size and location of the aerodynamic force produce a different **moment** (or *rotating effect)* in the pitching plane of the airplane, (this means that the airplane will want to rotate nose-up or nose-down to a new pitch attitude). The extent of this pitching moment depends on both the size of the aerodynamic force and the distance between the CP and the CG. You can normally balance this moment, and prevent the airplane from pitching nose-up or nose-down, by varying the aerodynamic force generated by the **horizontal stabilizer.** This is achieved by the forward and rearward movement of the control column, which controls the elevator (*see also* Chapter 2).

Past the stall angle, the significant rearward movement of the CP causes a nose-down pitching moment, and the nose of the airplane will drop, even with the control column held fully back (nose-up). This is a good safety feature because the nose-drop reduces the angle-of-attack below the stall angle. With appropriate stall recovery actions by the pilot, the angle-of-attack will remain below the critical (or stall) angle.

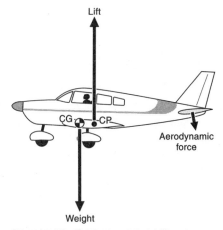

Figure 1-26. The horizontal stabilizer keeps the airplane in balance

Contamination on the Wings

Any contamination or damage to a wing, especially to its main lifting surface (the upper third rearward from the leading edge), will disrupt the smooth air flow over the airfoil and cause it to separate from the wing at a lower angle-of-attack than usual. This will cause decreased lift, increased drag, and may make it difficult, or even impossible, for the airplane to become airborne on takeoff.

If there is **frost, ice** or any other **contamination** (such as the remains of insects or a build-up of salt from sea-spray, for example) on the wings, then remove this contamination before flying. Ensure that the wings are clean and undamaged prior to flight, and that they remain so during the flight as much as possible.

Frost on a wing disturbs the air flow, reduces its lifting ability, and can prevent an airplane from becoming airborne.

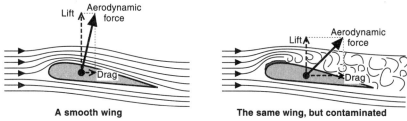

Figure 1-27. Contamination on the wings can seriously affect the lifting characteristics

✍ Now complete **Review 1, Part (b)** on page 32.

Drag

In flight, each part of the airplane exposed to the air flow will produce an aerodynamic force. This force can be split into two components: lift, which aids flight, and **drag,** which opposes it.

Drag is the aeronautical term for the air resistance experienced by the airplane as it moves through the air. It acts in the opposite direction to the motion of the airplane, and is the enemy of flight. Streamlining of shapes, flush riveting, polishing of surfaces and many design features are all attempts to reduce the drag force.

The main function of the **thrust** produced by the engine–propeller is to overcome the **drag.** The lower the drag, the less the thrust required to counteract it. The advantages of a lower thrust requirement are obvious: smaller (and possibly fewer) engines, lower fuel flows, less strain on the engine(s) and associated structures, and lower operating costs.

Drag opposes motion.

Figure 1-28. Low drag requires only low thrust to counteract it

Total Drag

The total drag is the sum total of the various drag forces acting on the airplane. A convenient way of studying these various types of drag forces is to break them up into two basic groups:

1. Those drag forces not directly associated with the development of lift—known as **parasite drag,** which includes form drag, skin friction and interference drag. (Form drag and skin friction are sometimes classified together under the name *profile drag.*)

2. Those drag forces associated with the production of lift, known as **induced drag** (manifested as vortices at the trailing edge of the wing and especially at the wingtips).

Total drag is the sum of induced drag and parasite drag.

Parasite Drag

Parasite drag comprises **skin friction, form drag** and **interference drag.**

Skin-Friction Drag. Friction forces between an object and the air through which it is moving produce skin-friction drag. The magnitude of this component of parasite drag depends on:

• the surface area of the airplane—the whole surface area of the airplane experiences skin-friction drag as it moves through the air;

• roughness on a surface (including ice-accretion)—flush riveting and polishing are attempts to smooth the surface and reduce skin-friction drag;

• airspeed—an increase in airspeed increases skin-friction drag.

Form Drag. When the air flow actually separates from the airfoil, disturbing the streamline flow and forming eddies, a turbulent wake is formed which increases drag. This is form drag.

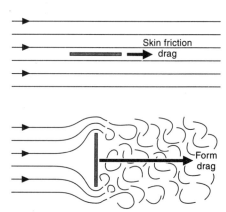

Figure 1-29. Skin friction (at top) and form drag

Perhaps the easiest way to distinguish form drag from skin-friction drag is to consider a flat plate in two different attitudes relative to the air flow. At zero degrees angle-of-attack, the drag is all skin friction. When the flat plate is perpendicular to the air flow, the drag is all form drag.

The point at which the streamline air flow separates from the airfoil and becomes turbulent is known as the **separation point.** As the wing's angle-of-attack increases, the separation point moves forward and the turbulent wake becomes deeper. The size of the wake (caused by an airfoil, or indeed the entire aircraft) indicates the magnitude of the form drag—the larger the wake the greater the form drag.

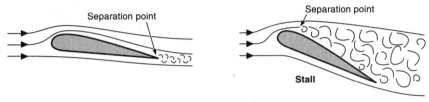

Figure 1-30. A stalled wing increases form drag substantially

Streamlining reduces form drag by decreasing the curvature of surfaces. This delays the separation of the air flow, and thereby reduces the size of the turbulent wake. The designer may choose an airfoil of different *fineness ratio* (wing thickness/chord) to achieve better streamlining.

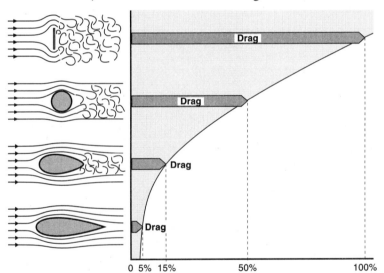

Figure 1-31. Streamlining, especially behind the shape, greatly reduces form drag

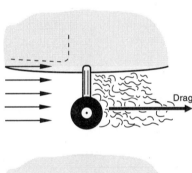

Figure 1-32. Streamlining reduces form drag

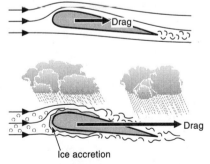

Figure 1-33. Ice accretion on the airframe will increase drag

Streamlining of other parts of the airframe can be achieved by adding *fairings*— parts of the skin (the external surface) of an airplane that encourage streamline flow, thereby reducing eddying and decreasing drag. *See* Figure 1-32.

Remember, streamlining may be ineffective if ice is allowed to form, as shown in Figure 1-33.

Interference Drag. The total parasite drag produced by an airplane is greater than the sum of the skin friction and form drag. Additional drag is caused by the mixing, or interference of air flows, which converge at the junction of various surfaces, such as at the wing-fuselage junctions and the tail section-fuselage junctions. This additional drag is referred to as interference drag. As it is not directly associated with the production of lift, interference drag is a component of parasite drag.

Smooth fairings at surface junctions reduce interference drag.

Parasite Drag and Airspeed

At zero airspeed there is no relative motion between the airplane and the air. Therefore there is no parasite drag. As the airspeed increases, the skin friction, form drag and interference drag (which together make up parasite drag) all increase.

Airspeed has a powerful effect on parasite drag. Doubling the airspeed gives four times (2-squared, or $2 \times 2 = 4$) the parasite drag, while tripling the airspeed would give $3 \times 3 = 9$ times the parasite drag. Parasite drag is therefore of greatest significance at high speeds and is small at low speeds. An airplane flying at a speed just above the stall may have only 25 percent of its total drag caused by parasite drag, with most of the total drag caused by induced drag.

Induced Drag

By definition lift is said to act at right angles to the remote free stream of air. The local average relative air flow about the wing is modified as the angle-of-attack is increased, causing an increase in downwash. The deflection of the air flow downward causes the wing to experience a local air flow (the average relative air flow), the direction of which is the average between the remote free air stream well ahead of the wing and the direction of the downwash immediately behind the wing.

The lift vector (*see* Figure 1-35) acts at right angles to the inclined local average relative air flow, which further inclines it rearward. The horizontal component acts as a drag component rearward—this is **induced drag**. It is a drag induced by the creation of lift.

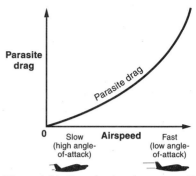

Figure 1-34. Parasite drag increases with airspeed

Induced drag occurs when lift is produced and is closely related to the angle-of-attack.

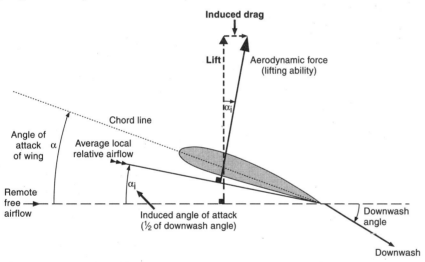

Figure 1-35. The effect of downwash creates an average relative air flow and tilts the aerodynamic force backwards

To produce upward lift, the static pressure on the upper wing surface will be less than that on the lower wing surface. The air flowing over the bottom surface of the wing has a higher pressure and tends to flow outward as well as rearward. The air flowing over the top surface of the wing has a lower pressure and tends to flow inward, toward the aircraft fuselage, as well as rearward.

When the two flows meet at the trailing edge they are flowing across, or at different angles to each other and a sheet of **trailing-edge vortices** rotating clockwise (when viewed from the rear) is formed. At the wingtips, where the spanwise flow is greatest, the strongest vortices are formed. These are known as **wingtip vortices**. A vortex is a whirling or twisting flow of air or some other fluid. Wingtip vortices are also discussed under *Wake Turbulence* in Chapter 10.

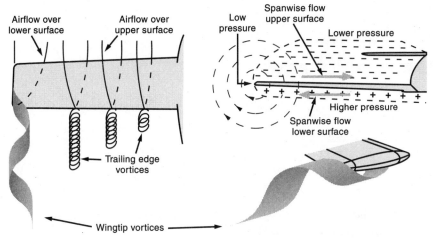

Figure 1-36. The production of lift creates wingtip vortices and induced drag

Angle-of-Attack. The greater the lift produced, the greater the induced drag. Induced drag is therefore most significant when the wing is at high angles-of-attack, such as during low-speed flight or maneuvering. Near the stall speed in level flight, induced drag could account for 75 percent of the total drag (parasite drag making up the rest), yet at high speed in level flight the induced drag might provide only 1 percent of the total drag.

Wing Design. Induced drag is affected by the span-to-chord ratio, known as the *aspect ratio*. Wings with a high aspect ratio—such as those on sailplanes— produce significantly less induced drag than short, stubby wings.

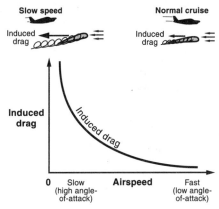

Figure 1-37. Induced drag is greatest at low speeds and high angles-of-attack

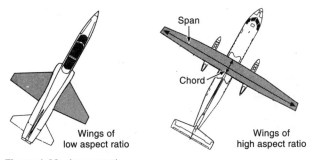

Figure 1-38. Aspect ratio

The Total Drag on an Airplane

Total drag is the total of all the drag forces. As we have seen, total drag has two components:

- **parasite drag;** and
- **induced drag** .

If we combine the graphs of parasite and induced drag as they vary with airspeed, we end up with a graph that illustrates the variation of total drag with airspeed (for a given airplane in level flight at a particular weight, configuration and altitude). This total drag graph (Figure 1-39) of drag versus airspeed (angle-of-attack) illustrates an extremely important relationship. It is a summary of all we need to know about drag.

The parasite drag increases with speed. The induced drag decreases as the speed increases. The graph shows how induced drag is predominant at low speed, while at high speed the parasite drag predominates. The total drag is least at the point where the parasite drag and the induced drag are equal. Many aspects of airplane performance are related to this **minimum-drag speed.**

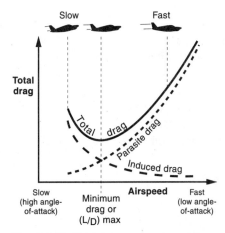

Figure 1-39. Total drag versus airspeed

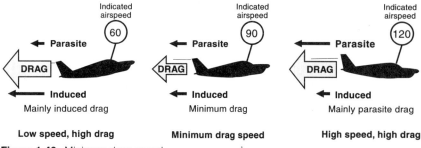

Figure 1-40. Minimum drag speed

Lift/Drag Ratio

To determine the performance and efficiency of an airfoil at a particular angle-of-attack (and airspeed), both the lift and the drag need to be considered. The size of lift compared to weight is the **lift/drag ratio** and is very important. (More detail on this appears in the *Commercial Pilot* section, later in the chapter.)

The most efficient angle-of-attack is the angle that gives the maximum or best lift/drag ratio, typically 10:1. In most airplanes you do not have an instrument to indicate angle-of-attack, but the airspeed indicator is a good guide because airspeed is related to angle-of-attack. High angles-of-attack in steady flight are associated with low airspeeds (and vice versa).

The angle-of-attack (and airspeed) for the best lift/drag ratio gives the required lift (to counteract the weight) for the minimum cost in total drag. At any other angle-of-attack there is a greater cost in terms of increased drag to obtain the same lift.

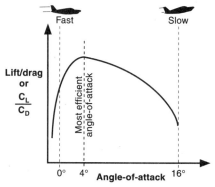

Figure 1-41. Lift/drag ratio versus angle-of-attack

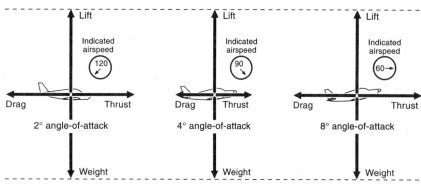

Figure 1-42. Same lift at a different cost in total drag

In steady flight drag is counteracted by thrust. If the lift required to counteract the weight is obtained at the minimum cost in drag, then thrust can be kept to a minimum with the resulting benefits—smaller engine–propeller combination, better economy through lower fuel and maintenance costs, and so on.

The L/D ratio is greatest when the drag is least—this occurs at about 4° angle-of-attack. For a propeller-driven airplane some important in-flight performance characteristics are obtained at the best L/D ratio, such as the maximum cruise range and the maximum power-off glide range.

Minimum drag means maximum L/D.

Changing Wing Area

Increasing the wing area allows the same lift to be produced at an even lower airspeed. Some flaps, such as Fowler flaps (which extend rearward as well as downward), increase the wing area as they are extended. Other less complex flaps simply change the cross-section of the wing, increasing camber, as they are lowered. All types of flaps change lift and drag, and consequently have an effect on the value of the L/D ratio.

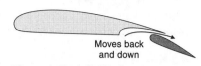

Figure 1-43. A Fowler flap

✍ Now complete **Review 1, Part (c)** on page 34.

Wing Flaps

The type of wing flaps fitted to most airplanes are those mounted on the trailing edge of the main wings. They serve two purposes: to increase the lifting ability of the wing, and to increase drag.

- Sometimes it is desirable to fly slowly, for instance when taking off and landing. The usual method to do this safely is to use the flaps to **increase the lifting ability** of the wing, enabling it to produce the required lift at a lower airspeed.
- At other times it is useful to have **increased drag**—to help reduce the airspeed, or to increase the rate of descent and allow a steeper descent angle without increasing the airspeed.

In straight-and-level flight the weight is counteracted by the lift:

> **Lift = the lifting ability of the wing × the airspeed squared × the wing area.**

Figure 1-44. Typical flap installation—a Cessna wing-flap system

Wing flaps allow the pilot to change the basic airfoil shape to one which has an increased lifting ability (and also an increased wing area, in the case of Fowler flaps), enabling the required lift to be generated at much lower speeds.

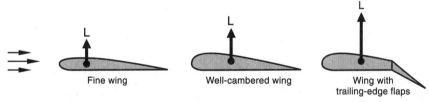

Fine wing | Well-cambered wing | Wing with trailing-edge flaps

Figure 1-45. Same airspeed: increased camber and/or wing flaps give higher lift

When the wing is near the stall angle-of-attack, the required lift with flaps extended will be generated at a much lower airspeed. When the stall angle is finally reached, the airspeed is much lower than that for flaps up. This means that all the other speeds which are factored from the stall speed, such as takeoff speed, approach speed and landing speed, can be lower—a safer situation that allows shorter takeoff and landing distances.

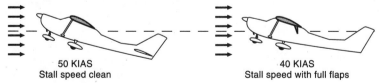

50 KIAS
Stall speed clean

40 KIAS
Stall speed with full flaps

Figure 1-46. Flaps lower the stall speed

Effects of the Flaps

Virtually all airplanes have trailing-edge flaps. The effects of flaps, be they desired or secondary, are outlined below.

Lift/Drag Ratio

When the flaps are lowered the lift increases, but so too does the drag. When we consider the angle-of-attack giving the best lift/drag ratio, the drag increase is proportionately greater than the lift increase, therefore the lift/drag (L/D) ratio decreases once the flaps are extended.

As a result of a lower L/D ratio, the airplane will not glide as far with flaps lowered as it would when *clean* (flaps up)—nor will it climb at as steep an angle. Also, if you cruise with flaps lowered, more fuel will be required to travel the same distance.

Think of the trailing-edge flaps at their early extension as *lift* flaps (when the lifting ability of the wings is increased significantly for a moderate cost in drag), and when fully extended as *drag* flaps. The latter stages of trailing-edge flap extension give only a small increase in lifting capability for a large increase in drag. In both cases the L/D ratio will reduce, however the L/D ratio will decrease greatly with full flaps extended.

When the flaps are extended, because the drag increases, the speed will decrease unless power is added or the rate of descent increased—or both.

Approach

When flaps are lowered the L/D ratio reduces, which enables the pilot to make a steeper approach without increasing airspeed.

Takeoff and Landing

One of the main functions of flaps, as previously stated, is to provide the same lift at a lower airspeed. This not only reduces takeoff and landing speeds (which is safer), but also shortens the length of runway required.

Ballooning

The initial effect of lowering the trailing-edge flaps is to produce an increased aerodynamic force because of the increased camber. With flaps extended, a lower pitch attitude is required to decrease the angle-of-attack, and prevent a short-lived climb called a **balloon.** It is only short-lived because the increased drag soon slows the airplane down, reducing the aerodynamic force. Conversely, raising the flaps can cause the airplane to *sink,* unless you raise the pitch attitude.

Trailing-edge flaps decrease the lift/drag ratio, and reduce glide range.

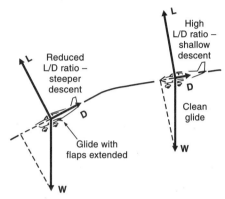

Figure 1-47. Effect of flaps on lift/drag ratio

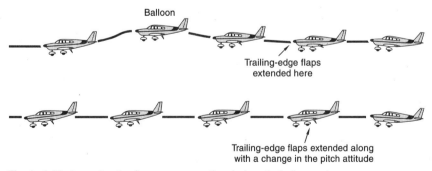

Figure 1-48. Lowering the flaps can cause the airplane to *balloon* unless you simultaneously adjust the pitch attitude

Pitch Attitude

Because the increased camber resulting from lowering the trailing-edge flaps occurs at the rear of the wing, the center of pressure moves rearward as the flaps are lowered. The resultant pitching effect will vary between airplane types. Elevator pressure will be required to hold the desired pitch attitude, but you can trim this steady pressure off.

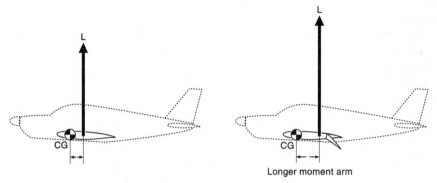

Figure 1-49. Extending the flaps may cause the nose to pitch

Leading-Edge Devices

As we have seen under *Airfoil Lift,* at high angles-of-attack the air flow separates from the wing's upper surface and becomes turbulent. This leads to a stalled condition that destroys much of the lifting ability of the wing.

Some airplanes have leading-edge devices that allow some of the high energy air from beneath the wing to flow through a slot and over the upper surface of the wing, thereby delaying separation and the stall, allowing the airplane to fly at a higher angle-of-attack and a lower airspeed. This can be achieved with **slats** which form part of the upper leading edge of the wing in normal flight, but can be extended forward and/or down to form a slot.

Some wings have fixed **slots** built in to the wing leading edge, but this is less common because they generate high drag at cruise speeds. On a high performance airplane this would be unacceptable, so the more complicated extendable slat would be fitted.

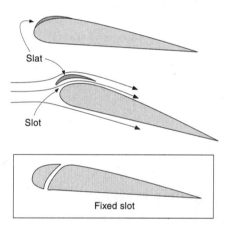

Figure 1-50. Slats and slots delay the stall

Spoilers

Most advanced jet transports and most gliders have **spoilers** on the upper surfaces of their wings. These are hinged control panels which, when extended, disturb the air flow over the upper lift-producing part of the wing, thereby decreasing lift and increasing drag. Pilots use spoilers to reduce airspeed and/ or steepen the descent path without increasing airspeed.

On large jet airplanes, pilots deploy the spoilers after touchdown to dump the lift and get all of the weight onto the wheels, thus making the wheel brakes more effective.

Spoilers increase drag and reduce the L/D ratio.

✍ Now complete **Review 1, Part (d)** on page 35.

Thrust from the Propeller

Thrust is one of the four main forces that act on an airplane. To maintain a steady straight-and-level speed, the thrust must equal the total drag of the airplane. To accelerate the airplane in level flight, thrust must be greater than drag; conversely, to decelerate in level flight, thrust must be less than drag.

A piston engine uses a propeller to convert the power output of the engine into thrust. Engine power is transmitted by a shaft to the propeller as *torque* or *turning effect.* This power is used to rotate the propeller, which converts most of the torque supplied by the engine into an aerodynamic force called *thrust.*

The propeller blades are **airfoils** that generate aerodynamic forces in a similar way to other airfoils, such as the wings, by modifying the air flow around them. Notice how the cross-section of a propeller blade resembles the cross-section of a wing.

As the propeller blade rotates through the air, the acceleration of the air flow over the front cambered surface of the blade causes a reduced static pressure ahead of the blade (Bernoulli's principle). The result is a forward thrust force on the propeller blade which pulls the airplane along. Air density affects the efficiency of a propeller, as it does a wing. In addition, the less dense the air, the less the mass of air accelerated rearward, and the less effective the propeller, such as at high altitudes or on very hot days.

Consider just one *blade section,* or *blade element* as it is sometimes called, at some radial distance from the hub or the centerline of the propeller rotation. The blade section is an airfoil and it has a leading edge, a trailing edge, a chord line and a camber just like any other airfoil.

The angle which the chord line of a propeller section makes with the plane of rotation is called the propeller **blade angle.** As we shall soon see, the blade angle varies from a large angle at the root near the hub, and gradually becomes less toward the propeller tip.

Propeller Motion

Rotational Velocity

If the airplane is stationary, the motion of the propeller section under consideration is purely rotational. The further out along the blade the section is, the faster its rotational velocity. Also, the higher the rpm (revolutions per minute) of the propeller, the faster the rotational velocity of the section.

Forward Velocity

As the airplane moves forward in flight, the propeller section will have a forward velocity as well as its rotational velocity. When this forward motion is combined with the rotational velocity, the overall *resultant velocity* of the propeller blade section through the air is obtained, as shown in Figure 1-53. The angle between the resultant velocity (and therefore relative air flow) of the propeller blade and the plane of rotation is called the **helix angle** or the *pitch angle* or the *angle-of-advance.*

Helical Motion

Each propeller blade section follows a corkscrew path through the air—called a **helix**—as a result of the combined rotational and forward velocities. The easiest way to picture it is to consider the helix as the path which the trailing edge of the propeller section follows.

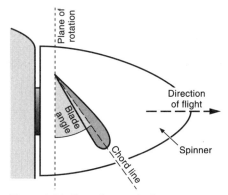

Figure 1-51. Propeller terminology

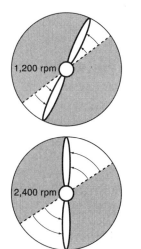

Figure 1-52. The speed of the blade section depends on the radius and rpm

The blade section experiences a relative air flow directly opposite its own path through the air. The angle between the chord line of the propeller blade section and the relative air flow is its **angle-of-attack.** Notice that the angle-of-attack plus the helix angle (pitch angle) make up the blade angle.

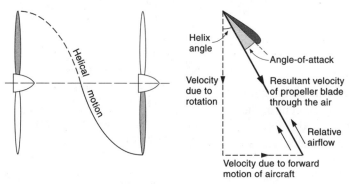

Figure 1-53. Each propeller blade-section follows its own path

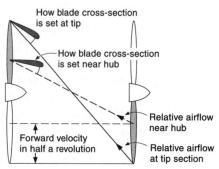

Figure 1-54. The propeller blade angle is made progressively larger from tip to hub to provide efficient angles-of-attack along its full length

When the airplane is in flight each propeller blade section will have the same forward velocity component. What will differ, however, is the rotational component of velocity—the further each blade section is from the propeller shaft the faster it is moving. If the blade angle was the same along the whole length of the propeller (which we know is not the case), then the angle-of-attack would be different at all points.

For a propeller with the same blade angle along its length, the angle-of-attack would vary with distance from the propeller shaft, causing thrust to be produced in an inefficient manner.

Like all airfoils, there is a most efficient angle-of-attack. If the propeller is designed to be most efficient at a certain airspeed of the airplane and rpm of the propeller, then the designer will aim to have this most efficient angle-of-attack along the whole length of the propeller blade when it is operating under the design airspeed and rpm conditions. To achieve this, the blade angle at the hub needs to be much greater than the blade angle at the tip. This is known as **blade twist** or *helical twist.*

A propeller has blade twist to maintain the same angle-of-attack along the length of the blade.

Forces on a Propeller Blade

When considering a wing, the total aerodynamic force is resolved into a lift component perpendicular to the relative air flow, and a drag component parallel to the relative air flow. For a propeller airfoil, however, each blade section has a different oriented relative air flow because of the different rotational velocities. It would therefore be complicated to resolve the aerodynamic forces into components parallel and perpendicular to the relative air flow. Therefore when considering the forces on a propeller blade it is much more convenient to resolve the total reaction into two components:

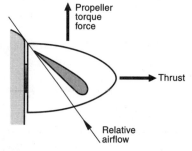

Figure 1-55. Forces on a propeller blade

- one in the plane of rotation called **propeller torque** (which is resistance to motion in the plane of rotation); and

- another in the direction perpendicular to the plane of rotation called **thrust.**

For a wing, drag must be overcome to provide lift. For a propeller, the propeller torque must be overcome or balanced by the engine for the propeller to provide thrust. Opening the throttle increases the engine power, overcomes the propeller torque, causes the propeller to rotate faster and generate more thrust.

Propeller Efficiency

An efficient propeller can convert a lot of the power produced by the engine (the brake horsepower) into thrust (that is, to thrust horsepower). A less-efficient propeller converts less of the engine power (brake horsepower or BHP) to thrust (thrust HP). Therefore:

$$\text{Propeller efficiency} = \frac{\text{thrust horsepower}}{\text{brake horsepower}}$$

Variation of Propeller Efficiency

Only part of the propeller blade is capable of producing thrust efficiently—this usually lies at some distance from the hub between 60 and 90 percent of the blade radius, with the greatest useful thrust produced at approximately 75 percent of the blade radius. Reference to blade angle, angle-of-attack, and so on, will refer to this most effective part of the propeller blade.

Now consider a well-designed fixed-pitch propeller blade. The term *fixed-pitch* means that the blade angle is fixed and unable to be changed, as on most training airplanes. If the propeller rpm is constant, then the direction of the relative air flow and the angle-of-attack will be determined by the forward speed.

As the forward airspeed increases, the angle-of-attack of a fixed-pitch propeller turning at a constant rpm will decrease. At some high forward speed, the angle-of-attack of the blades will be such that little or no thrust will be produced. For a given rpm, there will only be one airspeed at which the fixed-pitch propeller will operate at its most efficient angle-of-attack.

The designer chooses a fixed-pitch propeller whose most efficient airspeed/rpm combination fits the tasks for which the airplane is designed. For an airplane whose primary purpose is to lift heavy loads off short runways and operate at low airspeeds, a low-pitch propeller (small blade angle) is most suitable. Airplanes designed for agricultural spraying or fire-bombing are typical examples. For an airplane whose primary purpose is cruising long distances at high speeds, a propeller of higher pitch (large blade angle) is more suitable.

Although the fixed-pitch propeller can be designed for a specific role, its maximum efficiency is limited to just one airspeed/rpm combination. Faster or slower than this speed/rpm, propeller efficiency will reduce markedly.

The constant-speed propeller overcomes this problem by varying the blade angle so that it operates at an efficient angle-of-attack at any airspeed. Most pilots will fly constant-speed propeller airplanes early in their career.

Controllable-Pitch Propellers

An early development in improving propeller efficiency was the two-pitch propeller, which enabled the pilot to select a low pitch for takeoff and low-speed operations, and a high pitch for the higher airspeeds on the cruise and descent.

More recently the automatic **constant-speed propeller** was developed, with a blade angle that could take up any position between two in-flight limits at the **low** and **high** pitch ends of its range. This allows the propeller blade to maintain its most efficient angle-of-attack at all airspeed/rpm combinations.

At low airspeeds, the blade angle needs to be small for the angle-of-attack to be optimum. This is known as *low pitch*. As the forward speed increases, the blade angle needs to increase toward *high* pitch for the angle-of-attack to remain optimum. The device used to achieve this is the *governor*, whose function is to regulate the propeller rpm to that selected by the pilot. It does this by automatically adjusting the blade angle so that the rpm is maintained irrespective of the airspeed and the power delivered by the engine, hence the term constant-speed propeller.

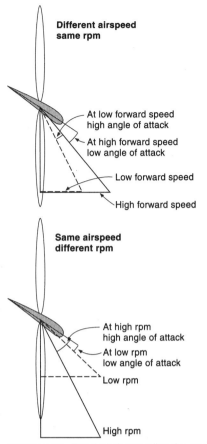

Figure 1-56. Fixed-pitch propeller–the angle-of-attack varies with forward speed and rpm

A fixed-pitch propeller is most efficient at only one airspeed and rpm.

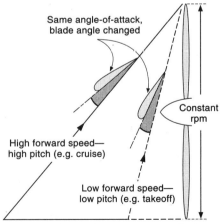

Figure 1-57. A constant-speed propeller maintains an efficient angle-of-attack over a wide speed/rpm range

The pilot sets the recommended rpm for the operation (climb, cruise or descent) with the propeller control. The aim is to have the propeller working close to its best angle-of-attack and maximum efficiency throughout its operating range, as advised by the manufacturer's operating procedures.

In the extreme case of low engine power, the blade angle will reduce until it reaches the minimum limit, known as the low-pitch stop. From then on, the propeller acts as a fixed-pitch propeller, with further power reductions causing a drop in rpm because the governor cannot reduce the blade angle any further to maintain the rpm.

Takeoff. Low pitch is used for takeoff so that the blade angle of the constant-speed propeller is at a small angle-of-attack. This enables the propeller to operate at maximum rpm as the throttle is advanced to the takeoff position, and so enable the engine to deliver maximum power.

Approach and Landing. When the airspeed and power are low, as on approach to land, the propeller blades are hard against the low-pitch stop, and the rpm changes with throttle movements.

In case a go-around is necessary, it is good airmanship to advance the prop control to high rpm on final approach so that the propeller can respond quickly and efficiently if the throttle is advanced.

Constant-Speed Propeller Controls

The pitch-changing mechanism is usually operated hydraulically by governor-regulated oil pressure. In contrast to fixed-pitch propellers, where the throttle alone is used to control engine power and rpm (and consequently propeller rpm), with a constant-speed propeller there are two controls:

- the **propeller control** to control propeller rpm; and
- the **throttle** to control the manifold pressure in the engine.

The desired power is achieved by selecting certain combinations of propeller rpm and manifold pressure (*see also* Chapter 7).

Main Advantages of the Constant-Speed Propeller

A constant-speed (or controllable-pitch) propeller enables the propeller to be at its most efficient angle-of-attack over a wide range of rpm and airspeed. In comparison, a fixed-pitch propeller only operates efficiently under the one set of rpm and airspeed conditions.

Other Advantages. More sophisticated constant-speed propellers have other significant features, including:

- **Beta range.** A range of very low pitch angles that reduce thrust and produce more drag for ground operations.
- **Reverse thrust.** Some propeller mechanisms can rotate the blades into reverse (or negative) pitch, which results in the propeller's thrust acting backwards. This provides a strong braking effect when power is applied.
- **Feathering.** Some controllable-pitch propellers, particularly on multi-engine airplanes, can be feathered in flight to stop a windmilling prop, reduce drag and prevent further engine damage following an engine failure.

Takeoff Effects of Propellers

Slipstream Effect

A clockwise-rotating propeller (as seen from the cockpit) will impart a clockwise rotation to the slipstream as it flows back over the airplane, following a corkscrew path. This causes an asymmetric air flow over the vertical stabilizer and rudder.

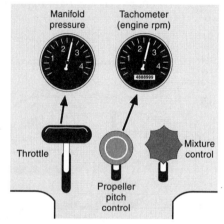

Figure 1-58. Constant-speed propeller controls

A constant-speed propeller is efficient over a range of rpm and airspeed conditions.

In the case of a single-engine airplane at high power, the slipstream will strike the left of the vertical stabilizer at an angle-of-attack, generating an aerodynamic force which pushes the tail to the right and makes the airplane **yaw left.** Some airplanes have an *offset vertical stabilizer* to help overcome this effect.

Propeller Torque Effect

If the propeller rotates clockwise (when viewed from behind), the torque reaction will tend to rotate the airplane counterclockwise, which means the airplane will **roll left.** This effect is most pronounced under conditions of high power and high propeller rpm, and at low airspeeds when fixed-pitch propeller blades have a large angle-of-attack—for example, during takeoff.

On the takeoff ground run, the tendency to roll left is absorbed by the left main-wheel, which will have to support more load. This will increase the friction force, tending to slow it down, and consequently the airplane will **yaw left.** Notice that on the ground run this effect yaws the airplane in the same direction as the slipstream effect. Use right rudder to keep straight.

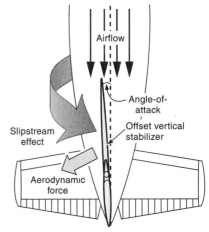

Figure 1-59. An offset fin helps counteract propeller-slipstream effect

SWING DUE TO GYROSCOPIC PRECESSION
Tail lifting on takeoff causes forces at (1). Fast spinning propeller follows gyro-precession principle. Effect occurs at (2), 90° in direction of rotation. Consequently, **nose yaws left.**

SWING DUE TO TORQUE REACTION
Engine rotates propeller clockwise as seen by pilot (on most modern aircraft)—torque. Torque reaction tries to twist engine and airframe the opposite way —counterclockwise. Downward force at (A) presses left wheel hard onto runway at (B). Resultant differential drag on the main wheels **swings nose left.**

SPIRAL SLIPSTREAM EFFECT
Clockwise spiral slipstream (from clockwise-rotating propeller) strikes vertical stabilizer on its left side. This tends to **yaw the nose left.**

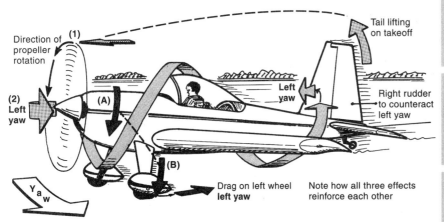

Figure 1-60. Takeoff swing resulting from the combined effects of slipstream effect, torque effect and gyroscopic precession

Gyroscopic Effect

Early in the takeoff run of a tailwheel airplane, the tail is lifted off the ground to place the airplane into a low drag and flying attitude. As the tail is being raised, a force is applied to the rotating propeller to tilt the rotating propeller disc forward. Because a rotating body tends to resist any attempt to change its plane of rotation, when such a change is imposed on it, a *gyroscopic precession* will be superimposed. *See* Chapter 8 for more on gyroscopic precession.

Gyroscopic effect causes any force applied to a spinning object to be displaced 90° in the direction of rotation. The action of **raising the tail** of the airplane on the takeoff run is like applying a forward force to the top of the rotating propeller disc. Gyroscopic precession causes an equivalent force to be applied 90° degrees in the direction of propeller rotation. With clockwise rotation, there will appear to be a force acting on the right side of the rotating propeller disc, causing the airplane to **yaw left.** The direction of yaw depends on the direction of propeller rotation. Right rudder must be applied to counteract this effect.

The extent of the gyroscopic effect depends on the propeller's *moment of inertia.* The moment of inertia depends on the mass of the propeller, how the mass is distributed along the blades and how fast the propeller is rotating. It also depends on how fast you try to change the plane of rotation—if you raise the tail quickly, the tendency to yaw left will be greater.

Gyroscopic effect is significant on the takeoff run in a tailwheel airplane as the tail is raised.

Raising the tail of a high-powered airplane like a P-51 Mustang on takeoff produces a much greater gyroscopic effect than raising the tail of a Piper Cub.

Asymmetric Propeller Blade Effect (P-Factor)

P-factor occurs for tailwheel airplanes on takeoff and for all airplanes when flying at high angles-of-attack (low speeds).

P-factor is present at high angles-of-attack (low airspeed) and high power.

During the first part of a tailwheel airplane's takeoff run, the tail is still on the ground, the propeller shaft is inclined upward and the plane of propeller rotation is not vertical. Because the airplane is moving horizontally, the downgoing propeller blade has a greater angle-of-attack than the upgoing blade. In addition, the downgoing blade also travels further (and therefore faster) through the air than the upgoing blade.

These two effects (greater angle-of-attack and higher blade velocity) combine to produce more thrust on the downgoing half of the propeller disc than on the upgoing half and the airplane will **yaw left.**

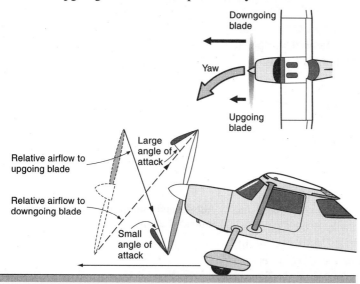

Figure 1-61. The downgoing propeller blade produces more thrust when the airplane is in a nose-high attitude, causing P-factor

P-factor is strongest at high power settings and high angles-of-attack, both on the ground and in flight. In normal cruise flight, the P-factor is insignificant because the upgoing and downgoing propeller blades produce similar amounts of thrust when the angle-of-attack is low.

Summary

On the takeoff ground run, the above four effects cause the airplane to **yaw left.** You can remain on the runway centerline by counteracting the yaw with right rudder.

Prevent unwanted yaw with rudder.

During flight, an increase in power will cause the airplane to yaw left due to slipstream effect and roll left due to the torque reaction. In addition, when flying slowly at a high angle-of-attack the airplane will yaw further left because of asymmetric blade effect.

✍ Now complete **Review 1, Part (e)** on page 35.

For Aspiring Commercial Pilots

Lift

Lift from a Typical Wing

Experimentally, it can be shown that the aerodynamic force, and therefore the lift, depends on:

- wing shape;
- angle-of-attack;
- air density (ρ or *rho*);
- velocity—true airspeed ($V \times V$, or V^2), and
- wing surface area (S).

Velocity of the air flow and air density (ρ) are combined in the expression for **dynamic pressure:** $\frac{1}{2}\rho V^2$, which is closely related to **indicated airspeed.** Putting this together with the wing surface area (S) we obtain the equation:

Lift = (some factor) $\times \frac{1}{2}\rho V^2 \times S$

We use some factor to cover the other variables, especially the wing shape and the angle-of-attack. "Some factor" is given the more technical sounding name of **coefficient of lift (C_L),** which is really the lifting ability of the wing at that particular angle-of-attack. Therefore:

$$\textbf{Lift} = \textbf{C}_\textbf{L} \times \textbf{1/2}\boldsymbol{\rho}\textbf{V}^\textbf{2} \times \textbf{S}$$

Apart from the extension of flaps, the wing shape is fixed by the designer, and any changes in C_L are caused by changes in angle-of-attack. If the C_L (lifting ability) of the wing is high at a particular angle-of-attack, then the same lift force to counteract the weight can be generated at a lower speed by increasing the angle-of-attack. This interrelationship between angle-of-attack (C_L) and airspeed is very important.

By using the equation: $L = C_L \frac{1}{2} \times \rho V^2 \times S$ and measuring L, V, ρ and S, we can calculate the value of C_L and develop a graph or curve of C_L versus angle-of-attack, known as the **lift curve** (Figure 1-62).

For a given wing, the angle-of-attack is the major controlling factor in the distribution of the static pressure around the wing. This determines the lift force that is generated. The actual value of C_L will therefore differ according to the angle-of-attack.

Each airfoil shape has its own particular lift curve which relates its C_L to angle-of-attack. We will consider an average cambered wing like that found on a typical training airplane such as a Cessna 172.

- At 0° angle-of-attack the cambered wing creates some lift and has a positive C_L.
- At about –4° angle-of-attack the lift is zero and $C_L = 0$. The airplane is rarely flown at the zero-lift angle-of-attack.
- As the angle-of-attack increases, the C_L increases proportionally up to about 12 or 13° angle-of-attack.

At higher angles-of-attack the curve starts to lean over, until at the stall angle (about 16° in this case) the C_L begins to decrease. This occurs when the air flow is unable to remain streamline over the wing's upper surface, separates from the wing surface and breaks up into eddies. Notice that the maximum C_L (the maximum lifting ability of the wing) occurs immediately prior to the stall.

Lift depends on the angle-of-attack and indicated airspeed.

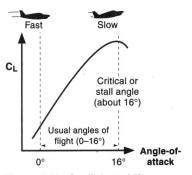

Figure 1-62. Coefficient of lift versus angle-of-attack; each angle-of-attack produces a particular C_L value

Lift from a Symmetrical Airfoil

Typical symmetrical airfoils are the vertical stabilizer and some horizontal stabilizers. The mean camber line of a symmetrical airfoil is a straight line because both surfaces have identical curvature. Therefore the chord line and mean camber line are identical.

The lift curve for a symmetrical airfoil will give a $C_L = 0$ (and zero lift) at 0° angle-of-attack, *see* Figure 1-64. This is because the streamlines follow mirror-image paths and therefore the air flow on both sides of the airfoil has the same velocity and static pressure. The center of pressure will *not* move as the angle-of-attack of a symmetrical airfoil is increased (whereas it moves forward on a cambered airfoil).

Changing Wing Area

Another factor that can alter lift is the wing area, *S*. If we could increase *S*, then we would obtain the same lift at a slower airspeed. Some flaps, such as Fowler flaps, increase the wing area as they are extended. Other basic flaps simply change the cross-section of the wing as they are lowered. All flaps cause changes in lift and drag, and consequently have an effect on the value of the L/D ratio.

Wing Loading

Both weight and balance must be considered by the pilot prior to flight. If any limitation is exceeded at any point in the flight, safety will be compromised. A detailed study of weight-and-balance appears in Chapter 12.

A useful means of describing the load that the wings carry in straight-and-level flight (when the lift from the wings supports the weight of the airplane) is **wing loading,** which is simply the weight supported per unit area of wing.

$$\text{Wing loading} = \frac{\text{Weight of the airplane}}{\text{Wing area}}$$

Example 1. An airplane has a maximum certificated weight of 2,600 pounds and a wing area of 200 square feet. What is its wing loading at maximum weight?

$$\text{Wing loading} = \frac{\text{Weight}}{\text{Wing area}} = \frac{2600}{200} = 13 \text{ pounds/square foot}$$

Drag

Drag from an Airfoil

At low speeds the total drag from the airfoil is high (because of induced drag) and at high speeds the total drag is high (because of parasite drag). A formula (similar to that for lift) can be developed for the drag produced by an airfoil:

$$\text{Drag} = C_D \times \tfrac{1}{2}\rho V^2 \times S$$

Where: > **coefficient of drag** (C_D) represents shape and angle-of-attack;
      > ρ (*rho*) is air density;
      > V is velocity (true airspeed)—(IAS is related to $\tfrac{1}{2}\rho V^2$),
      > S is the wing surface area.

A **drag curve** for the airfoil relating C_D to angle-of-attack can be developed. This is useful for comparison with the lift curve (C_L versus angle-of-attack). Note that at high angles-of-attack near the stall angle, the coefficient of drag for an airfoil is high and is a large factor in the formula $D = C_D \times \tfrac{1}{2}\rho V^2 \times S$.

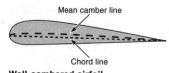
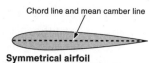

Figure 1-63. A cambered and symmetrical airfoil

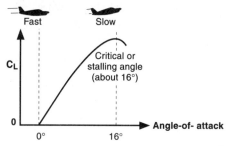

Figure 1-64. Lift curve for a symmetrical airfoil

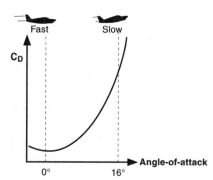

Figure 1-65. Coefficient of drag versus angle-of-attack

At low angles-of-attack, as during normal cruise, the coefficient of drag for the airfoil is small, but the airspeed (V) is high, which has a large effect in the formula. This is why the drag force (D) is high at both extremes of angle-of-attack (and airspeed). In between these extremes is an angle-of-attack (and airspeed) where the drag force is a minimum. The minimum C_D for a typical airfoil occurs at a small positive angle-of-attack.

Design Features that Minimize Induced Drag

Induced drag increases as the difference in pressure above and below the wing increases. This causes greater spanwise flow and larger vortices at the wingtips and trailing edges. In the history of airplane development, designers have made great advances in reducing induced drag by decreasing the amount of spanwise flow close to the wingtips. Design features to achieve this include:

- tapered or elliptical-shaped wings, *see* Figure 1-66a;
- wings of high aspect ratio (high span/chord ratio, as evident on sailplanes), *see* Figure 1-66b;
- wing washout (an built-in twist that causes a lower angle-of-attack at the wingtips compared with near the wing root), *see* Figure 1-66c;
- winglets (upward wingtip extensions—as on Boeing 747-400, McDonnell Douglas MD-11, Gulfstream IV), *see* Figure 1-66d.

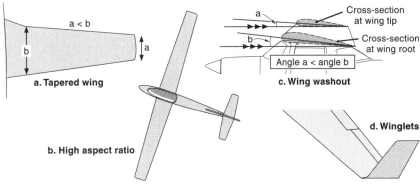

Figure 1-66. Design features that minimize induced drag

The Lift/Drag Ratio

We have already discussed the lift curve (C_L versus angle-of-attack) and the drag curve (C_D versus angle-of-attack).

The **lift curve** shows a steady increase in the coefficient of lift as the angle-of-attack is increased, up to the stall angle, beyond which C_L decreases.

The **drag curve** shows that drag is least at small positive angles-of-attack and increases either side as angle-of-attack is increased or decreased. As the stall angle is approached the drag increases at a greater rate. At the stall the separation of streamline air flow and the formation of a turbulent wake causes a large increase in drag.

Variation of the L/D Ratio with Angle-of-Attack

Lift is the benefit you obtain from an airfoil and drag is the price you pay for it. For a given amount of lift it is desirable to have the minimum amount of drag to gain the best possible lift/drag ratio.

If you require 2,400 pounds of lift and the cost is 200 units of drag from the airfoil, then $L/D = {}^{2,400}/_{200} = 12$, which means the lift is 12 times greater than the drag from the airfoil. If the 2,400 pounds of lift come with 400 units of drag from the airfoil, then the lift/drag ratio $= {}^{2,400}/_{400} = 6$ (the wing is much less efficient).

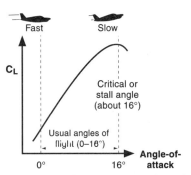

Figure 1-67. C_L versus angle-of-attack

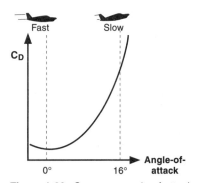

Figure 1-68. C_D versus angle-of-attack

An airfoil has the greatest lifting ability (C_L) at a high angle-of-attack, just prior to the stall angle-of-attack—approximately 16° (Figure 1-69). Unfortunately, near the stall angle, the airfoil generates a lot of induced drag.

The minimum C_D occurs at a fairly low angle-of-attack, in this case at about 0° angle-of-attack. Unfortunately, at low angles-of-attack, the lifting ability (C_L) of the wing is low.

Neither of these situations (high angle-of-attack or low angle-of-attack) is really satisfactory, because the ratio of lift to drag at these extreme angles-of-attack is low. What is required is the greatest lifting ability compared with the drag at the same angle-of-attack.

To find the **lift/drag ratio** we can divide the two equations:

$$\frac{\text{Lift}}{\text{Drag}} = \frac{C_L \times \frac{1}{2}\rho V^2 \times S}{C_D \times \frac{1}{2}\rho V^2 \times S} = \frac{C_L}{C_D}$$

For any angle-of-attack we can calculate the L/D ratio by dividing C_L by C_D. Developing a curve for L/D versus angle-of-attack shows that L/D increases rapidly up to about 4° angle-of-attack, where the lift is typically between 10 to 15 times the drag, depending on the airfoil used.

At angles-of-attack higher than about 4° the L/D ratio decreases steadily. Even though the C_L is still increasing, the CD increases at a greater rate. At the stall angle-of-attack the L/D ratio for this particular airfoil is about 5.

The curve shown in Figure 1-69 clearly shows the specific angle-of-attack at which the L/D ratio is a maximum, and this angle-of-attack is where the airfoil is most efficient—it gives the required lift for the minimum cost in drag.

In most airplanes you do not have an instrument to indicate angle-of-attack, but you can read airspeed, which is related to angle-of-attack. High angles-of-attack in steady flight are associated with lower airspeeds (and vice versa).

The angle-of-attack (and airspeed) for the best lift/drag ratio gives the required lift (to counteract the weight) for the minimum cost in drag. At any other angle-of-attack there is a greater cost in terms of increased drag to obtain the same lift.

In steady flight the drag is counteracted by the thrust. If the lift required to counteract the weight is obtained at the minimum drag cost, then thrust can be kept to a minimum. The benefits are clear—the engine–propeller can be smaller, fuel and maintenance costs can be lower, and economy improves.

Some important in-flight performance characteristics are obtained at the best lift/drag ratio, such as the maximum cruise range and the maximum power-off glide range. *See* Chapter 3.

Propellers

Pitch

Earlier in the chapter reference was made to "low pitch" and "high pitch" in constant-speed propellers. In summary, low pitch is associated with a small blade angle and slow flight, while high pitch is associated with a large blade angle and fast flight.

However, **pitch** is not a blade angle but a distance—the distance the propeller moves forward in one complete revolution. Normally during flight at low speeds you *select* low pitch to ensure the propeller is at the most efficient angle-of-attack. However the pitch (distance moved forward in one revolution) would have been small whether "low" or "high" pitch had been selected.

The angle-of-attack that gives the best lift/drag ratio is the most efficient angle-of-attack.

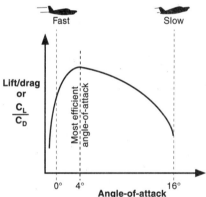

Figure 1-69. Lift/drag ratio versus angle-of-attack

Propeller Efficiency

There is a certain amount of slippage as a propeller blade moves through the air and pulls the airplane along, in the same way as a swimmer's hands or a rower's oars slip backward through the water. A propeller will therefore not advance as far through "fluid" air as a corkscrew would through a solid cork, where there is no slippage.

Geometric pitch is how far the propeller would theoretically advance in one revolution with no slippage. **Effective pitch** is how far the propeller *actually* advances through the air in one revolution. It is equal to geometric pitch minus propeller slippage. A propeller is more efficient in dense air than in thin air, because there is less slippage.

As a result of propeller slippage through the air, not all of the power generated by the engine will be converted to thrust by the propeller. We describe this as propeller efficiency, the ratio of useful power output (from the propeller) to actual power output (from the engine). Typical propeller efficiency varies between 50 percent and 85 percent lift-to-weight, depending on slippage.

Propeller efficiency is the ratio of thrust horsepower (propeller) to brake horsepower (engine).

✍ Now complete **Review 1, Commercial** on page 36.

✍ Review 1

Part (a)

1. The weight of an airplane can be considered as a single force acting through the _____.

➤ center of gravity

2. The force produced by the wings which supports the airplane in flight is called _____.

➤ lift

3. The force produced by the engine–propeller is called _____ .

➤ thrust

4. The force that resists the motion of the airplane through the air is called _____ .

➤ drag

5. Typically, lift and weight are (2/10/50/100) times greater than thrust and drag in straight-and-level flight at a constant airspeed.

➤ 10

6. What are the relationships between: lift and weight; and thrust and drag; when the airplane is flying straight-and-level at a constant airspeed?

➤ lift = weight, thrust = drag

7. For an airplane to accelerate, thrust must (equal/exceed) drag, and a state of equilibrium (will/will not) exist.

➤ exceed, will not

The Forces Acting on an Airplane

8. The four aerodynamic forces acting on an airplane in flight are in equilibrium:
   (a) during unaccelerated flight.
   (b) when the airplane is accelerating.
   (c) when the airplane is decelerating.

➤ (a)

9. The four aerodynamic forces acting on an airplane are:
   (a) lift, weight, thrust, and drag.
   (b) lift, gravity, thrust, and drag.
   (c) power, weight, velocity, and friction.

➤ (a)

Part (b)

1. A surface designed to create an aerodynamic lifting force as air flows over it is called an _____.

➤ airfoil

2. To produce a lift force to counteract the weight of the airplane in normal flight, the static pressure above the wing must be (equal to/less than/greater than) the static pressure beneath the wing.

➤ less than

3. A steady air flow around an airfoil, in which succeeding parcels of air follow each other, is called _____ flow. A disturbed flow with eddying is called _____ flow.

➤ streamline, turbulent

---

4. The point on an airfoil where the smooth boundary-layer flow separates from the airfoil surface and becomes turbulent is called the_____.

➤   separation point

5. Static pressure in the air is exerted (in all directions/down/up). _____pressure is the pressure caused by motion.

➤   in all directions, Dynamic

6. Bernoulli's principle describes the natural effect that, in a streamline flow, the *total* pressure energy (increases/decreases/remains constant).

➤   remains constant

7. Total pressure energy = _____pressure + _____ pressure.

➤   static + dynamic

8. In streamline flow, if dynamic pressure increases then the static pressure will _____.

➤   decrease

9. The velocity of the air flow and the air density (ρ) are combined in the one expression "$\frac{1}{2}\rho V^2$", which is called the _____.

➤   dynamic pressure

10. The line drawn half-way between the upper and lower surfaces of the wing, which gives an indication of its curvature, is called the_____ .

➤   mean camber line

11. The wing shape and the angle-of-attack determine the profile that the airfoil presents to the air flow and determines the _____ of the wing.

➤   lifting ability

12. The front and rear edges of a wing are called the _____ and _____ edges respectively.

➤   leading, trailing

13. The straight line joining the leading edge and the trailing edge of an airfoil section is called the _____.

➤   chord line

14. Drag is the component of relative air flow which is (horizontal/parallel to the longitudinal axis/parallel to the relative air flow).

➤   parallel to the relative air flow

15. The forces acting on an airfoil in flight as a result of the changes in static pressure around it may be considered to act through a point called the _____.

➤   center of pressure

16. The relative air flow is (parallel/perpendicular) to the flight path of the airplane, and in the (same/opposite) direction. The angle between the relative air flow and the chord of the airfoil is called the _____.

➤   parallel, opposite, angle-of-attack

17. If the angle-of-attack is increased gradually in normal cruise flight, the lifting ability of the wing (increases/decreases).

➤   increases

18. The term *angle-of-attack* is defined as the angle:
    (a) between the airplane's climb angle and the horizon.
    (b) between the wing chord line and the relative air flow.
    (c) formed by the longitudinal axis of the airplane and the chord of the wing.

➤   (b)

19. On a wing, the force of lift acts perpendicular to and the force of drag acts parallel to the:
    (a) chord line.
    (b) flight path.
    (c) longitudinal axis.

➤   (b)

20. By changing the angle-of-attack on a wing, the pilot can control the airplane's:
    (a) lift, airspeed, and drag.
    (b) airspeed, weight, and drag.
    (c) lift and airspeed, but not drag.

➤   (a)

21. The angle-of-attack of a wing directly controls the:
    (a) angle of incidence of the wing.
    (b) amount of air flow above and below the wing.
    (c) distribution of positive and negative pressure acting on the wing.

➤   (c)

22. As the angle-of-attack is gradually increased in the normal flight range, the lifting ability of the wing increases and the center of pressure (moves forward/stays in the same place/moves rearward) on the wing.

➤   moves forward

23. Beyond the stall angle-of-attack, the lifting ability of the wing (increases/decreases) significantly and the center of pressure moves (forward/rearward/remains stationary) on the wing.

➢ decreases, rearward

24. Frost on the wings is dangerous mainly because it:
   (a) causes early air flow separation with a loss of lift.
   (b) causes an increase in weight.
   (c) delays air flow separation from the wing resulting in a greater stall angle-of-attack.

➢ (a)

25. Frost or other contaminants on the wings (should/need not) be removed prior to flight, because they (may/will not) make it difficult or even impossible for the airplane to become airborne.

➢ should, may

26. How will frost on the wings of an airplane affect takeoff performance?
   (a) Frost will change the camber of the wing, increasing its lifting ability.
   (b) Frost will cause the airplane to become airborne with a higher angle-of-attack, decreasing the stall speed.
   (c) Frost will disrupt the smooth flow of air over the wing, adversely affecting its lifting ability.

➢ (c)

Part (c)

1. Drag (opposes/encourages) motion through the air.

➢ opposes

2. If drag can be kept low, then (lift/thrust) can be kept low.

➢ thrust

3. Total drag is considered in two basic groups:
   (a) that drag which comes about in the production of lift, called _____ drag, and
   (b) that drag which is *not* associated with the production of lift, called _____ drag.

➢ induced, parasite

4. Parasite drag consists of _____ , _____ and _____ .

➢ skin friction, form drag, interference drag

5. Flush riveting and polishing the surface of an airplane reduce (skin friction/induced drag/thrust).

➢ skin friction

6. As airspeed increases, drag caused by skin friction (increases/decreases).

➢ increases

7. Form drag occurs when the air flow _____ from the surface of the airfoil and becomes (smooth/turbulent).

➢ separates, turbulent

8. To reduce form drag, separation of the boundary layer air flow from the wing surface should be (delayed/encouraged) by _____ .

➢ delayed, streamlining

9. If you double the airspeed in level flight, the parasite drag will (increase/decrease) by a factor of (2/4/8).

➢ increase, 4

10. Air flows around the wingtips from the higher pressure area on the (upper/lower) surface of the wing into the area of lower pressure on the (upper/lower) surface of the wing. This forms wingtip _____ , and creates _____ drag.

➢ lower, upper, vortices, induced

11. The spanwise flow of air on the upper wing surface is (out toward the wingtip/in toward the wing root).

➢ in toward the wing root

12. The formation of wingtip vortices and induced drag is greatest at (high/low) angles-of-attack and (high/low) airspeeds.

➢ high, low

13. Wingtip vortices:
   (a) cause much of the drag at low speed;
   (b) cause much of the drag at high speed;
   (c) cause a decrease in drag.

➢ (a)

14. The total drag is minimum at (high speed/medium speed/low speed) where the parasite drag and induced drag are equal.

➢ medium speed

15. At high speeds and low angles-of-attack, because of the greater (induced/parasite) drag, the thrust requirement is (greater/less).

➢ parasite drag, greater

16. To maintain a steady speed straight-and-level, the thrust required is:
    (a) the same at all speeds.
    (b) greatest at normal cruise speed;
    (c) greater at a speed just above the stall than at cruise speed.

➤ (c)

17. The angle-of-attack that gives the best L/D ratio is the (most/least) efficient angle-of-attack.

➤ most

18. If you fly at the airspeed obtained at the best or maximum L/D ratio, then the required lift is obtained for the (minimum/maximum) drag.

➤ minimum

19. Minimum drag means (minimum/maximum) thrust to maintain airspeed.

➤ minimum

20. Lift/drag ratio:
    (a) describes the aerodynamic efficiency of the wing.
    (b) is the ratio of the lift produced from an airfoil compared with its area.
    (c) remains the same as the angle-of-attack of the airfoil changes.

➤ (a)

Part (d)

1. Lowering the flaps (increases/decreases/does not change) the camber of the wing.

➤ increases

2. With flaps extended, the required lift can be generated at a (higher/lower) airspeed and the stall speed will (increase/decrease/not alter).

➤ lower, decrease

3. Trailing-edge flaps not only increase lift, but also increase_____ .

➤ drag

4. The percentage increase in drag usually exceeds that in lift when the flaps are extended, therefore flaps (increase/decrease) the *lift/drag* ratio.

➤ decrease

5. The extension of flaps on a glide approach allows a (steeper/flatter) approach flight path at a constant speed.

➤ steeper

6. With flaps extended, the nose attitude of the airplane is (lower/higher).

➤ lower

7. Extending full flaps for landing enables (faster/slower) approach speeds and causes a (longer/shorter) landing run.

➤ slower, shorter

8. Wing flaps at the recommended takeoff setting:
   (a) increase lifting ability for a small penalty in drag.
   (b) increase lifting ability for a large penalty in drag.
   (c) significantly increase drag for a small decrease in lifting ability.

➤ (a)

9. Extending flaps in the approach phase enables you to:
   (a) decrease angle of descent without increasing airspeed.
   (b) touch down at a higher speed.
   (c) increase angle of descent without increasing airspeed.

➤ (c)

10. What is one purpose of wing flaps?
    (a) To enable the pilot to make steeper approaches to a landing without increasing the airspeed.
    (b) To relieve the pilot of maintaining continuous pressure on the controls.
    (c) To decrease wing area to vary the lift.

➤ (a)

11. Slots (increase/decrease) the angle-of-attack at which a wing stalls by (delaying/encouraging) the separation of the smooth air flow over the upper surface of the wing.

➤ increase, delaying

12. The primary purpose of wing spoilers is to decrease the (lift/drag) produced by the wing.

➤ lift

Part (e)

1. A propeller converts engine torque into _____.

➤ thrust

2. At high altitudes, when the air is (more/less) dense, a propeller will be (more/less) efficient.

➤ less, less

3. The angle that the propeller blade makes with the plane of its rotation is called the _____.

➤ blade angle

4. A propeller blade is twisted to ensure that it operates at its most efficient _____ along its full length.
➤ angle-of-attack

5. The blade angle is greatest near the (hub/tip) where the rotational velocity is (fast/slow).
➤ hub, slow

6. A fixed-pitch propeller is efficient at only one set of _____ and _____ conditions.
➤ rpm, airspeed

7. A *constant-speed* propeller has a (variable/constant) pitch angle and is efficient over a wide range of _____ and _____ conditions.
➤ variable, rpm and airspeed

8. As the forward speed of an airplane with a fixed-pitch propeller increases, with the rpm remaining constant, the angle-of-attack of the propeller blades:
    (a) decreases as forward speed increases.
    (b) increases as forward speed increases.
    (c) remains unaltered as forward speed increases.
➤ (a)

9. In an airplane with a clockwise rotating propeller, P-factor, or asymmetric blade effect, causes the airplane to yaw (left/right) at (high/low) angles-of-attack of the wing.
➤ left, high

10. At high angles-of-attack of the wings, the (downgoing/upgoing) propeller blade produces more thrust. This blade is on the (right/left) side of the propeller disc when viewed from the rear, and so will cause a tendency for the airplane to yaw to the (left/right).
➤ downgoing, right, left

11. In a single-engine airplane, torque effect is greatest at (high/low) power and (high/low) airspeed.
➤ high power, low airspeed

12. Raising the tail of a tailwheel airplane early in the takeoff roll causes a tendency to yaw left because of_____ .
➤ gyroscopic precession

13. During the takeoff roll of a single-engine airplane, the left tire will carry (more/less) load because of the propeller torque reaction, and the airplane will tend to yaw (left/right). You can keep the airplane tracking straight down the runway by applying (left/right) rudder.
➤ more, left, right

14. Under what flight conditions is torque effect the greatest in a single-engine airplane?
    (a) Low airspeed, high power, high angle-of-attack.
    (b) Low airspeed, low power, low angle-of-attack.
    (c) High airspeed, high power, high angle-of-attack.
➤ (a)

15. When does P-factor cause the airplane to yaw to the left?
    (a) When at low angles-of-attack.
    (b) When at high angles-of-attack.
    (c) When at high airspeeds.
➤ (b)

16. The left turning tendency of an airplane caused by P-factor is the result of the:
    (a) clockwise rotation of the engine and the propeller turning the airplane counterclockwise.
    (b) propeller blade descending on the right, producing more thrust than the ascending blade on the left.
    (c) gyroscopic forces applied to the rotating propeller blades acting 90 in advance of the point the force was applied.
➤ (b)

Commercial Review

1. If air flow velocity increases, static pressure _____.
➤ decreases

2. The *lifting ability* of the wing is given the technical name _____.
➤ coefficient of lift

3. Write down the lift formula, and identify each term.
➤ $L = C_L \frac{1}{2} \rho V^2 S$, where C_L is the coefficient of lift, ρ is air density, V is the airspeed, and S is the wing surface area.

4. The air flow around a well-cambered wing at zero angle-of-attack will still have to accelerate over the upper surface and, since increased velocity means decreased static pressure, there (will/will not) be some lift produced.
➤ will

5. As the angle-of-attack of a symmetrical airfoil is gradually increased from zero, the lifting ability (increases/decreases/stays the same).
➤ increases

6. When the angle-of-attack of a symmetrical airfoil is increased, the center of pressure will:
   (a) move aft (rearward).
   (b) move forward.
   (c) not move.
➤ (c)

7. A symmetrical airfoil moving through the air at zero degrees angle-of-attack:
   (a) will generate a low static pressure above the wing and a high static pressure beneath the wing.
   (b) will produce a high pressure above the wing and a low pressure beneath the wing.
   (c) will cause a similar acceleration of the air flow over both upper and lower surfaces, similar velocities of flow generating similar pressures and therefore no lift.
➤ (c)

8. The lift generated by an airfoil is:
   (a) proportional to the square of the velocity of the relative air flow.
   (b) inversely proportional to the air density.
   (c) inversely proportional to the wing surface area.
➤ (a)

9. Define *wing loading* in straight-and-level flight.
➤ wing loading = weight of the airplane/wing area

10. An airplane weighs 3,000 pounds and has a wing area of 150 square feet. What is its wing loading?
➤ 20 pounds per square feet

11. The airplane in question has burned off 150 pounds of fuel. It now weighs _____ pounds, and its wing loading is _____ .
➤ 2,850 pounds, 19 pounds per square feet

12. The designer can help minimize the formation of wingtip vortices and induced drag by using wings of (high/low) aspect ratio, _____, or wingtip modification.
➤ high, washout

13. A high aspect ratio wing has a (short/long) span and a (short/long) chord.
➤ long span, short chord

14. A wing with *washout* has a lower angle-of-attack at the (wingtip/wing root).
➤ wingtip

15. If you require 3,000 pounds of lift to support the airplane, and the drag is 250 pounds, then the L/D ratio is (10:1/12:1/120:1/5:1).
➤ 12:1

For Questions 16–18, refer to Figure 1-70.

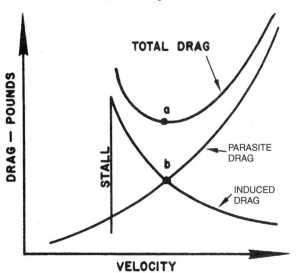

Figure 1-70. Drag versus velocity

16. The airspeed represented by point 'a' is the airspeed for (maximum/minimum) total drag.
➤ minimum

17. Flying faster than this minimum-drag airspeed, the total drag is (greater/less/the same), because of_____.
➤ greater, increased parasite drag

18. Flying slower than the minimum-drag airspeed, the total drag is (greater/less/the same), because of _____.
➤ greater, increased induced drag

19. Propeller efficiency is affected by propeller _____ .
➤ slippage

20. Propeller efficiency is the ratio of _____ power output to _____ power output, or (thrust/brake) horsepower to (thrust/brake) horsepower.
➤ useful, actual, thrust, brake

21. Consider an airplane with a constant-speed propeller. For high-speed cruise, compared with takeoff, you would select a (higher/lower) rpm that would provide a (greater/smaller) propeller blade angle.
➤ lower rpm, greater blade angle

22. A constant-speed propeller automatically adjusts the (rpm/blade angle) to maintain the selected (rpm/blade angle).

➤ blade angle, rpm

23. If you select a lower rpm, the blade angle of a constant-speed propeller will (increase/decrease).

➤ increase

24. The reason for blade twist along a propeller blade is that it permits a relatively constant (angle-of-attack/blade angle) along its length in cruise flight.

➤ angle-of-attack

For Questions 25–27, refer to Figure 1-71.

Note: The graphs in Figure 1-71 apply to a military fighter with swept wings. The angles-of-attack at which L/D and C_L are maximum are therefore higher than those you would expect for a training airplane.

25. At 4° angle-of-attack, C_L = (0.32/0.028/3.2), C_D = (0.32/0.028/3.2), the ratio C_L/C_D = _____ and L/D = _____.

➤ C_L = 0.32, C_D = 0.028, $C_L/C_D = \frac{0.32}{0.028} = 11.4$, L/D = 11.4

26. The airspeed for best L/D ratio occurs at _____ ° angle-of-attack, where L/D = _____.

➤ 6° angle-of-attack, L/D = 12.5

27. The L/D at 2° angle-of-attack on the low-airspeed side is _____ , which is the same as at _____ ° angle-of-attack on the high-airspeed side.

➤ L/D = 7.5, 16.5° angle-of-attack

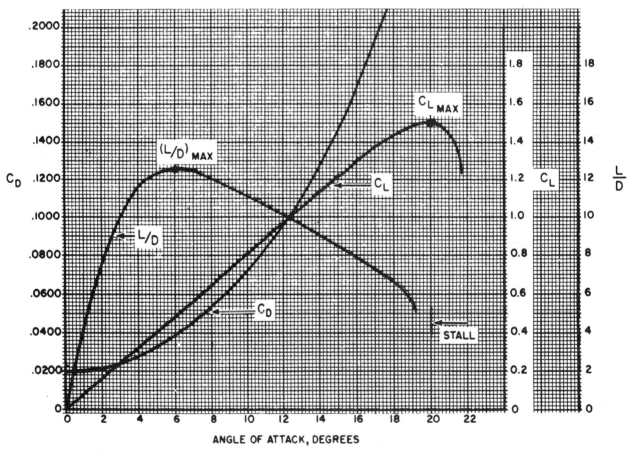

Figure 1-71.

Stability and Control 2

Stability

Stability is the natural ability of an airplane to return to its original position after being disturbed, without any action being taken by the pilot.

An inherently **stable** airplane will return to its original flight attitude after being disturbed from it without any specific action by the pilot.

An **unstable** airplane will move further away from its original attitude after being disturbed, making it more difficult for the pilot to control; this is also called *negative stability*.

A **neutrally stable** airplane will tend to remain in the disturbed position, unless the pilot does something about it.

The external force which most commonly displaces an airplane in flight is a gust of wind. A stable airplane will return to its original condition naturally—an unstable one will not, unless the pilot takes corrective action.

Figure 2-1. Stability of an airplane

Static and Dynamic Stability

Each type of stability—stable, unstable and neutral—can be further divided into *static* and *dynamic* stability, depending on the time when the stability is considered.

- **Static stability** refers to the instant when the airplane is no longer affected by the displacing force, and describes the initial movement tendency of the airplane in relation to its original attitude.
- **Dynamic stability** refers to the stability of an aircraft with respect to time.

If a wind gust causes the nose to drop, and the initial natural tendency is for it to rise of its own accord, then the airplane is said to exhibit positive static stability. If it rises a little above the original position, then falls a little beneath it, and finally settles after a number of decreasing oscillations, then it is said to exhibit positive dynamic stability (Figure 2-2a).

Continuing to oscillate without settling down is called neutral dynamic stability (Figure 2-2b), and continuing to oscillate with an increasing amplitude is called negative dynamic stability (Figure 2-2c), a characteristic that most designers make sure their airplanes do not exhibit.

Note that whenever an airplane oscillates the static stability is always positive because the initial movement tendency is to return to the undisturbed position or flight attitude.

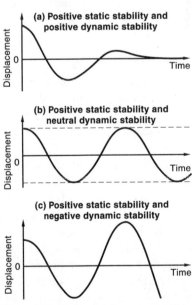

Figure 2-2. Static and dynamic stability

Stability and Maneuverability

An airplane with some positive stability is much easier to fly than an unstable airplane that shows a natural tendency to diverge from the trimmed flight attitude. The stability must not be so great, however, as to require unacceptably high control forces for maneuvering.

An unstable airplane is difficult to fly because of the continual need to apply control forces. A stable airplane can almost be flown hands-off and only requires guidance rather than second-to-second control inputs by the pilot.

The designer must achieve a compromise between stability and maneuverability, bearing in mind the qualities most desirable for the airplane's planned use. For instance, a passenger airplane would require more stability, whereas a fighter requires greater maneuverability.

Our examples so far have been drawn from the pitching plane, but stability in the other planes and about the other axes is just as important.

There is a trade-off between stability and maneuverability.

Airplane Equilibrium

An airplane is in a state of **equilibrium** when the sum of all forces and turning moments is zero. This means it will fly in a straight line at a steady airspeed. The airplane is **in trim** if all the moments in pitch, roll and yaw are zero.

As explained in the previous chapter, four main forces act on an airplane in flight: lift, weight, thrust and drag. For the airplane to remain in equilibrium in steady straight-and-level flight, the opposing forces must be equal so that they balance out, leaving an overall force of zero acting on the airplane. Therefore:

- lift is equal to weight and acts in the opposite direction; and

- thrust is equal to drag and acts in the opposite direction.

There is usually a considerable difference between the two pairs of forces, with lift and weight being much greater in magnitude than thrust and drag in normal flight. For example, lift and weight may each be 2,000 pounds, with thrust and drag each 200 pounds (that is, a lift/drag ratio of $^{2,000}/_{200} = 10{:}1$). The weight will gradually decrease as fuel is burned off, meaning that the lift required will also decrease. Thrust and drag will vary considerably depending on the angle-of-attack and airspeed.

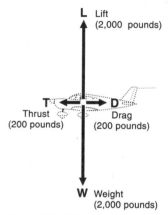

Figure 2-3. Lift counteracts weight, thrust counteracts drag in straight-and-level flight

Pitching Moments

The positions of the lift force acting through the center of pressure (CP), and the weight force acting through the center of gravity (CG), are not constant in flight. The basic CG position is established when the airplane is loaded, but will move as passengers or crew move around (noticeable in airliners as flight attendants walk down the cabin), if unsecured freight moves, and as fuel burns off. The CP changes position according to the angle-of-attack (and therefore airspeed).

Under most conditions of flight the CP and CG are not at the same point. The outcome is that the opposing forces of lift and weight, even though approximately equal in magnitude, will set up a *couple,* causing a nose-down pitching moment if the lift (CP) is behind the weight (CG), or a nose-up pitching moment if the CP is in front of the CG.

The different lines of action of the thrust force and the drag force produce another couple, causing a nose-up pitching moment if the drag line is above the thrust line, or a nose-down pitching moment if it is below the thrust line.

A *couple* is a pair of equal, parallel forces acting in opposite directions which tends to cause rotation because the forces are acting along different axes.

Ideally, the pitching moments from the two couples should neutralize each other in level flight so that there is no *residual* (remaining) moment that would cause the airplane to pitch nose-up or nose-down.

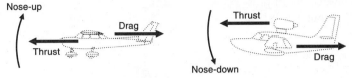

Figure 2-4. Thrust and drag form a pitching couple

In many airplanes the lines of action of the two couples are designed to be as shown in Figure 2-5. With this arrangement the thrust–drag couple produces a nose-up pitching moment which approximately cancels the nose-down pitching moment of the lift–weight couple.

There is a very good reason for the lift–weight couple to have a nose-down pitching moment balanced by the thrust–drag nose-up pitching moment. If thrust is lost after engine failure, the thrust–drag nose-up couple is weakened and therefore the lift–weight couple will pitch the airplane nose-down, without any action by the pilot. The airplane will then assume a glide attitude without a tendency to lose flying speed. The force generated by the horizontal stabilizer and elevator provides the final balancing force.

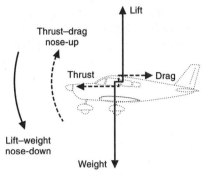

Figure 2-5. The lift–weight couple and the thrust–drag couple in balance

The Horizontal Stabilizer

The horizontal stabilizer counteracts the residual pitching moments from the two main couples. It is simply an airfoil that can generate an aerodynamic force by being positioned at an angle-of-attack relative to the local airflow. The lift component of the aerodynamic force can act upward or downward as required by the pilot, and because of this the horizontal stabilizer usually has a symmetrical section.

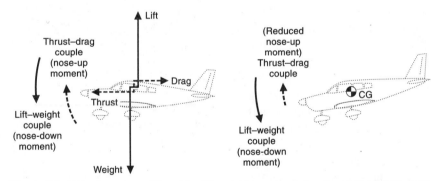

Figure 2-6. Following a loss of thrust the lift–weight couple pitches the airplane nose-down

If the residual moment from the four main forces is nose-down (as is most common), the horizontal stabilizer provides an aerodynamic force with a downward component on the tail section, which generates a nose-up pitching moment to balance the nose-down moment.

Because the horizontal stabilizer is situated some distance from the center of gravity, its moment-arm is quite long. The aerodynamic force provided by the horizontal stabilizer therefore needs only to be small to have a significant pitching effect. Consequently its size and aerodynamic capabilities are small compared with the wings.

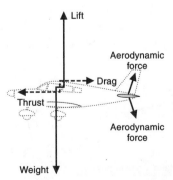

Figure 2-7. The horizontal stabilizer provides the final balancing moment

Many airplanes are designed to operate most efficiently at cruise speed. By designing the couples to be at least in approximate equilibrium when on the cruise, only small balancing aerodynamic forces are required from the horizontal stabilizer, thereby minimizing drag. Generally an airplane's center of pressure is designed to be aft of the center of gravity, with the horizontal stabilizer producing a small downward aerodynamic force.

The airplane will also pitch whenever the engine power setting is altered, because the speed of the slipstream over the horizontal stabilizer will change. When power is reduced, the slipstream over the horizontal stabilizer weakens, reducing the downward force and causing the nose to pitch down. Conversely, if the power is increased the slipstream over the horizontal stabilizer strengthens, increasing the downward force and causing the nose to pitch up. Therefore whenever power is changed you will need to retrim.

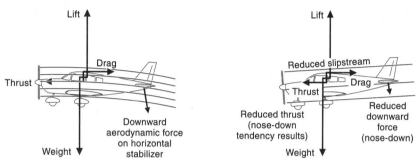

Figure 2-8. Thrust affects the force generated by the horizontal stabilizer

Angular Movement

We may consider the motion of the airplane to occur about each of three reference axes. Each axis passes through the center of gravity and is mutually perpendicular, or at right angles, to the other two.

The **longitudinal axis** runs from front to rear through the center of gravity. Movement around the longitudinal axis is known as rolling. Stability around the longitudinal axis is known as **lateral stability,** because it is concerned with movement in the lateral or rolling plane. *See* Figure 2-10.

The **lateral axis** passes through the center of gravity across the airplane from one side to the other. Movement around the lateral axis is called pitching (nose-up or nose-down). Stability around the lateral axis is called **longitudinal stability,** because it is concerned with stability in the longitudinal or pitching plane. *See* Figure 2-11.

The **normal axis** passes through the center of gravity and is perpendicular (normal) to the other two axes. Movement around the normal axis is called yawing. Stability around the normal axis is **directional stability,** because it is concerned with stability in the directional or yawing plane. *See* Figure 2-12. Normal axis is a better term than the commonly used vertical axis, since the axis is only vertical when the airplane is flying straight-and-level.

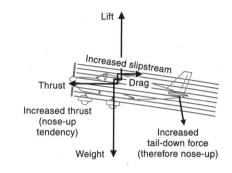

Figure 2-9. Angular movement can occur about three axes

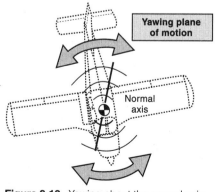

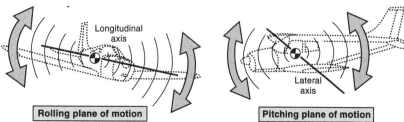

Figure 2-10. Rolling about the longitudinal axis

Figure 2-11. Pitching about the lateral axis

Figure 2-12. Yawing about the normal axis

Longitudinal Stability

Longitudinal stability is in the pitching plane and occurs about the lateral axis. To be longitudinally stable, an airplane must have a natural tendency to return to the same attitude in pitch after any disturbance. A longitudinally stable airplane tends to maintain the trimmed condition of flight and is therefore easy to fly in pitch.

The position of the center of gravity (CG) and the size of the horizontal stabilizer determines an airplane's longitudinal stability characteristics.

Let us consider a situation that is constantly occurring in flight, referring to Figure 2-13. If a disturbance, such as a gust (1), changes the attitude of the airplane by pitching it nose-up, the airplane, because of its inertia, will initially continue on its original flight path and therefore present itself to the relative airflow at an increased angle-of-attack (2). This will cause the horizontal stabilizer to produce a greater upward force (or decreased downward force) than before the disturbance. The increased aerodynamic force acting about the CG will produce a nose-down pitching moment, causing the airplane to return to its original trimmed condition (3).

Longitudinal stability is greatest with a large horizontal stabilizer and a forward CG.

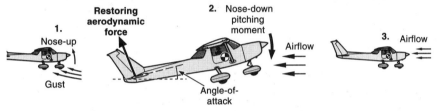

Figure 2-13. Longitudinal stability following an uninvited nose-up pitch

As shown in Figure 2-14, the horizontal stabilizer has a similar stabilizing effect following an uninvited nose-down pitch. In this way changes in the horizontal stabilizer's aerodynamic force lead to longitudinal stability.

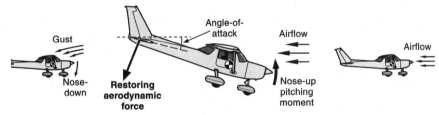

Figure 2-14. Longitudinal stability following an uninvited nose-down pitch

A good example of the stabilizing effect of a horizontal stabilizer is the flight of a dart or an arrow through the air, where the tail-fins act as a horizontal stabilizer to maintain longitudinal stability.

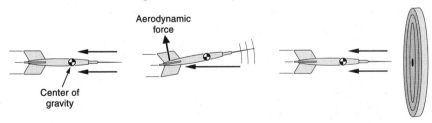

Figure 2-15. Longitudinal stability is provided by the tail-fins of a dart

The CG and Longitudinal Stability

The longitudinal stability of an airplane is determined by the size of the horizontal stabilizer and its distance from the airplane's CG. The pilot has a lot of control over the CG position when the airplane is being loaded. The further forward the CG, the greater the moment arm of the horizontal stabilizer, and therefore the greater the turning effect of the horizontal stabilizer aerodynamic force, and the greater the horizontal stability.

Limits are laid down for the range within which the CG must lie for safe flight. You must always load your airplane so that the actual CG position falls within the allowable CG range. If the CG is *behind* the legally allowable aft (rear) limit, the restoring moment of the horizontal stabilizer in pitch may be insufficient for satisfactory longitudinal stability, and the airplane may be difficult, or even impossible, to control. The further *forward* the CG, the greater the longitudinal stability.

Also, the more stable the airplane, the greater the control force you must exert to maneuver it, which can become tiring. If the CG is even further forward, beyond the allowable limit, the elevator may not be sufficiently effective at low speeds to flare the nose-heavy airplane for landing.

Design Considerations

Tailplane design features are very important to longitudinal stability. Horizontal stabilizer area, distance from the center of gravity, aspect ratio, angle-of-incidence, and *longitudinal dihedral* are considered by the designer. The aim is to generate a restoring force that is effective because of a long moment arm, leading to an airplane that is longitudinally stable.

At high angles-of-attack the wing may shield the horizontal stabilizer or cause the airflow over it to be turbulent, decreasing longitudinal stability.

Note: Longitudinal dihedral is the difference between the angle-of-incidence of the wing and the normally smaller angle-of-incidence of the horizontal stabilizer.

Directional Stability

Directional stability of an airplane is its natural tendency to recover from a disturbance in the yawing plane about the normal axis. It refers to an airplane's ability to weathercock or weathervane its nose into any airflow from the side.

If the airplane is disturbed from its straight path by the nose or tail being pushed to one side (yawed) by turbulence or by the pilot, then, because of its inertia, the airplane will initially keep moving in the original direction.

The airplane will now be moving somewhat sideways through the air, with its side surfaces, or keel surfaces, exposed to the airflow.

The vertical stabilizer is a symmetrical airfoil. As it is now positioned at an angle-of-attack to the relative airflow, it will generate a sideways aerodynamic force which acts about the CG and yaws the airplane back to its original position.

The position of the CG and size of the vertical stabilizer (fin) determine the directional stability. The greater the vertical stabilizer area and keel surface area behind the CG, and the greater the moment arm, the greater the directional stability of the airplane. Therefore, the further *forward* the CG, the greater the directional stability.

As well as being caused by turbulence, a yawing effect will also result from power changes, which cause changes in the slipstream over the vertical stabilizer and can lead to large changes in rudder requirements.

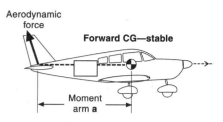

Forward CG—stable

Aerodynamic force

Moment arm **a**

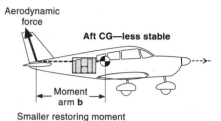

Aerodynamic force

Aft CG—less stable

Moment arm **b**

Smaller restoring moment

Figure 2-16. A forward CG—greater longitudinal stability

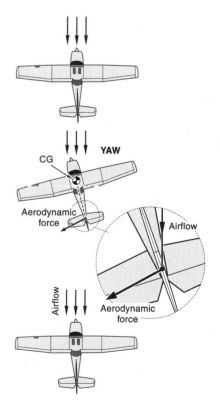

Figure 2-17. Directional stability following an uninvited yaw

Lateral Stability

Lateral stability is the natural ability of the airplane to recover from a disturbance in the lateral plane (that is, rolling about the longitudinal axis) without any pilot input.

Wing Dihedral

The wings can add lateral stability to an airplane if they have **dihedral**—a design feature where each wing is inclined upward from the fuselage to the wingtips.

When an airplane is disturbed in roll, the lift force is inclined and causes the airplane to **sideslip**. This sideslip combines a sideways and downward motion, which results in the relative airflow having a small upward and sideways component, as shown in Figure 2-19.

As the airplane sideslips, the lower wing, because of its dihedral, will meet the upcoming relative airflow at a greater angle-of-attack and produce increased lift. The upper wing will meet the relative airflow at a lower angle-of-attack and will produce less lift. The upper wing may also be shielded somewhat by the fuselage, causing even less lift to be generated. The rolling moment so produced, will tend to return the airplane to its original wings-level position.

Negative dihedral, or **anhedral** (where the wing is inclined downward from the fuselage) has an unstable effect.

Wing Sweepback and Lateral Stability

The wing can increase lateral stability if it has sweepback. As the airplane sideslips following a disturbance in roll, the lower sweptback wing generates more lift than the upper wing. This is because in the sideslip the lower wing presents more of its span to the airflow than the upper wing. Therefore the lower wing generates more lift and tends to restore the airplane to a wings-level position.

Figure 2-18. Wing dihedral

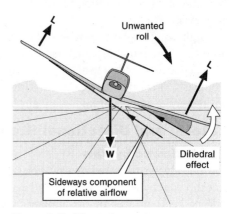

Figure 2-19. Dihedral corrects an uninvited roll

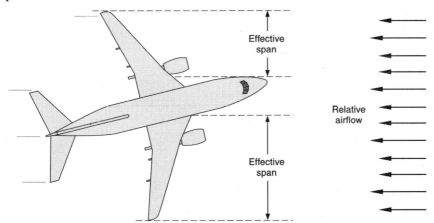

Figure 2-20. Sweepback corrects uninvited roll

High Keel Surfaces and Low CG

In the sideslip that follows a disturbance in roll, a high sideways drag line caused by high keel surfaces (high vertical stabilizer, a T-tail high on the vertical stabilizer, or high wings) and a low CG will give a restoring moment tending to raise the lower wing and return the airplane to the original wings-level position. *See* Figure 2-21.

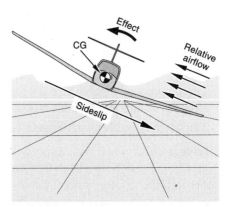

Figure 2-21. High keel surfaces and a low CG correct uninvited roll

High-Wing Airplanes

If a wind gust causes a wing to drop, the lift force is tilted, and the airplane will sideslip. The airflow striking the upper keel surfaces, including the high wings, will tend to return the airplane to the wings-level condition.

The increased stability of a high-wing airplane also comes from the pendulum effect when the airplane rolls. The CG is displaced from vertically beneath the CP and so a couple is established which tends to roll the airplane wings-level. Conversely, a low wing, below the airplane's CG, will be unstable. This is apparent when observing the difference in dihedrals of high- and low-wing airplanes.

High-wing airplanes have more lateral stability (by virtue of their wing position) than low-wing airplanes and therefore require significantly less, perhaps even negative, dihedral to achieve the required lateral stability. The McDonnell Douglas C-17, Lockheed C-141 Starlifter and British Aerospace 146 regional airliner are examples of high-wing airplanes with negative dihedral.

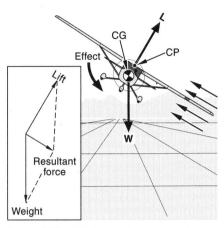

Figure 2-22. A high wing tends to level the wings

Lateral and Directional Stability Together

Roll Followed by Yaw

A roll is always followed by yaw. For lateral stability it is essential to have the sideslip which the disturbance in roll causes. This sideslip exerts a force on the side or keel surfaces of the airplane, which, if the airplane is directionally stable, will cause it to yaw its nose into the relative airflow. The roll has caused a yaw in the direction of the sideslip and the airplane will turn further off its original heading in the direction of the lower wing.

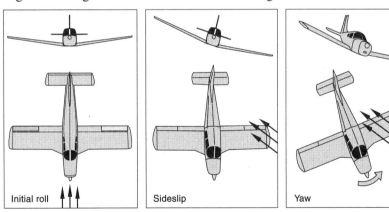

Initial roll | Sideslip | Yaw

Figure 2-23. Roll causes yaw

Note this interesting consequence: the greater the directional stability of the airplane, the greater the tendency to turn away from the original heading in the direction of the lower wing when the airplane is banked.

The lateral stability characteristics of the airplane, such as those resulting from wing dihedral, cause the lower wing to produce increased lift and to return the airplane to the wings-level position. There are two effects in conflict here.

1. The directionally stable characteristics (large vertical stabilizer) want to steepen the turn and drop the nose further.

2. The laterally stable characteristics (dihedral) want to level the wings.

If the first effect wins, with directional stability overriding lateral stability, (large vertical stabilizer and no dihedral), then the airplane will tend to bank further into the sideslip, toward the lower wing, with the nose continuing to drop, until the airplane is in a spiral dive (and all this without any input from the pilot). This is called **spiral instability.**

Most airplanes are designed with only weak positive lateral stability and have a slight tendency toward spiral instability. This is preferable to Dutch roll (*see* Figure 2-24).

If the lateral stability (dihedral) is stronger, the airplane will right itself to wings-level, and if the directional stability is weak (small vertical stabilizer) the airplane may have shown no tendency to turn in the direction of sideslip and may even turn away from the sideslip, causing a wallowing effect known as **Dutch roll,** which is best avoided.

Yaw Followed by Roll

If the airplane is displaced in yaw, it will initially continue in the original direction of flight because of its inertia, and therefore enter a sideslip. This sideslip will cause the lateral stability features of the airplane's wing such as dihedral, sweepback or a high-wing, to increase lift on the forward wing and decrease lift on the trailing wing. This causes a rolling moment that will tend to raise the forward wing, resulting in the airplane rolling toward the trailing wing and away from the sideslip. Yaw causes roll.

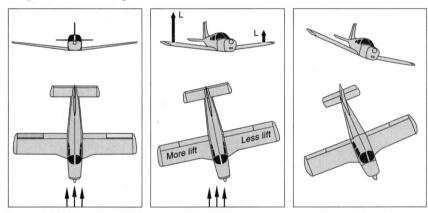

Figure 2-24. Yaw causes roll

Another point to note is that, as the airplane is actually yawing, the outer wing will move faster and produce more lift than the inner wing, giving a tendency to roll toward the inner wing. The airplane's inherent directional stability (from the vertical stabilizer) will tend to weathercock or yaw the airplane in the direction of the sideslip.

Note that a roll causes a yaw and a yaw causes a roll, and the two effects need to be studied together.

Stability on the Ground

On the ground, the center of gravity (CG) of an airplane must lie somewhere in the area between the three wheels at all times. The further away the CG is from any one wheel, the less the tendency for the airplane to tip over that wheel.

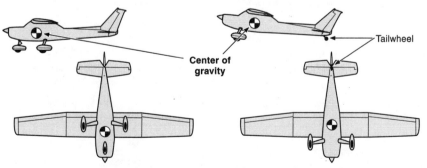

Figure 2-25. The CG must remain within the area bounded by the wheels

A low CG and widely spaced wheels reduces the tendency for the airplane to tip over on the ground when turning, braking the airplane, or when applying high power on takeoff.

A low thrust-line reduces the tendency for an airplane to pitch over on its nose when high power is applied (especially with brakes on). High keel surfaces and dihedral allow crosswinds to have a greater destabilizing effect.

You can keep moving in a straight line on the ground using the rudder pedals to maintain directional control and using the control wheel to prevent any crosswind from lifting the upwind wing. This is covered in Chapter 10.

✍ Now complete **Review 2, Part (a)** on page 56.

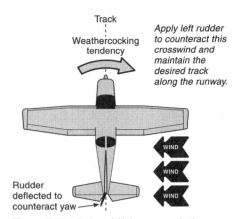
Figure 2-26. A destabilizing crosswind

Control

All airplanes have a control system to allow the pilot to maneuver the airplane in flight about each of the three axes. Airplanes normally have three **primary control** systems, and each one is equipped with its own control surface(s):

- the **elevators** for the longitudinal (pitch) control system, operated by forward and rearward movement of the control wheel or column;
- the **ailerons** for the lateral (roll) control system, operated by rotation of the control wheel or by sideways movement of the control column; and
- the **rudder** for the directional (yaw) control system, operated by movement of the two interconnected rudder pedals.

Ideally, each set of control surfaces should produce a moment about only one axis, but in practice *secondary* moments about other axes are often produced as well. For example, if an airplane yaws it will then start to roll.

The control surfaces work by deflecting airflow and changing the pressure distribution over the whole airfoil, not just over the control surface itself. The effect is to change the aerodynamic force produced by the total airfoil— control surface combination. The effectiveness of moving these control surfaces will partially determine the airplane's maneuverability.

As mentioned earlier, an airplane with too much stability designed into it (thereby making it very resistant to change) has poor maneuverability. Excessive stability opposes maneuverability.

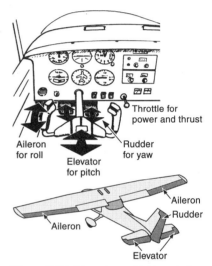
Figure 2-27. The primary flight controls: elevator, ailerons and rudder

The Elevator

The pilot controls the elevator by forward and rearward movement of the control column. A forward movement of the control column moves the elevator down which has the effect of pushing the nose of the airplane down. Rearward movement of the control column moves the elevator up, which has the effect of pulling the nose of the airplane up. These movements will become logical and instinctive to you.

When the control column is moved forward, the elevator moves down and the horizontal stabilizer section becomes cambered so that it provides an upward aerodynamic force. This creates an upward force on the tail section of the airplane and a moment about the airplane's CG that moves the nose down. A further effect of pitching the nose down with the elevator is a gradual increase in airspeed.

When the control column is pulled back, the elevator moves up and an extra downward aerodynamic force is produced by the horizontal stabilizer airfoil, causing the nose of the airplane to move up. The strength of the tail moment depends on the force produced by it and the length of the moment arm between it and the CG.

The primary control in the pitching plane is provided by the elevator.

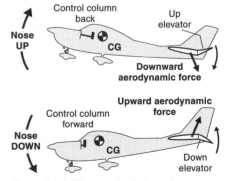
Figure 2-28. The elevator is the primary pitching control

CG Position

To retain satisfactory handling characteristics and elevator effectiveness throughout the airplane's entire speed range, the position of the CG must be kept within the prescribed range. If the **CG is too far forward,** the airplane will be too longitudinally stable because of the long moment arm to the horizontal stabilizer. Even with the control column pulled fully back there will be insufficient up-elevator to reach the high angles-of-attack and low speeds sometimes required in maneuvers such as flying slowly, taking off and landing. Therefore, the **forward allowable CG limit** is determined by the amount of pitch control available from the elevator. The **aft (rear) limit of the CG** is determined by the requirement for longitudinal stability.

Usually, the most critical situation for a nose-up requirement is in the flare and landing. A forward CG makes the airplane nose-heavy and resistant to changes in pitch. This may make it difficult to raise the nose during a landing, especially since the elevator will be less effective because of the reduced airflow over it due both to the slow landing speed and weak slipstream (low power).

If the CG is too far forward, the airplane will be too longitudinally stable. If the CG is too far aft the airplane will be longitudinally unstable.

Figure 2-29. Elevator control in the landing flare is critical

The Stabilator

Some designers combine the horizontal stabilizer and elevator into one airfoil and have the whole tailplane movable. A combined horizontal stabilizer/elevator combination is called a **stabilator.** Other terms include all-moving tail, all-flying tail and slab tail. When the control column is moved the entire slab moves. Forward movement of the control column increases the angle-of-attack of the stabilator, thereby generating a force that causes the tail to rise).

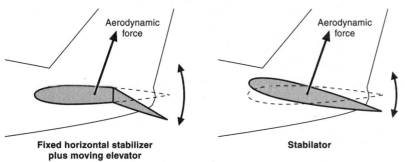

Figure 2-30. Separate horizontal stabilizer and elevator (left) and stabilator (right)

Butterfly or V-tail
Figure 2-31. A butterfly tail (early Beech Bonanza model)

Some airplanes have a V-tail (butterfly tail), which combines the functions of the elevator and rudder.

The Ailerons

The ailerons are usually positioned on the outboard trailing edges of the wings. The ailerons act in opposing senses, one goes up as the other goes down, so that the lift generated by one wing increases and the lift generated by the other wing decreases. The pilot operates the ailerons with rotation of the control wheel or sideways movement of the control column.

A resultant rolling moment is exerted on the airplane. The magnitude of this rolling moment depends on the distance the ailerons are from the airplane's CG (fixed at construction), and the magnitude of the differing lift forces (determined by the degree of aileron deflection and airspeed).

Note that the aileron on the upgoing wing is deflected downward. Conversely, the aileron on the downgoing wing is deflected upward.

The primary control in roll is provided by the ailerons.

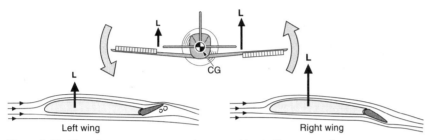

Figure 2-32. The ailerons–one up, one down–provide a rolling moment

Adverse Aileron Yaw

Adverse aileron yaw is caused by differential aileron drag. Deflecting an aileron down causes an effective increase in the camber of that wing section and an increase in the effective angle-of-attack. The lift from that wing increases, but unfortunately so does the drag. As the other aileron rises, the effective camber of that wing section is decreased and its angle-of-attack is less, therefore lift and drag from that wing is decreased. The differing lift causes the airplane to bank one way, but the differential aileron drag causes it to yaw the other way. This is known as *aileron drag* or *adverse aileron yaw* and is mainly a low airspeed problem that you would notice with a turn at low speed shortly after takeoff.

Adverse aileron yaw can be reduced by good design incorporating differential ailerons, Frise-type ailerons, or coupling the rudder to the ailerons.

Differential ailerons are designed to minimize adverse aileron yaw by increasing the drag on the downgoing wing. This is achieved by deflecting the upward aileron (on the descending wing) through a greater angle than the downgoing aileron (on the upgoing wing). The greater aileron deflection means that drag is increased on the downgoing wing, reducing (but not eliminating) the adverse yaw. The remaining unwanted yaw can be removed with rudder.

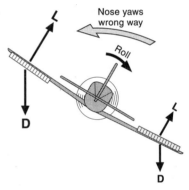

Figure 2-33. The rising wing has increased aileron drag, causing adverse aileron yaw

Differential ailerons overcome adverse aileron yaw.

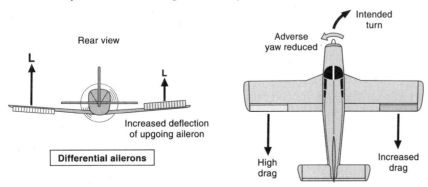

Figure 2-34. Differential ailerons reduce adverse yaw

Frise-type ailerons are shaped so that the drag from the descending wing is increased. The leading edge of the Frise aileron on the downgoing wing protrudes into the airstream beneath the wing causing increased drag on the downgoing wing. The leading edge of the upgoing aileron does not protrude into the airstream, causing no extra drag.

Frise-type ailerons can also be designed to operate differentially, thereby combining both effects.

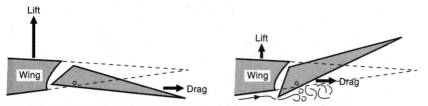

Figure 2-35. Frise-type ailerons equalize aileron drag and reduce adverse yaw

Coupled ailerons and rudder cause the rudder to move automatically and yaw the airplane into the bank, opposing the adverse yaw from the ailerons.

Note the interconnection between roll and yaw throughout this discussion. The primary effect of the ailerons is to roll the airplane, and the secondary effect is to yaw it. The primary effect of the rudder is to yaw the airplane, and the secondary effect is to roll it. Using the rudder to neutralize adverse yaw, with the ailerons deflected and the airplane rolling is one of the most important elements of airplane control by the pilot.

Roll is Followed by Yaw

When the airplane is banked using the ailerons, the lift force is tilted and the airplane will slip in the direction of the tilted lift force. As a result of the slip the airflow will strike the side of the airplane and the large keel surfaces (such as the vertical stabilizer), which are mainly behind the CG. This causes the nose of the airplane to yaw progressively in the direction of bank. Roll is followed by yaw.

Note: While the ailerons are deflected, there may be a small amount of adverse aileron yaw opposite to the direction of bank, but, once established in the bank with the ailerons neutral, the airplane will yaw progressively toward the lower wing. It will gradually enter a spiral descent and lose altitude unless the pilot does something about it, such as leveling the wings and exerting back pressure on the control column.

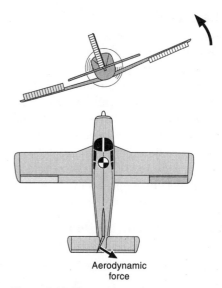

Figure 2-36. The rudder coupled to the aileron can reduce adverse yaw

The secondary effect of ailerons is to cause yaw.

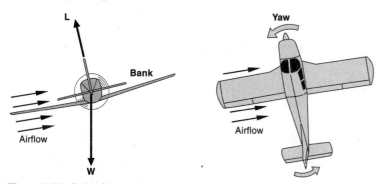

Figure 2-37. Roll is followed by yaw

The Rudder

To control and eliminate unwanted yaw, the airplane has a rudder. The rudder does not turn the airplane, it yaws it, which by itself, does not cause any change in flight path direction.

By pushing the left rudder pedal, the rudder will move left. This alters the vertical stabilizer–rudder airfoil section and a sideways aerodynamic force is created that moves the tail to the right and yaws the airplane to the left about the normal axis. Left rudder—the airplane yaws left.

Rudder effectiveness increases with airspeed, so large rudder deflections at low airspeeds and small deflections at high airspeeds are required to gain the same effect. In propeller-driven airplanes, any **slipstream** flowing over the rudder will increase rudder effectiveness.

Yaw is Followed by Roll

The primary effect of rudder is to yaw the airplane. This causes the outer wing to speed up, generate increased lift, and cause the airplane to roll. When it has begun to yaw, the airplane will continue on its original flight path for a brief period because of inertia. Any dihedral on the forward wing will cause it to be presented to the airflow at a greater angle-of-attack and therefore generate more lift. Consequently, having first yawed the airplane, the secondary effect of the rudder is to cause a roll.

Control Effectiveness

The size and shape of a control surface and its moment about the center of gravity primarily determine its effectiveness. Since the size and shape are fixed by the designer, and the CG (with the airplane loaded within limits) only moves a small amount, they can all be considered constant.

The variables in control effectiveness are **airspeed** and **control deflection.** For a given amount of control deflection, if the airspeed is doubled, the effect is squared ($2 \times 2 = 4$), so it quadruples. If the airspeed is halved, the same control surface deflection is only one-quarter as effective. Therefore, at low airspeeds, achieving a nominated change in attitude requires a much greater control-surface deflection (often referred to as *sloppy controls* or *less-effective controls*).

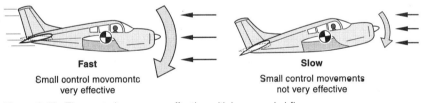

Figure 2-40. The controls are more effective with increased airflow

Slipstream Effect

Any factor that increases the speed of the airflow over a control surface will make it more effective. Such an increase in airflow does not necessarily have to be achieved by an increase in the airplane's forward speed. For instance, with high engine power set, the propeller slipstream (or *propwash*) of a single-engine airplane will flow strongly back over the empennage, making the elevators and rudder more effective, even at low airspeeds.

Approaching the stall with power on, the elevator and rudder will be more effective than the ailerons, because of the propeller slipstream flowing over them. The slipstream helps when taxiing single-engine tailwheel airplanes because power application increases rudder effectiveness.

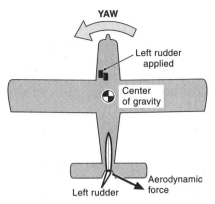

Figure 2-38. Left rudder pressure—the nose yaws left

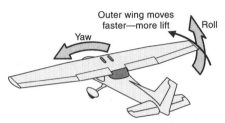

Figure 2-39. Yaw is followed by roll

Controls are more effective in a strong airflow.

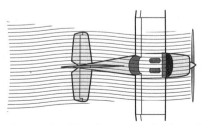

Figure 2-41. The slipstream only affects the elevator and rudder

Control Pressures on the Pilot

When a control surface is deflected, the aerodynamic force produced by the control surface itself opposes its own deflection. This causes a moment to act on the control surface about its hinge-line trying to return the control surface to its original faired (streamlined) position, and the pilot must overcome this to maintain the selected position. The pilot feels this as *stick force*.

Aerodynamic Balances

The stick force depends on the turning moment at the hinge-line of the control surface and the means by which the control column is linked to the control surface. If the control surface is hinged at its leading edge and trails from this position in flight, the stick forces required will be high, especially in heavy or fast airplanes. These forces can be made smaller by the designer adding an **aerodynamic balance,** which reduces the stick load on the pilot.

The designer may use an **inset hinge,** a **horn balance** or a **servo tab** to provide an aerodynamic force during control surface deflection that partially balances or reduces the hinge moment. The aerodynamic balance of a control surface is designed to reduce the control forces required from the pilot. The designer, however, must be careful not to over-balance the controls, otherwise the pilot will lose the important sense of feel.

An **inset hinge** reduces the distance from the hinge line to the control's center of pressure, which reduces the moment that the pilot feels as stick load. In addition, the part of the control ahead of the hinge protrudes into the airflow causing a turning moment which assists the pilot by reducing the stick load.

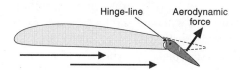

Figure 2-42. Hinge moment at the control surface

An aerodynamic balance on a control reduces the stick load on the pilot.

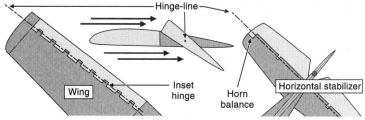

Figure 2-43. Inset hinge balance (at left) and horn balance (at right)

On conventional tailplanes it is quite common to have a **servo tab** incorporated as part of the elevator. It is mechanically connected to the elevator by a linkage that causes it to move in the opposite direction.

If the pilot exerts back pressure on the control column, the elevator is raised and the servo tab goes down. The elevator servo tab unit now generates a small upward aerodynamic force that acts to hold the elevator up, thereby reducing the control effort required from the pilot.

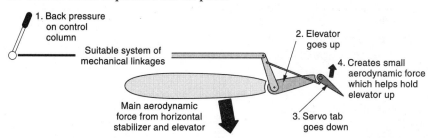

Figure 2-44. The servo tab

Note: The servo tab acts automatically as the elevator moves. This movement should be checked in the preflight inspection by moving the elevator one way and noting that the tab moves the other way.

Trim Tabs

An airplane is "in trim" in pitch, roll or yaw when it maintains a steady state of flight without the pilot having to exert any steady pressure on the particular control surface.

An airplane that you have trimmed properly is far more pleasant to fly than an untrimmed airplane. It requires control inputs only to maneuver and not to maintain an attitude or heading. The function of the **trim tab** is to reduce the moment at the hinge-line of the control surface to approximately zero, so that the present condition of flight can be maintained almost hands-off.

Almost all airplanes have an elevator trim, many light single-engine and all multi-engine airplanes have a rudder trim, and more sophisticated airplanes also have an aileron trim.

Trim tabs can differ in complexity, from metal strips that can only be altered on the ground, or springs that can apply a load to the control column, to trim tabs that the pilot can operate from the cockpit, usually by a trim wheel or trim handle, which may be mechanical or electrical.

The method of trimming is to hold the airplane in the attitude you want with control pressures and then trim these pressures out to zero. As you trim, the relevant control pressure can be gradually relaxed until it is zero. Do not use the trim to change the attitude of the airplane.

Although the control surface may be moved by the pilot to maneuver the airplane, the trim tab itself will remain in the same fixed position relative to the control surface until the pilot decides to retrim. There is a small proviso to this: some tabs perform a dual function, both as a trim tab and as an aerodynamic balance as the control surface moves. Its average position will be trimmed in by the pilot and it will vary about this mean position automatically to serve its other function of balancing control-surface movements. Such an arrangement is usually called a **trim-servo tab.**

The airplane will stay in trim until the power changes, the airspeed changes, or the CG position changes. You should then retrim. Airplanes with stabilators usually have the elevator trim incorporated so that trimming moves the entire slab.

Mass Balancing

At high speeds some control surfaces have a tendency to flutter. This is a vibration that results from the changes in pressure distribution over the surface as its angle-of-attack is altered. If part of the airframe structure starts to vibrate—control surfaces are particularly susceptible to this—then these oscillations can quickly reach structurally damaging proportions. To avoid this flutter, the designer may need to alter the mass distribution of the surface.

The **mass balance** is placed forward of the hinge-line to bring the CG of the control surface up to the hinge-line or even slightly ahead of it. On the inset hinge or horn balance this mass can easily be incorporated in that part ahead of the hinge line, but on others the mass must be placed on an arm that extends forward of the hinge-line. The distribution of mass on control surfaces is an important design consideration.

Note: The aim of mass-balancing is not for the control to be balanced in the sense of remaining level, but to alter the mass-distribution of the control to avoid flutter or vibration.

Anti-Servo Tab

Because of their combined function, stabilators have a much larger area than elevators and so produce a more powerful response to control input, and small movements can produce large aerodynamic forces. To prevent you from

Trim tabs are designed to remove the stick load on the pilot.

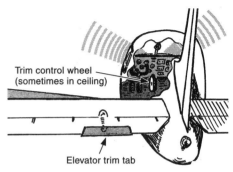
Trim control wheel (sometimes in ceiling)

Elevator trim tab

Figure 2-45. An elevator trim tab

A mass balance prevents flutter.

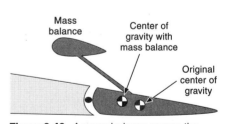
Mass balance

Center of gravity with mass balance

Original center of gravity

Figure 2-46. A mass balance moves the control's CG forward to prevent flutter

An anti-servo tab increases the stick load on the pilot to prevent overcontrolling.

moving the stabilator too far and overcontrolling the airplane (especially at high airspeeds), stabilators are often designed with **anti-servo tabs.**

An anti-servo tab moves in the *same* direction as the stabilator's trailing edge and generates an aerodynamic force that makes it harder to move the stabilator further, as well as providing feel for the pilot.

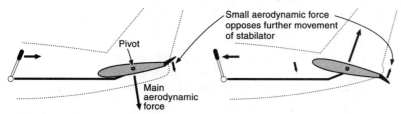

Figure 2-47. The anti-servo tab opposes further control deflection and provides feel

Correct operation of the anti-servo tab can be checked in the preflight inspection by moving the trailing edge of the stabilator and noting that the anti-servo tab moves in the same direction.

Summary of Controls

The **primary controls** are the elevator, ailerons and rudder. The elevator is used to control pitch, the aileron is used to control bank angle, and the rudder is used to eliminate unwanted yaw during coordinated flight and yaw the airplane during aerobatics or just prior to a crosswind touchdown.

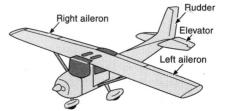

Figure 2-48. Airplane primary controls

Plane	Axis	Control	Primary Effect	Secondary Effect
pitch	lateral	**ELEVATOR**	pitch	airspeed change
roll	longitudinal	**AILERONS**	roll	yaw
yaw	normal	**RUDDER**	yaw	roll

Other controls available to the pilot include the throttle, propeller-pitch control (for constant-speed propellers), mixture control, carburetor heat, flaps (wing flaps and cowl flaps), and landing gear operating lever (for airplanes with retractable landing gear). These are covered in the next section of this volume.

Although the **throttle** is an ancillary control, it affects the airplane in flight sufficiently for us to consider it briefly here. The initial effect of applying throttle is to increase power and thrust. This in turn increases the thrust–drag nose-up turning moment and pitches the nose up. The increased slipstream over the horizontal stabilizer will increase its downward aerodynamic force, which unless opposed, will raise the nose. The corkscrewing slipstream effect on the vertical stabilizer will cause the airplane to yaw unless counteracted by rudder.

With a propeller rotating clockwise as seen from behind, applying power will raise the nose and yaw the airplane to the left (counteracted by forward pressure on the control column and application of right rudder). When the power is removed, the nose will tend to drop and yaw to the right (counteracted by holding the pitch attitude with back pressure and applying left rudder).

Control on the Ground

Directional control on the ground is achieved by use of the rudder, nosewheel steering (which may be connected to the rudder pedals), power and brakes. Airflow over the rudder increases its effectiveness. Use of the controls on the ground is covered in Chapter 10.

✍ Now complete **Review 2, Part (b)** on page 57.

✍ Commercial students complete **Review 2, Commercial** on page 58.

Part (a)

Stability and Control

1. Following a disturbance, an airplane that returns to its original position unassisted by the pilot is easier to control and is said to be inherently _____.

➤ stable

2. An inherently stable airplane is (easier/more difficult) to fly.

➤ easier

3. If the center of pressure is behind the center of gravity, the lift–weight couple will have a (nose-down/nose-up) pitching moment.

➤ nose-down

4. If the thrust line is lower than the drag line, then the thrust–drag couple will have a (nose-up/nose-down) pitching moment.

➤ nose-up

5. In Questions 3 and 4, if there was a sudden loss of thrust, the nose would (pitch up/pitch down/neither).

➤ pitch down

6. In most training airplanes, the center of pressure is (ahead of/behind/at the same position as) the center of gravity and the horizontal stabilizer produces (an upward/zero/a downward) aerodynamic force.

➤ behind, a downward

7. Most airplanes, other than T-tails, are designed so that the propeller slipstream strikes the horizontal stabilizer and elevators from (above/below), causing a (nose-up/nose-down) moment.

➤ above, nose-up

8. When power is reduced, the reduced propeller slipstream and reduced (upwash/downwash) over the horizontal stabilizer will cause the nose to (rise/drop).

➤ downwash, drop

9. Longitudinal stability refers to the motion of the airplane about its:
   (a) longitudinal axis.
   (b) lateral axis.
   (c) normal axis (sometimes called *vertical axis*).

➤ (b)

10. The axis that runs "across-ship" is called the _____ axis, and rotation about this axis is called _____ .

➤ lateral, pitching

11. The axis that is perpendicular or normal to the longitudinal and lateral axes is called the _____ axis, and rotation about it is called _____ .

➤ normal (or vertical), yawing

12. The most important factor contributing to longitudinal stability is the _____ .

➤ horizontal stabilizer

13. Longitudinal stability is greater with a (forward/aft) CG.

➤ forward

14. An airplane loaded with the CG too far aft will be (stable/unstable) at (slow/fast/all) speeds, and if stalled will be (difficult/easy) to recover.

➤ unstable, all, difficult

15. If the airplane is loaded incorrectly so that the CG is forward of the allowable range, then the elevator force required to flare the airplane for landing will be:
    (a) the same as usual.
    (b) greater than usual.
    (c) less than usual.

➤ (b)

16. A forward CG location will cause an airplane to be more (stable/unstable) at (high/low/all) speeds.

➤ more stable at all speeds

17. Directional stability is improved with a (large/small) _____ stabilizer.

➤ large vertical stabilizer

18. Lateral stability is increased if a wing has_____ or_____.

➤ dihedral, sweepback

19. If an airplane is yawed, then it will sideslip and the dihedral will cause it to _____ .

➤ roll

20. Roll and (pitch/yaw) are very closely interrelated.

➤ yaw

Part (b)

1. The primary control in pitch is provided by the _____.

➤ elevator

2. Nose movement up and down is in the _____plane. It involves angular movement around its center of gravity and its _____ axis.

➤ pitching, lateral

3. To raise the nose and lower the tail of the airplane, the trailing edge of the elevator moves (up/down).

➤ up

4. If you load the airplane incorrectly with the center of gravity beyond the forward limit, the airplane will be excessively (stable/unstable), which may make it (easy/difficult) to flare on landing.

➤ stable, difficult

5. If you load the airplane incorrectly with the center of gravity beyond the aft limit, the airplane will be excessively (stable/unstable), which may make it (difficult/easy) to fly smoothly.

➤ unstable, difficult

6. The primary control in roll is by the_____ .

➤ ailerons

7. Rolling is angular motion about the _____ axis running through the CG.

➤ longitudinal

8. For the right wing to rise, the pilot moves the control column to the _____ .

➤ left

9. At normal flight speeds, for the right wing to rise, the right aileron will go (down/up) and the left aileron will go (down/up).

➤ go down, up

10. The area below the wing has (higher/lower) static pressure than the area above the wing.

➤ higher

11. As an airplane is banking to the left for a left turn, the extra drag on the right aileron will tend to yaw the nose (in the direction of/away from) the turn.

➤ away from

12. Adverse aileron yaw can be reduced by the use of _____ or by _____-type ailerons.

➤ differential ailerons, Frise-type ailerons

13. If differential ailerons are used to counteract the effect of adverse aileron yaw, one aileron will rise by an amount (greater than/less than/the same as) the other aileron is lowered.

➤ greater than

14. The primary control in yaw is provided by the _____ .

➤ rudder

15. Yawing occurs about the _____ axis that passes through the CG. Another name for this axis is the _____ axis.

➤ normal, vertical

16. Yawing increases the speed of the outer wing causing its lift to (increase/decrease), leading to a _____ .

➤ increase, roll

17. Yaw also generates a sideslip, and the dihedral on the more forward wing will cause it to (rise/fall).

➤ rise

18. At high airspeeds the control surfaces are (more/less) effective than at low airspeeds.

➤ more

19. Slipstream from the propeller over the rudder and elevators (increases/decreases) their effectiveness.

➤ increases

20. An airplane designer may use *aerodynamic balance*, such as the _____, _____, or _____ to (reduce/remove) the control pressures required on a pilot.

➤ servo tab, horn balance, inset hinge, reduce

21. The correct method of using elevator trim is to:
   (a) change the attitude with elevator and/or the power with the throttle, allow the airplane to settle down, and then use the trim to remove steady control column pressure.
   (b) change the attitude with the trim.
   (c) change attitude, power and trim simultaneously.

➤ (a)

22. An anti-servo tab may be designed into a flight control surface to:
   (a) provide "feel" to the pilot and prevent excessive control movements.
   (b) prevent control surface flutter.
   (c) aerodynamically assist the pilot in moving the flight control surface.

➤ (a)

23. If the stabilator is moved in the preflight external inspection, then the anti-servo tab should:
    (a) move in the same direction.
    (b) move in the opposite direction.
    (c) not move.
➤ (a)

24. If the elevator is moved in the preflight external inspection, then the servo tab should:
    (a) move in the same direction.
    (b) move in the opposite direction.
    (c) not move.
➤ (b)

25. A mass balance is used to:
    (a) prevent control surface flutter in flight.
    (b) keep the control surface flared in flight.
    (c) relieve control pressures on the pilot.
➤ (a)

Commercial Review

1. The initial tendency of an airplane to return to its original attitude after being disturbed is called positive (static/dynamic) stability.
➤ positive static stability

2. If the airplane attitude remains in a new position after the control column is pressed forward and released, the airplane is said to display:
    (a) negative longitudinal static stability.
    (b) neutral longitudinal dynamic stability.
    (c) positive longitudinal static stability.
    (d) neutral longitudinal static stability.
➤ (d)

3. If the airplane attitude oscillates about its original position before gradually settling down after the control column is pressed forward and released, the airplane is said to display:
    (a) positive dynamic stability.
    (b) neutral static stability.
    (c) negative dynamic stability.
    (d) neutral dynamic stability.
➤ (a)

4. The longitudinal stability of an airplane is determined by:
    (a) the location of the CG with respect to the center of pressure.
    (b) the effectiveness of the horizontal stabilizer, rudder and rudder trim tab.
    (c) the relationship of thrust and lift to weight and drag.
    (d) the dihedral, sweepback angle, and the keel effect.
➤ (a)

5. Longitudinal dynamic instability in an airplane can be identified by:
    (a) bank oscillations becoming progressively steeper.
    (b) pitch oscillations becoming progressively steeper.
    (c) the need to apply continuous forward pressure on the control column.
➤ (b)

6. Longitudinal stability involves the motion of the airplane about its:
    (a) vertical axis.
    (b) lateral axis.
    (c) longitudinal axis.
➤ (b)

7. An airplane remains in a new attitude after the control column is pressed forward and released. The airplane displays:
    (a) neutral longitudinal static stability.
    (b) positive longitudinal static stability.
    (c) neutral longitudinal dynamic stability.
➤ (a)

Basic Flight Maneuvers **3**

Straight-and-Level Flight

In steady unaccelerated straight-and-level flight the airplane is in equilibrium. This means that all the forces acting on it cancel each other out and there is no resultant force to accelerate or decelerate it. Acceleration is a change in velocity, which means a change in speed or a change in direction, or both. In steady unaccelerated straight-and-level flight, the airplane is not forced to change either speed or direction.

The **four main forces** acting on the airplane are **lift, weight, thrust** and **drag.** We assume that thrust acts in the direction of flight, shown in Figure 3-1. Each of the four main forces has its own point of action:

- the **lift** through the **center of pressure;**
- the **weight** through the **center of gravity;**
- the **thrust** and the **drag** in opposite senses, parallel to the direction of flight, through points that vary with airplane attitude and design.

We make the assumption that the thrust force from the engine–propeller is acting in the direction of flight, even though this is not quite always the case. For instance, at a high angle-of-attack and slow airspeed the airplane has a nose-high attitude with the propeller shaft inclined upward to the horizontal direction of flight. This assumption that thrust acts in the direction of flight simplifies our discussion considerably.

In unaccelerated straight-and-level flight:

> **Lift = Weight** and **Thrust = Drag.**

The lift force is much larger than the drag force, usually by a ratio of about 10:1. For in-depth study and revision of each of these forces and their interaction, you should refer back to Chapter 1 and Chapter 2.

For straight-and-level flight at constant weight, the lift required will be constant. For a given airfoil, each angle-of-attack has a particular lifting ability. At low speed a high angle-of-attack (high lifting ability) is needed to maintain altitude, while at high speed only a small angle-of-attack (low lifting ability) is required.

Since we are considering level flight, the pilot *sees* the angle-of-attack as the pitch attitude of the airplane relative to the horizon—nose-up at low speeds and approximately nose-level at high speeds.

The Effect of Weight

In flight the weight gradually reduces as fuel is burned-off. If the airplane is to fly level, the lift produced must gradually decrease as the weight reduces. If there is a sudden decrease in weight, say by parachutists jumping out, then to maintain straight-and-level flight the lift must also reduce.

In Chapter 1 we said that if the airplane wing shape and area are kept constant by not using the flaps, then lift depends only on angle-of-attack and airspeed. Therefore to reduce lift either angle-of-attack or airspeed must be reduced.

In steady straight-and-level flight, lift equals weight and thrust equals drag.

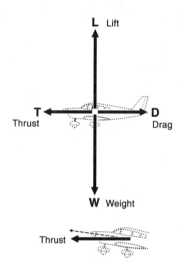

Figure 3-1. The four main forces

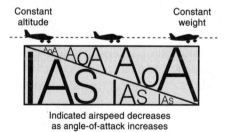

Indicated airspeed decreases as angle-of-attack increases

Figure 3-2. Indicated airspeed varies inversely with angle-of-attack

Suppose that an airplane is flying at a particular angle-of-attack, say at that for the best L/D ratio (about 4°). As weight gradually reduces, lift must also be reduced to remain equal to weight. If lift is to be reduced without altering the angle-of-attack, the airspeed must gradually be decreased. The power (thrust) will also need to be reduced because drag will decrease as lift decreases.

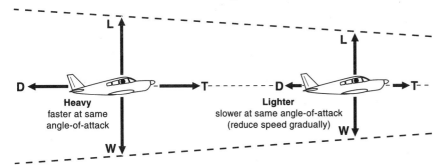

Figure 3-3. At a constant angle-of-attack, a lighter airplane must fly slower

If the power (thrust) is kept constant and you want to maintain altitude as the weight decreases, the lift must be decreased by lowering the angle-of-attack. The speed will then increase until the thrust produced by the engine–propeller is equal to the drag (which increases as the speed increases). This is the normal technique for the cruise in small training airplanes.

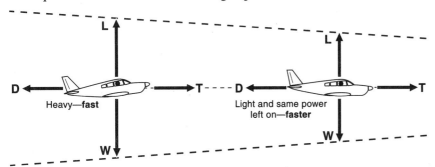

Figure 3-4. Same power–lighter airplane has a lower angle-of-attack and flies faster

If you want to keep the speed constant and maintain altitude, then as the weight reduces you must reduce the lift produced, and you do this by decreasing the angle-of-attack. In cruise flight this will mean less drag, and therefore the power required from the engine–propeller is less. If the power is not reduced as the weight decreases, the airspeed will increase.

   If your aim is to maintain a constant airspeed without reducing power, then you would need to slightly raise the nose to avoid the airspeed increasing. The airplane would then commence a climb and gradually a new set of equilibrium conditions (balance of forces) would establish themselves for a steady climb— no longer level flight. (This is covered in the next part of this chapter where we deal with *climbing and descending.*)

A very practical relationship to remember is that:

Power + Attitude = Performance (airspeed or rate of climb)

If you have excess power, you can adjust the pitch attitude so that altitude is maintained and airspeed increases; or you can maintain the pitch attitude and airspeed and accept a rate of climb.

✍ Now complete **Review 3, Part (a)** on page 88.

Climbing and Descending

Climbs

As an airplane climbs, it gains potential energy (the energy of position, in this case because of altitude). There are two ways an airplane can do this:

- by making a zoom climb;
- by a steady, long term climb.

Zoom climb. A zoom climb exchanges the kinetic energy of motion for potential energy by exchanging high velocity for an increase in altitude. Therefore, kinetic energy *reduces* while potential energy increases, and (kinetic + potential) energy remains the same. It is only a transient (temporary) process, as the velocity cannot be decreased below flying speed. Of course, the greater the speed range of the airplane the greater the capability of the zoom. For example, a jet fighter being pursued at high speed can gain altitude rapidly with a zoom, or an aerobatic glider that converts the kinetic energy of a dive into potential energy at the top of a loop. An airplane can zoom as long as it is above its stall speed.

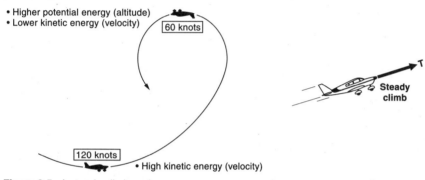

- Higher potential energy (altitude)
- Lower kinetic energy (velocity)

60 knots

Steady climb

120 knots
- High kinetic energy (velocity)

Figure 3-5. A steady climb and a zoom

Steady climb. In a steady climb, kinetic energy remains *constant* while potential energy increases. This increase in (kinetic + potential) energy is provided by the additional fuel which is burnt in the airplane engine during the climb. It is the steady climb that is of importance in day-to-day flying. To enter a steady climb, raise the nose (which temporarily increases the angle-of-attack) and add power. The airplane will quickly settle into a steady climb.

Forces in the Climb

In a steady en route climb the thrust force acts in the direction of flight, directly opposite to the drag force. The lift force acts perpendicular to the relative airflow and is no longer vertical. The weight force acts vertically, but note how, in the climb, it has a component that acts in the direction opposing flight. If you maintain a **steady climb** at a constant indicated airspeed, the engine–propeller must supply sufficient thrust to:

- overcome the drag force; and
- help lift the weight of the airplane at a vertical speed (known as rate of climb).

In a steady climb there is no acceleration. The forces are in equilibrium, with the up forces equaling the down forces, and the forward forces equaling the rearward forces. Consequently, the resultant force acting on the airplane is zero.

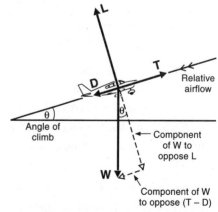

L

D

T

Relative airflow

θ

Angle of climb

θ

Component of W to oppose L

W

Component of W to oppose (T – D)

Figure 3-6. The four forces in equilibrium in a steady climb

Types of Climb

There are three types of climb, each with a different purpose.

- A **maximum angle climb** is used to clear obstacles, as it gains the greatest altitude for a given *horizontal distance.* By definition it is the steepest climb (maximum gradient) and is flown at a relatively slow airspeed, referred to as V_X. Because the slow airspeed results in reduced cooling and higher engine temperatures, it should only be used for short periods while clearing obstacles.

- A **maximum rate climb** is used to reach cruise altitude as quickly as possible, as it gains the greatest altitude in a given *time.* Maximum rate of climb speed is known as V_Y. The airspeed is faster than V_X and is usually somewhere near the speed for the best lift/drag ratio. It is a shallower climb than the maximum angle climb. Rate of climb is a vertical velocity and is indicated on the vertical speed indicator (VSI) in feet per minute (fpm).

- A **cruise climb** is a compromise climb that allows for a high speed (to expedite your arrival at the destination) as well as allowing the airplane to gain altitude and reach the cruise altitude without too much delay. It also allows for better engine cooling because of the faster speed, and better forward visibility because of the lower pitch attitude. The cruise climb is the shallowest climb at a higher airspeed compared with V_X and V_Y. For most airplanes it is the **normal climb.**

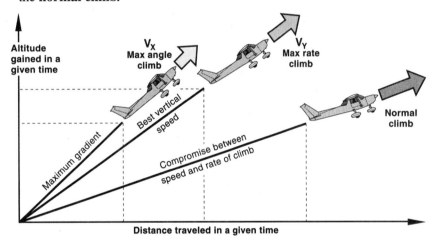

Figure 3-7. Maximum angle climb, maximum rate climb, cruise climb; use the one that suits the situation

Refer to your Pilot's Operating Handbook for the various climb speeds for your particular airplane. Typically, the best angle-of-climb speed V_X is about 10–15 knots less than the best rate-of-climb speed V_Y at sea level.

Climb Performance

Performance in the climb, be it angle or rate of climb, will:

- reduce when power is decreased;
- reduce when airplane weight is increased;
- reduce when temperature increases because of lower air density;
- reduce if you fly at the incorrect speed (either too fast or too slow); and
- reduce as altitude increases because of lower air density.

The power available from the engine and propeller decreases with altitude. The climb performance, rate-of-climb, and angle-of-climb capabilities all decrease with altitude.

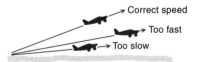

Figure 3-8. Fly at the correct climb speed for best performance

The altitude at which climb performance falls close to zero and a steady climb can no longer be maintained is called **ceiling**. The **service ceiling** is the altitude at which the steady rate of climb has fallen to just 100 feet per minute (fpm). The **absolute ceiling** is the slightly higher altitude at which the steady rate of climb achievable at climbing speed is zero. It is therefore almost impossible to climb to the absolute ceiling.

The airplane's Pilot's Operating Handbook will normally contain a table or graph with climb performance information.

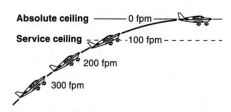

Figure 3-9. Climb performance decreases with altitude

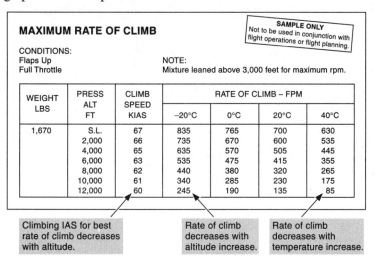

Figure 3-10. A typical climb performance table

The Effect of a Steady Wind on Climbing

Because rate of climb is a vertical velocity and wind normally acts horizontally, rate of climb will not be affected by a steady wind. Angle of climb through the air also will not be affected by a steady wind. However, if we consider the angle (or gradient) of climb over the ground—the airplane's flight path—a headwind increases the effective climb gradient over the ground and a tailwind decreases it. **Taking off upwind** has obvious advantages for obstacle clearance—it improves your clearance of obstacles on the ground.

A headwind increases climb gradient—a tailwind reduces it.

Wind does not affect rate of climb, but does affect angle of climb over the ground.

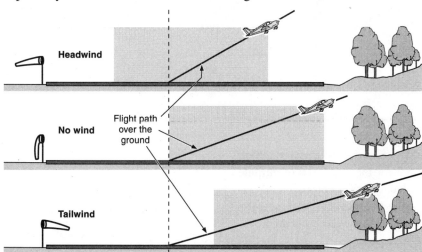

Figure 3-11. Wind affects the flight path achieved over the ground

The Descent

If an airplane is in a glide descent, with no thrust being produced by the engine and propeller, only *three* of the four main forces will be acting on the airplane: **weight, lift** and **drag.** In a *steady* glide these three forces will be in equilibrium as the resultant force acting on the airplane is zero.

Suppose that the airplane is in steady straight-and-level flight and the thrust is reduced to zero. The drag force is no longer opposed with an equal and opposite force, and will therefore decelerate the airplane—unless a descent is commenced where the component of the weight force acting in the direction of the flight path is sufficient to counteract the drag. This effect allows the airplane to maintain airspeed by descending and converting potential energy because of its altitude into kinetic energy (motion).

Resolving the forces in the direction of the flight path shows that a component of the weight force acts along the flight path in a descent, countering drag and contributing to the airplane's speed. The airspeed in the descent will remain constant when this component of weight is equal and opposite to the drag.

Resolving the forces vertically, you can see that, in a glide descent, the weight is counteracted by the total aerodynamic force, which is the resultant of the lift and drag.

Notice that the greater the drag force, the steeper the glide. The shallowest glide is obtained at the best lift/drag ratio when, for the required lift, the drag is least.

- **If the L/D ratio is high**, the angle of descent is shallow—a flat glide angle—and the airplane will glide a long way.

- **If the L/D ratio is low** (a poor situation), with a lot of drag being produced for the required lift, then the airplane will have a large angle of descent—a steep glide angle—and the airplane will therefore not glide very far.

In a steady glide lift, weight and drag are in equilibrium.

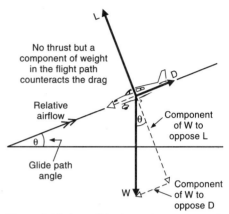

Figure 3-12. In a glide descent, a component of weight counteracts the drag

The maximum glide range is obtained if the airplane is at the best L/D ratio (minimum drag).

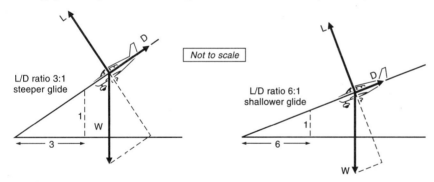

Figure 3-13. A smaller L/D ratio (increased drag) results in a steeper glide

Two points can be made here:

1. An aerodynamically efficient airplane is one which can be flown at a high lift/drag ratio. It is capable of gliding further for the same loss of altitude compared with an airplane that is flown with a lower L/D ratio.

2. The same airplane will glide furthest through still air when it is flown at the angle-of-attack (and airspeed) that gives its best L/D ratio. This angle-of-attack is usually about 4°.

Because you cannot read angle-of-attack in the cockpit, flying at the recommended best glide or descent speed (listed in the Pilot's Operating Handbook) will ensure that the airplane is somewhere near this most efficient angle-of-attack to achieve the best glide angle.

Factors Affecting Glide Angle

Airspeed

If the airplane is flown at a lower angle-of-attack (and therefore faster) than the optimum, the L/D ratio will be less and the airplane will not glide as far because it will dive toward the ground faster and at a steeper angle.

If the airplane is flown at a greater angle-of-attack (lower airspeed) than that for the best L/D ratio, the L/D ratio will be less and therefore the optimum glide angle will not be achieved. This may be deceptive for the pilot because the nose attitude may be quite high, but the airplane is descending steeply.

To glide the furthest in still air, fly at the recommended airspeed (and therefore angle-of-attack) that gives the best lift/drag ratio.

If you are gliding at the recommended airspeed and it looks like you will not reach the selected point, do not raise the nose to increase the glide distance. It will not work! The higher nose attitude may give the appearance of stretching the glide, but in fact it will decrease your glide distance.

The wrong airspeed (too fast or too slow) steepens the glide angle.

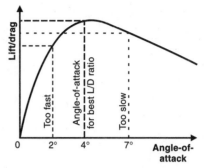

Figure 3-14. Angle-of-attack versus lift/drag ratio

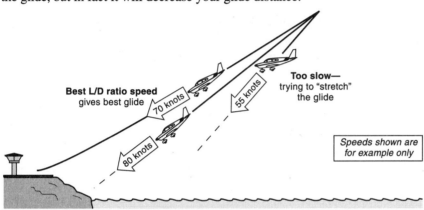

Figure 3-15. The flattest glide is achieved at the best L/D ratio

Flap Setting

Flaps will increase the drag more than the lift and consequently the L/D ratio will be lower. This gives a steeper glide.

Flaps reduce the L/D ratio and steepen the glide.

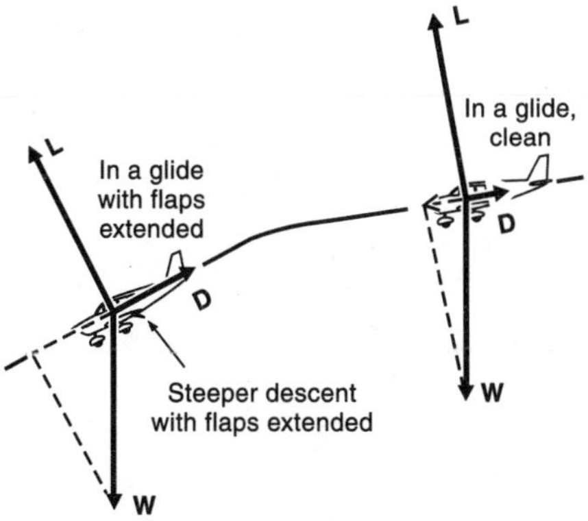

Figure 3-16. Steeper glide angle with flaps extended

Weight

If the airplane weight reduces, you can achieve the best glide angle by flying a slightly slower glide speed. By maintaining the angle-of-attack for the best L/D ratio (and therefore for the best glide), the airspeed will be lower but the glide angle the same. This also means that the rate of descent for the airplane when it is lighter will be less—it will glide the same distance through the air, but take longer to reach the ground because of the reduced airspeed.

The best glide speed reduces as weight decreases.

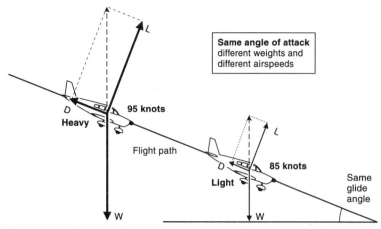

Figure 3-17. The best glide angle is the same at all weights (best L/D) but the airspeed must be lower at lower weights

The recommended glide speed (stated in the Pilot's Operating Handbook) is based on **maximum gross weight.** The variation in weight for most training airplanes is not large enough to significantly affect the glide if the recommended glide speed is used at all times—even though, theoretically, a slightly lower glide speed could be used when lightly loaded.

The recommended descent speed in your Pilot's Operating Handbook will be suitable for all permissible weights of your light training airplane.

Glide Distance over the Ground

A headwind reduces the glide distance over the ground, even though it does not affect the glide distance through the air, nor does it affect the rate of descent.

- **Glide angle** means relative to the *air mass* and is not affected by wind.
- **Flight path** means relative to the *ground* and is affected by wind.

The airplane "sees" only the air in which it is flying. In the case illustrated below we can see three identical glides through an air mass—same airspeed, same nose attitude, same angle-of-attack, same rate of descent (therefore same time taken to reach the ground) in all three cases. The only difference is that the air mass is moving over the ground in three different ways and carrying the airplane with it. The ground distance covered differs.

A tailwind increases the glide distance over the ground, even though it does not affect the glide distance relative to the air mass or the rate of descent.

A headwind reduces the glide distance over the ground—a tailwind increases it.

Wind does not affect rate of descent.

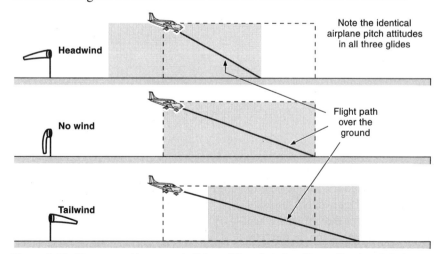

Figure 3-18. More ground is covered gliding with a tailwind and less with a headwind

Still Air Glide Distance

If you refer to Figure 3-19 of the forces acting in a glide you will see that the glide distance is furthest when the L/D ratio is at its maximum value. If the L/D ratio is 5:1, the airplane will glide 5 times as far as it will descend. If you are 1 nautical mile (nm) high (about 6,000 feet), you will glide for about 5 nautical miles. If you are at about 12,000 feet (2 nm), you will glide approximately 10 nm. An airplane with a L/D ratio of 12:1 will glide 12 times as far in still air as it will descend.

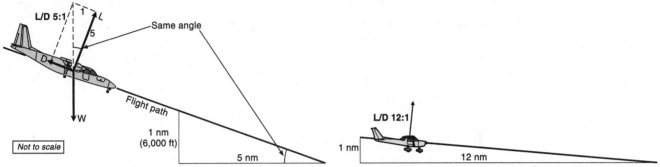

Figure 3-19. "Air distance/altitude" is the same ratio as "lift/drag"

Controlling the Powered Descent

If the engine and propeller is producing power, then the thrust force will help overcome part of the drag force. The result is that the airplane with power applied will have a shallower descent angle and a lower rate of descent than in the power-off glide. Of course, with sufficient power, the descent angle may be zero and the airplane will be flying level. With even more power, the airplane may climb.

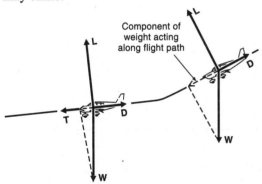

Figure 3-20. Add power to flatten the descent

If you are sinking *beneath* your desired flight path, the correct procedure is to apply some power and raise the nose (raising the nose alone simply worsens the situation by steepening the glide). Adding thrust, as shown in Figure 3-20, helps counteract the drag; the weight component required to counteract drag is less and a shallower flight path is possible. Any change in power will require some small adjustments to the nose attitude for the selected airspeed to be maintained—power and attitude together give you the desired performance.

Flatten the descent by increasing power.

If you are *above* your desired descent path, two things you can do are:
- reduce the thrust; and/or
- increase the drag by extending the wing flaps or lowering the landing gear.

Note: When you extend the flaps, a lower nose attitude is normally required.

Steepen the descent by reducing power or increasing drag.

✍ Now complete **Review 3, Part (b)** on page 88.

Turning and Load Factor

Forces in a Turn

For an object such as an airplane to turn, a force is required that acts toward the center of the turn. This turning force is known as the **centripetal force**.

Holding a string tied to a heavy object such as a stone, your hand supplies a lift force equal and opposite to the weight of the stone. If you swing the stone in a circle, however, your hand supplies not only a vertical force to counteract the weight but also a centripetal force to keep the stone turning. The total force exerted through the string is greater than the weight of the stone, and you will feel the increase.

The horizontal component of the lift force provides the centripetal force that pulls the airplane into a turn.

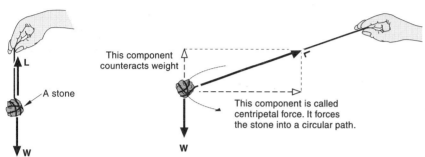

Figure 3-21. The centripetal force pulls a body into a turn

To turn an airplane, a centripetal force (toward the center of the turn) needs to be generated. This can be done by banking the airplane and tilting the lift force so that it has a sideways component.

Flying straight-and-level, the lift force from the wings counteracts the weight of the airplane. If you turn the airplane, the wings still need to supply a vertical force to counteract the weight (unless you want to descend) plus the centripetal force toward the center of the turn to keep the turn going. Consequently, the lift force in a level turn must be greater than the lift force when flying straight-and-level. To develop this increased lift force at the same airspeed, the angle-of-attack must be increased by applying backward pressure on the control column.

The steeper the bank angle in a level turn, the greater the lift force required. Note that you select the bank angle using the **ailerons** (to roll the airplane) and **elevator** to increase the angle-of-attack (and increase lift) to produce the centripetal force required to turn the airplane and maintain the selected altitude.

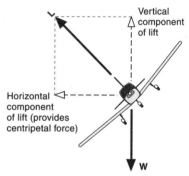

Figure 3-22. By banking, the tilted lift force has a horizontal component which provides the centripetal force

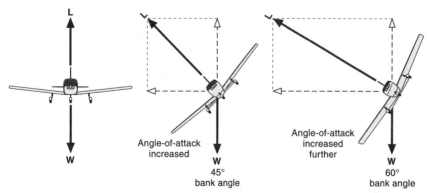

Figure 3-23. The steeper the bank, the greater the lift force required from the wings

The stability designed into the airplane, together with adverse aileron yaw, may resist it turning, and the application of a little rudder (left rudder for a left turn and vice versa) helps bring the tail around and yaw the nose into the turn—therefore the rudder is used to *coordinate* the turn by controlling yaw. You, of course, are forced into the turn along with the airplane and feel this as an increase in the force exerted by the seat; it feels like an *apparent* increase in your weight.

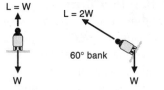

Figure 3-24. The steeper the bank angle, the greater the g-forces

Load Factor

The load factor on the wings is increased in a turn. Flying straight-and-level, the wing produces a lift force *equal* to the weight and L = W. The load factor is said to be 1. You experience a force from the seat equal to normal weight, and feel it as "1g."

In a banked turn of 60°, the wings produce a lift force equal to *double* the weight and L = 2W. This means the loading on the wings is doubled when compared with straight-and-level flight, or each square foot of wing has to produce twice as much lift in a 60° banked turn as it does in straight-and-level flight. You experience a force from the seat equal to twice your weight. This is 2g and the load factor is 2. This is true for all 60° banked turns, irrespective of airspeed, rate of turn or weight of airplane.

Load factor increases as bank angle increases.

The **load factor** is the ratio of the lift force produced by the wings compared with the weight force of the airplane.

$$\text{Load factor} = \frac{\text{lift}}{\text{weight}} = \frac{\text{wing loading in maneuver}}{\text{wing loading straight-and-level}}$$

At bank angles beyond 60°, the lift force generated by the wings must increase greatly so that its vertical component can counteract the weight, otherwise altitude will be lost.

Increased lift from the wings means increased wing loading and an increased load factor. We can show this in a curve of load factor versus bank angle.

Notes:

- In a 30° banked turn you will experience 1.15g load factor. The wings will produce 15% more lift than when straight-and-level, and you will feel 15% heavier.

- At 60° bank angle, the load factor is 2. The wings have to produce a lift force equal to double the weight to maintain altitude. The g-force is 2g, you will feel twice as heavy, and the wing will have to support double the weight.

- A 70° bank, the load factor is 3.

- A utility category airplane has a maximum allowable positive load factor of 4.4g, which is reached at approximately 77° bank angle (a normal category airplane is limited to 3.8g).

- In a 90° banked turn, the lift force is horizontal, and, even if of infinite size, would have no vertical component to counteract the weight. Therefore altitude cannot be maintained in a coordinated turn at 90° bank angle.

- For those who are mathematically minded, the load factor in a turn can be calculated from 1 divided by the cosine of the bank angle, or $\frac{1}{\cos\theta}$.

- The maximum weights permitted to be carried in a particular airplane (or compartments within an airplane) take into account load factor. A normal category airplane is stressed to 3.8g. If the baggage compartment is approved for 220 lb, then it will not be overstressed provided 3.8g is not exceeded.

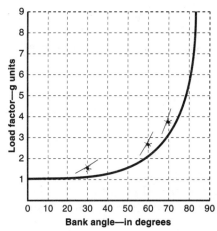

Figure 3-25. Load factor versus bank angle

Wing Loading in a Turn

In straight-and-level flight, the wings support a load that is the weight of the airplane. In a banked turn of 60°, the load factor is 2, and now each wing has to support twice the load that it did in straight-and-level. Wing loading is the load supported by the wings divided by their area.

For example, an airplane weighing 2,500 pounds (lb) with a wing area of 200 square feet has a wing loading of 12.5 lb/sq.ft in level flight. In a 60° banked turn the load factor is 2. Therefore the load that the wings are supporting is $2,500 \times 2 = 5,000$ lb. Wing loading $= \frac{\text{load}}{\text{wing area}} = \frac{5000}{200} = 25$ lb/sq.ft.

Like load factor, wing loading in a turn depends only on the bank angle. But wing loading is not only of concern for structural strength, it also affects minimum landing speeds, the smaller the wing, the higher the wing loading and the faster the minimum landing speed.

Wing loading increases as bank angle increases.

Thrust in a Turn

In a turn, increased lift from the wings is required to provide the centripetal force and to maintain altitude. This is achieved by applying back pressure on the control column to increase the angle-of-attack.

The steeper the bank angle, the greater the angle-of-attack and back pressure required. As we saw in our discussion on drag, an increase in the angle-of-attack will lead to an increase in the induced drag. If a constant airspeed is to be maintained in a level turn, an increase in thrust to counteract the increased drag in a turn is required (typically 50 rpm for a fixed-pitch propeller or $^1/_2$ in.Hg manifold pressure for a constant-speed propeller). In practice, however, the power is usually kept constant in medium turns and you accept a reduction in airspeed of approximately 5 knots.

If extra thrust is not added, the airspeed will reduce in a level turn. If required, airspeed could be maintained by allowing the airplane to lose altitude, trading potential energy for kinetic energy.

In a turn, extra thrust is required to maintain airspeed.

Steep Turns

A steep turn is one in which the bank angle exceeds 45° and airspeed is maintained by applying a significant increase in power. It is a high-performance maneuver that requires good coordination and positive control. A steep level turn requires a significant increase in lift so that:

- a strong horizontal component exists to pull the airplane into the turn; and
- the vertical component is sufficient to support the weight and allow altitude to be maintained.

Firm **back pressure** is needed on the control column to increase the lift force, and **increased power** is required to overcome the tendency to lose airspeed because of the increased drag. Ailerons must be used to maintain the selected bank angle as accurately as possible.

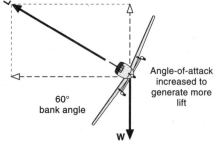

Figure 3-26. A steep level turn requires increased lift

The Stall in a Turn

In a turn, the angle-of-attack has to be greater than at the same speed in straight-and-level flight, to create the additional lift needed to turn the airplane as well as support its weight. This means that the stall angle-of-attack will be reached at a higher speed in a turn—the steeper the bank angle, the higher the airspeed at which the stall angle-of-attack is reached.

- At 30° bank angle, the stall speed is increased by 7% over the straight-and-level stall speed.
- At 45° bank angle, the stall speed is increased by 19%.
- At 60° bank angle, the stall speed is increased by 41%.
- At 75° bank angle, the stall speed is increased by 100%, or doubled.

For example, if your airplane stalls at 50 knots straight-and-level, then in a 60° banked turn it will stall at 71 knots (141% of 50 knots) which is a significant increase. In steep turns, you may feel the onset of the stall buffet because the margin between your speed and the stall speed has reduced.

Note: The stall speed increases by the square root of the load factor.

✍ Now complete **Review 3, Part (c)** on page 89.

Stalling and Spinning

A wing stalls when it reaches the *stall,* or *critical,* angle-of-attack, which is the point where the smooth airflow breaks down and becomes turbulent, thereby considerably reducing the lift generated. You can induce a stall on purpose by increasing the angle-of-attack using back pressure on the control column.

It is very easy both to prevent a stall, simply by ensuring that the critical angle-of-attack (about 16°) is not approached, and to recover from a stall, by easing the nose forward to decrease the angle-of-attack. Sometimes you want to approach the stall, for instance during the final stages of a landing.

Ideally the airflow around an airfoil would be streamline. In flight however, the streamline flow breaks away (or separates) at some point from the airfoil surface and becomes turbulent.

At low angles-of-attack this separation point is toward the rear of the wing and the turbulence is not significant. At higher angles-of-attack the separation point moves forward.

As the angle-of-attack is increased, a critical angle is reached beyond which the separation point will suddenly move well forward causing a large increase in the turbulence over the wing.

The separation of the airflow from the wing's upper surface and breakdown of the streamline flow reduces the magnitude of the low static pressure above the wing, greatly reducing the lift developed by the wing.

Conversely, as the angle-of-attack increases the small aerodynamic force produced by the airflow striking the wing's lower surface will increase slightly. The overall effect however, is a marked decrease in lift and the airplane will lose altitude. This reduction in the wing's lifting ability is shown in Figure 3-28.

The stall angle-of-attack occurs at higher airspeeds in a level turn.

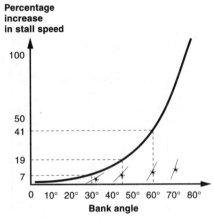

Figure 3-27. Percentage increase in stall speed versus bank angle

A stall occurs at the critical angle-of-attack.

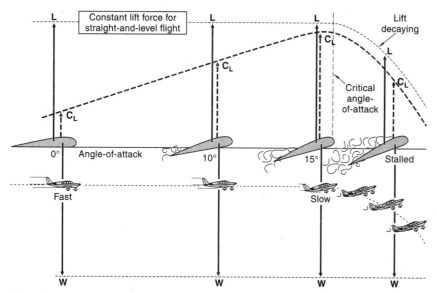

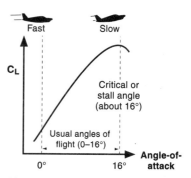

Figure 3-28. An airfoil reaches its maximum lifting ability at the critical angle-of-attack

Figure 3-29. Lift versus angle-of-attack

As the angle-of-attack increases up to the critical angle, the wing's lifting ability increases. Beyond the stalling or critical angle-of-attack, the lifting ability reduces as a result of the breakdown of streamline flow. This breakdown of streamline flow into turbulence is known as **stalling** the airfoil, or **the stall.** The **critical** or **stall angle-of-attack** is where the airfoil's lifting ability reaches its maximum value, and beyond which it markedly decreases.

Beyond the critical angle the center of pressure—which has been gradually moving forward as the angle-of-attack increased—suddenly moves *rearward* and there is also a rapid increase in drag.

Recognition of the Stall

Approaching the stall angle-of-attack, the streamline flow breaks down over parts of the wing and turbulent air flows back over the horizontal stabilizer. The airframe may shake or *buffet* as a result, known as **pre-stall buffet** or **control buffet.** Many airplanes have stall warning devices such as a buzzer or horn that will sound to warn the pilot that the wing is approaching the stall angle.

At the stall, the decrease in lift will cause the airplane to **sink.** The rearward movement of the center of pressure will cause the **nose to drop.**

There are natural and artificial warnings of an impending stall.

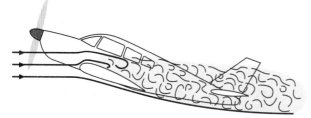

Figure 3-30. Turbulent flow over the horizontal stabilizer

Recovery from the Stall

To recover from a stall, the angle-of-attack must be reduced. This is achieved by releasing the back pressure on the control column and lowering the nose. If the airspeed is low, which is often the case, full power should also be applied to increase the airspeed as quickly as possible. Stall recovery should be initiated at the first indication of an impending stall.

To recover from a stall reduce the angle-of-attack by lowering the nose.

Stall and Angle-of-Attack

For most training airplanes, the stall angle-of-attack is about 15°–16°. This stalling or critical angle-of-attack is always the same regardless of airspeed, weight, loading, position of the center of gravity, load factor in maneuvers, altitude, and so on. The wing stalls at a particular angle-of-attack, and not at a particular airspeed.

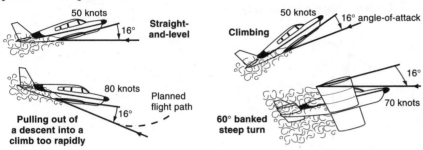

Figure 3-31. The stall occurs at the same stall angle in all phases of flight, but not necessarily at the same speed

Factors Affecting Stall Speed

A specific airfoil will stall at a particular angle-of-attack, however the stall may occur, for example, at:

- 50 knots straight-and-level for an airplane at maximum gross weight;
- 45 knots straight-and-level when it is light;
- 44 knots straight-and-level with flaps and gear down;
- 70 knots in a 60° banked turn; and
- 80 knots if you experience 3g pulling out of a dive.

(Do not bother learning these figures as they are only examples.)

There is, however, some connection between *angle-of-attack* and *indicated airspeed.* Their relationship depends on:

- lift produced by the airfoil;
- load factor;
- bank angle;
- weight;
- power; and
- flap setting (changes the airfoil's shape and lifting ability).

Load Factor

If the wing has to produce increased lift to maneuver the airplane at a particular airspeed, for instance in a turn or pulling out of a dive, then you will apply back pressure on the control column to increase the angle-of-attack. Lift will be increased, causing an increased load factor, and you will feel an increase in your g-loading.

Stall speed increases with load factor.

An increased angle-of-attack in maneuvers will bring the wing closer to the critical or stall angle, even though the airspeed has not changed, and, in the extreme case, if you increase the angle-of-attack to the critical angle, the wing will stall even though the airspeed is well above the 1g straight-and-level stall speed.

Stalling occurs at a critical angle-of-attack—not at any particular airspeed.

In *Airfoil Lift,* (Chapter 1) we saw that lift depends on angle-of-attack and airspeed squared. If lift depends on airspeed-squared then, conversely, airspeed is related to the square root of lift. This means that the actual stall speed when the critical angle-of-attack is reached will depend on the square root of the lift being produced.

If lift is increased by a factor of four in a strenuous maneuver, the stall speed will be doubled. If the straight-and-level 1g stall speed is 50 knots, then when pulling 4g the wing will stall at 100 knots. Note that 4g is outside the limits for most training airplanes.

If the load factor is doubled, for instance in a 60° banked turn, you will feel 2g (double your normal weight), and the stall speed will be 1.4 times greater (the square root of 2 is 1.4), which is 70 knots (1.4 × 50). This is illustrated in Figure 3-32 and Figure 3-33.

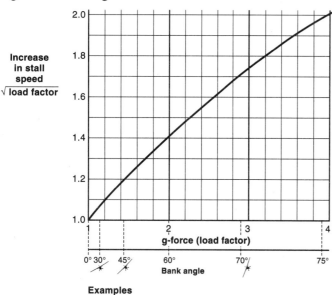

Examples

1. At 2g (load factor 2) the stall speed increases by 1.41, and at 3g by 1.73 times the level stall speed for the airplane.

2. In a 60° bank turn the load factor is 2 and the stall speed increase is by 1.41.

Figure 3-32. Stall speed increases with load factor

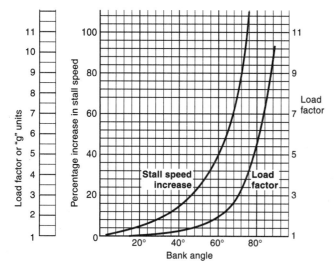

Figure 3-33. Relationship between stall speed, load factor and bank angle

Because the stall angle is reached in maneuvers at higher speeds than when flying under 1g conditions, these are known as **accelerated stalls.** Stall speed will be increased any time lift from the wings is increased, which will occur in turns, when pulling out of dives, in gusts and in turbulence.

Weight

In straight-and-level flight, sufficient lift must be generated to balance the weight. The heavier the airplane, the greater is the lift force required. Because the stall speed varies with the square root of lift, an increase in airplane weight will increase the stall speed—but not affect the stall angle-of-attack.

If the weight decreases 20% to only 0.8 of its original value, then the stall speed will decrease to 0.9 times its original value (0.9 is the square root of 0.8).

If the stall speed at maximum gross weight (say 2,000 pounds) was stated in the Pilot's Operating Handbook to be 50 knots, then at 1,600 pounds (only 80% of the maximum weight), the stall speed is only 90% of the original stall speed which is 45 knots. Conversely, an increase in weight will increase the stall speed.

The Pilot's Operating Handbook states various stall speeds. V_S is the minimum steady-flight speed at which the airplane is controllable, in straight-and-level flight, with the power off, at *maximum allowable gross weight*. Remember that whenever your airplane weighs less than its maximum weight it will stall at a speed slightly *below* that specified in the Pilot's Operating Handbook.

Stall speed increases with weight (stall angle-of-attack stays the same.)

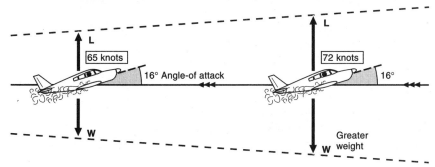

Figure 3-34. Stall speed is a function of weight

Power

With power on, the strong slipstream passes over the inner section of each wing as well as the empennage. The separation of the airflow from the upper surface of the inner section of each wing is thereby delayed, so a more positive stall occurs at a *lower* indicated airspeed, compared with power off.

In addition, as the stall angle is approached with power on, the high nose attitude allows the thrust to have a vertical component that will partially support the weight. Therefore, the wings are off-loaded a little and less lift is required from them. Less lift means a lowered stall speed.

Because the slipstream encourages the generation of lift from the inner parts of the wing, the outer sections of the wing may stall first. Any uneven production of lift from the outer sections of the two wings will lead to a rapid roll called a wing-drop. If a wing does drop close to the stall, do not correct by putting the aileron on the dropped wing down.

This will further increase the lower wing's effective angle-of-attack resulting in the wing becoming more stalled and dropping further. If a wing drops close to the stall, correct with rudder (the secondary effect of rudder is roll).

Stall speed is lower in a power-on stall.

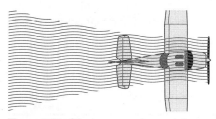

Figure 3-35. Slipstream can lower stall speed

A power-on stall may be more definite and accompanied by a wing-drop.

Altitude

The stall angle-of-attack will be reached (straight-and-level) at the same stall indicated airspeed irrespective of altitude. If the airplane has a 1g stall speed of 45 knots indicated airspeed (KIAS) at 1,000 feet MSL, its 1g stall speed at 5,000 feet MSL will also be 45 KIAS.

Stall indicated airspeed does not vary with altitude.

Ice, Frost and other Wing Contamination

Ice accretion has two effects:

- Ice increases weight, so the stall speed will be increased.

- Much more significantly, ice-accretion, frost, or other contamination on the wings (particularly the front half of the upper surface where most of the lift is generated) will disrupt the airflow over the wing, decreasing its lifting ability, and cause early separation of the airflow from the wing. The early separation of the airflow results in the breakdown of streamline flow at angles-of-attack well below the normal stall angle, and stalling will occur at higher speeds. In addition, the higher stall speeds will result in the takeoff speed increasing above the normal takeoff speed, and the takeoff distance increasing unexpectedly. Ice can prevent an airplane from becoming airborne.

Note: Any ice or frost at all, even if only the texture of very fine sandpaper, should be removed from the wing prior to flight, as should insects and salt from the wing leading edges.

Ice, frost or other wing contamination increases stall speed.

Flaps

Extending flaps gives us a new airfoil shape with increased camber and an **increased lifting ability.** This enables the wings to support the same load at a lower speed, and the airspeed can decrease to a lower value before the stall angle is reached.

Flaps reduce the stall speed.

The reduction of stall speeds is the main advantage of flaps. It makes for safe flight at lower speeds—very useful for takeoffs, landings (shorter fields) and low speed searches. Also, extending the flaps allows lower nose attitudes—not only is visibility increased, but also the stall angle will be reached at a lower nose attitude.

The stall with flaps extended may be accompanied by a wing-drop. Use rudder to correct the wing drop, not aileron. Because of the increased drag with flaps extended, any speed loss, especially with power-off, could be quite rapid, with little advance warning to the pilot of an impending stall.

In the stall with flaps down, turbulence over the horizontal stabilizer may cause very poor control from the elevator, known as *blanketing* of the elevator. Some training airplanes have a T-tail with the horizontal stabilizer high on the fin to avoid any such blanketing of the elevator in the stall.

Note: Some airplane manuals publish tables that show stall speed at various bank angles with power off and power on, with the airplane clean, and also with the airplane in the landing configuration (gear and flaps down).

Gross Weight 2,750 lb		Stall Speeds				SAMPLE ONLY not to be used for flight operations or flight planning
			Bank Angle			
		Level	30°	45°	60°	
Power		**Gear and Flaps Up**				
On	mph	62	67	74	88	
	kt	54	58	64	76	
Off	mph	75	81	89	106	
	kt	65	70	77	92	
		Gear and Flaps Down				
On	mph	54	58	64	76	
	kt	47	50	56	66	
Off	mph	66	71	78	93	
	kt	57	62	68	81	

Increasing bank angle increases stall speed

Adding power reduces stall speed

Extending flaps reduces stall speed

Figure 3-36. Examples of stall speeds in different situations

For example from Figure 3-36, the predicted stall speed:
- clean, power-off at 30° bank angle is 70 knots;
- gear/flaps down, power-on, level is 47 knots.

Stall Warning Devices

Most airplanes are equipped with a device such as a horn, flashing red light or whistle to warn of an impending stall. Such artificial devices are only secondary to the aerodynamic *stall warnings* that you must learn to recognize, such as stall buffet, decreasing speed, and less effective controls.

Wing Design and the Stall

If there is an uneven loss of lift from the outer sections of the wings near the tips, caused by one of them stalling first, then a strong rolling moment is set up because of the long moment arm from the outer sections of the wing to the CG. Also, the ailerons will become less effective because of the disturbed airflow around them.

Stalling at the wing roots is preferable because it allows the control buffet over the horizontal stabilizer (because of the turbulent air from the inner sections of the wing) to be felt, while the outer sections of the wings are still producing lift and the ailerons should still be effective. An uneven loss of lift on the inner sections, if one wing stalls before the other, does not have as great a rolling moment compared with when the outer sections of the wing stall first.

A *rectangular* wing, compared with other wing planforms, has a tendency to stall first at the wing root, and so provide adequate stall warning to the pilot while the ailerons are still effective. This is one reason why rectangular wings are common in basic training airplanes.

Stalling at the wing root first can also be achieved with a lower angle of incidence (and therefore a lower angle-of-attack) at the wingtip when compared with the wing root, which is known as **washout.** This means that the wing root will reach the stall angle prior to the wingtip. (Washout also helps to reduce the induced drag from wingtip vortices.) On other airplanes, small metal plates can be placed at the inboard leading edges to encourage the early onset of the stall at the wing root.

The Spin

A spin is a condition of stalled flight in which the airplane follows a spiral descent path. As well as the airplane being in a stalled condition, and yawing, one wing is producing more lift than the other, which results in a roll. The dropping wing is more deeply stalled than the other, and the greater drag from this wing results in further yaw, further roll, and so on. Upward pitching of the nose will also occur. You can induce a spin on purpose by yawing an airplane that is stalled, or just on the point of stalling.

In a spin, the airplane is in motion about all three axes. In other words, lots of things are happening in a spin! The airplane is:
- stalled;
- rolling;
- yawing;
- pitching;
- slipping; and
- rapidly losing altitude at a low airspeed (stalled).

Stalling first at the wing root is preferable to stalling first at the wingtip.

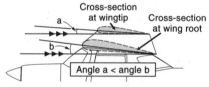

Figure 3-37. Built-in washout causes the wingtip to stall later than the root

To spin, an airplane must first be stalled.

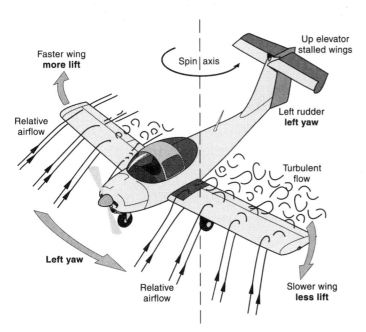

Figure 3-38. The airplane in a controlled spin

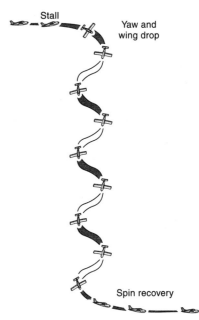

Figure 3-39. The flight path in a spin

In a spin the wings will not produce much lift, since they are stalled. The airplane will accelerate downward until it reaches a vertical rate of descent where the greatly increased drag, now acting upward, counteracts the weight. The altitude loss will be rapid as the airplane spins downward around the vertical spin axis but, because of the high angle-of-attack and the stalled condition, the airspeed in the spin will be quite low and fluctuating.

Characteristics of a developed spin include a **low airspeed** (which does not increase until recovery action is initiated), and a **high rate of descent**.

For a more detailed explanation of the spin *see* the Commercial Pilot section at the end of the chapter.

Spin Recovery

To recover from a spin you must oppose the yaw and unstall the wings. First note yaw direction and apply full opposite rudder, and then move the control column forward to unstall the wings. Once the airplane has stopped spinning, ease the airplane out of the dive and resume normal flight.

Misuse of Ailerons

Trying to raise a dropped wing with opposite aileron may have the reverse effect when the airplane is near the stall. If, as the aileron goes down, the stall angle-of-attack is exceeded, the wing may drop quickly instead of rising, resulting in a spin.

On some airplanes, misuse of the ailerons can cause a spin.

This is the spin entry technique used on some older airplane types; modern airplane designs, however, are required by the FAA to have ailerons that remain effective through a stall. This can be achieved with design features such as *washout*, which results in the inner part of the wing near the fuselage stalling before the wingtip/aileron area.

The application of aileron after a spin has developed may aggravate the spin. Discuss the spin characteristics of your particular airplane with your flight instructor.

The Spiral Dive

A maneuver that must not be confused with a spin is the spiral dive, which can be thought of as a steep turn that has gone wrong. In a spiral dive the nose attitude is low, and the rate of descent is high, but neither wing is stalled and the airspeed is high and rapidly increasing. A spiral dive is really just a steep descending turn. However, because the pilot may be disoriented it is often mistaken for a spin. The high and increasing airspeed will indicate that the airplane is in a spiral dive rather than a spin (when the airspeed would fluctuate at a low value).

Recovery from a spiral dive is simple. Roll wings level and pull gently out of the dive. Beware of overstressing the airplane by pulling too quickly out of the dive—remember the controls will be very effective because of the high airspeed.

✍ Now complete **Review 3, Part (d)** on page 90.

Do not confuse a spin (low airspeed and stalled) with a spiral dive (high airspeed and not stalled).

For Aspiring Commercial Pilots

Straight-and-Level Flight

Performance in Level Flight

As the thrust required for steady (unaccelerated) straight-and-level flight is equal to the drag (thrust equals drag), the thrust-required curve is identical to the familiar drag curve (shown opposite).

Points to be noted from the thrust-required or drag curve are:

- High thrust is required at high speeds and low angles-of-attack to overcome what is mainly *parasite* drag.

- Minimum thrust is required at the minimum-drag speed (which is also the best L/D ratio speed, since lift equals weight in straight-and-level flight and drag is at its minimum value).

- High thrust is required at low speeds and high angles-of-attack to overcome what is mainly *induced* drag (caused in the production of lift).

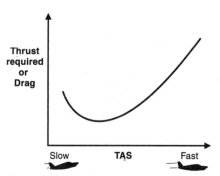

Figure 3-40. The thrust-required or drag curve

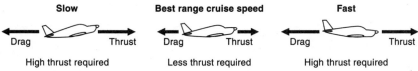

Figure 3-41. Both low speed and high speed require high thrust

The engine and propeller combination is a power producer (rather than a thrust producer like a jet engine). The fuel flow (in gallons per hour) of an engine–propeller combination is a function of power produced (rather than thrust produced).

Power is defined as the *rate* of doing work, or the speed at which an applied force moves a body. Therefore the power required for flight depends on the product of:

- thrust required; and
- flight velocity (true airspeed or TAS).

Power = thrust × TAS

We can develop a power-required curve from the thrust-required curve (shown previously) by multiplying:

the thrust required at a point on the curve × the TAS at that point

The graph of power-required to maintain steady straight-and-level flight is easy to understand if you take it slowly. If you want to fly at a particular velocity (TAS) then, by reading up from that TAS on the velocity axis, the power curve will tell you the power that the engine–propeller must deliver. This power will supply sufficient thrust to balance the drag and maintain the airspeed in straight-and-level flight.

These graphs may not be published for your airplane, and practically you would not refer to them. To achieve the minimum drag airspeed in straight-and-level flight, set the attitude for the selected airspeed (different airspeeds require different angles-of-attack) and adjust the power to maintain this speed.

Maximum Level-Flight Speed

If maximum power is applied, the airplane will accelerate and the drag will increase (mainly parasite drag). When the drag equals the thrust produced by the engine–propeller, the airplane will stop accelerating, and it will have reached its maximum level-flight speed.

Minimum Level-Flight Speed

At low speeds (slower than the minimum drag speed), higher power from the engine–propeller is required to provide thrust to counteract the higher drag (mainly induced drag).

The minimum level-flight speed is usually not determined by the power capabilities of the powerplant, but rather by the aerodynamic capabilities of the airplane. For most light airplanes, as airspeed reduces, the stall angle is reached, or some condition of instability or loss of control effectiveness occurs prior to any power limitation of the powerplant. This is the reason that the lines on the above graph stop on the low-speed side before they meet.

Maximum-Range Speed

For propeller-driven airplanes maximum range in still air is achieved at the TAS which allows:

- maximum **distance** for a given fuel burn-off $\left(\frac{distance}{fuel\ burn\text{-}off}\right)$; or conversely
- minimum fuel burn-off for a given air distance.

As stated above the **maximum-range** speed is achieved when $\left(\frac{fuel\ burn}{distance}\right)$ is maximum. This occurs when **drag is minimum.** On the drag curve (Figure 3-44) the maximum range speed will occur at the minimum drag point—which, as explained earlier—is also the point for the maximum L/D ratio.

Both the engine and propeller are most efficient at low altitude where the air is more dense. However for the same IAS, TAS increases with altitude, therefore a greater distance can be covered at altitude.

To achieve maximum $\left(\frac{distance}{fuel\ burn\text{-}off}\right)$ a compromise is required and the airplane should be flown at **full throttle height** (about 4,000 to 7,000 feet altitude) for maximum range. Ask your flight instructor how to achieve full throttle height for your airplane engine type.

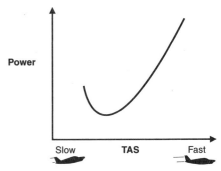

Figure 3-42. The power-required curve

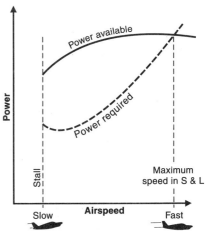

Figure 3-43. Maximum level flight speed

Maximum-range speed occurs at the TAS where drag is minimum and the L/D ratio maximum.

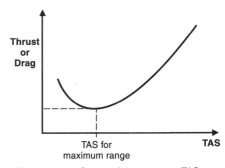

Figure 3-44. Graph of drag versus TAS

Maximum-Endurance Speed

Endurance refers to the **time** an airplane is airborne. The length of time airborne will depend on the amount of fuel in the tanks and the rate at which it is used. Maximum endurance means:

- the maximum time in flight for given amount of fuel $\left(\frac{time}{fuel\ used}\right)$; or
- a given time in flight for the minimum amount of fuel.

In both cases, for maximum endurance the rate of fuel use, which is known as **fuel flow,** must be *minimum.*

It is appropriate to fly at maximum-endurance speed when the speed over the ground is not significant, for instance, when:

- holding overhead or near an airport waiting to land; or
- carrying out a search in a specific area.

The speed for **maximum endurance** occurs when $\left(\frac{time}{fuel\ used}\right)$ is maximum and fuel flow is minimum. For a propeller-driven airplane this occurs when **power is minimum.**

At low altitude, because the engine and propeller are more efficient, fuel flow will be least. Therefore endurance is greatest at **low altitude.**

Speed Stability

Higher Speed Range. An increase in airspeed will increase the total drag, as can be seen from the drag curve, mainly because of an increase in parasite drag. This drag increase is not counteracted by the thrust from the propeller, so the airplane slows down.

A decrease in airspeed from a gust will decrease the total drag (due mainly to a decrease in parasite drag) and the thrust, which now exceeds the drag, will cause the airplane to accelerate back to its original speed.

In the normal flight range (above the minimum drag speed) you will not need to be very active on the throttle since the airplane is *speed stable* and, following any disturbance, will tend to return to its original equilibrium airspeed without further control inputs.

Lower Speed Range. At low airspeeds toward the stall angle it is a different matter. If a gust causes airspeed to decrease, the total drag increases (because of an increase in induced drag) and drag now exceeds thrust, causing the airplane to slow down even further unless you respond with more power.

If a gust causes airspeed to increase, the total drag decreases (because of a decrease in induced drag) and drag is now less than thrust, causing the airplane to accelerate further away from the original speed unless you react by reducing power.

Therefore, at low speeds near the stall angle you need to be fairly active with the throttle to maintain the required low speed accurately.

Straight-and-Level Flight at Altitude

At any altitude, if the airplane is in steady straight-and-level flight the lift must counteract the weight.

$$\text{Lift} = C_L \times {}^1\!/_2 \rho V^2 \times S$$

As altitude is increased, air density, ρ, decreases. One way to generate the required lift and compensate for the decreased density, ρ, is to increase the true airspeed (V) so that the value of ${}^1\!/_2 \rho V^2$ remains the same as before. This means that the decrease in density with altitude can be compensated for with an increase in V (the TAS).

Maximum-endurance speed occurs at the TAS where power is minimum.

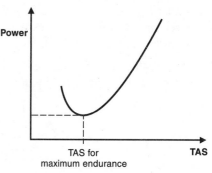

Figure 3-45. Graph of power versus TAS

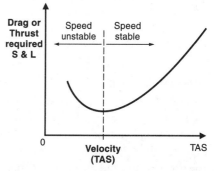

Figure 3-46. Speed stability

The term $^1/_2\rho V^2$ (dynamic pressure) is related to the indicated airspeed which you can read in the cockpit on the airspeed indicator. If $^1/_2\rho V^2$ remains the same, the indicated airspeed (IAS) remains the same and lift remains the same. (A further explanation of the difference between IAS and TAS is given in Chapter 8, under *Pressure Instruments.*)

Therefore as altitude increases the airplane will have the same lift at the same IAS, but an increased TAS.

Note: As altitude increases the indicated stall speed will also remain the same and the true stall speed will increase.

To produce the same lift as altitude increases, fly at the same indicated airspeed (true airspeed will increase).

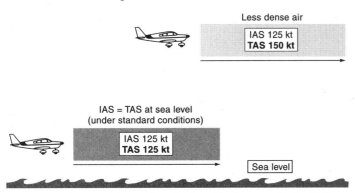

Figure 3-47. Same IAS (and lift) at a higher altitude means higher TAS

Climbing and Descending

Angle of Climb

The **angle of climb** (climb gradient) depends directly on the **excess thrust** (the thrust force in excess of the drag force). The angle of climb will therefore increase when thrust increases or drag decreases. When a maximum angle of climb is required, you will use full power, climb at the correct speed for maximum excess thrust and ensure the airplane is in a low drag configuration with flaps and gear up (where possible). This is a very important consideration for the climb-out after takeoff. Flaps for takeoff decrease the takeoff run prior to liftoff, but once in flight the angle of climb may be less because of the higher drag with flaps down.

Angle of climb depends on excess thrust.

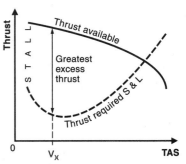

Figure 3-48. "Thrust required" and "thrust available" versus TAS

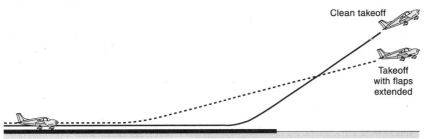

Figure 3-49. Climb gradient may be less with flaps extended

Rate of Climb

Rate of climb is the vertical velocity of the airplane in a climb. It is usually expressed in **feet per minute,** and abbreviated to **fpm** or **ft/min.** A rate of climb (RoC) of 500 fpm means that the airplane will gain 500 feet of altitude in one minute. Rate of climb is shown in the cockpit on the vertical speed indicator (VSI).

Rate of climb depends on excess power.

The **rate of climb** depends directly on the **excess power** (power is the rate of doing work which equals thrust velocity). Rate of climb will increase when power increases or the product of drag and TAS reduces. The maximum rate of climb usually occurs at a speed somewhere near that for the best *lift/drag* ratio, and is faster than the speed for maximum angle of climb (gradient). The maximum rate of climb speed will gain altitude in the shortest time.

Factors Affecting Climb Performance

Power

If full power is not used in a climb the power (and thrust) available will reduce, which will decrease the excess power and excess thrust and therefore the rate and angle of climb. During the initial climb it is important that you ensure that the correct climb power is set and maintained.

Weight

Compared to a light airplane, a heavy airplane will require more lift and therefore produce more drag. Thrust and power required for straight-and-level flight will therefore be increased, and excess thrust and excess power be reduced.

A heavier airplane weight therefore reduces angle and rate of climb.

Air Density

When temperature, humidity, or airplane altitude increase, the air density reduces. This causes the piston engine to produce less power and the propeller to produce less thrust. This reduction in thrust and power available results in excess thrust and excess power decreasing.

A reduction in air density therefore reduces angle of climb and rate of climb.

Incorrect Airspeed

If you fly faster or slower than the recommended speeds, (V_X and V_Y), excess thrust and excess power will reduce, decreasing the angle and rate of climb respectively.

✍ Now complete **Review 3, Commercial Part (a)** on page 91.

Turning and Load Factor

Rate of Turn

The rate of turn of an airplane in degrees per second is important. Instrument flying usually requires **standard-rate** turns of **3°/second.** This means that the airplane will turn through:

• 180° in 1 minute;

• 360° in 2 minutes.

A standard-rate turn at a higher airspeed requires a steeper bank angle.

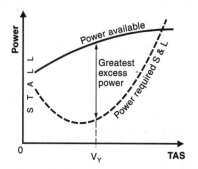

Figure 3-50. "Power required" and "power available" versus TAS

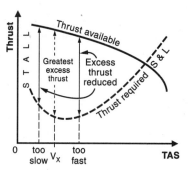

Figure 3-51. Flying the incorrect airspeed reduces excess thrust and angle of climb

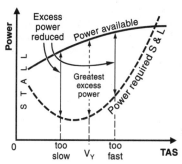

Figure 3-52. Flying the incorrect airspeed reduces excess power and rate of climb

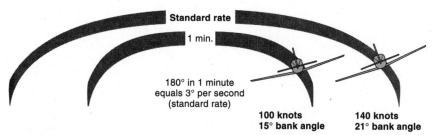

Figure 3-53. A standard-rate turn requires a steeper bank angle at a higher airspeed

An easy way to estimate the bank angle (in degrees) required for a standard-rate turn is:

> $^1/_{10}$ **of the airspeed in knots, plus** $^1/_2$ **the answer**

For example, at 140 knots, for a standard-rate turn,

bank angle is $^{140}/_{10} + ^1/_2$ the answer = $14 + 7 = 21°$.

Turn Performance

Constant-Angle Turn

An airplane in a 30° banked turn will travel around different circular paths depending on its airspeed. At low speed the turn is tighter (the radius of turn is smaller) than at high speed, *see* Figure 3-54.

At a constant bank angle, the slower airplane has an increased rate of turn. This is because the radius of turn will reduce by the square of airspeed. Therefore although the airplane is flying through the air at a slower speed than the faster airplane, its radius of turn is much smaller, and the overall rate of turn is greater.

In summary, if the bank angle is kept constant and the speed reduced, the radius of the turn will reduce and rate of turn increase.

Constant-Radius Turn

To fly a turn of the same radius at a higher speed requires a greater bank angle.

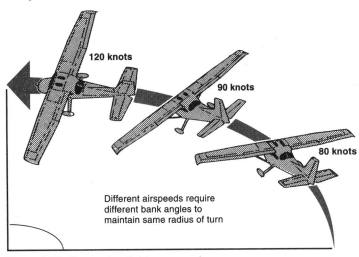

Figure 3-55. Constant-radius turn

Constant-Speed Turn

At a constant airspeed, the greater the bank angle, the tighter the turn (the smaller the radius of turn) and the greater the rate of turning (in degrees per second).

Notes:

- If airspeed and bank angle are kept constant, the turn radius (and rate) will remain the same regardless of airplane weight.
- For those who are mathematically minded, the relationship between bank angle (θ), turn radius (ρ) and airspeed (V) is $\tan \theta = \frac{V^2}{gr}$. If bank angle remains constant and airspeed doubles, the turn radius must increase four times. Similarly if airspeed remains constant and the turn radius is reduced, bank angle must increase.

At a constant bank angle a reduction in airspeed will reduce the turn radius and increase rate of turn.

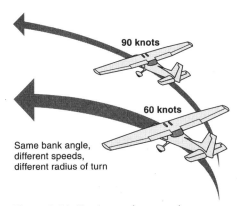

Same bank angle, different speeds, different radius of turn

Figure 3-54. Turning performance is increased at low airspeeds

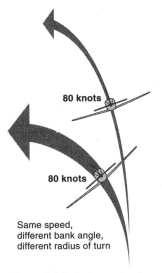

Same speed, different bank angle, different radius of turn

Figure 3-56. A steeper bank angle at constant speed increases turn performance

Flaps and Turning

If flaps are lowered before a level turn, the stall speed reduces allowing the airplane to turn at a slower airspeed. This has the advantage of allowing a smaller turn radius at the same bank angle.

Stalling

The Boundary Layer

We said earlier in this chapter that a wing stalls when it exceeds the critical angle-of-attack and the airflow separates from the wing's surface. To understand why this occurs it is important to study the boundary layer. The **boundary layer** is the thin ($\frac{1}{12}$ to $\frac{3}{4}$ inch) layer of air next to the wing's surface. Because of the air's viscosity, or stickiness, the speed of the air in the boundary layer is reduced below that of the main airflow.

In the boundary layer the air closest to the surface will be slowest. As the distance from the surface increases the relative speed of the air increases until it reaches that of the main airflow (free-stream flow). You may have noticed when watching water flow down a dam spillway that at the top the flow is thin and laminar, and then at some point it becomes thicker and turbulent. This is a visual picture that flow (in this case water) has two types, laminar and turbulent, separated by a transition point or region.

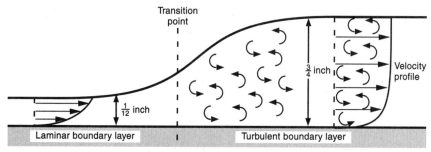

Figure 3-57. The boundary layer over a flat surface

The Adverse Pressure Gradient

Over a curved surface such as a wing, however, there is an additional factor that affects the boundary layer. As the airflow is fastest at the point of maximum curvature, the static pressure there will be lowest. Further aft the airflow's speed decreases and the static pressure, although still low, increases. This difference in static pressure causes a pressure gradient which acts in the opposite direction to the airflow. This is called an **adverse pressure gradient.**

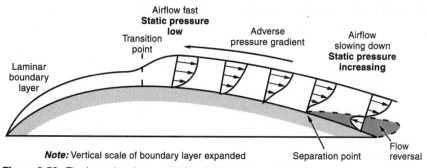

Figure 3-58. The boundary layer over the wing's upper surface

Close to the wing's surface the air is moving slowest and therefore has less kinetic energy to overcome this adverse pressure gradient. As the air in the boundary layer moves aft it slows, and at some point the adverse pressure gradient will be strong enough to stop it. This is the **separation point.** Note that aft of the separation point *flow reversal* occurs, where the air close to the wing is actually moving forward against the main flow.

Separation and the Stall

As the angle-of-attack increases, the static pressure at the point of maximum curvature will become even lower. The adverse pressure gradient now strengthens and the separation point moves further forward until the point is reached where the wing stalls.

Wing Contamination and Slats

If the adverse pressure gradient were kept constant, and the speed of the boundary layer altered, the separation point would also move. Ice, frost and other contamination on the wing slow down the speed of the thin boundary layer causing the separation point to move forward and the wing to stall at a lower angle-of-attack (which reduces the wing's lifting ability).

Slats, which introduce high speed air into the boundary layer near the leading edge, delay the forward movement of the separation point, so allowing the wing to fly at higher angles-of-attack (increasing the wing's lifting ability), *see* Figure 1-50.

Spinning

Autorotation

The two main features of the autorotation that occurs when a wing drops in stalled flight are:

- auto-roll—the more-deeply stalled dropping wing will generate even less lift, and so will want to keep dropping, causing the airplane to continue rolling; and
- auto-yaw—the dropping wing will generate increased drag, and want to yaw the nose of the airplane in the same direction as the roll.

If a wing drops in flight, perhaps from a gust or perhaps intentionally by the pilot's actions, the relative airflow will strike it more from below, and so its angle-of-attack will be greater. The rising wing, conversely, will have its angle-of-attack temporarily reduced.

In normal flight, at fairly low angles-of-attack well away from the stall, the increased angle-of-attack of the dropping wing will cause it to develop more lift. Conversely, the reduced angle-of-attack of the rising wing reduces its lift. The natural tendencies of the airplane in normal flight will therefore be for the airplane to roll wings level.

In stalled flight, however, the increased angle-of-attack on the dropping wing will cause it to be even more stalled, and develop even less lift. The result is that the dropping wing in a stalled condition will continue to drop, and the rolling motion will tend to continue. This will occur without any movement of the ailerons, so this characteristic may be thought of as **auto-roll.**

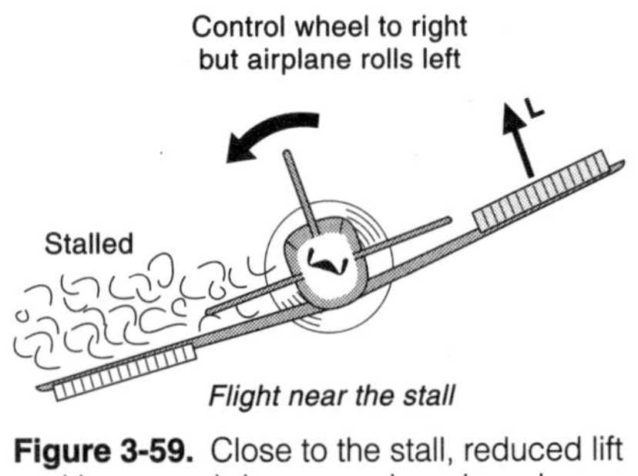

Control wheel to right but airplane rolls left

Stalled

Flight near the stall

Figure 3-59. Close to the stall, reduced lift and increased drag on a dropping wing cause autorotation

The *auto-roll* effect can be illustrated on the familiar *lift curve,* which shows lift increasing with angle-of-attack, but only up to the critical stall angle-of-attack beyond which lift decreases.

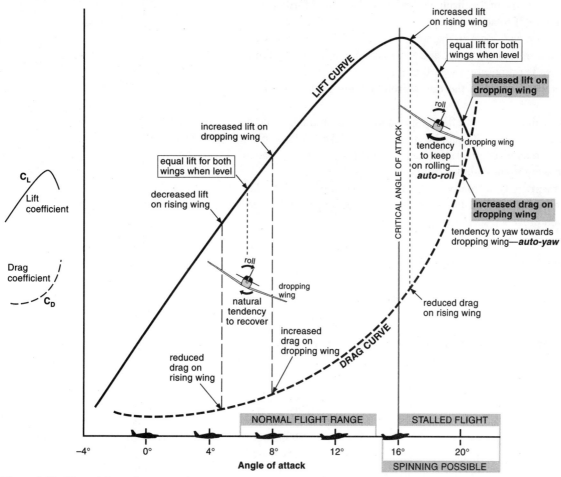

Figure 3-60. Lift and drag effects on a dropping wing

In normal flight, when lift on a wing increases, so does drag. In stalled flight, however, as we can see from the *drag curve* above, a dropping wing that is stalled not only experiences reduced lift, causing it to continue rolling (auto-roll), it also experiences increased drag which tends to yaw it in the direction of roll (auto-yaw).

In addition, the yawing motion in the same direction as the roll will *increase* the rolling tendency because the outside wing is traveling faster. This makes the rolling-yawing cycle self-sustaining, or automatic, in that the increased rolling velocity sustains or even increases the difference in the angle-of-attack on the two wings, strengthening the roll-yaw tendency. This natural tendency to *continue* rolling and yawing in the same direction when in the stalled condition is known as **autorotation.** Autorotation is the basis of the spin.

Rate of Rotation
The flatness of the spin will determine the rate of rotation. If the airplane adopts a higher nose attitude and the spin flattens:

• the rate of rotation will decrease; and
• the rate of descent will reduce (caused by increased drag from the higher angle-of-attack).

A spinning ice skater moves her arms in and out from her body to alter the rate of rotation. The same effect occurs in an airplane. In a steep nose-down attitude, the mass of the airplane is close to the spin axis and the rate of rotation is high. If the spin flattens, some of the airplane's mass is distributed further from the spin axis and the rate of rotation decreases.

If the nose pitches up and down in the spin, the rate of rotation will vary, becoming slower when the spin is flatter and faster when the nose position is steeper. Since the nose is purposely lowered in the recovery from a spin, you can expect a temporary increase in the rate of rotation until the recovery is complete.

A **rearward CG** will encourage a flatter spin and it will be more difficult to lower the nose in the recovery. This applies to straight stalls as well as spins, and is a very important reason for ensuring that you never fly an airplane loaded outside its approved weight-and-balance limits.

Conversely, a **forward CG** normally results in a steeper spin with a higher rate of descent and a higher rate of rotation. It may make recovery much easier and, in fact, may even prevent a spin occurring.

A rearward CG makes a spin recovery more difficult.

Spin Direction

Spin direction is determined by the direction of yaw. This can be found from the turn coordinator. Do not use the inclinometer to determine direction of yaw as it will indicate the same regardless of turn direction depending on where it is mounted.

✍ Now complete **Review 3, Commercial Part (b)** on page 92.

✍ Review 3

Part (a)

1. In steady straight-and-level flight;
   (a) lift is greater than drag and thrust equals weight.
   (b) weight equals lift and drag equals thrust.
   (c) lift equals weight and thrust is greater than drag.

   ➤ (b)

2. In steady-state flight the sum of the opposing forces acting on an airplane is equal to:
   (a) zero.
   (b) the thrust plus total lift.
   (c) the total weight of the airplane plus the total drag.

   ➤ (a)

3. If indicated airspeed is decreased, then for the airplane to remain in straight-and-level flight, the angle-of-attack must be (increased/reduced).

   ➤ increased

4. Low indicated airspeeds are associated with (high/low) angles-of-attack and a (high/low) nose attitude.

   ➤ high, high

Basic Flight Maneuvers

5. If the weight decreases, then, for straight-and-level flight to continue, the lift must _____. This is achieved by (increasing/decreasing) the angle of attack or (increasing/decreasing) the airspeed.

   ➤ decrease, decreasing, decreasing

6. Ice or frost on the wings is hazardous because:
   (a) it changes the aerodynamic shape of the airfoils, thereby decreasing lift.
   (b) it causes the airflow to slow, decreasing control surface effectiveness.
   (c) it disrupts the smooth airflow over the wings, decreasing the lifting ability.

   ➤ (c)

Part (b)

1. In a steady climb, when the airplane is not accelerating or decelerating, the four main forces (are/are not) in equilibrium.

   ➤ are

2. An airplane that climbs 700 feet in 2 minutes has a rate of climb of (50/260/350/700) fpm.

   ➤ 350 fpm

---

3. An airplane will clear obstacles by a greater margin at the (best angle-of-climb speed/best rate-of-climb speed/cruise-climb speed).

➤ best angle-of-climb speed

4. During the transition from straight-and-level flight to a climb, the angle-of-attack is:
   (a) increased but lift is decreased.
   (b) increased but lift remains the same.
   (c) increased and lift is momentarily increased.

➤ (c)

5. To climb 1,200 feet in 2 minutes, your rate of climb needs to be _____ fpm.

➤ 600 fpm

6. Rate of climb is shown in the cockpit on the _____.

➤ vertical speed indicator

7. An airplane will reach a given altitude in the minimum time if it climbs at the (best angle-of-climb speed/best rate-of-climb speed/cruise-climb speed).

➤ best rate-of-climb speed

8. A prolonged en route climb is best flown:
   (a) at a relatively low airspeed to gain height quickly.
   (b) at a relatively low airspeed for better engine cooling and improved visibility.
   (c) at a relatively high airspeed for better engine cooling.

➤ (c)

9. The angle of climb of the same airplane carrying the pilot and three passengers will be (greater/less) than the angle of climb when only the pilot is on board.

➤ less

10. The altitude at which the climb performance of an airplane falls to zero is called its _____ .

➤ absolute ceiling

11. If the airplane is climbing into a headwind after takeoff, the climb angle relative to the ground obstacles on the ground, will be (the same/steeper/shallower).

➤ steeper

12. The takeoff ground run may be shortened by using a small flap extension, but once in flight, the climb angle through the air is (steeper/flatter/the same) when compared with a clean (flaps up) airplane.

➤ flatter

13. Climb performance reduces if:
    (a) weight, altitude and temperature reduce.
    (b) weight, temperature and altitude increase.
    (c) power and weight increase.

➤ (b)

14. In a steady glide the airplane (is/is not) in equilibrium, with weight counteracted by _____ and _____ .

➤ is, lift, drag

15. Adding power, while maintaining the same airspeed, will (increase/decrease/not alter) the rate and angle of descent.

➤ decrease

16. If flaps are lowered, the drag (increases/decreases) and the descent becomes (steeper/shallower).

➤ increases, steeper

17. Flying faster than the correct descent speed will (steepen/flatten) the descent angle through the air.

➤ steepen

18. If the same angle-of-attack is maintained, a heavy airplane will glide (further/not as far/the same distance) compared with when it is light. To glide the same distance as when it is heavy, a light airplane will need (a higher/a lower/the same) airspeed on descent.

➤ the same distance, a lower airspeed

19. A tailwind will (increase/decrease) glide distance over the ground.

➤ increase

20. If you have a rate of descent of 500 fpm, how long will it take you to descend 3,000 feet in a 20 knot headwind?

➤ 6 mins (wind does not affect rate of climb or descent)

21. If an airplane is flown in a glide at an airspeed where the L/D ratio is 8:1, for each 1,000 feet of altitude lost it will glide an air distance of _____ feet.

➤ 8,000 feet

22. How much altitude would an airplane lose in gliding 1 statute mile in still air at an airspeed providing a L/D ratio 10:1? (1 statute mile is 5,280 feet.)

➤ 528 feet

Part (c)

1. Load factor is the ratio of _____ /_____ .

➤ lift/weight

2. For an airplane to turn, a _____ force is required. This is provided by the _____ component of the _____ force.

➤ centripetal, horizontal, lift

3. To retain a vertical component of lift to counteract the weight, the lift force required in a level turn must be (greater than/equal to/less than) the lift required when flying straight-and-level.

➤ greater than

4. An airplane turns as the result of:
(a) the horizontal component of a tilted lift force.
(b) equilibrium between the four main forces.
(c) ailerons.

➤ (a)

5. To maintain airspeed in a turn, the pilot must apply _____ to overcome the increased (parasite/induced) drag.

➤ power, induced

6. The load factor in a turn depends on:
(a) bank angle.
(b) airspeed.
(c) bank angle and airspeed.

➤ (a)

For Questions 7–9, refer to Figure 3-25 on page 69.

7. In a 60° banked turn at a constant altitude, the load factor is _____, and the wings must generate a force equal to (3/2/1) times the weight of the airplane.

➤ 2, 2

8. If an airplane weighs 3,300 pounds, the approximate 'load' that the airplane structure is required to support in a 30° banked turn while maintaining altitude is _____ pounds.

➤ 3,960 pounds approximately (3,300 × 1.2)

9. If an airplane weighs 5,400 pounds, the approximate 'load' that the airplane structure is required to support in a 55° banked turn while maintaining altitude is _____ pounds.

➤ 9,180 pounds approximately (5,400 × 1.7)

Part (d)

1. Stalling occurs at a (high/low) angle-of-attack when the airflow around the airfoil is unable to remain streamline, and separates from the airfoil surface and becomes _____.

➤ high, turbulent

2. Beyond the stall angle, the lift produced by the wing (increases/decreases), and the center of pressure moves (rearward/forward), causing the nose to (raise/drop).

➤ decreases, rearward, drop

3. If the wings stall, the turbulent airflow over the horizontal stabilizer may cause control _____.

➤ control buffet

4. The stall angle on a typical light training airplane could be (0/4/16)° angle-of-attack.

➤ 16°

5. An airplane wing can be stalled:
(a) only when the nose is high and the airspeed is low.
(b) at any airspeed and in any flight attitude, provided that the critical angle-of-attack is reached.

➤ (b)

6. Indicated stall speed is affected by changes in (temperature/density/altitude/load factor).

➤ load factor (stall IAS is not affected by air density)

7. At higher weights, the airplane will stall at (a higher/a lower/the same) angle-of-attack.

➤ the same

8. If the airplane approaches the stall angle with a lot of power on, the slipstream adds a lot of kinetic energy to the airflow, and so separation and stalling is delayed. The stall speed power on is (less than/the same as/greater than) the power-off stall speed.

➤ less than

9. Attempting to pick-up a dropped wing with aileron near the stall on some airplanes can:
(a) stall the dropped wing by increasing its angle-of-attack beyond the stall angle.
(b) stall the upper wing by increasing its angle-of-attack beyond the stall angle.
(c) stall the upper wing by decreasing its angle-of-attack.

➤ (a)

10. Washout designed into a wing causes the (inner/outer) section of the wing to stall first.

➤ inner

11. In what flight condition must an aircraft be placed in order to spin?
(a) Partially stalled with one wing low.
(b) In a steep diving spiral.
(c) Stalled.

➤ (c)

12. During an approach to a stall, an increased load factor caused by turning or turbulence will make the airplane:
    (a) stall at a higher airspeed.
    (b) have a tendency to spin.
    (c) more difficult to control.
➤ (a)

13. How does frost and ice affect the lifting surfaces of an airplane on takeoff?
    (a) Frost and ice will change the shape of the wing, increasing lift at takeoff.
    (b) Frost and ice on the wing may delay the takeoff to a higher airspeed than normal.
    (c) Frost and ice on the wing may cause the airplane to become airborne at a lower than normal airspeed.
➤ (b)

Commercial Review

Commercial Part (a)

1. To achieve the minimum fuel burn-off for a given air distance, you should fly at the airspeed for maximum (endurance/range).
➤ range

2. Maximum-range cruise airspeed is minimum (thrust/power) airspeed; maximum-endurance airspeed is minimum (thrust/power) airspeed.
➤ thrust, power

3. The airspeed at which minimum drag occurs is also the cruise airspeed at which minimum (thrust/power) occurs.
➤ thrust

4. Minimum thrust for steady cruise flight occurs at:
    (a) maximum cruise speed.
    (b) minimum cruise speed.
    (c) the speed for minimum total drag.
➤ (c)

5. The maximum-range airspeed is the airspeed where minimum (drag/power) occurs.
➤ drag

6. Minimum fuel flow for an airplane powered by a piston engine and propeller occurs at the airspeed for minimum (power/thrust). The lower the fuel flow in gallons/hour, the greater the (range/endurance).
➤ power, endurance

7. As weight reduces, the maximum range airspeed, which is the airspeed for minimum drag, (increases/reduces/stays the same).
➤ reduces

8. An airplane is *speed stable* (above/below) the minimum-drag airspeed.
➤ above

9. An airplane that climbs 250 feet in 30 seconds has a rate of climb of _____ fpm.
➤ 500 fpm

10. Rate of climb depends on _____ .
➤ excess power

11. Angle of climb depends on:
    (a) maximum lift.
    (b) excess thrust
    (c) excess power.
➤ (b)

12. Climb performance on a hot day is (better/worse) than on a cold day.
➤ worse

For Questions 13–17, refer to Figure 1-71 on page 38.

13. To achieve the best glide range in this airplane, you would glide it at the airspeed for _____ °angle-of-attack, where (L/D ratio/C_L/C_D) is at its maximum value.
➤ 6° angle-of-attack, L/D ratio maximum

14. If flown at an angle-of-attack of 10°, the airplane will have a lift/drag ratio of _____:1.
➤ 11:1

15. If the airplane glides at an angle-of-attack of 10°, it will descend _____ feet in 1 statute mile.
➤ 480 feet (L/D = 11:1, $\frac{5280}{11} = 480$)

16. How much altitude will this airplane lose in 3 miles of gliding at an angle-of-attack of 8°?
    (a) 440 feet.
    (b) 880 feet.
    (c) 1,320 feet.
➤ (c) (L/D = 12, $\frac{3 \times 5280}{12} = 1,320$)

17. The L/D at 2° angle-of-attack, which is at a high airspeed, is approximately the same as at _____° angle-of-attack, which is at a low airspeed.
➤ 16.5° angle-of-attack

For Questions 18–19, refer to Figure 1-70 on page 37.

18. At the airspeed represented by point "a", in steady flight the airplane will:
    (a) have its maximum L/D ratio.
    (b) have its minimum L/D ratio.
    (c) be developing its maximum coefficient of lift.

    ➤ (a)

19. At the airspeed represented by point "b", in steady flight the pilot can expect to obtain the airplane's maximum:
    (a) endurance.
    (b) glide range and cruise range.
    (c) coefficient of lift.

    ➤ (b)

Commercial Part (b)

1. To increase rate of turn at a constant airspeed, you would have to _____ bank angle.

   ➤ increase

2. To decrease radius of turn at a constant airspeed, you would have to _____ bank angle.

   ➤ increase

3. To increase rate of turn at a constant bank angle, you would have to _____ airspeed.

   ➤ reduce

4. To reduce radius of turn at a constant bank angle, you would have to _____ airspeed. The rate of turn would _____ .

   ➤ reduce, increase

5. If bank angle is kept constant, but airspeed in the turn is varied, the wing loading will (vary/remain constant).

   ➤ remain constant

6. In a turn wing loading and load factor depend only on (bank angle/airspeed).

   ➤ bank angle

7. Turning though 120° at standard rate, would take _____ seconds. The bank angle required to achieve this at 100 knots would be _____.

   ➤ 40 seconds, 15°

8. A normal category airplane is stressed to _____ g. If a baggage compartment weight limit is 80 lb, what is the maximum baggage weight you can put in the compartment if you intend to fly up to 3g.

   ➤ 3.8g, 80 lb

For Question 9, refer to Figure 3-36 on page 76.

9. Determine the stall speed in KIAS at gross weight 2,750 pounds under the following conditions:
   (a) Gear and flaps up, wings level, power on.
   (b) Gear and flaps up, 30° bank angle, power on.
   (c) Gear and flaps up, 45° bank angle, power off.
   (d) (d)Gear and flaps down, 30° bank angle, power off.

   ➤ (a) 54 KIAS; (b) 58 KIAS; (c) 77 KIAS;
   (d) 62 KIAS

10. To increase rate of turn and at the same time decrease turn radius, the pilot should:
    (a) maintain the bank and decrease airspeed.
    (b) steepen the bank and increase airspeed.
    (c) steepen the bank and decrease airspeed.

    ➤ (a)

11. While maintaining a constant bank angle and altitude in a coordinated turn, an increase in airspeed will:
    (a) decrease the rate of turn resulting in a decreased load factor.
    (b) decrease the rate of turn resulting in no change in load factor.
    (c) increase the rate of turn resulting in no change in load factor.

    ➤ (b)

12. Turbulent air can cause an increase in stall speed by:
    (a) abrupt increases in the angle-of-attack and load factor.
    (b) abrupt decreases in the angle-of-attack and load factor.
    (c) abrupt increases in weight.

    ➤ (a)

13. It is more difficult to recover from a stall or spin when the airplane is loaded with a (forward/mid-range/aft) center of gravity.

    ➤ aft

14. Which is true regarding the use of flaps during turns?
    (a) The addition of flaps increases the stall speed.
    (b) The addition of flaps decreases the stall speed.
    (c) In any given degree of bank, the addition of flaps has no effect on stall speed.

    ➤ (b)

15. A rectangular wing, as compared to other wing shapes, has a tendency to stall first at the:
    (a) wingtip, providing adequate stall warning.
    (b) wing root, providing adequate stall warning.
    (c) wing root, providing inadequate stall warning.

    ➤ (b)

The Airplane Section Two

Airframes 4

Airplane Components

The major components of an airplane are:

- the fuselage;
- the wings;
- the empennage (tail section);
- the flight controls;
- the landing gear (or undercarriage);
- the engine and propeller.

Fuselage

The fuselage forms the body of the airplane to which the wings, empennage, engine and landing gear are attached. It contains a cabin with seats for the pilot and passengers, plus the cockpit controls and instruments, and may also contain baggage lockers.

The fuselage of many modern training airplanes is of **semi-monocoque** construction, a light framework covered by a skin (usually aluminum) that carries much of the stress. It is a combination of the best features of a **strut-type** structure, in which the internal framework carries almost all of the stress, and a **monocoque** structure which, like an eggshell, has no internal structure and the stress is carried by the skin.

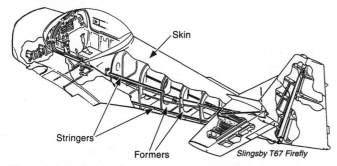

Figure 4-1. Typical semi-monocoque construction

Wings

The wings are designed to cope with the flight loads of lift and drag. They also may support other external devices such as engines and flaps.

Wings generally have one or more internal **spars** which are attached to the fuselage and extend to the wingtips. The spars carry the major loads, which are upward bending because of the lift, and downward bending because of wing-mounted engines and fuel.

The wings in most airplanes also contain **fuel tanks** installed between the curved upper and lower surfaces. This is an efficient use of the space available, and the weight of the fuel in the tanks also provides a downward force on the wing structure that reduces the upward bending effect of the lift forces.

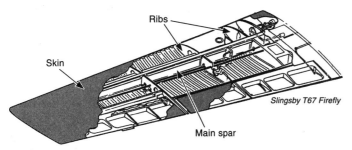

Figure 4-2. Spars, ribs and formers in the wing

In addition to the spar(s), some wings also have external **struts** connecting them to the fuselage to provide extra strength by transmitting some of the wing loads to the fuselage.

Ribs, roughly perpendicular to the wing spar(s), assisted by stringers running parallel to the spars, provide the airfoil shape and stiffen the skin which is attached to them. The ribs transmit loads between the skin and the spar(s).

Monoplanes are designed with a single set of wings placed so that the airplane is known as a high-wing, low-wing, or mid-wing monoplane. Biplanes, such as the Pitts Special, are designed with a double set of wings. The Cessna 172 is a high-wing monoplane; the Piper Warrior is a low-wing monoplane.

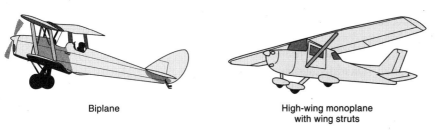

Biplane

High-wing monoplane
with wing struts

Low-wing monoplane

Figure 4-3. A biplane, high-wing monoplane and low-wing monoplane

Empennage

The empennage is the tail section of the airplane. It is generally constructed like the wings and consists of a fixed **vertical stabilizer** (or fin) to which is attached a movable **rudder,** and a fixed **horizontal stabilizer** with a movable **elevator** hinged to its trailing edge.

There are variations in design, some airplanes have a stabilator (all-moving tailplane), others have a ruddervator (combined rudder and elevator) in the form of a butterfly tail, and yet others have a high T-tail, with the horizontal stabilizer mounted on top of the vertical stabilizer.

Flight Controls

The main flight control surfaces are the **elevator, ailerons** and **rudder.** They are operated from the cockpit by moving the control column and rudder pedals. In a typical airplane, movement of the control column or rudder pedals operates an internal system of cables and pulleys that then moves the relevant control surface. Turnbuckles may be inserted in the cables to allow the cable tension to be adjusted by qualified personnel.

There are usually stops to protect the control surfaces from excessive movement in flight and on the ground. Stops in the flight control system may be installed to limit control column movement.

Flight controls are fully covered in Section 1.

Landing Gear

The landing gear (or undercarriage) supports the weight of the airplane when it is on the ground, and may be of either the tricycle type (with a nosewheel) or the tailwheel type. Most tricycle landing gear airplanes are equipped with **nose-wheel steering** through the rudder pedals, and almost all airplanes have **main wheel brakes.**

Main Wheels

The main wheels carry most of the load when the airplane is on the ground, especially during the takeoff and landing, and so are more robust than the nose-wheel (or tailwheel). They are usually attached to the main airplane structure with legs in the form of:

- a very strong spring leaf of steel or fiberglass;
- struts and braces; or
- an oleo strut.

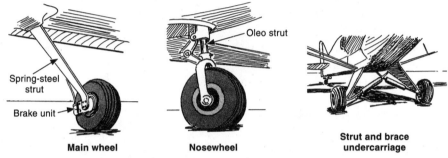

Figure 4-4. Various means of attaching the landing gear

The **oleo strut** acts as a shock absorber, and is of telescopic construction, with a piston that can move within a cylinder against an opposing pressure of compressed air. The piston is attached to the wheel by an oleo strut and the cylinder is attached to the airframe.

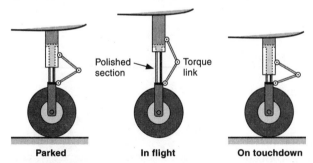

Figure 4-5. The oleo strut

The greater the load on the strut, the more the air is compressed by the piston. While the airplane is running along the ground, the load will be varying, and so the strut will move up and down as the compressed air absorbs the loads and shocks, preventing jarring of the main airplane structure.

Special oil is used as a **damping agent** to prevent excessive in-and-out tele-scoping movements of the oleo strut and to damp its rebound action.

When the airplane is stationary, a certain length of polished oleo strut should be visible (depending to some extent on how the airplane is loaded), and this should be checked in the preflight external inspection. Items to check are:

- correct extension when supporting its share of the airplane's weight;
- the polished section of the oleo strut is clean of mud or dirt (to avoid rapid wearing of the seals during the telescoping motion of the strut); and
- there are no fluid leaks.

Nosewheel

The nosewheel is of lighter construction than the main wheels and is usually attached to the main structure of the airplane near the engine firewall.

A **torque-link** is used on nosewheel assemblies to correctly align the nosewheel with the airframe. It links the cylinder assembly attached to the airplane structure with the nosewheel assembly, and is hinged to allow for the telescopic extension and compression of the oleo.

Most airplanes have **nosewheel steering,** achieved by moving the rudder pedals which are attached by control rods or cables to the nosewheel assembly, thereby allowing the pilot greater directional control when taxiing.

Some airplanes have **castoring nosewheels** which are free to turn, but are *not* connected by controls to the cockpit. The pilot can turn the airplane by using the rudder when it has sufficient airflow over it (from either slipstream or airspeed) or with differential braking of the main wheels.

Nosewheel oleo struts are prone to **nosewheel-shimmy,** an unpleasant and possibly damaging vibration set up when the nosewheel oscillates a few degrees either side of center as the airplane runs along the ground. To prevent this, most nosewheel assemblies are equipped with a **shimmy-damper,** a small piston-cylinder unit that dampens out the oscillations and prevents the vibration. If nosewheel-shimmy does occur, it could be because the shimmy-damper is insufficiently pressurized or the torque link has failed.

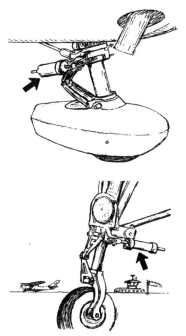

Figure 4-6. The shimmy-damper

Tires

Airplane tires must be inflated to the correct pressure for them to function as designed. Vibration during taxiing, uneven wear and burst tires may result from a pressure that is too high; damage to the tire structure and a tendency for the tire to creep with respect to the rim will occur if the pressure is too low. Correct **inflation** is important in achieving a good service life from a tire.

Creep will occur in normal operations because of the stresses during landing, when a stationary tire is forced to rotate on touching the ground and has to "drag" the wheel around with it, and will also occur when the airplane is braking or turning. To monitor creep, there are usually paint marks on the wheel flange and on the tire which should remain aligned. If any part of the two creep marks is still in contact, that amount of creep is acceptable, but if the marks are separated, then the inner tube may suffer damage and the tire should be inspected and serviced. This may require removal and reinstallation, or replacement.

Tire **strength** comes from its carcass which is built up from casing cords and then covered with rubber. The ply rating is a measure of its supposed strength. Neither the rubber sidewalls nor the tread provide the main strength of the tire; the sidewalls protect the sides of the tire carcass, and the rubber tread provides a wearing surface at the contact points between the tire and the runway.

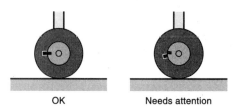

OK   Needs attention

Figure 4-7. "Creep" marks on the tire and wheel flange enable visual checks for creep

Shallow cuts or scores in the sidewalls or on the tread, or small stones embedded in the tread, will not be detrimental to tire strength. However, any large cuts (especially if they expose the casing cords) or bulges (that may be external indications of an internal casing failure) should cause you to reject the tire prior to flight.

The condition of the tires should be noted during the preflight external inspection, especially with respect to:

- inflation;
- creep;
- wear, especially flat spots caused by skidding;
- cuts, bulges (especially deep cuts that expose the casing cords); and
- damage to the structure of the sidewall.

Wheel Brakes

Most training airplanes are equipped with **disc brakes** on the main wheels. These are hydraulically operated by the **toe brakes** which are situated on top of the rudder pedals. Pressing the left toe brake will slow the left main wheel down and pressing the right toe brake will slow the right main wheel down. Used separately, they provide differential braking, which is useful for maneuvering on the ground. Used together, they provide normal straight line braking.

A typical system consists of a separate master cylinder containing hydraulic fluid for each brake. As an individual toe brake is pressed, this toe pressure is hydraulically transmitted via the master cylinder to a **slave cylinder** which closes the brake friction pads (like calipers) onto the brake disc. The brake disc, which is part of the wheel assembly, then has its rotation slowed down.

Most airplanes have a **parking brake** (usually hand-operated, sometimes in conjunction with the toe-brakes) that will hold the pressure on the wheel brakes and can be used when the airplane is parked.

During the preflight external inspection, you should check the brakes to ensure that they will function when you need them, ensuring that:

- there are no leaks of hydraulic brake fluid from the brake lines;
- the brake discs are not corroded or pitted;
- the brake pads are not worn-out; and
- the brake assembly is firmly attached.

A severely corroded or pitted disc will cause rapid wear of the brake pads, as well as reducing their effectiveness, and, in an extreme case, the disc may even fail structurally. Fluid leaks from the brake lines or cylinders indicate a faulty system that may in fact provide no braking at all when it is needed. Any brake problems should be rectified prior to flight.

Following a satisfactory external inspection, you should still test the brakes immediately after the airplane first moves, by closing the throttle and gently applying toe brake pressure. **Brake wear** can be minimized by judicious use of the brakes during ground operations.

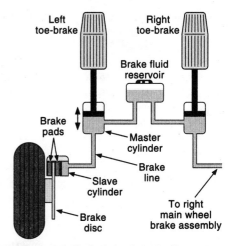

Figure 4-8. Typical simple hydraulic braking system

Engine and Propeller

The engine is usually mounted on the front of the airplane, and separated from the cockpit by a **firewall.** In most training airplanes, the engine drives a **fixed-pitch propeller,** although more advanced airplanes will have a **constant-speed propeller** with blades whose pitch can vary. The engine and its attachments are considered in detail in the next few chapters.

✍ Now complete **Review 4** on page 100.

✍ Review 4

Airframes

1. The main structural component of the wing is the (rib/strut/spar/skin).
   ➤ spar

2. Name the four major components of the empennage.
   ➤ vertical stabilizer and rudder, horizontal stabilizer and elevator

3. The airfoil shape of the wing surface is formed by the (spar/ribs/ailerons).
   ➤ ribs

4. Airplanes designed with only one set of wings are called _____ planes.
   ➤ monoplanes

5. The most usual form of fuselage construction in training airplanes, in which the skin covers a light structure and carries much of the stress, is called _____ .
   ➤ semi-monocoque

6. A cracked or severely corroded landing gear strut found during your preflight inspection (should/need not) be inspected by a qualified engineer before the airplane flies.
   ➤ should

7. The damping agent used to dampen the rebound action in the oleo strut following a shock is the (compressed air/oil).
   ➤ oil

8. The oleo strut will extend (further/the same/less) in flight than on the ground.
   ➤ further

9. Why should mud or dirt noticed in a preflight inspection be cleaned off the polished section of an oleo strut prior to taxiing?
   ➤ to avoid rapid wearing of the seals during taxiing and ground maneuvers as the strut telescopes in and out

10. The nosewheel is held aligned with a _____ link and nosewheel oscillations either side of center are damped by a _____ .
    ➤ torque link, shimmy-damper

11. The relative movement between the tire and the wheel flange is called _____ .
    ➤ creep

12. A nosewheel which is free to turn, but is not connected to the cockpit by any control rods or cables for turning is said to be of the _____ type.
    ➤ castoring

13. Nosewheel steering in light airplanes is usually operated by:
    (a) control rods or cables operated by the rudder pedals.
    (b) a steering wheel.
    (c) the brakes.
    ➤ (a)

14. A castoring nosewheel can be made to turn by:
    (a) a steering wheel.
    (b) differential braking.
    ➤ (b)

15. If a tire has moved so that the creep marks are out of alignment, then:
    (a) the tire is serviceable.
    (b) the tire should be inspected and possibly reinstalled or replaced.
    (c) tire pressure should be checked.
    ➤ (b)

16. A tire that has some shallow cuts in the sidewalls and a number of small stones embedded in its tread (should/need not) be rejected by a pilot.
    ➤ need not

17. A tire that has a deep cut that exposes the casing cords or a large bulge in the sidewall (should/need not) be rejected for further flight.
    ➤ should

18. Most light airplane braking systems are operated:
    (a) by cables.
    (b) pneumatically.
    (c) hydraulically.
    ➤ (c)

19. Hydraulic fluid leaks from the brake lines or other parts of the brake system (are/are not) acceptable.
    ➤ are not

20. Wheel brakes (should/should not) be tested early in the taxi.
    ➤ should

The Engine

Airplanes can be powered by a variety of engines, and the two fundamental types are **reciprocating** or **piston engines** and **gas turbines** (jets). The jet engine will not be considered in this manual.

The piston engine can be designed in various ways, many of which are suitable for airplanes. Older engine types often had the cylinders arranged **radially** around the crankshaft, for example the radial powerplants in the Stearman, Douglas DC-3, North American T-6, de Havilland Canada Beaver and Cessna 195.

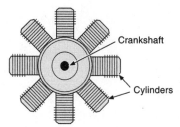

Figure 5-1. Radial engine

The de Havilland Canada Beaver and the Grumman Ag-Cat are two types with radial engines that are still in widespread commercial use today. These engines have an excellent power/weight ratio in the high power range required for operations such as agricultural spraying.

Some airplanes have **in-line engines,** where the cylinders are arranged in one line—the same basic design as in many automobiles. Some of the earliest airplanes had upright, in-line engines, with the cylinder head at the top of the engine and the crankshaft/propeller shaft at the bottom, but this caused some design problems. Raising the thrust line to a suitable position, because of aerodynamic design requirements, put the cylinders and the main body of the engine in a very high position. This obscured the pilot's vision and prevented effective streamlining.

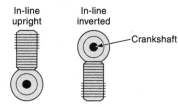

Figure 5-2. In-line engine and inverted in-line engine

Another problem with a low crankshaft/propeller shaft was the ground clearance of the propeller, requiring long struts for the main wheels. The easiest way to solve this problem was to invert the engine and have the crankshaft/ propeller shaft at the top of the engine, quite different to automotive engine design where the crankshaft is always at the bottom. Many airplanes have these *inverted* in-line engines.

There are other possibilities as well, such as V-engines and H-engines (V and H describes the layout of the cylinders), which were used in military airplanes such as the P-40 Kittyhawk and P-51 Mustang, types which required high horsepower (2,000–3,000 horsepower) from a compact engine.

The usual powerplant found in the modern light airplane is the **reciprocating engine,** with the cylinders (4, 6 or 8 of them) laid out in a **horizontally opposed** manner.

Figure 5-3. Horizontally opposed engine

The most common light airplane engine is the horizontally opposed reciprocating engine.

Basic Principles

The reciprocating engine has a number of cylinders within which pistons move back and forth (hence the name reciprocating engine). In each cylinder a fuel/ air mixture is burned, and the heat energy causes gases to expand and push the piston down the cylinder. A two-stage energy-conversion process is therefore involved, whereby chemical energy (in the fuel) is initially converted to heat energy in the cylinder, and then finally converted to mechanical energy by the action of the piston.

The piston is connected by a rod to a crankshaft, which it turns. This connecting rod, or conrod, converts the back-forth motion of the piston into a rotary motion of the crankshaft, which transmits the power generated by the engine to the propeller. Light airplanes with fixed-pitch propellers (and most with constant-speed propellers) have the propeller directly attached to the crankshaft, in which case the crankshaft is also the propeller shaft. The propeller produces the thrust force necessary for powered flight.

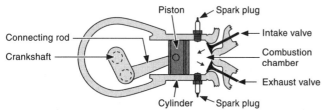

Figure 5-4. Parts of a typical reciprocating engine

Four-Stroke Engine Cycle

A complete cycle of this type of piston engine comprises four strokes of the piston traveling within the cylinder, hence the name **four-stroke engine.** The German engineer, Nicholas Otto, developed this engine, so the four-stroke cycle is also known as the **Otto cycle.** The four strokes are: **(1)** **intake** (or induction); **(2)** **compression**; **(3)** **power** (or expansion); **(4)** **exhaust.**

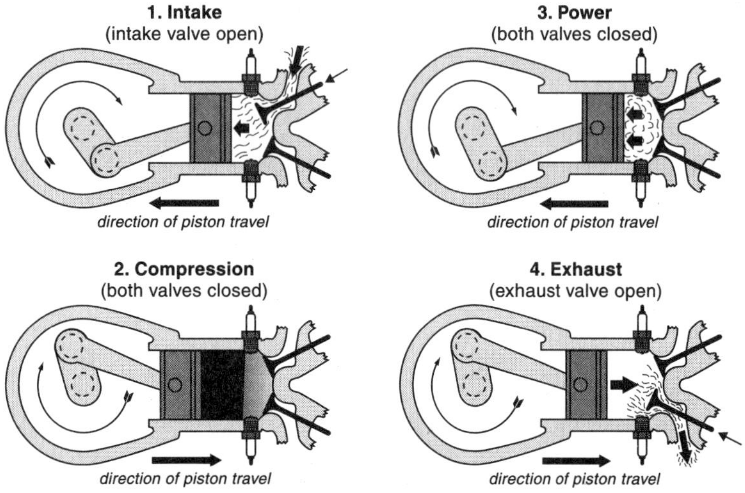

The four-stroke cycle comprises intake, compression, power and exhaust.

1. Intake
(intake valve open)

direction of piston travel

2. Compression
(both valves closed)

direction of piston travel

3. Power
(both valves closed)

direction of piston travel

4. Exhaust
(exhaust valve open)

direction of piston travel

Figure 5-5. The four strokes of a reciprocating engine

In the **intake** (or *induction)* stroke, the fuel/air mixture is "sucked" or induced to flow into the top of the cylinder. The piston, moving from the top to the bottom of the cylinder, decreases the pressure in the cylinder by increasing the volume of the space between the piston and the top of the cylinder. The decreased pressure draws air in through the induction system and, as the air passes through the carburetor prior to reaching the cylinder, fuel is metered into the airflow to provide a fuel/air mixture. A charge of this fuel/air mixture of gases is drawn into the cylinder during each induction stroke via the intake manifold and the temporarily open intake valve. The **intake manifold** is a pipe system distributing from a single input (the carburetor) to multiple outlets which are fed to the cylinder inlet ports.

Early in the **compression stroke,** the intake valve is closed and the piston moves back toward the top (or the head) of the cylinder. This increases the pressure of the fuel/air mixture, and because of the compression, the temperature of the fuel/air mixture rises.

As the piston is completing the compression stroke, the fuel/air mixture is ignited by an electrical discharge between the electrodes of a spark plug and a controlled burning commences. This causes the gases to expand rapidly and exert a strong pressure on the piston. The piston, which has now passed the top of its stroke, is pushed back down the cylinder in the **power stroke.**

Just prior to the completion of the power stroke, the exhaust valve opens and then, as the piston returns to the top of the cylinder in the **exhaust stroke,** the burnt gases are forced out of the cylinder to the atmosphere via the exhaust manifold, a pipe system that collects gases from the cylinder outlets and feeds them through an exhaust pipe to the atmosphere.

As the piston is approaching the cylinder head again, while the last of the burnt gases is being exhausted, the intake valve opens in preparation for the next induction stroke. And so the cycle continues.

In a single-cylinder Otto-cycle engine involving four strokes of the piston (down—*induction,* up—*compression,* down—*power,* up—*exhaust),* only one stroke provides power for each two rotations of the crankshaft (which carries the power to the propeller).

To increase the power developed by the engine and to allow smoother operation, the engine has a number of cylinders whose power strokes occur at different positions during the revolution of the crankshaft. The spacing of these power strokes is equal, so that evenly spaced impulses are imparted to the crankshaft. So, in a full Otto cycle of a six-cylinder engine, the crankshaft would, in two revolutions, receive the power from six different power stokes—one per cylinder.

An engine with four cylinders (common in light airplanes) would receive four impulses of power in two revolutions of the crankshaft. The more evenly these impulses of power from each of the cylinders are spread, the more efficient the transfer of power, the smoother the running of the engine and the less the vibration.

Valves and Valve Timing

The intake valve, through which the fuel/air mixture is taken into the cylinder, and the exhaust valve, through which the burned gases are exhausted, must open and close at the correct times during the four-stroke cycle of each piston. To achieve this, there is a **camshaft,** which is usually gear-driven by the crankshaft of the engine. The camshaft rotates at half-crankshaft speed, operating rocker arms and push rods which push the appropriate valve open (against spring pressure) at what has been determined by the design engineers to be the most suitable moment in the cycle.

A typical engine speed while cruising is **2,400 revolutions per minute (rpm).** Since the intake valve and exhaust valve of each cylinder must each open and close once during the four piston strokes of each complete cycle, the camshaft must rotate at half-crankshaft speed. At an engine speed of 2,400 rpm, each valve will have to open and close 1,200 times—1,200 times in 60 seconds means 20 times a second—quite amazing!

The power that the engine can develop depends on how much fuel/air mixture can be induced through the intake valve during the intake stroke, which, as we have seen, is extremely short. Opening the intake valve just prior to the piston reaching the top of its stroke, or **top-dead-center (TDC),** and not closing it until the piston has gone just past **bottom-dead-center (BDC)** following the induction stroke, allows maximum time for the intake of the fuel/air mixture to occur. This is called **valve lead** and **valve lag.**

Power is increased by increasing the amount of fuel/air mixture entering the cylinder by extending the time of the intake stroke using valve lead and valve lag.

Similarly, the exhaust valve opens just prior to the piston reaching bottom-dead-center on the power stroke and remains open until a little after the piston passes top-dead-center for the exhaust stroke and commences the induction stroke.

Notice that, for a brief period at the start of the induction stroke, the burned gases are still being exhausted through the still-open exhaust valve while a fresh charge (or slug) of fuel/air is commencing induction through the just-opened intake valve. This brief period when both the intake and the exhaust valves are open together is called **valve overlap.**

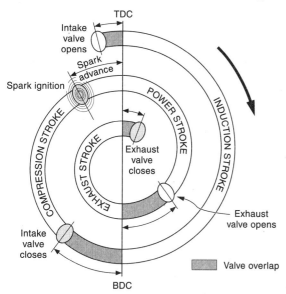

Figure 5-6. Typical valve timing in the four-stroke cycle

Ignition

A high voltage (or high tension) spark occurs in the cylinder just prior to the piston reaching top-dead-center, shortly before commencing the power stroke. This slightly advanced spark is to enable a controlled flame front to start moving through the fuel/air mixture that has been compressed in the cylinder. The purpose of the ignition system is to provide this correctly timed spark.

Most airplane engines have **dual** (and independent) **ignition** systems running in parallel with one another, with the magneto of each ignition system supplying one of the two **spark plugs** per cylinder.

A dual ignition system:

- is safer, in the event of failure of one ignition system; and
- results in more even and more efficient fuel combustion.

The necessary high-tension electrical current for the spark plugs comes from self-contained generation and distribution units called the **magnetos.** Each of the dual ignition systems has its own magneto which is mechanically driven by the engine.

The magneto consists of a magnet that is rotated (within the magneto housing) near a conductor which has a coil of wire wound around it. The rotation of the magnet induces an electrical current to flow in the coil. Around this primary coil is wound a secondary coil of many more turns of wire, which transforms the primary voltage into a much higher voltage. This arrangement of primary and secondary coils is known as a transformer. The higher voltage is fed to each spark plug at the appropriate time, causing a spark to jump between the two electrodes. This spark ignites the fuel/air mixture.

Dual ignition is safer and results in improved fuel combustion.

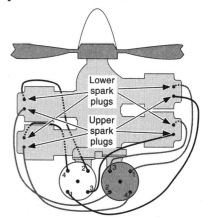

Cylinder firing order 1-3-2-4

Left magneto	**Right magneto**
its distributor fires right top and left bottom plugs	its distributor fires left top and right bottom plugs

Figure 5-7. A typical ignition system

The timing of the spark is critical. The magneto has a set of **breaker points** which are forced open and closed by a small cam that is part of the rotating magnet-shaft connected indirectly to the crankshaft. The points are in the circuit of the primary coil and, when they open, the electrical current in the primary coil stops flowing. This sudden collapse of the primary current (aided by a condenser or capacitor placed across the points) induces a high voltage in the secondary coil. The spark plug is in the circuit of the secondary coil and the large voltage (approximately 20,000 volts) across its electrodes causes a spark to jump between them.

As each cylinder is operating out of phase with the others, the current must be distributed to each spark plug at the correct moment (just prior to commencement of the power stroke). The **distributor,** which is part of the magneto, does this.

Each cylinder fires once in every two revolutions of the crankshaft and the distributor has a **finger** (distributor rotor) which is geared to the crankshaft in such a way that it turns only once for every two turns of the crankshaft. Therefore the distributor finger turns once in every complete four-stroke cycle. Once during each turn of the distributor finger it transfers the high-tension secondary current to each cylinder, in the correct firing order of the cylinders.

Separate leads to each of the spark plugs belonging to that ignition system (one per cylinder) emanate from different electrodes of the distributor case. These leads are often bound together, forming an **ignition harness.**

Leakage of current from the ignition harness will lead to rough running. One item of the preflight inspection is a visual check for chafing and heat cracking of those parts of the ignition harness easily seen.

While the engine is running, the magneto is a completely self-sufficient source of electrical energy and it operates independently of all the other electrical power sources. All it needs is a little mechanical energy from the engine to rotate the magnet.

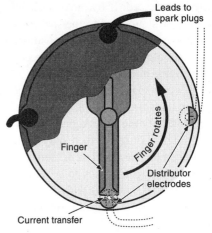

Figure 5-8. Distributor finger

Starter

Most modern training airplanes have an **electric starter motor** that is powered by the battery and activated by turning the ignition key to the *START* position.

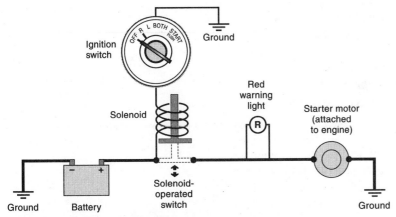

Figure 5-9. The electric starter system

Starting the engine causes a very high current to flow between the battery and the starter motor, and this requires heavy-duty wiring. If the ignition switch in the cockpit was directly connected to the starter circuit, heavy-duty wiring to the cockpit switch would be required.

Such an arrangement would have a number of disadvantages, including the additional weight of the heavy cable, a significant loss of electrical energy over the additional length, and high electrical currents through the cockpit environment (which would introduce an unnecessary fire risk). To avoid these disadvantages, the starter circuit connecting the battery to the starter motor is remotely controlled from the cockpit using a solenoid-activated switch.

Moving the ignition key to *START* causes a small current to flow through the starter key circuit and energize a **solenoid** (an electromagnet with a movable core). The energized solenoid operates a heavy-duty switch that closes the heavy-duty circuit between the battery and starter motor. High current flows through this circuit, activating the starter motor which turns the engine over. Electric starters often have an associated **starter warning light** in the cockpit that glows while the starter is engaged. It should extinguish immediately the starter is released. If by any chance the starter relay sticks (so that electrical power is still supplied to the starter motor even though the starter switch has been released from the *START* position) the warning light will remain on. The engine should be stopped (mixture control to *IDLE CUT-OFF*) to avoid damage to the engine and/or starter motor.

Only one spark per cylinder is necessary for start-up, so when the ignition key is in the *START* position, the right magneto system is automatically de-energized and only the left magneto system provides a high-tension supply to the spark plugs. (For this reason, only the left magneto is equipped with an impulse coupling, a device which aids the starting process—*see* below.) After start-up, switching the ignition key to *BOTH* activates the right magneto system as well, and the engine now runs with dual ignition in each cylinder.

Older airplanes with the starter switch separate to the magneto switches should have only the left magneto switch *ON* for start-up. Once the engine is started, you should switch the other magneto on as well.

There are two design limitations of magnetos that significantly affect starting an engine.

1. When the starter motor turns the engine over, the engine rotates comparatively slowly (approximately 120 rpm as against 800 rpm at idle speed). Because the magneto rotates at half crankshaft speed (to supply one spark per cylinder every two revolutions of the crankshaft), magneto speed at start-up is very slow, up to about 60 rpm. To generate a spark of sufficiently high voltage to ignite the fuel/air mixture requires a magneto speed of about 100–200 rpm, so some device must be incorporated in the system to overcome this slow magneto speed when starting the engine.

2. When the engine is running (800–2,700 rpm is a typical operating range) the spark occurs at a fixed number of degrees *prior* to the piston reaching top-dead-center at the commencement of the power stroke. This is known as **spark advance.** On start-up, with only very low revs occurring, unless the spark is **retarded** (delayed) until the piston is at or past top-dead-center, ignition of the gases could push the piston down the cylinder prematurely, causing the crankshaft to turn in the wrong direction. This is called **kick-back.**

To overcome these two difficulties special devices have been developed for installation in the magneto; the most common in small airplane engines is the **impulse coupling.**

Impulse Coupling

The impulse coupling initially delays the magnet from rotating as the engine is turned over. Energy from the initial part of the engine rotation is stored by winding up a coiled spring. When a certain amount of energy is stored, the coupling releases, and the spring accelerates the magnet rapidly. This generates a current of sufficient strength to create a spark across the electrodes of the spark plug. It also retards the spark sufficiently to allow the burning fuel/air mixture to drive the crankshaft in the correct direction.

Once the engine is started and is running at its usual rpm, the magnet's driveshaft accelerates away from the coiled spring, which has no further effect. The spark is then produced normally (by the engine rotating the magnet), and the timing is no longer retarded but operates normally, with the spark occurring just prior to commencement of the power stroke.

Notice that, as the impulse coupling does not depend on any electrical power source, the engine can be started by swinging the propeller. (This should only be done by trained and qualified personnel.) If you use an electric starter powered by the airplane battery to start the engine then, once the engine is running, disconnecting the battery will not stop the engine. It will, however, prevent the battery from being recharged.

Ignition Switch

There are two separate ignition systems for safety in the event of failure of one of them, as well as for more efficient burning of the fuel/air mixture with two sparks in the cylinder instead of one. Older airplanes often have separate switches for each magneto, while most modern airplanes have rotary switches operated by the ignition key. With these, you can select either the left system *L*, the right system *R*, or *BOTH*. *BOTH* is selected for normal engine operation. Airplanes with a separate starter button are usually started on the left magneto.

The engine will run on just one magneto, but not as smoothly as on two, and with a slight drop in rpm. With one spark instead of two, there will be only one flame-front advancing through the fuel/air mixture in the cylinder instead of two. This increases the time for full combustion to occur and decreases the efficiency of the burning.

If *L* is selected, only the left magneto system supplies a spark. The *R* magneto is grounded (or earthed), which means its current runs to ground and no spark is generated. Switching from *BOTH* to *L* should cause a drop in rpm and possibly slightly rougher running. If a slight drop in rpm does not occur, then either the *R* system is still supplying a spark or else the *R* magneto was not working previously when *BOTH* was selected.

The pilot will normally check both left and right magneto systems in this way as part of the pre-takeoff power check, switching from *BOTH* to *L*, noting the rpm drop and returning to *BOTH*, when the rpm originally set should be regained. Then the pilot will switch from *BOTH* to *R*, noting the rpm drop, and back to *BOTH*.

Comparisons are made between the two rpm drops, which should be within certain limits (*see* the Pilot's Operating Handbook for your particular airplane). Some typical figures are: check at 1,600 rpm on *BOTH*, magneto drop 125 rpm maximum on either *L* or *R* with a difference between these two drops not to exceed 50 rpm.

It is important to remember that placing the ignition switch to *OFF* grounds the primary winding of the magneto system so that it no longer supplies electrical power. This means that with a particular magneto's ignition switch *OFF*, the system is supposed to be grounded and unable to supply a spark.

Impulse coupling generates a high voltage and retards the ignition timing to start the engine.

Figure 5-10. The ignition switch in the cockpit

Always treat a propeller as live.

With a loose or broken wire, or some other fault, switching the ignition to *OFF* may not ground both of the magnetos. Therefore, a person moving the propeller could inadvertently start the engine, even though the ignition is switched off. It *has* happened, often with fatal results, and is still happening.

The pilot has no visual method of checking that the magneto systems, although switched off, are actually de-activated. Just before shutting an engine down, some pilots do a system function test at idle rpm, checking *BOTH, L, R*. This is followed by a dead-cut, where the ignition is switched to *OFF* (a sudden loss of power should be apparent) and rapidly back to *BOTH* to allow the engine to run normally. The engine is then shut down normally using the idle cut-off function of the mixture control. Some manufacturers/instructors advise against a dead-cut check as it may damage the engine. Refer to your Pilot's Operating Handbook.

If the ignition switch is momentarily switched off and the engine continues to run, this indicates that the system is not grounded, which is a dangerous situation.

Exhaust System

The burnt gases leave the engine cylinders and are carried out to the atmosphere via the exhaust system. It is important that there is no leakage of exhaust gas into the cabin because it contains carbon monoxide, a colorless and odorless gas that is difficult to detect, but can cause loss of consciousness and death.

✍ Now complete **Review 5, Part (a)** on page 118.

The Carburetor

Gasoline needs to be mixed with oxygen in the correct ratio to burn properly. The correct **fuel/air** ratio is about 1 part of fuel to 12 parts of air by **weight**. The device commonly used to mix fuel with air in an engine is called the **carburetor**.

The carburetor mixes fuel with air.

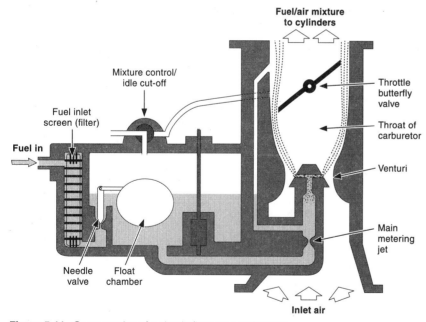

Figure 5-11. Cross-section of a simple float-type carburetor

The carburetor works on the principle that the airflow through the throat of the carburetor will have its pressure reduced by the venturi effect. This causes the fuel to flow through the main metering jet and into the airstream, because of the atmospheric pressure in the float chamber being greater. The fuel vaporizes and mixes with the air. The fuel/air mixture then flows through to the cylinders in preparation for burning. The pilot can vary the airflow using the **throttle lever** in the cockpit. The fuel/air mixture can be varied, if necessary, using the **mixture control.**

Combustion can occur in the cylinders when the fuel/air ratio is between approximately 1:8 **(rich mixture)** and 1:20 **(lean mixture).** The ideal or chemically correct mixture of fuel/air is one in which the fuel and the oxygen are perfectly matched so that, after burning, all of the fuel and all of the oxygen have been used. The chemically correct mixture may be referred to as the *ccm* or the *stoichiometric* mixture.

If the mixture is rich, there is *excess* fuel and, after burning, some unburned fuel will remain. If the mixture is lean, there is a *shortage* of fuel in the sense that, after all of the fuel has burned, there will still be some oxygen remaining.

A simple carburetor, like that in Figure 5-11, has a venturi through which the amount of airflow is controlled by a **throttle valve** (or **butterfly**). The venturi has fuel jets positioned in it so that the correct amount of fuel by weight is metered into the airflow. The butterfly valve is controlled with the throttle lever in the cockpit.

It is important that you move the throttle smoothly so that unnecessary stress is not placed on the many moving parts in the engine. To open or close the throttle fully should take about the same time as a "1-2-3" count.

A simple float-type carburetor has a small chamber that requires a certain level of fuel. If the level is too low, the float-valve opens and allows more fuel from the fuel tanks to enter. This is happening continually as fuel is drawn from the float chamber into the venturi of the carburetor. The air pressure in the float chamber is atmospheric, while the air pressure near the metering jet is reduced by the venturi effect.

The acceleration of the airflow through the carburetor venturi causes a decreased static pressure (Bernoulli's principle—increased velocity, decreased static pressure). The higher atmospheric pressure in the float chamber forces fuel through the main metering jet into the venturi airflow. The faster the airflow, the greater the differential pressure and the greater the quantity of fuel discharged to the airflow. Therefore the *weight* of fuel that flows through the carburetor is controlled by the airflow through the carburetor venturi.

Accelerator Pump

When you fully open the throttle, the butterfly valve is fully opened and does not restrict the airflow through the venturi. The airflow therefore increases.

If the throttle is opened quickly, the airflow initially increases at a rate greater than the fuel flow, producing an insufficiently rich (lean) mixture. This would cause a lag in the production of power if it were not for the **accelerator pump.** The accelerator pump is therefore used to prevent a weak-cut when the throttle is rapidly opened.

The accelerator pump is a small plunger within the float chamber, connected to the throttle linkage so that it gives an extra spurt of fuel as the throttle is opened.

Vary the fuel/air mixture with the mixture control.

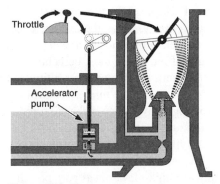

Figure 5-12. The accelerator pump

Idling System

When the engine is idling with the butterfly valve almost closed, the pressure differential between the venturi and the float chamber is not great enough to force fuel through the main jet. To allow for this, there is a small **idling jet** with an inlet near the butterfly valve, where a small venturi effect is caused when the valve is almost closed. This provides sufficient fuel to mix with the air to keep the engine idling at low rpm.

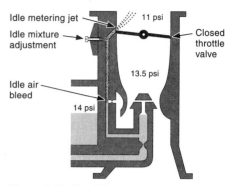

Figure 5-13. The idling system

Fuel/Air Mixture Control

The **fuel/air ratio** is the ratio between the weight of fuel and the weight of air mixed together and entering the cylinders where the combustion process is to occur. The carburetor is the device used to mix the fuel and the air, and it is designed in its most basic form to function best under mean sea level conditions at standard temperature +15°C (59°F).

Under other conditions when the air density is significantly less, such as at high altitudes or with high temperatures, the basic operation of the carburetor must be modified by the pilot to maintain a suitable fuel/air ratio.

Using the Mixture Control for Climbs and Descents

As altitude is gained in a climb, the volume of air flowing through the carburetor remains the same, but the weight of air is less because of its lower density (fewer molecules in the same volume). The same weight of fuel is drawn into the airstream, however, which means that the fuel/air mixture is now richer with fuel. This may lead to rough running, fouling of the spark plugs, increased fuel consumption, and a loss of power (loss of rpm for a fixed-pitch propeller and loss of manifold pressure for a constant-speed propeller).

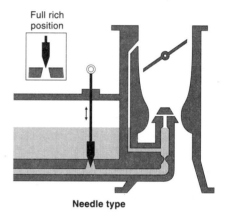

A **mixture control** is provided to keep the fuel/air ratio roughly constant. To return to a correct mixture, you can reduce the amount of fuel entering the carburetor venturi by moving the mixture control back out slightly toward lean. This moves a small needle in the carburetor which restricts the fuel flow through the main metering jet, thereby **leaning** the mixture, or making it less rich. The mixture control in the cockpit is usually a red knob. It should be moved smoothly and gradually, to avoid leaning the mixture too far and perhaps even stopping the engine by starving it of fuel. When climbing above approximately 5,000 feet MSL, if rough running is present, the mixture should only be leaned sufficiently to return the engine to smooth running. Normally, an engine is leaned if less than 75 percent power is being used.

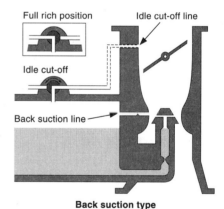

Figure 5-14. Mixture control systems

Conversely, as an airplane descends the air becomes more dense, and so the weight of air in each charge increases while the weight of fuel remains the same. This causes the fuel/air mixture to become leaner. The correct procedure on descent is to move the mixture control in toward the *RICH* position, which (for a given throttle position) will provide additional fuel to match the increased weight of air. Since most descents are made with low power set from cruise altitude until reaching pattern altitude at the destination airport, it is common practice to move the mixture control to the rich position at the top of descent, or to progressively richen the mixture (if descending from high altitude), so that the mixture control is correctly positioned for the approach and landing phase, when full power should be available in case of a go-around.

The mixture control is usually in *FULL RICH* for takeoff, unless you are operating at a high-elevation airport, possibly with high temperatures, where the air density as a consequence is very low (see below). Usually, the mixture remains in *FULL RICH* for the climb, unless it is an extended climb to altitudes in excess of 5,000 feet MSL.

As you climb with the mixture in *FULL RICH* the resulting excess fuel as the fuel/air mixture gradually becomes richer acts as a cooling agent for the cylinder walls and piston tops to help prevent abnormal combustion. Some of the more sophisticated engines require leaning during the climb, but for training airplanes this is not generally the case.

Using the Mixture Control at Cruise Altitude

On the cruise, and with cruise power set, you should consider leaning the mixture to regain a more chemically correct fuel/air ratio. This ensures more efficient burning of the gases in the cylinders, more efficient operation of the engine (slightly higher rpm for a fixed-pitch propeller) and better fuel economy. In some light airplanes correct leaning on the cruise can reduce the fuel consumption by over 25 percent compared with full rich, allowing greatly improved range and endurance performance.

The mixture should be slightly on the rich side of the chemically correct mixture, provided the cruise power setting is less than 75 percent of maximum continuous power (MCP). Normal cruise for most airplanes is about 55–65 percent MCP, and so leaning the mixture is advisable.

At high power settings (in excess of 75 percent) a full-rich mixture is necessary to provide excess fuel as a coolant. The Pilot's Operating Handbook contains information on how to achieve the best power mixture and how to achieve the best economy mixture.

To lean the mixture, slowly move the mixture control toward the lean position. As a chemically correct fuel/air ratio is regained, the rpm for a fixed-pitch propeller will increase. Eventually, with further leaning, the rpm will decrease slightly and the engine will show signs of rough running. The mixture control should then be gently pushed back in a small amount to regain the best rpm (indicating a chemically correct mixture) and smoother running. The mixture control is then moved further in to a slightly richer position to ensure that the engine is operating on the rich side of the chemically correct mixture. This must be repeated when either cruise altitude or power-setting is changed.

Some airplanes are equipped with an **exhaust gas temperature (EGT) gauge** which indicates peak EGT when there is a chemically correct mixture, and this can assist you in leaning the mixture correctly.

For a constant-speed propeller, the leaning is normally done with reference to a **fuel flow gauge** (to obtain minimum fuel flow for smooth running) or the exhaust gas temperature gauge. Refer to your Pilot's Operating Handbook.

The principles of leaning the mixture apply to both carburetor-equipped and fuel-injected engines (to be discussed shortly).

Note: Above 5,000 feet density altitude, a normally aspirated (not turbocharged) engine *cannot* achieve more than 75 percent maximum continuous power (even at full throttle).

Using the Mixture Control for Takeoff and Landing

During takeoff (and landing, when high power may be required in case of a go-around), the mixture control should normally be in *FULL RICH*.

In conditions where the air density is very low, however, such as at a very high elevation airport with high outside air temperatures (say 6,000 feet MSL and 100°F), you should consider if there is a need to lean the mixture. The reduced air density, sometimes referred to as a **high density altitude,** may result in too little air for the normal fuel flow, and an excessively fuel-rich mixture. When the engine runs too rich it is unable to provide its best power for takeoff.

An excessively rich mixture may be indicated on the ground by slightly rough running that is made worse during the carburetor heat check, when hot and even less-dense air enters the carburetor, starving the engine of air and further richening the fuel/air mixture.

You should discuss leaning the mixture for high density altitude takeoffs with your flight instructor, and refer to the Pilot's Operating Handbook.

Rich and Lean Mixtures

The mixture is usually slightly rich to protect against abnormal combustion and overheating in the cylinders. These damaging events are more likely to occur at power settings above 75 percent maximum continuous power than at the normal cruise power settings (55–65 percent), when leaning is advisable.

An over-rich mixture will cause a loss of power, rough running, high fuel consumption, fouling of the spark plugs and formation of lead deposits (from unburned fuel) on the piston heads and valves. The extra fuel in a rich mixture causes cooling within the cylinders by its evaporation which absorbs some of the heat produced in the combustion chamber. A lean mixture will therefore have higher cylinder head temperatures.

An excessively lean mixture will cause excessively high cylinder head temperatures, leading to abnormal combustion (detonation or preignition). The pilot is then faced with a loss of power and quite possibly complete engine failure. If you suspect that conditions are conducive to detonation, richen the mixture and check engine temperatures. A high cylinder head temperature could be an indication of detonation. Too rich is preferable to too lean.

> Too rich a mixture is preferable to too lean a mixture.

Idle Cut-Off (or Idle Cut-Out)

The **idle cut-off** position of the mixture control is the normal means of shutting the engine down. In a typical system, when the mixture control is moved fully out to the idle cut-off position by the pilot, a small needle moves to cut off the fuel flow between the float chamber and the venturi. The supply of fuel to the fuel jets is then cut off.

The engine will continue running until all of the fuel/air mixture in the inlet manifold and the cylinders is burned. This leaves no combustible fuel/air mixture anywhere in the system, which would not be the case if the engine was stopped simply by turning the ignition *OFF*.

Abnormal Combustion

There are two kinds of abnormal combustion and both should be avoided:

- detonation—explosive combustion; and
- preignition—early ignition ahead of the spark.

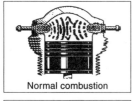
Normal combustion

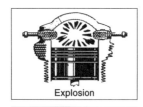
Explosion

Normal burning

Detonation

Figure 5-15. A comparison between normal combustion and detonation

Detonation

Correct progressive burning of the fuel/air mixture should occur as the flame-front advances through the combustion chamber. This causes an increase in pressure which smoothly forces the piston down the cylinder in the power stroke.

When a gas is compressed, it experiences a rise in temperature. You can feel this if you hold your hand over a bicycle pump outlet during the compression stroke. If the pressure and the temperature rise is too great for the fuel/air mixture in the cylinders, the burning will not be progressive, but explosive, spontaneous combustion of the unburned charge after normal spark ignition.

Detonation is the instantaneous, explosive combustion of the unburned charge in the cylinder.

This explosive increase in pressure is called **detonation** and can cause severe damage to the pistons, valves and spark plugs, as well as causing a decrease in power and quite possibly complete engine failure. Detonation cannot normally be detected by a pilot, although an indication of excessively high cylinder head temperature is a warning that conditions conducive to detonation may exist.

Detonation can be caused by:

- a lower fuel grade than recommended;
- a time-expired fuel;
- an over-lean mixture;
- excessive manifold pressure;
- an over-heated engine; or
- excessive temperature of the air which is passing through the carburetor.

Airplane engines are normally operated a little on the rich side, the extra fuel acting as a coolant to prevent the mixture becoming too hot and to cool the cylinder walls by evaporation.

If detonation conditions are expected, for instance by an excessively high cylinder head temperature:

- richen the mixture;
- reduce pressures in the cylinders (throttle back); or
- increase airspeed to assist in reducing cylinder head temperatures.

Preignition

Preignition, while involving a progressive combustion of the fuel/air mixture, is an ignition that commences before the spark from the plug. This early ignition (or preignition) can be caused by a hot-spot in the cylinder (from a carbon or lead deposit) becoming red-hot and igniting the mixture before the spark plug fires, causing peak pressures in the cylinder at the wrong point in the cycle.

Preignition is the uncontrolled firing of the fuel/air charge before the spark ignition.

The results of preignition are:

- rough running;
- possibly back-firing;
- a sudden rise in the cylinder head temperature; and
- possible engine damage such as a burnt piston, broken cylinder head, scuffed cylinder wall, and damage to valves and spark plugs.

Preignition can be caused by:

- carbon or lead deposits in the cylinder;
- using high power when the mixture is too lean (no extra fuel for cooling); or
- overheated spark plugs (possibly as a result of detonation).

Preignition may occur in one cylinder only, where a hot-spot exists, whereas detonation will normally occur in all cylinders.

Preignition is a function of the condition of a particular cylinder or cylinders (such as a hot spot) whereas detonation is a function of the fuel/air mixture that is being supplied to all cylinders (too lean and/or too hot).

Both detonation and preignition can be prevented, provided the correct fuel is used and the operating limitations of the engine are observed. This information is available to you in the Pilot's Operating Handbook.

Carburetor Ice

The expansion of the air as it accelerates through the carburetor venturi causes it to drop in temperature. Even quite warm air can cool to below zero and, if it contains moisture, ice can form. This will seriously degrade the functioning of the carburetor, even to the point of stopping the engine!

The first sign of carburetor ice in an airplane equipped with a fixed-pitch propeller is a loss of rpm.

Fuel-injected engines do not have a carburetor and are less susceptible to ice.

Impact Ice

Impact ice will occur when water droplets, which are below freezing point (in the intake air), contact the metal surfaces of the inlet air scoop and duct to the carburetor, immediately forming ice. (This can happen even in a fuel-injected system as well as in a normal carburetor system.)

Impact ice can occur when the outside air temperature is near or below zero, or if the inlet surfaces themselves are below zero and the airplane is in visible moisture such as cloud, rain or sleet. This may be the case if the airplane is on descent from high altitudes, where the temperature is below the freezing level, into areas of visible moisture.

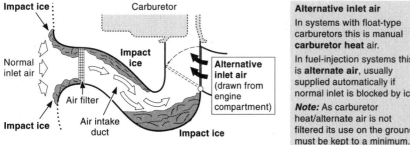

Alternative inlet air

In systems with float-type carburetors this is manual **carburetor heat** air.

In fuel-injection systems this is **alternate air**, usually supplied automatically if normal inlet is blocked by ice.

Note: As carburetor heat/alternate air is not filtered its use on the ground must be kept to a minimum.

Figure 5-16. Impact ice

Fuel Ice

When fuel is introduced into the carburetor airstream, the temperature of the resulting fuel/air mixture is lowered substantially because of the latent heat absorption that occurs during fuel vaporization. You can feel this effect when water or perspiration evaporates off your skin on a hot day.

Fuel ice will form downstream of the metering jet in the throat of the carburetor if the temperature of the fuel/air mixture drops to between 0°C to –8°C (32°F to 16°F). The water will precipitate from the incoming air (if it is moist) and freeze onto any surface it encounters, such as the inlet manifold walls and the throttle butterfly valve. This ice will seriously restrict the airflow and thus reduce the engine's power output.

Fuel ice can occur in ambient air temperatures well above freezing, even as high as 30°C (85°F) when the relative humidity exceeds about 50 percent.

Note: Fuel ice is sometimes called refrigeration ice, since it is caused by the vaporizing of a liquid—the same process that is used in most refrigerators.

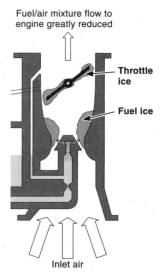

Figure 5-17. Throttle and fuel ice

Throttle Ice

As the fuel/air mixture accelerates past the throttle valve, there is a decrease in static pressure and a consequent drop in temperature. This process can cause ice to form on the throttle valve. The acceleration and resulting temperature drop is greatest at small throttle openings because the throttle butterfly restricts the airflow at these low power settings, creating a substantial pressure drop. Therefore, there is a greater likelihood of carburetor ice at low throttle settings.

Formation of Carburetor Ice

Both fuel ice and throttle ice can occur even when the *outside* air temperature is high. Any time the outside air temperature is within the approximate range (20°F to 70°F) and especially if the relative humidity is high, you should remain alert for signs of carburetor ice, caused by cooling in the carburetor venturi.

Carburetor ice is most likely when the temperature is between −10°C to +20°C (20°F to 70°F) and the relative humidity is high.

Note: Visible moisture is not necessary for the formation of throttle ice.

All of this carburetor ice can have a very serious effect on the running of the engine. The size and shape of the carburetor passages are altered by the ice, the airflow is disturbed, and the fuel/air mixture ratio is affected. These factors all lead to rough running, a loss of power and possibly a total stoppage of the engine unless prompt corrective action is taken.

Typical symptoms of carburetor ice formation are:
- a power loss (a drop in rpm for a fixed-pitch propeller, and a drop in manifold pressure for a constant-speed propeller), resulting in poorer performance (a loss of airspeed or a poorer rate of climb); and
- rough running.

Carburetor Heat

Most modern airplanes have a carburetor heat system to prevent and remove carburetor ice. This usually involves heating the induction air prior to intake into the carburetor by passing the air close to the (hot) exhaust system of the engine. The density of this *heated air* passing through the carburetor will be less, therefore making the fuel/air mixture too rich. The initial effect of applying carburetor heat will be to decrease the power from the engine (seen as an initial drop in rpm for a fixed-pitch propeller or an initial drop in manifold pressure for a constant-speed propeller), possibly by as much as 10–20 percent.

The **carburetor heat control** is usually located near the throttle in the cockpit. By pulling it fully out, heated air is passed into the carburetor. It is usual, if carburetor ice is suspected, to apply full carburetor heat. As the hot air passes through the carburetor venturi, it will melt the ice. If there has been a large ice build-up in the carburetor, the engine may run extremely roughly, especially as the melted ice (now water) passes through the cylinders along with the fuel/air mixture, but this roughness will quickly disappear.

When the ice clears from the carburetor, the engine will begin running smoother and there will be an increase in power. The rpm of a fixed-pitch propeller will rise as the ice clears, as will the manifold pressure of a constant-speed propeller. Following this, carburetor heat may be removed and cold air again used, at which time there will be a further slight increase in power.

If carburetor ice re-forms, then this operation will have to be repeated. Full carburetor heat must be re-applied until the carburetor ice melts. You may find that, under some conditions, full carburetor heat is required not only to remove carburetor ice, but also to prevent it from re-forming.

Some engines have a **carburetor air temperature gauge,** which may be used to keep the carburetor air temperature out of the icing range. It may allow you to use only partial carburetor heat to prevent further formation of ice once the initial ice has been removed with full carburetor heat. If carburetor ice still forms, immediately re-apply full carburetor heat to remove it, and then try a higher setting of partial heat to prevent its formation.

Caution: Partial use of carburetor heat may raise the temperature of the induction air into the temperature range which is most conducive to the formation of carburetor ice, thereby increasing the risk of ice build-up rather than decreasing it. Monitor the engine power gauges and be alert for any rough running.

On descent with low power, particularly in high humidity, it is usual to apply carburetor heat to ensure that no carburetor ice forms or is present. The small throttle butterfly openings needed for low power increase the chance of carburetor ice forming.

On short final approach to land, the carburetor heat is usually returned to *COLD,* just in case full power is required in the event of a go-around.

Avoid using carburetor heat on the ground because the hot air is taken from around the engine exhaust manifold (in most airplanes) and, unlike the normal inlet air, is unfiltered. This will avoid introducing dust and grit into the carburetor and the engine itself, which could lead to unnecessary wear and damage.

Fuel Injection Systems

Many sophisticated engines have fuel directly metered into the induction manifold and then into the cylinders without using a carburetor. This is known as **fuel injection.**

A venturi system is still used to create the pressure differential. This is coupled to a **fuel control unit (FCU),** from which metered fuel is piped to the **fuel manifold unit** (fuel distributor). From here, a separate fuel line carries fuel to the **discharge nozzle** in each cylinder head, or into the inlet port prior to the inlet valve. The mixture control in the fuel injection system controls the idle cut-off.

With fuel injection, each individual cylinder is provided with a correct mixture by its own separate fuel line. (This is unlike the carburetor system, which supplies the same fuel/air mixture to all cylinders. This requires a slightly richer-than-ideal mixture to ensure that the leanest-running cylinder does not run too lean.)

Advantages of Fuel Injection

- Freedom from fuel ice (no suitable place for it to form).
- More uniform delivery of the fuel/air mixture to each cylinder.
- Improved control of fuel/air ratio.
- Fewer maintenance problems.
- Instant acceleration of the engine after idling with no tendency for it to stall.
- Increased engine efficiency.

Disadvantages of Fuel Injection

- Starting an already hot engine that has a fuel injection system may be difficult because of vapor locking in the fuel lines. Electric boost pumps that pressurize the fuel lines can help alleviate this problem.
- Having very fine fuel lines, fuel injection engines are more susceptible to any contamination in the fuel such as dirt or water.

- Correct fuel management is imperative! Know the fuel system of your particular airplane!
- Surplus fuel provided by a fuel injection system will pass through a **return line** which may be routed to only one of the fuel tanks. If the pilot does not remain aware of where the surplus fuel is being returned to, it may result in uneven fuel loading in the tanks or fuel being vented overboard (thus reducing flight fuel available).

Correct fuel management is imperative! Know the fuel system of your airplane!

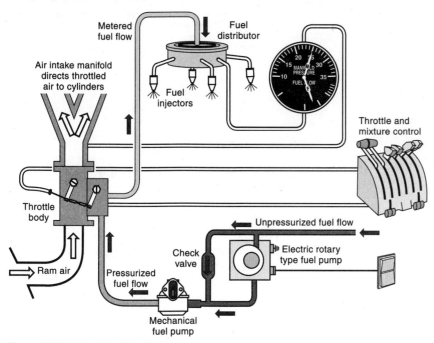

Figure 5-18. Typical fuel injection system

✍ Now complete **Review 5, Part (b)** on page 118.

✐ Review 5

Part (a)

1. Name the four strokes of a piston engine commencing with the stroke intake.

   ➤ intake (or induction), compression, power (or expansion), exhaust

2. During most of the compression stroke the intake valve is (open/closed) and the exhaust valve is (open/closed).

   ➤ closed, closed

3. During most of the exhaust stroke the intake valve is (open/closed) and the exhaust valve is (open/closed).

   ➤ closed, open

4. The period when both intake and exhaust valves are open simultaneously is called _____.

   ➤ valve overlap

5. To ignite the fuel/air mixture in the cylinder, just prior to top-dead-center and the commencement of the _____ stroke there is a high-voltage _____.

   ➤ power, spark

6. If one of the magneto switches is turned to OFF, there (should/should not) be an engine rpm drop.

   ➤ should

7. Two separate ignition systems provide a higher level of _____ and more efficient _____ in the combustion chamber.

   ➤ safety, combustion

8. Switching the ignition OFF connects the magneto systems to ground. (true/false)?

   ➤ true

9. If a magneto ground wire comes loose in flight, the engine (will/will not) stop.

   ➤ will not

10. The spark plugs in a piston engine are provided with a high energy (or high tension) electrical supply from:
    (a) the battery at all times.
    (b) the magnetos.
    (c) the battery at start-up, and then the magnetos.

    ➤ (b)

11. The most probable reason an engine continues to run after the ignition switch has been turned off is:
    (a) carbon deposits glowing on the spark plugs.
    (b) a magneto ground wire is in contact with the engine casing.
    (c) a broken magneto ground wire.

    ➤ (c)

12. Because of the very low revs as you start the engine, the spark needs to be delayed. This is done automatically in some magnetos by an _____.

    ➤ impulse coupling

13. If the ground wire between the magneto and the ignition switch becomes disconnected, the engine:
    (a) will not operate on one magneto.
    (b) cannot be started with the switch in the BOTH position.
    (c) could accidentally start if the propeller is moved with fuel in the cylinder.

    ➤ (c)

Part (b)

1. The carburetor mixes _____ and _____ to the correct ratio to burn properly in a piston engine.

   ➤ fuel, air

2. The principle of a simple carburetor is to (increase/decrease) the pressure as air flows through a venturi throat, and draw fuel into the passing airstream.

   ➤ decrease

3. The fuel/air ratio is the ratio between the (volume/weight) of the fuel and the (volume/weight) of the air entering the (cylinders/carburetor).

   ➤ weight, weight, carburetor

4. The pilot controls the fuel/air ratio with the:
   (a) throttle.
   (b) manifold pressure.
   (c) mixture control.

   ➤ (c)

5. Following combustion of a rich mixture, excess _____ remains; following combustion of a lean mixture, excess _____ remains.

   ➤ fuel, air

6. To ensure sufficient fuel is fed to the cylinders when idling at low rpm, the carburetor has an _____ .
➤ idling jet

7. The *best-power mixture* is that fuel/air ratio which provides the (most/least) power for any given throttle setting.
➤ most

8. As air density decreases, the weight of fuel introduced into the cylinder needs to be (increased/reduced) to match the decreased weight of air. This is done from the cockpit using the _____, which is usually a _____ colored knob.
➤ reduced, mixture control, red

9. An over-rich mixture can cause (detonation/fouling of the spark plugs).
➤ fouling of the spark plugs

10. For takeoff at a sea level airport on a cool day, the mixture control should normally be in (full rich/lean/idle cut-off).
➤ full rich

11. What will occur if no leaning is made with the mixture control as the flight altitude increases?
    (a) The volume of air entering the carburetor decreases and the amount of fuel decreases.
    (b) The density of air entering the carburetor decreases and the amount of fuel increases.
    (c) The density of air entering the carburetor decreases and the amount of fuel remains constant.
➤ (c)

12. The correct procedure to achieve the best fuel/air mixture when cruising at altitude is to move the mixture control toward *LEAN* until the engine rpm:
    (a) drops to a minimum value.
    (b) reaches a peak value.
    (c) passes through a peak value at which point the mixture control is returned to a slightly richer position.
➤ (c)

13. The extra fuel in a rich mixture causes extra (heating/cooling) in the cylinders by its evaporation.
➤ cooling

14. While cruising at 9,500 feet MSL, the fuel/air mixture is properly adjusted. What will occur if a descent to 4,500 feet MSL is made without readjusting the mixture?
    (a) The fuel/air mixture may become excessively lean.
    (b) There will be more fuel in the cylinders than is needed for normal combustion, and the excess fuel will absorb heat and cool the engine.
    (c) The excessively rich mixture will create higher cylinder head temperatures and may cause detonation.
➤ (a)

15. Detonation is an (explosive/progressive) combustion of the fuel/air mixture in the cylinders.
➤ explosive

16. Detonation may be caused by using a (higher/lower) than specified grade of fuel and/or excessively (high/low) engine temperatures.
➤ lower, high

17. Detonation may be caused by the mixture being too (lean/rich).
➤ lean

18. The uncontrolled firing of the fuel/air charge in advance of normal spark ignition is known as:
    (a) combustion
    (b) preignition.
    (c) detonation.
➤ (b)

19. If a pilot suspects that the engine (with a fixed-pitch propeller) is detonating during climb-out after takeoff, the initial corrective action to take would be to:
    (a) lean the mixture.
    (b) lower the nose slightly to increase airspeed.
    (c) apply carburetor heat.
➤ (b)

20. Hot-spots in a combustion chamber are likely to cause (preignition/detonation).
➤ preignition

21. A great danger to correct functioning of the carburetor, especially in moist conditions, is _____.
➤ carburetor ice

22. The remedy for suspected carburetor ice is to apply_____.
➤ carburetor heat

23. One of the first indications of carburetor ice forming in an airplane equipped with a fixed-pitch propeller is a (loss/increase) of power, which will be indicated by a (decrease/increase) in rpm.

➤ loss, decrease

24. The hotter air entering the engine after carburetor heat is applied will be (more/less) dense, which means that (more/less) air by weight for the same weight of fuel enters the cylinders. Applying carburetor heat will therefore result in a (richer/leaner) mixture.

➤ less dense, less air by weight, richer mixture

25. At a high-elevation airport, on a hot day, you note a slight engine roughness that is not affected by the magneto check but gets worse during the carburetor heat check. This may be caused by the mixture being (too rich/too lean).

➤ too rich (The air density is already low, making the mixture too rich. Carburetor heat worsens the situation.)

26. Leaving the carburetor heat on while taking off:
   (a) leans the mixture for more power on takeoff.
   (b) will decrease the takeoff distance.
   (c) will increase the ground roll.

➤ (c)

27. The pressure drop (and consequent temperature drop) near the throttle butterfly is greatest at (large/small) throttle openings, causing a greater likelihood of carburetor ice forming.

➤ small

28. The presence of carburetor ice in an aircraft equipped with a fixed-pitch propeller can be verified by applying carburetor heat and noting:
   (a) an increase in rpm, then a gradual decrease in rpm.
   (b) a decrease in rpm, then a constant rpm indication.
   (c) a decrease in rpm, then a gradual increase in rpm.

➤ (c)

29. Which condition is most favorable to the development of carburetor icing?
   (a) Any temperature below freezing and a relative humidity of less than 50 percent.
   (b) Between 32°F and 50°F and low humidity.
   (c) Between 20°F and 70°F and high humidity.

➤ (c)

30. Normally you should avoid using carburetor heat during ground operations because the hot air source is_____ .

➤ unfiltered

31. The principles of leaning the mixture by reducing the fuel flow to match the lower density air as altitude is gained (do/do not) apply to fuel-injected engines.

➤ do

32. With regard to carburetor ice, float-type carburetor systems in comparison to fuel injection systems are generally considered to be:
   (a) more susceptible to icing.
   (b) equally susceptible to icing.
   (c) susceptible to icing only when visible moisture is present.

➤ (a)

Systems 6

The Fuel System

The function of a fuel system is to store fuel and deliver it to the carburetor (or fuel injection system) in adequate quantities at the proper pressures. It should provide a continuous flow of fuel under positive pressure for all normal flight conditions, including:

• changes of altitude;

• changes of attitude; and/or

• sudden throttle movements and power changes.

Fuel is stored in **fuel tanks,** which are usually installed in the wing. A sump and a drain point at the lowest point of the tank allows heavy impurities (such as water or sediment) to gather, be inspected and drained off. The tanks often contain **baffles** to prevent the fuel surging about in flight—especially during large attitude changes or uncoordinated maneuvers, or in turbulence.

The fuel supply line (pipe) inlet is higher than the sump to prevent impurities (water or sludge) from entering the fuel lines to the carburetor, even though there is a **fuel filter** in the line to remove any small impurities from the fuel as it passes down the supply line. Because the fuel enters the supply line through a standpipe at the bottom of the tank, there will always be some **unusable fuel** in the tanks.

The top of the fuel tank is vented to the atmosphere so that the air pressure above the fuel in the tank remains the same as outside as altitude is changed. Reduced pressure in the tank caused by ineffective venting could reduce the rate of fuel flow to the engine and also cause the fuel tanks to collapse inward. **Fuel vents** should be checked in the preflight external inspection to ensure that they are not blocked or damaged.

An **overflow drain** prevents excessive pressure building up if fuel volume increases because the full tanks have been warmed in the sun.

A high-wing airplane with the tanks in the wings will generally allow the fuel to be **gravity-fed** to the carburetor without the need for a **fuel pump.** If there is no carburetor as with a fuel injection system, then electric **boost pumps** are necessary.

In a low-wing airplane, the tanks, being lower than the engine, need a fuel pump to lift the fuel to the carburetor. Prior to start-up, an electric auxiliary (boost) pump is used to prime the fuel lines and to purge any vapor from them. Once the engine is started, the engine-driven mechanical fuel pump takes over. Pump function can be monitored on the fuel pressure gauge.

All engines have an engine-driven fuel pump.

For many airplanes, the Pilot's Operating Handbook recommends that the electric fuel pump be switched on for critical maneuvers such as the takeoff, landing and low flying. This prevents fuel starvation in the event the engine-driven mechanical fuel pump fails.

Some engines (such as those in low-wing airplanes) also have an electric auxiliary fuel boost pump.

It is important that the fuel strainer drain valve in a low part of the fuel system is checked closed during the preflight external inspection. If it is not closed, the engine-driven fuel pump may not be able to draw sufficient fuel into the engine (sucking air instead), and the engine may be starved of fuel unless the electric fuel pump is used.

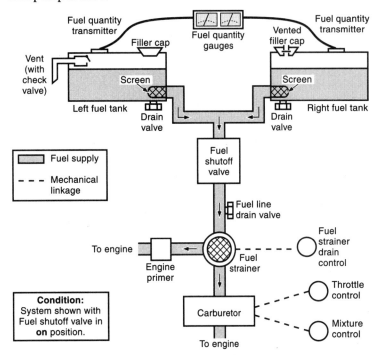

Figure 6-1. Simple carburetor fuel system

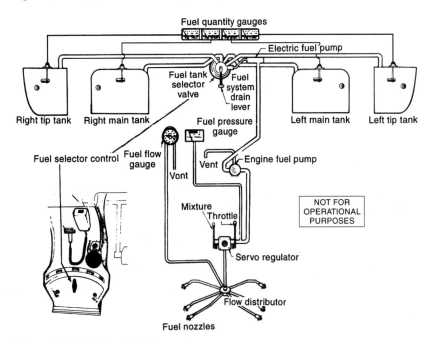

Figure 6-2. Typical fuel injection system

The Priming Pump

The fuel primer is a hand-operated pump in the cockpit which the pilot uses to pump fuel into the induction system of the engine in preparation for engine start-up. This fuel does not pass through the carburetor, but is hand-pumped directly into the inlet manifold just before the cylinders.

Priming the engine is especially useful when starting a cold engine on a cold day, when the fuel in the carburetor is reluctant to vaporize.

The primer must be locked when the engine is running to avoid excessive fuel being drawn through the priming line into the cylinders, especially at low power settings, which could stop the engine if the fuel/air mixture is too rich.

A priming pump sends fuel directly into the engine prior to start-up.

Fuel Selection

A fuel line runs from each tank to a selector valve in the cockpit, which the pilot uses to select the tank from which fuel will be taken or to shut the fuel off. Incorrect fuel tank selection can result in fuel starvation, and has been the cause of many accidents—so study your Pilot's Operating Handbook very closely on this matter. The sounds of silence while you still have fuel in one tank, but not the tank that you have incorrectly selected, can be very loud indeed!

You should not run a tank dry in flight before switching tanks, because the fuel pump may draw air into the fuel lines, causing a vapor lock which may stop the fuel flow, even from another tank, into the engine. Once a vapor lock has formed, it may be very difficult to restart the engine.

It is advisable when changing tanks to switch on the electric auxiliary or booster fuel pump (if installed) to guarantee fuel pressure to the carburetor, and then to positively monitor the fuel pressure as the tanks are changed.

Any sudden and unexpected loss of power should bring two possible causes immediately to mind:

- lack of fuel to the engine; or
- carburetor icing.

If the cause is incorrect fuel selection, your actions should include:

- close the throttle (to avoid a sudden surge of power as the engine restarts);
- set the mixture control to full-rich;
- turn the electric fuel pump on; and
- check fuel tank selection and tank quantity—change tanks if necessary.

If the cause of the engine problem is carburetor ice, then apply full carburetor heat. Refer to your Pilot's Operating Handbook for the correct actions to be taken in the event of any power loss.

Know your fuel system and always select a tank that contains fuel.

Fuel Boost Pumps (or Auxiliary Pumps)

The reasons for installing **electric fuel boost pumps** are to:

- provide fuel at the required pressure to the carburetor or to the fuel metering unit of a fuel injection system;
- purge the fuel lines of any vapor to eliminate the possibility of a vapor lock;
- prime the cylinders of fuel-injected engines for start-up; and
- supply fuel if the engine-driven pump fails.

If an electric fuel pump is installed, it is usual to also have a **fuel pressure gauge** to monitor its operation.

Fuel Gauges

Most light airplanes have fuel gauges in the cockpit, which may be electrical, so the master switch will have to be *ON* for them to register. Some older airplanes have direct-reading fuel gauges which do not require electrical power.

It is good airmanship not to rely on the fuel gauges, since they can read quite inaccurately, especially when the airplane is not straight-and-level. Always carry out a visual check of the contents in the fuel tanks during the preflight external inspection by removing the fuel caps, visually checking the contents of the tanks, and then replacing the caps securely.

The fuel consumption rate specified in the Pilot's Operating Handbook assumes **correct leaning of the mixture** which, if not done, could lead to a fuel burn around 20% in excess of the 'book-figures,' and the fuel gauges consequently reading much less than expected because of excessive fuel burn.

Do not rely on the fuel gauges—they can be inaccurate. Always check the contents of the fuel tanks visually before takeoff.

Fueling

For safety during fueling, the airplane should be positioned well away from other airplanes and from buildings, the engine should not be running, and the ignition switches and parking brake should be in the *OFF* position. The location of any firefighting equipment should be noted in case it is needed. A **no-smoking** rule should be enforced and passengers should be kept well clear.

To prevent the possibility of a spark of static electricity igniting the fuel vapor that is present in any fueling operations, you should connect ground wires between the airplane, the fueling equipment and the ground to ensure that they are all at the same electrical potential. This should be done before you start fueling—even before you remove the fuel caps, when fuel vapor could be released into the atmosphere.

Before fueling, the airplane must be electrically grounded to minimize the risk of fire.

Fuel Grades

AVGAS (AViation GASoline) comes in various grades to cater for different types of piston engines. These different grades of AVGAS are **color-coded** to aid you in checking that the correct fuel is on board. Normal fuel for light airplanes is blue-colored 100LL (low lead) or green-colored 100/130 octane.

The most important thing is to ensure that you are loading the correct fuel type into the airplane tanks. Jet fuel (kerosene) is required for gas turbine engines (jets) and AVGAS for piston engines. Jet fuel is straw-colored or clear, has a distinctive smell, and must not be used in piston engines.

The **fueling equipment** has color-coded labeling:

- jet-fuel decals have a black background with Jet-A written in white letters.
- AVGAS decals have a red background with white letters, (100/130 or AVGAS).

There are additional small labels on the fuel hoses or nozzles colored the same as the fuel grade, for both AVGAS and jet fuel.

Fuel should possess **anti-detonation** (or anti-knock) qualities, which are described by their **grade** (octane rating or performance number). The higher the grade, the greater the compression that the fuel/air mixture can take without detonating. High grade fuels have a higher lead content, which improves their anti-detonation qualities.

The higher grade indicates the power possible (compared with the standard reference fuel) before a rich mixture would detonate, and the lower grade indicates the power possible before the same fuel leaned-out would detonate. Certain engines require certain fuel—make sure you know which one your engine requires and use it, and make sure that the fuel already in the tanks is the same as that being loaded.

Fuel Grade	Color
100LL	BLUE (low lead)
100/130	GREEN
80/87	RED

Figure 6-3. Fuel grades

Do not use jet fuel (kerosene) in piston engines. AVGAS decals on fueling equipment have a red background with white letters.

If you use fuel of a *lower* grade than specified, or fuel that is date-expired, excessive engine temperatures and detonation may occur, especially at high power settings, with a consequent loss of power and possible engine damage.

If you use fuel of a higher grade than specified, the spark plugs can be fouled by lead deposits, and also the exhaust valves and their sealing faces can be eroded during the exhaust cycle.

Note: A *higher* grade of fuel than specified is usually less dangerous than using a lower grade. If the recommended grade of fuel is not available, you could consider using the next higher grade of fuel on a short term basis, but not a lower grade. Refer to the manufacturer's handbook and your flight instructor.

Auto Gasoline

AVGAS comes in batches with tight quality control. Ordinary auto gasoline from the gas station does *not* have such tight quality control and has different burning characteristics to AVGAS. In an airplane engine, auto gasoline would cause a lower power output, lead fouling of the spark plugs and a strong possibility of detonation. Auto fuel is more volatile and vaporizes more readily than AVGAS, which might cause vapor locks in the fuel system and starve the engine of fuel.

Do not use auto gasoline in an airplane engine unless it is specifically authorized by the manufacturer and in accordance with an FAA Supplemental Type Certificate (STC).

Fuel Checks

Fuel which is about to be loaded should be checked first for contamination. The most common contamination is water. It can leak into ground fuel tanks, and from there be loaded into the fuel truck and into the tanks of an airplane.

Fuel must be checked for water and other contaminants.

Fuel naturally contains a small amount of water and this can condense with a drop in temperature, contaminate the fuel system, block the fuel passages in the carburetor, and possibly cause a loss of engine power.

There are certain **fuel test pastes** and **fuel test papers** available which react when water is present, and the fueling agent will use these on a regular basis to guarantee the purity of the fuel in his storage tanks.

Other impurities besides water can also cause problems in the fuel. Rust, sand, dust and micro-organisms can cause problems just like water. Filtering or straining the fuel should indicate the presence of these and hopefully remove them prior to fueling.

Be especially careful when fueling from drums because they may have been standing for some time. Always check drum fuel with water-detection paste, for date of expiry, and for correct grade of fuel. Additionally, it is a good idea to check the release note for the fuel. Filter the fuel through a chamois cloth prior to loading into the airplane tanks if the drum pump has no filter.

Water, because it is more dense than fuel, will tend to gather at the low points in the airplane fuel system. After fueling has been completed, a small quantity of fuel should be drained from the bottom of each tank and from the **fuel strainer drain valve** to check for impurities, especially water, which will sink to the bottom of the glass. Fuel drains are usually spring-loaded valves at the bottom of each fuel tank, and the fuel strainer drain is usually found at the lowest point in the whole fuel system.

There is usually a drop in air temperature overnight and, if the space above the fuel in the airplane's fuel tanks is large, the fuel tank walls will become cold and there will be a lot more condensation than if the tanks were full of fuel. The water, as it condenses, will accumulate at the bottom of the fuel tanks.

If the tanks are kept full when the airplane is not being used for some days, or overnight if low temperatures are expected, condensation will be minimized. However, the disadvantages of fueling overnight include:

- If the airplane has a takeoff weight restriction the following day, it may have to be partially defueled to reduce the weight or adjust the balance.
- If the tanks are full and the temperature rises, the fuel will expand and some could overflow from the tank, creating a possible fire hazard on the tarmac. This is an operational choice—check with your flight instructor.

It is good practice to carry out a check for water in the airplane fuel system:

- prior to the first flight of the day;
- following each fueling; and
- any time you suspect fuel contamination.

In general terms, if you find a large quantity of water in the tanks, the following procedures should be included in your actions:

- the mechanic should be informed;
- drain the tanks until all the water has been removed;
- rock the wing to allow any other water to gravitate to the fuel strainer drain valve;
- drain off more fuel and check for water at *all* drain points.

Fuel Management

- Ensure that the airplane has the correct grade of fuel on board and that it is free of impurities.
- Ensure that sufficient fuel for the flight plus an adequate reserve is on board. Do not rely only on the fuel gauges as they are often inaccurate. Calculate the fuel required and be sure to check the tanks visually prior to flight for sufficient fuel. Remember that some of the fuel in the tanks will be unusable fuel.
- Carry out a fuel drain if required or if you think it is advisable.
- Ensure that there are no leaks, that fuel caps are replaced, and that tank vents are clear and unobstructed. Fuel tank caps are usually on the upper surface of the wing, which is a low pressure area in normal flight. **Fuel can be siphoned out very quickly in flight if the tank caps are not secured.** With high-wing airplanes especially, where the tank caps are not visible easily from the ground or when in flight, extra care should be taken.

Be familiar with, and follow, the procedures recommended in the Pilot's Operating Handbook for your airplane. Understand the fuel system, especially the functioning of the fuel selector valves. When selecting a new tank, ensure that the selector valve is moved firmly and positively into the correct detent.

Do not change tanks unnecessarily immediately prior to takeoff or landing, or at low altitude. If possible, verify prior to takeoff that fuel is being drawn from the appropriate tank(s). If operation is possible from more than one tank at the one time, this is usually preferred for operations near the ground. If boost pumps are installed, their use for takeoff is generally advised.

When changing tanks, check that there is fuel in the tank about to be selected; if an electric fuel pump is installed, switch it on and if a fuel pressure gauge is installed, monitor fuel pressure during and after the transfer, and when you switch off the electric boost pump.

✍ Now complete **Review 6, Part (a)** on page 142.

Full fuel tanks minimize condensation in low temperatures.

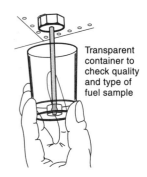

Transparent container to check quality and type of fuel sample

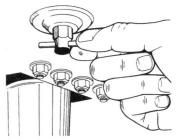

Figure 6-4. Fuel drains are located at the lowest point of the fuel tanks

Fuel planning and good management are vital tasks.

The Oil System

The purpose of the oil system is to circulate oil around the engine, to:

Oil lubricates, clears, and cools and seals.

- lubricate the moving parts so that they can move smoothly;
- prevent high temperatures by reducing friction between the moving parts;
- provide a seal between the cylinder walls and the pistons, increasing the effectiveness of the expanding gases in the combustion process;
- assist in cooling the engine by carrying some of the heat generated by combustion away from the pistons; and
- carry away contaminants which are then removed in an oil filter.

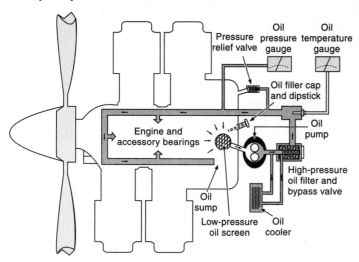

Figure 6-5. A typical oil system

Sufficient quantity of oil of the correct grade is absolutely essential. An oil dipstick to check oil quantity is generally found under a small cowl above the engine, along with an oil filling point if more oil is required. Always check that the oil filler cap has been firmly replaced prior to flight.

Indication of correct operation of the oil system is provided in the cockpit by an **oil pressure gauge,** an **oil temperature gauge** and, in some aircraft, a **cylinder-head temperature gauge.**

The Functions of Engine Oil

Friction

If a small film of oil separates two metal surfaces, it will allow them to slide over each other without actually touching. There will be only low friction forces and consequently, high temperatures will not be generated in the metal. The metallic friction will be replaced by internal friction in the lubricating oil, which will heat up to some extent. Engine components subjected to high loads, such as the bearings at either end of the connecting rods and the crankshaft (or *big end)* bearings, need to be cushioned by a layer of oil so that the mechanical shock on them is reduced.

Oil reduces friction.

Without oil there would be high friction forces, causing very high temperatures to develop quickly in the metal, with extreme wearing of the metal surfaces and, very likely, subsequent mechanical failure.

Cooling

The pistons absorb a lot of heat from the combustion chamber and are cooled by oil splashed or sprayed onto them from below. Lubrication and cooling of the bearings and pistons is the main function of the oil system.

Oil cools the hot sections of the engine.

Heat generated by internal friction in the oil and the heat absorbed from the hot sections of the engine is removed by the oil continually being circulated. The hot oil is carried away and cooled in a component known as the **oil cooler,** which is exposed to the airflow.

Removal of Contaminants

Oil circulating through an engine can carry away dirt and other foreign material, thereby reducing abrasive wear on the moving parts of the engine. This contamination is removed from the oil as it passes through the **oil filter.** If the filter is not kept clean (by correct maintenance or replacement at the recommended service intervals) it may become blocked, causing dirty oil to bypass the filter and circulate within the engine's lubrication system. Dirty oil has poorer cooling and lubricating qualities and so the engine will suffer. There will be an increased wear rate which will shorten the life of the engine.

Oil carries away contaminants.

Sealing Qualities

Oil also provides a seal between the cylinder walls and the pistons as they move up and down within the cylinders, preventing the compressed gases (burning fuel/air) escaping past the piston rings into the crankcase, and so increasing the effectiveness of the compressed gases in forcing the piston down the cylinder.

Oil provides a seal.

Oil Properties

Oil must have appropriate **viscosity** over the operating temperature range of the engine—it must flow freely, but not be too thin. An oil of high viscosity (stickiness) flows slowly; an oil of low viscosity flows more easily. High temperatures make oil less viscous and cause it to flow more freely. The oil must remain sufficiently viscous under the wide range of operating temperatures and bearing pressures found in aviation engines.

Excessively high temperatures affect the lubricating qualities of oil, impairing its effectiveness, so keep an eye on the oil temperature gauge.

The owner or operator of the airplane may decide to use an oil of lower viscosity than normal in a severely cold climate. Likewise, an oil of higher viscosity could be used if the airplane is to be operated in a continually hot climate. Be aware of the oil grade being used and **do not mix oil grades.**

Use only recommended type and grade of oils. Do not mix grades.

The oil must also have a sufficiently **high flash point** and fire point to ensure that it will not vaporize excessively or catch fire easily. It must also be chemically stable and not change its state or characteristics.

Maintenance

Since the same oil in an engine is continually circulated, over a period of time it will become contaminated because the filters cannot clean it perfectly. Chemical changes will also occur in the oil in the form of:

- oxidation caused by contamination from some of the byproducts of the fuel combustion in the engine; and
- absorption of water that condenses in the engine when it cools after shutdown.

Consequently the **oil must be changed at regular intervals,** as required by the maintenance schedule.

Note: The airplane's Pilot's Operating Handbook will usually show the oil grade as an SAE rating (Society of Automotive Engineers), but commercial aviation oil has a *commercial aviation number* which is **double** the SAE rating:

- 80 grade oil—SAE 40;
- 100 grade oil—SAE 50.

There are different types of oils designed for different operating conditions. Use only the correct type of oil as directed in the Pilot's Operating Handbook and **do not use turbine (jet) oil in piston engines.**

A Typical Oil System

After doing its work in the engine, the oil gathers in the **sump,** which is a reservoir attached to the lower part of the engine casing.

A **wet sump** engine has a sump attached to it in which the oil is stored. Most light aircraft engines are wet sump engines.

A **dry sump** engine has scavenge pumps that scavenge the oil from the sump attached to the lower part of the engine casing and pump it back into the oil tank, which is separate from the engine. It is usual to have a dry sump on aerobatic airplanes for continuous lubrication in extreme attitudes. Radial engines such as in the Grumman Ag-Cat, DC-3 and DHC Beaver have dry sump oil systems.

There is usually an **engine-driven oil supply pump** that supplies oil from the sump or the tank through oil lines, passages and galleries to the moving parts of the engine. Within the oil pump is a spring-loaded **oil pressure relief valve.** If the pressure set on the pressure relief valve is exceeded, it will open and relieve the pressure by allowing oil to be returned to the pump inlet.

An **oil pressure gauge** in the cockpit indicates the oil pressure provided by the oil pump. The oil pressure sensor is situated after the oil pump and before the oil does its work in the engine.

Oil filters and screens are placed in the system to remove any foreign matter such as dirt or carbon particles in the circulating oil. The oil filters should be inspected and replaced at regular intervals, as required in the maintenance schedule. The foreign matter collected may give an indication of the condition of the engine—for instance, small metal particles might indicate an impending engine failure.

Within the oil filter housing is the **oil filter bypass valve.** This permits the oil to bypass the filter in the event of the filter becoming clogged. Dirty and contaminated oil is preferable to no oil at all.

Because the oil absorbs engine heat, the cooling that occurs in the sump is often insufficient, so most engines have an **oil cooler.** The oil is pumped from the sump through the oil filter to the oil cooler. If the oil is already cool, a thermally operated valve allows it to bypass the oil cooler, as further cooling is unnecessary. If the oil is hot (as it is when the engine has warmed-up), the thermally operated valve directs the oil through the cooler. Should the cooler become blocked, a **pressure bypass valve** allows the oil to bypass the cooler.

The oil cooler is usually positioned in the system so that the oil cools a little in the sump and then passes through the oil cooler for further cooling just prior to entering the main parts of the engine.

As part of your **daily/preflight inspection** you should check the condition of the oil cooler for:

- freedom from insects, birds' nests and other contamination, to ensure free air passages; and
- any oil leakage or fatigue cracks.

There is an **oil temperature gauge** in the cockpit. It is connected to a temperature probe that senses the temperature of the oil after the oil has passed through the oil cooler and before its use within the hot sections of the engine. Also, some airplanes have a **cylinder-head temperature (CHT) gauge** to provide another indication of engine temperature, this time in the cylinder head.

Malfunctions in the Oil/Lubrication System

Incorrect Oil Type

The **incorrect type of oil** will possibly cause poor lubrication, poor cooling and engine damage. Oil temperature and oil pressure indications may be abnormal. For instance, mixing detergent and mineral oils can lead to engine damage.

Incorrect Oil Quantity

The **oil level** should be checked and corrected if necessary prior to flight. There will be an **oil dipstick** in the tank for this purpose. The dipstick is calibrated to show maximum and minimum oil quantities. If the oil quantity is below the minimum, then you will find that the oil overheats and/or the oil pressure is too low or fluctuates. If the oil quantity is too great, then the excess oil may be forced out through various parts of the engine, such as the front shaft seal.

The oil quantity needs to be checked before each flight, as it gradually decreases because of:

- being burned with the fuel/air mixture in the cylinders;
- loss as a mist or spray through the oil breather; and
- leaks.

Low Oil Pressure

At normal power a low oil pressure may indicate an impending engine failure caused by:

- insufficient oil;
- lack of oil because of a failure in the oil system;
- a leak in the oil tank or oil lines;
- failure of the oil pump;
- a problem in the engine, such as failing bearings; or
- the oil pressure relief valve (PRV) stuck open.

Where an indication of low or fluctuating oil pressure occurs and is associated with a rise in oil temperature while in flight—play it safe and land as soon as possible, as it could indicate a serious problem in the lubrication system.

High Oil Temperature

Too little oil being circulated will also be indicated by a high oil temperature, therefore a rising oil temperature may indicate a decreasing oil quantity. Prolonged operation at excessive cylinder head temperatures will also give rise to a high oil temperature indication. This would be most likely to occur in situations of high power, low airspeed (climbing), especially in high ambient air temperatures.

Gradual Loss of Oil

If the engine is gradually losing oil, the oil temperature will gradually rise as less oil is available for cooling and lubricating the engine. If oil is lost, the oil pressure will probably be maintained, until the oil quantity reaches a critically low level. This may be indicated by rapidly rising oil temperature with a sudden drop in oil pressure occurring just before engine seizure.

If you suspect a problem concerning oil, then you should plan a landing before the time you estimate the oil problem will become serious. This is a matter of judgment, especially if the choice of nearby landing areas is not great.

Lack of oil will cause an engine seizure and an immediate loss of power.

Faulty Oil Pressure Gauge

Sometimes of course, the oil pressure gauge may be faulty. A low oil pressure indication may be recognized as a faulty indication—and not a genuine low pressure—by noting that the oil temperature remains normal over a period of time. Keep your eye on both gauges.

High Oil Pressure

A pressure relief valve in the system should ensure that the oil does not reach an unacceptably high oil pressure. A high oil pressure may cause some part of the system to fail, rendering the whole oil system inoperative.

✎ Now complete **Review 6, Part (b)** on page 142.

The Cooling System

The engine cooling system is designed to keep the engine temperatures within those limits designed by the manufacturer. The burning of the fuel/air mixture in the engine's cylinders, and the friction of its moving parts, results in the engine heating up. Engine temperatures are kept within acceptable limits by:

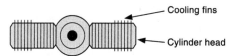

Figure 6-6. Cooling fins

- the oil that circulates within the engine;
- expulsion of much heat energy in the exhaust gases; and
- the air cooling system that circulates fresh air around the engine compartment.

Most modern light airplane engines are **air-cooled** by exposing the cylinders and their cooling fins to an airflow. The fins increase the exposed surface area to allow better cooling.

As the airflow passes around a cylinder it may become turbulent and break away in such a manner that uneven cooling occurs, forming local poorly cooled hot-spots. To avoid this uneven cooling, cowling ducts at the front of the engine capture air from the high-pressure area behind the propeller, and then baffles distribute it as evenly as possible around the cylinders. After cooling the engine, the air flows out holes at the bottom rear of the engine compartment.

Air cooling is least effective at high power and low airspeed, for instance on takeoff or go-around. The high power produces a lot of heat, and the low airspeed provides only a reduced cooling airflow. At high airspeed and low power, for instance on descent, the cooling might be too effective.

Some airplanes have movable cooling **cowl flaps** that can be operated (electrically or manually) from the cockpit, giving the pilot more control over the cooling of the engine. Open cowl flaps permit more air to escape from the engine compartment. This causes increased airflow over and around the engine. The open cowl flaps cause parasite drag to increase.

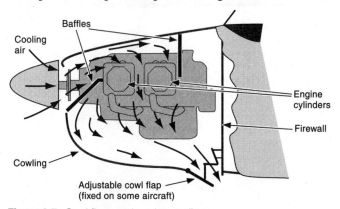

Figure 6-7. Cowl flaps and engine cooling

Cowl flaps are normally open for takeoff, partially open or closed on climb and cruise, and closed during a power-off descent. They will be open on final in readiness for a go-around, when high power at a low airspeed will be required. Cowl flaps should be open when taxiing to help dissipate the engine heat.

The deciding factor for the pilot in where to position the cowl flaps is the cylinder head temperature, or the anticipated cylinder head temperature, and this may be indicated in the cockpit by a **cylinder-head temperature (CHT) gauge.**

Excessive engine temperatures may be caused by:
- high power (greater heat generation);
- low airspeed (less air cooling);
- incorrect fuel (lower-than-specified grade);
- a too-lean mixture (no excess fuel to evaporate and cool the cylinders); or
- a low oil level.

You should monitor the cylinder-head temperature gauge throughout the flight, and also on the ground when air-cooling will be poor. The Pilot's Operating Handbook will give advice on satisfactory temperatures.

Monitor CHT and adjust engine cooling if necessary.

If excessive cylinder-head temperatures are noted in flight, the cooling of the engine can be improved by:
- opening the cowl flaps fully (to allow greater airflow around the engine);
- making the mixture richer (extra fuel has a cooling effect in the cylinders because more fuel is evaporated, so a rich mixture cools better than a lean mixture);
- reducing the engine power (so that less heat is produced); or
- increasing the airspeed (for greater air cooling).

Just how you achieve the latter two is a matter of judgment. In a climb, you could increase speed by reducing the rate of climb. In a cruise (straight-and-level) at normal cruise speeds, you could maintain the power and increase the airspeed by commencing a descent, unless terrain prevents this.

Other factors influencing engine cooling and over which the pilot has little control during flight include:
- **Condition of the oil cooler.** A dirty and inefficient oil cooler will not allow the best cooling of the circulating oil. The oil, if warmer than optimum, will be unable to carry as much heat away from the engine, and its viscosity and lubricating qualities will be reduced, which will lead to higher engine temperatures.
- **Outside air temperature.** Obviously, warm air will not cool the engine as well as cool air.

Note: On some airplanes the propeller **spinner** is part of the airflow director for the cooling air, so these airplanes should *not* be operated without the spinner installed. If you find yourself in such a situation, refer to the Flight Manual or a mechanic to establish what is allowable for your airplane.

✍ Now complete **Review 6, Part (c)** on page 142.

The Electrical System

A typical modern light airplane has a **direct current (DC)** electrical system. The electric current is produced by an **alternator** when the engine is running, or from a **battery** or **external power source** when the engine is not running.

The current runs through wires and the **bus bar** to the electrical unit requiring power, does its work there and then runs to ground through a **ground wire** attached to the airplane structure (which is the return path of the electrical current).

Typical Electrical Systems

The Pilot's Operating Handbook for each airplane will contain a diagram of its electrical system and the services to which electrical power is supplied. It is good airmanship to be aware of what powers the vital services and instruments in your particular airplane. Electrical systems vary greatly between airplanes, but certain important services that may be powered electrically include:

- some, or all, gyroscopic flight instruments (turn coordinator, attitude indicator and heading indicator)—a common arrangement is electrically powered turn coordinator with vacuum-driven attitude indicator and heading indicator to reduce the possibility of all gyroscopic instruments failing simultaneously; (note that the pitot-static instruments—airspeed indicator, altimeter, vertical speed indicator—are not electrically powered);
- the fuel quantity indicators, and perhaps an oil temperature gauge, or carburetor air temperature gauge;
- the starting system;
- landing lights, beacon, strobe, cabin lights, instrument lights; and
- radios.

Check the electrical system diagram for your particular airplane. A schematic diagram of a typical light airplane electrical system follows.

The Bus Bar

The **bus bar** is the main conductor and the distribution center in the electrical system. Electrical power is supplied to the bus bar by the alternator (or generator) and a battery, from where it is distributed to the circuits and electrical components that require power.

The Battery

The **battery** provides the initial electrical power to turn the engine over and start it with an **electric starter motor,** and also provides back-up or emergency electrical power at all times. Once the engine is running, it is self-sustaining and no longer needs electrical power from the battery. In fact the alternator (or generator), which is driven by the engine, provides current to recharge the battery after the engine has been started.

The battery provides emergency electrical power and electrical power for engine start.

Most light airplanes have a **lead-acid battery** that creates an electrical current (measured in amps) by a chemical reaction between lead plates immersed in weak **sulfuric acid** that acts as an electrolyte. To prevent corrosion from any spillage of the acid, the battery is usually housed in its own compartment. The battery needs to be vented to exhaust the hydrogen and oxygen formed when it is being charged.

The battery is classified according to the voltage across its terminals (usually 12 or 24 volts) and its capacity to provide a current for a certain time (amp-hours). For instance, a 30 amp-hour battery is capable of steadily supplying a current of 1 amp for 30 hours (or 6 amps for 5 hours; 3 amps for 10 hours).

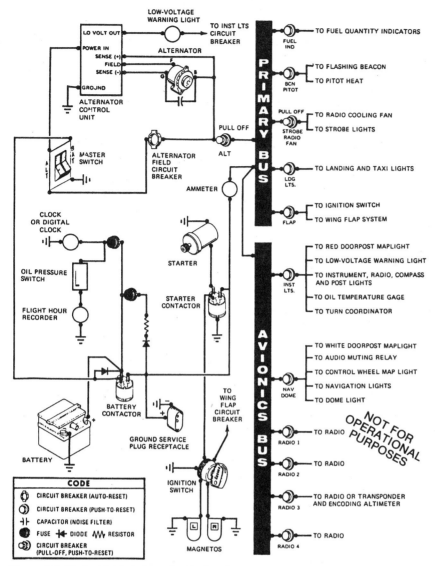

Figure 6-8. Typical light airplane electrical system

If its electrical energy is depleted, as it is in an engine start, the battery needs to be recharged. This normally occurs after the engine is running, when the battery absorbs power produced by the alternator. The largest current draw on the battery is during start-up, when it supplies electrical power to the starter motor to turn the engine over, so the greatest rate of battery recharging will normally occur immediately after the engine is started.

The electrolytic level in the battery should be checked periodically, to ensure that the plates are covered. If the level is well below the top of the plates, the battery will not retain its full charge for very long, and the ammeter will indicate a high charging rate in flight. Leaks, connections and security of the battery should also be checked. This is carried out in the regular maintenance schedule by the mechanics.

Do not start a flight with an uncharged (flat) battery—it could result in you having no electrical power in flight if the engine-driven alternator fails. If the battery is flat, replace it or have it recharged before flight.

The battery should recharge after engine start.

Do not start the engine with radios and other unnecessary electrical equipment switched on. Large voltage fluctuations when the starter is engaged may severely damage sensitive electronic circuits. Turn on this ancillary electrical equipment after the engine is started, and after you have checked that the alternator is charging the battery. For the same reasons, turn off ancillary electrical equipment before shutting down the engine.

The Alternator

The electrical power in most modern light airplanes is usually supplied by an **alternator.** On older airplanes, the electrical power may be produced by a **generator.**

Both alternators and generators initially produce **alternating current (AC)**—an electric current that flows in alternate directions. Since most airplanes require **direct current (DC)**—electric current that flows in only one direction—the AC has to be rectified to DC. The AC within the alternator is rectified into DC electronically with diodes, whereas within the generator an electromechanical device known as the commutator performs this function. Also, the diodes in the alternator prevent any reverse current flow out of the battery, whereas a generator requires a reverse current relay.

As well as providing the power for lights, radios and other services, a very important function of the generator/alternator is to recharge the battery so that it is ready for further use. Most airplane electrical systems are direct current of 14 or 28 volts. Note that these voltages are marginally higher than the battery voltages to allow the battery to be fully recharged by the electrical system.

The Advantages of an Alternator

Alternators:

- are lighter than generators because alternators do not contain as heavy electromagnets and casings, and have a simpler and lighter brush assembly;
- have a relatively constant electrical voltage output, even at low rpm; and
- are easier to maintain (because of their simpler brush assembly and the absence of a commutator).

The Disadvantage of an Alternator

Unlike a generator, an alternator requires an initial current from the battery to set up a magnetic field, which is necessary before the alternator can produce an electrical current. Therefore an airplane with an alternator must have a serviceable battery. A flat battery must be replaced or recharged.

> An aircraft with an alternator must have a serviceable battery.

If the propeller is hand-swung to start the engine, the alternator will *not* come on-line unless the battery has at least some residual voltage. The advantages of an alternator outweigh this disadvantage.

Voltage Regulator

The correct output voltage from the generator/alternator is maintained by a **voltage regulator**, over which the pilot has no direct control.

Overvoltage Protector

Some airplanes have **overvoltage protectors** (or overvoltage relays). Refer to your Pilot's Operating Handbook for information.

The Ammeter

The **ammeter** measures the electrical current (amps) flowing into or out of the battery. (In some airplanes a **voltmeter** is provided to measure the electromotive force available to deliver the current.)

There are two quite distinct types of ammeter presentation and you should understand exactly what this important instrument is telling you.

Left-Zero Ammeter

A **left-zero** ammeter measures only the output of the alternator or generator. It is graduated from zero amperes on the left end of the scale and increases in amperes to the right end of the scale, or it may be shown as a percentage of the alternator's rated load.

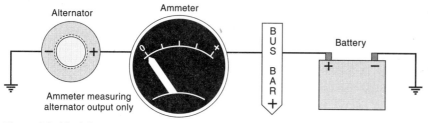

Figure 6-9. The left-zero ammeter

As the left-zero ammeter indicates the electrical load on the alternator, this type of ammeter can be referred to as a **loadmeter**.

- With the battery switch *ON* and the engine not running, or, with the engine running and the alternator switch *OFF,* the ammeter will show zero.
- If the engine is started and the alternator is turned *ON,* the ammeter will then show the **alternator output.**

During start-up, the battery discharges electrical power, so immediately after start-up the ammeter indication will be quite high during the initial battery recharging.

When the battery is fully charged, and the alternator is operating, the ammeter should show a reading slightly above the zero graduation if all the other electrical circuits are switched off. As these extra circuits are switched on (lights, radios), the ammeter reading will increase.

If the ammeter reading drops to zero in flight, it probably means an alternator failure. Some electrical systems have a red warning light that illuminates when the alternator fails to supply electrical power. You should be familiar with the procedures for electrical failure in your Pilot's Operating Handbook, which may allow you to restore electrical power.

Generally, it is advisable to reduce electrical load to a minimum if the alternator fails, since only the battery will be supplying electrical power. Land as soon as practicable to have the problem corrected.

Center-Zero Ammeter

The **center-zero** ammeter measures the flow of current (amperage) into and out-of the battery.

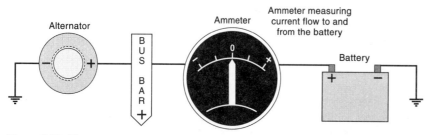

Figure 6-10. The center-zero ammeter

- Current into the battery is **charge,** with the ammeter needle deflected right of center.
- Current out of the battery is **discharge,** with the ammeter needle deflected left of center.
- No current flow either into or out of the battery is shown by the needle being in the center-zero position.
- With the battery switch *ON* and no alternator output, the ammeter will indicate a *discharge* from the battery, because the battery is providing current for the electrical circuits that are switched on. The ammeter needle is to the left (discharge) side of center-zero.
- With the alternator *ON* and supplying electrical power, if the electrical load required to power the circuits switched on is less than the capability of the alternator, the ammeter will show a *charge,* because there will be a flow of current to the battery.
- If the alternator is *ON,* but incapable of supplying sufficient power to the electrical circuits, the battery must make up the balance and there will be some flow of current from the battery. The ammeter will show a discharge. If this continues, the battery could be drained or "flattened." In this case, reduce the load on the electrical system by switching off unnecessary electrical equipment until the ammeter indicates a charge, (a flow of current from the alternator into the battery).

The Master Switch

The **master switch** (or battery switch/alternator switch) controls all of the airplane's electrical system, with one very important exception—it does not control the ignition system which gets electrical power directly from the engine-driven magneto. This statement is not completely true if the airplane has an electric clock, which will draw a very small amount of electrical power at all times whether the master switch is on or not.

Figure 6-11. The master switch (battery switch/alternator switch)

The master switch needs to be *ON* for any other electrical system to receive power or for the battery to be recharged when the engine is running. It should be turned *OFF* after stopping the engine, to avoid the battery discharging by powering electrical equipment connected to it.

In airplanes with an alternator installed, the master switch is a **split switch** (with two halves that can be switched on and off separately):

- one half for operating the **battery switch** (or master relay for the electrical systems), which connects battery power to the bus bar (electrical load distribution point or bar); and
- the other half, the **alternator switch,** for energizing the alternator. It connects the alternator field to the bus bar, thus providing the alternator with battery power.

Both switches must be *ON* for normal operation of the electrical system. If either switch has to be turned *OFF* due to malfunction in flight then you should consider terminating the flight as soon as possible. They can be switched on separately, but only the alternator can be switched off separately—switching the battery *OFF* will automatically switch the alternator off as well.

Fuses, Circuit Breakers and Overload Switches

Fuses, circuit breakers and **overload switches** are provided to protect electrical equipment from current overload. If there is an electrical overload or short-circuit, a fuse-wire will melt or a circuit breaker (CB) will pop out and break the circuit so that no current can flow through it. It may prevent the circuit from overheating, smoking or catching fire.

It is normal procedure (provided there is no smell or other sign of burning or overheating) to reset a circuit breaker once only, by pushing it back in or resetting it. If a circuit breaker pops again, you can be fairly sure there is an electrical problem, and so it should not be reset a second time. Similarly, a fuse-wire should not be replaced more than once (with the correct amperage first checked on the replacement fuse-wire). Spare fuses of the correct type and rating should be available in the cockpit.

Only reset a circuit breaker once.

A fuse wire should not be replaced more than once.

Do not replace a blown fuse with one of a higher rating (15 amp is a higher rating than 5 amp), as this may allow excessive current to flow through the electrical circuit that it is supposed to protect. An electrical fire could result.

Do not replace a blown fuse with one of a higher rating.

Overload switches are combined *ON-OFF* switches and *overload protectors*. Overload switches will switch themselves off if they experience an electrical overload. The pilot can switch them back on like a resettable circuit breaker.

Some airplane handbooks recommend a delay of a minute or two prior to resetting, to allow for cooling of the possibly overloaded circuit. If you detect fire, smoke or a burning smell, then caution is advised. Resetting the circuit breaker or replacing the fuse in such cases is not advisable.

Relays

A **relay** is a device in an electrical circuit that can be activated by a current or voltage to cause a change in the electrical condition of another electrical circuit.

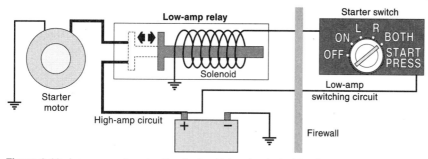

Figure 6-12. Low-amp relay circuit activates high-amp starter circuit

Instead of having high currents and heavy wiring running to where the switches are in the cockpit (with consequent current losses and fire danger from arcing), a low amperage current operated by a switch in the cockpit can be used to close a remote relay and complete the circuit for a much higher amperage circuit in the engine compartment, the starter motor for example.

A relay is usually operated on the **solenoid** principle. A solenoid is a metal bar or rod with a coil of wire wound around it. If a current passes through the coil, it establishes a magnetic field that can move the metal rod, which can then perform some mechanical task, such as making or breaking a contact in another electrical circuit.

A typical relay consists of a contact held open by a spring, thereby interrupting an electrical circuit. Around the stem of the relay is wound a coil of wire. If a current is made to pass through this coil, a magnetic field is set up that will move the relay to the closed position, thereby completing the circuit and allowing current to flow in it.

The current that activates the relay is in a completely different circuit to the relay. Occasionally a relay will stick even though its activating current has been removed, and an unwanted current will flow through the circuit. Many electric starters have an associated red warning light that will stay illuminated to warn the pilot of the starter relay sticking and the starter motor still operating even though the starter has been selected to *OFF*. (In this situation, the engine could be stopped by starving it of fuel—mixture control to *IDLE CUT-OFF*.)

External Power Sockets or Ground Servicing Receptacle

The more sophisticated light airplanes and most large airplanes have provision for a suitable external power source to be plugged into the airplane's electrical system. The external power source provides ground power over an extended period when the engine or engines are not running or conserves the airplane battery during an engine start.

On some airplane types external power can be plugged in but will not connect in to the airplane electrical system. A small current from the battery is needed to operate the relay that connects the plugged-in external power to the airplane circuit, hence a serviceable battery is required to use external power. There are other systems that operate differently to this, so refer to your Pilot's Operating Handbook. Ensure a ground power unit (GPU) of the correct voltage is used. (Connecting a 28V GPU on a 12 volt airplane will severely damage the radios and other electrical equipment.)

Electrical Malfunctions

An electrical overload will normally cause a fuse-wire to melt or a circuit breaker to pop. This protects the affected circuit. Allow two minutes to cool and, if no indication of smoke, fire or a burning smell, replace the fuse or reset the circuit breaker—**but reset once only.** If the circuit breaker pops or the fuse melts again—do not reset or replace a second time.

The ammeter should be checked when the engine is running to ensure that the alternator is supplying sufficient current (amps) for the electrical services and to recharge the battery. The ammeter usually indicates the rate at which current is flowing into the battery and recharging it.

With the engine running, the ammeter can indicate two faults:

1. Insufficient current to charge the battery.
2. Too much current.

With insufficient current from the alternator, or none at all, nonessential electrical equipment should be switched off to conserve the battery, and thought should be given to making an early landing. Most airplane batteries cannot, on their own, supply all electrical equipment for a long period.

With too much current and an excessive charge rate, the battery could overheat and the electrolyte (which may be sulfuric acid) begin to evaporate, possibly damaging the battery. If the cause of the excessive current is a faulty voltage regulator, equipment such as the radio could be adversely affected. Many airplanes have an overvoltage sensor that would, in these circumstances, automatically shut-down the alternator and illuminate a red warning light in the cockpit to alert the pilot.

Note: Operations of an alternator-powered electrical system with a partially charged battery that is unable to turn the engine over are not recommended for the above reasons.

If the alternator fails (indicated in most airplanes by either the ammeter indication dropping to zero and/or a red warning light), the battery will act as an emergency source of electrical power. To extend the period for which the battery can supply power following failure of the alternator, the electrical load should be reduced. This can be done by switching off nonessential services such as unnecessary lights and radios. Consideration should be given to terminating the flight at a nearby suitable airport while electrical power is still available.

✍ Now complete **Review 6, Part (d)** on page 143.

The Vacuum System

The gyroscopes in the flight instruments may be spun electrically or by a stream of high-speed air directed onto buckets cut into the perimeter of the rotor. The vacuum system (which sucks this high-speed air into the gyro instrument cases and onto the gyro rotors, causing them to spin very fast) needs a little explaining.

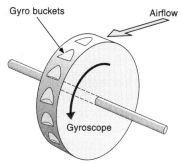

Figure 6-13. Gyroscope buckets

The Engine-Driven Vacuum Pump

Most modern vacuum systems use an engine-driven vacuum suction pump. Some airplanes are equipped with an electrically driven system. The vacuum suction pump evacuates the cases of the gyroscopic-driven instruments creating a partial vacuum (low pressure). The required suction is typically 4.5 to 5.4 inches of mercury, which creates a pressure 4.5–5.4 in.Hg *less* than atmospheric, indicated in the cockpit on a suction gauge.

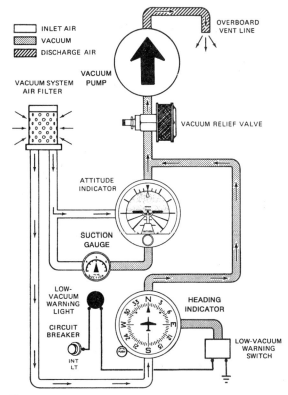

Figure 6-14. A typical vacuum system

Filtered air is continuously drawn in at high speed through a nozzle directed at the gyro buckets, causing the gyro to spin at high speed, often in excess of 20,000 rpm. This air is continuously being sucked out by the suction pump and exhausted into the atmosphere.

The effects of various malfunctions in the vacuum system are summarized below.

- If the air filter blocks, or the vacuum system fails, the reduced airflow may allow the gyroscopes to gradually run down and the vacuum-operated instruments will eventually indicate erratically or incorrectly, or respond slowly. A lower suction will be indicated on the gauge.

- Failure of the vacuum pump will be indicated by a zero reading on the suction gauge. It may be that the gyroscopes have sufficient speed to allow the instruments to read correctly for a minute or two before the gyros run down following failure of the vacuum pump.

- A zero reading on the suction gauge could also mean a failure of the gauge (rather than a failure of the vacuum pump), in which case the instruments should continue to operate normally.

- If the vacuum pressure is too high, the gyro rotors may spin too fast and suffer mechanical damage. To prevent this, a vacuum relief valve (or vacuum regulator) in the system will admit air from the atmosphere to reduce the excessive suction.

When the gyros are not being used, they should normally be **caged** (if provision is made to do this). Caging a gyro locks it in a fixed position. Caging the gyros is also recommended in the Pilot's Operating Handbook of some airplanes when performing aerobatic maneuvers.

Vacuum Provided by a Venturi Tube

Some airplanes (especially older ones) have their vacuum system operated by a **venturi tube.** This is a shaped tube on the outside of the airframe, which replaces the engine-driven vacuum pump. When air flows through the venturi tube, and speeds up because of the shape of the venturi, the static pressure decreases (Bernoulli's principle). This low pressure area, if connected to the gyro instrument cases, will draw air through each instrument via an internal filter and spin the gyroscopes, as in the engine-driven system.

Before the venturi-powered vacuum system can work there must be an appreciable airflow through the venturi tube. This is normally created by the forward motion of the airplane through the air with sufficient airflow being provided at flying speeds. It may be several minutes after takeoff before the gyroscopes are spinning fast enough for the instrument indications to be reliable. This is a significant disadvantage compared with the engine-driven system.

Other disadvantages are the increased drag caused by the externally mounted venturi-tube, and the possibility of ice affecting it (like in a carburetor, where the reduced pressure causes a reduced temperature).

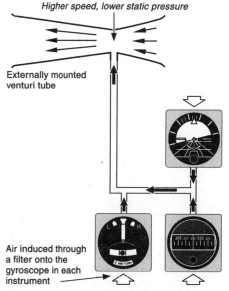

Higher speed, lower static pressure

Externally mounted venturi tube

Air induced through a filter onto the gyroscope in each instrument

Figure 6-15. Air flowing through a venturi tube can create a "suction", and power a vacuum system

Figure 6-16. A typical venturi tube

✐ Now complete **Review 6, Part (e)** on page 143.

✍ Review 6

Part (a)

1. Some airplanes have auxiliary fuel boost pumps to provide fuel at the required _____, to purge the fuel lines of any _____, to _____ a fuel-injected engine for start-up, and to supply fuel if the _____-driven fuel pump fails.

➤ pressure, vapor, prime, engine-driven

2. A cold engine needs to be primed for start-up. The fuel priming pump operated by the pilot delivers fuel:
   (a) through the carburetor to the induction manifold or inlet valve ports.
   (b) through the carburetor and directly into each of the cylinders.
   (c) to the induction manifold or intake valve ports, bypassing the carburetor.

➤ (c)

3. What type of fuel can be substituted in an aircraft if the recommended octane is not available?
   (a) The next higher octane aviation gas.
   (b) The next lower octane aviation gas.
   (c) Unleaded automotive gas of the same octane rating.

➤ (a)

4. You should not use fuel of a lower grade than specified because it could lead to _____ and engine damage.

➤ detonation

5. Auto gasoline (may/should not) be used in an airplane engine.

➤ should not

6. Fuel should be checked for contamination, especially water, prior to the _____ , and after _____ .

➤ first flight of the day, each fueling

7. Water tends to collect at the (highest/lowest) points in the fuel system.

➤ lowest

8. Aviation gasoline can be distinguished from aviation turbine fuel (kerosene) by _____ and _____.

➤ color and smell

9. 100/130 fuel is colored _____ .
   100 LL (low lead) fuel is colored _____ .

➤ green, blue

Systems

10. Filling the fuel tanks after the last flight of the day is considered a good operating procedure because this will:
    (a) force any existing water to the top of the tank away from the fuel lines to the engine.
    (b) prevent expansion of the fuel by eliminating airspace in the tanks.
    (c) prevent moisture condensation by eliminating airspace in the tanks.

➤ (c)

11. AVGAS fueling equipment decals should normally be colored _____ , while jet fuel equipment decals should normally be colored _____ .

➤ AVGAS—red; jet fuel—black

12. If you allow a fuel tank to run dry in flight before changing tanks, you run the risk of:
    (a) air being drawn into the fuel lines and causing a vapor lock.
    (b) overheating the fuel pump, leading to failure.
    (c) pumping foreign matter into the fuel lines.

➤ (a)

Part (b)

1. Oil lowers friction between moving parts and so prevents high (pressures/temperatures), and what heat is formed can to some extent be carried away by circulating (oil/water/fuel).

➤ temperatures, oil

2. Oil grades (may/may not) be mixed.

➤ may not

3. Impurities in the oil are removed by the _____ .

➤ oil filter

4. With too little oil, you may observe a (high/low) oil temperature and/or a (high/low) oil pressure.

➤ high oil temperature, low oil pressure

5. If the oil filter becomes blocked, then the unfiltered oil is forced through an _____ valve. Dirty and contaminated oil is (better/worse) than no oil at all.

➤ oil filter bypass valve, better

Part (c)

1. Most airplane engines have cooling _____ to aid in cooling.

➤ fins

2. For internal cooling, reciprocating aircraft engines are especially dependent on:
   (a) a properly functioning thermostat.
   (b) air flowing over the exhaust manifold.
   (c) the circulation of lubricating oil.
   ➤ (c)

3. What action can a pilot take to aid in cooling an engine that is overheating during a climb?
   (a) Reduce rate of climb and increase airspeed.
   (b) Reduce climb and increase rpm.
   (c) Increase climb speed and increase rpm.
   ➤ (a)

4. Excessively high engine temperatures will:
   (a) cause damage to heat-conducting hoses and warping of the cylinder cooling fins.
   (b) cause loss of power, excessive oil consumption, and possible permanent internal engine damage.
   (c) not appreciably affect an aircraft engine.
   ➤ (b)

Part (d)

1. Normal in-flight electrical power is provided by an _____ or _____ .
   ➤ alternator, generator

2. A distribution point for electrical power to various services is called a:
   (a) circuit breaker.
   (b) distributor.
   (c) bus bar.
   ➤ (c)

3. Electrical power for start-up and as an emergency source of electrical power is the _____ .
   ➤ battery

4. An alternator requires an initial current from the _____ to activate it.
   ➤ battery

5. A center-zero ammeter measures _____ in and out of the _____, whereas a left-zero ammeter measures only the _____ of the alternator. It has zero amps on the _____ end of the scale and increases in amps to the right end of the scale.
   ➤ current, battery, output, left

6. Immediately after start-up, ammeter indication will be (high/low) as the battery is recharged.
   ➤ high

7. Fuses and circuit breakers are protection against excessive electrical (current/voltage).
   ➤ current

8. The battery master switch should be turned to *OFF* after the engine is stopped to avoid the battery discharging through:
   (a) the magnetos.
   (b) the alternator or generator.
   (c) electrical services connected to it.
   ➤ (c)

9. A fully charged battery rated at 15 amp-hours is capable of providing 5 amps for a period of _____ hours without recharging.
   ➤ 3 hours

10. Which of the following instruments and gauges would normally be electrically powered? Airspeed indicator, altimeter, vertical speed indicator, attitude indicator, turn coordinator, heading indicator, fuel quantity gauges, engine rpm gauge, oil temperature gauge.
    ➤ ASI, altimeter and VSI are pitot-static instruments and are not typically electrically powered (although there may be an electrical pitot heater to avoid icing); the gyroscopic instruments (AI, TC and HI) may be electrically powered or powered from the vacuum system—a typical arrangement is a vacuum-powered AI and HI with an electrical TC; the fuel quantity gauges and oil temperature gauge (if installed) will probably be electrically powered; the rpm gauge (tachometer) is self-powered directly off the engine. (In addition, check for your airplane).

Part (e)

1. The suction (or vacuum) gauge reads the pressure (above/below) atmospheric pressure.
   ➤ below

2. The vacuum pump, if installed on a modern airplane, is most likely to be (electrically/engine/hydraulically)-driven.
   ➤ engine-driven

3. Air-driven gyro rotors are prevented from spinning too fast by the _____ .
   ➤ vacuum relief valve

4. Insufficient suction (may/will not) cause gyroscopic instruments (such as the artificial horizon or the heading indicator) to indicate incorrectly, erratically, or respond slowly.
   ➤ may

Engine Operation

Operating the Engine

Having gained a knowledge of the engine and its main associated systems, you now need to bring this knowledge together in your day-to-day operation of the airplane. The correct procedures will be laid down in your Pilot's Operating Handbook, and general principles are covered in detail in our *Flight Training* manual.

Starting the Engine

Ensure that adequate **safety precautions** are always taken prior to engine start.

- Prior to start, position the aircraft so that it is clear of obstructions, other aircraft, open hangar/workshop doors, and fueling installations.
- Set the parking brakes on, or chock the main wheels, to avoid the embarrassing and dangerous situation of the airplane commencing its own taxiing. Chocking the nosewheel is *not* advisable because of its proximity to the propeller and the consequent risk to a person walking into the rotating propeller when removing a nosewheel chock.
- Be aware of the location of firefighting equipment—just in case of fire. Ensure no open flames, cigarettes or fuel spillages in the vicinity.
- Most importantly **check** the immediate area is clear of people and then **warn** any nearby persons (especially those you may not be able to see) of the impending danger of a spinning propeller by making a loud warning call of "*CLEAR!*" or "*CLEAR PROP!*" The aircraft red rotating beacon should be turned on just prior to starting the engine. Be prepared to discontinue the start immediately if a problem develops or if someone approaches the danger area near the propeller.

Your first action after starting the engine should be to adjust for proper rpm and check for the desired indications on the engine gauges, especially the oil pressure gauge which should show an increase within 30 seconds.

If it is necessary to handprop an airplane engine (an extremely hazardous procedure) it is important that a competent pilot be at the airplane controls and that the person turning the propeller has sufficient training.

Starting a Cold Engine

Starting in cold conditions usually requires some *priming* (providing an initial charge of fuel to the cylinders). Many aircraft have a priming pump (electrical or manual) in the cockpit for this purpose—it is used only prior to startup, and should be locked at all other times.

Know the procedures recommended in your Pilot's Operating Handbook. These differ from airplane-to-airplane, engine-to-engine and situation-to-situation. You should understand the reasons why a certain procedure is recommended and when it is appropriate to vary it slightly. An over-primed (flooded) engine or restarting a hot engine, for example, will require different techniques to starting a cold engine in a cold climate.

Note: On start-up of a cold engine, the oil pressure should normally rise within 30 seconds, to ensure adequate lubrication of the engine and its moving parts. If the oil pressure rise is not indicated within this time, shut down the engine to avoid possible damage. If the engine is warm, the oil pressure should rise more quickly. In cold climates, it is normal for the oil pressure rise to take up to 60 seconds—*see* your Pilot's Operating Handbook.

Starting an Engine that has been Over-Primed

Most over-primed engines will start more easily with the mixture control in *IDLE CUT-OFF* so that no more fuel enters the cylinders until the engine has actually started. When the mixture in the cylinders reaches the right balance as air-only is drawn in, the engine should fire, at which stage the mixture control should be moved quickly to *FULL RICH* to provide a continuing fuel supply.

If the engine does *not* fire, the rotations may have cleared the cylinders of fuel. Therefore move the mixture control to rich to allow fresh fuel to be drawn into the cylinders. This technique applies to both carbureted and fuel-injected engines. Refer to your Pilot's Operating Handbook.

Starting a Hot Engine

Usually a hot carbureted engine will start satisfactorily using the normal procedure for a cold engine if you do not prime it or pump the throttle.

When starting a hot fuel-injected engine, the hot air and vapor in the very narrow fuel lines may cause a vapor lock and prevent the flow of any fuel. To prevent this, switch on the fuel boost pumps. This will pressurize the fuel lines up to the fuel control unit, removing any vapor in that part of the system. Leave the mixture control in *IDLE CUT-OFF* so that fuel does not reach the cylinders but is recycled back into the tank.

Some engines require the throttle to be opened for the boost pumps to work in *HIGH*. After 15 to 20 seconds, the narrow fuel lines to the fuel injectors should have been purged of vapor and be full of fuel. Because a small amount of fuel will probably have found its way into the fuel nozzles near the cylinders, a start can be made without priming (with throttle at idle or open about $1/2$ inch).

Stopping the Engine

A brief **cooling period** at 1,000 rpm is usually recommended to allow gradual cooling. During this time check for any abnormal indications and perform a systems check of the ignition system for *OFF*, (described in the *magneto/ignition system* in Chapter 16.)

Most engines are shut down from a low power position (usually 1,000 rpm) by moving the mixture control to *IDLE CUT-OFF*, thus allowing the cylinders to be purged of fuel. All switches are usually moved to *OFF*.

It is a good practice to:

• leave the mixture control in the idle cut-off position;

• leave the throttle in the closed position in case someone turns the propeller and firing occurs because the magneto system is still *live*.

Changing Power Settings with a Constant-Speed Propeller

While almost all training airplanes have a **fixed-pitch propeller** whose rpm is controlled with the throttle, more advanced airplanes which you may soon fly are equipped with a **constant-speed propeller** with blades that can vary their pitch angle.

The controls in the cockpit for a constant-speed propeller are:
- the **propeller control** (or pitch knob) to control **rpm;** and
- the **throttle** to control fuel flow and **manifold pressure (MP).**

The pilot selects the desired rpm of the engine and propeller using the **propeller control** (also known as the *pitch control* or *rpm control*). The propeller blades will then automatically change their pitch angle or blade angle to absorb the power available and maintain the selected rpm. For instance, if you have selected a cruise rpm of 2,400 with the propeller control and then move the throttle to increase manifold pressure from 22 to 23 in. Hg, the propeller pitch will increase to absorb the extra power by increasing the blade angle and providing increased thrust.

Conversely, if power is reduced, the propeller blade angle will reduce to maintain rpm. The constant-speed unit in the propeller operates automatically—usually the blade movement to a new pitch angle is hydraulically operated by a governor sensitive to rpm.

There is a mechanical limit to how far the propeller pitch or blade angle can reduce, known as the **low-pitch stop.** With the blades back on the low-pitch stop, the propeller will behave like a fixed-pitch propeller.

The pilot selects the desired power with various combinations of rpm and manifold pressure. **Manifold pressure** is the pressure in the intake manifold of the engine, and is normally measured in inches of mercury (in. Hg). Manifold pressures higher than those recommended by the manufacturer can lead to high cylinder pressures and possibly detonation, and must be avoided. This can occur if high manifold pressures are set at low rpm.

Increasing power:

To avoid high MP and low rpm:
- **first increase rpm** with the propeller control. The MP will drop automatically as a result of less time per cycle being available for the fuel/air mixture to be induced into the cylinder, hence a smaller charge in the cylinder for combustion;
- **then increase MP** to desired value with the throttle.

Decreasing power:

To avoid high MP and low rpm:
- **first reduce MP** with the throttle;
- **then reduce rpm** with the propeller control. The MP will rise a little automatically—as a result of more time for cycle for the fuel/air mixture to be induced into the cylinder, hence a larger charge in the cylinder for combustion. After the reduction of rpm, some minor readjustment of MP will be necessary.

Air pressure falls by about 1 in. Hg per 1,000 feet as altitude is gained, and so will the manifold pressure in an unsupercharged engine if you do not adjust it with the throttle. In this situation the rpm would remain the same, but the power would reduce gradually. Superchargers and turbochargers are used in more sophisticated engines to boost the air pressure to the engine, thereby increasing the power available at altitude.

Note: The propeller governor that controls rpm is operated by engine oil, which is another very good reason for regular oil changes. Dirty oil could have an adverse effect on propeller operation.

Change rpm with the propeller control.

Change MP with the throttle.

Never exceed the recommended manifold pressure.

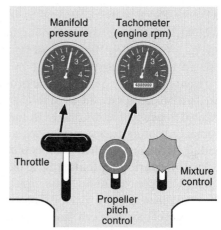

Figure 7-1. With a constant-speed propeller, the propeller control controls rpm and the throttle determines the manifold pressure

When increasing power increase rpm before MP.

When decreasing power reduce MP before rpm.

Engine Handling

At all times, follow recommended procedures found in the manufacturer's handbook. This will ensure correct operation of the engine, avoid spark plug fouling and over-stressing the engine components, and achieve best fuel economy. Know the manufacturer's engine limitations and do not exceed them.

When the engine is operating, you should monitor the **oil temperature gauge** (and the *cylinder-head temperature gauge* if installed). An abnormally high engine oil temperature could indicate insufficient oil in the engine. High engine temperatures, either in the air or on the ground, will cause:

- loss of power;
- excessive oil consumption; and
- possible permanent internal engine damage.

In flight, you could consider cooling the engine by opening the air-cooling cowl flaps (if installed), richening the mixture, reducing power, or lowering the nose and increasing airspeed.

Avoid running the engine **on the ground** for prolonged periods if possible but, if unavoidable, face the aircraft into wind for better cooling and, if they are installed, open the cowl flaps. If the limiting red-line temperatures are approached during ground operations, consider taxiing clear of the runway and shutting the engine down to allow cooling.

Prevent **spark-plug fouling** by avoiding operating the engine at very low rpm for long periods. At low idling rpm, deposits can form on the spark plugs which will increase their electrical conductivity and may lead to misfiring.

Misuse of controls can lead to detuning of engine crankshaft counterweights and engine damage. Opening the throttle by ramming it forward can produce an incorrect fuel/air mixture in the carburetor and cause the engine to cut-out, or encourage detonation. Rough handling of the throttle can also cause de-tuning of the crankshaft counterweights, which will permanently reduce the efficiency of the engine as a power-producer. As a guide you should take about three seconds to open the throttle from idle to full. Similarly when reducing power, do so slowly.

Advance and retard the throttle smoothly.

On a prolonged descent at low power, it is good airmanship to smoothly open the throttle for brief periods to avoid the engine becoming too cool. Closing cowl flaps, if installed, also helps. This will avoid a sudden temperature shock to the engine when it is returned to high power at the end of the descent.

Use the mixture control correctly. A too-lean mixture at high power and low altitudes can cause detonation. It is usual to lean the mixture when cruising at altitude, depending on the manufacturer's recommendations. On a very hot day, even at only 1,000 feet MSL the atmosphere may have a density altitude of several thousand feet, and leaning may be required for efficient operation (*see* Chapter 9).

Rough Running

The Engine

Engine rough running can be continuous or intermittent. If the engine starts running roughly, immediately refer to the engine instruments to see if they indicate the cause. In all cases, follow the procedures laid down in the Pilot's Operating Handbook. A thorough knowledge of these is essential.

Rough running can be caused by:

- **An inadequate fuel supply.** Check the fuel quantity gauge and if it indicates empty immediately select another tank. If the gauges show sufficient fuel suspect low fuel pressure caused by a blocked filter and switch on the fuel boost pumps to ensure a steady fuel pressure.

- **Carburetor ice.** The formation of ice in the carburetor causes a loss of power and possibly rough running. Remember that carburetor ice can form when the outside air temperature is as high as 70°F if the humidity is high enough.

- **An incorrect mixture.** If the mixture is not leaned correctly, a prolonged climb will gradually lead to a richening of the mixture as the air density falls, with consequent rough running. A prolonged descent will require the pilot to move the mixture control towards the rich position.

- **A faulty magneto.** If you suspect a faulty magneto is causing the engine to run roughly, select a low cruise power, and then check each magneto individually by switching the other one off. If the engine runs smoothly on one particular magneto, but roughly on both or on the other magneto, then select the single magneto system that gives smoother running. Consideration should be given to landing at the nearest suitable airport, the airplane engine will still operate satisfactorily on only one ignition system, but a failure of the second magneto would leave you with none.

- **A faulty ignition system.** Fouling of the spark plugs can cause faulty ignition. Sometimes this can be cured by leaning the mixture to raise the temperature and perhaps burn the residue off the plug, or by changing the power setting. Leakage of the **ignition current,** which can sometimes occur around the ignition leads could be the cause, however this cannot be remedied in flight. This leakage may be worse at high altitude/high power settings and in wet weather.

The Propeller

Vibration or rough running usually indicates a problem or impending problem. An out-of-balance propeller can cause vibration.

An out-of-balance propeller can cause vibration.

If the vibration is caused by a damaged propeller, possibly an out-of-balance propeller due to nicks, then a change of rpm or a change of airspeed should reduce the vibration. This, of course, is only a temporary remedy and the nicks should be repaired on landing. Nicks in the propeller blade degrade its performance considerably and are liable to cause cracks which can ultimately lead to blade failure in flight, with disastrous results. Propeller nicks and other damage should be brought immediately to the attention of a mechanic.

If the vibration does not diminish, but worsens, it could indicate that the bolts attaching the propeller to the shaft are loosening. In this case, shutting down the engine is advisable. If you suspect this defect in a single-engine airplane, a landing as soon as possible (a forced landing, if necessary) should be contemplated. Ice on the propeller blades may also cause vibration.

Cross-Checking Engine Instruments

If one engine instrument indicates a problem, verify this, if possible, by checking against another instrument. For instance, an oil pressure gauge that suddenly shows zero could indicate that all the oil has been lost out of the system, or it could be just a faulty gauge. Cross-reference to the oil temperature gauge should establish the fault. A normal oil temperature would indicate sufficient oil is still circulating, whereas a rapidly increasing oil temperature would indicate that loss of oil has occurred.

If you are in flight, a serious loss of oil will mean an engine shutdown, so in a single-engine airplane you should prepare to land as soon as possible. With a faulty gauge, the engine will continue to operate normally.

Taxiing

Do not taxi over rough ground because the propeller could hit long grass, obstructions or the ground, damaging the propeller and possibly bending the engine crankshaft, a very costly lack of common sense.

Avoid engine runups or taxiing on stony or gravel surfaces where possible. The strong airflow and vortices around a propeller pick up stones, damaging the propeller and airframe and hitting other aircraft and people. Good airmanship involves looking after your airplane and thinking of others.

Emergencies

Engine Failure in Flight

Due to improved manufacturing and operating procedures, mechanical engine failure is becoming a rare event, but **fuel starvation** as a cause of engine stoppage is not as uncommon as it should be. Fuel starvation will of course stop an engine and can be caused by:

- insufficient fuel;
- mishandling of the fuel tank selection;
- incorrect use of the mixture control;
- ice forming in the carburetor; or
- contaminated fuel (such as water in the fuel).

If the **mixture control** is left in *LEAN* for descent (instead of being moved to *RICH*), the fuel/air mixture will gradually become more and more lean as the airplane descends into denser air, possibly resulting in the engine stopping. **Carburetor ice** can also be a problem, especially on descent when the engine is idling and not producing much heat. **Electrical failure** in both magneto systems will also cause the engine to stop.

In all these cases, the airflow past the airplane may cause the propeller to windmill and turn the engine over, even though it is not producing power.

Mechanical failure, such as the break-up of pistons or valves, will probably be accompanied by mechanical noise and the engine and propeller may be unable to rotate. In such cases any attempt to restart the engine is not advisable.

Irrespective of whether you decide to glide down for a landing or attempt to restart the engine, you must ensure that flying speed is maintained.

Some obvious items to be considered in an attempted engine restart are:

- **a fuel problem:**
  - change fuel tanks;
  - fuel pump on (if installed);
  - mixture *RICH;*
  - primer locked;
- **an ignition problem:**
  - check magneto switches individually *(BOTH–LEFT–RIGHT)*. If the engine operates on one magneto as a result of a fault in the other magneto system, then operate using the one good ignition system, otherwise return to *BOTH;*
- **an icing problem:**
  - carburetor heat *FULL HOT.*

Engine Fire in Flight

Engine fire is also a rare event, but you should always be prepared to cope with it. The firewall at the back of the engine is designed to protect the structural parts of the airframe from damage and the cockpit occupants from injury if a fire breaks out in the engine bay, provided the fire is extinguished without delay.

To check for the presence of fire, the pilot should yaw the nose left and look rearward and to the left for any trailing smoke.

The initial reaction to an engine fire in flight should be as per the Pilot's Operating Handbook. This usually involves turning off the fuel (fuel selector *OFF* or mixture control to *IDLE CUT-OFF)* and allowing the engine to run itself dry of fuel and stop. The engine and induction system will then be purged of fuel and the fire should extinguish. At this point, the ignition should be switched off and a forced landing carried out.

Throughout any emergency procedure in flight, remember that your main task is to **fly the airplane** (maintain flying speed and avoid collisions)—and the secondary task is to resolve the emergency.

Engine Fire on Startup

If a fire starts in the engine air intake during startup, a generally accepted procedure to minimize the problem is:

- **continue cranking** the engine with the starter (to keep air moving through);
- move the mixture control to *IDLE CUT-OFF* (to remove the source of fuel); and
- **open the throttle** (to maximize the airflow through the carburetor and induction system, and purge the system of fuel).

The fire will probably go out, but if it does not, then further action would be taken:

- Fuel—*OFF;*
- Switches—*OFF;*
- Brakes—*OFF.*
- Evacuate the airplane, taking the fire extinguisher.

You should refer to the Pilot's Operating Handbook for the correct procedure for your particular airplane.

✎ Now complete **Review 7** on page 151.

✎ Review 7

Engine Operation

1. The engine fuel primer is used (only prior to startup/ during normal in-flight operations).

➤ only prior to startup

2. The pilot should monitor _____ when an engine is started up. If the engine is cold prior to start-up, it should be shut down if the oil pressure does not rise within _____ seconds after start-up.

➤ oil pressure, 30

3. Prior to takeoff, you (should/need not) check each of the two ignition systems with a magneto check.

➤ should

4. As you apply power with the throttle during the takeoff run, you should observe the rpm increase, and note that the correct power is achieved early in the takeoff run. For a fixed-pitch propeller, power is indicated by _____ . For an engine equipped with a constant-speed propeller, power is indicated by_____ and _____ .

➤ rpm; manifold pressure and rpm

5. A fixed-pitch propeller achieves its best efficiency:
   (a) over a wide operating range of airspeed and rpm.
   (b) at only one airspeed and rpm.

➤ (b)

Chapter 7 **Engine Operation**

6. A constant-speed propeller, with cruise rpm selected, automatically adjusts its blade angle to absorb the power available. (true/false)?

➤ true

7. A constant-speed propeller achieves its best efficiency:
   (a) over a wide operating range of airspeed and rpm.
   (b) at only one airspeed and rpm.

➤ (a)

8. Increasing power with a constant-speed propeller, you should increase _____ first, followed by

_____ .

➤ rpm, manifold pressure

9. When decreasing power with a constant-speed propeller, decrease _____ first, followed by _____ .

➤ manifold pressure, rpm

10. For an engine equipped with a constant-speed propeller, fuel flow and consequently power output is controlled by the (throttle/propeller control/mixture control). The power output is registered on the (rpm/manifold pressure/carburetor temp) gauge.

➤ throttle, manifold pressure gauge

11. In an airplane with a constant-speed propeller, which of the following procedures should be used?
    (a) When power is decreased, reduce rpm before manifold pressure.
    (b) When power is increased, increase rpm before manifold pressure.
    (c) When power is increased or decreased adjust manifold pressure before rpm.

➤ (b)

12. When operating a constant-speed propeller:
    (a) avoid high rpm setting with high manifold pressures.
    (b) avoid low rpm settings with high manifold pressures.
    (c) always use a rich mixture with high rpm settings.

➤ (b)

13. A detuning of engine crankshaft counterweights is a source of overstress that may be caused by:
    (a) rapid opening and closing of the throttle.
    (b) carburetor ice forming on the throttle valve.
    (c) operating with an excessively rich fuel/air mixture.

➤ (a)

14. As altitude is gained when climbing in an airplane equipped with a constant-speed propeller, the rpm will (increase/decrease/stay the same), and the manifold pressure will (increase by about 1 in. Hg per 1,000 feet/ decrease by about 1 in. Hg per 1,000 feet/stay the same) unless you adjust the throttle.

➤ rpm will stay the same, MP will decrease by about 1 in. Hg per 1,000 feet

15. If you are cruising at 8,000 feet MSL, you (will/will not) achieve better fuel efficiency by leaning the mixture, which will (increase/reduce) the amount of fuel to match the (increased/reduced) weight of air.

➤ will, reduce, reduced

16. The usual method of shutting an engine down is to:
    (a) switch the magnetos off.
    (b) move the mixture to idle cut-off.
    (c) switch the master switch off.
    Note: Explain your answer, and the reasons why the other alternatives are incorrect.

➤ (b)—in a carbureted engine, it clears the induction manifold and engine cylinders of fuel; with a fuel-injected engine it clears fuel lines and cylinders of fuel. *Not (a)*—stopping the engine by removing the spark ignition would leave fuel in the fuel lines and engine. *Not (c)*—this would only turn off aircraft electrical services such as lighting, radios, etc., but would have no effect at all on the engine or engine ignition.

17. If the oil quantity gauge suddenly drops to zero in flight, you should immediately check the _____ gauge.

➤ oil temperature gauge

18. If the oil temperature gauge shows a rapid increase in temperature then suspect _____. Consideration should be given to (an immediate landing/a landing at the next suitable airport which is say a half-hour away).

➤ a serious loss of oil, an immediate landing

19. If the oil temperature gauge and the cylinder head temperature gauge are both reading higher than their normal operating range, a possible cause is:
    (a) an over-rich mixture and too much power.
    (b) a too-lean mixture and too much power.
    (c) fuel with a higher-than-specified fuel rating.

➤ (b)

Flight Instruments 8

Airplane Flight Instruments

The first impression most people have of an airplane cockpit is of the number of instruments. However when you analyze the instrument panels of even the largest jet transport airplanes, you will find that the instrumentation is not all that complicated. In fact, the basic instruments will be very similar to those found in the smallest training airplane.

Airplane flight instruments fall into three basic categories:
- pressure instruments—which use variations in air pressure;
- gyroscopic instruments—which use the properties of gyroscopic inertia; and
- magnetic instruments—which use the earth's magnetic field.

Pressure Instruments

The basic flight instruments that inform the pilot of airspeed (airspeed indicator), altitude (altimeter) and rate of change of altitude (vertical speed indicator) are **pressure instruments.**

As we saw in Chapter 1 there are two aspects of air pressure that can be considered—**static pressure** and **dynamic pressure.** If these terms are a little hazy reread pages 7 to 9 in Chapter 1 before continuing.

Static Pressure

At any point in the atmosphere static pressure is exerted equally in all directions. It is the result of the weight of all the air molecules above that point pressing down. As its name implies, static pressure does not involve relative movement of the air. Static pressure is measured on the surface of an airplane through a **static vent** or **static port** (*see* Figure 8-4).

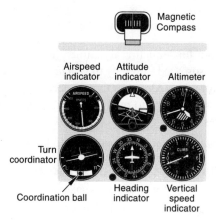

Figure 8-1. The flight instruments

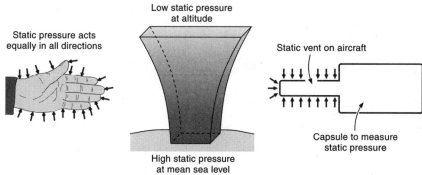

Figure 8-2. Static pressure

Dynamic Pressure

If you hold your hand up in a strong wind or out of the window of a moving automobile, you feel extra pressure (over static pressure) because of the air impacting your hand. This extra pressure, over and above the static pressure is called dynamic pressure, the pressure that results from relative movement.

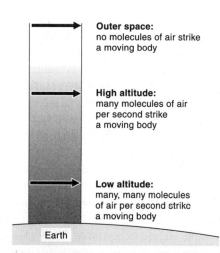

Figure 8-3. Dynamic pressure depends on air density

Dynamic pressure is expressed as $\frac{1}{2}\rho V^2$ and therefore depends on the air's density (ρ) and relative speed (V). The faster the airflow or the denser the air, the stronger the dynamic pressure, because of the greater number of air molecules that impact per second.

Total Pressure

In Chapter 1 we looked at Bernoulli's principle and noted that the total air pressure equals static pressure plus dynamic pressure.

static pressure		**dynamic pressure**		**total pressure**
measured by static vent	+	$\frac{1}{2}\rho V^2$	=	measured by pitot tube

From this equation dynamic pressure can be found by subtracting the static pressure (measured by the static vent) from the total pressure (measured by the pitot tube). Although the airspeed indicator (ASI) indicates dynamic pressure, it is calibrated to read in units of speed (usually knots) rather than in units of pressure.

Note: Dynamic pressure is also known as **impact pressure.**

The Pitot-Static System

Three flight instruments make use of pressure readings:

• the **altimeter** which converts static pressure to altitude;

• the **vertical speed indicator** which relates the rate of change of static pressure to a rate of climb or descent; and

• the **airspeed indicator** which relates the difference between total pressure and static pressure to the indicated airspeed.

The **pitot tube** mounted on the airplane is the source of total pressure and the airplane's static vent is the source of static pressure. There are two common arrangements of the pitot-static sensing system:

• a combined pitot-static head; or

• a pitot tube (possibly on the wing) and a static vent (or two) on the side of the fuselage.

The pitot tube must be positioned where the free airflow is not greatly disturbed by changes in static pressure, often forward of, or beneath the outer section of one wing. Otherwise the airspeed indicator system will suffer from significant errors. In addition, pitot heaters are sometimes provided as a precaution against ice blocking the pitot tube. They usually consist of electrical elements built into the pitot tube, and are operated by a switch from the cockpit.

Some airplanes have two **static vents,** one on each side of the fuselage, so that the reading for static pressure, when averaged, is more accurate, especially if the airplane is slipping or skidding.

There is often an **alternative static source** that can measure pressure inside the cabin, in case of ice or other matter obstructing the external vents. Cabin pressure is usually slightly less than the external atmospheric pressure and will cause the instrument readings to be slightly in error when the alternate static source is being used.

It is vital that the pitot tube and static vent(s) are not damaged or obstructed, otherwise false readings from the relevant flight instruments could degrade the safety of the flight. They should be carefully checked in the preflight external inspection. The pitot cover, used to prevent water or insects accumulating in the tube, should be removed. They should not be tested by blowing in them, since very sensitive instruments are involved.

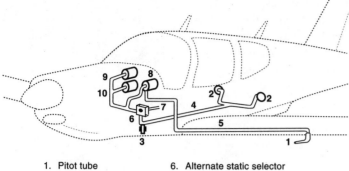

1. Pitot tube
2. Static vents
3. Static drain
4. Static line
5. Pitot line

6. Alternate static selector
7. Alternate static pressure
8. Airspeed indicator
9. Altimeter
10. Vertical speed indicator

Figure 8-4. Typical pitot-static installation

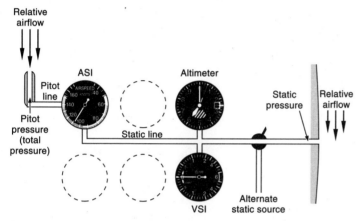

Figure 8-5. The pitot-static system

Airspeed Indicator (ASI)

The airspeed indicator displays indicated airspeed (IAS), which is related to dynamic pressure.

We can find dynamic pressure by subtracting the static vent measurement from the pitot tube measurement. This is easily done by having a diaphragm with total pressure from the pitot tube being fed onto one side of it and static pressure from the static line being fed onto the other side of it. The diaphragm and pointer connected to it will move according to the difference between the total pressure and the static pressure.

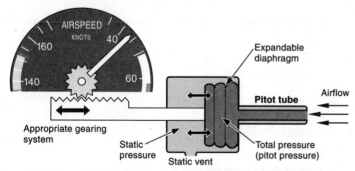

Figure 8-6. The airspeed indicator measures dynamic pressure

As airspeed increases, the dynamic pressure increases, but the static pressure remains the same. The difference between the total pressure (measured by the pitot tube) and the static pressure (measured by the static vent or static port) gives us a measure of the dynamic pressure (which is related to indicated airspeed). This difference between total and static pressures causes the diaphragm to reposition itself, and the pointer to indicate a higher airspeed.

Color Coding on the Airspeed Indicator

To assist the pilot, ASIs in modern airplanes have certain speed ranges and certain specific speeds marked according to a conventional color code.

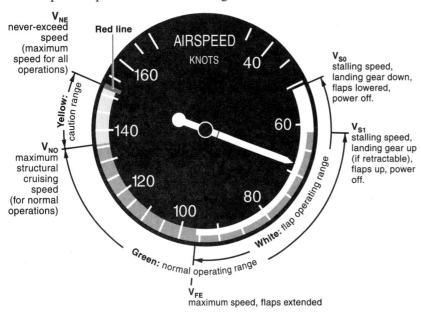

Figure 8-7. The airspeed indicator

- **Green arc:** denotes the **normal-operating speed range,** from stall speed V_{S1} at maximum gross weight (flaps up, wings level) up to V_{NO} (normal-operating limit speed or maximum structural cruise speed) which should not be exceeded except in smooth air. Operations at indicated airspeeds in the green arc should be safe in normal flying conditions. The best airspeed to use in turbulence (V_B), should be specified in the Pilot's Operating Handbook.

- **Yellow arc:** denotes the **caution range,** which extends from V_{NO} (normal-operating limit speed) up to V_{NE} (the never-exceed speed). The airplane may be operated at indicated airspeeds in the caution range **only in smooth air,** and then only with small control inputs.

- **White arc:** denotes the **flaps operating range,** from stall speed at maximum gross weight in the landing configuration V_{S0} (full flaps, landing gear down, wings level, power-off) up to V_{FE} (maximum flaps-extended speed).

- **Red radial line:** denotes V_{NE}, the **never-exceed speed.** It is the maximum speed at which the airplane may be operated.

Note 1: ASI markings refer to indicated airspeed (IAS) and not true airspeed (TAS). Where weight is a factor in determining limit speeds, such as stall speeds, the value marked is for the maximum gross weight situation.

Note 2: One important speed not marked on the airspeed indicator is the maneuvering speed (V_A)—the maximum speed at which the limit load factor can be imposed (either by gusts or by full control deflection) without overstressing or causing structural damage.

Indicated Airspeed (IAS) and True Airspeed (TAS)

The fact that indicated airspeed (IAS) and true airspeed (TAS or V) are usually different seems to worry many student pilots, but it need not. IAS is closely related to dynamic pressure ($\frac{1}{2}\rho V^2$), and is of aerodynamic importance.

When we discuss the flight performance of the airplane—lift, drag, stall speed, takeoff speed, maximum speeds and climb speeds—we talk in terms of **indicated airspeed** (IAS). The indicated airspeed is vital performance information for the pilot, as the aerodynamic qualities of the airplane depend on it.

The **true airspeed** (TAS) is the actual speed of the airplane relative to the air. TAS (or V) is important for navigational purposes, to describe speed through the air (TAS). By incorporating wind, we can calculate speed over the ground.

Indicated airspeed (IAS) is important aerodynamically.

True airspeed (TAS) is important for navigation.

True Airspeed Usually Exceeds Indicated Airspeed

In a climb it is usual for the pilot to maintain the same indicated airspeed. As the airplane gains altitude it climbs into less dense air because air density (ρ) decreases with increasing altitude.

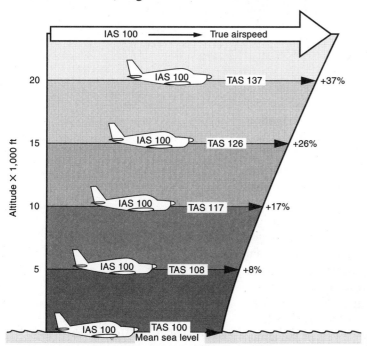

Figure 8-8. With IAS constant, TAS increases with increase in altitude

For IAS to remain the same, the value of dynamic pressure ($\frac{1}{2}\rho V^2$) must remain constant. Because air density (ρ) decreases with increasing altitude, a constant IAS ($\frac{1}{2}\rho V^2$) can only be maintained by increasing the value of V (TAS). Therefore, climbing to a higher altitude with the airspeed indicator showing a constant IAS, will mean TAS is gradually increasing. You can calculate true airspeed from indicated airspeed, pressure altitude and temperature using a flight computer (*see* Chapter 24).

On hot days and at high airports, to generate sufficient lift for takeoff the airplane must be accelerated to a higher V (TAS) to compensate for the decreased air density. (IAS shown on the ASI will remain the same.) This, coupled with possible reduced performance from the engine–propeller, will mean a longer takeoff distance—this is discussed in detail in Chapter 10.

ASI Errors Caused by a Blocked Static Vent

A blockage or ice buildup in either the static vent(s) or pitot tube will cause the pressure to be trapped in that particular line to the pressure instruments.

If you are climbing and the static vent ices over, then the static pressure trapped in the line will be higher than the actual static pressure at the altitude the airplane has climbed to. The measured difference between pitot (total) pressure and static pressure will be less than actual and the ASI will read low, (show a lower indicated airspeed than actual).

On a descent, the reverse would be the case, a blocked static vent would cause the ASI to read high, (show an indicated airspeed higher than actual). This is a dangerous situation if the pilot does not recognize it and reduces speed, because the airplane will actually be flying at a lower speed than indicated.

If the static vent(s) become blocked the ASI will read low in a climb, and high in a descent.

ASI Errors Caused by a Blocked Pitot Tube

If the pitot tube becomes blocked, say by ice, the total pressure trapped in the pitot tube (which remains constant) will be fed to the ASI, to be compared to the varying static pressure from the static vent.

Therefore in a climb, the outside static pressure reduces, hence the airspeed indicator will read higher than it should. Conversely, on descent below the altitude where icing occurred, it will read a lower airspeed than it should.

A blocked pitot tube will cause the ASI to read high in a climb, and low in a descent.

Altimeter

Unlike an automobile, an airplane must be navigated and its position known in three dimensions, not only left and right (or west and east), but also up and down. The altimeter is the most important instrument for **vertical navigation** and **vertical separation** between yourself and the ground or other aircraft. You must use it correctly and understand exactly what it is telling you.

A very important reference point for vertical navigation and for charts is **mean sea level (MSL),** the average height of the sea surface calculated from hourly tide readings taken over many years.

The altimeter relates the static pressure at the level of the airplane to a height in the **International Standard Atmosphere (ISA),** a theoretical "average" atmosphere which acts as a convenient hypothetical yardstick. The main purpose of the International Standard Atmosphere is to calibrate altimeters. Standard pressure at mean sea level (MSL) is 29.92 inches of mercury. (Its metric (SI) equivalent is 1013.2 hectopascals, usually written 1013 hPa.)

Atmospheric pressure reduces by approximately 1 in. Hg (one inch of mercury) for each 1,000 feet gain in altitude in the lower levels of the atmosphere (up to about 5,000 feet).

Atmospheric pressure reduces by approximately 1 in. Hg for each 1,000 feet gain in altitude.

The altimeter converts this reduction in atmospheric pressure to a gain in altitude. For instance, if the pressure falls by 0.45 in. Hg, the altimeter will indicate a gain in altitude of 450 feet.

How the Altimeter Works

The altimeter contains sealed, but expandable, aneroid capsules that are exposed within the instrument case to the current static pressure that enters through the static port. As the airplane climbs and static pressure decreases, the sealed capsules expand and drive pointers, via a mechanical linkage, around the altimeter scale. These indicate the increased height above the selected pressure level. There may be a short time lag before changes in altitude are actually indicated on the altimeter.

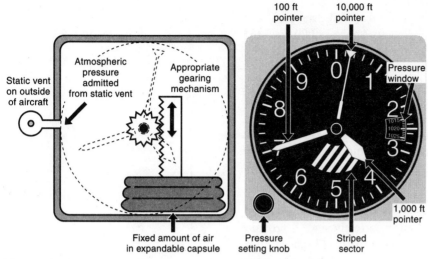

Figure 8-9. The altimeter is a pressure-sensitive instrument

Unfortunately for altimeters, the real atmosphere existing at a particular place and time can differ significantly from the standard atmosphere. Atmospheric pressure at MSL will vary from place-to-place and from time-to-time as weather pressure patterns move across the country. If an altimeter is to measure altitude from any particular level, such as mean sea level (MSL), then it must be designed so that the appropriate MSL pressure setting can be selected.

The Pressure Window

The altimeter incorporates a small adjustable pressure subscale that allows the pilot to select the pressure level from which altitude will be measured. This subscale is known as the pressure window. If you want to measure the altitude of the airplane above the 29.92 in. Hg standard pressure level, then you set 29.92 in the pressure window.

If you want to measure the height of the airplane above the 30.10 in. Hg pressure level, then you set 30.10 in the pressure window. If 30.10 in. Hg happens to be the current MSL barometric pressure, then the altimeter will be indicating the altitude of the airplane.

For flight operations in the United States below 18,000 feet MSL, the level from which height is measured is mean sea level (MSL). Although 29.92 inches of mercury is standard MSL pressure, the existing MSL pressure will usually differ, often significantly, from this value.

The MSL pressure at a particular place and time is called the **local altimeter setting** and, when this is set in the pressure window, the altimeter will display what is known as the **indicated altitude** (*see* Figure 8-9).

When the setting in the pressure window is changed by winding the pressure setting knob, the altimeter needle will also move around the dial. This is because it measures height above the selected pressure level and the selected level is being changed.

A one inch decrease in pressure in the lower levels of the atmosphere indicates approximately 1,000 feet gain in altitude. Therefore, increasing the setting in the pressure window will increase the altimeter reading. This can be remembered as "Wind on inches, wind on altitude."

The pressure window allows the pilot to set the current MSL pressure.

Wind on inches, wind on altitude.

Pressure Settings Above 18,000 feet MSL

When flying in the United States at or above 18,000 feet MSL, standard pressure 29.92 in. Hg should be set in the pressure window. Above 18,000 feet MSL there is adequate terrain clearance above the highest mountains, so vertical separation from other aircraft is the main concern.

Having a common setting of 29.92 in. Hg gives all high-flying aircraft a common pressure level from which their flight level is measured, avoiding any conflict caused by altimeter settings from different geographic locations.

With standard pressure 29.92 set, the altimeter indicates **pressure altitude.** It is usual to remove the last two zeros of a pressure altitude and refer to it as a **flight level.** For example, an altimeter reading 21,000 feet with 29.92 in. Hg set, is referred to as FL210 (flight level two one zero).

Different Altimeter Presentations

You must be able to interpret the altimeter reading correctly since it provides absolutely vital information. Lives have been lost in the past because pilots have misread the altimeter by 10,000 feet. Learn how to read them accurately right at the beginning!

The most common altimeter presentation consists of **three pointers** of varying shapes and sizes:

- The pointer with a long, fine needle and a splayed tip indicates 10,000s of feet. If it is on 1 (or just past it), it is indicating 10,000 feet. This pointer is particularly easy to misread. Note that some altimeters have a very short, medium thickness 10,000 feet pointer, rather than the usual long, fine needle.

- The short, fat pointer indicates 1,000s of feet. It will move once around the dial for a change of 10,000 feet. If it is on 4 (or just past it), it is indicating 4,000 feet. To reinforce that the airplane is below 10,000 feet, a striped sector is visible which gradually becomes smaller as 10,000 feet is approached.

- The long, medium-thickness pointer indicates 100s of feet. It will move once around the dial for each 1,000 feet change in altitude. If it is on 7, it means $7 \times 100 = 700$ feet.

All taken together, the altimeter shown in Figure 8-11 reads 4,700 feet.

| 10,000-foot pointer | 1,000-foot pointer | 100-foot pointer | **4,700 feet** |

Figure 8-11. Altimeter presentation

Check Altimeter Accuracy on the Ground

The altimeter uses air pressure to measure altitude above (or below) the reference pressure level selected in the pressure window. The only place you can check the accuracy of an altimeter is while the airplane is on the ground at an airport where the elevation is accurately known. With the local altimeter setting in the pressure window, the altimeter should indicate approximate airport elevation (to within ±75 feet).

During this check, allow for the fact that the published airport elevation is the height above MSL of the highest point on any of the usable runways. If you have any doubts about the accuracy of the altimeter, refer it to an appropriately rated repair station for evaluation and possible correction.

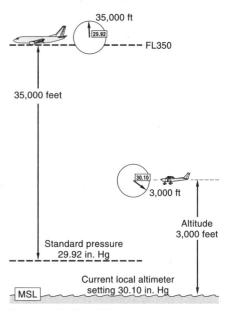

Figure 8-10. The altimeter measures height above the pressure level set in the pressure window

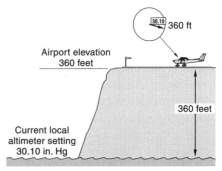

Figure 8-12. On the ground, the altimeter should read airport elevation

Whenever the current local altimeter setting is set in the pressure window, the altimeter will indicate the altitude—the approximate height of the airplane above MSL. This will enable the pilot to fly at an altitude that is well separated vertically both from terrain and other aircraft

If you are flying at a constant indicated altitude from a high-pressure area toward a low-pressure area, and you neglect to set the lower altimeter settings periodically given by a local FSS or ATC, then the airplane will be gradually descending even though the altimeter reading is not changing. This could be dangerous. Remember, "From high to low look out below!"

"From high to low—look out below!"

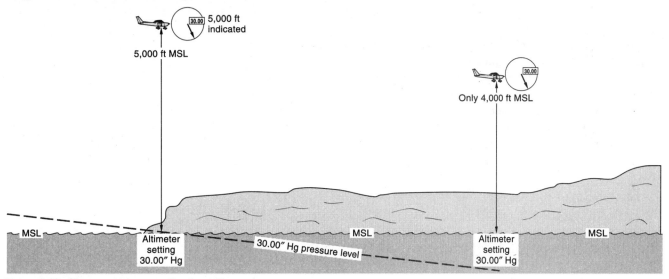

Figure 8-13. Always update your altimeter setting

Note: The pilot reads indicated altitude on the altimeter. For the reading to be correct, the altimeter setting must be correct.

Altimeter Errors

A number of errors are evident in altimeters.

Instrument errors. Imperfections in the design, manufacture, installation and maintenance of the individual altimeter will cause errors.

Instrument lag. Because the altimeter takes a second or two to respond to rapid pressure changes, the indicated altitude will lag behind the actual altitude.

Position error. Poor design may place the static vent in a position where the static pressure is not representative of the free atmosphere in that vicinity, resulting in an inaccurate altimeter reading.

Blockages of the static vent. If ice or insects (or anything) block the static vent completely, then that static pressure will remain fixed in the line to the altimeter. A constant altitude will be indicated, even though the airplane may be changing altitude.

If ice forms over the static vent on a climb-out, the altimeter will continue to read the altitude at which the static vent froze over, and not indicate the higher altitude that the airplane is actually at.

Similarly on a descent, a blocked static vent will cause the altimeter to indicate a constant altitude which is higher than the actual altitude, a dangerous situation.

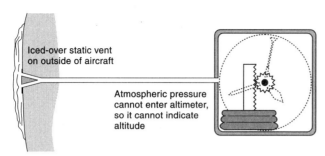

Figure 8-14. A blocked static vent—altimeter indication constant irrespective of airplane altitude

Temperature Error. The altimeter is calibrated to read the height above the pressure level selected in the pressure window as if the characteristics of the existing atmosphere (temperature, density and humidity) are identical to the International Standard Atmosphere. Since this is rarely the case, the altimeter indication will differ by some extent from the real or true altitude. Normally, this does not present a problem, since all airplanes in the one area will have their altimeters affected identically, and so vertical separation between aircraft will not be affected.

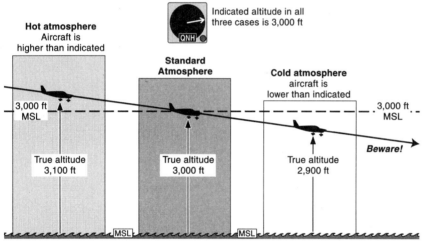

Figure 8-15. Temperature error often causes indicated altitude to differ from true altitude

While the temperature error is of little significance for most flight operations, it may occasionally require some consideration during precision instrument approaches.

In very warm air, the density will be less than standard and the pressure levels will be expanded. Therefore a given pressure level will be higher in a warm atmosphere compared with the standard atmosphere. After climbing a *true* 1,000 feet, the altimeter will sense less than 1,000 feet difference in pressure in the thinner air and will *indicate* a climb of less than 1,000 feet, and the altimeter will read low. This is easily remembered as **HI–LO** (higher temperature than standard—lower altimeter reading).

The altimeter in warmer air will read low.

Conversely, in air colder than ISA, the altimeter will indicate higher than the airplane actually is, a hazardous situation. Remember **LO–HI** (lower temperature than standard—higher altimeter reading) or the saying "from high to low, look out below."

An altimeter in colder air will read high—"from high to low, look out below."

The Various "Altitudes"

Indicated altitude is what you read on your altimeter when the **local altimeter setting** is set in the pressure window, as is the case when you are operating at or below 18,000 feet MSL in the United States. Indicated altitude is approximate height above MSL.

Pressure altitude is what you read on your altimeter when **standard pressure (29.92 in. Hg or 1013.2 hPa)** is set in the pressure window, as is the case when you are operating above 18,000 feet MSL in the United States.

True altitude is the actual altitude above MSL, and cannot be determined in flight by the altimeter alone. It is rarely required in flight. True altitudes of airports, mountains, radio masts, and so on are measured by survey and shown on charts. The difference between indicated and true altitude is usually no more than 100 feet.

Absolute altitude means height above ground level or **height AGL.** To determine this, you need to know both airplane altitude MSL and ground elevation.

Density altitude is one means of describing air density, and is used in performance calculations. It is computed from pressure altitude and air temperature (*see* Chapter 9).

Encoded altitude is not seen by the pilot, but by the radar controller—the aircraft's encoding altimeter sends altitude information to the aircraft's transponder which transmits position and altitude information to radar stations.

Vertical Speed Indicator (VSI)

While you can form some idea of how fast you are changing altitude by comparing the altimeter against a stopwatch, the vertical speed indicator provides a direct readout of the rate of change of altitude. The VSI converts a rate of change of static pressure to a rate of change of altitude, which is expressed in hundreds of feet per minute (fpm or ft/min).

If you begin a descent, the airplane will be moving into air with a progressively increasing static pressure. The new and higher pressure at the lower level is fed directly from the static vent into a flexible capsule inside the VSI case. The same pressure is also fed into the casing that surrounds this capsule, but via a metering valve that introduces a slight delay to the increase in pressure. This means there is a small differential pressure within the instrument. The capsule therefore expands and drives a pointer around the VSI scale (graduated in fpm) to indicate a rate of descent, such as 500 fpm. It will take some seconds before a stabilized rate is indicated, because of the inherent lag in the VSI.

If the **static vent** became iced-over or **blocked,** then the two pressure areas (inside the capsule and surrounding it) would equalize and the VSI would read zero, even though the airplane's altitude might be changing.

Figure 8-16. The vertical speed indicator

✍ Now complete **Review 8, Part (a)** on page 174.

Gyroscopic Instruments

Gyroscopes

A gyroscope is basically a rotating wheel, mounted so that its axis is free to move in one or more directions. A characteristic of rotating masses, such as gyroscopes, is their tendency to maintain their original alignment in space despite what goes on around them, a property referred to as **rigidity in space.**

This means that a gyro is able to remain stable in space while the airplane in which it is mounted moves around it. Gyroscopes are therefore useful as the basis for indicators that show direction and attitude.

The degree of rigidity of a gyroscope depends on the mass of the rotor, the speed at which it is rotating, and the radius at which the mass is concentrated. A large mass concentrated near the rim and rotating at high speed provides the greatest directional rigidity.

A gyroscope has another characteristic called **precession.** If a force is applied to the gyroscope, the change in direction brought about by the force is not in line with the force, but is displaced 90° further on in the direction of rotation. This gyroscopic effect is quite common (you use it every time you lean your bicycle over to turn a corner).

There are various ways of mounting a gyroscope on one or more axis of rotation *(gimbals)*, depending on the information required from that gyroscopic instrument. Gyroscopes are used in the turn coordinator/turn indicator, the attitude indicator and the heading indicator.

Figure 8-17. Gyroscopes are rotating masses

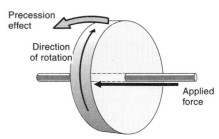

Figure 8-18. Gyroscopic precession

Vacuum-Driven Gyroscopes

Many gyroscopes are operated by a vacuum system which draws high-speed air through a nozzle and directs it at the gyro rotor blades. A vacuum pump that draws air through is generally preferable to a pressure pump that blows air through, since the air may pick up contaminants such as oil from the pressure pump which could affect the very sensitive rotor.

The amount of suction is shown on a gauge in the cockpit and is approximately 4.5 to 5.4 inches of mercury, which is 4.5 to 5.4 in. Hg *below* atmospheric pressure. If the *numerical* vacuum reading is too small, the air flow will be reduced, the rotor(s) will not be up-to-speed, and the gyros will be unstable or will only respond slowly. If the numerical vacuum reading is too high, the gyro rotors may spin too fast and be damaged.

The vacuum in most airplanes is provided by an engine-driven vacuum pump, but some older airplanes may have the vacuum provided by an externally mounted venturi-tube (making the gyroscopic instruments unusable until after several minutes at flying speed following takeoff).

Electrically Driven Gyroscopes

When the electrical master switch first goes on, you will probably hear the electrically driven gyroscopes start to spin up. They should self-erect and red power-failure warning flags (if provided on the instrument face) should disappear.

If the master switch is left on, when the engine is shut down on the ground, these instruments will be drawing power from the battery and the battery will gradually discharge. So ensure that there is no power to the electrically driven gyroscopes when leaving the airplane for any length of time.

Errors in Gyroscopic Instruments

If the gyroscope is not up-to-speed, the instrument may indicate erratically, respond only slowly to changes in attitude and/or heading, or indicate incorrectly.

- Check for a **red power-failure warning flag** on *electrically driven* instruments, and check for correct **suction** on *vacuum-driven* instruments. In many airplanes the attitude indicator and the heading indicator are driven by suction, but the turn coordinator is driven electrically. This guards against the loss of all three instruments simultaneously.

- Check that the heading indicator is aligned with the magnetic compass during steady straight-and-level flight. Check that the attitude indicator, if it has a caging (locking) device, has been uncaged. Do this in steady straight-and-level flight or in a level attitude on the ground.

Turn Coordinator/Turn Indicator

The turn coordinator and turn indicator both use **rate gyros.** The rotating mass has freedom to move about two of its three axes and is designed to show the rate of movement of the airplane about the third axis (in this case turning about the normal axis). This rate of movement is indicated in the cockpit on one of two possible types of presentation—either a **turn coordinator** (which has a symbolic airplane), or a **turn indicator** (which has a vertical needle or "bat").

Both the turn coordinator and turn indicator show the airplane's **rate of turn,** which is not bank angle. However, because the gyro in the turn coordinator is mounted slightly differently to that in the turn indicator, the *turn coordinator* will also show **roll rate.** It will respond when an airplane banks, even before the turn actually commences. Note that the symbolic airplane on the turn coordinator (even though it resembles that on an attitude indicator) does not give pitch information.

If the airplane is turning to the left, the gyroscope will experience a turning force, (*see* Figure 8-20). However this force will precess through a further 90° in the direction of rotation and will cause the gyro to tilt. The greater the turning force, the greater the tendency to tilt.

Figure 8-19. The modern turn coordinator (top), and the older turn indicator, each indicating standard-rate turns to the left

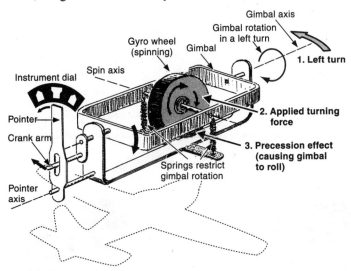

Figure 8-20. Workings of the turn indicator

The tilting of the gyroscope stretches a spring, which makes the gyro precess with the airplane turn until the rates match up, when further tilt ceases. A pointer moved by the action of the gimbal tilting indicates the rate of turn against a scale.

The scale is graduated to show a **standard-rate** turn of 3° per second. You can check the accuracy of the turn indicator by timing yourself through a steady indicated standard rate turn of 180° and see if it takes 60 seconds (3° per second).

The gyroscope may be rotated at high speed by an electric motor, or it may be spun by a small jet of air generated by a vacuum system, and directed at small "buckets" cut into the edge of the gyro wheel. Preflight checks for the serviceability of the turn coordinator should include:

- a check of the gyro rotation speed (whirring sound and no failure flags if electrically driven, correct vacuum if pressure-driven); and

- correct indications in a turn while taxiing ("turning left, skidding right— turning right, skidding left"), and, if in any doubt, a timed turn in flight.

Coordination Ball or Inclinometer

The coordination ball is a simple device that is usually incorporated into the turn coordinator/turn indicator. It is a useful mechanical device that indicates the direction of the g-forces—the combined effect of the earth's gravity force and any turning force. It has no power source. It is also known as the inclinometer, the slip-skid indicator, the balance ball or the coordination ball.

The coordination ball is simply a small ball, free to move like a pendulum bob, except that it moves in a curved cylinder filled with damping fluid. In straight flight it should appear at the lowest point in the curved cylinder (like a pendulum bob hanging straight down), and the airplane is said to be coordinated, or in balance.

In a **skid,** the ball will move to one side in the same way as a pendulum bob would swing out, and you will feel a force pushing you outward. In a **slip,** the ball will fall to one side, and you will feel as if you are falling inward.

In a coordinated turn, you will feel no sideways forces, nor will the ball, which should remain centered. Any sideways force (either a *slip* in toward the turn or a *skid* out away from the turn) will be shown by the coordination ball and felt by you.

If the ball is out to the right, apply right rudder pressure to center it. Use same-side rudder pressure to center the ball. Some instructors say, "Step on the ball."

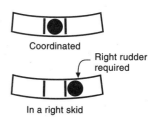

Figure 8-21. The coordination ball

For coordinated flight, "Step on the ball."

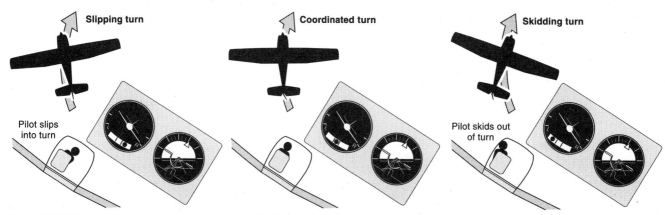

Figure 8-22. Slipping turn; more right rudder required (left). A comfortable and coordinated turn (center). A skidding turn (right)

Attitude Indicator (AI)

As the airplane changes its attitude, the **earth gyro** that is the basis of the attitude indicator (AI) retains its alignment (rigidity) at right angles to the earth's surface. This means that the airplane moves around the gyro rotor of the attitude indicator which has a vertical spin axis.

Attached to the gyroscope is a picture of the horizon, around which the airplane (and the instrument panel) moves. The attitude of the airplane to the real horizon is symbolized by the artificial horizon line attached to the gyro and a small symbolic airplane attached to the instrument dial. This small model airplane is referred to as the miniature airplane or index airplane.

The attitude indicator shows **pitch attitude** and **bank angle.** Pitch attitude is indicated by the position of the center dot of the miniature airplane relative to the artificial horizon. Bank attitude is indicated by the relationship of the wings of the miniature airplane to the artificial horizon.

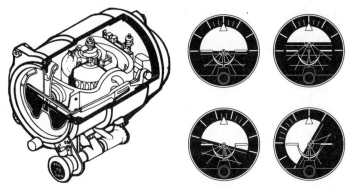

Figure 8-23. The attitude indicator displays pitch attitude and bank angle

The AI shows a picture of the airplane's attitude, but tells you nothing about the performance of the airplane. For instance, a nose-high attitude could occur in a steep climb or in a stalled descent—to know the performance of the airplane you need to refer to the airspeed indicator, altimeter and vertical speed indicator.

You should always check the power source of the attitude gyro. Some attitude indicators, especially the vacuum-driven ones, have limits of pitch and bank which, if exceeded, may cause the gyro to tumble and give erroneous readings. The miniature airplane should be aligned with the artificial horizon on the instrument when the airplane is in straight-and-level flight or on the ground. The small knob at the base of the AI adjusts the miniature airplane alignment. Some older types of gyroscope need to be caged when not being used.

The attitude indicator is also called the **artificial horizon** and **gyro horizon.**

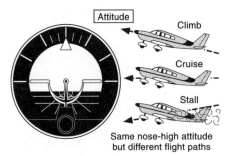

Figure 8-24. Pitch attitude displayed on the AI does not reflect climb/descent performance

Heading Indicator (HI)

The magnetic compass is the primary indicator of direction in most airplanes. It is, however, difficult to read in turbulence and subject to acceleration and turning errors, making it a difficult instrument to fly by accurately.

The heading indicator (HI) is a gyroscopic instrument that you should keep aligned with the magnetic compass in flight. Although it takes its directional reference from the compass, it is not subject to the same acceleration and turning errors. This makes accurate turns and a constant heading possible.

Figure 8-25. The heading indicator

There are mechanical factors present in the HI (mainly friction) that will cause it to drift off its original alignment with magnetic north because of gyroscopic precession. This is called mechanical drift. In addition, because the airplane is flying over a rotating earth, a line in space from the airplane to north will steadily change. This causes apparent drift. Both mechanical and apparent drift can be corrected by simply realigning the HI with the magnetic compass periodically, as described below.

You should check the power source of the HI prior to flight and, when taxiing, check the correct turn indications on the HI ("turning right, heading increases—turning left, heading decreases").

The HI has a **slaving knob** that enables the pilot to realign the HI with the magnetic compass, correcting for both mechanical drift and apparent drift. This should be done every 10 or 15 minutes. Some older heading indicators have to be uncaged after realigning with the magnetic compass. Advanced airplanes have HI gyros that are aligned automatically.

Manually Aligning HI with Magnetic Compass

- Choose a reference point directly ahead of the airplane, aim for it and fly steadily straight-and-level.
- Keep the nose precisely on the reference point, and then read the magnetic compass heading (when the compass is steady).
- Maintain the airplane's heading toward the reference point and then refer to the HI, adjusting its reading (if necessary) to that taken from the magnetic compass.
- Check that the airplane has remained steadily heading toward the reference point during the operation (if not, repeat the procedure).

✍ Now complete **Review 8, Part (b)** on page 176.

The Magnetic Compass

In most light airplanes, the magnetic compass is the primary source of direction information, to which other direction indicators are aligned. In steady straight-and-level flight, the reference line of the magnetic compass indicates the **magnetic heading** of the airplane.

Magnetic compass readings will not be accurate while the airplane is accelerating or turning, or when entering a climb or descent, nor will they be accurate if magnetic objects are placed near the compass.

The Earth's Magnetic Field

The earth acts like a very large and weak magnet. The surface of the earth is surrounded by a weak magnetic field, consisting of lines of magnetic force that begin deep within the earth near Hudson Bay in Canada and flow toward a point deep within the earth near South Victoria Land in Antarctica.

Because of their proximity to the north and south geographical poles which are known as **true north pole** and **true south pole,** the magnetic poles are referred to as the **north magnetic pole** and the **south magnetic pole.**

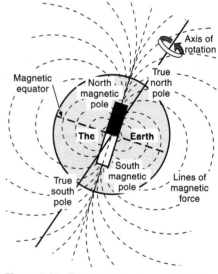

Figure 8-26. The earth has a magnetic field

Direction

There are two common ways to describe direction: using the cardinal points of north, south, east and west; or by using a graduated circle of 360 degrees going clockwise from true or magnetic north.

Direction is almost always expressed as a three-figure group such as 251, 340, or 020. The only exception is runway direction, where the numbers are rounded off to the nearest 10°. A runway bearing 247° magnetic would be referred to as RWY 25, and its reciprocal, bearing 067°M, would be RWY 7.

A bar magnet that is freely suspended horizontally will swing so that its axis points roughly north–south. The end of the magnet that points toward the earth's **north magnetic pole** is called the north-seeking pole of the magnet.

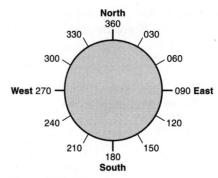

Figure 8-27. Direction

Magnetic Variation

The latitude-longitude grid shown on charts is based on *true* north and *true* south. Our small compass magnet, however, does not point exactly at true north but at the north magnetic pole. The angular difference between true north and magnetic north at any particular point on the earth is called **variation.** If the magnet points slightly east of true north, then the variation is said to be east. If the compass points to the west of true north, then the variation is west. Magnetic variation is the same for all aircraft in a given vicinity.

Isogonic Lines

On charts, as well as the lines forming the latitude-longitude grid, there are dashed lines joining places that have the same magnetic variation, known as **isogonic lines** or **isogonals.** For example, the 10° east isogonic line is drawn through all the places having a variation of 10°E. If you are anywhere on this line, magnetic north will be 10° east of true north. As you can see from the left inset in Figure 8-29, a magnetic heading of 105° will correspond to a true heading of 115°. The line joining places where the variation is zero is called the **agonic line.**

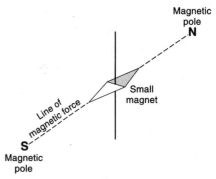

Figure 8-28. A simple bar magnet

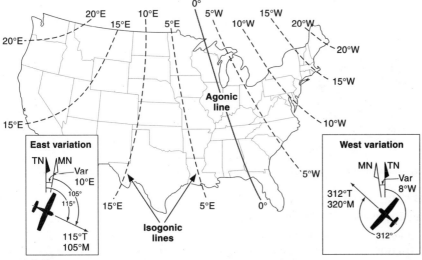

Figure 8-29. Variation is the angle between true and magnetic; isogonic lines join places of equal magnetic variation

Two easy ways to remember the relationship between true and magnetic are:
- "Variation east, magnetic least; variation west, magnetic best."
- "East is least; west is best."

Variation east, magnetic least; variation west, magnetic best.

Example 1. If the magnetic variation in your area is 10° east and your airplane is heading 295 on the magnetic compass, what is your true heading?

 Variation east, magnetic least: so 295°M is 295 + 10 = 305° true.

Example 2. If your compass indicates due east, and the magnetic variation where you are is 4° west, what is your heading related to true north?

 Variation west, magnetic best: so 090 – 4 = 086° true.

Deviation

Unfortunately, the magnet in each compass is affected not only by the magnetic field of the earth, but also by any other magnetic field it is exposed to.

Metal airframe components, the rotating parts of an engine, and electrical equipment all generate their own magnetic fields. The combined effect of these fields in a particular airplane on its magnetic compass is called **deviation.** Deviation causes the compass to deviate, or deflect, from precisely indicating magnetic north. The precise deviation can only be established once the compass is installed in the particular airplane, and test measurements made with the airplane on different headings.

In each airplane is a small placard, known as the **deviation card,** which shows the pilot the corrections to be made to the compass reading to obtain the magnetic direction. This correction usually involves only a few degrees and is an easy mental calculation to do in flight.

The deviation card is filled out by a mechanic to reflect the deviation present when the compass was tested. If any other magnetic influences are introduced into the airplane at a later time, they will not be allowed for, even though they may significantly affect the compass. Therefore, ensure that no metal or magnetic materials are placed anywhere near the compass. Many pilots have become lost as a result of random deviations in the compass readings caused by these extraneous magnetic fields.

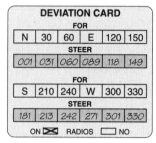

Figure 8-30. Deviation card

Do *not* place these cockpit items near the magnetic compass:
• headphones
• ferrous metals
• portable radios
• calculators
• books with metal binders

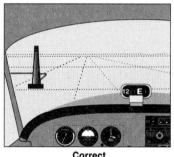 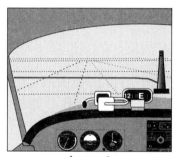

Correct
Heading 095

Incorrect
Pilot thinks heading is still 095
but in reality it is now 040

Figure 8-31. Keep foreign objects away from the magnetic compass

Compass Construction and Serviceability

The modern airplane has a direct-reading compass, usually filled with a liquid in which a float partially supporting a bar magnet is pivoted. The liquid supports some of the weight, decreases the friction on the pivot and, most importantly, dampens the oscillations of the magnet and float during flight. This allows the compass to give a steadier indication and makes it easier to read.

Attached to the pivot is the combined magnet and compass card. The compass card is graduated in degrees and can be read against a reference line which is attached to the bowl of the compass, and therefore to the rest of the airplane. Remember that it is the airplane that turns around the magnet, while the magnet continues to point to magnetic north at all times.

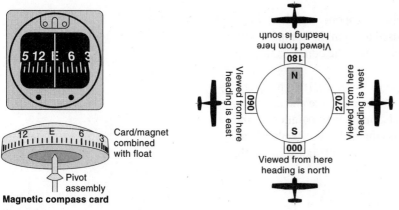

Card/magnet combined with float

Pivot assembly

Magnetic compass card

Viewed from here heading is south

Viewed from here heading is east

Viewed from here heading is west

Viewed from here heading is north

Figure 8-32. The magnetic compass

Pilot Serviceability Checks

Preflight, you should check that the compass is securely installed and can be easily read. The liquid in which the magnet is suspended should be free of bubbles and should not be discolored. The glass should not be broken, cracked or discolored, and it should be secure. Then locate the position of the compass deviation card in the cockpit.

When you are taxiing out prior to takeoff, check the compass is working correctly by turning the airplane left and right and note the response of the magnet. In addition, before takeoff cross-check the compass reading with the runway direction. Runway 18 will point approximately 180° magnetic.

Figure 8-33. Always cross-check compass direction

Magnetic Dip and Compass Errors

Near the magnetic equator, the lines of magnetic force are parallel to the surface of the earth. As the magnetic poles are approached, the lines of magnetic force dip toward them and any magnet bar will also try to dip down and align itself with these lines of force.

The angle of dip, called **magnetic dip,** is approximately 70° in the United States. Magnetic dip is zero at the magnetic equator and increases to 90° at the magnetic poles.

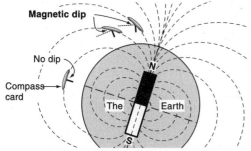

Figure 8-34. Magnetic dip is strongest nearest the poles

Magnetic Dip Effect

The earth's **magnetic field** can be resolved into two components: a horizontal one parallel to the surface of the earth (which is used to align the compass with magnetic north), and a vertical component, which causes the compass magnet to dip down.

At the magnetic equator, the horizontal component of the earth's magnetic field is at its strongest and so the magnetic compass is very stable and accurate.

However, at higher latitudes, the horizontal component parallel to the surface of the earth is weaker, making the compass magnet less effective as an indicator of horizontal direction. At latitudes higher than 60° north or south, the magnetic compass is not very reliable.

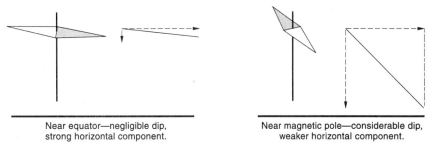

Near equator—negligible dip, strong horizontal component.

Near magnetic pole—considerable dip, weaker horizontal component.

Figure 8-35. Dip is caused by the vertical component of the earth's magnetic field

Compass Design to Minimize Dip Effect

To keep the magnet as close to horizontal as possible, the airplane compass is cleverly designed so that the point from which the magnet is suspended is well above its center of gravity. As the magnet aligns itself with the earth's magnetic field, the more it tries to dip down, the further out its center of gravity is displaced. This sets up a balancing couple which reduces the remaining dip, which is known as residual dip, to less than 5° from the horizontal.

Acceleration Errors

If you change airspeed, either by accelerating or decelerating, transient indication errors occur with a magnetic compass, especially on easterly and westerly headings. They disappear after the speed stabilizes.

As the airplane accelerates, it takes the compass and the pivot along with it. The compass magnet, being suspended like a pendulum, is left behind because of its inertia. Its weight, not being directly under the pivot, will cause the compass magnet to swing away from the correct magnetic direction as the pivot accelerates away. The compass card attached to the magnet rotates a little and indicates a new direction, even though there has been no change in direction.

Once a new steady speed is maintained, the magnet will settle down and the compass will read correctly once again.

Accelerating east or west. Accelerating toward the east or west, the center of gravity of the magnet, near the south-seeking end, is left behind. This swings the compass card so that it indicates an *apparent turn to the north.* After acceleration is completed you should allow the compass to settle down before adjusting the airplane heading (if necessary).

Decelerating east or west. Decelerating toward the east or west, the pivot slows down with the rest of the airplane and the center of gravity of the magnet, because of its inertia, tries to advance. The compass card rotates to indicate an *apparent turn to the south.*

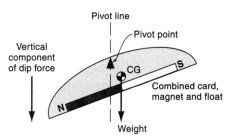

Pivot line

Pivot point

Vertical component of dip force

CG

Combined card, magnet and float

Weight

Figure 8-36. Magnet suspension

Accelerating north and south. Accelerating and decelerating (toward the north or south) will *not* cause apparent turns, because the pivot and the CG of the magnet will lie in the same N–S line as the acceleration or deceleration. On other headings, the acceleration errors will be greater the closer you are to due east or west.

Note: These effects are valid only for the Northern Hemisphere. In the Southern Hemisphere, the effects are reversed. Also, the closer to the magnetic poles you are, the greater the effect because the dip is greater. Magnetic dip is the major source of compass indication errors.

Remember: Acceleration and deceleration errors on easterly and westerly headings in the Northern Hemisphere may be summarized by the mnemonic "A N D S." Accelerate—apparent turn North; Decelerate—apparent turn South. The situation in the Southern Hemisphere is reversed.

When accelerating or decelerating on an easterly or westerly heading, use: "A N D S:" Accelerate—apparent turn North; Decelerate—apparent turn South.

Turning Errors

Turning is also an acceleration, because of the change in direction. In a turn, a centripetal force acts on the compass pivot, which is attached to the airplane, and accelerates it toward the center of the turn. The compass magnet (and compass card), being suspended like a pendulum, is left behind because of inertia. This leads to a transient error in the direction indicated by the compass, which will gradually disappear after the wings have been leveled. The result is that when turning through north the compass lags behind.

Turning through north. For example, when turning from 310° to 040° you should level the wings at about 020°, before reaching 040°. This is because once the airplane stops turning the compass reading will continue rotating for a few seconds because of the lag.

Turning through south. When turning through south the compass heading turns ahead of the airplane. If you turn from 130° to 210° you should level the wings at about 230°. Once the compass settles down it should read 210°.

Remember: Turning errors of the magnetic compass may be summarized by the mnemonic "U N O S:" Undershoot heading through North; Overshoot heading through South.

When turning onto a heading use: "U N O S:" Undershoot heading through North; Overshoot heading through South.

A magnetic compass only reads accurately in straight unaccelerated flight.

Note: Do not align the heading indicator with the magnetic compass if you are changing speed or direction, or entering a climb or descent, as the magnetic compass will be experiencing acceleration or turning errors. When aligning the heading indicator with the compass keep the wings level and maintain a constant speed.

One of the advantages of a heading indicator is that it is *not* subject to turning or acceleration errors. However its accuracy depends on it being correctly aligned with magnetic north.

✍ Now complete **Review 8, Part (c)** on page 177.

✍ **Review 8**

Part (a)

1. Static pressure is collected by the (pitot tube/static vent/static tube).

➤ static vent

2. The pitot tube collects (total/static/dynamic) pressure.

➤ total pressure

3. As a precaution against ice forming in the pitot tube some airplanes are fitted with an electrical _____ .

➤ pitot heater

4. The VSI measures the rate of change of _____ pressure.

➤ static

5. The ASI uses _____ pressure and _____ pressure to find dynamic pressure, to which indicated airspeed is closely related.

➤ pitot, static

6. For which instrument(s) does the pitot tube/static vent provide total or impact pressure?

➤ the airspeed indicator only

7. Will the altimeter be affected if the pitot tube becomes clogged, but the static vents remain clear?

➤ no

8. Will the airspeed indicator be affected if the pitot tube becomes clogged, but the static vents remain clear?

➤ yes

9. Which instrument(s) will be affected if the static vents become clogged?

➤ airspeed indicator, altimeter, VSI

10. If a static vent ices over, the altimeter during a climb will show (an increasing/a decreasing/the same) altitude.

➤ the same

11. The caution airspeed range of an airplane is indicated by a _____-colored arc on the airspeed indicator.

➤ yellow or amber

12. The normal-operating airspeed range of an airplane is indicated on the airspeed indicator with a _____ -colored arc.

➤ green

Flight Instruments

13. The normal flap-operating range of an airplane is indicated on the airspeed indicator with a _____ -colored arc.

➤ white

14. Which color on the ASI identifies the never-exceed speed?
    (a) Lower limit of the yellow arc.
    (b) Upper limit of the white arc.
    (c) The red radial line.

➤ (c)

15. Which color on the ASI identifies the power-off stalling speed with wing flaps and landing gear in the landing configuration?
    (a) Upper limit of the green arc.
    (b) Upper limit of the white arc.
    (c) Lower limit of the white arc.

➤ (c)

16. The stall speed, with wings-level and full flaps extended, is indicated on the ASI as the (high/low)-speed end of the (white/green/yellow) arc.

➤ low, white

17. The stall speed, with wings-level and no flaps extended, is indicated on the ASI as the (high/low)-speed end of the (white/green/yellow) arc.

➤ low, green

18. It (is/is not) permissible to fly at speeds in the yellow caution range in smooth air.

➤ is

19. The maximum flaps-extended speed corresponds to the high-speed end of the (white/green/yellow) arc.

➤ white

20. The maximum structural cruise speed is the maximum speed for normal operations and is indicated by the high-speed end of the (white/green/yellow) arc.

➤ green

21. The altimeter is a (gyro/pressure) instrument.

➤ pressure

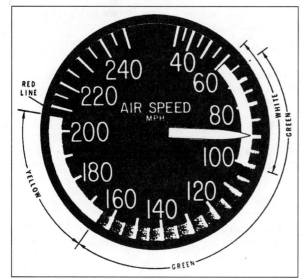

Figure 8-37. Airspeed indicator

For the questions 22 to 24 refer to Figure 8-37.

22. What is the caution range of the airplane?
    (a) 0 to 60 mph.
    (b) 100 to 165 mph.
    (c) 165 to 208 mph.
    ➤ (c)

23. What is the full flap operating range for the airplane?
    (a) 60 to 100 mph.
    (b) 60 to 208 mph.
    (c) 65 to 165 mph.
    ➤ (a)

24. What is the maximum flaps-extended speed?
    (a) 65 mph.
    (b) 100 mph.
    (c) 165 mph.
    ➤ (b)

25. Standard MSL pressure is _____ in. Hg. This equates to _____ hectopascals.
    ➤ 29.92 in. Hg, 1013.2 hPa

26. If 30.05 is set in the pressure window, then the altimeter will indicate the height of the airplane above _____ .
    ➤ the 30.05 in. Hg pressure level

27. If the current altimeter setting is set in the pressure window, then the altimeter will indicate the height of the airplane above (ground/mean sea level).
    ➤ mean sea level

28. If the current airport altimeter setting is set in the pressure window, then the altimeter, when the airplane is on the runway, will indicate _____ .
    ➤ field elevation (approximately)

29. What is absolute altitude?
    (a) The altitude read directly from the altimeter.
    (b) The vertical distance of the aircraft above the surface.
    (c) The altitude above the standard datum plane.
    ➤ (b)

30. What is density altitude?
    (a) The altitude above the standard datum plane.
    (b) The pressure altitude corrected for non-standard temperature.
    (c) The altitude read directly from the altimeter.
    ➤ (b)

31. Prior to takeoff and landing you must ensure that (the correct local altimeter setting/29.92) is set in the pressure window of the altimeter.
    ➤ the correct local altimeter setting

For questions 32 to 34 refer to Figure 8-38.

32. Altimeter A depicts _____ ?
    ➤ 10,500 feet

33. Altimeter B depicts _____ ?
    ➤ 14,500 feet

34. Altimeter C depicts _____ ?
    ➤ 9,500 feet

Figure 8-38. Altimeter presentation

35. If you are departing from an airport where you cannot obtain an altimeter setting, you should:
    (a) set 29.92 in.Hg in the pressure window of the altimeter.
    (b) set the altimeter to read field elevation.
    (c) set the altimeter to read zero.
    ➤ (b)

36. When cruising below 18,000 feet in the United States it is usual to set _____ in the pressure window so that the altimeter reads _____ .
    ➤ local altimeter setting, height above sea level

37. For every 1,000 feet of altitude gained in the lower levels of the atmosphere, atmospheric pressure decreases by approximately _____ in.Hg.
    ➤ 1 in.Hg

38. If a pilot changes the altimeter setting from 30.11 to 22.96, what is the approximate change in indication?
    (a) The altimeter will indicate 15 in.Hg higher
    (b) The altimeter will indicate 150 feet higher
    (c) The altimeter will indicate 150 feet lower
    ➤ (b)

39. If you change the setting in the pressure window of an altimeter from 29.92 to 29.98, the indicated altitude will (increase/decrease) by approximately _____ feet.
    ➤ increase by approximately 60 feet

40. The current altimeter setting is 30.32 in.Hg. If an airplane is flying at an altitude of 6,500 feet MSL, what is its approximate pressure altitude?
    ➤ 6,100 feet

41. A cruising level of FL230 is a (true/pressure/calibrated/density) altitude of _____ feet.
    ➤ pressure altitude, 23,000 feet

42. If you fly from an area of high pressure into an area of low pressure without adjusting the altimeter setting, and maintain a constant indicated altitude, the airplane will be (higher than/lower than/at) the indicated altitude.
    ➤ lower than

43. On warmer than standard days, the pressure and density levels are raised, causing the indicated altitude to be (greater/less) than the true altitude.
    ➤ less than

44. What conditions are required for the pressure altitude to be equal to the true altitude?
    ➤ standard atmospheric conditions must exist.

45. Under what condition will true altitude be higher than indicated altitude?
    ➤ in warmer than standard temperature

46. The altimeter will indicate a lower altitude than actually flown (true altitude) when the air temperature is (higher/lower) than standard.
    ➤ higher

47. If the outside air temperature increases during a flight at constant power and at a constant indicated altitude, the true altitude will (increase/decrease).
    ➤ increase

48. An encoding altimeter sends electronic altitude information to the _____ .
    ➤ transponder

Part (b)

1. The (miniature airplane/horizon bar) of an AI is adjustable.
   ➤ miniature airplane

2. During a turn to the left, the left wing of the miniature airplane will appear (above/below/on) the horizon bar of the AI.
   ➤ below

3. The turn indicator gives you (turn/roll/turn) information.
   ➤ turn

4. The turn coordinator gives you (turn/roll/turn and roll) information.
   ➤ turn and roll.

5. The turn coordinator (gives/does not give) pitch information.
   ➤ does not give

6. Most turn coordinators have markings to indicate a standard-rate turn left or right, which is at _____ per second.
   ➤ 3° per second,

7. The gyroscopic heading indicator should be regularly realigned with the magnetic _____ .
   ➤ compass

8. A vacuum pump fitted to an airplane may operate the (ASI/VSI/AI/HI/compass/turn coordinator).
   ➤ AI, HI, turn coordinator

9. Slip or skid is indicated on the:
   (a) turn coordinator.
   (b) coordination ball.
   (c) attitude indicator.
   ➤ (b)

10. Failure of the electrical supply to an electrically driven attitude indicator may be indicated by:
   (a) a low ammeter reading.
   (b) a red warning flag.
   (c) low suction.
   ➤ (b)

11. The turn coordinator and turn indicator provide information resulting from the precession of a gyro that has a (vertical/horizontal) spin axis.
   ➤ horizontal

12. The attitude indicator has a gyro with a (vertical/horizontal) spin axis.
   ➤ vertical

13. Some airplanes have an electrically driven turn coordinator with the other gyroscopic instruments being vacuum-driven. This is to _____ .
   ➤ guard against a loss of all gyroscopic instruments simultaneously

14. Which instrument provides direct pitch attitude information?
   ➤ the attitude indicator

15. Which instrument provides rate of turn information?
   ➤ the turn coordinator (or turn indicator)

16. To receive accurate indications during flight from a heading indicator, the instrument must be:
   (a) set prior to flight on a known heading.
   (b) calibrated on a compass rose at regular intervals.
   (c) periodically realigned with the magnetic compass as the gyro precesses.
   ➤ (c)

17. The proper adjustment to make on the attitude indicator during level flight is to align the:
   (a) horizon bar to the level-flight indication.
   (b) horizon bar to the miniature airplane.
   (c) miniature airplane to the horizon bar.
   ➤ (c)

Part (c)

1. The earth rotates about its axis. The points where this axis intersects the surface of the earth are known as the geographic or (true/magnetic) north and south poles.
   ➤ true

2. The points to which the lines of magnetic force surrounding the earth flow are known as the (true/magnetic) north and south poles.
   ➤ magnetic

3. The difference between true north and magnetic north at any point on earth is called magnetic _____ which (is constant/varies) over the earth.
   ➤ variation, varies

4. If, at a particular point on earth, a perfect magnetic compass points 10° to the right of true north, the magnetic variation is said to be 10° (east/west).
   ➤ 10° east variation

5. Your airplane is headed due east, (090° true or TH 090). Magnetic variation at that position on earth is 10° east. The compass will indicate MH _____ . (Sketch a diagram to help visualize this, and remember, "Variation east—magnetic _____")
   ➤ MH 080, variation east—magnetic least

6. Your airplane is headed due east, (090° true or TH 090). Magnetic variation at that position on earth is 4° east. The compass will indicate MH _____.
   ➤ MH 086

7. Your airplane is headed due east, (090° true or TH 090). Magnetic variation at that position on earth is 5° west. The compass will indicate MH _____.
   ➤ MH 095

8. Lines drawn on charts joining places of equal magnetic variation are known as _____ lines. The line joining places where the variation is zero, (where the directions to true north and magnetic north coincide) is called the _____ line.
   ➤ isogonic lines, agonic line

9. A heading of magnetic south may be written as MH (000/090/180/360).
   ➤ MH 180

10. A heading of south-west may be written as MH (045/135/225/315).
   ➤ MH 225

11. Magnetic variation is the result of:
    (a) the earth's magnetic poles being positioned away from the true geographic poles.
    (b) magnetic fields within a particular airplane distorting the lines of magnetic force.

➤ (a)

12. Deviation in a magnetic compass is caused by:
    (a) the earth's magnetic poles being positioned away from the true geographic poles.
    (b) magnetic fields within a particular airplane distorting the lines of magnetic force.

➤ (b)

13. Deviation varies with the airplane's (heading/position on earth).

➤ heading

14. During flight, the indications of a magnetic compass are accurate:
    (a) in straight-and-level unaccelerated flight.
    (b) if the airspeed is constant, even in turns.
    (c) in straight-and-level flight, even if accelerating.

➤ (a)

15. The reference line of the magnetic compass indicates:
    (a) the magnetic heading of the airplane.
    (b) the true heading of the airplane.
    (c) the track of the airplane over the ground.

➤ (a)

16. Runway 32 at a particular airport could have a bearing of approximately:
    (a) 032°M.
    (b) 322°M.
    (c) 032°T.

➤ (b)

17. In the Northern Hemisphere, if you accelerate on an easterly heading, the magnetic compass will indicate an apparent turn toward the (north/south/east/west).

➤ north

18. In the Northern Hemisphere, if you decelerate on a westerly heading, the magnetic compass will indicate an apparent turn toward the (north/south/east/west).

➤ south

19. In the Northern Hemisphere, accelerating on an easterly or westerly heading will cause the compass to indicate an apparent turn to the (north/south/east/west). Decelerating will have the (same/opposite) effect.

➤ north, opposite

20. Acceleration errors for a magnetic compass are greatest on (easterly or westerly/northerly or southerly) headings.

➤ Acceleration errors occur on easterly or westerly headings, and do not occur on northerly or southerly headings.

21. You are heading MH 010 in the Northern Hemisphere and want to make a left turn to a heading of MH 300. You should (overshoot/undershoot) this heading on the magnetic compass, and roll out wings-level when the compass initially indicates (280/300/320), because the compass will (lag behind/be ahead of) the actual turn.

➤ undershoot, 320, lag behind

22. You are heading MH 210 in the Northern Hemisphere, and want to make a left turn to MH 160. You should (overshoot/undershoot) this heading on the magnetic compass, and roll out wings-level when the compass initially indicates (140/160/180), because the compass will (lag behind/be ahead of) the actual turn.

➤ overshoot, 140, be ahead of

23. The amount of magnetic dip depends on (latitude/longitude/time of day).

➤ latitude

24. Turning and acceleration errors of the magnetic compass will be greater in (Alaska/Florida), because of the (greater/smaller) magnetic dip.

➤ Alaska, greater

25. In the Northern Hemisphere, a magnetic compass may initially indicate a turn toward the east if:
    (a) it decelerates while on a southerly heading.
    (b) it accelerates while on a northerly heading.
    (c) it turns left from a northerly heading.

➤ (c)

26. During flight, when are the indications of a magnetic compass accurate?
    (a) Only in unaccelerated flight.
    (b) As long as the airspeed is constant.
    (c) During turns if the bank does not exceed 18°.

➤ (a)

27. In the Northern Hemisphere, a magnetic compass will normally indicate a turn toward the north if:
    (a) a right turn is entered from an east heading.
    (b) a left turn is entered from a west heading.
    (c) the aircraft is accelerated while on an east or west heading.

➤ (c)

Airplane & Section Three
Pilot Performance

Airplane Performance Factors 9

Airworthiness

When a new type or model of airplane is designed and built, the manufacturer applies for and, after suitable tests on the original test airplanes have been passed, is granted a Certificate of Type Approval. This document is issued to the manufacturer by the aviation authority in the country of manufacture (Federal Aviation Administration (FAA) in the United States).

Engineering and safety requirements, reliability and many other factors are considered in detail, and many inspections and flight tests are carried out prior to the issue of a Type Certificate. Once it is obtained, the manufacturer commences production and a new airplane type comes on to the market.

The pilot does not see the Type Certificate, which is retained by the manufacturer.

The airworthiness requirements for airplanes are specified in the Federal Aviation Regulations. A large number of documents are involved in the airworthiness system, but those of most immediate importance to the individual pilot are the:

- Certificate of Registration (Part 91);
- Certificate of Airworthiness (Part 91); and
- approved Flight Manual (Part 91).

Certificate of Registration

The Federal Aviation Regulations require that an American-owned or operated airplane be on the Register of Aircraft. When this is done for an individual airplane, the FAA issues a Certificate of Registration to the owner.

The airplane is given a registration number to follow the letter "N," which is the United States nationality marking, for example, N4713P, and this must be displayed prominently on the airplane in specific sizes and positions. Examples of other aircraft nationality markings are: "D-" for Germany (Deutschland), "F-" for France and "G-" for Great Britain.

The Certificate of Registration must be carried and prominently displayed in the airplane. Before flight you should verify that the airplane is registered.

Certificate of Airworthiness

The Certificate of Airworthiness is issued by the FAA for an individual airplane. This may be American or an American approval of a foreign certificate. The Certificate of Airworthiness is normally granted for an unlimited period—its validity being subject to regular inspections. However, in some cases, the Certificate of Airworthiness may be issued for only a specified period. It should be carried in the airplane and prominently displayed.

The Certificate of Airworthiness is issued by the FAA for an individual airplane to operate in a particular category, provided it complies with the appropriate airworthiness requirements. Categories and their authorized purposes include: transport; experimental; normal; limited; utility; restricted; acrobatic; and provisional.

Figure 9-1. Examples of airplane registrations

A private pilot is likely to fly airplanes in the following categories, which are defined in Part 23 of the Federal Aviation Regulations.

- **Normal category**:
  - below 12,500 pounds and non-acrobatic maneuvers limited to stalls (but not whip stalls), lazy eights, chandelles and steep turns of 60°. Typical limit load factors are +3.8g and –1.52g.
- **Utility category:**
  - as for a normal category, plus limited acrobatics (aerobatics), which may include spins. Typical limit load factors are +4.4g and –1.76g. Note that some airplanes in the normal category may be allowed to operate in the utility category within certain specified weight-and-balance limits, usually with fuel/passenger restrictions.
- **Acrobatic category**:
  - airplanes in this category are fully aerobatic, but may have some limitations based on flight test results. Typical limit load factors are +6.0g and –3.0g.

Never intentionally carry out inappropriate maneuvers for the category of your airplane—structural damage or destruction is a very real possibility.

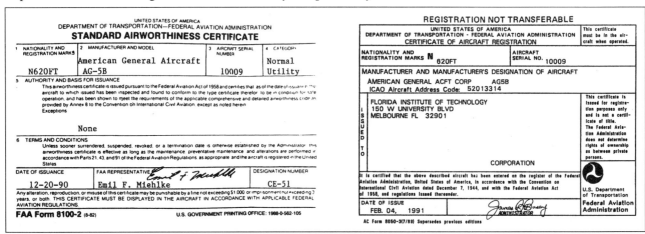

Figure 9-2. Certificate of Airworthiness and Certificate of Registration

The Certificate of Airworthiness has other documents associated with it, in particular, the approved Flight Manual.

Approved Flight Manual (AFM)

The Flight Manual for each airplane must be approved by the FAA. The AFM comes in various forms, including the Pilot's Operating Handbook (POH) for modern airplanes, and the Owner's Manual for older aircraft. These documents must contain the latest valid information for the airplane.

The information in the Flight Manual is presented in a standard format, as follows:

1. General Section;
2. Limitations Section;
3. Emergency Procedures;
4. Normal Procedures;
5. Performance;
6. Weight-and-Balance;
7. Description and Operation of the Airplane and its Systems;

8. Handling, Service and Maintenance; and

9. Supplements (optional systems and equipment not provided with the standard airplane).

The pilot must comply with all of the requirements, procedures and limitations with respect to the operation of the airplane as set out in its approved Flight Manual. Placards placed in the cockpit will often reflect the Flight Manual limitations, and have the same status.

Maintenance

The owner or operator of an airplane is responsible for maintaining it in an airworthy condition. Specific FAA requirements for maintenance may be found in Parts 91 and 43 of the Federal Aviation Regulations.

✐ Now complete **Review 9, Part (a)** on page 193.

Airframe Limitations

Weight Limitations

The gross weight (GW) of the airplane is subject to certain limitations. Some of the limitations are structural in nature, as the airplane is designed and built to perform certain tasks and carry certain loads, up to a maximum. Other limitations stem from the performance limitations of the airplane—certain conditions of temperature, pressure, runway conditions, and wind, may limit allowable weights for takeoff, landing and so on.

Maximum Takeoff Weight (MTOW)

This is a structural limitation. The MTOW is the maximum gross weight, according to the Flight Manual and approved weight-and-balance documents, at which that airplane is permitted to takeoff.

Note: The takeoff weight (TOW) for a particular takeoff must not exceed the structural MTOW or the weight as limited by airplane performance and runway considerations.

Maximum Landing Weight (MLW)

This is also a structural limitation. The MLW is the maximum gross weight, according to the Flight Manual and approved weight-and-balance documents at which that airplane is permitted to land.

Note: The landing weight (LW) for a particular landing should not exceed the structural MLW or the weight as limited by airplane performance and runway considerations. The MLW is usually less than the MTOW because of the greater stresses expected in landing compared with taking off.

Maximum Zero Fuel Weight (MZFW)

Although not generally applicable to light airplanes, you should be aware that most large airplanes have a **structurally limited zero fuel weight (MZFW)**. This limit is imposed to ensure that stresses on the wing caused by the upward lift forces in flight are not excessive. The fuel load carried in the wing tanks exerts a downward force which helps to relieve these stresses. Any load above MZFW *must* be usable fuel in the wings.

Maximum Ramp Weight

The **maximum ramp weight** is the maximum gross weight permitted prior to taxiing. It may exceed the *maximum take-off weight* by the taxi fuel allowance. While this is not specified for many light airplanes, you may come across it.

Speed Limitations

The airplane should only be flown in a specific operating speed range, limited by certain high and low speeds. Sometimes *aerodynamic* considerations provide the reason for the limit (the stall speed V_S is the lower speed limit), and sometimes *power* considerations limit the speeds, (the maximum speed on the cruise is limited by the amount of power available to overcome the increasing parasite drag). More important are the structural speed limitations. There might be sufficient power available for a very high speed cruise or dive, but the airframe may not be designed to withstand these stresses.

The speed limitations range from the structural limit of the never-exceed speed (V_{NE}) on the high side to the aerodynamic limit of stall speed (V_S) on the low side. Within these extreme limits are other more cautious limits, such as the normal-operating limit speed (V_{NO}), and the stall buffet.

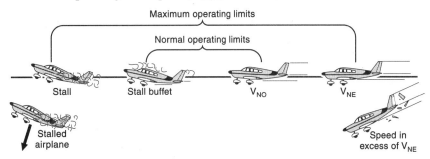

Figure 9-3. The speed range of an airplane

The Never-Exceed Speed—V_{NE}

V_{NE} is the absolute maximum speed at which the airplane may be flown. It is indicated on the airspeed indicator (ASI) by a red line. Any gusts or maneuvering at speeds approaching V_{NE} may cause unacceptable load factors leading to airframe deformation and failure. A sensible pilot would not allow the airplane to approach this speed under normal operations.

The Normal-Operating Limit Speed—V_{NO}

V_{NO} is known as the normal-operating limit speed, or the maximum structural cruising speed, and is the maximum speed at which the airplane should be flown under normal operating conditions. You should not exceed V_{NO}, because while it may be safe in smooth air, any gusts could overstress the airframe.

The normal-operating speed range is indicated on the ASI by a green arc. Above V_{NO} (normal-operating limit speed) is a yellow or orange caution arc, extending to the limiting red line at V_{NO}.

The Maneuvering Speed—V_A or V_{MAN}

When the pilot is maneuvering the airplane, the control surfaces (ailerons, elevators and rudder), the wings and the empennage are all subjected to increased loading. Maneuvering speed (V_A) is the maximum speed for maneuvers at which full application of the primary flight controls cannot overstress the airframe. This is because below V_A the airplane will always stall before the limiting load factor is reached. V_A is not marked on the airspeed indicator.

Note: The airplane Flight Manual may specify varying speeds for V_A because, at light weights, V_A is slower than at higher weights.

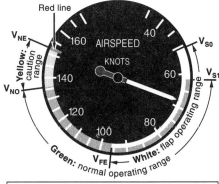

V_{S0}	Stall speed at max weight, landing gear down, flaps down, power off
V_{S1}	Stall speed at max weight, landing gear up (if retractable), flaps up, power off
V_{FE}	Maximum speed, flaps extended
V_{NO}	Maximum structural cruising speed (for normal operations)
V_{NE}	Never-exceed speed (max speed, all ops.)

Figure 9-4. Color coding on the airspeed indicator

Flying in Turbulence

Turbulent air or gusts can change the direction of the local relative airflow and the angle-of-attack almost instantaneously. Flying slowly (at a high angle-of-attack), an upward gust could increase the angle-of-attack causing the wing to stall. Flying slowly through gusts therefore decreases the stresses on the airplane, but exposes it to the possibility of a stall. Flying fast through turbulence gives a bumpier ride and puts more stress (higher load factors) on the structure that could exceed the structural load factor limits.

The **turbulence-penetration speed** (V_B or V_{TURB}), or the rough-air speed (V_{RA}), are the recommended target speeds for flying through turbulence. They are compromise speeds to avoid the stall on the low-speed side and excessive wing loading on the high-speed side. Not every airplane Flight Manual will specify a V_B or V_{RA}. In this event, you should use the maneuvering speed (V_A) to avoid structural damage. V_{NO} should not be exceeded in turbulence.

Other Maximum Speeds Specified

V_{FE}. As the flaps are lowered, drag increases and the airframe is subjected to extra stresses and so a maximum flaps-extended speed (V_{FE}) is usually specified.

V_{LO}, V_{LE}. For airplanes with retractable landing gear (also known as retractable undercarriage) one or two speed limitations will be specified according to system design. The maximum speed for operating (extending or retracting) the landing gear (V_{LO}) may be slower than the airspeed at which you may fly with the gear extended (V_{LE}). This is because, while the landing gear is extending and retracting, some gear doors may open outward into the airstream and be subjected to air loads. With those systems in which the doors close again once the gear is extended, the faster airspeed V_{LE} is permitted. Also, the landing gear system may include small locking devices which strengthen the landing gear structure when it is fully extended.

Load Factor Limitations

In straight-and-level flight, the airframe is subjected to 1g forces. You also experience a force of 1g exerted on your body by the seat, equal and opposite to your weight. This force, both on the airframe and you, will change in maneuvers. Any maneuvering, such as turning, pulling out of a dive or performing aerobatics will increase or decrease this load on the airplane structure and you. For example, a 60° banked turn increases the structural load to 2g, and pulling out of a dive at a fast airspeed could easily achieve a load factor of 3 or 4g.

It is important when recovering from the more unusual flight attitudes (steep turns, steep dives, spiral dives) that you avoid pulling excessive "g", because this may overstress the airframe.

As well as the static load factor or g-forces, there are dynamic strength considerations, such as dynamic instability of the airplane in high-speed flight, flutter in the control surfaces, which, if allowed to develop, can lead to structural failure.

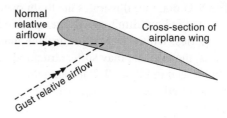

Figure 9-5. Gusts can increase or decrease the angle-of-attack, cause high wing loadings, or cause the wing's critical angle-of-attack to be exceeded (stall)

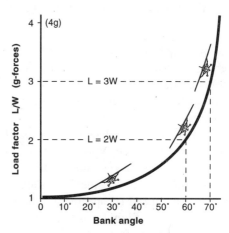

Figure 9-6. Load factor versus bank angle

The Velocity/Load Factor or V-G Diagram

The V-G diagram illustrates the flight operating strength of an airplane. Limit load factors and limit speeds are specified by the FAA for different airplane categories, within which the airplane must be operated. Taken beyond these limits, the airplane may suffer structural damage or even structural failure. As can be seen in Figure 9-7, the amount of excess load (in excess of 1g) that can be imposed on the wings without causing structural damage depends on airspeed.

The high-speed limit is V_{NE}, the never-exceed speed, and the low-speed limit is the stall. The stall speed is affected by the load factor, occurring at higher speeds when g is being pulled.

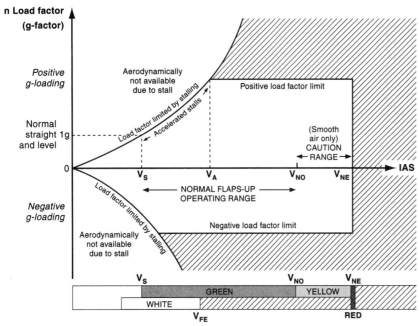

Figure 9-7. A typical V-G diagram related to ASI markings

Full backward movement of the control column will increase the g-loading but, at low speeds, the stall occurs before the limit load factor is reached. At speeds above V_A, however, the wing is at a small angle-of-attack, and so lots of excess lift is available by pulling the control column back. This could cause the limit load factor to be exceeded, therefore you must not apply full back stick at high speeds.

Gusts also cause changes in the load factor and care should be taken when flying in turbulence. V_{NO}, the normal-operating limit speed, should not be exceeded except in very smooth air, when V_{NE} becomes the absolute limit. In strong turbulence, consideration should be given to flying at the turbulence penetration speed (if specified), otherwise at the maneuvering speed V_A, to avoid excessive flight loads causing damage to the airplane structure.

The limit load factor should never be intentionally exceeded, because of the risk of structural damage. The load factor at which the structure will actually break is called the ultimate load factor and it is greater than the limit load factor.

Above V_A you should avoid making any abrupt or large control movements.

Checks Following Excessive Stress on the Airframe

While you must not knowingly exceed the airframe limitations, excessive stress can be caused by unexpected severe turbulence or a particularly heavy landing. In both cases, the wing structure may be heavily loaded and, in the case of a heavy landing, the landing gear and the areas to which it is attached to the airframe will have been heavily loaded.

One of the responsibilities of being a pilot is to ensure that following pilots will be presented with an airworthy airplane. The occurrence of heavy stress must be referred to an A&P (airframe and powerplant) mechanic. There could be damage not immediately apparent to you during an inspection, quite apart from those items already mentioned. For this reason, if an airplane has been overstressed, you must ensure that an A&P mechanic carries out an inspection prior to the next flight.

Many light airplanes are of semi-monocoque construction, where the loads are carried, not only by the internal structure, but also by the skin. Damage to either of these will weaken the overall structure.

In carrying out an inspection, the A&P mechanic will look for indications of stress on the airframe, the main external items being:

- distortion of the structure;
- cracks;
- popped or sheared rivets; and
- wrinkles in the skin, especially in the areas surrounding the main structural attachments for the engine, wing, wing struts, landing gear attachments and tailplane.

Severe overload can distort or break the wings and associated struts or braces. In the case of a heavy landing, checks of the landing gear and the areas surrounding its attachment points would be made, for example, the engine fire-wall to which a nosewheel may be attached.

Structural damage can exist even without external indications. If you overstress an airplane you must ensure an A&P mechanic checks it.

✍ Now complete **Review 9, Part (b)** on page 193.

Air Density

Pressure and temperature are extremely important factors in the operation of airplanes, and affect both the performance of the airframe and the engine. The critical element is air density, which decreases as pressure falls and temperature rises. On a hot day, the air is less dense and the performance capabilities of the airplane will be reduced. Similarly, if the pressure is low (for example, on take-off at an airport of high elevation), the air will be less dense, and airplane performance will suffer. Of the two factors, temperature has the most effect.

The **power** delivered by the engine depends on the weight of the fuel/air charge—the less dense the air, the lower the power-producing capability of the engine.

The **aerodynamic qualities** of the airframe depend on air density. If air density decreases, then aerodynamic qualities decrease, and the airplane will have to move faster through the air to create the same aerodynamic forces. High temperatures and low pressures (at altitude) cause a decrease in air density, as does high humidity (moisture content).

Performance reduces when air density reduces.

Factors Affecting Air Density

Altitude

The atmosphere consists of a mixture of gases that surround the earth and are held to it by the force of gravity. The pressure that the air exerts at any point depends on the weight of air pressing down from above; therefore pressure decreases with altitude. If the pressure is reduced, then the air expands and becomes less dense. Since both engine and aerodynamic performance depend on air density, airplane performance is poorer at high altitudes.

Performance reduces as altitude increases.

Temperature

Heating of an air mass to a higher temperature causes it to expand and its density to decrease, resulting in a reduction in both engine and aerodynamic performance. Airplane performance is therefore poorer on hot days. Temperature generally decreases with altitude (the nominal standard rate is approximately 2°C/1,000 feet). Although cooling of an air mass increases its density, the effect of this, as altitude is gained, is not as great as that of the decreased pressure—the overall effect is still a decrease of density at higher altitudes.

Performance reduces as air temperature increases.

Humidity

The mixture of gases that we call *air* consists mainly of:

- nitrogen (78%);
- oxygen (21%); and
- water vapor.

The other 1% consists of argon, carbon dioxide and other gases.

The presence of water vapor in the air is called **humidity.** Because water molecules are very light, a high humidity will cause the air density to be slightly less, but no account of this effect is taken in performance charts. You should be aware, however, that high humidity will cause reduced performance that is *not* allowed for on the performance charts.

Performance reduces as humidity increases.

Just how much water a parcel of air can hold depends on its temperature—warm air is able to hold more water than cold air. If a parcel of air is holding 70% of its maximum capacity of water vapor, then it has a relative humidity of 70%. As it cools, its capacity to hold water vapor becomes less and, even though the actual amount of water does not change, the relative humidity increases.

Relative humidity is defined as the amount of water vapor present in a parcel of air compared to the maximum amount that it can support (when saturated) at the same temperature. High relative humidity means poorer airplane performance.

The Standard Atmosphere

The continual changes in temperature and pressure which take place in the atmosphere make major difficulties for engineers and meteorologists, who need a fixed standard reference for calculations such as airplane performance, instrument calibration, and determination of cloud heights. As a result a **standard atmosphere** has been derived with specific values of temperatures and pressures. The important values for pilots are as follows:

- a surface temperature of 59°F (15°C) and a surface pressure of 29.92 inches of mercury (1013.2 millibars—mb) at sea level;
- a temperature lapse rate of approximately 2°C per 1,000 feet up to approximately 36,000 feet, where the temperature of –56.6°C is assumed to remain constant up to approximately 80,000 feet. (*See also* Chapter 14.)

Note: It is still common practice to use °F for surface temperatures, but °C are used almost exclusively for temperatures aloft.

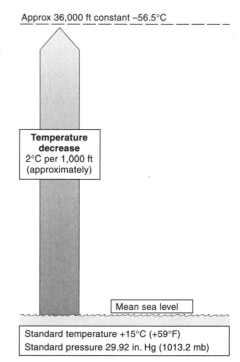

Figure 9-8. The standard atmosphere

The standard atmosphere described above is essentially the same as that established by the International Civil Aviation Organization (ICAO). The ICAO Standard Atmosphere (always referred to as ISA) is in general use throughout the world, and you will find reference to both it and the standard atmosphere during your aviation career. For instance, you may be told that on a "standard day" a takeoff run of 2,000 feet is required. Similarly, you may be told that the temperature deviation is "ISA+10°C" or "10° warmer than standard."

Pressure Altitude

The standard mean sea level pressure is 29.92 in.Hg, and this decreases at about 1 inch of mercury per 1,000 feet increase in altitude (up to about 5,000 feet).

At 2,000 feet, the standard pressure will have decreased by approximately 2 in.Hg, (from 29.92 in.Hg to 27.92 in.Hg). If the point where your airplane is located has a pressure of 27.92 in.Hg, then we say it has a pressure altitude of 2,000 feet, which means it is 2,000 feet above the 29.92 in.Hg pressure level.

Pressure altitude is the altitude in the standard atmosphere above the 29.92 in.Hg pressure level at which the pressure equals that of the point under consideration.

The easiest way to read pressure altitude in the cockpit is to set 29.92 in the pressure window—the altimeter will then indicate pressure altitude. Knowing the pressure altitude allows us to compare the airplane performance against a known standard.

Example 1. An airplane is flying at 5,000 feet with altimeter setting 30.34. How can you find the pressure altitude in flight? (Figure 9-9.)

Answer:

The altimeter measures altitude above or below the particular pressure level set in the pressure window. To quickly estimate pressure altitude, simply wind 29.92 into the pressure window. Winding off inches, winds off altitude.

Pressure altitude can also be estimated (using a decrease of 1 in.Hg per 1,000 feet gain in altitude), or found using the pressure altitude conversion factors on a density altitude chart (*see* Figure 9-13).

Example 2. If local altimeter setting is 29.42 in.Hg, find the pressure altitude of an airport with an elevation of 20 feet (Figure 9-10).

Answer:

Since pressure decreases with altitude, the standard pressure level of 29.92 in.Hg must be below sea level.

To find pressure altitude (altitude above the standard 29.92 in.Hg level), we first find the altitude difference between MSL (with a setting of 29.42) and the 29.92 in.Hg level. The 0.5 in. Hg difference is equivalent to (0.5 × 1,000) = 500 feet.

The airport is a further 20 feet above this, therefore it is 520 feet above the 29.92 in.Hg pressure level. The pressure altitude is 520 feet.

Example 3. The altimeter setting is 30.50 in.Hg at an airport with an elevation of 20 feet. Find the pressure altitude of the airport (Figure 9-11).

Answer:

The standard pressure level of 29.92 in.Hg must be above MSL on this particular day. The pressure difference of 0.58 in.Hg (30.5 – 29.92) means that the altitude difference is about (0.58 × 1,000) = 580 feet.

From Figure 9-11 we can see that the airport is 560 feet below the standard 29.92 in.Hg pressure level. Thus, its pressure altitude is –560 feet.

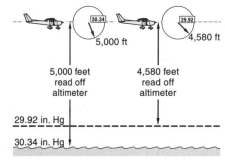

Figure 9-9. Example 1

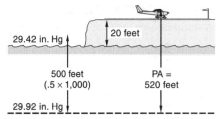

Figure 9-10. Example 2

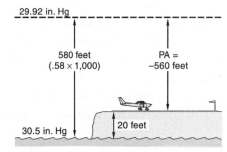

Figure 9-11. Example 3

More Accurate Calculation of Pressure Altitude

As an alternative to estimating pressure altitude by using the approximation of 1 in. Hg per 1,000 feet change in altitude, the pressure altitude data given in the density altitude chart in Figure 9-13 can be used. This will give a more accurate answer than the approximations used in Examples 2 and 3 above.

In Figure 9-13, to the right of the chart, there are two columns. The left-hand column shows the altimeter settings, and the right-hand column the pressure altitude conversion factor, which is the correction (in feet) which must be added or subtracted from the indicated altitude, which is based on the local altimeter setting to obtain pressure altitude. For example, with a local altimeter setting of 28.80 in. Hg, you would add 1,053 feet to the indicated altitude to obtain the pressure altitude. Similarly, if the altimeter setting was 30.40 in. Hg, you would have to subtract 440 feet.

For in-between altimeter settings that are not tabulated, such as 29.45 in. Hg, you will need to interpolate, or estimate, the in-between number. In this case, the correction number lies halfway between the 485 for 29.4 and the 392 for 29.5. The difference in altitude is (485 – 392) = 93, half of this is 47 which we can add to 392 (or subtract from 485) to give +439 feet correction.

Example 4. Using the same data as in Example 3, find the pressure altitude using Figure 9-13.

From the chart, the pressure altitude conversion factor for an altimeter setting of 30.50 in. Hg is –531 feet. Field elevation is 20 feet, so pressure altitude is: 20 – 531 = –511 feet (compared with –560 feet using the approximation of 1 in. Hg = 1,000 feet).

Temperature

The higher the temperature the lower the air density—and the poorer the airplane performance.

Standard (ISA) sea level temperature is +15°C and it falls at approximately 2°C per 1,000 feet gain in altitude.

- At 1,000 feet in the ISA, the temperature will have fallen to +13°C.
- At 2,000 feet in the ISA, the temperature will have fallen to +11°C.
- At 3,000 feet in the ISA, the temperature will have fallen to +9°C.

To Calculate ISA (Standard) Temperature

ISA temperature in °C at any altitude = 15 – (2 × number of thousands of feet).

Example 5.

$$ISA \text{ at } 9,000 \text{ feet} = 15 - (2 \times 9)$$
$$= 15 - 18 = -3°C$$

Example 6.

$$ISA \text{ at } 13,500 \text{ feet} = 15 - (2 \times 13.5)$$
$$= 15 - 27 = -12°C$$

Note: Temperature is usually expressed in °C. To allow for occasions when you have to use a performance chart that is still using °F, standard MSL temperature is +59°F (the equivalent of +15°C) and the temperature lapse rate is approximately 3.6°F/1,000 feet.

Example 7.

$$ISA \text{ in } °F \text{ at } 9,000 \text{ feet} = 59 - (3.6 \times 9)$$
$$= 59 - 32.4 = 26.6°F$$

Fahrenheit and Celsius Conversions

There are two main temperature scales used in aviation at present. If you are flying in foreign countries, it may be necessary to convert from one to the other. The Fahrenheit and Celsius scales both use the boiling point and freezing point of water as set temperatures—the difference between them is 180°F or 100°C as shown in Figure 9-12.

Each 1°C is larger than 1°F by a ratio of $^{180}/_{100}$ or $^9/_5$. The starting point of both scales is the freezing point of water, 0°C or 32°F. These can be combined into one relationship connecting °F and °C:

$$F = ^9/_5\, C + 32. \qquad C = ^5/_9\,(F - 32).$$

Example 8. Convert 20°C to °F.

°F = $(^9/_5 \times 20°C) + 32 = 36 + 32 = 68°F$.

To reverse the relationship, simply subtract 32 from both sides and then multiply both sides by $^5/_9$ to obtain:

°C = $^5/_9$ (°F – 32).

Convert 68°F to °C:

°C = $^5/_9$ (68°F – 32) = $^5/_9 \times 36 = 20°C$.

Note: In practice, the easiest method of converting temperatures is to use the flight computer (*see* Chapter 24).

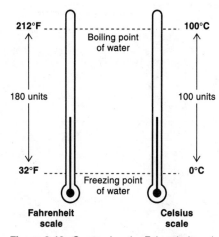

Figure 9-12. Comparing the Fahrenheit and Celsius temperature scales

To Calculate Deviations from ISA (Standard) Temperature

Temperature at an altitude is often expressed as an ISA deviation, which is the difference between the standard, or ISA, temperature at that altitude and the actual temperature at that altitude. For instance, at 9,000 feet the ISA temperature is –3°C. If the actual temperature at 9,000 feet today happens to be –8°C, the actual temperature is 5°C colder than the ISA temperature, which is described as ISA – 5.

Example 9. Express an actual temperature of +16°C at a pressure altitude of 3,000 feet as an ISA deviation.

ISA at 3,000 feet = 15 – (2 × 3) = 15 – 6 = +9°C

16°C at 3,000 feet is 7° warmer than the ISA temperature +9°C = ISA+7

Density Altitude

Airplane and engine performance depend on air density. It is impracticable for you to have the equipment necessary to measure air density, so we use two pieces of information already available in the cockpit and on which air density depends—pressure altitude and temperature.

By considering pressure altitude and temperature, we are really considering density. Most performance charts allow us to enter with pressure altitude and temperature, therefore there is usually no need to calculate density directly.

The term density altitude is simply one means of describing air density—it is the altitude in the standard atmosphere that has an identical density as the air we are considering. If temperature or pressure are nonstandard (which is almost always the case), then density altitude will differ from the airplane's true altitude MSL:

• the lower the pressure, the higher the density altitude;
• the higher the temperature, the higher the density altitude.

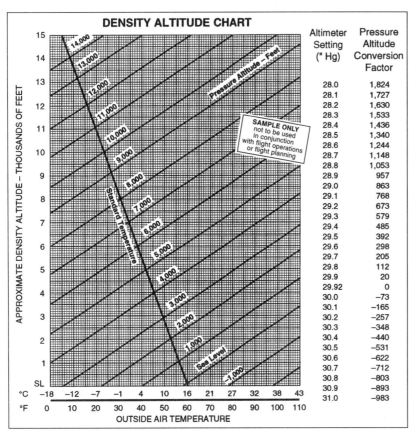

Figure 9-13. Density altitude chart

To Calculate Density Altitude

The main reason for calculating density altitude is to determine airplane performance—and you may allow for its effect unknowingly if you enter performance charts or graphs with pressure altitude and temperature. Sometimes however, you need to calculate density altitude specifically, and this is done in two steps:

1. Determine pressure altitude as discussed previously, by:
   (a) setting 29.92 in pressure window and reading altimeter;
   (b) by using the 1 in.Hg/1,000 feet approximation; or
   (c) by using the tabulated pressure altitude conversion factor.

2. Adjust pressure altitude for temperature by:
   (a) mental arithmetic (each deviation of 1°C above the temperature in the standard atmosphere, or ISA, will increase density altitude by approximately 120 feet, or 70 feet for each 1°F deviation); or
   (b) graph (*see* density altitude chart in Figure 9-13); or
   (c) light computer (*see* Chapter 24).

Example 10. Using the density altitude chart in Figure 9-13. What is the density altitude if the altimeter reads 5,000 feet with 28.30 in.Hg in the pressure window, and the true outside air temperature is 90°F?

1. Pressure altitude = 5,000 + 1,533 (from table) = 6,533 feet.
2. Enter graph at bottom with 90°F and proceed up to your estimate of the 6,533 feet (say 6,500 feet) sloping pressure altitude line, and then read across horizontally from this intersection to obtain the answer: 10,000 feet density altitude.

Indicated Airspeed and Performance

We stated earlier that indicated airspeed (shown on the airspeed indicator in the cockpit) is related to dynamic pressure, which is dependent on air density and velocity ($\frac{1}{2}\rho V^2$).

Therefore, to create the same aerodynamic forces that are required, for instance, to achieve takeoff, you need to fly the airplane at the same indicated airspeed regardless of density altitude. The consequence of this is that if air density ρ is low, then V (true airspeed) must be greater. Therefore when air density is low, to achieve the required indicated airspeed, the true speed of the airplane through the air must be greater. This leads to longer takeoff and landing distances at high elevation airports and/or under high temperature conditions.

Indicated airspeed is not affected by changes in density.

As density altitude increases TAS increases for a constant IAS.

✍ Now complete **Review 9, Part (c)** on page 195.

✍ Review 9

Airplane Performance Factors

Part (a)

1. The document that verifies registration is the
   _____ .
   ➤ Certificate of Registration

2. The document issued by the FAA to indicate that a particular airplane complies with the airworthiness requirements is the _____ .
   ➤ Certificate of Airworthiness

3. The Pilot's Operating Handbook (may/will not) be approved by the FAA as the approved Flight Manual for the airplane.
   ➤ may

Refer to your own POH for the following questions:

4. The maximum takeoff weight for my airplane is specified in Section _____ and Section _____ of the POH.
   ➤ Sections 1 and 2

5. Emergency procedures, such as for engine failure immediately after takeoff, are described in Section _____ of the POH.
   ➤ Section 3

6. Takeoff and landing performance charts or tables are found in Section _____ of the POH.
   ➤ Section 5

7. A description of the airplane fuel system, or any other system, may be found in Section _____ of the POH.
   ➤ Section 7

8. A particular area navigation (RNAV) system is an option that does not come with the basic airplane. Information on this system may be found in Section _____ of the POH.
   ➤ Section 9

9. If the operational category of an airplane is listed as "utility", it would mean that this airplane could be operated in which of the following maneuvers?
   (a) All types of acrobatics.
   (b) Limited acrobatics, including spins.
   (c) Any maneuver except acrobatics or spins.
   ➤ (b)

10. Who is primarily responsible for maintaining an aircraft in an airworthy condition?
    (a) Owner only.
    (b) Pilot-in-command.
    (c) Operator or owner of the aircraft.
    ➤ (c)

Part (b)

Define the following:

1. Maximum landing weight.
   ➤ *see* page 183

2. Never-exceed speed.
   ➤ *see* page 184

3. Turbulence-penetration speed.
   ➤ *see* page 185

---

4. At speeds in excess of the maneuvering speed (V_A), the pilot should avoid abrupt or large control movements mainly because:
   (a) the airplane will stall.
   (b) the limit load factor may be exceeded.
   (c) the airplane will be out-of-balance.
   ➤ (b)

5. The normal-operating limit speed (V_NO) should:
   (a) only be exceeded in smooth air.
   (b) never be exceeded.
   (c) be less than the maneuvering speed (V_A).
   ➤ (a)

6. It is easier to accidentally exceed limit load factors at (low/medium/high) airspeeds.
   ➤ high

7. Which V-speed represents maximum landing gear extended speed?
   (a) V_LE.
   (b) V_LO.
   (c) V_FE.
   ➤ (a)

8. V_NE is represented on the airspeed indicator by the:
   (a) red line.
   (b) green arc.
   (c) white arc.
   ➤ (a)

For questions 9 and 10 refer to Figure 9-14.

9. The horizontal dashed line from point C to point E represents the:
   (a) ultimate load factor.
   (b) positive limit load factor.
   (c) airspeed range for normal operations.
   ➤ (b)

10. The vertical line from point D to point G is represented on the airspeed indicator by the maximum speed limit of the:
    (a) green arc.
    (b) yellow arc.
    (c) white arc.
    ➤ (a)

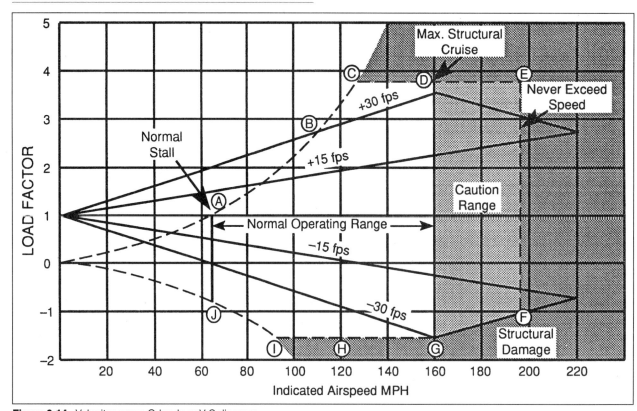

Figure 9-14. Velocity versus G-loads or V-G diagram

Part (c)

1. Performance tables and graphs are based on (true/pressure/density) altitude.

➤ density altitude

2. Air density may be accounted for by considering both air _____ and air _____ .

➤ air pressure and air temperature

3. A water molecule weighs (less/more) than the average "air molecule."

➤ less

4. Humidity (increases/decreases) the air density, and (improves/degrades) performance.

➤ decreases, degrades

5. In less dense air at high pressure altitudes, (more/less) air is processed by the propeller than at sea level, which (increases/decreases) its efficiency.

➤ less, decreases

6. A quick method to determine pressure altitude when you are in the cockpit is to set _____ in. Hg in the pressure window and then read the altimeter.

➤ 29.92 in. Hg

7. Standard values for mean sea level temperature and pressure are _____ °C and _____ in. Hg.

➤ 15°C, 29.92 in. Hg

8. Which of the following would increase the density altitude at a given airfield?
   (a) An increase in barometric pressure.
   (b) An increase in ambient temperature.
   (c) A decrease in relative humidity.

➤ (b)

9. If the outside air temperature (OAT) at a given altitude is warmer than standard, the density altitude is:
   (a) equal to pressure altitude.
   (b) lower than pressure altitude.
   (c) higher than pressure altitude.

➤ (c)

10. Which combination of atmospheric conditions will reduce airplane takeoff and climb performance?
    (a) Low temperature, low relative humidity, and low density altitude.
    (b) High temperature, low relative humidity, and low density altitude.
    (c) High temperature, high relative humidity, and high density altitude.

➤ (c)

11. Estimate the approximate pressure altitude of an airport with elevation 3,000 feet MSL if the altimeter setting is 28.90 in. Hg.

➤ 4,000 feet

12. Express +9°C at 7,000 feet as an ISA deviation.

➤ ISA+8

13. Express +1°C at 10,000 feet as an ISA deviation.

➤ ISA+6

14. To achieve the same dynamic pressure, and create the same aerodynamic forces, the airplane must fly at (a higher/a lower/the same) indicated airspeed irrespective of altitude. In the thinner air at higher altitudes, the true airspeed will be (higher/lower/the same) compared with its value at sea level.

➤ the same indicated airspeed, a higher true airspeed

15. An airplane is to approach for landing at 60 KIAS. Landing at a high elevation airport, compared with landing at a sea level airport, the true airspeed of the airplane at touchdown will be (the same/greater/less), and so its ground roll will be (the same/longer/shorter).

➤ greater, longer

For Questions 16–24 use Figure 9-13 on page 192.

16. What is the pressure altitude at an airport with elevation 3,000 feet MSL if the altimeter setting is 29.60 in. Hg?

➤ 3,298 feet pressure altitude
(pressure less than standard, so add 298 feet conversion factor found from table)

17. What is the pressure altitude at an airport with elevation 3,563 feet MSL if the altimeter setting is 29.96 in. Hg?

➤ 3,526 feet pressure altitude (3,563 − 37)

18. The indicated altitude is 1,380 feet with an altimeter setting of 28.22 in.Hg. What is the pressure altitude?

➤ 2,991 feet pressure altitude (1,380 + 1,611)
   Interpolation:

 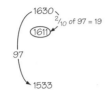

19. From the density altitude chart, what is the density altitude if the pressure altitude is 5,000 feet and the temperature is:
    (a) 42°F (i.e. standard temperature at 5,000 feet).
    (b) 50°F.
    (c) 4°C.
    (d) 21°C.

➤ (a) 5,000 feet, (b) 5,500 feet, (c) 4,850 feet,
   (d) 6,800 feet

20. What is the effect of a temperature increase from –1°C to +16°C on the density altitude if the pressure altitude remains at 5,000 feet?

➤ 1,950 feet increase (6,150 – 4,200)

21. What is the effect on the density altitude of a temperature decrease and a pressure altitude decrease from +4°C and 3,000 feet to –7°C and 2,500 feet?

➤ 1,850 feet decrease (2,300 to 450 feet, a decrease of 1,850 feet)

22. Determine the density altitude for the following conditions:
    Altimeter setting .... 29.25 in.Hg
    Runway temperature .... +27°C
    Airport elevation .... 5,250 feet

➤ 8,500 feet (pressure altitude = 5,250 + 626 = 5,876)

23. What is the effect of a temperature increase from 25 to 50°F on the density altitude if the pressure altitude remains at 5,000 feet.
    (a) 1,200-foot increase.
    (b) 1,400-foot increase.
    (c) 1,650-foot increase.

➤ (c)

24. What is the effect of a temperature decrease and a pressure altitude increase on the density altitude from 90°F and 1,250 feet pressure altitude to 60°F and 1,750 feet pressure altitude.
    (a) 500-foot increase.
    (b) 1,300-foot decrease.
    (c) 1,300-foot increase.

➤ (b)

For Questions 25 to 27, calculate the density altitude and cross-check your answers using Figure 9-13 on page 192 and your flight computer.

25. Refer to Figure 9-13. Determine the density altitude given:
    Indicated altitude .... 5,000 feet
    Pressure setting .... 28.30 in.Hg
    Temperature .... ISA +10°C

➤ 7,700 feet

$$
\begin{aligned}
\text{Indicated altitude} &= 5,000 \\
\text{Correction (Figure 9-13)} &= +1,533 \\
\text{Therefore PA} &= \underline{6,5333} \\
\text{ISA temp at PA 6,500 ft} &= 15 - (2 \times 6.5) \\
&= +2°C \\
\text{Temp deviation} &= +10 \\
\text{ISA temp at PA 6,500 ft} &= 15 - (2 \times 6.5) \\
&= +12°C
\end{aligned}
$$

Calculation methods:
(a) Using Figure 9-13, DA = 7,700 feet.
(b) Using 120 feet/1°C difference from ISA
$$
\begin{aligned}
\text{correction} &= 12 \times 10 \\
&= 1,200 \\
\text{PA} &\underline{6,500} \\
\text{therefore DA} &= 7,700 \text{ ft}
\end{aligned}
$$
(c) Using flight compute: 7,700 feet (approx).

26. Calculate density altitude given:
    Pressure altitude .... 15,000 feet
    True air temperature .... –35°C

➤ 12,600 feet
   Check: ISA = 15 – (2 × 15) = –15°C
   therefore temp –35°C at PA 15,000 feet = ISA–20
   $$
   \begin{aligned}
   \text{correction} &= -20 \times 120 = -2,400 \\
   \text{PA} &\underline{15,000} \\
   \text{DA} &\ 12,600 \text{ ft}
   \end{aligned}
   $$

27. Calculate density altitude given:
    Pressure altitude .... 15,000 feet
    True air temperature .... –5°C

➤ 16,000 feet
   Check: ISA = 15 – (2 × 15) = –15°C
   therefore temp –5°C at PA 15,000 feet = ISA+10
   $$
   \begin{aligned}
   \text{correction} &= 10 \times 120 = +1,200 \\
   \text{PA} &\underline{15,000} \\
   \text{DA} &\ 16,200 \text{ ft}
   \end{aligned}
   $$

Takeoff and Landing Performance 10

Takeoff Performance

Takeoff and landing are perhaps two of the most labor intensive tasks involved in piloting an airplane, and they start long before the wheels leave the ground.

Takeoffs involve much more than smooth piloting skills; they involve careful planning and preparation. A very smooth takeoff is of little value if the airplane, once airborne, is faced with obstacles impossible to avoid. The takeoff performance of the airplane needs to be matched to the runway and the surrounding obstacles prior to actually taking off.

Definitions

The **ground roll** is the distance an airplane will travel on the takeoff run, from a standing start until it leaves the ground. The **takeoff distance** is the distance established on a paved, level, dry runway for the airplane to clear a 50-foot obstacle from a standing start, at maximum takeoff power. The **takeoff safety speed (TOSS),** which provides a 20% margin over the stall speed, should be achieved by the 50-foot point.

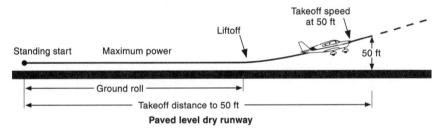

Figure 10-1. Takeoff distance

Factors Affecting Takeoff Performance

Weight

A heavier airplane will require an increased ground run and takeoff distance to clear a 50-foot obstacle because of the slower airplane acceleration and increased takeoff speed. In addition, the greater weight on the wheels during the ground run increases the friction, further reducing acceleration and increasing the distance to reach a set takeoff speed.

A heavier airplane results in a greater takeoff distance.

Increased Takeoff Speed

A heavier airplane will have a faster stall speed. Because the liftoff speed is related to the stall speed, any increase in stall speed also means an increase in liftoff speed. After liftoff, the greater weight will also reduce the airplane's climb performance (rate of climb and angle of climb) and so the distance required for the initial climb to 50 feet above the runway will be greater. This climb is still part of the takeoff distance, hence there is a corresponding increase in the takeoff distance extracted from the performance chart.

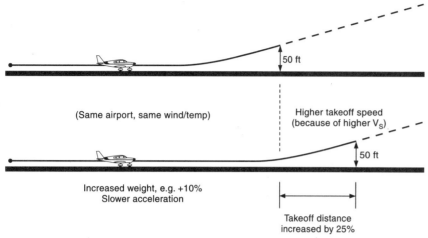

(Same airport, same wind/temp)

Higher takeoff speed
(because of higher V_S)

50 ft

50 ft

Increased weight, e.g. +10%
Slower acceleration

Takeoff distance
increased by 25%

Figure 10-2. Increased weight decreases takeoff performance

The overall effect of a 10% increase in weight may be to increase the takeoff distance by 25%.

Air Density

An increase in density altitude results in a longer ground run and takeoff distance to clear a 50-foot obstacle. A decrease in air density can be caused by a number of factors.

A **lower air pressure** will decrease the density and this can occur as a result of a different ground-level ambient pressure or as a result of a higher airport elevation. This effect is covered by pressure altitude, which relates the actual pressure experienced by the airplane to a level in the standard atmosphere that has an identical pressure. High-elevation airports lead to longer takeoff distances.

A **higher air temperature** will also decrease the air density, reducing airplane and engine performance.

If the air density decreases, the engine–propeller combination will not produce as much power and so the takeoff distance will increase. As well as the power-producing performance of the engine–propeller decreasing, the aerodynamic performance of the airplane will also decrease as air density becomes less.

To produce the required lift force (L = Lifting ability $\frac{1}{2}\rho V^2 \times S$), a decrease in air density (ρ) means that for the same required indicated airspeed, an increase in the velocity (true airspeed, V) is required and a longer takeoff distance will result. Not only does a lower air density affect the aerodynamic performance of the airframe (controlled by $\frac{1}{2}\rho V^2$), it also decreases the weight of the fuel/air mixture in the engine cylinders, causing a decrease in engine power.

The effects of pressure and temperature are accounted for in your takeoff performance charts. However, one effect that is *not* accounted for is humidity. Air is a mixture of gases, mainly oxygen and nitrogen, whose molecules are reasonably heavy. When there is **high humidity,** some of these heavier molecules are replaced by very light water molecules, which has the effect of lowering the air density.

A high airport elevation results in decreased airplane and engine performance.

High temperatures decrease airplane and engine performance.

High humidity decreases airplane and engine performance.

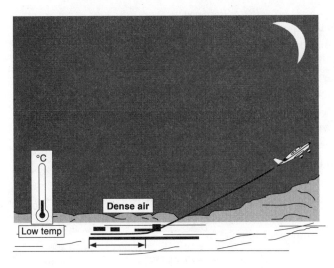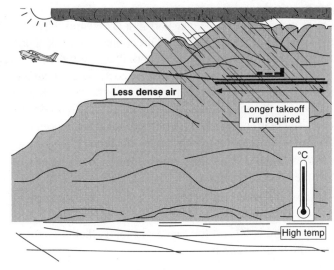

Figure 10-3. Hot, high and humid means decreased performance

Headwinds and Tailwinds

A headwind reduces the ground roll and takeoff distance to clear a 50-foot obstacle. For flight, the airplane requires a certain speed relative to the air in which it is flying. An airplane stopped at the end of the runway and facing into a 20-knot headwind is already 20 knots closer to the liftoff indicated airspeed, compared with the no-wind situation.

In a **headwind** takeoff the airplane therefore reaches liftoff indicated airspeed at a lower groundspeed, and so less ground run is required. Once in the air, the angle or gradient relative to the ground is increased by a headwind, making for better obstacle clearance.

In a **tailwind**, the effect is to lengthen the ground run and to flatten the climb-out. Tailwinds in excess of 5 knots are normally not considered suitable for takeoff. Obviously, a takeoff into the wind shows better airmanship.

A headwind reduces the takeoff distance.

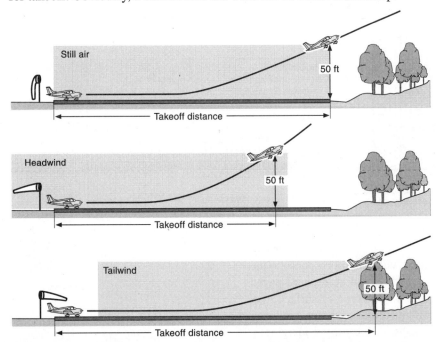

Figure 10-4. A headwind reduces the ground run and takeoff distance to clear a 50-foot obstacle

Crosswinds

The airplane must not be taken off in a **crosswind** that exceeds the maximum crosswind limit for the airplane. Directional control is a problem. The aerodynamic force from the rudder is potentially not sufficient to overcome the effect of the keel surfaces wanting to weathercock the airplane into the wind. Lateral control is an additional problem, because the crosswind will generally try to lift the into the wind wing, which then has to be held down with aileron.

In calculating the strength of a crosswind component we will consider a 10-knot wind blowing from various directions:

- If the wind is 30° off the runway heading, then the crosswind component is $\frac{1}{2}$ the wind strength.
- If the wind is 45° off the runway heading, then the crosswind component is $\frac{2}{3}$ the wind strength.
- If the wind is 60° off the runway heading, then the crosswind component is $\frac{9}{10}$ the wind strength.
- If the wind is 90° off the runway heading, then it is all crosswind.

Note: Flight computers have the facility for calculating crosswind (and head/tail wind components), *see* Chapter 24. Sometimes a **crosswind corrections graph** is provided in the Pilot's Operating Handbook.

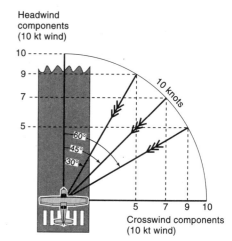

Figure 10-5. Estimating crosswind and headwind components

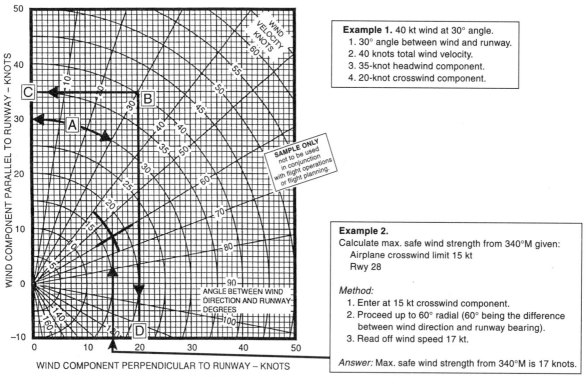

Example 1. 40 kt wind at 30° angle.
1. 30° angle between wind and runway.
2. 40 knots total wind velocity.
3. 35-knot headwind component.
4. 20-knot crosswind component.

SAMPLE ONLY
not to be used
in conjunction
with flight operations
or flight planning.

Example 2.
Calculate max. safe wind strength from 340°M given:
   Airplane crosswind limit 15 kt
   Rwy 28

Method:
1. Enter at 15 kt crosswind component.
2. Proceed up to 60° radial (60° being the difference between wind direction and runway bearing).
3. Read off wind speed 17 kt.

Answer: Max. safe wind strength from 340°M is 17 knots.

Figure 10-6. A typical crosswind corrections graph

Runway Surface

The length of the ground roll, at any given weight, will vary in response to the friction caused by the runway surface during the takeoff roll. A dry hard-paved runway causes the least amount of friction, and so this type of surface may serve as a datum, or reference surface, on takeoff performance charts. A runway with a short dry-grass surface, based on firm subsoil, has only a marginally higher retarding effect.

Soft ground or long grass (especially if wet) will reduce the acceleration, and this will result in a greater takeoff distance by as much as 25%. Gravel is considered to have the same effect as a short dry-grass surface. Pools of water on any type of runway surface can significantly retard the acceleration, and takeoff under such conditions requires very careful consideration. Soft, wet ground or a soft, sandy surface might make acceleration to the liftoff speed impossible, no matter what runway length is available.

Poor runway surfaces increase takeoff ground run.

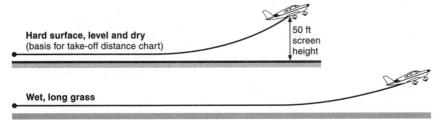

Figure 10-7. Poor surfaces may increase the ground run

Flaps

The use of small flap settings decreases the length of the ground run. Flaps have the effect of lowering the stall speed, which reduces the liftoff speed. Provided that the flap setting used for takeoff is small (so that the drag is not greatly increased), the slower liftoff speed after a shorter ground run may enable a shorter runway to be used. If the ground surface is rough, using a small flap setting for takeoff will allow you to get off the ground sooner.

The use of small flap settings decreases the ground run.

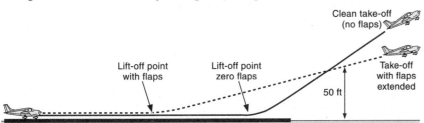

Figure 10-8. Use of takeoff flaps reduces the ground run

Notice we have used the words "ground run" rather than "takeoff distance to clear a 50-foot obstacle." While the ground run will be less when small flap settings are used, the takeoff distance to clear a 50-foot obstacle may not be reduced significantly. This is because flaps, as well as increasing lift, increase drag, thus reducing the excess thrust and thereby the angle of climb. This is the main reason for only using small flap settings for takeoff. A larger flap setting, even though it might reduce the stall speed, would greatly increase the aerodynamic drag during the ground run, causing a slower acceleration and then, once airborne, would significantly degrade the climb-performance.

We cannot generalize too much in our statements here, as the precise effect of the use of flaps on the takeoff of a particular airplane depends on many things, including the flap setting, the engine–propeller combination and the airspeed flown. You must become familiar with your own airplane type.

Runway Slope

Takeoff distance is calculated for a level runway, and some takeoff charts allow for the effect of runway slope. A downslope of 2-in-100 or 2% down will allow the airplane to accelerate faster and so will decrease the ground roll. An upslope of 2-in-100 or 2% up will make it more difficult for the airplane to accelerate and so the ground roll will be greater. A 2% upslope may increase the takeoff distance to 50 feet by approximately 20%.

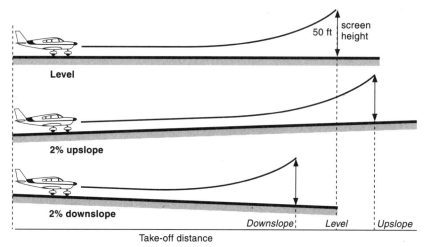

Figure 10-9. An upward-sloping runway will increase the ground roll and takeoff distance to 50 feet

Note: Runway slope is calculated using the elevations at either end. Therefore a runway with downslope may have a hump (involving upslope) somewhere along its length.

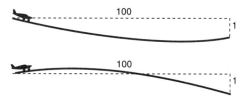

Figure 10-10. Each of these runways has a downslope of 1%

The Takeoff Distance Graph

Many manufacturers present performance data in the form of graphs and tables. The most common is the graph, and an example is shown in Figure 10-11. This performance graph has been prepared for a full-throttle takeoff with flaps up. Using this graph you can apply corrections for:

- air density (using temperature, and pressure altitude);
- airplane takeoff weight; and
- headwind or tailwind component (note that the tailwind must not exceed 10 knots).

It allows you to determine:

- the takeoff distance from the starting point to a point 50 feet above the runway;
- the length of the ground roll prior to liftoff; and
- the liftoff speed and takeoff speed at 50 feet.

1. The air density correction is made in the first (left) section of the graph where you enter at the bottom with **temperature,** and move up to the appropriate **pressure altitude** line. Then move horizontally to the right until you meet the reference line. The higher the pressure altitude and/or temperature, the longer the takeoff distance.

Note: The line sloping upward to the left intersects the pressure altitude lines at standard temperature for those altitudes, eliminating the need for you to calculate the numerical figure for temperature if it is given to you as standard.

TAKEOFF DISTANCE

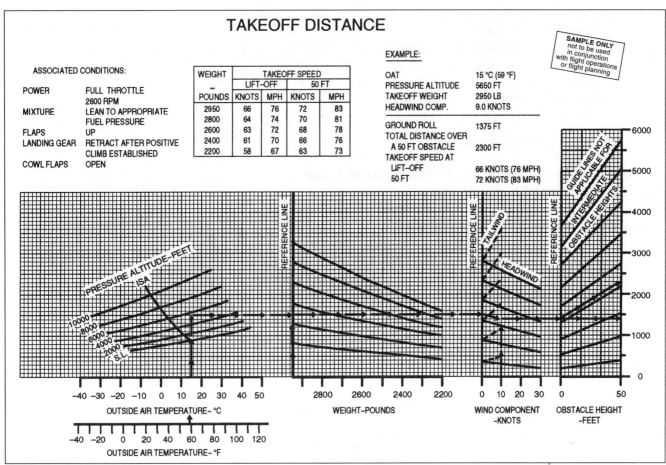

ASSOCIATED CONDITIONS:

POWER	FULL THROTTLE 2600 RPM
MIXTURE	LEAN TO APPROPRIATE FUEL PRESSURE
FLAPS	UP
LANDING GEAR	RETRACT AFTER POSITIVE CLIMB ESTABLISHED
COWL FLAPS	OPEN

WEIGHT	TAKEOFF SPEED			
	LIFT-OFF		50 FT	
~ POUNDS	KNOTS	MPH	KNOTS	MPH
2950	66	76	72	83
2800	64	74	70	81
2600	63	72	68	78
2400	61	70	66	76
2200	58	67	63	73

EXAMPLE:

OAT	15 °C (59 °F)
PRESSURE ALTITUDE	5650 FT
TAKEOFF WEIGHT	2950 LB
HEADWIND COMP.	9.0 KNOTS
GROUND ROLL	1375 FT
TOTAL DISTANCE OVER A 50 FT OBSTACLE	2300 FT
TAKEOFF SPEED AT	
LIFT-OFF	66 KNOTS (76 MPH)
50 FT	72 KNOTS (83 MPH)

Figure 10-11. Takeoff distance graph

2. The **airplane weight correction** is made in the next section of the graph. If the airplane is at maximum takeoff weight of 2,950 pounds (represented by the reference line), then you continue straight across horizontally; if not, you should follow the guidelines down to the right until you intersect a line drawn upward from the weight, from which point you should move horizontally right to the next reference line.

3. The **wind correction** section of the graph comes next. This allows you to correct for a headwind, which will shorten the takeoff distance, or a tailwind, which will increase the takeoff distance. Follow the appropriate guidelines (up for a tailwind, down for a headwind) until you meet the wind component line drawn up from the bottom. Then move horizontally across to the final reference line. This last section of the graph allows you to determine:

   (a) the **ground roll** (from starting point to just on liftoff at 0 feet above the runway) shown at the reference line; and

   (b) the **takeoff distance to 50 feet** from the starting point on the runway, by following the guidelines up to the right to the 50 feet line.

4. The **liftoff speed** and the **takeoff speed** at 50 feet are found in a small table above the graph. At 2,800 pounds takeoff weight, for instance, you would lift the wheels off at 64 knots and fly away from the ground at a rate that allows you to reach 70 knots by 50 feet above the runway.

Note: It is possible to use this graph somewhat in reverse if you have a short runway and wish to determine the maximum takeoff weight permitted. This would be known as the **performance-limited takeoff weight.** You would enter the graph from the left and the right with the known information, following the same pattern of lines until the left line and right line intersect in the weight section. Then drop a vertical line to find the maximum permissible weight.

✎ Now complete **Review 10, Part (a)** on page 221.

Different Presentations of Performance Data (for Commercial Students only)

You must become familiar with the various methods of presentation of data. Refer to the performance documents for the airplane you are flying.

Although the takeoff and landing charts in the Commercial Pilot Written Test are not identical to those used in the Private Pilot Written Test, the same principles apply. The commercial review at the end of the chapter includes questions on the commercial written test takeoff and landing charts to test your understanding and to increase your confidence.

✎ Commercial students complete **Review 10, Commercial Part (a)** on page 225.

Landing Performance

The total **landing distance** is the distance established from a point where the airplane is 50 feet over the runway threshold (assumed to be a paved, level dry runway) to the point where the airplane reaches a full stop, assuming a steady, full flaps approach, with power off at 50 feet and maximum braking once the wheels are on the ground.

Note: This is the certification technique—you are not required to carry out all landings and stops exactly like this in practice.

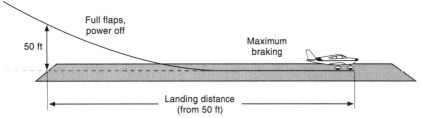

Figure 10-12. Landing distance

Factors Affecting Landing Performance

Weight

A heavier airplane will need a greater ground roll and total landing distance. A heavier weight has a number of effects:

- The stall speed is increased, so the approach speed must be greater.
- The higher approach speed results in the airplane possessing greater kinetic energy ($\frac{1}{2}mV^2$) which has to be absorbed by the brakes, increasing the length of the landing run. (There will, however, be a slight increase in the retarding friction force because of the extra weight on the wheels.)

A heavier airplane will need a greater landing distance.

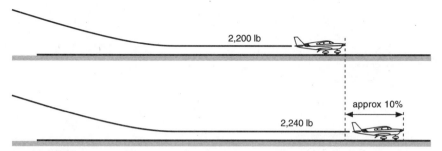

Figure 10-13. A 10% increase in weight requires a 10% increase in landing distance (approximately)

Air Density

An increased density altitude results in a longer landing distance. Low ambient pressure, high elevation and high ambient temperatures decrease the air density (ρ), giving a higher density altitude.

A decreased air density (ρ) means an increased V (TAS) is needed to provide the same lift force. Even though you see the same indicated airspeed ($\frac{1}{2}\rho V^2$) in the cockpit, the true airspeed is higher in air of lower density.

At high density altitudes the true airspeed will be greater than for lower density altitudes, and the touchdown groundspeed will be higher. Therefore the amount of kinetic energy to be dissipated in the ground roll is greater—hence a longer ground run and total landing distance is required.

An increased density altitude results in a longer landing distance.

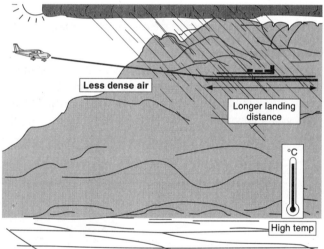

Figure 10-14. High temperatures and high altitudes result in a longer landing distance

The Effect of Wind

A headwind reduces the landing distance because the groundspeed is reduced by the headwind for the same true airspeed (V). A tailwind means that the groundspeed will exceed the true airspeed, and so the touchdown speed relative to the ground is higher and a longer landing distance will be required.

A headwind reduces the ground run and landing distance.

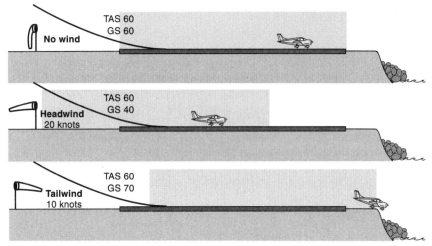

Figure 10-15. Headwind reduces landing distance

Runway Surface

A smooth or wet runway surface will not allow good braking to occur and so the landing distance required will be longer. On a wet surface, hydroplaning may occur, which will greatly increase the stopping distance. Conversely a dry grass runway with increased friction will reduce the landing distance.

Hydroplaning is the phenomenon of a tire skating along on a thin film of water and not rotating, even though it is free to do so. Wheel braking therefore has no effect. Friction forces are practically zero.

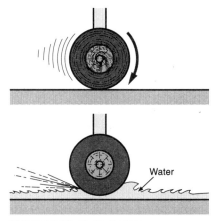

Figure 10-16. Hydroplaning

Runway Slope

A downslope will result in a longer total landing distance. It will take longer for the airplane to touch down from 50 feet above the runway threshold, because the runway is falling away beneath the airplane, and airplane braking while going downhill will not be as effective as on a level or upward sloping runway.

A downslope will result in a longer landing distance.

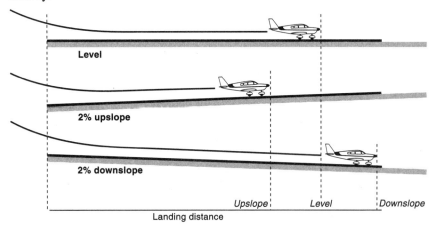

Figure 10-17. Downslope increases landing distance

Flaps

Higher flap settings reduce the stall speed and therefore the approach speed, which provides a 30% buffer over the stall speed, is lower. High flap settings also give additional aerodynamic drag that helps to slow the airplane down, but only in the initial stages of the landing roll, after which they lose their effect.

Increased flap settings decrease the landing distance.

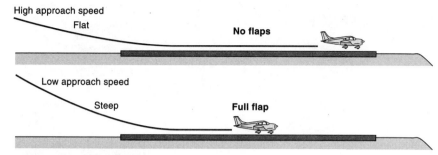

Figure 10-18. Increased flaps—slower and steeper

Fast Approach Speeds

The landing performance charts are based on **specified approach speeds.** If you approach for a landing at a speed higher than that specified, the landing distance will exceed that predicted by the chart. This is because of the greater kinetic energy of the airplane and the tendency of the airplane to float at the round-out because of ground effect (*see* page 214).

The Landing Distance Graph

Many manufacturers present performance data in the form of a graph, rather than a table of figures. The landing performance graph in Figure 10-19 is an example.

This graph has been prepared for a flaps-down landing, on a paved, level, dry surface, followed by maximum braking. However in normal practice it is not good airmanship to use maximum braking on every landing, since uncomfortable stops for the passengers and excessive brake wear will occur. Only use maximum braking when necessary on short runways. The landing performance graph allows you to apply corrections for:

- air density (using temperature and pressure altitude);
- airplane landing weight; and
- headwind or tailwind component (tailwind must not exceed 10 knots).

It allows you to determine:

- total landing distance from an obstacle 50 feet above runway threshold;
- ground roll; and
- approach speed.

First the air density correction is made in the left-hand section of the graph where you enter at the bottom with **temperature** and move up to the appropriate **pressure altitude** line. Then mark a horizontal line to the reference line. The higher the pressure altitude and/or temperature, the longer the final distances.

The **airplane weight correction** is then made by starting at the point on the reference line where the air density line intersected it, and moving parallel to the guidelines that slope down to the right until you intersect the airplane weight line drawn up from the bottom. At this point mark a horizontal line across to the next reference line. The lower the weight, the shorter the final distances.

Note: For maximum takeoff weight 2,950 pounds, which is represented by the first reference line, you would not need to follow the guidelines down but just keep moving across horizontally to the second reference line.

The **wind correction** part of the graph allows you to correct for either a headwind (which will shorten the landing distance) or a tailwind (which will increase the landing distance). Follow the appropriate guidelines (up for a tailwind, down for a headwind) until you meet the wind component line drawn up from the bottom. Then move horizontally across to the final reference line.

LANDING DISTANCE

ASSOCIATED CONDITIONS:

POWER	RETARDED TO MAINTAIN 900 FT/on FINAL APPROACH
FLAPS	DOWN
LANDING GEAR	DOWN
RUNWAY	PAVED, LEVEL, DRY SURFACE
APPROACH SPEED	IAS AS TABULATED
BRAKING	MAXIMUM

WEIGHT ~ POUNDS	SPEED AT 50 FT	
	KNOTS	MPH
2950	70	80
2800	68	78
2600	65	75
2400	63	72
2200	60	69

EXAMPLE:

OAT	25 °C (77 °F)
PRESSURE ALTITUDE	3965 FT
WEIGHT	2814 LB
WIND COMPONENT	9.0 KNOTS (HEADWIND)

GROUND ROLL	1080 FT
TOTAL OVER 50 FT OBSTACLE	1700 FT
APPROACH SPEED	68 KNOTS (78 MPH)

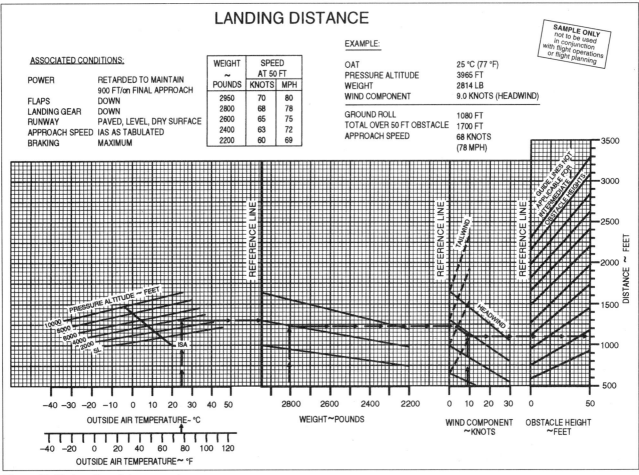

Figure 10-19. Landing distance graph

This last section of the graph allows you to determine:

(a) the **ground roll,** where your line intersects the reference line (which is marked as 0 feet); and

(b) the total **landing distance from 50 feet,** by following the guidelines up to the right (marked 50 feet) to give a significantly greater distance, since much of the landing from 50 feet consists of air distance before the wheels touch down.

The **approach speed** is shown in a small table above the graph. At 2,800 pounds for instance, you would approach with flaps down at 68 knots.

The graph can also be used in reverse if you have a **short runway** and wish to determine the maximum landing weight permitted. The steps are:

1. As before, enter from the left with temperature and pressure altitude, then from the reference line move down the guidelines to a so far unknown weight.

2. Enter from the far right with runway length. Following the original pattern, move to the left down the guidelines to the reference line. Next move horizontally across to intersect with the appropriate headwind or tailwind line, and follow the guidelines up to the reference line. Then move horizontally across to the left until you intersect the line you marked in during (a).

3. From this intersection point, drop a line vertically to give you the maximum permissible weight, known as the **performance-limited landing weight.**

The Landing Distance Table

Some manufacturers present performance data in the form of a table, rather than a graph. The landing performance table in Figure 10-20 is an example.

——— LANDING DISTANCE ———

FLAPS LOWERED TO 40 ° - POWER OFF
HARD SURFACE RUNWAY - ZERO WIND

GROSS WEIGHT LB	APPROACH SPEED, IAS, MPH	AT SEA LEVEL & 59 °F		AT 2500 FT & 50 °F		AT 5000 FT & 41 °F		AT 7500 FT & 32 °F	
		GROUND ROLL	TOTAL TO CLEAR 50 FT OBS	GROUND ROLL	TOTAL TO CLEAR 50 FT OBS	GROUND ROLL	TOTAL TO CLEAR 50 FT OBS	GROUND ROLL	TOTAL TO CLEAR 50 FT OBS
1600	60	445	1075	470	1135	495	1195	520	1255

NOTES: 1. Decrease the distances shown by 10% for each 4 knots of headwind.
2. Increase the distance by 10% for each 60 °F temperature increase above standard.
3. For operation on a dry, grass runway, increase distances (both "ground roll" and "total to clear 50 ft obstacle") by 20% of the "total to clear 50 ft obstacle" figure.

Figure 10-20. Landing distance table

This table has been prepared for a 40° flaps landing, power off, on a dry and level hard-surface runway with zero wind, at specific pressure altitudes at standard temperatures. Both the total distance to land from 50 feet over the runway threshold, and the ground roll, are published. For instance, at pressure altitude 2,500 feet and standard temperature 50°F, the landing distance from 50 feet is 1,135 feet and the ground roll is 470 feet.

When the pressure altitude is between the values given in the table, you will need to interpolate to find the landing distance and ground roll.

For example, the pressure altitude 6,250 feet is halfway between the published pressure altitudes 5,000 feet and 7,500 feet, so the distances will also be halfway between the published figures. To find the "landing distance from 50 feet", take the 5,000 feet pressure altitude figure of 1,195 feet, and to this add one-half of the *difference* between it and the figure for 7,500 feet pressure altitude (1,255 – 1,195 = 60 feet, $\frac{1}{2}$ of 60 = 30), to give an answer of **1,225 feet** (1195 + 30). Ground roll is 495 + $\frac{1}{2}$ of (520 – 495) = 495 + 12.5 = 507.5, say **508 feet.**

Once the ground roll and landing distance to clear a 50-foot obstacle have been found for a given pressure altitude, apply the following corrections, if applicable:

• headwind component;
• high temperatures (60°F above standard); and
• a dry grass runway (instead of a hard surface).

Headwind component correction—for each 4 knots of headwind, you may reduce the distances by 10%. You can calculate this 10% and then subtract, but a faster method is simply to take 90% of the distance, by multiplying it by 0.9. For a headwind of 12 knots (3 × 4 knots), you may reduce the distance by 30%, or multiply it by 0.7. If the airport is at sea level then the corrected distance would be 1,075 × 0.7 = 752.5, say **753 feet.**

High temperature correction—for extremely high temperatures (at least 60°F above the standard temperature for that altitude) you should increase the distance by 10%. If the OAT at 5,000 feet was 105°F (more than 60°F above standard at 6,250 feet altitude), the corrected distance would now be 1,195 × 1.1 = 1,315 feet (increasing by 10% is the same as multiplying by 1.1).

Dry grass runway correction—on this surface both the ground roll and landing distance must be increased by 20% of the total distance to land from 50 feet. The logic for this is that the retarding effect of the grass does not occur before touchdown, hence the same increase for both distances.

At 2,500 feet for example, the correction for a dry grass surface is 20% of 1,135 feet = 227 feet. Therefore, the corrected landing distance from 50 feet = 1,135 + 227 = 1,362 feet, and the corrected ground roll is 470 + 227 = 697 feet.

✍ Now complete **Review 10, Part (b)** on page 222.

✍ Commercial students complete **Review 10, Commercial Part (b)** on page 226.

Wake Turbulence

As a wing produces lift, the higher static pressure area beneath the wing causes an airflow around the wingtip to the lower pressure area above. The greater the difference in pressure, the greater the flow around the wingtips. (If it is some time since you have read Section 1 we suggest that you now reread *Induced Drag* on page 16 to refresh your memory.)

At the high angles-of-attack necessary to produce the required lift force at low speeds, very large and strong trailing vortices are formed. High angles of attack are required when an airplane is heavy and flying slowly (particularly if flaps are not extended). As a large and heavy airplane is rotated for takeoff or flared for landing, the angle-of-attack is also large. The trailing wingtip vortices formed at these high angles-of-attack can be strong enough to rapidly roll a following airplane if it flies into them. This hazardous trail of wingtip vortices behind an airplane is known as **wake turbulence.**

The wake turbulence behind a Boeing 747 can significantly affect a 737 and cause a lighter airplane to become uncontrollable. The induced rolling motion may exceed the rolling capability of the airplane affected, making it impossible for the pilot to hold the wings level. The rolling effect will be greatest when the affected airplane is aligned with the flight path of the airplane generating the vortices.

To avoid wake turbulence accidents and incidents, Air Traffic Control may delay the operation of light airplanes on runways behind heavy jets for up to five minutes to allow the vortices to drift away and dissipate.

Every pilot should have an awareness of wake turbulence because the Air Traffic Control procedures may occasionally provide insufficient separation from the wingtip vortices behind another airplane. Remember that pilots have the ultimate responsibility for the safety of their airplanes—so learn to visualize the formation and movement of invisible wingtip vortices.

Wingtip vortices tend to *lose height* slowly (typically at approximately 500 fpm), slowly *move apart* and drift *downwind*. To be able to avoid these invisible danger areas, you must visualize the movement of the vortices and take steps to avoid them.

Helicopters also produce wake turbulence. The helicopter blades act as a wing to produce lift and, as the helicopter proceeds, a trail of wingtip vortices will be left behind, just the same as for a fixed-wing aircraft. The heavier and slower the helicopter, the stronger the wake turbulence behind it.

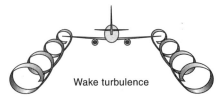
Figure 10-21. Wake turbulence from a large, slow-flying airliner

Wake turbulence will be strongest behind a heavy aircraft flying slowly with its flaps up.

The main danger from wake turbulence is loss of control because of induced roll.

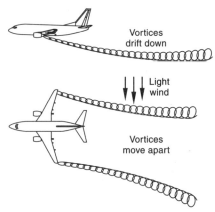
Figure 10-22. Wingtip vortices slowly lose height, move apart and drift downwind

Avoiding Wake Turbulence

The main aim of wake-turbulence avoidance is to avoid passing through it at all. This is accomplished by flying *above* and *upwind* of the flight path of the aircraft producing wake turbulence.

Avoid wake turbulence by flying above and upwind of the path of other aircraft.

Takeoff

When taking off behind a large airplane which has itself just taken off, commence your takeoff at the end of the runway so that you will become airborne in an area well before where the heavy airplane rotated, or to where its vortices may have drifted with the wind. If in doubt, delay your takeoff. Once airborne, maneuver to avoid the vortices in flight by turning away from where you think the wake turbulence is.

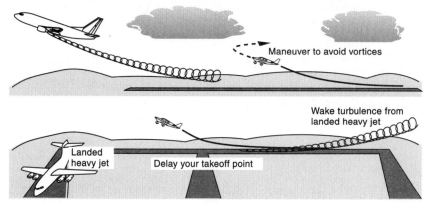

Figure 10-23. Avoid wake turbulence on your takeoff

When taking off after a heavy airplane has landed, plan to become airborne well past the point where it flared and landed.

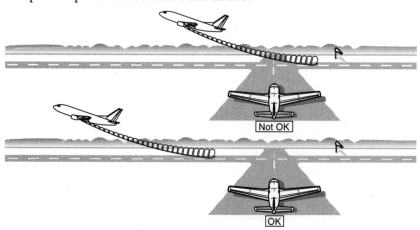

Figure 10-24. Awareness of wake turbulence for your takeoff

If a heavy airplane has taken off on a different runway and you expect to be airborne prior to the intersection of the runways, check to ensure that the heavy airplane was still on the ground until well past the intersection, before you commence your takeoff. This is because unless an airplane is flying and therefore producing lift, it will not be producing wake turbulence.

In the Traffic Pattern

Avoid flying below and behind large airplanes. Fly a few hundred feet above them, a thousand feet below them or upwind of them. Calm days, where there is no turbulence to break up the vortices, are potentially the most dangerous.

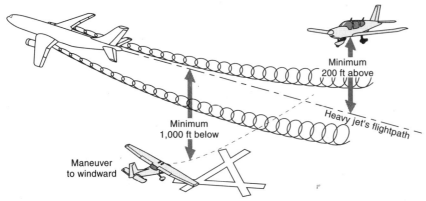

Figure 10-25. Avoidance of wake turbulence in the traffic pattern area

Approach to Land

When following a preceding landing airplane, fly above the approach path of the heavy airplane and land well beyond his touchdown point. This is usually possible in a light airplane landing on a long runway where heavy airplanes are landing. Be very cautious in light, quartering tailwinds, which may drift the vortices of the preceding airplane forward into your touchdown zone.

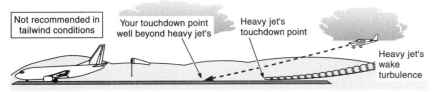

Figure 10-26. Avoidance of wake turbulence on approach

If a preceding heavy airplane has discontinued its approach and gone around, its turbulent wake will be a hazard to a following airplane. You must consider changing your flight path in these circumstances.

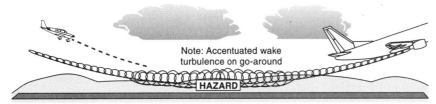

Figure 10-27. Making an approach behind a heavy airplane that has gone around

Jet Blast

Do not confuse wake turbulence (wingtip vortices) with jet blast, which is the high velocity air exhausted from a jet engine. Jet blast can be dangerous to a light airplane taxiing on the ground behind a jet, so always position your airplane when taxiing or when stopped to avoid any potential jet blast.

Do not confuse jet blast with wake turbulence.

Figure 10-28. Jet blast and wake turbulence

✍ Now complete **Review 10, Part (c)** on page 222.

Ground Effect

An airplane's flight characteristics change when it is very close to the ground or any other surface, because:

• it can fly at a slower speed than when it is at altitude; and

• it can fly at the same speed using less thrust than when it is at altitude.

This increased performance of an airplane flying just above a surface is known as **ground effect**. Ground effect is greatest when the aircraft is just airborne and least when the aircraft is at an altitude above the ground approximately equal to one wing span. In Section 1 we considered the airplane to be flying well away from the ground. There was no restriction to the downwash of the airflow behind the wings, nor to the upwash ahead of the wings. There was also no restriction to the formation of wingtip vortices.

When the wing is just above the ground, the ground modifies the downwash and the angle is reduced, thus reducing the effect on the local average relative wind. In other words, the relative wind angle about the wing will be closer to the remote free stream. This keeps drag at a minimum and the wingtip vortices at a minimum.

As the aircraft gradually climbs and increases its altitude above the ground, the downwash angle steepens and increases the induced drag, all without an aircraft attitude change. When at one wing span height above the ground, ground effect ceases to affect the downwash or wingtip vortices and induced drag is at its maximum.

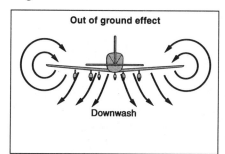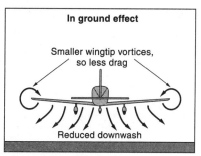

Figure 10-29. Near the ground, the upwash and downwash are restricted and the formation of wingtip vortices is restricted.

Reduced Drag

In Chapter 1 we divided the total drag on an airplane into two main types: **induced drag,** which is a by-product of the production of lift; and **parasite drag,** which is not directly associated with the production of lift.

Wingtip vortices, and trailing vortices behind the trailing edge, are the major cause of induced drag. So when a nearby surface, such as the ground, restricts their formation, the induced drag will be less, and therefore the total drag on the airplane will be less.

You are aware that, in level flight, drag is counteracted by thrust. The reduction in drag when near the ground or water means that the same airspeed can be maintained using less thrust. Therefore, under-powered airplanes may be able to maintain flying speed while in ground effect, even if they cannot maintain that speed in free air, well away from the ground.

Ground effect becomes noticeable when the airplane is at a height above the surface of less than one wingspan. The effect is greater the closer the wing is to the surface.

Ground effect limits the size of wingtip vortices which reduces induced drag.

Ground Effect during Landing

On an approach to land, as the airplane enters ground effect at about one wing-span high, the pilot will experience a floating sensation—a result of the extra lift (from the increased lifting ability of the wing) and the slower deceleration (because of less drag).

In most landings there is no desire to maintain speed—indeed the aim is to lose speed. It is therefore usually important at flare height and in ground effect to ensure that the power is throttled back, especially considering the reduction in drag because of ground effect.

Excess speed at the beginning of the landing flare and the better flyability of an airplane in ground effect may incur a considerable **float** distance prior to touchdown. This is not desirable, especially on short landing strips.

Ground Effect on Takeoff

As the airplane climbs out of ground effect on takeoff the lifting ability of the wing will decrease for the same airplane pitch attitude. In addition the induced drag will increase because of the greater wingtip vortices and line vortices. Thus the airplane will not perform as well in free air as it will in ground effect. You will feel a sagging in climb-out performance as the airplane flies out of ground effect. You will need to increase the angle-of-attack to generate the same lift as you fly out of ground effect, and either increase thrust to overcome the additional induced drag or accept a reduced climb performance.

It pays to bear this in mind if you are ever operating on very short runways, or runways which finish on the edge of a cliff (or aircraft carrier). Ground effect may allow the airplane to become airborne before reaching the recommended takeoff speed. Once away from the takeoff surface the climb performance will be less—a good reason for not forcing the airplane to become airborne at too low a speed. It might manage to fly in ground effect, but it will be unable to climb out of it.

✍ Now complete **Review 10, Part (d)** on page 223.

Windshear

The study of windshear and its effect on airplanes, and what protective measures can be taken to avoid potentially dangerous results, is still in its infancy and much still remains to be learned. What is certain is that every airplane and every pilot will be affected by windshear—usually the light windshears that occur in everyday flying, but occasionally a moderate windshear that requires positive recovery action from the pilot. On rare occasions, severe windshears can occur from which a recovery may even be impossible. A little knowledge can help you understand how to avoid significant windshear, and how best to recover from a windshear encounter.

Windshear Terminology

A **windshear** is defined as a change in wind direction and/or wind speed in space. This includes updrafts and downdrafts. Any change in the wind velocity (be it a change in speed or in direction) as you move from one point to another is a windshear. The stronger the change and the shorter the distance within which it occurs, the stronger the windshear.

Updrafts and **downdrafts** are the vertical components of wind. The most hazardous updrafts and downdrafts are usually those associated with a thunderstorm.

Windshear is a change in wind speed and/or wind direction.

The term **low-level windshear** is used to specify any windshear occurring along the final approach path prior to landing, along the runway and along the takeoff/initial climb-out flight path. Windshear near the ground (below 3,000 feet) is often the most critical in terms of safety for the airplane.

Turbulence is eddy motions in the atmosphere which vary both with time and from place to place.

The Effects of Windshear on an Airplane

So far our studies have considered an airplane flying in still air or a steady wind. However, an actual air mass does not move in a totally steady manner—there will be gusts and updrafts and changes of wind speed and direction, which the airplane will encounter as it flies through the air mass. These windshears will have a *transient effect* on the flight path of an airplane.

Even when the wind is relatively calm on the ground, it is not unusual for the light and variable surface wind to suddenly change into a strong and steady wind at a level only a few hundred feet above the ground. If we consider an airplane making an approach to land in these conditions, we can see the effect the windshear has as the airplane passes through the shear.

An airplane flying through the air will have a certain *inertia* depending on its mass and its velocity relative to the ground. Its inertia makes it resistant to change. If the airplane has an airspeed of 80 knots and the headwind component is 30 knots, then the inertial speed of the airplane over the ground is (80 − 30) 50 knots.

When the airplane flies down into the calm air, the headwind component reduces reasonably quickly to, say, 5 knots. The inertial speed of the airplane is still 50 knots, but the new headwind of only 5 knots will mean that its airspeed has suddenly dropped back to 55 knots.

The normal reaction is to add power and/or to lower the nose to regain airspeed, and to avoid undershooting the desired flight path. The stronger the windshear, the greater the changes in power and attitude that will be required. Any fluctuations in wind will require adjustments by the pilot, and this is why you have to work so hard sometimes, especially when approaching to land.

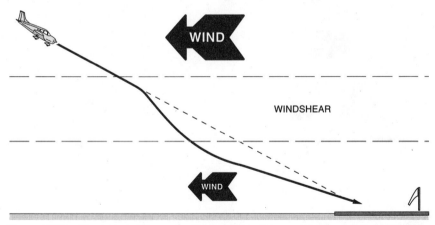

Figure 10-30. A typical windshear situation—calm on the ground with a wind at altitude

In gusty wind conditions, a power-on approach and landing should be used so that the engine can respond more quickly when required. In addition, if turbulence is encountered during the approach to land you should increase the airspeed to slightly above the normal approach speed to allow for sudden changes in indicated airspeed.

In gusty conditions, use a power-on approach and landing and consider adding a few knots to the approach speed.

Overshoot and Undershoot Effect

The effects of windshear on an airplane's flight path depend on the nature and location of the shear, as follows.

Overshoot Effect

Overshoot effect is caused by a windshear that results in the airplane flying above the desired flight path and/or an increase in indicated airspeed. The nose of the airplane may also tend to rise. Overshoot effect may result from flying into an increasing headwind, a decreasing tailwind, from a tailwind into a head-wind, or an updraft.

Undershoot Effect

Undershoot effect is caused by a windshear that results in an airplane flying below the desired flight path and/or a decrease in indicated airspeed. The nose of the airplane may also tend to drop. Undershoot effect may result from flying into a decreasing headwind, an increasing tailwind, from a headwind into a tailwind, or into a downdraft.

The actual effect of a windshear depends on:

- the nature of the windshear;
- whether the airplane is climbing or descending through that particular windshear; and
- the direction in which the airplane is proceeding.

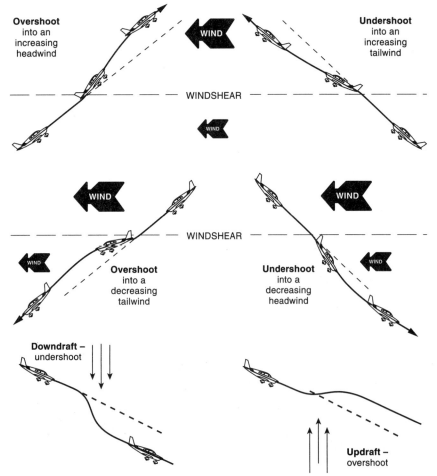

Figure 10-31. Six common windshear situations

Windshear Reversal Effect

Windshear reversal effect is caused by a windshear which results in the initial effect on the airplane being reversed as the airplane proceeds further along the flight path. It is an overshoot effect followed by undershoot, or undershoot followed by overshoot effect, as appropriate.

Windshear reversal effect is a very common phenomenon that pilots often experience on approach to land, when things are usually happening too fast to analyze exactly what is taking place in terms of wind. The pilot can, of course, observe undershoot and overshoot effect and react accordingly with changes in pitch attitude and/or power to maintain the desired flight path and airspeed.

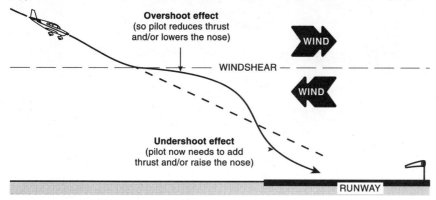

Figure 10-32. Windshear reversal effect

Crosswind Effect

Crosswind effect is caused by a windshear that requires a rapid change of airplane heading to maintain a desired track (not uncommon in a crosswind approach and landing because the crosswind component changes as the ground is neared). On crosswind landings, at the moment of touchdown the direction of the airplane's motion and its longitudinal axis must be parallel to the runway. If this is not the case the airplane will skip sideways on landing imposing large side loads on the landing gear.

Figure 10-33. Crosswind effect

The Causes of Windshear

There are many causes of windshear. They include: obstructions and terrain features which disrupt the normal smooth wind flow; localized vertical air movements associated with thunderstorms, cumulonimbus and large cumulus clouds; low-level temperature inversions; and sea breezes. These will be discussed in section 4.

✍ Now complete **Review 10, Part (e)** on page 224.

Taxiing

Control on the Ground

Directional control on the ground is achieved by use of the rudder, nosewheel steering (which may be connected to the rudder pedals), power and brakes. Airflow over the rudder increases its effectiveness.

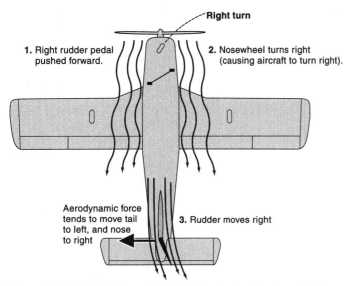

Figure 10-34. The rudder pedals, nosewheel and rudder in a right turn

Do not turn too sharply, especially when taxiing fast—a high CG, a narrow wheelbase, or an unfavorable wind effect may all combine to roll you onto the outer wingtip. In addition any wind will tend to weathercock the airplane into the wind—so take care when taxiing in crosswinds and tailwinds.

Speed is controlled on the ground by use of power and brakes. Applying power with the throttle is generally used to accelerate the airplane and, once moving, the power can usually be reduced. Air resistance, ground friction and wheel brakes will slow the airplane. Do not use power against brakes.

Hard braking, especially in a tailwheel airplane, may cause it to nose-over. Braking a tailwheeler may destabilize it directionally—the CG (because of inertia) will try to move ahead of the main wheels on which the brakes are being applied. In a nosewheel (tricycle landing gear), airplane braking will not cause the airplane to yaw.

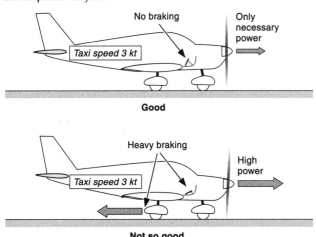

Figure 10-35. Avoid using power against brakes

Taxiing in a Strong Wind

When taxiing, you should hold the flight controls in a position to avoid either the tail or a wing being lifted by a strong wind.

When taxiing into a strong **headwind,** hold the control wheel either neutral or back. This holds the elevator neutral or up, and the tail down, and takes the load off the nosewheel. For a tricycle-gear airplane, it is better to hold the control wheel neutral (elevator neutral) so that the weight carried by the nosewheel is neither too little (causing steering difficulties) nor too much. For a tailwheeler, it is better to hold the control wheel back (elevator up), holding the tailwheel firmly on the ground.

When taxiing with a strong **tailwind,** hold the control wheel forward to move the elevator down. This stops the wind lifting the tailplane from behind.

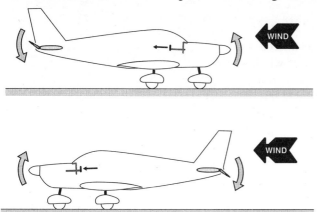

Figure 10-36. Taxi into the wind with the control wheel neutral or back, and taxi downwind with the control wheel forward

A **crosswind** will try to weathercock the airplane into the wind because of the large keel surfaces behind the main wheels. This weathercocking tendency is greater in tailwheel airplanes than in those with a nosewheel.

The rudder pedals, especially if nosewheel steering is fitted, should provide adequate directional control to steer a straight path even in a strong crosswind, but, if not, use differential braking to assist. The weathercocking tendency caused by a crosswind also makes is easier to turn the airplane upwind and harder to turn it downwind.

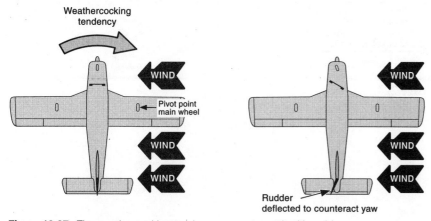

Figure 10-37. The weathercocking tendency—counteract it with rudder (and differential braking if necessary)

To avoid a **quartering headwind** from lifting the upwind wing, raise its aileron by moving the control wheel or control column into the wind. This also applies for a direct crosswind—hold the control wheel into the wind.

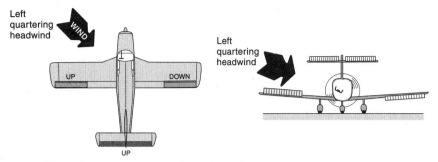

Figure 10-38. Taxiing with a left-quartering headwind

To avoid a **quartering tailwind** lifting the upwind wing, lower its aileron, so that the wind cannot get under it, by moving the control wheel out-of-wind. A quartering tailwind from behind the airplane and to one side is the most difficult and hazardous taxiing condition. Hold the control wheel forward and out-of-wind, and maintain directional control with the rudder pedals, using differential toe brake when necessary. Avoid any sudden braking or any sudden power increases.

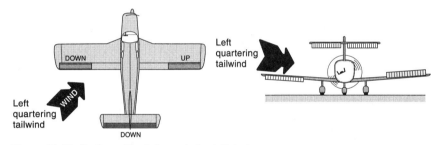

Figure 10-39. Taxiing with a left-quartering tailwind

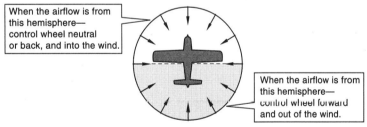

Figure 10-40. Summary of the use of controls when taxiing in windy conditions

✍ Now complete **Review 10, Part (f)** on page 224.

✍ Review 10

Takeoff and Landing Performance

Part (a)

For questions 1–4, refer to Figure 10-6 on page 200.

1. A 20 knot wind at 30° off the runway heading gives a (0/ 5/10) knot crosswind component.

   ➤ 10 knots

2. What is the crosswind component for a landing on Runway 18 if the tower reports the wind as 220° at 30 knots?
   (a) 19 knots.
   (b) 23 knots.
   (c) 30 knots.

   ➤ (a)

3. In crosswind conditions, the headwind or tailwind component (should/need not) be applied when calculating the takeoff or landing distances.

   ➤ should

4. Your airplane has a crosswind limit of 12 knots. What is the maximum wind strength you can tolerate from 30° off the runway direction (such as runway 18 with the wind from 150°)? What headwind component would this wind give you?

   ➤ 25 knots, headwind component 22 knots

For questions 5–16, refer to Figure 10-11 on page 203.

5. As pressure altitude increases, takeoff distance (increases/decreases/stays the same).

   ➤ increases

6. What effect does an uphill runway slope have on takeoff performance?
   (a) It increases takeoff speed.
   (b) It increases takeoff distance.
   (c) It decreases takeoff distance.

   ➤ (b)

7. As headwind component increases, takeoff distance (increases/decreases/stays the same).

   ➤ decreases

8. A greater headwind component will (increase/decrease/ not affect) the indicated airspeeds at which you should liftoff and reach 50 feet. At the point of liftoff, the groundspeed of the airplane will be (higher/lower/the same) compared with calm wind conditions.

   ➤ not affect, lower

9. Takeoff distance is measured from the start point on the runway to the point where the airplane reaches (0/50/ 100/500) feet above the runway.

   ➤ 50 feet

10. The takeoff distance performance graph is for a takeoff with a flaps setting of _____ .

    ➤ flaps up

11. The maximum pressure altitude allowed for in this graph is _____ feet. The maximum takeoff weight for this airplane is _____ pounds.

    ➤ 10,000 feet, 2,950 pounds

12. What is the liftoff speed and the takeoff speed at 50 feet if the takeoff weight is 2,400 pounds? Answer in knots.

    ➤ 61 KIAS, 66 KIAS

13. What is ISA (standard) temperature at 10,000 feet? Answer in degrees Celsius and degrees Fahrenheit.

    ➤ – 5°C, 23°F

14. True outside air temperature (OAT) 100°F, pressure altitude 2,000 feet, takeoff weight 2,750 pounds, headwind component calm. Determine the total distance for a takeoff to clear a 50-foot obstacle and the ground roll distance under the following conditions. What are the takeoff speeds?

    ➤ Takeoff distance to 50 feet is 1,800 feet, ground roll is 1,100 feet, liftoff at 64 KIAS, reach 50 feet at takeoff speed 70 KIAS

15. Conditions are standard temperature, pressure altitude 4,000 feet, takeoff weight 2,800 pounds, headwind component calm. Determine takeoff distance, ground roll, liftoff speed, speed at 50 feet, and OAT in both °C and °F.

    ➤ 1,750 feet, 1,050 feet, 64 KIAS, 70 KIAS, 7°C and 46°F

16. Determine the approximate ground roll distance required for takeoff.
    OAT ....90°F
    Pressure altitude ....2,000 feet
    Takeoff weight...................................2,500 pounds
    Headwind component........................20 knots
    (a) 650 feet.
    (b) 850 feet.
    (c) 1,000 feet.

    ➤ (a)

Part (b)

For questions 1 to 4 refer to Figure 10-19 on page 208.

1. The landing performance chart provided is for an approach with flaps (up/down).

➤ down

2. Conditions are OAT 90°F, pressure altitude 4,000 feet, weight 2,800 pounds, tailwind 10 knots.
   What is the landing distance from over a 50-foot obstacle, the expected ground roll, and the approach speed at 50 feet?

➤ 2,750 feet, 1,900 feet, 68 KIAS

3. Determine the total distance required to land.
   OAT ....90°F
   Pressure altitude ....3,000 feet
   Takeoff weight....................................2,900 pounds
   Headwind component..........................10 knots
   Obstacle ....50 feet
   (a) 1,450 feet
   (b) 1,550 feet
   (c) 1,725 feet

➤ (c)

4. Determine the approximate distance required to land.
   OAT ....32°F
   Pressure altitude ....8,000 feet
   Takeoff weight....................................2,600 pounds
   Headwind component..........................20 knots
   Obstacle ....50 feet
   (a) 850 feet.
   (b) 1,440 feet.
   (c) 1,750 feet.

➤ (b)

For questions 5 to 11 refer to Figure 10-20 on page 209.

5. The landing distance performance table provided is for a landing made with flaps setting _____°.

➤ 40°

6. Conditions are sea level, standard temperature (59°F), headwind 4 knots.
   What is the total landing distance over a 50-foot obstacle, and the approximate ground roll?

➤ 968 feet (1,075 reduced by 10% = 1,075 × 0.9 = 967.5), 401 feet (445 reduced by 10% = 445 × 0.9 = 400.5)

7. Conditions are elevation 2,500 feet, 48°F, headwind 8 knots.
   What is the total landing distance over a 50-foot obstacle, and the approximate ground roll?

➤ 908 feet (1,135 × 0.8), 376 feet (470 × 0.8)

8. Conditions are pressure altitude 3,750 feet, headwind 12 knots, temperature standard.
   What is the total landing distance over a 50-foot obstacle, and the approximate ground roll?

➤ 815 feet (3,750 feet is halfway between 2,500 feet and 5,000 feet, so distance is halfway between 1,135 and 1,195, i.e. 1,135 + $\frac{1}{2}$ of 60 = 1,135 + 30 = 1,165, multiplied by 0.7 to allow for 12 knots HWC = 815), 338 feet (470 + $\frac{1}{2}$ of 25 = 470 + 12.5 = 482.5, multiplied by 0.7 to allow for 12 knots HWC = 338)

9. Conditions are pressure altitude 1,250 feet, headwind 12 knots, temperature 55°F, dry grass runway.
   What is the total landing distance over a 50-foot obstacle, and the approximate ground roll?

➤ 929 feet (pressure altitude correction 1,075 + $\frac{1}{2}$ of 60 = 1,075 + 30 = 1,105, wind correction 1,105 × 0.7 = 774, dry grass runway correction—add 20% of 774 = 774 + 155 = 929)
   476 feet (pressure alt. correction 445 + $\frac{1}{2}$ of 25 = 445 + 13 = 458, wind correction 458 × 0.7 = 321, dry grass runway correction = 321 + 20% of 774 = 321 + 155 = 476)

10. Determine the approximate distance required to land over a 50-foot obstacle.
    Pressure altitude .... 7,500 feet
    Headwind component .... 8 knots
    Temperature .... Standard
    Runway .... Dry grass
    (a) 1,004 feet.
    (b) 1,205 feet.
    (c) 1,506 feet.

➤ (b)

11. Determine the approximate distance required to land over a 50-foot obstacle.
    Pressure altitude .... 5,000 feet
    Headwind component .... 8 knots
    Temperature .... 41°F
    Runway .... Hard surface
    (a) 837 feet.
    (b) 956 feet.
    (c) 1,076 feet.

➤ (b)

Part (c)

1. The static air pressure beneath a wing is (greater than/less than) the static air pressure above the wing. The air beneath a wing of an airplane in flight tends to leak around the wingtip and into the lower static pressure area above the wing. This leaves a trail of invisible _____ behind which is the cause of _____ .

➤ greater than, wingtip vortices, wake turbulence

2. Wingtip vortices tend to drift _____ and _____ .

➤ down and outward

3. The greatest vortex strength occurs when the generating aircraft is:
   (a) light, dirty (flaps down), and fast.
   (b) heavy, dirty, and fast.
   (c) heavy, clean (flaps up), and slow.

➤ (c)

4. Wake turbulence is more likely to be encountered (above/below/on) the flight path of the large airplane generating the turbulence.

➤ below

5. When you are departing behind a heavy airplane, you should avoid its wake turbulence by maneuvering your airplane (above/below) and (upwind/downwind) of its flight path.

➤ above, upwind

6. Choose the correct statement regarding wake turbulence.
   (a) Vortex generation begins with the initiation of the takeoff roll.
   (b) The primary hazard is loss of control because of induced roll.
   (c) The greatest vortex strength is produced when the generating airplane is heavy, clean and fast.

➤ (b)

7. The wind condition that requires maximum caution when avoiding wake turbulence on landing is a:
   (a) light, quartering headwind.
   (b) light, quartering tailwind.
   (c) strong headwind.

➤ (b)

8. A heavy jet airplane has landed on the runway you intend to use for takeoff. There is a light headwind blowing. You should become airborne (at/before/beyond) its touchdown point.

➤ beyond

9. Which procedure should you follow to avoid wake turbulence if a large jet crosses your course from left to right approximately 1 mile ahead and at your altitude?
   (a) Make sure you are slightly above the path of the jet.
   (b) Slow your airspeed to V_A and maintain altitude and course.
   (c) Make sure you are slightly below the path of the jet and perpendicular to the course.

➤ (a)

10. Vortices created by a helicopter:
    (a) only descend downward in the propwash.
    (b) do not exist.
    (c) trail behind it and descend gradually, like from fixed-wing aircraft.

➤ (c)

11. During a takeoff made behind a departing large jet airplane, the pilot can minimize the hazard of wingtip vortices by _____ .

➤ being airborne prior to reaching the jet's flight path until able to turn clear of its wake.

Part (d)

1. What is ground effect?
   (a) The result of the interference of the surface of the earth with the airflow patterns about an airplane.
   (b) The result of an alteration in airflow patterns increasing induced drag about the wings of an airplane.
   (c) The result of the disruption of the airflow patterns about the wings of an airplane to the point where the wings will no longer support the airplane in flight.

➤ (a)

2. An airplane leaving the ground will:
   (a) experience a reduction in ground friction and require a slight power reduction.
   (b) experience an increase in induced drag.
   (c) require a lower angle-of-attack to maintain the same lift coefficient.

➤ (b)

3. If the same angle-of-attack is maintained in ground effect as when out of ground effect, lift will:
   (a) increase, and induced drag will decrease.
   (b) decrease, and parasite drag will increase.
   (c) increase, and induced drag will increase.

➤ (a)

4. After climbing out of ground effect immediately after takeoff, the induced drag will (increase/decrease/stay the same), leading to (increased/decreased/the same) performance capability.

➤ increase, decreased

5. Floating during a landing can be caused by ground effect when within (1/2/3) wingspans height above the ground.

➤ 1

6. Ground effect is most likely to result in which problem?
   (a) Settling to the surface abruptly during landing.
   (b) Becoming airborne before reaching recommended takeoff speed.
   (c) Inability to get airborne even though airspeed is sufficient for normal takeoff needs.

➤ (b)

Part (e)

1. Any change in the wind speed and/or the wind direction as you move from one point to another is called a

   _____ .

➤ windshear

2. The effect of a windshear that causes an airplane to fly above the desired flight path and/or to increase its speed is called (over/under)shoot effect.

➤ overshoot effect

3. If the initial effect of a windshear is reversed as the airplane travels further along its flight path (say on approach to land), then the overall influence of the windshear on the airplane is called a windshear _____ effect.

➤ windshear reversal effect

4. A sudden decrease in headwind will cause the airplane to briefly show a (gain/loss) of airspeed equal to the decrease in wind velocity. On approach to land, this could be (more/less) dangerous than an increase in headwind.

➤ loss, more

5. Which type of approach and landing is recommended during gusty wind conditions?
   (a) A power-on approach and power-on landing.
   (b) A power-off approach and power-on landing.
   (c) A power-on approach and power-off landing.

➤ (a)

6. When turbulence is encountered during the approach to a landing, what action is recommended and for what primary reason?
   (a) Increase the airspeed slightly above normal approach speed to attain more positive control.
   (b) Decrease the airspeed slightly below normal approach speed to avoid overstressing the airplane.
   (c) Increase the airspeed slightly above normal approach speed to penetrate the turbulence as quickly as possible.

➤ (a)

7. A proper crosswind landing on a runway requires that, at the moment of touchdown, the:
   (a) direction of motion of the airplane and its lateral axis be perpendicular to the runway.
   (b) direction of motion of the airplane and its longitudinal axis be parallel to the runway.
   (c) downwind wing be lowered sufficiently to eliminate the tendency for the airplane to drift.

➤ (b)

Part (f)

1. When taxiing a tricycle-gear airplane in a headwind, you should hold the control column (forward/back/neutral) so that the nosewheel does not carry too much or too little weight.

➤ neutral

2. When taxiing a tricycle-gear airplane in a strong headwind, holding the control column back may tend to put (too much/too little) weight on the nosewheel.

➤ too little

3. Which wind condition would be most critical when taxiing a nosewheel equipped airplane?
   (a) Quartering tailwind.
   (b) Direct crosswind.
   (c) Quartering headwind.

➤ (a)

4. When taxiing with strong quartering tailwinds, which aileron positions should be used?
   (a) Aileron down on the downwind side.
   (b) Ailerons neutral.
   (c) Aileron down on the side from which the wind is blowing.

➤ (c)

5. How should the flight controls be held while taxiing a tricycle-gear equipped airplane into a left quartering headwind?
   (a) Left aileron up, elevator neutral.
   (b) Left aileron down, elevator neutral.
   (c) Left aileron up, elevator down.

➤ (a)

6. Refer to Figure 10-41, area C. How should the flight controls be held while taxiing a tricycle-gear equipped airplane with a left quartering tailwind?

   (a) Left aileron up, elevator neutral.

   (b) Left aileron down, elevator down.

   (c) Left aileron up, elevator down.

➤ (b)

7. Refer to Figure 10-41, area B. How should the flight controls be held while taxiing a tailwheel airplane into a right quartering headwind?

   (a) Right aileron up, elevator up.

   (b) Right aileron down, elevator neutral.

   (c) Right aileron up, elevator down.

➤ (a)

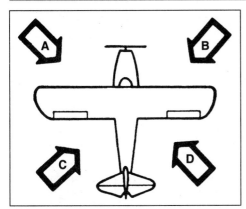

Figure 10-41.

Commercial Review

Commercial Part (a)

For questions 1–6 refer to Figure 10-42.

1. The takeoff performance graph provided is only for takeoff with a flap setting of _____ °.

➤ 20°

2. The ground roll may be calculated by taking _____ % of the takeoff distance to 50 feet found on the performance graph. Therefore if the takeoff distance was 2,000 feet, the ground roll would be _____ feet.

➤ 73%, 1,460 feet

3. What is the liftoff speed and takeoff speed at 50 feet for a takeoff weight of 3,100 pounds?

➤ 64 KIAS, 64 KIAS

4. OAT 75°F, pressure altitude 6,000 feet, takeoff weight 2,900 pounds, 20-knot headwind component. Determine the total distance required for a takeoff to clear a 50-foot obstacle for the situation given. What is the ground roll distance? What is the liftoff speed and the required takeoff speed at 50 feet?

➤ 1,400 feet, 1,020 feet, 62 KIAS, 62 KIAS.

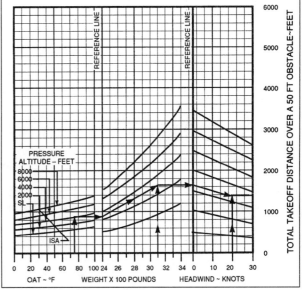

ASSOCIATED CONDITIONS:

POWER	TAKEOFF POWER SET BEFORE BRAKE RELEASE
FLAPS	20°
RUNWAY	PAVED, LEVEL, DRY SURFACE
TAKEOFF SPEED	IAS AS TABULATED

NOTE: GROUND ROLL IS APPROX. 73% OF TOTAL TAKEOFF DISTANCE OVER A 50 FT OBSTACLE

EXAMPLE:

OAT	75 °F
PRESSURE ALTITUDE	4000 FT
TAKEOFF WEIGHT	3100 LB
HEADWIND	20 KNOTS
TOTAL TAKEOFF DISTANCE OVER A 50 FT OBSTACLE	1350 FT
GROUND ROLL (73% OF 1350)	986 FT
IAS TAKEOFF SPEED LIFT-OFF	74 MPH
AT 50 FT	74 MPH

WEIGHT POUNDS	IAS TAKEOFF SPEED (ASSUMES ZERO INSTR. ERROR)			
	LIFT-OFF		50 FEET	
	MPH	KNOTS	MPH	KNOTS
3400	77	67	77	67
3200	75	65	75	65
3000	72	63	72	63
2800	69	60	69	60
2600	66	57	66	57
2400	63	55	63	55

Figure 10-42. Obstacle takeoff graph

5. Given:

   Temperature .... 30°F

   Pressure altitude .... 6,000 feet

   Weight .... 3,300 pounds

   Headwind .... 20 knots

   What is the total takeoff distance over a 50-foot obstacle?

   (a) 1,100 feet.

   (b) 1,300 feet.

   (c) 1,500 feet.

➤ (c)

6. Given:

Temperature................................100°F
Pressure altitude ....4,000 feet
Weight..3,200 pounds
Headwind......................................Calm

What is the ground roll required for takeoff over a 50-foot obstacle?

(a) 1,180 feet.

(b) 1,450 feet.

(c) 1,850 feet.

➤ (b) (73% of takeoff distance 2,000 feet)

Commercial Part (b)

For questions 1–5 refer to Figure 10-43.

1. The landing distance chart provided is for an approach made with flaps (up/down).

➤ down

2. At maximum weight the approach speed is _____ KIAS.

➤ 78 KIAS

3. This chart applies to what type of runway surface?

➤ a paved, level dry surface

4. Given:

Temperature ....50°F
Pressure altitude ....Sea level
Weight ....3,000 pounds
Headwind ....10 knots

Determine the approximate ground roll.

(a) 425 feet.

(b) 636 feet.

(c) 836 feet.

➤ (b) (53% of landing distance 1,200 feet)

5. Given:

Temperature ....80°F
Pressure altitude ....4,000 feet
Weight ....2,800 pounds
Headwind ....24 knots

What is the total landing distance over a 50-foot obstacle?

(a) 1,125 feet.

(b) 1,250 feet.

(c) 1,325 feet.

➤ (a)

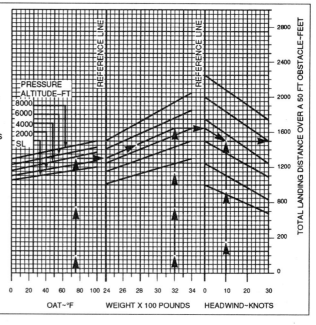

ASSOCIATED CONDITIONS:

POWER — AS REQUIRED TO MAINTAIN 800 FT/MIN DESCENT ON APPROACH

FLAPS — DOWN

RUNWAY — PAVED, LEVEL, DRY SURFACE

APPROACH SPEED — IAS A TABULATED

NOTE: GROUND ROLL IS APPROX. 53% OF TOTAL LANDING DISTANCE OVER A 50 FT OBSTACLE.

EXAMPLE:

OAT	75 °F
PRESSURE ALTITUDE	4000 FT
LANDING WEIGHT	3200 LB
HEADWIND	10 KNOTS
TOTAL LANDING DISTANCE OVER A 50 FT OBSTACLE	1475 FT
GROUND ROLL (53% OF 1475)	782 FT
IAS APPROACH SPEED	87 MPH IAS

WEIGHT POUNDS	IAS APPROACH SPEED (ASSUMES ZERO INSTR. ERROR)	
	MPH	KNOTS
3400	90	78
3200	87	76
3000	84	73
2800	81	70
2600	78	68
2400	75	65

OAT~°F   WEIGHT X 100 POUNDS   HEADWIND~KNOTS

Figure 10-43. Normal landing chart

En Route Performance 11

En route performance is an important consideration, especially in high-performance airplanes. The incorrect selection of power settings, cruise speed and cruise altitudes can significantly affect the efficiency and economics of operating your airplane.

While you are required to extract only cruise performance data for the Private Pilot FAA Knowledge Exam, we recommend that, at some stage, you read through the commercial pilot section of this chapter which includes climb performance data, as well as different presentations of cruise performance data. The additional knowledge gained will lead to improved practical operation of your airplane.

Cruise Altitude and Power Setting

Choice of **cruise altitude** depends on:

- distance to destination;
- terrain;
- airplane gross weight;
- weather (visibility and cloud base);
- wind at various altitudes; and
- ATC and airspace requirements.

To level off at cruise altitude leave climb power set until the airplane has accelerated to the desired cruise speed in level flight. The power is then reduced to **cruise power,** and the mixture is *leaned* as recommended in the Pilot's Operating Handbook.

The cruise speed maintained is determined by the power set. Cruise power settings are usually specified as a percentage of **maximum continuous power (MCP).** Typical cruise figures are in the range 55–75% MCP (or 55–75% BHP, where BHP means brake horsepower). It is possible, of course, to set higher power for the cruise, even 100% MCP as the name maximum continuous power implies, but the consequences will be very high fuel consumption and increased engine wear.

After cruise power is set, you should lean the mixture according to the procedures in the Pilot's Operating Handbook. Most engine manufacturers recommend that you lean the mixture only when the power setting is 75% MCP or less—full rich is used at higher power settings. Usually you would lean for *best power,* so that there is a slight excess of fuel compared with the chemically correct mixture. This will give the best speed at that power setting, and the small amount of excess fuel will help cool the cylinders. Correct leaning procedure is important for long engine life.

From a performance point of view, the engine–propeller combination is most efficient at the altitude where the desired percentage power is obtained with the throttle fully open, known as the full throttle height.

> The cruise speed maintained is determined by the power set.

> Lean the mixture for best fuel consumption.

Indicated and Outside Air Temperature

The temperature shown in the cockpit on the outside air temperature gauge is the **indicated outside air temperature (IOAT).** As the airspeed increases, the air moving past the outside air temperature probe will be compressed. When air is compressed, it warms, and this will cause a slight increase in the temperature detected and displayed in the cockpit.

As airspeed increases the IOAT will be slightly higher than the actual outside air temperature.

The actual temperature of the outside air is called the **outside air temperature (OAT)** and can be obtained from a weather forecast or report. When operating high-speed airplanes a correction factor can be applied to the IOAT to obtain OAT.

Although you will find both IOAT and OAT in performance tables and graphs, in the Private and Commercial Knowledge Exams, it is normal to find a simple reference to "temperature" in the question setting.

Presentation of Performance Data

Manufacturers present performance data in different ways, the most common being tables and graphs. The following examples are typical of the data for Piper and Cessna airplanes.

Piper Warrior Performance Data

To use the graph in Figure 11-1, simply enter with the temperature and pressure altitude, move across to the desired percentage power and then down to find the cruise TAS.

Note: On the graph in Figure 11-1, at higher cruise altitudes, the maximum power available in terms of percentage MCP is limited by the full throttle position.

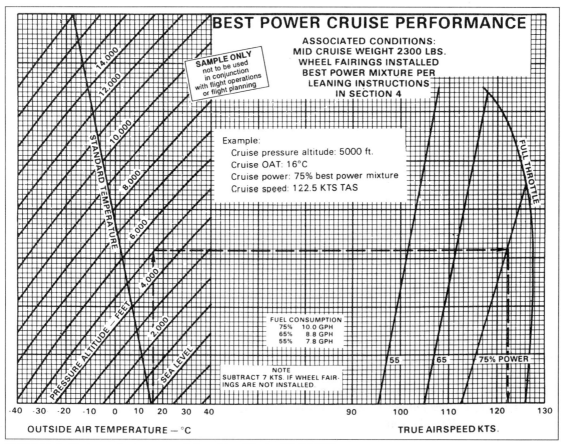

Figure 11-1. Cruise performance graph for a Piper Warrior (PA-28-161)

Cessna 172 Performance Data

To use the table in Figure 11-2, simply extract the figures. For instance, at 4,000 feet pressure altitude at standard temperature and with 2,400 rpm set, you would be cruising at 65% BHP, and would achieve 108 knots true air speed (KTAS) with a fuel flow 7.3 gph.

SECTION 5
PERFORMANCE

CESSNA
MODEL 172P

CRUISE PERFORMANCE

SAMPLE ONLY
not to be used
in conjunction
with flight operations
or flight planning

CONDITIONS:
2400 Pounds
Recommended Lean Mixture (See Section 4, Cruise)

NOTE:
Cruise speeds are shown for an airplane equipped with speed fairings which increase the speeds by approximately two knots.

PRESSURE ALTITUDE FT	RPM	20°C BELOW STANDARD TEMP			STANDARD TEMPERATURE			20°C ABOVE STANDARD TEMP		
		% BHP	KTAS	GPH	% BHP	KTAS	GPH	% BHP	KTAS	GPH
2000	2500	- - -	- - -	- - -	76	114	8.5	72	114	8.1
	2400	72	110	8.1	69	109	7.7	65	108	7.3
	2300	65	104	7.3	62	103	6.9	59	102	6.6
	2200	58	99	6.6	55	97	6.3	53	96	6.1
	2100	52	92	6.0	50	91	5.8	48	89	5.7
4000	2550	- - -	- - -	- - -	76	117	8.5	72	116	8.1
	2500	77	115	8.6	73	114	8.1	69	113	7.7
	2400	69	109	7.8	65	108	7.3	62	107	7.0
	2300	62	104	7.0	59	102	6.6	57	101	6.4
	2200	56	98	6.3	54	96	6.1	51	94	5.9
	2100	51	91	5.8	48	89	5.7	47	88	5.5
6000	2600	- - -	- - -	- - -	77	119	8.6	72	118	8.1
	2500	73	114	8.2	69	113	7.8	66	112	7.4
	2400	66	108	7.4	63	107	7.0	60	106	6.7
	2300	60	103	6.7	57	101	6.4	55	99	6.2
	2200	54	96	6.1	52	95	5.9	50	92	5.8
	2100	49	90	5.7	47	88	5.5	46	86	5.5
8000	2650	- - -	- - -	- - -	77	121	8.6	73	120	8.1
	2600	77	119	8.7	73	118	8.2	69	117	7.8
	2500	70	113	7.8	66	112	7.4	63	111	7.1
	2400	63	108	7.1	60	106	6.7	58	104	6.5
	2300	57	101	6.4	55	100	6.2	53	97	6.0
	2200	52	95	6.0	50	93	5.8	49	91	5.7
10,000	2600	74	118	8.3	70	117	7.8	66	115	7.4
	2500	67	112	7.5	64	111	7.1	61	109	6.8
	2400	61	106	6.8	58	105	6.5	56	102	6.3
	2300	55	100	6.3	53	98	6.0	51	96	5.9
	2200	50	93	5.8	49	91	5.7	47	89	5.6
12,000	2550	67	114	7.5	64	112	7.1	61	111	6.9
	2500	64	111	7.2	61	109	6.8	59	107	6.6
	2400	59	105	6.6	56	103	6.3	54	100	6.1
	2300	53	98	6.1	51	96	5.9	50	94	5.8

Figure 11-2. Cruise performance table for a Cessna 172

Note: All performance graphs and tables will have various notes printed on them, giving details of the conditions which apply and information governing the use of the data. You should pay particular attention to these notes, and be aware that they will be different for each graph or table.

Performance Data used for the Private Pilot Knowledge Exam

The table of **cruise power settings** used in the Private Pilot Knowledge Exam is shown in Figure 11-3. It is based on an airplane gross weight of 2,800 pounds with 65% maximum continuous power set, or full throttle at higher altitudes.

CRUISE POWER SETTINGS
65% MAXIMUM CONTINUOUS POWER (OR FULL THROTTLE)
2800 POUNDS

SAMPLE ONLY not to be used in conjunction with flight operations or flight planning

| PRESS ALT. | ISA –20 °C (–36 °F) | | | | | | | | STANDARD DAY (ISA) | | | | | | | | ISA +20 °C (+36 °F) | | | | | | | |
| | IOAT | | ENGINE SPEED | MAN. PRESS | FUEL FLOW PER ENGINE | | TAS | | IOAT | | ENGINE SPEED | MAN. PRESS | FUEL FLOW PER ENGINE | | TAS | | IOAT | | ENGINE SPEED | MAN. PRESS | FUEL FLOW PER ENGINE | | TAS | |
FEET	°F	°C	RPM	IN HG	PSI	GPH	KTS	MPH	°F	°C	RPM	IN HG	PSI	GPH	KTS	MPH	°F	°C	RPM	IN HG	PSI	GPH	KTS	MPH
SL	27	-3	2450	20.7	6.6	11.5	147	169	63	17	2450	21.2	6.6	11.5	150	173	99	37	2450	21.8	6.6	11.5	153	176
2000	19	-7	2450	20.4	6.6	11.5	149	171	55	13	2450	21.0	6.6	11.5	153	176	91	33	2450	21.5	6.6	11.5	156	180
4000	12	-11	2450	20.1	6.6	11.5	152	175	48	9	2450	20.7	6.6	11.5	156	180	84	29	2450	21.3	6.6	11.5	159	183
6000	5	-15	2450	19.8	6.6	11.5	155	178	41	5	2450	20.4	6.6	11.5	158	182	79	26	2450	21.0	6.6	11.5	161	185
8000	-2	-19	2450	19.5	6.6	11.5	157	181	36	2	2450	20.2	6.6	11.5	161	185	72	22	2450	20.8	6.6	11.5	164	189
10000	-8	-22	2450	19.2	6.6	11.5	160	184	28	-2	2450	19.9	6.6	11.5	163	188	64	18	2450	20.3	6.5	11.4	166	191
12000	-15	-26	2450	18.8	6.4	11.3	162	186	21	-6	2450	18.8	6.1	10.9	163	188	57	14	2450	18.8	5.9	10.6	163	188
14000	-22	-30	2450	17.4	5.8	10.5	159	183	14	-10	2450	17.4	5.6	10.1	160	184	50	10	2450	17.4	5.4	9.8	160	184
16000	-29	-34	2450	16.1	5.3	9.7	156	180	7	-14	2450	16.1	5.1	9.4	156	180	43	6	2450	16.1	4.9	9.1	155	178

NOTES: 1. Full throttle manifold pressure settings are approximate.
            2. Shaded area represents operation with full throttle.

Notice that maximum TAS for a given percentage MCP occurs at full throttle altitude.

Figure 11-3. Airplane power setting table used in the Private Knowledge Exam

Enter this table on the left-hand side with **pressure altitude,** and **temperature** using either ISA deviation at the top of the table when planning, or with IOAT when in flight.

Note: You will see that the IOAT values are slightly higher than the OAT. For instance at sea level, the ISA temperature is +15°C, whereas the IOAT for a TAS of 150 knots is +17°C.

Now you can find:

• **power setting** to achieve 65% MCP in terms of **rpm** and **manifold pressure (MP);**

• **fuel flow** in gallons per hour (gph), with the expected fuel pressure gauge indication in pounds per square inch (psi); and

• **true airspeed (TAS)** in knots or in miles per hour (mph).

For example, at 4,000 feet pressure altitude with standard temperature (ISA), you can extract:

(a) power setting 2,450 rpm, MP 20.7 in. Hg;

(b) fuel flow 11.5 gph (expected fuel pressure 6.6 psi); and

(c) TAS 156 knots (or 180 mph).

Interpolation

Often the figures you require lie somewhere between the tabulated figures, and so you must interpolate.

Example 1. Refer to Figure 11-3. The IOAT at 6,000 ft is –5°C, what is the TAS?

From the table in the margin, you can see that at 6,000 ft, an IOAT of –15°C gives a TAS of 155 knots. Since –5°C is halfway between –15 and +5°C, the TAS is $155 + \left(\frac{158-155}{2}\right) = 155 + 1.5 = 156.5$ knots.

Press Alt	IOAT °C	TAS kt	IOAT °C	TAS kt
6,000	–15	155	+5	158

Fuel Consumption

Once the flight distance has been measured and the TAS and fuel flow found from the performance graph or chart, the fuel consumption for the flight can be calculated.

- First find the flight time by dividing the flight distance by the TAS. For example, to cover 240 nautical miles (nm) at 90 KTAS will take $^{240}\!/_{90} = 2.67$ hours.

- Find the fuel consumption by multiplying the flight time by the fuel flow. For example, if the fuel flow was 6.6 gph over 2.67 hours the fuel consumption would be $6.6 \times 2.67 = 17.6$ gallons.

Note: These calculations can be done either on an electronic calculator or on a flight computer (*see* Chapter 11).

Example 2. Referring to Figure 11-13, what is the expected fuel consumption for a 420 nm flight in no-wind conditions at 65% MCP under the following conditions? Specify the power settings.

Pressure altitude . . . . 6,000 feet

Forecast temperature . . . . –15°C

Wind. . . . . calm

Answer.

First find which ISA column to use.

ISA at 6,000 feet is $[15 - (6 \times 2)] = 3$°C. Therefore –15°C is equivalent to ISA–18°C. This is closest to ISA–20°C, so we can extract:

- power setting: 2,450 rpm, MP 19.8 in. Hg;

- TAS 155 knots;

- 11.5 gph.

Step 1. Time calculation: Time $= \frac{\text{distance}}{\text{TAS}} = \frac{420}{155} = 2.71$ hours.

Step 2. Fuel calculation: Fuel $=$ time $\times$ fuel flow $= 2.71 \times 11.5 = 31.2$ gallons.

Effect of Wind in Cruise

Normally in the cruise there is a wind that will affect the distance covered over the ground. If there is a headwind, the air in which the airplane is flying will be moving backward over the ground and therefore in a given time the ground distance covered, measured in ground nautical miles (gnm), will reduce. Conversely a tailwind will increase the ground distance covered in a set time. However the distance flown through the air, measured in air nautical miles (anm), will remain the same.

Because the effect of wind will alter the time to cover a set ground distance, such as between two airports, it will also affect the amount of fuel required. A strong headwind will markedly increase your flight time and fuel consumption, a hazardous situation if you had planned your fuel requirements on no wind.

Example 3. Using the information in Example 2, what will be the flight time and fuel consumption if there is now a 30-knot headwind?

Answer.

Step 1. Time $= \dfrac{\text{ground distance}}{\text{groundspeed}} = \dfrac{420}{(\text{KTAS} - \text{headwind})} = \dfrac{420}{(155 - 30)} = 3.36$ hours

Step 2. Fuel = time × fuel flow = $3.36 \times 11.5 = 38.7$ gallons.

✍ Now complete **Review 11, Part (a)** on page 238.

For Aspiring Commercial Pilots

The Commercial Pilot Knowledge Exam requires that you have a knowledge of climb performance as well as cruise performance, and that you can apply some basic navigation and flight planning knowledge, such as wind effect increasing or decreasing your groundspeed.

Climb Performance

There are three types of climb that you may use at the start of a cross-country flight:

1. The **maximum angle climb** at speed V_X allows you to gain the maximum altitude in the shortest *distance*. It is normally used only immediately after the takeoff to provide a steep climb-out gradient over any obstacles, after which the airplane nose is lowered slightly and the airspeed allowed to increase to normal climb speed. Since this type of climb is only of short duration, no performance tables (in terms of fuel flow and distance covered) are provided.

2. The **maximum rate of climb** at speed V_Y allows you to gain the maximum altitude in the shortest *time*. This climb speed is used when you want to reach cruise altitude as quickly as possible. Performance charts or tables, such as that shown Figure 11-5, are provided, since this type of climb may be prolonged and used all the way up to cruise altitude. The important figures from a flight planning point of view are the time, fuel and distance to top of climb. A wind will not affect the time, fuel and air distance to reach the required altitude, but it will affect the *ground* distance covered.

3. The **normal climb** at the specified climb speed is somewhat faster than the maximum rate climb speed, and is sometimes called a *cruise* climb. Performance tables or charts are provided.

For all climb types the fuel required from start-up to cruise altitude will be the climb fuel plus a fuel allowance for start, taxi and takeoff.

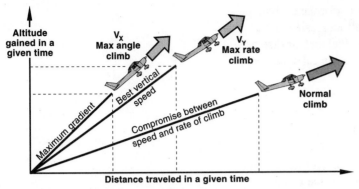

Altitude gained in a given time

V_X
Max angle climb

V_Y
Max rate climb

Best vertical speed

Compromise between speed and rate of climb

Normal climb

Maximum gradient

Distance traveled in a given time

Figure 11-4. The different types of climb

Maximum Rate of Climb

Figure 11-5 shows a maximum rate of climb performance table. To see how simple it is to use, follow this explanation.

Consider a **maximum rate climb** from a sea level airport to 8,000 feet under ISA conditions, with takeoff weight 3,700 pounds.

From the table you can read that you should climb at 2,600 rpm, 35 in. Hg MP and the fuel flow will be 162 pounds per hour (pph).

MAXIMUM RATE OF CLIMB

WEIGHT LBS	PRESS ALT FT	RATE OF CLIMB FPM	FROM SEA LEVEL		
			TIME MIN	FUEL USED POUNDS	DISTANCE NM
4000	S.L.	605	0	0	0
	4000	570	7	14	13
	8000	530	14	28	27
	12,000	485	22	44	43
	16,000	430	31	62	63
	20,000	365	41	82	87
3700	S.L.	700	0	0	0
	4000	665	6	12	11
	8000	625	12	24	23
	12,000	580	19	37	37
	16,000	525	26	52	53
	20,000	460	34	68	72
3400	S.L.	810	0	0	0
	4000	775	5	10	9
	8000	735	10	21	20
	12,000	690	16	32	31
	16,000	635	22	44	45
	20,000	565	29	57	61

CONDITIONS:
Flaps Up
Gear Up
2600 RPM
Cowl Flaps Open
Standard Temperature

NOTES:
1. Add 16 pounds of fuel for engine start, taxi and takeoff allowance.
2. Increase time, fuel and distance by 10% for each 10°C above standard temperature.
3. Distances shown are based on zero wind.

PRESS ALT	MP	PPH
S.L. TO 17,000	35	162
18,000	34	156
20,000	32	144
22,000	30	132
24,000	28	120

Figure 11-5. Climb performance table

Under standard conditions, it should take 8 minutes to climb from MSL to 8,000 feet, and you will cover 13 air nautical miles (anm). Fuel used on the climb will be 21 pounds (plus the 16 pounds for start-up, taxi and takeoff, making a total of 37 pounds used from start-up to top of climb). Initial rate of climb will be approximately 1,060 fpm, decreasing to approximately 1,020 fpm by 4,000 feet MSL, and 975 fpm as you approach 8,000 feet MSL.

If the temperature is **warmer than standard,** climb performance will be poorer (*see* Note 2), with time, fuel, and air distance all increasing. Rate of climb will be poorer. Under **ISA+10°C** conditions, time, fuel and air distance must be increased by 10% to 110% of the ISA figures—we can calculate these by multiplying the tabulated figures by 1.1 to obtain:

8 min × 1.1 = 8.8, say 9 min;

13 anm × 1.1 = 14.3 anm;

21 lb × 1.1 = 23.1 gal (+16 = 39.1 gal).

If temperature is **colder than standard,** use the tabulated figures.

Remember, a **headwind** will reduce the ground distance covered on the climb. For instance, an average 30-knot headwind acting for the estimated 9 minutes of climb would have an effect of $-30 \times \frac{9}{60} = -4.5$ nm, with 14.3 anm becoming 14.3 – 4.5 = 9.8 gnm. (This method is quicker than working out the TAS and then finding the groundspeed.) Conversely, a **tailwind** will increase the ground distance covered.

Climbing from a High-Elevation Airport

The technique for calculating a climb to cruise altitude following takeoff from a high-elevation airport is:

1. Determine the climb figures from sea level to cruise pressure altitude.
2. Subtract the climb figures for an imaginary climb from sea level to airport pressure altitude.

Example 4. Using Figure 11-5, determine the climb figures for a maximum rate climb to 12,000 feet pressure altitude where the temperature is +1°C from an airport with pressure altitude 4,000 feet. There is a 20-knot headwind on the climb. Airplane weight is 3,700 pounds.

First find the ISA deviation. At 12,000 feet, ISA = 15 – (2 × 12) = –09°C. Therefore +1°C is equivalent to ISA+10°C. A temperature correction will therefore be required.

	Time (min)	Fuel (lb)	Distance (anm)
Climb from sea level to 12,00 ft (#1)	12	33	21
Climb from sea level to 4000 ft (#2)	4	10	6
Climb from 4000 ft to 12,000 ft (#1–#2)	8	23	15
Correction for temperature deviation ISA+10°C, so increase figures by 10%, i.e. multiply by 1.1)	9 (8.8)	26 (25.3)	17 (16.5)
Startup, taxi, takeoff allowance	–	16	–
Totals	**9 min**	**42 lb**	**17 anm**
Wind effect: $-20 \times \frac{9}{60}$ =			–3
			14 gnm

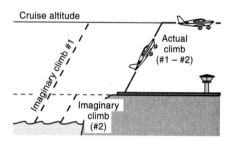

Figure 11-6. Climb to cruise altitude from a high-elevation airport

Answer.

The answer is: 9 min, 42 lb, 17 anm, 14 gnm.

Note: Fuel has been rounded-up to the next whole gallon to be on the safe side.

The Cruise or Normal Climb

Figure 11-7 shows a typical climb performance chart. To use this chart, enter with the temperature at the cruise level and read vertically up to the pressure altitude at the top of climb. Then move horizontally to cut the fuel, time and distance curved lines, and read vertically down to extract fuel, time and distance.

Next, enter with the temperature at the start of climb and read vertically to the departure pressure altitude. Then move horizontally to extract the fuel, time and distance values as before. The difference between the two sets of figures is the actual climb data. *See* the example on the chart.

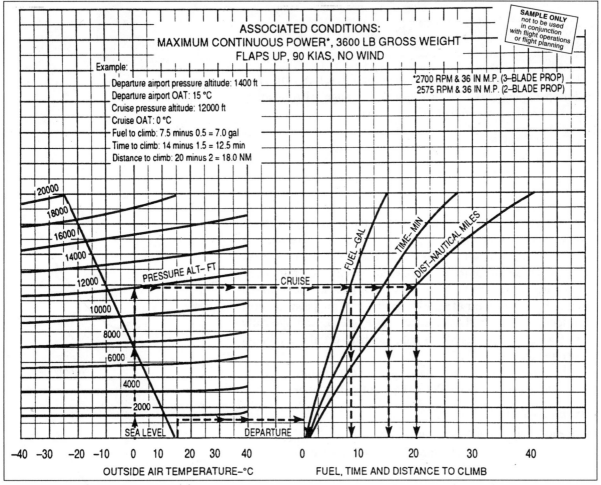

Figure 11-7. A climb performance chart

Cruise Performance

This part of the chapter looks at the cruise in greater depth. If it is some time since you read Chapter 3, we suggest that before continuing you refresh your memory on range and endurance. *See* pages 79–82.

Fuel Reserves

Fuel reserves for VFR (Visual Flight Rules) flights are specified in the Federal Aviation Regulations, Part 91. Reserve fuel is designed not to be used. It is a safety reserve, available in unplanned-for situations, such as unexpected closure of your destination airport due to a runway obstruction, or unforecast poor weather. Reserve fuel is fuel in your tanks that you should not plan on using—think of it as an emergency reserve.

The reserves specified in Part 91 are:

(a) VFR day reserve: 30 minutes at normal cruising speed; and

(b) VFR night reserve: 45 minutes at normal cruising speed.

Specific Range

Specific range is the distance traveled per unit of fuel burned. It may be expressed in various units, such as anm/pound or anm/gallon for specific air range (SAR), or gnm/pound or gnm/gallon for specific ground range (SGR).

$$\text{Specific range} = \frac{\text{nautical miles}}{\text{fuel}} = \frac{\text{nautical miles}/\text{time}}{\text{fuel}/\text{time}} = \frac{\text{airspeed}}{\text{fuel flow}}$$

$$\textbf{SAR} = \frac{\textbf{TAS}}{\textbf{fuel flow}} \quad \text{and} \quad \textbf{SGR} = \frac{\textbf{GS}}{\textbf{fuel flow}}$$

Example 5. With a given power setting, you can achieve 150 KTAS with a fuel flow of 9 gallons per hour (gph). Calculate specific air range. Also calculate specific ground range if a headwind of 30 knots exists.

$$\text{SAR} = \frac{150 \text{ KTAS}}{9 \text{ gph}} = 16.7 \text{ anm/gal.}$$

$$\text{SGR} = \frac{120 \text{ knots groundspeed}}{9 \text{ gph}} = 13.3 \text{ gnm/gal.}$$

Flying for Range

Normal cruise speed takes into account time-to-destination as well as fuel burn. However sometimes you will want to keep fuel used over a set flight distance as low as possible, which reduces fuel costs. This is achieved by flying at the correct speed for maximum range and keeping fuel and therefore weight to a minimum.

The maximum-range speed occurs where the wing is most efficient, which occurs at the airspeed for **minimum drag.** Maximum range airspeed for most airplanes is considerably slower than normal cruise speed, and typically requires about 45% MCP. As weight reduces with fuel burn-off, the maximum range airspeed also reduces.

Efficiency on the cruise requires that you *lean* the fuel/air mixture correctly according to procedures specified in the Pilot's Operating Handbook.

To achieve maximum range:

• keep airplane loaded weight to a reasonable minimum;

• fly at "full throttle" altitude if possible (throttle butterfly fully open, causing less restriction to the airflow through the carburetor);

• use the correct power setting and airspeed (usually the highest recommended "high MP/low rpm" combination for maximum engine efficiency);

• lean the mixture as recommended in the Pilot's Operating Handbook;

• avoid continuous use of carburetor heat if possible; and

• minimize drag (ensure in-trim, gear up and flaps up).

Wind Effect on Range

The maximum range airspeed in no-wind conditions was illustrated in Figure 11-8. A **tailwind** will increase the range over the ground, and this range can be further increased by flying a little slower than the no-wind maximum range airspeed, which gives the wind more time to carry the airplane further.

Conversely, a **headwind** will reduce the range over the ground, but this reduction can be minimized by flying a little faster than the no-wind maximum airspeed, giving the wind less time to act on the airplane. Typical increases or decreases in airspeed for strong wind conditions are 5%.

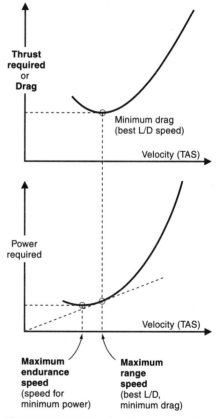

Figure 11-8. Maximum-endurance speed and maximum-range speed

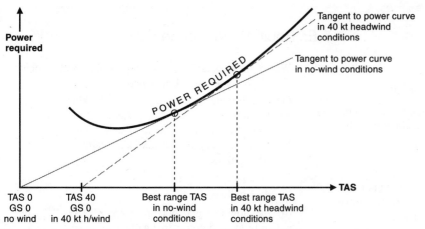

Figure 11-9. Graphical explanation of increased best-range TAS for strong winds

Whereas specific air range is air nautical miles per unit of fuel, **specific ground range (SGR)** is *ground* nautical miles per unit of fuel. Best range will be achieved at the airspeed that provides the best specific ground range—the maximum number of ground nautical miles per pound of fuel burned.

Example 6. Some typical cruise performance figures extracted from Figure 11-11 on page 240, for a particular airplane type at 6,000 feet and standard temperature are shown below. Consider the effect of an 80-knot headwind on specific ground range at these power settings.

% BHP	rpm	MP	KTAS	pph (lb per hr)	SAR (TAS/pph)	W/C	GS	SGR (GS/pph)
75% BHP	2500	24	171	95	1.80	−80	91	.96
63% BHP	2400	22	159	79	2.01	−80	79	1.00
48% BHP	2200	20	138	62	2.22	−80	58	0.94

In no-wind conditions, SAR and SGR will be the same, and best range performance in the above case is 2.22 gnm/lb, obtained at the low speed of 138 KTAS.

You can see that an 80-knot headwind has a very significant effect on specific ground range, reducing it to only 0.94 gnm/lb at speed 138 KTAS. Note that the maximum specific ground range of 1.00 gnm/lb is achieved at the higher speed of 159 KTAS in strong headwind conditions.

Flying for Endurance

Occasionally you might want to remain in flight for the longest time possible without any consideration of the distance covered, for instance when holding over a fix and waiting for an ATC clearance to proceed. The airspeed at which you would hold is known as the **best endurance airspeed.** To achieve this you need to keep the fuel flow as low as possible.

Fuel consumption of a piston engine depends on the power it produces. Therefore, for best endurance, you should select an indicated airspeed near the **minimum power speed** from the performance charts. Best endurance airspeed is slower than best range airspeed (*see* Figure 11-8).

At the appropriate endurance IAS, the power required is lowest at **low altitudes**—so, for maximum endurance in a piston-engine airplane, fly at a low (but safe) altitude at the speed for minimum power.

✍ Commercial students complete **Review 11, Commercial** on page 238.

✍ Review 11

Part (a)

For Questions 1 to 10, use Figure 11-3 on page 230.

1. What true airspeed can you expect with 65% maximum continuous power, at 8,000 feet pressure altitude, with a temperature of 20°C below standard?

➤ TAS 157 knots or 181 mph

---

2. What true airspeed can you expect with 65% maximum continuous power, at 9,500 feet pressure altitude, with a temperature of ISA −20°C? Give your answer in knots and mph.

➤ TAS 159 knots or 183 mph (Interpolate between the TAS values for 8,000 and 10,000 feet)

---

3. To achieve 65% maximum continuous power at 4,000 feet pressure altitude, with 2,450 rpm set, what would be the manifold pressure, if the temperature was ISA −20°C?

➤ 20.1 in. Hg

---

4. Determine the approximate manifold pressure setting with 2,450 rpm, to achieve 65% maximum continuous power at 7,000 feet, with a temperature of 36°F higher than standard.
    (a) 20.9 in. Hg.
    (b) 20.8 in. Hg.
    (c) 21.0 in. Hg.

➤ (a)

---

5. What fuel flow in gph can you expect cruising at 10,000 feet pressure altitude, on a standard day (ISA temperatures), with 65% maximum continuous power? What true airspeed in knots would you expect to achieve?

➤ 11.5 gph, 163 KTAS

---

6. What fuel flow in gph can you expect cruising at 11,000 feet pressure altitude, on a standard day (ISA temperatures), with 65% maximum continuous power? What true airspeed in knots would you expect to achieve?

➤ 11.5 gph, 163 KTAS

---

7. Approximately what true airspeed should a pilot expect with 65% maximum continuous power, at 9,500 feet, with a temperature of 36°F below standard?
    (a) 178 mph.
    (b) 181 mph.
    (c) 183 mph.

➤ (c)

En Route Performance

8. What is the expected fuel consumption for a 500 nautical mile flight under the following conditions?
    Pressure altitude .... 4,000 feet
    Temperature .... +29°C
    Manifold pressure .... 21.3 in. Hg
    Wind.. calm
    (a) 31.4 gallons.
    (b) 36.2 gallons.
    (c) 40.1 gallons.

➤ (b) (fuel flow 11.5 gph, 500 nm @ 159 KTAS = $^{500}/_{159}$ hr = 3.14 hr @ 11.5 gph = 36.2 gallons)

---

9. What is the expected fuel consumption for a 450 nm flight under the following conditions: 12,000 feet pressure altitude, IOAT −6°C, manifold pressure 18.8 in. Hg, and a 10-knot headwind?

➤ 32.1 gallons
    (10.9 gph, TAS 163 knots, headwind 10 knots = GS 153 knots for 450 nm = 2.94 hr @ 10.9 gph = 32.1 gal)

---

10. What is the expected fuel consumption for a 1,000 nautical mile flight under the following conditions: 8,000 feet pressure altitude, indicated temperature −19°C, manifold pressure 19.5 in. Hg, and wind calm?

➤ 73.3 gallons
    (fuel flow 11.5 gph, TAS 157 knots for 1,000 nm = $^{1,000}/_{157}$ hr = 6.37 hr @ 11.5 gph = 73.24, say 73.3 gal)

Commercial Review

1. As altitude is gained, the rate of climb will (increase/decrease/stay the same).

➤ decrease

---

2. At 6,000 feet pressure altitude, ISA+10°C is equivalent to _____ °C.

➤ +13°C
    (ISA at 6,000 feet is [15 − (2 × 6)] = 3°C, therefore ISA+10 = 13°C)

---

3. A headwind will (increase/decrease/not affect) the amount of fuel burned in the climb to a given altitude.

➤ not affect

---

4. Higher gross weights will (increase/decrease/not affect) climb performance.

➤ decrease

5. If fuel flow is 54 pounds/hr at 210 KTAS, express fuel consumption in anm/pound.

➤ 3.89 anm/pound

6. If fuel flow is 6.6 gph at 161 KTAS, express fuel consumption in anm/gallon. What is SGR in 30-knot headwind conditions, and in 30-knot tailwind conditions?

➤ 24.4 anm/gallon, 19.8 gnm/gallon, 28.9 gnm/gallon

7. Which maximum range factor decreases as weight decreases?

  (a) Maximum range altitude.

  (b) Maximum range airspeed.

  (c) Maximum range angle-of-attack.

➤ (b)

```
                NORMAL CLIMB – 110 KIAS

CONDITIONS:
Flaps Up
Gear Up                          SAMPLE ONLY
2500 RPM                         not to be used
30 Inches Hg                     in conjunction
120 PPH Fuel Flow                with flight operations
Cowl Flaps Open                  or flight planning
Standard Temperature

NOTES:
1.  Add 16 pounds of fuel for engine start, taxi and takeoff allowance.
2.  Increase time, fuel and distance by 10% for each 7 °C above standard temperature.
3.  Distances shown are based on zero wind.
```

WEIGHT LBS	PRESS ALT FT	RATE OF CLIMB FPM	FROM SEA LEVEL		
			TIME MIN	FUEL USED POUNDS	DISTANCE NM
4000	S.L.	605	0	0	0
	4000	570	7	14	13
	8000	530	14	28	27
	12,000	485	22	44	43
	16,000	430	31	62	63
	20,000	365	41	82	87
3700	S.L.	700	0	0	0
	4000	665	6	12	11
	8000	625	12	24	23
	12,000	580	19	37	37
	16,000	525	26	52	53
	20,000	460	34	68	72
3400	S.L.	810	0	0	0
	4000	775	5	10	9
	8000	735	10	21	20
	12,000	690	16	32	31
	16,000	635	22	44	45
	20,000	565	29	57	61

Figure 11-10. Fuel, time, and distance to climb table

For Questions 8 to 13, use Figure 11-10.

8. For the normal climb in this airplane you should:

  (a) set power _____ rpm and _____ MP;

  (b) climb with flaps (up/down) and gear (up/down) at an (indicated/true) airspeed of _____ knots, with the cowl flaps (open/closed).

➤ (a) 2,500 rpm, 30 in. Hg MP

  (b) flaps up, gear up, indicated airspeed, 110 KIAS, cowl flaps open

9. Under ISA+14°C conditions you would need to (increase/decrease) the climb figures by _____ %, best achieved by (multiplying/dividing) through using a factor of _____ .

➤ increase, 20%, multiplying, 1.2

10. What is the fuel allowance for engine start, taxi and takeoff?

➤ 16 pounds

11. Complete the following using Figure 11-10.

  (a) The climb figures in no-wind conditions from SL to 12,000 feet under ISA conditions for an airplane weighing 4,000 pounds are _____ min, _____ pounds, _____ anm, _____ gnm.

  (b) If there is an average tailwind component of 24 knots, the climb figures will be _____ min, _____ pounds, _____ anm, _____ gnm.

  (c) What fuel is required from engine start through to top of climb?

➤ (a) 22 min, 44 pounds, 43 anm, 43 gnm

  (b) 22 min, 44 pounds, 43 anm, 34 gnm ($\frac{22}{60} \times 24 = 8.8$, say 9; $43 - 9 = 34$)

  (c) 60 pounds (engine start, taxi, takeoff allowance 16 pounds + climb fuel 44 pounds)

12. Calculate the fuel burn from engine start at a sea level airport to top of climb at pressure altitude 14,000 feet under ISA conditions, for an airplane with gross weight 4,000 pounds.

➤ 69 pounds (44 pounds to 12,000 feet; 62 pounds to 16,000 feet; by interpolation, use $\frac{1}{2}$ of the 18 pounds difference to climb $\frac{1}{2}$ of the 4,000 feet difference; i.e. 44 + 9 = 53 pounds to climb + 16 pounds start, taxi and takeoff allowance)

13. Given:

  Aircraft weight .... 3,700 pounds
  Airport pressure altitude .... 4,000 feet
  Temperature at 4,000 feet .... 21°C

  Using a normal climb under the given conditions, how much fuel would be used from engine start to a pressure altitude of 12,000 feet?

  (a) 30 pounds.

  (b) 37 pounds.

  (c) 46 pounds.

➤ (c)

  21°C = ISA+14, therefore apply 20% correction to climb fuel from 4,000 feet to 12,000 feet, (37 – 12) = 25 × 1.2 = 30 + 16 pounds start and taxi = 46 pounds

| PRESSURE ALTITUDE 6,000 FEET | CONDITIONS: Recommended Lean Mixture 3800 Pounds Cowl Flaps Closed |

SAMPLE ONLY not to be used in conjunction with flight operations or flight planning

RPM	MP	20 °C BELOW STANDARD TEMP -17 °C			STANDARD TEMPERATURE 3 °C			20 °C ABOVE STANDARD TEMP 23 °C		
		% BHP	KTAS	PPH	% BHP	KTAS	PPH	% BHP	KTAS	PPH
2550	24	---	---	---	78	173	97	75	174	94
	23	76	167	96	74	169	92	71	171	89
	22	72	164	90	69	166	87	67	167	84
	21	68	160	85	65	162	82	63	163	80
2500	24	78	169	98	75	171	95	73	172	91
	23	74	166	93	71	167	90	69	169	87
	22	70	162	88	67	164	85	65	165	82
	21	66	158	83	63	160	80	61	160	77
2400	24	73	165	91	70	166	88	68	167	85
	23	69	161	87	67	163	84	64	164	81
	22	65	158	82	63	159	79	61	160	77
	21	61	154	77	59	155	75	57	155	73
2300	24	68	161	86	66	162	83	64	163	80
	23	65	158	82	62	159	79	60	159	76
	22	61	154	77	59	155	75	57	155	72
	21	57	150	73	55	150	71	53	150	68
2200	24	63	156	80	61	157	77	59	158	75
	23	60	152	76	58	153	73	56	154	71
	22	57	149	72	54	149	70	53	149	67
	21	53	144	68	51	144	66	49	143	64
	20	50	139	64	48	138	62	46	137	60
	19	46	133	60	44	132	58	43	131	57

Figure 11-11. Cruise performance table

For Questions 14 to 18, use Figure 11-11.

14. What fuel flow can you expect at 6,000 ft pressure altitude, temperature ISA+10°C, with a power setting of 2,400 rpm and 23 in. Hg MP?

➤ 82.5 lb/hr

15. What is the maximum available flight time (no reserves) under the conditions stated? What is it with VFR night reserve?

Pressure altitude .... 6,000 ft
Temperature .... –17°C
Power.. 2,300 rpm, 23″ Hg
Usable fuel available .... 370 lb

➤ 4 hr 31 min, 3 hr 46 min
(370 lb @ 82 lb/hr = 4.51 hr = 4 hr 31 min, minus 45 min = 3 hr 46 min)

16. What is the maximum available flight time (no reserves) under the conditions stated? What is it with VFR night reserve?

Pressure altitude .... 6,000 ft
Temperature................................... –17°C
Power.. 2,400 rpm, 23″MP
Usable fuel available .... 505 lb

➤ 5 hr 48 min, 5 hr 03 min
(505 lb @ 87 lb/hr = 5.80 hr = 5 hr 48 min, minus 45 min = 5 hr 03 min)

17. What cruise performance in terms of true airspeed and fuel flow (in lb/hr) can you expect at 6,000 ft pressure altitude and ISA (i.e. 3°C) if you set the following power? In each case, calculate the distance in air nautical miles per 1 lb of fuel burned.

(a) 2,550 rpm, 22 MP.
(b) 2,500 rpm, 22 MP.
(c) 2,400 rpm, 22 MP.
(d) 2,300 rpm, 22 MP.
(e) For this range of power settings with 22 MP, the lower the rpm, the (greater/smaller) the range for a given quantity of fuel.

➤ (a) 166 KTAS, 87 lb/hr, 1.91 anm/lb
(b) 164 KTAS, 85 lb/hr, 1.93 anm/lb
(c) 159 KTAS, 79 lb/hr, 2.01 anm/lb
(d) 155 KTAS, 75 lb/hr, 2.07 anm/lb
(e) greater

18. What is the maximum available flight time (no reserves) under the conditions stated? What is it with VFR night reserve?

Pressure altitude .... 6,000 ft
Temperature .... +3°C
Power .... 2,300 rpm, 22″MP
Usable fuel available .... 465 lb

➤ 6 hr 12 min, 5 hr 27 min
(465 lb @ 75 lb/hr = 6.2 hr = 6 hr 12 min, minus 45 min = 5 hr 27 min)

PRESSURE ALTITUDE 18,000 FEET

CONDITIONS:
4000 Pounds
Recommended Lean Mixture
Cowl Flaps Closed

NOTE

For best fuel economy at 70% power or less, operate
at 6 PPH leaner than shown in this chart or
at peak EGT.

RPM	MP	20 °C BELOW STANDARD TEMP -41 °C			STANDARD TEMPERATURE -21 °C			20 °C ABOVE STANDARD TEMP -1 °C		
		% BHP	KTAS	PPH	% BHP	KTAS	PPH	% BHP	KTAS	PPH
2500	30	---	---	---	81	188	106	76	185	100
	28	80	184	105	76	182	99	71	178	93
	26	75	178	99	71	176	93	67	172	88
	24	70	171	91	66	168	86	62	164	81
	22	63	162	84	60	159	79	56	155	75
2400	30	81	185	107	77	183	101	72	180	94
	28	76	179	100	72	177	94	67	173	88
	26	71	172	93	67	170	88	63	166	83
	24	66	165	87	62	163	82	58	159	77
	22	61	158	80	57	155	76	54	150	72
2300	30	79	182	103	74	180	97	70	176	91
	28	74	176	97	70	174	91	65	170	86
	26	69	170	91	65	167	86	61	163	81
	24	64	162	84	60	159	79	56	155	75
	22	58	154	77	55	150	73	51	145	65
2200	26	66	166	87	62	163	82	58	159	77
	24	61	158	80	57	154	76	54	150	72
	22	55	148	73	51	144	69	48	138	66
	20	49	136	66	46	131	63	43	124	59

Figure 11-12. Cruise performance table

For Questions 19 to 22, use Figure 11-12.

19. What flight time is available, allowing for VFR day fuel reserve, under the following conditions if the mixture is leaned correctly?

Pressure altitude .... 18,000 ft
Temperature .... –21°C
Power .... 2,400 rpm, 28″MP
Usable fuel .... 425 lb

➤ 4 hr 01 min
(425 lb @ 94 lb/hr = 4.52 hr = 4 hr 31 min, minus day VFR reserve 30 min = 4 hr 01 min)

20. What flight time is available, allowing for VFR night fuel reserve, under the following conditions if the mixture is leaned correctly?

Pressure altitude .... 18,000 ft
Temperature .... –41°C
Power .... 2,500 rpm, 26 MP
Usable fuel .... 318 lb

➤ 2 hr 28 min
(318 lb @ 99 lb/hr = 3.21 hr = 3 hr 13 min, minus night VFR reserve 45 min = 2 hr 28 min)

21. What flight time is available, allowing for VFR day fuel reserve, under the following conditions if the mixture is leaned correctly?

Pressure altitude .... 18,000 ft
Temperature .... –1°C
Power .... 2,200 rpm, 20″MP
Usable fuel .... 344 lb

Note: Calculate flight time first for (a) the tabulated figures, then (b) for 'best fuel economy' as mentioned in the note.

➤ (a) 5 hr 20 min
(344 lb @ 59 lb/hr = 5.83 hr = 5 hr 50 min, minus VFR day reserve 30 min = 5 hr 20 min)
(b) 5 hr 59 min
(for best fuel economy at 70% power or less, operate at 6 lb/hr leaner, i.e. at 53 lb/hr. Therefore 344 lb @ 53 lb/hr = 6.49 hr = 6 hr 29 min – 30 min = 5 hr 59 min)

22. What manifold pressure would you set with the throttle to achieve 76% power at 18,000 ft under ISA conditions, with 2,500 rpm set with the propeller control? What true airspeed and what fuel flow could you expect to achieve?

➤ 28″MP, 182 KIAS, 99 lb/hr

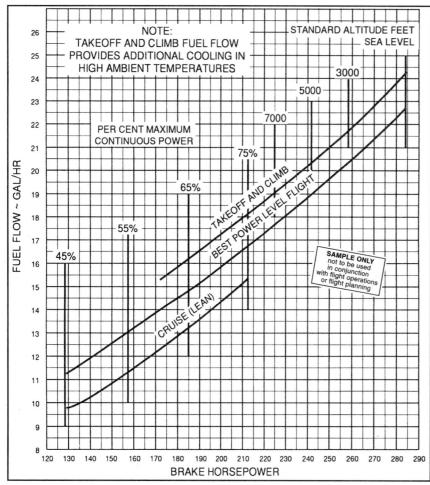

Figure 11-13. Fuel consumption versus brake horsepower graph

For Questions 23 to 27, use Figure 11-13.

23. What flight time is available, allowing for 45 minutes reserve (calculated at cruise rate), if the usage fuel on board is 47 gallons, and you set 55% cruise (lean) power?

   ➤ 3 hr 22 min (from graph, fuel flow is 11.4 gph. Total time $= \frac{47 \text{ gallons}}{11.4 \text{ gph}} = 4.12$ hr = 4 hr 7 min, minus 45 min reserve = 3 hr 22 min flight time.)

24. You have 65 gallons of usable fuel. Power setting is 55% best power level flight. How much flight time would be available with a 30 minute reserve remaining?

   ➤ 4 hr 30 min (from graph, fuel flow is 13.0 gph. Total time $= \frac{65 \text{ gallons}}{13.0 \text{ gph}} = 5.0$ hr, minus 30 min reserve = 4 hr 30 min flight time.)

25. How many gallons of fuel is consumed during takeoff and climb at 70% power for 10 minutes?

   ➤ 2.9 gallons (by interpolation on graph, fuel flow = 17.3 gph for 10 min = $17.3 \times \frac{10}{60} = 2.9$ gallons)

26. With 38 gallons of fuel aboard, and cruising (lean) at 55 percent power, how much flight time is available with a 45 minute fuel reserve still remaining?

   ➤ 2 hr 35 min (from graph, fuel flow = 11.4 gph.
   Total time $= \frac{38 \text{ gallons}}{11.4 \text{ gph}} = 3.33$ hr = 3 hr 20 min, minus 45 min reserve = 2 hr 35 min flight time.)

27. What is the fuel flow in gallons per hour if you cruise with 75% best power level flight set?

   ➤ 16.7 gph

28. If fuel flow is 80 lb/hr at 160 KTAS, express fuel consumption in anm/lb.

   ➤ 2 anm/lb

29. If fuel flow is 6.6 gph at 161 KTAS, express fuel consumption in anm/lb. What is SGR in 30-knot headwind conditions, and in 30-knot tailwind conditions?

   ➤ 4.07 anm/lb (6.6 gph = 39.6 lb/hr), 3.31 gnm/lb, 4.82 gnm/lb

Weight and Balance **12**

Airframe Limitations

An airplane must only be flown within certificated limits of weight and balance to ensure that it remains controllable, performs adequately and is not over-stressed. Correct weight and balance means:

- maximum allowable weight not exceeded; and
- center of gravity (CG) within a specified range.

Weight

The main force created to counteract the weight and allow the airplane to be maneuvered is lift. In straight-and-level flight the lift will be approximately equal to the weight. In certain maneuvers it may considerably exceed the weight—increased lift means an increase in wing loading and load factor (*see* pages 69 and 70).

For instance, in a 2g maneuver such as a 60° banked turn, where the load factor is 2, the load on the wings is double the weight. If the airplane weighs 3,000 pounds, the wings will be carrying a load of 6,000 pounds.

The heavier an airplane is, the poorer its performance will be. In particular, it will have:

- a higher stall speed;
- a higher takeoff speed and a longer takeoff run;
- poorer climb performance (poorer climb angle and climb rate);
- a lower cruising level;
- less maneuverability;
- higher fuel consumption, and less range and endurance;
- reduced cruise speed for a given power setting;
- a higher landing speed and a longer landing distance; and
- greater braking requirements when stopping.

This is not to suggest that following a takeoff at maximum permissible weight, the airplane will not perform perfectly safely; it simply draws attention to the effect of weight on performance.

On the other hand, if the airplane is actually *overweight,* that is above any weight limitations imposed by the manufacturer, then not only will it perform poorly but it will also be difficult to control. If turbulence is encountered, or other than gentle maneuvers performed, the resulting wing loading may be so great that structural damage will result.

On a more mundane (but possibly expensive) level, operating an overloaded airplane may render your insurance invalid.

Never fly an overloaded airplane!

Besides the limiting weights of maximum takeoff weight, maximum landing weight, maximum zero fuel weight and maximum ramp weight, discussed in Chapter 9, for weight and balance purposes we need to take account of the following weights.

Empty Weight

The **empty weight** of an airplane is a precise, measured weight for that particular airplane. It is included in its weight and balance documents as the licensed empty weight.

The empty weight includes:
- the airframe and the powerplant;
- all permanently installed operating equipment (such as radios);
- all nondrainable fluids (including unusable fuel, hydraulic fluid, and undrainable oil—*see* note below).

Note: For some airplanes, the certificated empty weight specifically includes full oil. You should check this point carefully in all your weight and balance problems—if full oil is *not* included, then you must add its weight and moment.

Items that the empty weight does *not* include are:
- pilot(s) and their equipment and baggage;
- passenger(s);
- baggage, cargo and temporary ballast added for balance; and
- full oil (unless specifically included).

If the airplane has new equipment installed (such as a new GPS receiver), then a qualified person should amend the empty weight, and the empty-weight CG position and moment, in the weight and balance documents.

Gross Weight (GW)

The **gross weight** is the actual total weight of the airplane and its contents at any particular time. In other words, gross weight is the empty weight plus pilot(s), payload (passengers and cargo), added ballast and fuel load.

The gross weight should not exceed the maximum weight permissible for any particular maneuver. On **takeoff,** it must not exceed the structural maximum takeoff weight or the performance-limited takeoff weight; on **landing,** gross weight must not exceed the structural maximum landing weight or the performance-limited landing weight. If you wish to operate the airplane in the utility category, rather than in the normal category, you must ensure that the lower maximum permissible gross weight for the utility category is not exceeded.

The Weight of Fuel and Oil

- One gallon of AVGAS weighs 6 pounds (lb).
- One liter of AVGAS weighs 1.56 lb (0.71 kg).
- One gallon of oil weighs 7.5 pounds (so 8 quarts or 2 gallons weighs 15 pounds).

Caution: Be careful when ordering fuel in foreign countries—some places measure fuel quantity in units such as liters rather than US gallons.

Other Weight Limitations

There may be other weight restrictions specified in your airplane's weight and balance documents or on placards in the airplane—for instance, a maximum baggage compartment load, or a maximum zero fuel weight (ZFW).

Be familiar with your airplane's weight limitations.

The more familiar you are with the weight limitations applicable to your airplane, the easier weight and balance problems will become. In the following table, we show the important data for the loading of any airplane, and you should consider using this for any airplane you fly.

MTOW (structural)	= .... lb
MLW (structural)	= .... lb
Empty weight	= .... lb (with/without oil)
Maximum fuel load	= .... gal = ... lb
Taxi allowance	= .... lb
Maximum number of passengers	= .... gal = ... lb
Maximum baggage compartment load	= .... lb
Maximum fuel ...... gallons (total)	Mains .... gal = ... lb Aux .... gal = ... lb

Note: In many small airplanes, it is *not* possible to carry both a full fuel load and a full passenger-and-baggage load and remain within the maximum permissible gross weight.

✍ Now complete **Review 12, Part (a)** on page 267.

Balance

The Moment of a Force

The **moment** of a force is its **turning effect,** and it depends on two things:

- the **size** (magnitude) of the force; and
- its moment **arm,** which is the distance from the point at which the force is applied to the pivot point (or fulcrum).

If the force being applied (weight) is measured in pounds (lb) and the arm is in inches (in.), then the moment is expressed in **pound-inches (lb-in)**, or **inch-pounds (in-lb).**

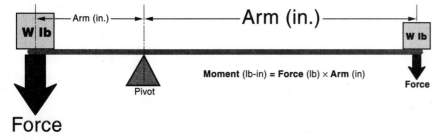

Figure 12-1. Force, arm and moment

We are all familiar with the effect of a lever—the longer the lever arm, the smaller the force required to achieve the same turning effect. In the case of an airplane, we are not trying to rotate it, but to balance it—to stop it rotating or pitching. This is like a balanced beam, where the moments trying to turn it clockwise are perfectly balanced by the moments wanting to turn it counter-clockwise.

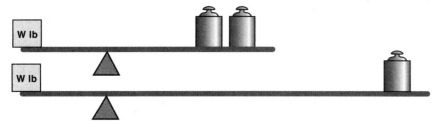

Figure 12-2. Balancing (or turning) moment depends on weight and moment arm

We can see in Figure 12-2 that the same turning effect (moment) is achieved by placing half the original weight at double the distance. For instance:

- a 2 pound weight, with an arm of 10 inches, has a moment of $2 \times 10 = 20$ lb-in;
- a 1 pound weight, with an arm of 20 inches, has a moment of $1 \times 20 = 20$ lb-in.

Balancing a Loaded Beam (or Airplane)

To balance a loaded beam (or airplane), we need to provide a supporting force at the point where the total weight may be considered to be concentrated, and where the counterclockwise turning moments are balanced by the clockwise turning moments. This position is called the **center of gravity (CG).** The magnitude of the supporting force will need to equal the total weight. For a beam, the supporting force may be provided by a pivot or by a rope; for an airplane, the supporting force is provided by the lift.

To balance a beam, we need to provide a supporting force at its central position.

We need to reduce this situation ...

supporting rope

6 lb

CG (balance point)

30″

... to this situation.

3 lb

Total weight 9 lb

6 lb

CG (balance point)

10″   20″

Figure 12-3. Finding the total weight and CG position

In this case you have probably already estimated the position of the CG to be closer to the 6 pounds weight, in fact about 10 inches from it. If the supporting force is provided at this CG position, the beam will balance.

For an airplane to be in balance, its CG must lie somewhere near the point where the lift is produced by the wings.

Finding the Position of the CG

To calculate the position of the CG (rather than just estimate it), we need to calculate the total moment—the sum of the turning effects of the individual weights. Then we find the position (CG arm) where a *single* weight (equal to the sum of the individual weights) will have the same total moment. The CG arm can be found using the equation:

Total weight $\times$ CG arm = total moment

To do this we need to know the individual moment arms as measured from an appropriate datum. It does not matter which point we choose as the datum—the results for the CG position will always be the same. We will take time out to illustrate this important point. By convention, moment arms to the left of the chosen datum are negative; arms to the right of the datum are positive.

The CG position remains the same regardless of datum position.

(a) Using the Estimated CG Position as Datum

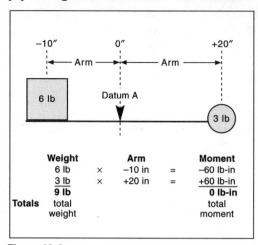

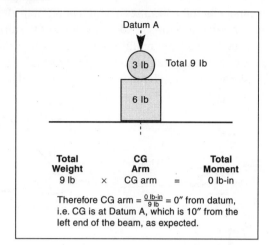

	Weight		Arm		Moment
	6 lb	×	−10 in	=	−60 lb-in
	3 lb	×	+20 in	=	+60 lb-in
	9 lb				0 lb-in
Totals	total weight				total moment

Total Weight		CG Arm		Total Moment
9 lb	×	CG arm	=	0 lb-in

Therefore CG arm = $\frac{0 \text{ lb-in}}{9 \text{ lb}}$ = 0″ from datum, i.e. CG is at Datum A, which is 10″ from the left end of the beam, as expected.

Figure 12-4.

(b) Using Another Datum, the Left End of the Beam

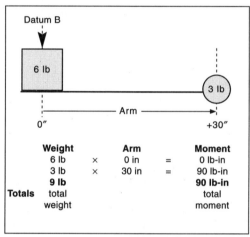

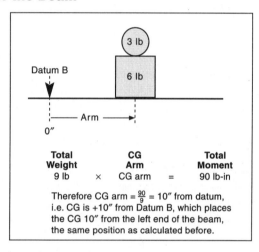

	Weight		Arm		Moment
	6 lb	×	0 in	=	0 lb-in
	3 lb	×	30 in	=	90 lb-in
	9 lb				90 lb-in
Totals	total weight				total moment

Total Weight		CG Arm		Total Moment
9 lb	×	CG arm	=	90 lb-in

Therefore CG arm = $\frac{90}{9}$ = 10″ from datum, i.e. CG is +10″ from Datum B, which places the CG 10″ from the left end of the beam, the same position as calculated before.

Figure 12-5.

(c) Using an External Datum, 20 inches Left of the Beam

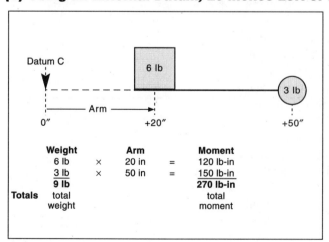

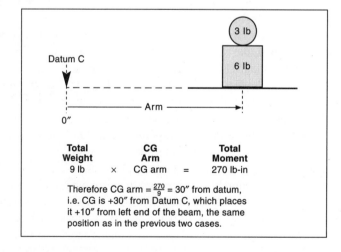

	Weight		Arm		Moment
	6 lb	×	20 in	=	120 lb-in
	3 lb	×	50 in	=	150 lb-in
	9 lb				270 lb-in
Totals	total weight				total moment

Total Weight		CG Arm		Total Moment
9 lb	×	CG arm	=	270 lb-in

Therefore CG arm = $\frac{270}{9}$ = 30″ from datum, i.e. CG is +30″ from Datum C, which places it +10″ from left end of the beam, the same position as in the previous two cases.

Figure 12-6.

Conclusion: The choice of datum makes no difference to the results for CG position.

Airplane Datums

In the case of airplanes, the manufacturer specifies a datum point in the weight and balance data supplied. Some manufacturers choose the nose of the airplane as the datum; others choose the firewall behind the engine; and others choose an external point along the extended longitudinal axis, ahead of the nose. The datum point for your particular airplane will be stated in its weight and balance documents.

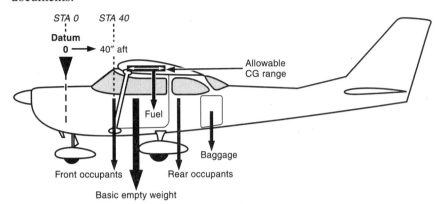

Figure 12-7. The datum can be at any convenient point on the longitudinal axis

The position of the datum is often referred to as "station zero" (or STA 0). Other positions may be specified relative to the station zero datum—for instance, a point 40 inches aft of the datum is called "STA 40." If the datum is behind the nose, then all weights forward of this datum will have a negative arm and a negative moment. The advantage of having a datum at or forward of the nose is that all moments are positive, making the calculations easier.

Effect of CG Position on Airplane Handling

The CG of an airplane is on the longitudinal axis and must lie within a specified range for the airplane to be controllable and to fly safely (and legally).

The main supporting force in flight counteracting the total weight of the loaded airplane is the lift generated by the wings. It is considered to be concentrated at the center of pressure (CP), usually situated somewhere on the forward section of the wing—its position varies depending on angle-of-attack and other factors. A small balancing force (usually downward) is provided by the horizontal stabilizer.

If loaded with the **CG well forward,** the horizontal stabilizer has a long moment arm, the airplane will be very stable longitudinally, and resist any pitching moment. The forward position of the CG is limited to ensure that the elevator has sufficient turning moment to overcome the nose-heaviness and excessive longitudinal stability, ensuring that you are able to rotate the airplane for takeoff and flare it for landing at relatively low airspeeds.

If the **CG is well aft,** the airplane will be tail-heavy and less stable longitudinally, because of the shorter moment arm from the CG to the horizontal stabilizer, and the shorter moment arm between the CG and the CP. The aft position of the CG is limited to ensure that the airplane remains sufficiently stable so that a reasonably steady nose position can be held without excessive and frequent control movements being necessary, and so that the elevator-feel experienced through the control column remains satisfactory.

With a CG that is too far aft, the airplane will be very tail-heavy, will be difficult to control, and tend to stall and/or spin more easily—a situation from which it may be more difficult (or even impossible) to recover.

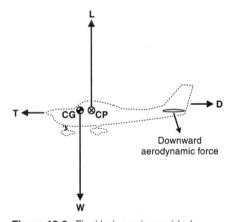

Figure 12-8. Final balance is provided by the horizontal stabilizer

A Simple Layout for Weight and Balance Calculations

The CG is the position through which all of the weights, combined into a gross weight (or total weight), may be considered to act. The total weight should have the same turning moment as the sum of the individual moments.

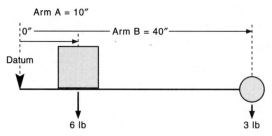

Figure 12-9. The actual situation

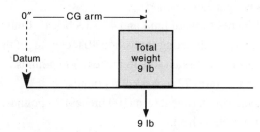

Figure 12-10. The modified situation

Sum of individual moments = total moment = total weight × its moment arm

$$(6 \times 10) + (3 \times 40) \quad = \quad 180 \text{ lb-in} \quad = \quad 9 \text{ pounds} \times \text{CG arm}$$

The CG position can now be found by dividing the total moment by the total weight.

$$\text{CG arm} = \frac{\text{total moment}}{\text{total weight}} = \frac{180 \text{ lb-in}}{9 \text{ lb}} = 20 \text{ inches}$$

Therefore the CG position is 20 inches aft of the datum. This can be neatly laid out in tabular form, which is the way we do many of our airplane weight and balance problems.

	Weight (lb)	Arm (in)	Moment (lb-in)
	6	10	60
	3	40	120
Totals	9	**20** **CG position**	180

Take particular note when doing these problems, that you **cannot add the individual arms** to obtain the location of the CG. This answer can be found only by dividing the sum of all the moments by the total weight.

To help you visualize the method by which you can solve this type of problem, the figure below shows the pattern of the steps to be taken—and this pattern can be applied to almost all airplane weight and balance problems.

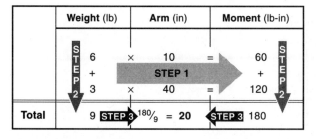

To find the CG position:

1. Calculate the individual moments.

2. Calculate the total weight and the total moment.

3. Find the CG arm = $\dfrac{\text{total moment}}{\text{total weight}}$

Figure 12-11. How to find CG position

Finding the CG for a Loaded Airplane

Using a tabulated layout, like that suggested above, will make all airplane weight and balance problems easy to do, and easy to check.

Example 1. Given the following information regarding a loaded airplane, calculate: (a) total moment; (b) CG position.

- Maximum gross weight 2,400 pounds.
- CG limits are 35 inches forward limit and 47.3 inches aft limit.
- Empty weight 1,200 pounds acting at position 40 inches aft of the datum.
- Pilot and passenger in front seat (arm 36 inches) 300 pounds.
- Passengers in rear seat (arm 72 inches) 400 pounds.
- Baggage in baggage compartment (arm 100 inches) 35 pounds.
- Fuel 30 gallons (arm 50 inches).
- Oil 8 quarts (arm – 10 inches).

Note:

1. Oil is obviously in front of the datum, since it has a negative arm (it may be that the datum on this airplane is the firewall behind the engine).
2. A calculator will help you in these weight and balance problems.
3. Setting out your calculations in tabular form will keep things neat.
4. A diagram of the airplane is not necessary, but we show one here to help you visualize the situation.

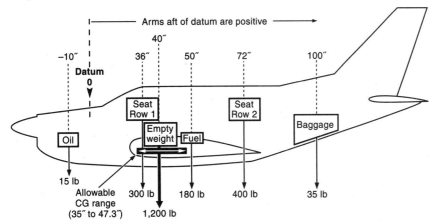

Figure 12-12. The loaded airplane

Item	Weight (lb)	Arm (in)	Moment (lb-in)
Empty weight	1200	40	48000
Pilot + front passenger	300	36	10800
Rear passengers	400	72	28800
Baggage	35	100	3500
Fuel: 30 gal (× 6 lb)	180	50	9000
Oil: 8 qt (2 gal × 7.5 lb)	15	–10	–150
Totals	2130	46.9	99950

Total moment (99,950 lb-in) = total weight (2,130 pounds × CG arm

therefore, CG arm = $\frac{99,950 \text{ lb-in}}{2,130 \text{ lb}}$ = 46.9 in aft of datum.

With every weight and balance problem, you should always check that:
- no weight limit is exceeded; and
- the CG is within limits.

For this airplane, maximum gross weight is 2,400 pounds, so 2,130 pounds is OK. Center of gravity limits are 35 inches forward limit and 47.3 inches aft limit, which means the CG must lie between 35 and 47.3 inches aft of the datum, so 46.9 inches is OK. Therefore this airplane is loaded correctly.

Weight and/or CG Outside Limits

If the airplane was shown to be loaded incorrectly, then you would have to reorganize the loading so that it is within the weight and CG limits.

- If the airplane is **too heavy,** then you must remove some of the load, which is baggage, passenger(s) or fuel. Make your choice!
- If the airplane is **out of balance,** with the CG outside the specified limits, then you must move the CG position. There are three ways in which this can be done:

1. **Shift the load.** For example, move the CG forward by moving baggage forward from the baggage compartment to an empty seat (where you would need to restrain it).
2. **Remove some of the load.** For example, move the CG forward by removing some baggage from the baggage compartment, or by leaving one of the rear passengers behind.
3. **Add ballast.** For example, move the CG aft by adding ballast to the baggage compartment.

Later in this chapter we will show how to ensure that the CG position is within the allowable CG range, and that it remains between the forward and aft limits throughout the flight as fuel is used.

Index Units

When calculating the weight and balance of an airplane, the moments are often quite large numbers, such as 28,800 lb-in. The size of these numbers can be reduced, for instance by dividing them by 1,000 to give *moment/1,000* and 28,800 lb-in would therefore equal 28.8 index units, where 1 index unit = 1,000 lb-in.

In some cases, you will see the moment divided by 100 to give *moment/100* and 28,800 lb-in would then equal 288 index units, where 1 index unit = 100 lb-in.

Example 2. If you are given moment/1,000 = 93.2 lb-in/1,000, then the moment = 93,200 lb-in (found by multiplying the index unit by 1,000 in this case).

Example 3. If you are given moment/100 = 1,617 lb-in/100, then the moment = 161,700 lb-in (found by multiplying the index unit by 100 in this case).

✍ Now complete **Review 12, Part (b)** on page 267.

Graphical Presentation of Weight and Balance Data

To eliminate the need to calculate moments or index units, some airplane manufacturers provide a small loading graph that you can use to find the moment in index units. Enter with the weight in pounds on the left-hand side of the graph, move across horizontally to the appropriate guideline (for front seat position, fuel position, and so on), and then vertically down to read off the moment in index units (in this case moment/1,000).

Note: In this graph, you will notice provision is made to use weight in kilograms and moment in kg-mm. Make sure you use the correct scales.

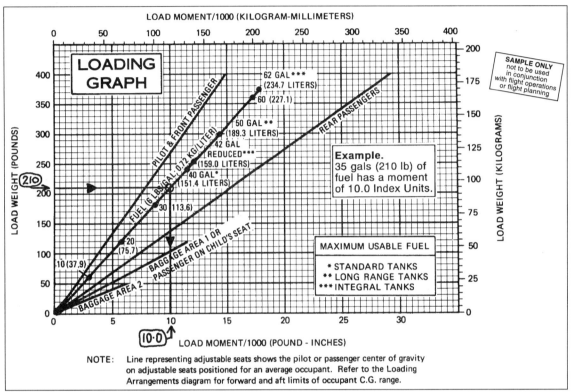

Figure 12-13. Graphical weight and balance data. See table below for calculations.

Sample Loading Problem	Weight (lb)	Mom/1000 (lb-in./1000)
1. Basic empty weight (includes unusable fuel and full oil)	1463	56.9
2. Usable fuel: 35 gal	210	10.0
3. Pilot and front passenger	390	14.5
4. Rear passengers	260	19
5. Baggage Area 1	54	5.0
6. Baggage Area 2	—	—
7. Ramp weight and moment	2377	105.4
8. Fuel allowance for start, taxi & runup	–7	–0.3
9. **Takeoff Weight and Moment**	2370	105.1

Given figures entered in white boxes. Calculated figures in the gray boxes.

35 gal @ 6 lb/gal = 210 lb. Enter Loading Graph with 210 lb; go across to fuel line, and then read down to get 10.0 mom/1000.

Add items 1 to 6.

Plot on CG Moment Envelope Graph in Figure 12-14 on the following page

Having found the total weight and moment, we can check either of the next two graphs to ensure that:

- the weight is within limits; and
- the airplane is balanced correctly.

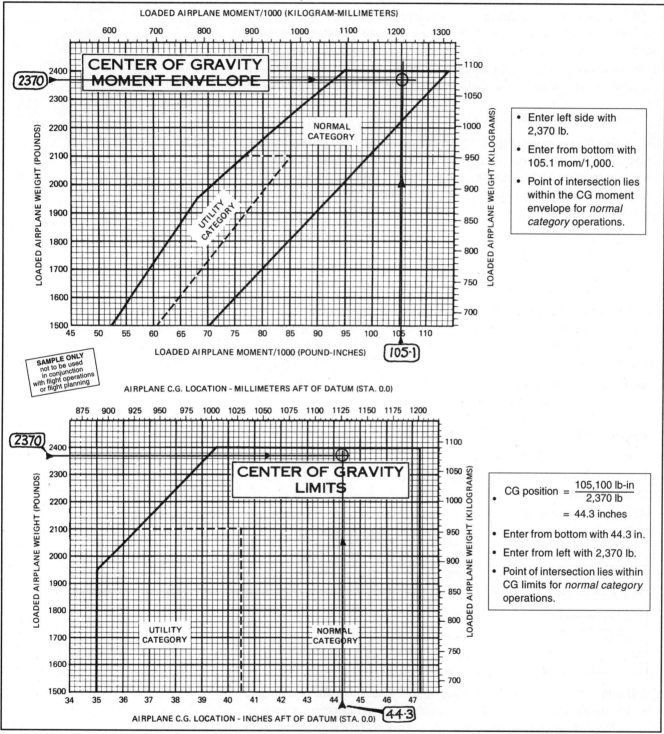

Figure 12-14. Cessna 172 weight and balance data

The two graphs (Figure 12-14) tell us the same thing, albeit in a slightly different manner. You need refer to only one of them.

The maximum weight is specified on both graphs: 2,400 pounds for normal category operations; and 2,100 pounds for utility category operations.

- The total weight should not exceed the specified maximum weight;
- If the total moment lies within the CG moment envelope (top graph), then the airplane is in balance with the CG within limits (even though you may not have calculated the actual position of the CG, but only the total moment); or
- If the center of gravity lies within the CG limits (on the lower graph), then the airplane is in balance—but finding the CG involves the extra calculation:

$$\text{CG position} = \frac{\text{total moment}}{\text{total weight}}$$

Note: Using the top graph (Figure 12-14) avoids the need to calculate the CG position. To illustrate this point, notice that total weight 2,400 pounds and total moment 113,500 pound-inches places the airplane on the extreme limit of the CG moment envelope. If you go ahead and calculate the CG position for this case:

$$\text{CG position} = \frac{113,500 \text{ lb-in}}{2,400 \text{ lb}} = 47.3 \text{ inches}$$

This puts you at the extreme limit of the CG limits graph, which is the same message in a slightly different form.

Weight and Balance for the Private Knowledge Exam

The airplane weight and balance graphs used in the Private Pilot Knowledge Exam are used in exactly the same way as the Cessna 172 weight and balance data. The following example uses these graphs, shown in Figure 12-15.

Example 4. Using the graphs in Figure 12-15, determine the airplane loaded moment and aircraft category with the following data.

	Weight (lb)	Mom/1,000
Empty weight	1,350	51.5
Pilot and front passenger	340	—
Fuel (standard tanks)	Full (38 gal)	—
Oil, 8 qt	—	—

Answer. 74.8 pound-inches, utility category.

	Weight (lb)	Mom/1000 (lb-in/1000)
Empty weight	1350	51.5
Pilot and front passenger	340	12.5
Full fuel (standard tanks)	228	11
Oil, 8 quarts	15	−0.2
Gross weight	1933	74.8

1. Fill in the table as far as possible. Read the notes carefully. The bottom note states that the empty weight does not include oil and therefore it must be considered separately. Note 2 gives the oil's weight and moment index units. (Do not omit the minus in the index unit.)

    The maximum usable fuel in standard tanks is shown in the top graph and is 38 gallons at 6 lb/gal. The fuel therefore weighs 38 × 6 = 228 lb and has an index unit of 11 pound inches. Similarly, to find pilot and front passenger index unit move horizontally across at 340 lb until you meet the pilot and front passenger line and then vertically down to read off the moment index of 12.5.

2. Add up the gross weight and its index unit. Then using the bottom center of gravity moment index, plot the gross weight and moment index unit to discover it falls within the envelope in the utility category.

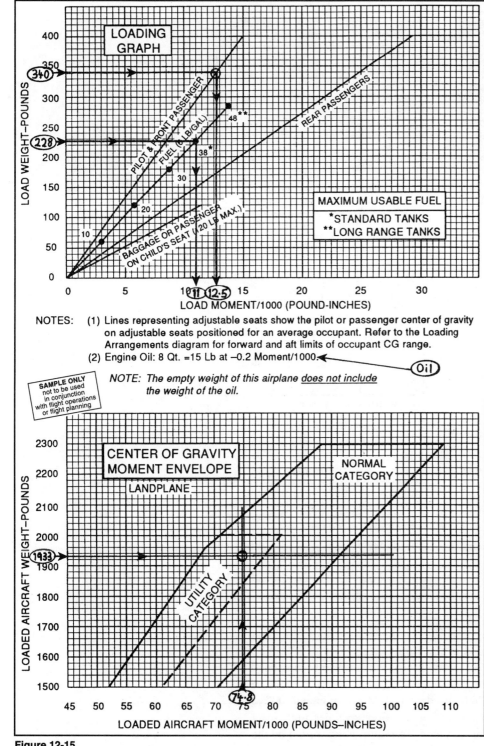

NOTES: (1) Lines representing adjustable seats show the pilot or passenger center of gravity on adjustable seats positioned for an average occupant. Refer to the Loading Arrangements diagram for forward and aft limits of occupant CG range.
(2) Engine Oil: 8 Qt. =15 Lb at −0.2 Moment/1000.

NOTE: The empty weight of this airplane *does not include* the weight of the oil.

SAMPLE ONLY
not to be used
in conjunction
with flight operations
or flight planning

Figure 12-15.

Tabular Presentation of Weight and Balance Data

Some manufacturers present their weight and balance data, not in graphical form, but in the form of tables as shown in Figures 12-16a and 12-16b.

USEFUL LOAD WEIGHTS AND MOMENTS

OCCUPANTS

FRONT SEATS ARM 85		REAR SEATS ARM 121	
Weight	Moment/100	Weight	Moment/100
120	102	120	145
130	110	130	157
140	119	140	169
150	128	150	182
160	136	160	194
170	144	170	206
180	153	180	218
190	162	190	230
200	170	200	242

USABLE FUEL

MAIN WING TANKS ARM 75

Gallons	Weight	Moment/100
5	30	22
10	60	45
15	90	68
20	120	90
25	150	112
30	180	135
35	210	158
40	240	180
44	264	198

BAGGAGE OR 5TH SEAT OCCUPANT ARM 140

Weight	Moment/100
10	14
20	28
30	42
40	56
50	70
60	84
70	98
80	112
90	126
100	140
110	154
120	168
130	182
140	196
150	210
160	224
170	238
180	252
190	266
200	280
210	294
220	308
230	322
240	336
250	350
260	364
270	378

AUXILIARY WING TANKS ARM 94

Gallons	Weight	Moment/100
5	30	28
10	60	56
15	90	85
19	114	107

*OIL

Quarts	Weight	Moment/100
10	19	5

*Included in basic Empty Weight

SAMPLE ONLY not to be used in conjunction with flight operations or flight planning

Empty Weight ~ 2015

MOM / 100 ~ 1554

MOMENT LIMITS vs WEIGHT

Moment limits are based on the following weight and center of gravity limit data (landing gear down).

WEIGHT CONDITION	FORWARD CG LIMIT	AFT CG LIMIT
2950 lb (takeoff or landing)	82.1	84.7
2525 lb	77.5	85.7
2475 lb or less	77.0	85.7

Figure 12-16a.

From Figure 12-16a, the empty weight is 2,015 pounds (the * indicating that full oil, 10 quarts, has been included in the empty weight), with an empty weight moment of 1,554 mom/100 (155,400 lb-in). Since full oil is included here, there is no need to consider it separately in your calculations. The columns for your calculations should be headed "weight and moment/100".

Figure 12-16a allows you to extract the moment (as an index unit) for a series of weights at each station, without having to multiply the weight by the arm. This tabular presentation saves time and is sufficiently accurate.

MOMENT LIMITS vs WEIGHT (Continued)

Weight	Minimum Moment 100	Maximum Moment 100	Weight	Minimum Moment 100	Maximum Moment 100
2100	1617	1800	2600	2037	2224
2110	1625	1808	2610	2048	2232
2120	1632	1817	2620	2058	2239
2130	1640	1825	2630	2069	2247
2140	1648	1834	2640	2080	2255
2150	1656	1843	2650	2090	2263
2160	1663	1851	2660	2101	2271
2170	1671	1860	2670	2112	2279
2180	1679	1868	2680	2123	2287
2190	1686	1877	2690	2133	2295
2200	1694	1885	2700	2144	2303
2210	1702	1894	2710	2155	2311
2220	1709	1903	2720	2166	2319
2230	1717	1911	2730	2177	2326
2240	1725	1920	2740	2188	2334
2250	1733	1928	2750	2199	2342
2260	1740	1937	2760	2210	2350
2270	1748	1945	2770	2221	2358
2280	1756	1954	2780	2232	2366
2290	1763	1963	2790	2243	2374
2300	1771	1971			
2310	1779	1980	2800	2254	2381
2320	1786	1988	2810	2265	2389
2330	1794	1997	2820	2276	2397
2340	1802	2005	2830	2287	2405
2350	1810	2014	2840	2298	2413
2360	1817	2023	2850	2309	2421
2370	1825	2031	2860	2320	2428
2380	1833	2040	2870	2332	2436
2390	1840	2048	2880	2343	2444
			2890	2354	2452
2400	1848	2057	2900	2365	2460
2410	1856	2065	2910	2377	2468
2420	1863	2074	2920	2388	2475
2430	1871	2083	2930	2399	2483
2440	1879	2091	2940	2411	2491
2450	1887	2100	2950	2422	2499
2460	1894	2108			
2470	1902	2117			
2480	1911	2125			
2490	1921	2134			
2500	1932	2143			
2510	1942	2151			
2520	1953	2160			
2530	1963	2168			
2540	1974	2176			
2550	1984	2184			
2560	1995	2192			
2570	2005	2200			
2580	2016	2208			
2590	2026	2216			

At 2,950 lb, the total moment must lie between 2,422 and 2,499 mom/100.

This table shows the **moment limits**, which is another measure of **CG limits**.

Weight × fwd CG arm = minimum moment

Weight × aft CG arm = maximum moment

Figure 12-16b.

Finding the Moment Index for an Item

To find the mom/100 for any item, there are two ways to proceed. For example, find the mom/100 for a pilot weighing 180 pounds in the front seats.

    (a) **Using tabular data:**
        from front-seat table, enter with 180 pounds and extract 153 mom/100.

    (b) **Mathematically:**
        moment = weight 180 lb × arm 85 in. = 15,300 lb-in, or 153 mom/100.

Nontabulated Weights

For nontabulated weights, it will be necessary to interpolate when using the tabular data. For example, find the mom/100 for a passenger weighing 177 pounds in the rear seat. There are several ways of interpolating, as follows:

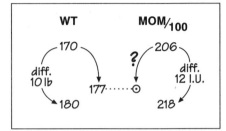

Figure 12-17.

- For a difference of 10 pounds between 170 pounds and 180 pounds, there is a mom/100 difference of 12. A moment/100 difference of 12 for 10 pounds = 1.2 per pound; therefore, for 7 pounds = 7 × 1.2 = 8.4 mom/100, plus the 206 gives 214 mom/100.

- Alternatively, for a difference of 7 pounds between 170 pounds and 177 pounds, there will be a mom/100 difference of $\frac{7}{10}$ of 12 = 8.4 (say 8). For a weight of 177 pounds, the mom/100 = 206 + 8 = 214.

Note: For nontabulated weights, or for weights outside the table, it is easier to use the mathematical method to find the moment index.

    Moment = weight 177 pounds × arm 121 inches = 21,417 lb-in, or 214.17 mom/100.

✎ Now complete **Review 12, Part (c)** on page 268.

Weight-Shift Calculations

If, after calculating the weight and balance, you find that the CG is outside the limits of the CG range, it will be necessary to *shift* some weight to bring the CG position back within limits.

Note: The tabulated method shown here does not require the use of a formula. Some instructors prefer to use a formula for weight-shift and weight-change problems. We discuss the formula method at the end of this chapter in the section for commercial pilots.

Example 5. You have calculated the total weight to be 4,000 pounds with the CG located at 100 inches aft of datum. What is the new CG position if you shift 50 pounds of baggage from the rear baggage area at station 200 to the forward baggage area at station 50?

Answer. 98.13 inches aft of datum. Remember: **Moment ÷ Weight = Arm.** You cannot add the arm values to derive total arm.

	Weight (lb)	Arm (in)	Moment (lb-in)
Original totals	4000	00	400000
Rear baggage out	−50	200	−1000
Forward baggage in	+50	50	+25000
New totals	4000	**98.13**	392500

Example 6. You have calculated the total weight to be 4,000 pounds with the CG located 100 inches aft of datum. You wish to move the CG to 98 inches aft of datum, by shifting some baggage from the rear baggage area at station 200 to the forward baggage area at station 50. How much should you shift (to the nearest pound)?

Answer. 53.3 lb. Assume that you shift "w" lb.

	Weight (lb)	Arm (in)	Moment (lb-in)
Original totals	4000	100	400000
Rear baggage *out*	−w	200	−200w
Forward baggage *in*	+w	50	+5w
New totals	**4000**	98	**400000 − 150w**

$$\text{CG position} = \frac{\text{total moment}}{\text{total weight}}$$

$$98 = \frac{400,00 - 15\,w}{4,000}$$

Multiply both sides of the equation by 4,000

$$4,000 \times 98 = 400,000 - 150\,w$$
$$392,00 = 400,000 - 150\,w$$
$$150\,w = 400,000 - 392,000 = 8,000$$
$$w = \frac{8,000}{150} = \textbf{53.5 lb}$$

You should do a quick check as follows:

$$\text{New moment (lb-in)} = 400,000 - 15\,w$$
$$\text{therefore new moment} = 400,000 - (150 \times 53.3) = 392,005$$
$$\text{therefore new arm} = \frac{392,005}{4,000\ (wt)} = 98 \text{ inches}$$

Weight-Change Calculations

Having calculated the weight and balance, you may decide to *change* the weight, perhaps because the airplane is overweight (reduce the load), perhaps because the airplane is below maximum weight (you can add extra load), or perhaps because the CG is out of limits and you want to shift it (by removing weight or adding ballast). You can work out a formula to assist in this calculation, but the simplest approach is to follow your now-familiar tabular pattern.

Example 7. Your airplane total weight is 4,100 lb with the CG located at 100 inches aft of datum. Maximum permissible weight is 4,000 lb, so you decide to remove 100 lb of baggage from the baggage compartment at station 200. What is the new CG position?

Answer. 97.5 inches aft of datum.

Item	Weight (lb)	Arm (inches)	Moment (lb-inches)
Original totals	4100	100	410000
Baggage change	−100	200	−20000
Revised totals	4000	97.5	390000

Example 8. You have calculated the total weight to be 2,400 lb with the CG located at 73.5 inches, which is 1.5 inches outside the aft limit of 72 inches. Maximum permissible weight is 2,400 lb and the airplane is fully loaded, with no possibility of shifting the load. What is the minimum baggage (to the next pound) you must remove from station 150 to bring the CG within limits for takeoff?

Answer. 47 lb. Set up the table and assume you remove "w" lb of baggage.

	Weight (lb)	**Arm** (in)	**Moment** (lb-in)
Original totals	2400	73.5	400000
Baggage charge	−w	150	−150w
Revised totals	**2400 − w**	72.0	**176400 − 150w**

$$\text{New CG position } 72.0 = \frac{\text{total moment}}{\text{total weight}}$$

$$72.0 = \frac{176{,}400 - 150\,w}{2{,}400 - w}$$

Multiplying both sides by (2,400 − w)

$$72 \times (2{,}400 - w) = 176{,}400 - 150\,w$$

Note that the (2,400 − w) cancels out on side of the equation.

$$172{,}800 - 72\,w = 176{,}400 - 150\,w$$
$$150\,w - 72\,w = 176{,}400 - 172{,}800$$
$$78\,w = 3{,}600$$
$$w = \frac{3{,}600}{78} = 46.15$$

which, to the next pound to be on the safe side, is **47 lb**.

Weight-Shift/Change Calculations

A more usual occurrence is for there to be a change in both the location and weight of passengers, fuel or baggage.

Example 9. You have calculated the TOW to be 2,800 lb, with the CG moment at 2,296 mom/100 index units. Before departure you are advised that a passenger weighing 180 lb and seated at STA 85.0 will not be traveling, and will be replaced by another person weighing 200 lb and carrying 40 lb of luggage. This passenger will be seated at STA 85.0 and the accompanying luggage stowed at STA 140.0. Calculate the new CG moment in index units, and how far the CG has moved forward or aft.

	Weight (lb)	**Arm** (in)	**Moment** (lb-in)
TOW	2800	82.0	2296
Passenger OUT	−180	85.0	−153
New totals	2620	–	2143
Passenger IN	+200	85.0	+170
Baggage IN	+40	140.0	+56
New TOW	2860	82.83	2369

Answer. The new mom/100 = 2,369, and the CG has moved (82.83 − 82.0) = 0.83 inches aft.

CG Movement

Up to this point, we have ignored the fact that during flight, the gross weight of the airplane decreases as fuel is used. This change in weight will cause the position of the CG to move gradually. The amount of movement of the CG will

The center of gravity moves during flight as fuel is used.

depend on the location, and therefore the moment arm of the fuel tanks. The airplane designer ensures that the fuel tanks are positioned so that their effective arms, when full and empty, are not much displaced from the fore-and-aft CG limits of the airplane.

To be precise in your weight and balance calculations, you should confirm that the CG position (or total moment) is within limits throughout the flight. This is done by checking that the CG is within limits at both the **takeoff weight (TOW)** and **zero fuel weight (ZFW)**.

Note: If you considered weight and balance at the landing weight (rather than at the zero fuel weight), and found that the CG was right on the rear limit, then any further fuel burn-off (say for an emergency diversion) may take you out of the CG envelope. Therefore, it is better to consider the moment at the ZFW, rather than at the LW. Despite this, you may be asked in the Knowledge Exam to compute the weight and balance at landing, and some airplane loading data may require it (*see* the note on Figure 12-20).

Figure 12-18. Zero fuel weight

Figure 12-19. Gross weight

Example 10. You have calculated the loaded weight and moment of your airplane to be 3,400 lb and 180 lb-in/1,000. The fuel on board is 60 gallons. Is the airplane loaded satisfactorily? If not, offer a suggestion. (Refer to the graphs in Figure 12-20.)

Answer.

	Weight (lb)	**Mom/1000** (lb-in/1000)	
Takeoff weight	**3400**	180	◄—— OK—just within limits
Fuel: 60 gal	−360	−15.5	◄—— Moment from top graph
Zero fuel weight	**3040**	**164.5**	◄—— NOT OK—outside limits

At takeoff, the total moment is right on the rear limit. As fuel burns off, however, the CG moment position on the graph will move toward the ZFW CG moment position, which is **outside limits.** Therefore this flight should *not* commence unless the airplane is loaded differently—a solution could be to shift passengers or baggage forward if possible. Then you should recalculate the weight and balance to confirm within limits.

Suppose you decide to move a 150 lb passenger from a rear seat to an empty center seat. Total weight will be unchanged, but the moment for this passenger will change from 15.0 in the rear seat to 10.7 in the center seat, a decrease of 4.3 lb-in/1,000. Now recalculate the weight and balance.

	Weight (lb)	**Mom/1000** (lb-in/1000)	
Original TOW and Moment	3400	180	
Adjustment—move 150 lb passenger from rear to center	0	−4.3	
New TOW Moment	**3400**	**175.7**	◄—— OK—within limits
Fuel: 60 gal	−360	−15.5	
Now ZFW and Moment	**3040**	**160.2**	◄—— OK—within limits

To help in deciding how much weight you have to move in order to bring the ZFW within the CG limits, you can easily establish the required minimum change in moment from the graph. In this example we find:

ZFW 3040, actual moment   684.5 mom/1,000

for ZFW 3,040, limiting rear moment   <u>160.5</u>

therefore minimum **change required in moment** = **4.0 mom/1,000**

Since 164.5 is outside the rear limit, this required change must be forward. Moving from the rear seat to the center gives a moment change of 4.3; this is slightly more than the minimum and is therefore acceptable.

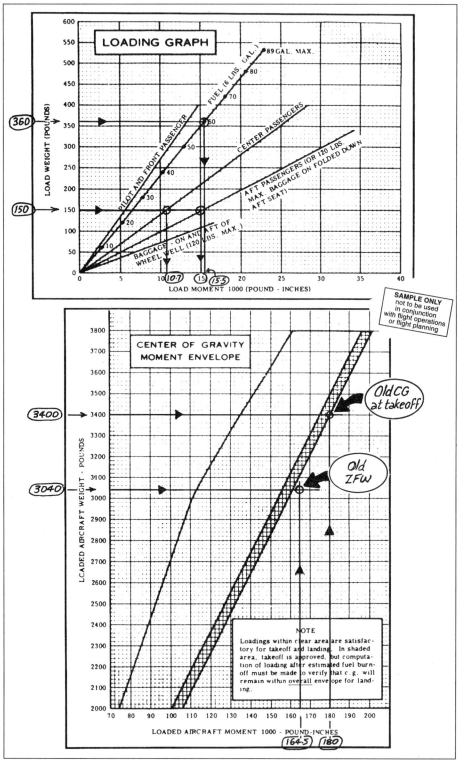

Figure 12-20. Example 10

Example 11. State if the CG is within the allowable CG envelope for the following load configuration. (*See* Figure 12-20.)

Empty weight (oil included) ....2,260 lb

Empty weight moment......................93.2 lb-in/1,000

Pilot + front seat passenger..............380 lb

Center passengers ....240 lb

Aft passengers................................220 lb

Baggage ....120 lb

Fuel ....75 gal

Note: A convenient way to tabulate your answer is to calculate the ZFW and moment (without fuel) and then add the fuel weight and moment to find the takeoff weight and moment.

Answer. Yes, the CG is within limits throughout the flight.

	Weight (lb)	Mom/1000 (lb-in/1000)	
Empty weight	2260	93.2	
Pilot and front seat passenger	380	14.0	
Center passengers	240	17.0	
Aft passengers	220	22.0	
Baggage	120	16.5	
ZFW	3220	162.7	◄ — OK
Fuel: 75 gal	450	19.2	
Total weight	3670	181.9	◄ — OK

✍ Now complete **Review 12, Part (d)** on page 270.

Note for Commercial Students. The weight and balance graphs used in the Commercial Knowledge Exam are shown in Figure 12-28. Practice questions using these graphs are in the Commercial Review at the end of the chapter.

Weight-Shift and Weight-Change by Formula

Weight-shift and weight-change problems may be easily solved using our standard tabulated layout, without the need to remember any formulas. Some pilots, however, prefer to use a formula for these problems, and so we now include this method, which is based on:

> **Any change in individual moments = the change in total moments**

Weight-Shift

Suppose weight "w" is shifted from the aft baggage compartment to the forward baggage compartment (Figure 12-21). This will have the effect of shifting the CG forward. Since weight is shifted (not changed), airplane gross weight remains the same.

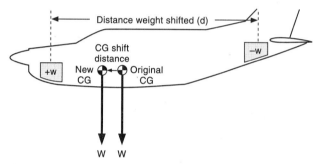

Figure 12-21. Shifting weight forward moves the CG forward

Change in individual moments = change in total moment
Therefore:

> **Weight shifted × distance shifted = airplane GW CG shift**

Example 12. Your loaded airplane weighs 4,000 lb with CG at station 91.0. How much baggage must be shifted from the rear baggage area (station 150) to the forward baggage area (station 30) in order to move the CG to station 89.0?

$$\begin{aligned}
\text{weight shifted} \times \text{distance shifted} &= \text{GW} \times \text{CG shift}\\
\text{w} \times (150 - 30) &= \text{GW} \times (91.0 - 89.0)\\
\text{w} \times 120 &= 4{,}000 \times 2\\
\text{w} &= \frac{4{,}000 \times 2}{120} = 6.7 \text{ lb}
\end{aligned}$$

Weight-Change

If weight "w" is added to the forward baggage compartment (Figure 12-22), it will have the effect of shifting the CG forward, as will removing weight from aft of the CG. Conversely, reducing weight ahead of the CG will shift the CG rearward, as will adding weight aft. Weight added to shift the CG is known as *ballast*.

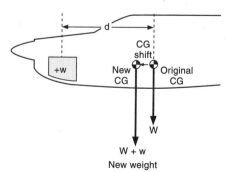

Figure 12-22. Adding weight forward moves the CG forward

Change in individual moments = change in total moment

Therefore:

Weight shifted × distance shifted = new GW CG shift

Example 13. Your airplane weighs 4,000 lb with the CG located at station 85.0. The fuel tanks are at station 84.0, and the fuel consumption is 10 gph. What is the CG position after 2 hours of flight?

Answer.

Fuel burn = 2 hr @ 10 gph = 20 gal = 20 × 6 lb = 120lb

therefore the new GW = 4,000 – 120 = 3.880 lb

As the fuel forward of the CG reduces, the CG will move aft.

$$\text{Change in individual moments} = \text{change in total moment}$$
$$120 \times 1.0 = 3,880 \times \text{CG shift}$$
$$\text{CG shift} = \frac{120 \times 1.0}{3,880} = 0.03$$

Therefore new position of CG is (85.0 + 0.03) = 85.03 inches aft of the datum (Figure 12-23).

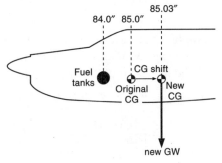

Figure 12-23. Removing weight forward of the CG, shifts the CG aft

Mean Aerodynamic Chord

The mean aerodynamic chord (MAC) is the chord of an imaginary rectangular wing that has the same aerodynamic characteristics as the actual wing. In effect, this replaces the actual wing (which may have a quite different and more complicated plan form) for calculation purposes with a theoretical simplified, rectangular average wing.

The MAC is the chord of this theoretical rectangular wing and its main use is as a reference for longitudinal stability characteristics (such as balance). The MAC of the airplane illustrated in Figures 12-24 and 12-25 is:

• length of MAC 60.00 inches;

• location of leading edge of MAC 80.00 inches aft of reference datum.

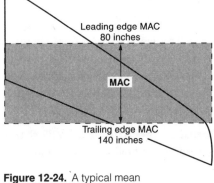

Figure 12-24. A typical mean aerodynamic chord

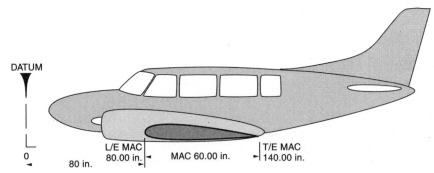

Figure 12-25. MAC in relation to the airplane

This concept of MAC is used by designers when they determine stability characteristics of the airplane, bearing in mind that any turning moments generated by the lift–weight and thrust–drag couples will have to be balanced by a force (usually downward) from the horizontal stabilizer.

Calculating CG Position as a "Percentage MAC"

The greatest forces acting on an airplane are weight and lift. It is important that the distance between them is not too great to ensure that their turning moment is kept within limits.

Since the lift force will act somewhere along the mean aerodynamic chord, it is common for the CG to be specified as a position on the MAC, usually as a percentage aft of the MAC leading edge.

$$\text{CG position as \% MAC} = \frac{\text{distance aft of MAC leading edge}}{\text{MAC}} \times \frac{100}{1} \text{ \% MAC}$$

Example 14. Convert a CG of 100.00 inches aft of reference datum to a percentage MAC. CG at 100.00 inches aft of datum is (100.00 – 80.00) = 20.00 inches aft of the MAC leading edge.

$$\% \text{ MAC} = \frac{\text{distance aft of MAC leading edge}}{\text{MAC}} \times \frac{100}{1}$$

$$= \frac{20.00}{60.00} \times \frac{100}{1} = 33.3\% \text{ MAC}$$

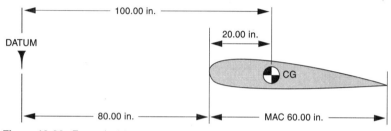

Figure 12-26. Example 14

Note: The center of pressure (CP), through which the lift force may be considered to act, is, for most airplanes in normal flight, somewhere on the forward half of the wing chord. The CG (through which the weight force may be considered to act) should be forward of the CP so that, if power fails, the nose will drop.

Relating the Allowable CG Range to the MAC

The weight and balance documents for a certain airplane specify the position and length of the mean aerodynamic chord (MAC leading edge 219.0 inches aft of datum; length of MAC 190.0 inches), which allows us to relate the allowable CG range to the MAC.

For this airplane, at all weights, the **aft CG limit** is 268.0 inches, which is (268.0 – 219.0) = 49.0 inches aft of the MAC leading edge:

$$\% \text{ MAC} = \frac{49.0}{190.0} \times \frac{100}{1} = 25.79 \text{ \% MAC}.$$

However the **forward CG limit** often depends on the airplane weight. Below a certain low weight, the forward CG limit is at 240.0 inches, which is (240.0 – 219.0) = 21.0 inches aft of the MAC leading edge:

$$\% \text{ MAC} = \frac{21.0}{190.0} \times \frac{100}{1} = 11.05 \text{ \% MAC}.$$

At the maximum gross weight, the forward CG limit is 256.0 inches, which is (256.0 – 219.0) = 37.0 inches aft of the MAC leading edge:

$$\% \text{ MAC} = \frac{37.0}{190.0} \times \frac{100}{1} = 19.47 \text{ \% MAC}.$$

Between these weights the forward limit progressively moves aft as weight increases. These are quite typical figures, in that the CG range for most conventional airplanes lies somewhere between 10% and 30% MAC. Provided that the CG lies within the CG limits for that particular gross weight, the in-flight stability and control characteristics of the airplane will be acceptable.

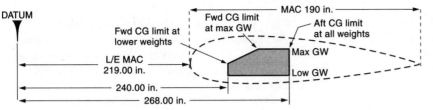

Fwd CG limit at lower weights

Fwd CG limit at max GW

MAC 190 in.

Aft CG limit at all weights

L/E MAC 219.00 in.

Max GW

Low GW

240.00 in.

268.00 in.

DATUM

Note: The shaded area represents the CG envelope position on the wing at certain weights.

Figure 12-27. The CG range related to MAC

The allowable CG range is quite restricted (28.0 inches maximum, covering only some 15% of the forward part of the MAC) because the lift and weight forces are so large. Small movements in the position of the CG or the center of pressure will produce large alterations of turning moments, because of the magnitude of the forces involved.

✍ Commercial students complete **Review 12, Commercial** on page 272.

✍ **Review 12**   Weight and Balance

Part (a)

1. The maximum allowable gross weight permitted for takeoff is the _____ .
   ➤ maximum takeoff weight

2. A short runway may not allow us to land at the MLW (structural), but at a lighter _____ landing weight.
   ➤ performance-limited

3. Landing weight = takeoff weight minus _____ .
   ➤ fuel burn-off

4. The empty weight of an airplane includes which of the following items: airframe, powerplant, permanently installed equipment, full fuel, unusable fuel, full oil, unusable oil, hydraulic fluid, pilots, passengers, baggage?
   ➤ airframe, powerplant, permanently installed equipment, unusable fuel, unusable oil (unless it is specifically stated that full oil is included), hydraulic fluid

5. One gallon of AVGAS weighs _____ pounds.
   26 gallons of AVGAS weighs _____ pounds.
   ➤ 6, 156

6. An aircraft is loaded 110 pounds over maximum certificated gross weight. If fuel (AVGAS) is drained to bring the aircraft weight within limits, how much fuel should be drained?
   (a) 15.7 gallons.   (b) 16.2 gallons.   (c) 18.4 gallons.
   ➤ (c)

Part (b)

1. If the CG is located at the rear limit, the airplane will be (less/very) stable longitudinally.
   ➤ less

2. The longer the moment arm from the CG, the (greater/smaller) the turning effect of a given force.
   ➤ greater

3. The CG of an aircraft may be determined by:
   (a) dividing total arms by total moments.
   (b) dividing total moments by total weight.
   (c) multiplying total weight by total moments.
   ➤ (b)

4. If all index units are positive when computing weight and balance, the location of the datum would be at the:
   (a) centerline of the main wheels.
   (b) nose, or out in front of the airplane.
   (c) centerline of the nose or tailwheel, depending on the type of airplane.
   ➤ (b)

5. If 1 index unit = 100 lb-in, what is the moment for 176 index units?
   ➤ 17,600 lb-in

6. What is the maximum amount of fuel (in pounds and gallons) that you can carry if the maximum takeoff weight is 2,400 lb? Tank capacity is 50 gallons. *(No need to consider CG position.)*

    Empty weight .... 1,432 lb
    Front seat occupants .... 320 lb
    Rear seat occupants .... 340 lb
    Baggage .... 20 lb
    Oil .... 8 qt 15 lb

➤   273 lb (2,400 – 2,127), 45.5 gal

Empty weight	1432 lb
Front seat	320
Rear seat	340
Baggage	20
Oil	15
ZFW	2127
MTOW	2400
Fuel	**273 lb**

← This is the zero fuel weight for these condition. Note that it is not a limiting weight.

7. What is the maximum weight of baggage that can be carried when the airplane is loaded as follows for a takeoff that is performance-limited to 2,910 lb, because of a high elevation airport and high temperatures? *(No need to consider balance.)*

    Basic empty weight (incl. full oil) ...... 2,015 lb
    Front seat occupants .... 369 lb
    Rear seat occupants .... 267 lb
    Fuel (36 gal) .... —

➤   43 lb

Basic empty weight (incl. oil)	2015 lb
Front seat	369
Rear seat	267
Fuel: 36 gal @ 6 lb/gal	216
ZFW	2867
Max allowed TOW	2910
Therefore, max. baggage is:	**43 lb**

8. Where is the CG located in the following situation? (No mention of oil, so assume full oil in empty weight.)

	Wt (lb)	Arm (in)	Mom (lb-in)
Empty weight	1,495.0	101.4	151,593.0
Pilot & passengers	380.0	64.0	—
Fuel (30 gal usable)	—	96.0	—

    (a) 92.44
    (b) 94.01
    (c) 119.8

➤   (b)

	Weight (lb)	Arm (in)	Moment (lb-in)
Empty weight	1495.0	101.4	151593.0
Pilot & passenger	380.0	64.0	24320.0
Full fuel 30 gal usable	180.0	96.0	17280.0
Total	2055.0	94.1	193193.0

Part (c)

For Questions 1 to 3, use the loading graphs in Figure 12-15 on page 255.

1. Calculate the loaded index units (moments/1,000) of the airplane loaded as follows, and determine in which category you may operate it.

	Weight (lb)	Mom/1,000
Empty weight	1,350	51.5
Pilot and front passenger	310	—
Rear passengers	96	—
Fuel (38 gal)	—	—
Oil (8 qt)	—	–0.2

➤   80.8, utility category

Item	Weight (lb)	Moment (mom/1,000)
Empty weight	1350	51.5
Pilot & front passenger	310	11.5
Rear passengers	96	7.0
Fuel: 38 gal	228	11.0
Oil, 8 quarts	15	–0.2
Gross weight	**1999**	**80.8**

Using the center of gravity moment envelope 1,999 lb and 80.8 inches lie just within the envelope in the utility category.

2. Calculate the loaded moment (normal category) and determine if it is within limits. Where is the CG?

	Weight (lb)	Mom/1,000
Empty weight	1,350	51.5
Pilot and front passenger	380	—
Fuel (48 gal)	—	—
Oil (8 qt)	—	—

➤ 79.2, 38.9 inches aft of datum. The weight and moment index of the oil is given in the graph at Note 2.

Item	Weight (lb)	Moment (mom/1,000)
Empty weight	1350	51.5
Pilot & front passenger	380	14.2
Fuel: 48 gal = 288 lb	288	13.7
Oil, 8 qt	15	–0.2
Gross weight	2033	79.2

Using the center of gravity moment envelope 2,033 lb and 79.2 lie within the envelope in the normal category.

$$\text{CG position} = \frac{\text{total moment}}{\text{total weight}}$$

$$= \frac{79,200}{2,033} = \textbf{38.9} \text{ inches aft of datum}$$

3. Calculate the maximum amount of fuel that may be in the tanks when the airplane is loaded as follows:

	Weight (lb)	Mom/1,000
Empty weight	1,350	51.5
Pilot and front passenger	340	—
Rear passengers	310	—
Baggage	45	—
Oil (8 qt)	—	—

(a) 24 gallons.

(b) 32 gallons.

(c) 40 gallons.

➤ (c)

1. Fill in the table as far as possible.

2. Calculate weight and moments as far as possible—without the fuel, since it is an unknown quantity.

3. Add up the actual weights and, from the known maximum gross weight (2,300 lb shown on CG envelope for the normal category), calculate the maximum possible fuel from a weight point of view (no balance as yet), and check that it does not exceed fuel tank limits (48 gal = 288 lb).

4. Add the fuel weight and moment to table, find new totals, and check they lie inside the CG envelope.

5. Convert pounds of fuel to gallons (1 gal = 6 lb).

Item	Weight (Lb)	Moment (Mom/1,000)
Empty weight	1350	51.5
Pilot & front passenger	340	12.5
Rear passengers	310	22.5
Baggage	45	4.0
Oil, 8 qt	15	–0.2
ZFW	2060	90.3
Maximum fuel (2300 – 2060)	240	11.5
Maximum gross weight (from CG envelope)	2300	101.8 OK

For questions 4–6, use the tables in Figures 12-16a and 12-16b (on page 256 and page 257).

4. Calculate the maximum weight of baggage that can be carried when the airplane is loaded as follows:

Front seat occupants .... 387 lb
Rear seat occupants .... 293 lb
Fuel .... 35 gal

➤ 45 lb

Item	Weight (lb)	Moment (mom/1,000)
Empty weight	1350	51.5
Front seats (200 +187)	387	330 (170 + 160)
Rear seats (140 + 153)	293	355 (169 + 186)
Fuel: 35 gal	210	158
Gross weight (no baggage)	2905	2397
Baggage	45	63
Gross weight (with baggage)	2950	2460
Maximum weight	2950 OK	2422-2499 OK

Note: The empty weight and moment is stated in Figure 12-16a.

5. Determine the weight and balance, and calculate if the CG and weight of the airplane are within limits.

Front seat occupants .... 350 lb
Rear seat occupants .... 325 lb
Baggage .... 27 lb
Fuel 35gal

➤ Weight is 2,927 lb, CG is 83.39 inches aft of datum, weight and balance is within limits.

Note: "Determine weight and balance" means: "calculate the weight, calculate the moments, and also calculate the position of the CG".

Item	Weight (lb)	Mom/100
Empty weight	2015	1554
Front seats (200 + 150)	350	298 (170 + 128)
Rear seats (200 + 125)	325	393 (242 + 151)
Baggage	27	38
Fuel: 35 gal	210	158
Gross weight	**2927** OK	**2441** OK, within the range 2399–2483 at the very close weight of 2930 lb

To calculate the CG position:

mom/100 = 2,441

moment = 244,100 lb-in
= 2,927 lb × CG arm

CG arm = $\frac{79,200}{2,033}$ = **83.39** inches aft of datum

6. Is the following weight and balance within limits?

Front seat occupants .... 415 lb
Rear seat occupants .... 110 lb
Baggage .... 32 lb
Fuel .... 63 gal

➤ The weight is within limits (right on maximum), but the CG is out of limits (because the mom/100 lies outside the allowable range at that weight).

Item	Weight (lb)	Mom/100
Empty weight	2015	1554
Front seats (215 + 200)	415	353 (183 + 170)
Rear seats	110	133
Baggage	32	45
Fuel: mains 44 gal aux 19 gal	264 114	198 107
Gross weight	**2950** OK (max wt)	**2390** NOT OK, 2422–2499 is the CG range at 2950 lb

Part (d)

For Questions 1 to 5 refer to Figures 12-16a and 12-16b (pages 256 and 257).

1. Which action can adjust the airplane's weight to the maximum gross weight and the CG located within limits for takeoff, when it is loaded as follows?

Front seat occupants .... 425 lb
Rear seat occupants .... 300 lb
Fuel (main tanks) .... 44 gal

(a) Drain 12 gallons of fuel.

(b) Drain 9 gallons of fuel.

(c) Transfer 12 gallons of fuel from the main tanks to the auxiliary tanks.

➤ (b) Drain 9 gallons of fuel.

Item	Weight (lb)	Mom/100
Empty weight	2015	1554
Front seats (225 + 200)	425	362 (192 + 170)
Rear (150 + 150)	300	364 (182 + 182)
Fuel: mains 44 gal	264	198
Gross weight	**3004** NOT OK, max wt 2950 lb	**2478**

Need to reduce gross weight by (3,004 – 2,950) = 54 lb = $\frac{54}{6}$ gal = 9 gal.

Shifting fuel changes the CG, but not the weight; balance is not the problem, but weight is; so answer (c) is not correct.

Answers (a) and (b) are correct from the weight point of view, since draining 9 or more gallons of fuel will bring the weight within limits; so now we need to check the balance. Try the 9 gal first, since the less we have to drain the better, and if this doesn't work, try the balance after draining 12 gal.

Item	Weight (lb)	Mom/100
Empty weight	2015	1554
Front seats (225 + 200)	425	362 (192 + 170)
Rear seats (150 + 150)	300	364 (182 + 182)
Fuel: mains 35 gal	210	158
Gross weight	**2959** OK	**2438** OK, 2422-2499 is allowable range

In these workings, we have shown how the weight values (and associated mom/100) have been sub-divided and necessary interpolations made. With practice, you will be able to do this without having to lay out your workings in this way. Remember, you can always use **weight arm** to derive the moment.

2. On landing, the front passenger (180 lb) departs the airplane. A rear passenger (204 lb) moves to the front passenger position. What effect does this have on the CG if the airplane weighed 2,690 lb and the mom/100 was 2,260 prior to the passenger transfer?

    (a) The CG moves forward approximately 3 inches.

    (b) The weight changes, but the CG is unaffected.

    (c) The CG moves forward approximately 0.1 inch.

➤ (a)

This question is best solved by following the **tabulation method** shown in Example 9 on page 260. The following is the sequence of steps.

    (a) Deduct the front passenger and derive the new gross weight and moment.

    (b) Deduct the rear passenger and derive the new gross weight and moment.

    (c) Add rear passenger (204 lb) to front seat and derive final gross weight and moment.

    (d) Check that weight and moment are within limits.

    (e) Calculate original and new CG locations and determine the CG movement.

Step	Item	Wt (lb)	Arm (in)	Mom/100
(1)	Gross weight	2690	84.01	2260
	Front seat (OUT)	−180		−153
(2)	New GW	2510	–	2107
	Rear seat (OUT)	−204		−247
(3)	New GW	2306	–	1860
	Front seat (IN)	+204		+173
(4)	Final GW	2510	81.00	2033
	Both GW and moment (mom/100) are within limits.			

    (f) Orig. CG = 84.01 in. aft of datum (226,000/2,690)
    New CG = 81.00 in. aft of datum (203,300/2,510)
    CG movement 84.01 – 81.00 = **3.01 inches** forward (say 3 inches)

---

3. With the following loading, can you carry 100 lb of baggage and, if not, what action could you take to carry the baggage? What is the final CG position?

Pilot .... 180 lb
2 passengers on rear seats .... 2 × 170 lb
Minimum fuel required .... 30 gal

➤ Yes, you can carry 100 lb but must move one passenger to front seat. Final CG is at 82.84 inches aft of datum.

Item	Weight (lb)	Mom/100
Empty weight	2015	1554
Pilot: front seat	180	153
2 × rear seat @ 170 lb	340	412
Baggage	100	140
Minimum fuel: 30 gal	180	135
Gross weight	**2815**	**2394** *CG outside aft limit*
1 × rear passenger OUT	−170	−206 *to move CG fwd*
New GW	2645	2188
1 × passenger to front	+170	+144
Final GW	2815	2332 *OK*

As loaded initially, CG is outside aft limits of 2,393 mom/100 (by interpolation). So, 1 passenger must move from rear seat to front seat (rear arm 121, front arm 85). CG limits for 2,815 lb are 2,271 – 2,393 mom/100, so the new CG location is well within.

CG location = 2,332 index units

           $= \dfrac{233{,}200 \text{ lb-in}}{2{,}815}$

           = **82.84 inches aft of datum**

---

4. What effect does a 35 gal fuel burn have on the weight and balance, if the airplane weighs 2,890 lb and the mom/100 is 2,452 at takeoff?

    (a) Weight reduced by 210 lb, and CG is aft of limits.

    (b) Weight reduced by 210 lb, and CG is unaffected.

    (c) Weight reduced to 2,680 lb, and CG moves forward.

➤ (a) Burning 35 gallons will reduce gross weight by 210 lb, which will reduce the mom/100 by 158 (find this on table, or work it out as 210 lb arm 75 in. = 15,750 lb-in = 157.5 mom/100; say 158). New gross weight = 2,890 – 210 = 2,680 lb
New mom/100 = 2,452 – 158 = 2,294; but allowable limits are 2,123 to 2,287; therefore, weight is OK, but mom/100 is too great, which means CG is aft of limits.

---

5. Can you take off under the following conditions and, if not, what ballast must be added in the baggage locker? Also, calculate the landing weight and CG location.

Pilot & passenger (front) .... 300 lb
Passenger (rear) .... 180 lb
Baggage .... 60 lb
Fuel (44 mains + 15 aux) .... 59 gal
Planned fuel burn-off to landing .... 35 gal
(assume auxiliary fuel used first).

➤ Yes, takeoff is permitted and no ballast is required; landing weight 2,699 lb, CG 82.25 inches aft of datum.

Item	Wt (lb)	Mom/100
Empty weight	2015	1554
Front seat	300	256
Rear seat	180	218
Baggage	60	84
ZFW	2555	2112 *OK; 1990 limit*
Fuel: mains 44 gal aux 15 gal	264 90	198 85
Planned TOW	2909 *OK*	2395 *OK; 2377 limit*
Burn-off: aux 15 gal	−90	−85
	2819	2310 *OK*
mains 20 gal	−120	−90
Landing weight	2699	2220 *OK; 2144 limit*

$$\text{CG at landing} = \frac{222{,}000 \text{ lb-in}}{2{,}699 \text{ lb}} = \textbf{82.25 inches aft of datum}$$

Commercial Review

1. Calculate the position of the CG for the following weights at the given locations.

   Weight A ....165 lb at 135 in. aft of datum.
   Weight B ....125 lb at 115 in. aft of datum.
   Weight C ....75 lb at 85 in. aft of datum.

   ➤ CG is 117.9 inches aft of datum

	Weight (lb)	Arm (in. aft of datum)	Moment (lb-in)
A	165	135	22275
B	125	115	14375
C	75	85	6375
Totals	365	117.9	43025

2. Determine the CG under these conditions.

   Empty weight ....857 lb, arm +29.07 in.
   Pilot (fwd seat) ....145 lb, arm −45.30 in.
   Passenger (aft seat).........175 lb, arm +1.60 in.
   Ballast.............................15 lb, arm −45.30 in.

   ➤ CG is 15.05 inches aft of datum (at +15.05 in.)

	Weight (lb)	Arm (in. aft of datum)	Moments (lb-in)
Empty weight	857	29.07	24913.0
Pilot (fwd)	145	−45.30	−6568.5
Passenger (aft)	175	+1/60	+280.0
Ballast	15	−45.30	−679.5
Totals	1,192	+15/05	+17945.0

For Questions 3 and 4, refer to Figure 12-28.

3. Given:

   Empty weight (oil included) ....1,271 lb
   Empty weight moment..................102.04 lb-in/1,000
   Pilot + copilot..............................400 lb
   Rear seat passenger ....140 lb
   Cargo...100 lb
   Fuel ....37 gal

   Is the airplane loaded within limits?

   (a) Yes, the weight and CG is within limits.
   (b) No, the weight exceeds the maximum allowable.
   (c) No, the weight is acceptable, but the CG is aft of the aft limit.

   ➤ (a)

Item	Weight	Moment/1,000
Empty weight	1271	102.04
Pilot and copilot	400	36.0
Rear seat passenger	140	17.5
Cargo	100	11.5
Fuel: 37 gal	222	20.0
Gross weight	**2,133**	**187.04**

   Plotting 2,133 lb against 187.04 index units on the bottom graph, it falls within the envelope in the normal category.

4. Given:

   Empty weight (oil is included)...........1,271 lb
   Empty weight moment (in-lb/1,000)..102.04
   Pilot and copilot ....360 lb
   Cargo...340 lb
   Fuel ....37 gal

   Will the CG remain within limits after 30 gallons of fuel have been used in flight?

   (a) Yes, the CG will remain within limits.
   (b) No, the CG will be located aft of the CG limit.
   (c) Yes, but the CG will be located in the shaded area of the CG envelope.

   ➤ (a) Fuel remaining is 37 gal (start) − 30 gal (burned) = 7 gal = 7 × 6 lb = 42 lb

Item	Weight	Moment/1,000
Empty weight	1271	102.04
Pilot and copilot	360	32.5
Cargo	340	39.5
Fuel (7 gal. × 6 lb/gal)	42	4.0
Totals	**2,013**	**178.04**

   The intersection of total weight of 2,013 lb and total moment of 178.04 in-lb is within the CG moment envelope.

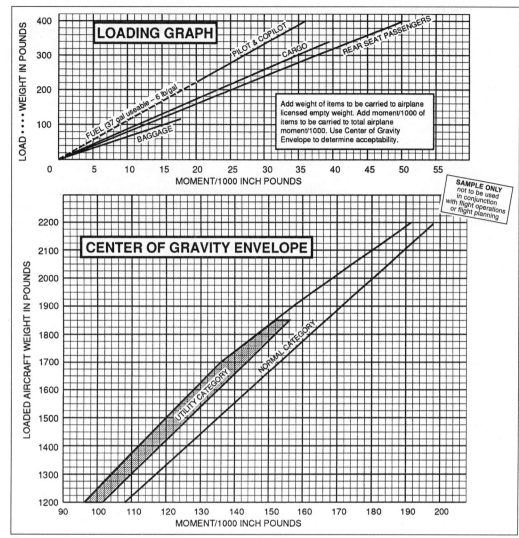

Figure 12-28. Commercial Knowledge Exam weight and balance graphs

For Questions 5 and 6, solve using tabular method.

5. The airplane is loaded to a gross weight of 5,000 lb, with three pieces of luggage in the rear baggage compartment. The CG is 98 inches aft of datum, which is 2 inches aft of the permissible rear limit. If you move two pieces of luggage weighing a total of 100 lb from the rear baggage compartment (145 inches aft of datum) to the front compartment (45 inches aft of datum), what is the new CG?

➤ 96 in aft of datum

	Weight (lb)	Arm (in)	Moment (lb-in)
Original tools	5000	98	490000
Rear baggage OUT	−100	145	−14500
Front baggage IN	+100	45	4500
New tools	5000	96	48000

6. Determine the position of the CG after 1 hr 45 min of flight time, given the following data:

Total weight .... 4,037 lb
CG location station 67.8
Fuel consumption .... 14.7 gph
Fuel tanks .... station 68.0

➤ 67.79 inches aft of datum

Weight change = fuel burn in 1 hr 45 min

= $\frac{105}{60}$ hours × 14.7 gph × 6 lb/gal

= 154.35 lb

	Wt (lb)	Arm (in)	Moment (lb-in)
Original tools	4037.0	67.8	273708.6
Fuel change	−154.35	68.0	−10495.8
New tools	3882.65	**67.79**	263212.8

7. Given:

    Total weight ....4,137 lb
    CG location station 67.8
    Fuel consumption ....13.7 gph
    Fuel tanks station 68.0

    After 1 hour 30 minutes of flight time, the CG would be located at station:

    (a) 67.79.

    (b) 68.79.

    (c) 70.78.

➤   (a) *Working:*

    Wt change = 1.5 hours @ 13. 6 lb/gal 123.3 lb from aft of original CG, which will move the CG forward.

    $$\text{Change in individual moments} = \text{change in total moment}$$
    $$\text{weight change} \times \text{arm} = \text{change in total moment}$$
    $$123.3 \times (68 - 67.8) = (4{,}137 - 123.3) \times \text{CG shift}$$
    $$= \frac{123.3 \times 0.2}{4{,}013.7} = 0.006 \text{ fwd}$$
    $$\text{new CG position} = 67{,}800$$
    $$\underline{-0.006}$$
    $$67.794$$

8. Given an airplane loaded with a ramp weight of 3,650 lb and having a CG of 94.0, approximately how much baggage would have to be moved from the rear baggage area at station 180, to the forward baggage area at station 40, in order to move the CG to 92.0?

    (a) 52.14 lb.

    (b) 62.24 lb.

    (c) 78.14 lb.

➤   (a) *Working:*

    $$\text{weight shifted} \times \text{distance shifted} = \text{GW} \times \text{CG shift}$$
    $$\text{weight shifted} \times (180 - 40) = 3{,}650 \times (94.0 - 92.0)$$
    $$\text{weight shifted} \times 140 = 3{,}650 \times 2$$
    $$\text{weight shifted} = \frac{23.3 \times 0.2}{140} = 52.14$$

9. Given:

    Total weight ....2,017 lb
    CG location.........58.5 in. aft of datum
    CG limits ....between 60 and 68 in. aft of datum

    What minimum weight must be added as ballast in the rear baggage compartment (120 inches aft of datum), to bring the CG within limits?

➤   50.43 lb

Working:

Add "**w**" lb as ballast, to shift CG aft to at least 60 in.

$$\text{wt change} \times \text{dist from CG} = \text{new GW} \times \text{CG shift}$$
$$w \times (120 - 58.5) = (2{,}017 + w) \times (60 - 58.5)$$
$$w \times 61.5 = (2{,}017 \times 1.5) \times 1.5$$
$$= (2{,}017 \times 1.5) + 1.5\,w$$
$$61.5\,w - 1.5\,w = 2{,}017 \times 1.5$$
$$60\,w = 2{,}017 \times 1.5$$
$$w = \frac{2{,}017 \times 1.5}{60}$$
$$= 50.43 \text{ lb}$$

10. Using the *Moment Limit versus Weight* table in Figure 12-16b (page 257), express the fwd (minimum) and rear (maximum) CG limits as % MAC for an airplane with a gross weight of 2,700 lb. The leading edge of the MAC is 75 inches aft of the datum, and the length of the MAC is 40 inches.

➤   fwd limit 11% MAC, rear limit 25.73% MAC

    Working:
    From Figure 12-16b, for GW 2,700 lb the total moments lie between 2,144 mom/100 and 2,303 mom/100. The forward limit of the CG is therefore:

    $$\frac{214{,}400}{2{,}700} = 79.4''$$

    and the aft limit is at:

    $$\frac{230{,}300}{2{,}700} = 85.3''$$

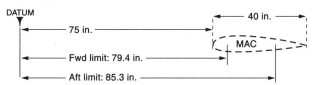

    The forward limit is therefore (79.4 – 75) inside the leading edge, which gives:

    $$\frac{(79.4 - 75)}{40} \times \frac{100}{1} \text{ % MAC} = 11\% \text{ MAC}$$

    and the aft limit is at:

    $$\frac{(85.3 - 75)}{40} \times \frac{100}{1} \text{ % MAC} = 25.75\% \text{ MAC}$$

11. The leading edge of the MAC is 75 inches aft of the datum, and the length of the MAC is 40 inches. What are the CG limits expressed in inches aft of datum if the MAC limits are: forward 13.75%, rear 25.07%?

➤   fwd limit 80.50 inches, rear limit 85.03 inches

Flight Physiology 13

Am I Fit to Fly?

Before each flight you must ask yourself, "Am I fit to fly? Do I feel well? Am I able to perform the physical and mental tasks that may be required of me as pilot-in-command?"

Fitness alone will not be sufficient protection against aeromedical problems. While fitness and good health are advantageous, you must be familiar with the potential problems that you may encounter and their effect on you and flight safety, such as low temperatures, lack of oxygen, an excess of oxygen, decompression sickness, food poisoning, fatigue and carbon monoxide poisoning.

You must also learn good judgement and decision-making skills if you intend to fly safely. If you learn to manage the obvious stresses that come from being pilot-in-command you will be a good pilot.

Physical Fitness

Physical fitness helps you cope better with stress, fatigue and the reduced availability of oxygen at higher levels in the atmosphere. Keeping fit requires regular exercise. If you are grossly unfit or obese, obtain medical supervision to advise you on a suitable exercise program and diet.

Mental Fitness

Flying an airplane involves physical activity but the main workload on a pilot is mental. Mental fitness is vital to safe flying, but it can be degraded by:

- medication;
- drugs, including alcohol and nicotine;
- excessive stress;
- personal or family problems;
- lack of sleep or poor eating habits; and
- fatigue or allowing oneself to become over-tired.

Pilots who are not mentally fit cannot make good decisions before or during a flight. **Aeronautical decision making** is the process by which pilots assess the risk of a particular flight or a particular maneuver during flight and judge the consequences. Pilots who lack good decision making skills can fall into dangerous traps including peer pressure, mind set, get-there-itis, duck-under syndrome, scud running, VFR into IFR, low fuel, poor preflight planning and flying outside the airplane's envelope.

The FAA defines five types of hazardous mental attitudes for pilots. They include:

- **Antiauthority (don't tell me!).** People who don't like others to tell them what to do are often resentful of wise advice and prone to disregarding the rules. *The antidote to antiauthority is: Follow the rules; they are usually right.*

Stress management includes:
1. Identifying hazardous attitudes.
2. Learning to modify your behavior.
3. Recognizing and coping with stress.
4. Developing a method to assess risks.
5. Using all your resources.
6. Being able to evaluate your performance.

Pilots must assess the risks involved in any flight. Good judgment and decision-making skills can be learned.

- **Impulsivity (do something, quickly!).** People who don't stop to think before they act are impulsive. They often do the first thing that comes to mind. *The antidote is: Not so fast. Think first.*

- **Invulnerability (it won't happen to me).** We all know accidents happen, but some feel it could never happen to them. They are far more likely to take chances and risks. *The antidote is: It could happen to me.*

- **Macho (I can do it).** Now, here's a person with something to prove and he or she will probably take risks to show off. *The antidote is: Taking chances is foolish.*

- **Resignation (what's the use?).** Resigned pilots figure that the flight went well because they were lucky. If the flight goes poorly, however, it isn't their fault, there's nothing they can, or will do to change things. *The antidote to this attitude is: I'm not helpless. I can make a difference.*

Pilots can avoid all of these dangerous mental attitudes by using a simple mnemonic checklist when making decisions about flying.

1. **D**etect. Notice that a change in the flight has occurred.
2. **E**stimate. Assess your need to counter or react to the change.
3. **C**hoose. Pick the successful outcome you want for the flight.
4. **I**dentify. Sort out actions that can successfully control or counter the change in flight.
5. **D**o. Take action to effect a change back to the flight you had in mind.
6. **E**valuate. Assess whether the flight is now where you want it. If not, start the steps over again.

In short, **DECIDE.** You'll find that your cockpit stress is significantly lowered if you use these steps to make good decisions before and during a flight. You'll also learn to recognize a dangerous attitude and change it, before it takes you on a journey you may not have intended.

Keep stress down by: avoiding high risk flights; knowing your personal limits; staying proficient in your aircraft; concentrate on flying the aircraft, first and foremost.

Medical Checks

Regular checks by an aviation medical examiner are required to monitor your general health, both physical and mental. Major items in the medical test include checks of the central nervous system (including eyesight), the cardio-vascular system (including heart and blood pressure), normal functioning of the kidneys (using a urine test), hearing ability and, finally, the respiratory system (ears, nose, throat and lungs), especially the Eustachian tubes for their ability to allow pressures to equalize either side of the eardrums.

Regular medical checks verify your general health and fitness, but occasional bouts of sickness or injury may make you temporarily unfit to fly. Pilots carry a heavy responsibility to themselves and to the general community.

A minor complaint on the ground (such as the common cold) may have serious effects under the stress of flying and high altitudes. In addition, pharmaceutical drugs taken to treat an illness may further impair flying ability and physical comfort in flight. The Federal Aviation Regulations (FARs) require you to ground yourself at any time you do not meet the conditions required for the issue of your medical certificate.

Good dental care is also important. Air or other gases trapped in cavities may expand and cause pain as cabin pressure drops.

Do not assume that because you have a physical disability you may not be able to hold a pilot certificate. There are many people with disabilities who are permitted to fly. Check with an aviation medical examiner.

Medication

Until cleared by a doctor, you must assume that *any* drug or medication will temporarily ground you. Common medications considered incompatible with flying include:

- antibiotics (for example, penicillin) used to combat infection;
- tranquilizers, antidepressants and sedatives;
- stimulants (amphetamines) used to maintain wakefulness or suppress appetite;
- antihistamines, often used to combat colds and hay fever;
- drugs to control high blood pressure;
- analgesics to relieve pain;
- anesthetics (used for local, general or dental purposes) usually require about 24 hours before you may return to flying.

Upper Respiratory Tract Problems

The common cold, hay fever, sinusitis, tonsillitis or any similar condition can lead to blocked ears, which is a problem for a pilot.

Each eardrum has ambient pressure from the outer ear on one side and air pressure in the middle ear on the other side—the middle ear being an air-filled cavity connected indirectly to ambient air via the Eustachian tube. The function of each Eustachian tube is to allow the air pressure in the middle ear to equalize with ambient pressure. When air is unable to pass through the Eustachian tubes and equalize pressures either side of the eardrums, great pain and ultimately permanent damage to the eardrums can be caused.

During a climb, atmospheric pressure on the outer parts of the body decreases. The differential pressure within the inner ear forces the eardrum out and also causes air to flow from the inner ear through the Eustachian tubes into the throat to equalize the pressures.

Most training airplanes only have a low rate of climb (about 500 fpm), allowing adequate time for pressure equalization to occur through the Eustachian tubes, which means that ear problems during the climb are generally not serious. During descent, however, difficulties with the ears may be more serious due to high rates of descent and problems with pressure equalization.

As atmospheric pressure on the outer parts of the body increases during a descent, it pushes the eardrums in. Ideally, some air will flow from the throat and nasal passages through the Eustachian tube into the inner ear and equalize the pressure. However the nature of the Eustachian tubes is such that air will not move into them from the nasal passages as readily as it moves out and so any swelling or blocking can lead to problems. High rates of descent worsen the situation and the pain can be very severe.

Blocked ears can sometimes be cleared by holding your nose and blowing hard (a technique known as the *Valsalva technique),* by chewing, swallowing or yawning. The best advice is, however, if you have a cold, do not fly.

Problems can also arise in the sinuses. Blockages can cause great pain, especially during descent. Do not fly with sinus problems.

"Recreational drugs" such as, marijuana, cocaine and LSD must *never* be mixed with flying. Persons who are dependent on such drugs are not permitted to hold a pilot certificate.

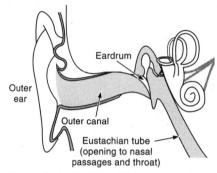

Figure 13-1. The Eustachian tubes equalize pressure either side of the ear drums

If you have a cold, do not fly.

Corrective Lenses

If you are required by the aviation medical examiner to wear glasses or contact lenses to correct your sight, then you should wear them as required. It is also good practice to carry a spare pair of glasses whenever you are flying, and this may be required by your medical certificate. If flying in bright sunlight, especially above clouds, it is good practice to wear a good set of sunglasses.

Food Poisoning

Food poisoning may result from eating improperly prepared food. Its onset may be almost immediate following consumption of the food, or it may not become evident for some hours but, even then, its onset may be very sudden. The stomach pains, nausea, diarrhea, vomiting, and so on, that accompany food poisoning can make it physically impossible for you to perform your pilot duties.

It is a good practice, for the half day prior to flight, to avoid foods that are often associated with food poisoning, including shellfish, fish, mayonnaise, creams, over-ripe and thin-skinned fruits, uncooked foods, and old food (for example, food that has been cooked and stored for some time). If you suspect that some effects of food poisoning are imminent from something bad that you have eaten, do not fly!

Alcohol

A pilot who is under the influence of alcohol is obliged not to fly. The regulations preclude flying within 8 hours of consuming alcohol.

Do not fly under the influence of alcohol.

Even small quantities of alcohol in the blood can impair your performance, with the added danger of relieving anxiety so that you think you are performing marvelously. Alcohol severely affects judgment and ability. High altitude, where there is less oxygen, worsens the effect.

Figure 13-2. Alcohol and flying should never be mixed!

It takes time for the body to remove alcohol and after heavy drinking, alcohol may still be in the blood up to 30 hours later. Sleep will not speed up the removal process, in fact it slows the body processes down and the removal of alcohol may take even longer.

Persons who are dependent on alcohol (alcoholics) are not permitted to hold a pilot certificate.

Smoking

Smoking is detrimental to good health, both in the short and long term.

In the short term—carbon monoxide, which is present in cigarette smoke, is absorbed into the blood in preference to oxygen. This reduces the body's ability to produce energy (including in the brain). The diminished supply of oxygen to the body and brain becomes very noticeable at higher altitudes where cigarette smoke in the cabin can significantly decrease your performance.

In the long term—it is now known that cigarette smoking causes cardiovascular and other diseases. If you want to live a long and healthy life, then you should not smoke.

Cigarette smoking in the cockpit is banned by many captains. In some countries, smoking by everyone including passengers is banned in flight.

Smoking in the airplane should be discouraged.

Fatigue and Sleep Deprivation

Fatigue, tiredness and sleep deprivation can lower your mental and physical capacity quite dramatically. The nature of flying is such that you must train yourself to cope with moderate levels of these complaints and to recognize when your **personal limits** are being approached. However, if you are deeply fatigued you should not be flying!

Do not fly when fatigued. It shows poor judgement.

Fatigue can become deep-seated and chronic if psychological or emotional problems are not solved, resulting in deep rest or sleep not occurring over a prolonged period. Chronic fatigue will be cured when the problems are solved, or at least being coped with, and the person can relax and unstress. A pilot should prohibit himself or herself from flying until this is the case.

Short-term fatigue is caused by overwork, mental stress, an uncomfortable body position, noise, a recent lack of sleep, living it up a bit too much, lack of oxygen or lack of food. Sleep and rest are essential!

To guard against fatigue, you should:

- have your psychological and emotional life under control;
- be reasonably fit;
- eat regularly;
- ensure that you are not deprived of adequate sleep;
- ensure that cockpit comfort is optimized and that energy foods and drink are available on long flights; and
- exercise your limbs occasionally.

Blood Donation

It is recommended that active pilots do not donate blood. While it is a very worthwhile contribution to the community, it does reduce, at least temporarily, the ability to move energy-giving oxygen around the body.

Low Temperatures

Low temperatures can decrease pilot performance, and in extreme cases, cause **hypothermia,** an abnormally low body temperature.

Hypothermia is an abnormally low body temperature.

On average the temperature falls about 2°C (3.5°F) for every 1,000 feet gained in altitude. This means that even though the temperature might be quite warm on the ground, it is likely to be well below freezing at 10,000 feet. Ensure that you take adequate clothing on every flight in case the heater fails. If your airplane does not have a heater think carefully about what clothing you should wear in flight.

✍ Now complete **Review 13, Part (a)** on page 292.

Respiration

Respiration brings oxygen into the body and removes carbon dioxide. By muscular action of the diaphragm, the lungs are expanded and air is drawn in through the nose and mouth and into the lungs. The oxygen diffuses across the membranes in the millions of small air sacs in the lungs and becomes attached to hemoglobin in the red blood corpuscles.

The diffusion across the lung membranes depends on the *partial pressure* of oxygen, and when it is low (for example, at high altitudes), less oxygen enters the blood. The blood transports this oxygen throughout the body where it is used to produce energy.

Carbon dioxide is produced as a waste product in the energy-production process in the body cells, and it is transported back to the lungs in the blood and is then exhaled in the breath. The concentration of waste carbon dioxide in the returning blood is sensed by the brain, which responds by altering the respiration (breathing) rate.

The average capacity of the lungs is about 5 liters and the average breath when at rest is only about $1/2$ liter. This uses only a fraction of the lung capacity to provide about 8 liters/minute with approximately sixteen breaths a minute. Strenuous activity may increase this to 60 liters/minute.

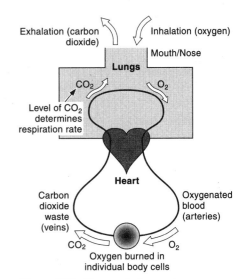

Figure 13-3. The respiration cycle

Increased Altitude

As an airplane climbs, the air pressure drops and therefore *less* pressure is exerted on the human body. The partial pressure of oxygen will also reduce resulting in each "lung-full" of air containing fewer molecules of oxygen.

Therefore at higher altitudes, fewer oxygen molecules will diffuse across the lung membranes and attach themselves to the hemoglobin in the red blood corpuscles. Less oxygen is then transported around the body and less energy is generated (including in the brain). In this oxygen-deficient condition, a pilot is less able to think clearly and less able to perform physically.

Air pressure decreases with altitude, resulting in less oxygen per breath.

Hypoxia

Hypoxia is a state of oxygen deficiency in the body sufficient to impair functions of the brain and other organs.

Above 8,000 feet cabin altitude, the effects of oxygen deprivation may start to become apparent in some pilots, especially if the pilot is active or under stress. At 10,000 feet, most people can still cope with the diminished oxygen supply, but above 10,000 feet supplemental oxygen is required (for example, oxygen supplied through a mask) if a marked deterioration in performance is not to occur.

At 14,000 feet without supplemental oxygen, performance will be very poor and at 18,000 feet the pilot may become unconscious—this will occur at lower altitudes if the pilot is a smoker, is unfit or fatigued.

The initial symptoms of hypoxia may hardly be noticeable to the sufferer, and in fact, they often include feelings of euphoria. The brain is affected quite early, so a false sense of security and well-being may be present. Physical movements will become clumsy, but the pilot may not notice this.

Drowsiness, giddiness, a headache, deterioration of vision, a high pulse rate, blue lips and blue fingernails may all follow, ending in unconsciousness and death. Throughout all of this the pilot will probably feel euphoric and imagine that there is no problem. Hypoxia is subtle and it sneaks up on you!

Hypoxia is a deficiency of oxygen in the body.

Depressurization

Advanced airplanes have pressurized cabins that allow the cabin to hold air at a higher pressure than in the outside atmosphere. For instance, an airplane flying at 30,000 feet may have a cabin that is pressurized (pumped up) to the same pressure level found at 4,000 feet in the outside atmosphere, eliminating the need for the pilot and passengers to wear oxygen masks—a significant improvement in comfort and convenience.

If the airplane depressurizes for some reason and the cabin air escapes, the partial pressure of oxygen in the cabin air is reduced. Supplemental oxygen will then be required by the pilot and passengers, and is obtained through a mask. When the pilot descends to a lower altitude (below 10,000 feet) and there is sufficient oxygen available, supplemental oxygen is no longer required.

The Time of Useful Consciousness

If a person is suddenly deprived of an adequate supply of oxygen, unconsciousness will follow. This is a very important consideration for a high-flying pressurized aircraft that suffers depressurization.

The time available for you to perform useful tasks *without* a supplemental oxygen supply is known as the time of useful consciousness, which gets shorter the higher the altitude. You *must* get the mask on and receive oxygen well within this period if you are to save your life and those of your passengers.

Consciousness of the pilot is paramount, even if the passengers become unconscious for a short period. You must think of yourself first, since the safety of all on board depends on your well-being.

Depressurization of a pressurized cabin can cause hypoxia.

Altitude (feet) Above Sea Level	Sudden Failure of Oxygen Supply	
	Moderate Activity	Minimal Activity
22,000	5 minutes	10 minutes
25,000	2 minutes	3 minutes
28,000	1 minute	$1\frac{1}{2}$ minutes
30,000	45 seconds	$1\frac{1}{4}$ minutes
35,000	30 seconds	45 seconds
40,000	12 seconds	15 seconds

Figure 13-4. Time of useful consciousness following failure of oxygen supply

How to Avoid Hypoxia

To avoid hypoxia it is best to be reasonably fit, to have no cigarette smoke in the cockpit, and to ensure that you use supplemental oxygen above 10,000 feet. Remember that lack of oxygen can lead to a feeling of euphoria and a lack of judgment (a similar effect to alcohol). Self-discipline must be imposed and the oxygen mask donned when the altitude approaches 10,000 feet in unpressurized aircraft.

Avoid hypoxia by using supplemental oxygen at high cabin pressures.

Carbon Monoxide Poisoning

Carbon monoxide is produced during the combustion of fuel in the engine and is present in cigarette smoke, both of which can sometimes be found in the cockpit. Susceptibility to carbon monoxide poisoning increases as cabin altitude increases.

Carbon monoxide is a colorless, odorless and tasteless gas for which hemoglobin in the blood has an enormous affinity. The prime function of hemoglobin is to transport oxygen from the lungs throughout the body to act as fuel. If carbon monoxide molecules are present in the air inhaled into the lungs, then the hemoglobin will transport the carbon monoxide in preference to oxygen, causing the body and the brain to suffer oxygen starvation even though oxygen is present in the air.

The symptoms of carbon monoxide poisoning may include headache, dizziness, nausea, deterioration in vision, slower breathing rate, loss of muscular power, convulsions, coma, and eventually, death. If carbon monoxide is suspected in the cabin, shut off cabin heat, stop all smoking, increase the supply of fresh air through vents, and don oxygen masks if available. Recovery, even on pure oxygen, may take several hours.

Carbon monoxide poisoning is serious and can be fatal!

Many cabin heating systems use warm air from around the engine and the exhaust manifold as their source of heat. Any leaks in the exhaust system can allow carbon monoxide to enter the cabin in the heating air and possibly through open windows and cracks. To minimize the effect of any carbon monoxide that enters the cockpit in this way, fresh air should always be used in conjunction with cabin heat. Regular checks and maintenance are essential. Even though carbon monoxide is odorless, it may be associated with other exhaust gases that do have an odor.

Engine smells in the cabin are a warning that carbon monoxide may be present.

Carbon monoxide poisoning will seriously impair human performance, and if not remedied, could be fatal.

Hyperventilation

The body normally regulates the rate of breathing according to the amount of waste carbon dioxide in the blood. If carbon dioxide levels rise, for instance because of muscular exertion, then the body responds by breathing faster to clear the blood of the excess carbon dioxide.

When subject to psychological stress such as a fright or anxiety, however, the body responds by producing adrenalin and readying the body for possible sudden action. The heart rate increases, the body perspires, blood is diverted to muscles, and the *breathing rate increases*. This flushes an excessive amount of carbon dioxide out of the blood, resulting in a severe shortage of carbon dioxide in the blood. The balance of oxygen and carbon dioxide in the body is upset, causing symptoms similar to those of hypoxia to occur.

Hyperventilation is an involuntary and inappropriate increase in breathing rate, and is usually a symptom of psychological distress.

A person experiencing hyperventilation will over-breathe at a fast rate, and may experience a feeling of suffocation (and a need to breathe fast), a higher pulse rate, giddiness, sweating, coolness, nausea, blurred vision, numbness or tingling or a crawling feeling in the lips, fingers and toes, muscle spasms, drowsiness, and unconsciousness.

If these symptoms occur, it is essential to establish whether the problem is hyperventilation (over-breathing) or hypoxia (a lack of oxygen). To do this you must check your altitude. Below 10,000 feet cabin altitude, when oxygen is plentiful hyperventilation is most likely. Consciously slow down your breathing rate—talking is a good way of doing this. Alternatively, breath into and out of a bag which will raise the percentage of carbon dioxide inhaled and increase your blood's carbon dioxide level back toward normal.

The remedy for hyperventilation is to calm down, slow the breathing rate (by talking), and increase the amount of carbon dioxide in the blood (by breathing in and out of a bag).

Above 10,000 feet where oxygen is less-plentiful you *must* initially assume hypoxia rather than hyperventilation is the problem and use oxygen. Remember hypoxia is fatal but hyperventilation is not.

Decompression Sickness

Scuba diving and flying do not mix well. When the body is deep under water it is subjected to strong pressures, and certain gases, such as nitrogen, are absorbed into the blood. The deeper and longer the diving, the more this absorption occurs.

If the pressure on the body is then reduced—for example, by returning to the surface from a great depth or, even worse, by flying in an airplane at high cabin altitudes—the gases may come out of the blood solution as bubbles. You can see the same effect caused by a suddenly reduced pressure when the top is removed from gaseous drinks and bubbles of gas come out of solution.

Gas bubbles in the blood will cause great pain and immobilization in the shoulders, arms and joints. This serious complaint is known as decompression sickness or *the bends*. The remedy is to return the body to a region of high pressure for a lengthy period of time (in a decompression chamber), and then gradually return it to normal lower pressures over a period of hours or days.

Scuba diving at depths below 20 feet, for long periods, should *not* be considered in the 24 hours prior to flying. Snorkeling will not cause decompression sickness.

✍ Now complete **Review 13, Part (b)** on page 292.

Decompression sickness can follow scuba diving.

Figure 13-5. Do not fly within 24 hours of scuba diving.

Balance

Sensing Acceleration

The human body does not sense motion in a straight line at a steady (unaccelerated) speed, except by visual means, since muscular sensations and the balance organs of the inner ear do not sense motion unless it involves acceleration or deceleration.

Sometimes, when you are a passenger on one of two trains traveling on parallel tracks, it is difficult to know whether your train is moving, the other train is moving, or both trains are moving—even with your eyes open. This is because the muscles and inner ear balance organs are not sensitive enough to detect very slow accelerations or straight-line unaccelerated motion.

The "seat of the pants" sensations and inner ear balance organs will however sense accelerations caused by a change in either speed or direction.

For instance, as an elevator accelerates upward, you experience more than 1g and feel heavier than normal, reverting to your normal weight once the elevator has reached a steady speed. As it slows down, you tend to keep on going, experiencing less than 1g and feeling lighter than usual. You revert to normal 1g feeling once the elevator has stopped. Your body also reacts to changes in angular speed, such as when you roll into a banked turn.

The g-force changes in normal flight are small compared with those experienced by flying aerobatic maneuvers such as loops, or steep turns. Forces of +4g or more for a sustained period, can be experienced during such maneuvers, and will have a significant effect on your body. The blood will be forced toward the lower extremities and away from the brain, causing a loss of vision because of the lack of oxygen, leading to *grayout* and, eventually, *blackout*. If *negative* g-forces are experienced, the blood rushes to the head. In an extreme case of negative g, the lower eyelids will move up and cover the eyes, resulting in *redout*.

Your body can sense accelerations (g-forces).

The Inner Ear Balance Mechanism

The inner ear contains a balance organ consisting of three **semicircular canals** connected at a sac. They contain fluid and small sensory hairs that detect any movement of the fluid. The three semicircular canals are at right angles to each other, like the pitch-roll-yaw planes of an airplane, and can detect angular accelerations (in pitch, roll and yaw). During the angular acceleration, the fluid is more or less left behind in the relevant semicircular canal, causing the sensory hairs to move and send an angular acceleration message to the brain.

Once the angular acceleration has ceased, and a steady angular speed is maintained, the fluid ends up moving with the canal so the sensory hairs on the canal wall no longer bend.

Gravity and linear accelerations or decelerations are detected in a similar fashion by sensory hairs in the sac, which are sometimes known as the **static organ.** The hairs bend while there is linear acceleration up or down, sideways, or forward or back, and return to their normal position once the body is moving at a steady speed (which may be zero). These hairs also detect the direction of g-forces, which are usually down toward the center of the earth in the normal everyday 1g situation, but will not be vertical in a banked turn. These hairs cannot differentiate between the two situations (gravity and other g-forces), and this is the reason why, with your eyes closed, it is sometimes difficult to know if you are level or in a banked turn.

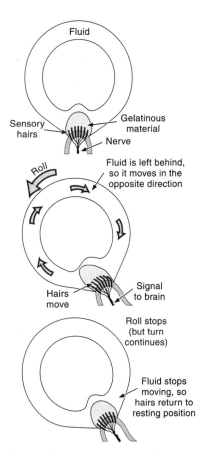

Figure 13-6. Angular acceleration

Motion Sickness

Air sickness is generally caused by the balance mechanisms of the inner ear continually being over-stimulated by accelerations. This can be caused by turbulence, or maneuvers such as steep turns or spins, in which forces other than the normal 1g that the body is used to will be experienced.

Psychological aspects can also affect the onset of motion sickness, for instance a fear of flying or apprehension at seeing the horizon at different angles.

Many pilots have experienced airsickness, especially early in their training when stress levels are higher than normal, and when unusual attitudes and g-forces are encountered.

To avoid airsickness:

- fly the airplane smoothly and in-balance;
- avoid maneuvers involving unusual g-forces;
- avoid areas of turbulence;
- ventilate the cabin with a good supply of fresh air;
- involve a potentially airsick passenger in the operation of the flight, especially if this involves looking outside the airplane and into the distance (for example, to help identify ground references);
- as a last resort, recline the airsick passenger's seat to reduce the effect of the vertical accelerations and keep an airsickness bag handy; and
- land as soon as is practical if necessary.

Vertigo

Vertigo is generally experienced as a feeling of rotation, when in fact no rotation is actually occurring.

Vertigo can be caused by disease, by accelerations that disturb the delicate balance mechanisms in the inner ear, and by sudden pressure changes in the inner ear. Strong blowing of the nose or sneezing can do this quite violently, and bring on a spell of dizziness.

If you want to experience vertigo on the ground, you can bring it on by spinning around about 20 times with your head held low, and then try to walk in a straight line. Similar forces on your body occur when an airplane is maneuvering, especially when high g-loadings are pulled in aerobatics and steep turns. This can cause vertigo, especially if there is no visual reference to the horizon.

Spatial Disorientation

Spatial disorientation occurs when pilots are unsure of their precise attitudes in space, for example, where is up and where is down. Dizziness caused by vertigo need not necessarily be present although it may be.

Spatial disorientation is a state of confusion resulting from misleading information being sent to the brain from various sensory organs. Humans normally rely mainly on sight and the natural horizon for spatial orientation, supported by the balance organs in the inner ear and "seat of the pants" sensations. Spatial disorientation can occur when any pilot (regardless of experience) loses reference to the natural horizon by flying into clouds, by flying over sloping terrain or a sloping cloud layer, or when flying in restricted visibility. Flashing strobe lights or the sun flashing through the propeller can also have a destabilizing effect and cause a pilot to become disoriented or suffer vertigo. Abnormal g-forces in planned or unplanned maneuvers are also destabilizing.

To help avoid spatial disorientation, you should avoid flying in the above conditions, avoid looking directly at the sun or any strobe light, and you should gain some basic expertise at flying on instruments. The flight instruments will allow you to spatially orient yourself even when your normal sensory cues (sight and balance) obtained from the outside world are abnormal. However, you must never fly in non-VFR conditions unless you are a current qualified instrument-rated pilot.

Avoid spatial disorientation by looking outside or by looking at the flight instruments. Do not rely on body signals.

Sensory Illusions Can Lead You Astray

Most people live in a 1g situation, with their feet on the ground. *One-g* means the force of gravity. Some variations to 1g, however, do occur in everyday life, such as when driving an automobile. Accelerating an automobile, hard braking, or turning on a flat bend will all produce g-forces on the body different to the 1g of gravity alone. A passenger with closed eyes could perhaps detect this by bodily feel or with sense of balance.

A right turn on a flat road, for instance, could be detected by the feeling of being thrown to the left—but it might be more difficult to detect if the curve was perfectly banked for the particular speed. A straight road sloping to the left (and causing the passenger to lean to the left) might give the passenger the false impression that the automobile is turning right, even though it is in fact not turning at all.

The position-sensing systems of the body, using nerves all over the body to transmit messages of feel and pressure to the brain, can be fooled in this and other ways.

The organs within the inner ear, used for balance and to detect accelerations, can also be deceived. For instance, if you are sitting in an automobile traveling around a suitably banked curve, the sensing system in your ears *falsely* interprets the g-force holding you firmly and comfortably in the seat as a vertical force, as if you were moving straight ahead rather than in a banked turn.

The inner ear organs also have other limitations, one being that a constant velocity is not detected, nor is a gradual change in velocity.

Figure 13-7. Turning right–or simply leaning?

False impressions of motion can also be caused by unusual g-forces—for instance, by rapid head motion, or by lowering the head. If you happen to drop your pencil while flying, don't just lower your eyes and lean down to look for it in one motion—take it very carefully step by step to avoid any feeling of vertigo.

Because an airplane moves in three dimensions, it is able to accelerate and decelerate in three dimensions, and this can lead to more complicated illusions. Pulling up into a steep climb, for instance, holds you tightly in your seat, which is exactly the same feeling as in a steep turn. With your eyes closed, it is sometimes difficult to recognize which maneuver it is.

Other examples are: decelerating while in a turn to the left may give a false impression of a turn to the right; and accelerating in a straight line can give the illusion of climbing. Be aware that your senses of balance and bodily feel can lead you astray in an airplane. The one sense that can resolve most of these illusions is **sight.** If the automobile passenger could see out, or if the pilot had reference to the natural horizon and landmarks, then the confusion would be easily dispelled.

Accelerating can give the illusion of climbing.
Decelerating can give the illusion of descending.

Unfortunately, in instrument flight in clouds and on dark nights you do *not* have reference to ground features, but you can still use your vital sense of sight to **scan the instruments,** and obtain substitute information. Therefore, an important instruction to the budding instrument pilot is: believe your eyes and what the instruments tell you.

While sight is the most important sense, and must be protected at all costs, also make sure that you avoid anything that will affect your balance or position sensing systems. Do not fly when you are medically unfit. In the cockpit, avoid sudden head movements. Avoid lowering your head or turning around, especially when you are in a turn.

✍ Now complete **Review 13, Part (c)** on page 293.

Vision

Your eyes are the most important sensory organ for flight, although their messages to the brain are backed up by other sensory organs.

Structure of the Eye

Each eye acts like a camera lens. Its pupil widens in dark conditions or narrows in bright conditions to admit a suitable amount of light. The appropriate amount of light then passes through the pupil and is focused by the lens onto the retina, which is a light-sensitive layer at the back of the eye. Messages from the retina pass via the optic nerve to the brain.

The retina contains two types of light-sensitive cells:

- **Cones**—which are concentrated around the central section of the retina, especially the foveal area directly opposite the lens. Cones are very sensitive to color, small details, and distant objects, and are most effective in daylight, and less effective in darkness.

- **Rods**—which are concentrated in a band outside the central foveal area, and are sensitive to movement, but not to detail or color, and so see only in black, white and gray. Rods are effective in daylight and darkness, and are responsible for your peripheral vision and night vision.

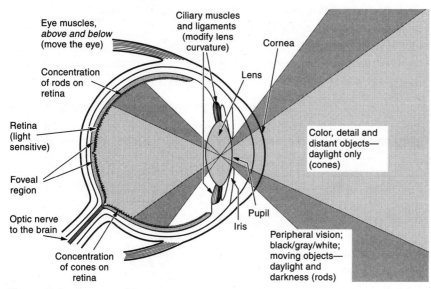

Figure 13-8. Structure of the eye

Adaptation of Eyes to Darkness

At night, there are some special considerations regarding your vision. Since your attention during night flying will be both inside and outside the cockpit, care should be taken to ensure that your eyes can continuously function at near maximum efficiency. It takes the eyes some minutes to adapt to a dark environment, as most of us have experienced when walking into a darkened cinema, and stumbling across other patrons in an attempt to find an empty seat.

The rate at which dark adaptation of the eyes occurs depends to a large extent on the contrast between the brightness of light previously experienced, and the degree of darkness of the new environment.

Whereas the cones adjust quickly to variations in light intensity, the rods (which are most important for night vision) take some 30 minutes to adapt fully to darkness. It is good airmanship to assist night adaptation by **avoiding bright white lights** (landing lights, strobes, flashlights and so on) in the 30 minutes prior to night flight, and also while in flight. Exposure to bright light, even for just a second or two, can cause a loss of night adaptation that will then require many minutes to return.

Adapt your eyes to darkness before night flying by avoiding bright lights for at least 30 minutes before flight.

Night vision can also be affected by a lack of oxygen, so ensure that you use oxygen when flying above 10,000 feet MSL. In addition, do not permit cigarette smoke in the cockpit at night, since it will displace oxygen in your blood to an appreciable extent, reducing your night vision by an amount comparable to an extra 5,000 feet in altitude. In the long term, a good diet containing foods with Vitamins A and C can improve your night vision.

Since bright lights will impair your outside vision at night, it is good airmanship to keep the cockpit lighting at a reasonably low level, but not so low that you cannot see your charts, or locate switches.

Cockpit lighting should be dimmed at night.

There are some occasions, however, when bright cockpit lighting can help preserve your vision. This can occur on an instrument flight, for instance, if flying in the vicinity of electrical storms. Nearby lightning flashes can temporarily degrade your dark adaptation and your vision, particularly if it is in contrast to a dim cockpit. Bright lighting in the cockpit can minimize this effect and, although your external vision will not be as good as with dim cockpit lighting, you will avoid being temporarily blinded by the lightning flashes.

Flying near electrical storms is not recommended. They should be avoided by at least 20 miles. If you are not an instrument-rated pilot in a suitably equipped airplane then you should stay on the ground at night if there are storms in your proximity.

Scanning for Other Aircraft by Day

The central (foveal) region of the retina provides the best vision, but only during daylight, and not in darkness. Airplanes and other objects are best seen by day if you can focus their image on the foveal region, and you do this by looking directly at them.

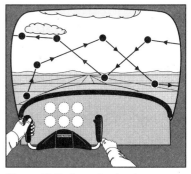

Figure 13-9. Scanning by day

In hazy conditions, objects may be closer than they appear.

The most effective method of scanning for other aircraft for collision avoidance during daylight hours is to use a series of short, regularly spaced eye movements to search each 10 degree sector of the sky. Systematically focusing on different segments of the sky for short intervals is a better technique than continuously sweeping the sky.

You may be on a collision course with another aircraft if there is no apparent relative motion between your aircraft and the other aircraft, especially if the other aircraft appears to be getting bigger and bigger in the windshield.

In hazy or low visibility conditions, your ability to see other aircraft and objects will be diminished and, if you can see them, they may *appear* to be further away than their actual distance.

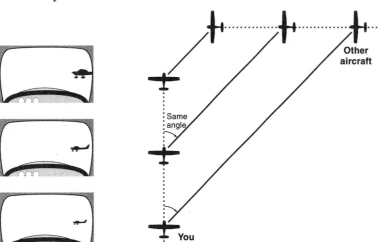

Figure 13-10. A potential collision

Scanning for Other Aircraft by Night

Because the central foveal region of the retina containing mainly cones is *not* effective by night, you need to rely to a greater extent on your peripheral vision, which is provided by the rods in the outer band of the retina. An object at night will be more readily visible when you are looking to the side of it, rather than directly at it.

The most effective way to use your eyes during night flight is to scan small sectors of sky more slowly than in daylight, to permit off-center viewing of objects in your *peripheral vision.*

At night, scan slowly using your peripheral vision.

Because you may not be able to see the aircraft shape at night, you will have to determine its direction of travel, from its visible lighting:

- the flashing red beacon;
- the red navigation light on the left wingtip;
- the green navigation light on the right wingtip; and
- a steady white light on the tail.

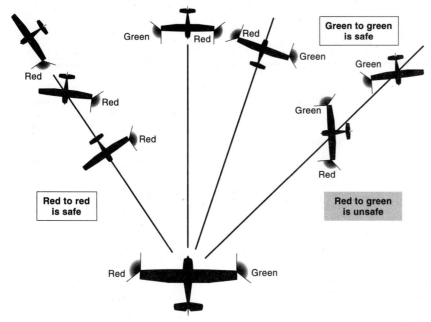

Figure 13-11. Using navigation lights to avoid collision

The visual illusion of **autokinesis** (self-motion) can occur at night if you stare continuously at a single light against a generally dark background. It will appear to move after only a few seconds of staring at it, even though in fact it is stationary, and you could lose spatial orientation if you use it as your single point of reference. You can guard against autokinesis at night by maintaining movement of your eyes in normal scanning, and by monitoring the flight instruments frequently to ensure correct altitude.

Unless you have a distant object in view at night, your eyes will tend to focus at a point about 5 feet ahead of you, especially if you are an older person with "tired eyes", and you may miss sighting distant objects. This is known as **empty field myopia** (near-sightedness), which you can combat by searching for *distant* lights and focusing on them.

Also guard against **false horizons** formed at night by lines of lights, say a well-lit road or city lights on a shoreline or hillside, by referring periodically to the flight instruments.

Visual Illusions on Approach

Most runways are of standard width and on flat ground. On every approach, you should try to achieve the same flight path angle to the horizontal, and your eyes will become accustomed to this, by keeping your view of the runway through the windshield in standard perspective.

If you are approaching a **sloping runway**, however, the perspective will be different. A runway that slopes *upward* will look shorter, and you will feel that you are high on slope, when in fact you are right on slope. The tendency will be for you to go lower and make a shallower approach.

A runway that slopes *downward* will look longer, and you will feel that you are low on slope, when in fact you are right on slope. The tendency will be for you to go higher and make a steeper approach.

If you know the slope of the runway, you can allow for it in your visual estimation of whether you are high or low on slope.

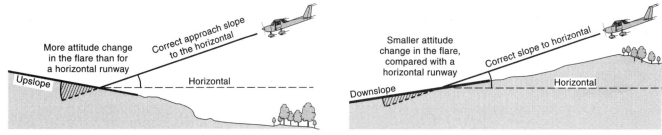

Figure 13-12. An upward sloping runway creates a "too-high" illusion. A downward sloping runway creates a "too-low" illusion

A **wide runway**, because of the angle at which you view it periphally in the final stages of the approach and landing, will cause an illusion of being too low, and you may flare and hold-off too high as a result, leading to "dropping-in" for a heavy landing.

Conversely, a **narrow runway** will cause an illusion of being too high, and you may delay the flare and make contact with the runway earlier (and harder) than expected.

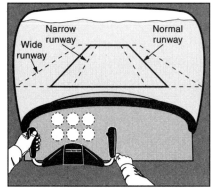

Figure 13-13. How runways of different widths should appear at the same point on final

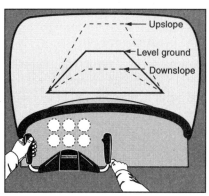

How runways of different slope should appear at the same point on final

If you know that the runway is wider or narrower than what you are familiar with, then you can allow for this in your visual judgment of the round-out.

In hazy conditions, you may be closer to the runway than you appear to be, an illusion that may lead to an unnecessarily hard landing if you are not aware of the effect of haze on your vision.

The Night Approach

At night, a powered approach is preferable to a glide approach, because it provides a normal, well-controlled approach at normal speeds. In modern training aircraft, the powered approach is generally used by day also. Power gives the pilot more control, a lower rate of descent and, therefore, a less steep approach slope. The approach to the aiming point should be stable, using any available aids, such as the runway lighting and a VASI (visual approach slope indicator system).

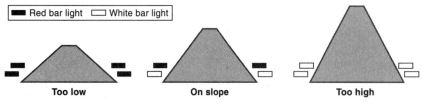

Figure 13-14. Perspectives on approach using a VASI

Using the runway edge lighting only, correct tracking and slope is achieved when the runway perspective is the same as in daylight. For correct tracking, the runway should appear symmetrical in the windshield. Guidance on achieving the correct approach slope is obtained from the apparent spacing between the runway edge lights.

If the airplane is low on slope, the runway lights will appear to be closer together. If the airplane is flying above slope, then the runway lights will appear to be further apart. Attention should also be paid to the airspeed indicator throughout the approach, to ensure that the correct airspeed is being maintained.

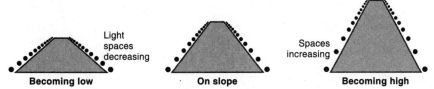

Figure 13-15. Perspectives on approach using runway edge lighting

A VASI will provide correct slope guidance day or night, but the perspective provided by runway edge lighting may be slightly misleading if you do not allow for any runway slope.

✍ Now complete **Review 13, Part (d)** on page 293.

✎ Review 13

Flight Physiology

Part (a)

1. Can a cold cause you discomfort while flying?
   ➤ yes

2. If you have consumed a small amount of alcohol, you should not fly for at least _____ hours.
   ➤ 8 hours

3. If you are on medication, the effect of which you are unsure, then you (may/should not) fly.
   ➤ should not

4. Which is true regarding the presence of alcohol in the human body?
   (a) A small amount of alcohol increases vision activity.
   (b) An increase in altitude decreases the adverse effect of alcohol.
   (c) Judgment and decision-making abilities can be adversely affected by even small amounts of alcohol.
   ➤ (c)

5. A person suffering from an abnormally low temperature has _____ .
   ➤ hypothermia

6. The FAA prescribes a method for evaluating risk and reducing stress. What is it?
   ➤ DECIDE, which stands for: Detect, Estimate, Choose, Identify, Do, Evaluate. The six-step process is a logical way to make decisions while flying or flight planning.

7. There are level 4 thunderstorms blocking your route. You're in a hurry, though, and you need to get where you're going soon. You are at risk for which dangerous attitude?
   ➤ Impulsivity. You feel pressured to do something immediately, without thinking first.

8. What should you do if you feel like you need to prove yourself in the air?
   ➤ Label that thought as "macho," then apply the antidote.

9. List at least two ways you can keep your stress level down when planning or during a flight.
   ➤ know your personal limits; use all available resources; avoid hazardous attitudes; learn to modify your behavior; develop methods to assess risk.

Part (b)

1. The amount of oxygen available (increases/decreases/remains the same) as altitude is gained.
   ➤ decreases

2. A lack of oxygen can affect a pilot dramatically and this is known as _____ .
   ➤ hypoxia

3. Hyperventilation is (overbreathing/underbreathing) and causes a low (carbon dioxide/oxygen) level in the blood. It is often caused by (exercise/psychological distress).
   ➤ overbreathing, carbon dioxide, psychological distress

4. The percentage content of oxygen in the air (does/does not) decrease significantly as altitude is gained.
   ➤ does not

5. Good flights begin and end with_____ .
   ➤ good decisions

6. In an unpressurized airplane, at high altitudes, the amount of oxygen that diffuses across the lung membranes and into the blood is:
   (a) decreased because of the low partial pressure of oxygen.
   (b) decreased because of the lower temperatures.
   (c) unchanged to that at sea level.
   ➤ (a)

7. At higher altitudes where air density is less, each breath by the pilot in an unpressurized airplane will contain (more/less/approximately the same number of) oxygen molecules compared with a breath at sea level.
   ➤ less

8. Loss of muscular power (is/is not) an indication of possible carbon monoxide poisoning.
   ➤ is

9. Which statement best defines hypoxia?
   (a) An abnormal increase in the volume of air breathed.
   (b) A state of oxygen deficiency in the body.
   (c) A condition of gas bubble formation around the joints or muscles.
   ➤ (b)

10. A faulty exhaust system may be dangerous because of the possibility of _____ poisoning.
    ➤ carbon monoxide

11. Carbon monoxide in an aircraft cabin is:
    (a) easily recognizable because of its peculiar odor.
    (b) easily recognizable because of its peculiar color.
    (c) difficult to recognize because it is odorless and colorless.
➤ (c)

12. Susceptibility to carbon monoxide poisoning increases as:
    (a) air pressure increases.
    (b) altitude decreases.
    (c) altitude increases.
➤ (c)

13. Rapid or deep breathing, especially when using oxygen can lead to _____ .
➤ hyperventilation

14. To overcome the symptoms of hyperventilation, a pilot should:
    (a) swallow or yawn.
    (b) slow the breathing rate.
    (c) increase the breathing rate.
➤ (b)

15. Hyperventilation may be caused by (alcohol/stress/slow breathing).
➤ stress

16. To help overcome hyperventilation you should (slow/increase) the breathing rate.
➤ slow

17. Hypoxia susceptibility due to inhalation of carbon (monoxide/dioxide) from a faulty exhaust or heating system (increases/decreases) as altitude increases.
➤ carbon monoxide, increases

18. A common symptom of hyperventilation is (slow breathing/euphoria/tingling sensations in the hands and feet).
➤ tingling sensations in the hands and feet

Part (c)

1. A state of temporary confusion resulting from misleading information being sent to the brain by various sensory organs is called _____ .
➤ spatial disorientation

2. To interpret airplane attitude in poor visibility conditions you should rely on your (body signals/flight instruments).
➤ flight instruments

3. To best overcome the effects of spatial disorientation, a pilot should:
    (a) rely on body sensations.
    (b) increase the breathing rate.
    (c) rely on aircraft instrument indications.
➤ (c)

Part (d)

1. The retina contains _____ , which are concentrated around the central section of the retina, and _____ , which are concentrated in the outer parts of the foveal area.
➤ cones, rods

2. Cones are most effective in the (day/night).
➤ day

3. Rods (are color-sensitive/see only in black-and-white).
➤ see only in black-and-white

4. Your peripheral vision is provided by (cones/rods).
➤ rods

5. The most effective method of scanning for other aircraft in daylight is to use (peripheral vision/continuous sweeping/successive eye movements).
➤ successive eye movements

6. In daylight, other aircraft are most clearly seen in your (central/peripheral) vision.
➤ central

7. Another aircraft remains in view in the same position in your windshield. There (is/is not) a possibility that you are on a collision course.
➤ is

8. At night, other aircraft are most clearly seen in your (central/peripheral) vision.
➤ peripheral

9. The most effective method of scanning for other aircraft for collision avoidance during nighttime hours is to use:

   (a) regularly spaced concentration on the 3, 9, and 12 o'clock positions.

   (b) a series of short, regularly spaced eye movements to search each 30-degree sector.

   (c) peripheral vision by slowly scanning small sectors and utilizing offcenter viewing.

   ➤ (c)

10. How can you determine if another aircraft is on a collision course with your aircraft?

    (a) The nose of each aircraft is pointed at the same point in space.

    (b) The other aircraft will always appear to get larger and closer at a rapid rate.

    (c) There will be no apparent relative motion between your aircraft and the other aircraft.

    ➤ (c)

11. In hazy conditions, another object may be (closer/further away) than it appears to be.

    ➤ closer

12. Prior to night flight, try to avoid bright lights during the preceding _____ minutes.

    ➤ 30

13. During a night flight, you observe a steady red light and a flashing red light ahead and at the same altitude. What is the general direction of movement of the other aircraft?

    (a) The other aircraft is crossing to the left.

    (b) The other aircraft is crossing to the right.

    (c) The other aircraft is approaching head-on.

    ➤ (a)

14. During a night flight, you observe a steady white light and a flashing red light ahead and at the same altitude. What is the general direction of movement of the other aircraft?

    (a) The other aircraft is crossing to the left.

    (b) The other aircraft is crossing to the right.

    (c) The other aircraft is flying away from you.

    ➤ (c)

15. An upward sloping runway gives the illusion that the correct approach path is (too steep/too shallow) and that the runway is (shorter/longer) than it is.

    ➤ too steep, shorter

16. A narrow runway may give the illusion that you are (higher/lower) than you really are, resulting in the airplane (stalling above the runway/flying into the runway).

    ➤ higher, flying into the runway

Weather Section Four

Heating Effects in the Atmosphere 14

The Atmosphere

The Earth is surrounded by a mixture of gases held to it by the force of gravity. This mixture of gases we know as **air,** and the space it occupies around the earth we call the **atmosphere.** The atmosphere is of particular importance to pilots because it is the medium in which we fly.

Air Density

The force of gravity attracts the air molecules toward the surface of the earth, causing them to squeeze closer together in the lower levels of the atmosphere than at higher altitudes. The number of molecules in a cubic foot of air at 40,000 feet altitude is only one-half that at sea level where the air is much more dense.

Air density is important to pilots because:
- the airplane's lift force is generated by the flow of air around the wings;
- engine power is generated by burning fuel and air; and
- we need to breathe air in order to live.

If the air is more dense:
- the required airfoil lift force can be generated at a lower true airspeed (V);
- greater engine power is available because of the greater mass of each fuel/air charge taken into the cylinders; and
- breathing is easier, since a greater mass of oxygen is taken into the lungs during each breath.

The Subdivision of the Atmosphere

The atmosphere is divided into layers based on temperature—the *troposphere,* the *stratosphere,* the *mesosphere* and the *thermosphere.* Most flying occurs in the troposphere, although high-flying jets may cruise in the stratosphere—the boundary between the two regions is known as the **tropopause.**

The temperature usually falls with a gain in altitude in the troposphere until the tropopause is reached, above which it remains somewhat constant at a fairly low value (typically −57°C). The rate of change of temperature with altitude is called the **temperature lapse rate.**

The earth spins on its axis, carrying the atmosphere with it and tends to throw the air in the lower part of the atmosphere to the outside. This, plus strong heating in tropical areas, causes the troposphere to extend further into space above the equator than above the poles. The tropopause occurs at a an altitude of about 20,000 feet over the poles, and at about 60,000 feet over the equator. It is higher in each region in summer than in winter. On average, the tropopause is assumed to occur at approximately 36,000 feet.

Air density decreases with altitude.

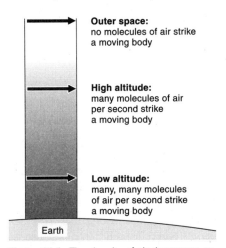

Figure 14-1. The density of air decreases as altitude is gained

Most flying occurs in the troposphere.

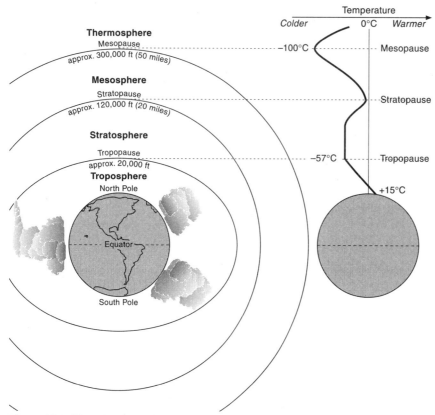

Figure 14-2. The subdivision of the atmosphere is based on temperature

Most weather occurs in the troposphere, including clouds, precipitation (rain, snow, and so on) and wind—especially the vertical air currents that cause the strong vertical development of convective clouds. Sometimes this vertical development is so strong that large thunderstorm clouds, known as *cumulo-nimbus,* burst through the tropopause into the stratosphere.

Because almost all flight occurs in the troposphere and the lower levels of the stratosphere, we concentrate on these areas in this manual.

Differences between the Troposphere and Stratosphere
Significant differences between the troposphere and the stratosphere include:

- Temperature decreases with altitude in the troposphere, with an abrupt change in temperature lapse rate at the tropopause, above which it is constant.

- A marked vertical movement of air in the troposphere, with warm air rising and cool air descending on both large and small scales, whereas there is little vertical movement of air in the stratosphere.

- Almost all the water vapor in the atmosphere is contained in the troposphere, and so cloud formation rarely extends beyond the tropopause.

Air is a Mixture of Gases
In its dry state, air is a mixture of atmospheric gases—the two main constituents are nitrogen (78%) and oxygen (21%). The remaining (1%) gases include argon, neon, helium and carbon dioxide. *See* Figure 14-3.

Air in the troposphere nearly always contains some **water vapor,** varying from almost zero to 5% by volume. This is most important, because it is water vapor that condenses to form clouds from which we get the precipitation (rain, snow, hail, and so on) that is vital to life on earth. As the content of water vapor in a parcel of air increases, the other gases decrease proportionately.

The Composition of Air	
Gas	**Volume (%)**
Nitrogen	78%
Oxygen	21%
Other gases (argon, carbon dioxide, neon, helium, etc.)	1%
Total	100%

Figure 14-3.

Maritime and Continental Air Masses

Air over an ocean (known as *maritime air*) will absorb moisture from the body of water and will, in general, contain more water vapor than the air over a continent (known as *continental air*), particularly if the land mass consists largely of desert areas. In other words, a maritime air mass is more moist than a continental air mass. An air mass moving in across the United States from over the Caribbean Sea, for instance, is likely to carry more moisture than an air mass originating in continental Canada.

Maritime air is more moist than continental air.

The Standard Atmosphere

In Chapter 9 we briefly discussed the standard atmosphere and its values. To refresh your memory, these are repeated below:

- mean sea level (MSL) pressure is 29.92 in. Hg;
- mean sea level temperature is +15°C (or 59°F);
- temperature lapse rate is 1.98°C/1,000 feet up to approximately 36,000 feet above which temperature is assumed to remain constant at 56.5°C.

Note: For forecasting purposes, pressure is usually expressed in *millibars (mb)*, and the standard MSL pressure is 1013.2 mb. You will see millibars plotted as lines (isobars) on weather charts to indicate places of the same surface pressure.

The Actual Atmosphere

The actual atmosphere can differ from the standard atmosphere in many ways, and in reality almost always does. The pressure at sea level varies from day-to-day, indeed from hour-to-hour, and the temperature fluctuates between wide extremes at all levels.

The variation of ambient pressure throughout the atmosphere—both horizontally and vertically, is of great significance to pilots as it affects the operation of the altimeter, as well as causing wind.

One difference between the actual atmosphere and the theoretical standard atmosphere, which is very important for high-flying jet pilots, is that the real tropopause is much higher over equatorial latitudes than over polar latitudes. This means that weather, such as cumulonimbus clouds, will exist to higher levels in tropical regions. Also, the tropopause is not a continuous sheet, but has some breaks in it, within which high-speed jetstream tubes of wind blowing from west to east develop.

✍ Now complete **Review 14, Part (a)** on page 306.

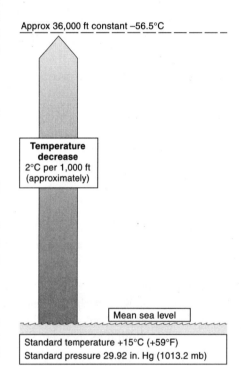

Approx 36,000 ft constant –56.5°C

Temperature decrease 2°C per 1,000 ft (approximately)

Mean sea level

Standard temperature +15°C (+59°F)
Standard pressure 29.92 in. Hg (1013.2 mb)

Figure 14-4. The International Standard Atmosphere (ISA)

The actual atmosphere differs from the ISA.

Heat Exchange Processes

The Sun

The main source of energy on earth is the sun, which radiates electromagnetic energy in the form of infrared radiation, light rays, radio waves, ultraviolet radiation, and so on. We experience this solar radiation as **heat** and **light.**

The wavelengths of solar radiation are such that a large percentage penetrates the earth's atmosphere and is absorbed by the earth's surface, causing its temperature to increase. How much the surface temperature rises depends on its nature—land shows a greater temperature rise than water for the same amount of solar energy. The earth's surface, in turn, heats the air closest to it and if that parcel of air is warmer than the surrounding air, it will rise.

Heat exchanges and temperature variations in the atmosphere create air movements within the atmosphere, resulting in changes in the weather.

The sun radiates energy and heats the earth.

All weather processes result from, or are accompanied by a heat exchange.

Seasonal Variations

The earth orbits around the sun once every year and, because the earth's axis is tilted, this gives rise to the four seasons. The solar radiation received at a place on earth is more intense during its summer than in winter, when its surface is presented to the sun at a more oblique angle.

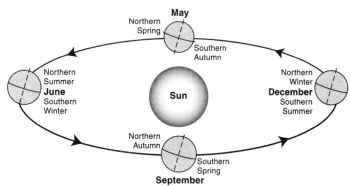

Figure 14-5. Solar radiation received at the earth's surface is more intense in summer

Solar Heating

Solar radiation is like a flashlight beam that produces more intense light on a perpendicular surface than on an oblique surface. Since solar radiation strikes tropical regions from directly overhead, or almost so, right through the year, the heating is quite intense. In contrast, the sun's rays strike polar regions of the earth at an oblique angle and, during winter (the northern summer is shown in Figure 14-6), they do not strike the polar regions at all.

Heating from solar radiation is greatest in the tropics.

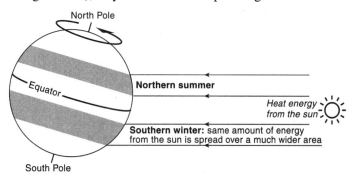

Figure 14-6. Surface heating is greatest in the tropics and least at high latitudes

Terrestrial Re-Radiation

Heat energy in the earth's surface is re-radiated into the atmosphere but, because its wavelength is longer than solar radiation, it is more readily absorbed in the atmosphere, especially by water vapor and carbon dioxide. It is this absorption of heat from the earth that is the main heat exchange that causes weather.

In summary:

• Solar radiation penetrates the atmosphere and heats the earth's surface; then

• The earth re-radiates this energy and heats the lower levels of the atmosphere; this indirect heating of air by solar heating causes thermals.

General Circulation

Large vertical circulations of air occur in the troposphere caused by unequal heating of the different regions of the earth. The tropics for instance, receive much more energy than the polar regions.

    The surface air in the tropics becomes very warm, causing it to expand and rise. This thermally induced vertical motion is called **convection.** The rising air leaves behind an area of lower pressure near the surface known as the **equatorial trough.** New surface air moves as a result of the pressure differential that has been created, and replaces the air that has risen. (These surface winds flowing into the equatorial trough are the trade winds, which were so important to sailing ships in the old days.) Meanwhile, the tropical air rising above the equatorial trough cools as it rises, and spreads out in the upper atmosphere.

    In contrast, the cooler air over the polar regions sinks, causing a higher pressure at the surface and spreads out, moving toward areas of lower pressure. This sinking polar air together with the rising air in warmer regions creates a large scale **general circulation** pattern in the troposphere. You would expect the general circulation to be a single large cell in each hemisphere, but an effect produced by the earth's rotation—known as the **Coriolis effect**—leads to *three* main circulation cells existing over each hemisphere of the earth:

• the polar cell;

• the mid-latitude cell; and

• the tropical (or Hadley) cell.

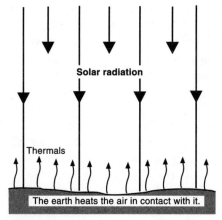

Figure 14-7. Indirect heating of the atmosphere by the sun

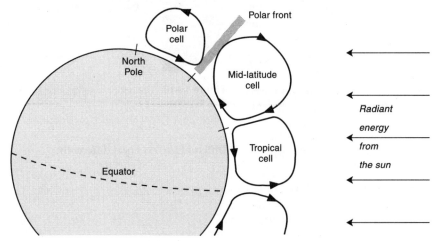

Figure 14-8. The general circulation pattern

The cold surface air moving southward from the north polar region is "left behind" by the rotation of the earth, effectively turning right and becoming easterly by about latitude 60°. Further southward movement of the surface air is blocked. As this air is warmed, it rises, spreads out, and so the **polar circulation cell** is formed.

Meanwhile, the warm upper air flowing out from the equator "moves ahead" of the rotating earth, effectively turning right and becoming westerly by about latitude 30°. Further movement is blocked because, as this air cools, it subsides (descends) to form the subtropical high-pressure belt at about latitude 30°. Surface air diverges from this area and forms the **tropical circulation cell.**

Note that the Coriolis force (from earth rotation) causes air movement to turn right in the Northern Hemisphere and left in the Southern Hemisphere. The Coriolis force will be further explained in Chapter 15.

Most weather occurs in the mid-latitudes. In this area, the rising air spreading out in the upper levels of the troposphere near latitude 60° and the descending air spreading out in the lower levels near latitude 30° cause an intermediate or **mid-latitude circulation cell** between latitudes 30° and 60°. Sometimes large masses of very cold polar air break through the barrier near 60° and move toward the equator, and sometimes large masses of warm air move from the tropics into this area—the result being that the mid-latitudes have moving storms and ever-changing weather.

The generalized circulation is an idealized version of the real situation of constantly changing large masses of cold and warm air pushing their way around, responding to pressure differentials caused by uneven surface heating.

The situation in the Southern Hemisphere, with its great ocean areas, is less complicated than in the Northern Hemisphere, where the large continental land masses with their uneven surface heating and cooling cause many variations and complicated weather patterns.

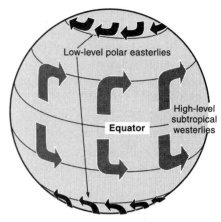

Figure 14-9. The north–south flow of air is *blocked* at latitudes around 60° and 30°

Local Heating and Cooling

Daily variations in heating are caused by the earth's rotation. The earth makes one complete rotation on its axis every 24 hours, causing the *apparent* motion of the sun across the sky, and day and night on earth.

Solar heating of the earth's surface occurs only by day, but terrestrial re-radiation of heat energy from the earth occurs continually, both day and night. The net result is that the earth's surface heats up by day, reaches its maximum temperature about mid-afternoon (3:00 p.m.) and cools by night, reaching its minimum temperature typically an hour after sunrise. This continual heating and cooling on a daily basis is called the **diurnal variation** of temperature— a typical daily pattern of heating and cooling that is most extreme in desert areas and more moderate (in some cases almost nonexistent) over the oceans.

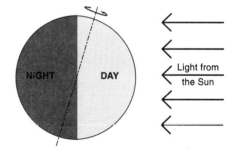

Figure 14-10. The earth's rotation causes day and night

Surface Heating

The heating of various surfaces and the temperatures that they reach depends on a number of factors:

- **The specific heat of the surface.** Water requires more heat energy to raise its temperature by one degree Fahrenheit than does land, therefore land areas will heat more quickly during the day than sea (and also cool more quickly at night). Compared with the sea, land is warmer by day and cooler by night. Scientifically we say that water has a higher *specific heat* than land.

- **The reflectivity of the surface.** If the solar radiation is reflected by a surface, it is not absorbed. There is less heating of reflective surfaces, such as snow and water compared with absorbent surfaces, such as plowed fields.

Different surfaces heat differently.

- **The conductivity of the surface.** Heat energy does not readily pass through soil into the lower levels, whereas ocean currents carry heat energy with them, causing the sea to be heated to a greater depth than a land surface.

Cloud Cover

Cloud coverage by day prevents some of the solar radiation penetrating to the earth's surface, resulting in reduced heating of the earth and lower temperatures on cloudy days compared with sunny days. By night, however, cloud cover causes the opposite effect and prevents some of the heat energy escaping from the earth's surface. The atmosphere beneath the clouds experiences less cooling, and so cloudy nights are not as cool as clear nights.

Cloud cover can affect surface heating and cooling.

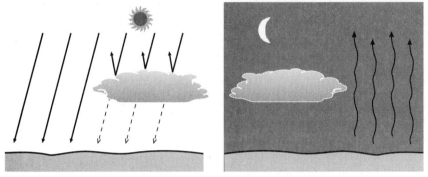

Figure 14-11. Clouds reduce surface heating by day and cooling by night

The Transfer of Heat Energy

Heat energy may be transmitted from one body to another, or redistributed within the one body by a number of means, including:

- **Radiation.** All bodies transmit energy in the form of electromagnetic radiation, the higher the temperature of the body, the shorter the wavelength of the radiation. Radiation from the sun is therefore of shorter wavelength than the much cooler re-radiation from the earth.

- **Absorption.** Any body in the path of radiation will absorb some of its energy. How much is absorbed depends on both the body and the radiation. A rocky desert area will absorb more solar radiation than snow-covered mountains.

- **Conduction.** Heat energy may be passed or conducted within the one body, or from one body to another in direct contact with it, by conduction. Iron is a good conductor of heat. Wood is not a good conductor, nor is air. A parcel of air heated by contact with the earth's surface will not transfer this heat energy to neighboring parcels of air. It will, however, carry its heat energy if it moves—a very significant factor in the development of weather systems.

- **Convection.** A mass of air that is heated at the earth's surface will expand, become less dense, and rise, carrying its heat energy higher into the atmosphere, a process known as *thermal convection*. A small mass of rising air is called a **thermal**. These are common over open terrain on sunny afternoons with light winds.

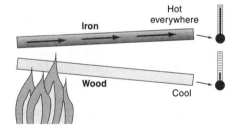

Figure 14-12. Some things are good conductors of heat; others are not

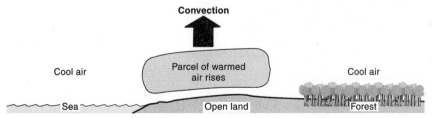

Figure 14-13. Convection

- **Advection.** The horizontal motion of air is known as advection. An air mass moving horizontally by advection, for instance the surface air moving in to replace air that has risen by convection, will of course bring its heat energy and moisture content with it. Advection is simply another term for winds.

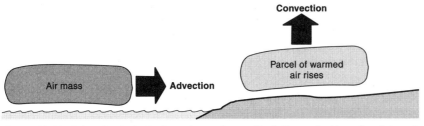

Figure 14-14. Advection is the horizontal transfer of air and heat energy

Convection is the vertical transfer of air and heat energy

Local Air Movements

The Sea Breeze by Day

Circulation patterns can be large scale, like the general circulation pattern just discussed—or they can be on a small scale, like sea breezes and land breezes.

Sea breezes occur on sunny afternoons after the land has warmed. The land heats the surface air in contact with it, causing it to rise, and to leave behind a localized area of low pressure. Cool air from over the sea moves in, lowering the temperature on the beach, and a small circulation pattern is set up. The vertical extent of a sea breeze is usually only 1,000 or 2,000 feet.

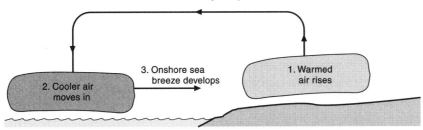

Figure 14-15. The sea breeze—a small circulation cell

Sea breezes may have a significant effect on airports near a coastline. If the sea breeze opposes the general wind pattern, it is quite possible that the wind velocity at traffic pattern altitude will be quite different from that at ground level. Windshear and some turbulence may be experienced as the airplane passes from one body of air to the other. Also, a sea breeze may carry a sea fog inland, causing visibility problems for pilots.

Sometimes you can determine the position of the sea breeze front over the land by the differences in visibility either side of it, or by a line of small cumulus clouds if the warm inland air moving upward at the cold sea breeze front is moist enough to form clouds.

The Land Breeze by Night

By night, the land cools more quickly than the sea, causing the air above it to cool and subside (descend). The air over the sea is warmer and will rise. A small **land breeze** circulation pattern is set up, with surface air moving out to sea and upper air moving inland. The land breeze may reach maximum strength just after dawn when the land is at its minimum temperature.

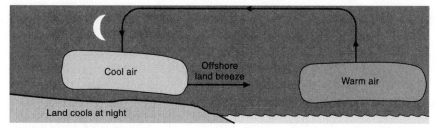

Figure 14-16. The land breeze blows offshore at night

Sometimes a land breeze holds a sea fog offshore early in the day but, as the land warms, the land breeze dies out and a sea breeze develops, bringing the sea fog inland and causing visibility problems at coastal airports.

Katabatic Winds

During night time the earth's surface loses heat energy through terrestrial radiation and cools down, particularly on clear, cloudless nights. The air in contact with the surface then cools down.

Air that is cooled by contact with a mountain slope at night becomes denser than air at the same altitude but further from the slope. The cooler parcels of air start to flow down the slope and into the valleys, creating what is called a **katabatic wind,** a **mountain wind,** or a **drainage wind** flowing down and out of the valleys. In certain areas, katabatic winds can build up during the night and, by sunrise, be flowing down the slopes of large mountains and into the valleys at speeds in excess of 30 knots.

As you will see in the next chapter, air that is descending becomes warmer and drier, and so what starts out as a cool katabatic wind may become relatively warm as it flows down mountain slopes.

Anabatic Winds

Solar heating of a mountain slope causes the air mass in contact with it to become warmer than air at the same altitude but further from the slope, decreasing its density and causing it to flow up the slope. This local upslope wind is known as an **anabatic wind,** or as a **valley wind** since it flows up and out of valleys. Uphill flow is opposed by gravity, so the anabatic wind, which flows up the slope, is generally a weaker wind than the nighttime downslope katabatic wind.

Temperature Inversions

Temperature normally decreases with altitude. In the standard atmosphere the temperature is assumed to decrease by approximately 1.98°C for each 1,000 feet climbed in a stationary air mass. In practice, we can assume a decrease, or temperature lapse rate, of 2°C per 1,000 feet.

In some layers of air in the actual atmosphere, however, air temperature may increase with altitude (an inverted temperature structure), and a temperature **inversion** is said to exist. This often happens near ground level on cold, clear nights when the earth's surface loses heat by terrestrial radiation and cools down. The air near the ground is cooled by conduction, and tends to sink and not mix with air at the higher levels. This leads to the air at ground level being cooler than the air at altitude, and a temperature inversion will exist.

Katabatic winds blow down mountain slopes and valleys at night.

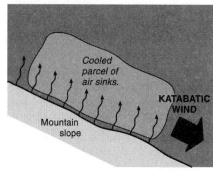

Figure 14-17. The katabatic wind

Anabatic winds drift up mountain slopes by day.

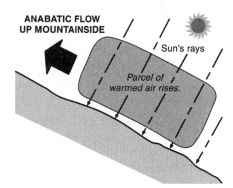

Figure 14-18. The anabatic wind

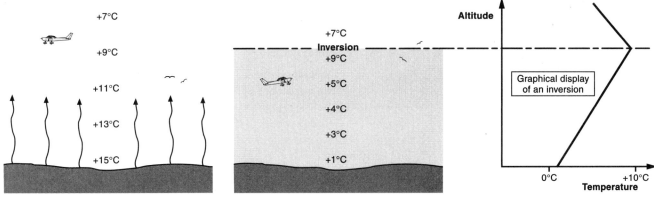

Figure 14-19. Normal temperature situation (left) and a temperature inversion

Air that has no tendency to rise is called **stable air,** as is the case in a temperature inversion, and this generally means smooth flying conditions. Visibility may be a problem, however, because there will be no upward convective currents to carry particles in the air away, so any fog, haze, smoke, smog or low clouds will stay beneath the inversion layer and restrict visibility.

A phenomenon known as **windshear** (in which the wind strength or direction changes from place-to-place) may exist at the upper boundary of the inversion if there are overlying strong winds. An airplane may experience an airspeed change or some turbulence as it flies through the inversion level from one air mass to another. (Windshear is covered in Chapter 18.)

Over desert areas, the upper level of an inversion can sometimes be identified by a layer of dust with clear air above it. Inversions also occur at altitude in warm fronts, when a warm current of air overruns a lower colder layer. A danger for pilots in this situation is freezing rain, which is liquid rain falling out of warmer air above into below-freezing air beneath, where it can quickly form a great deal of ice on an airplane's structure.

✍ Now complete **Review 14, Part (b)** on page 307.

✍ Review 14

Heating Effects in the Atmosphere

Part (a)

1. The atmosphere is divided into four layers based on (temperature/pressure/density/water vapor content).
    ➤ temperature

2. The layer of the atmosphere closest to the earth and in which weather occurs is called the _____ .
    ➤ troposphere

3. The troposphere extends further into space above the (equator/poles).
    ➤ equator

4. The second layer of the atmosphere is called the _____ , and the boundary between it and the troposphere is called the _____ .
    ➤ stratosphere, tropopause

5. There is an abrupt change in (air density/temperature lapse rate) as you climb through the tropopause.
    ➤ temperature lapse rate

6. Which feature is associated with the tropopause?
    (a) Constant height above the earth.
    (b) Abrupt change in temperature lapse rate.
    (c) Absolute upper limit of cloud formation.
    ➤ (b)

7. The main gases that form the atmosphere, in approximate proportions, are _____ (78%), _____ (21%), other gases (1%), and a variable amount of _____ vapor.

➤ nitrogen, oxygen, water vapor

8. Most of the water vapor in the atmosphere is contained in the:
   (a) tropopause.
   (b) troposphere.
   (c) stratosphere.

➤ (b)

9. Air density generally (increases/decreases/stays the same) as altitude is gained.

➤ decreases

10. Temperature generally (increases/decreases/stays the same) as altitude is gained in the troposphere.

➤ decreases

11. There is marked vertical movement of air in the troposphere. (True/False?)

➤ True

12. An air mass that passes over an ocean is likely to be (more/less) moist than an air mass that passes over a continent.

➤ more

13. A body of air over an ocean is referred to as:
   (a) maritime air.
   (b) polar air.
   (c) oceanic air.

➤ (a)

14. Temperature at sea level in the standard atmosphere is _____ °C, which is equivalent to _____ °F.

➤ +15°C or +59°F

15. Standard pressure at sea level is _____ in.Hg, which is equivalent to _____ hPa.

➤ 29.92 in.Hg, 1013.2 hPa

16. Standard temperature theoretically decreases by approximately _____ °C for each 1,000 feet gained in the lower levels of the atmosphere.

➤ 28C/1,000 feet

17. The rate of decrease of temperature with altitude in the actual atmosphere is called the temperature (lapse/change) rate.

➤ temperature lapse rate

18. Above approximately 36,000 feet in the theoretical International Standard Atmosphere, the temperature ceases to decrease and remains constant at approximately _____ °C.

➤ – 56.5°C

19. What are the standard temperature and pressure values for sea level?
   (a) 15°C and 29.92 in.Hg.
   (b) 59°C and 1013.2 millibars.
   (c) 59°F and 29.92 millibars.

➤ (a)

Part (b)

1. The air surrounding the earth is mainly heated (directly by the sun/from below by the earth's surface).

➤ from below by the earth's surface

2. Heating of the earth is greatest in the (tropics/ temperate mid-latitude zones/polar regions).

➤ tropics

3. Every physical process of weather is accompanied by or is the result of:
   (a) a heat exchange.
   (b) the movement of air.
   (c) a pressure differential.

➤ (a)

4. Warmed air (rises/sinks) and cooled air (rises/sinks).

➤ rises, sinks

5. Terrestrial radiation is:
   (a) the direct heating of the earth by the sun.
   (b) the re-radiation of heat from the earth.

➤ (b)

6. Solar heating of the earth occurs:
   (a) only by day.
   (b) continually.

➤ (a)

7. Terrestrial re-radiation occurs:
   (a) only by day.
   (b) continually.
   (c) only at night.

➤ (b)

8. The sea heats (more/less) rapidly than land, and cools (more/less) rapidly than land.

➤ less, less

9. Generally the sea is (warmer/cooler) by day, and (warmer/cooler) by night, than the land.
➤ cooler, warmer

10. Water has a (higher/lower) specific heat than land.
➤ higher

11. Cloud coverage (reduces/increases/does not affect) the heating of the earth's surface.
➤ reduces

12. Cloud coverage (reduces/increases/does not affect) the cooling of the earth's surface by the terrestrial re-radiation of heat.
➤ reduces

13. The transfer of heat as electromagnetic waves is called the process of (radiation/absorption/conduction/convection/advection).
➤ radiation

14. The transfer of heat from body to body by direct contact is called the process of (radiation/absorption/conduction/convection/advection).
➤ conduction

15. The transfer of heat by the horizontal motion of an air mass is called (radiation/absorption/conduction/convection/advection).
➤ advection

16. The transfer of heat by the vertical motion of an air mass is called (radiation/absorption/conduction/convection/advection).
➤ convection

17. The development of thermals depends upon:
   (a) a counterclockwise circulation of air.
   (b) temperature inversions.
   (c) solar heating.
➤ (c)

18. A sea breeze blows (offshore/onshore) during the late afternoon.
➤ onshore

19. A sea breeze front can sometimes be identified by a line of (cumuliform/stratiform) clouds just inland.
➤ cumuliform

20. Convective circulation patterns associated with sea breezes are caused by:
   (a) warm, dense air moving inland from over the water.
   (b) water absorbing and radiating heat faster than the land.
   (c) cool, dense air moving inland from over the water.
➤ (c)

21. The wind that flows down mountain slopes at night due to cooling is called a _____ wind.
➤ katabatic

22. The wind that flows up mountain slopes by day due to heating is called an _____ wind.
➤ anabatic

23. Upslope winds are usually (stronger/weaker) than downslope winds due to the force of _____ .
➤ weaker, gravity

24. If the air at the earth's surface is cooler than that above, a temperature _____ is said to exist.
➤ inversion

25. An inversion means that the temperature (increases/decreases/stays constant) as altitude increases.
➤ increases

26. A ground-based inversion is most likely to form on (clear/cloudy) nights.
➤ clear

27. Air beneath a ground-based inversion will be (stable/unstable), and will tend to (rise/not rise).
➤ stable, not rise

28. Flying conditions beneath an inversion are likely to be (smooth/turbulent), with (good/poor) visibility.
➤ smooth, poor

Wind 15

What is Wind?

The term **wind** refers to the flow of air over the earth's surface. This flow is almost completely horizontal, with only about one one-thousandth of the total flow being vertical.

Despite being only a small proportion of the overall flow of air in the atmosphere, vertical airflow is extremely important to weather and to aviation, since it leads to the formation of clouds. Some vertical winds are so strong, like those in or below a cumulonimbus stormcloud, that they are a hazard to aviation and can destroy airplanes. In general, however, the term wind is used in reference to the horizontal flow of air.

It is pressure differences in the atmosphere (usually resulting from temperature differences) that causes winds.

How Wind Is Described

Both the direction and strength of a wind are significant and are expressed thus:

- **wind direction** is the direction *from* which the wind is blowing and is expressed in degrees, measured clockwise from north;
- **wind strength** is expressed in knots (abbreviated kt).

Direction and strength together describe the **wind velocity,** which is usually written in the form 27035 or 270/35—in other words, a wind blowing from 270° at a strength of 35 knots. Meteorologists relate wind direction to *true* north, so all winds that appear on forecasts are expressed in degrees true (°T). Thus 34012KT on a forecast or observation means a wind strength of 12 knots from a direction of 340°T.

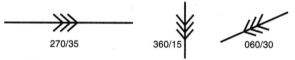

Figure 15-1. Examples of wind velocity

Airport runways, however, are described in terms of their *magnetic* direction, so when an airplane lines up on a runway for takeoff, its magnetic compass and the runway direction should agree, at least approximately.

The wind direction relative to the runway direction is extremely important when taking off and landing. For this reason, winds passed to the pilot by the Tower have direction expressed in degrees *magnetic*. This is also the case for the recorded messages on the automatic terminal information service (ATIS) that a pilot can listen to on the radio at some airports.

Veering and Backing

A wind whose direction is changing in a clockwise direction is called a **veering** wind. For example, following a change from 080/20 to 120/25, the wind is said to have veered.

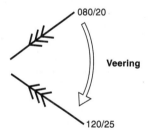

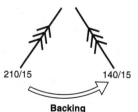

Figure 15-2. A veering wind (top) and a backing wind

A wind whose direction is changing in a counterclockwise direction is called a **backing** wind. A change from 210/15 to 140/15 is an example of a wind that has backed.

What Causes a Wind to Blow?

A change in velocity (speed and/or direction) is called acceleration. Acceleration is caused by a force (or forces) being exerted on an object, be it an airplane, an automobile or a parcel of air.

The combined effect of all the forces acting on a body is known as the net (or resultant) force, and determines the acceleration of the body. If all of the forces acting on a parcel of air balance each other so that the resultant force is zero, then the parcel of air will not accelerate, but will continue to move in a straight line at a constant speed (or stay still). A steady wind velocity is known as **balanced flow.**

The Pressure-Gradient Force

The force that is usually responsible for starting the movement of a parcel of air is known as the **pressure-gradient force.** This acts to move air from areas of *high* pressure to areas of *low* pressure.

Places on the earth's surface where the air pressure is the same are shown on weather charts by lines called **isobars.** The pressure-gradient force acts at right angles to the isobars, in the direction from high to low pressure. Strong pressure gradients are indicated by closely spaced isobars.

If the pressure gradient force was the only force acting on a parcel of air, it would continue to accelerate toward the low pressure, getting faster and faster, and eventually the high and low pressure areas would disappear. This, of course, does not occur, and the reason is that there is another force acting on the air. This force, which is created by the earth's rotation, is known as the Coriolis effect.

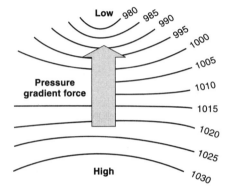

Figure 15-3. The pressure-gradient force starts a parcel of air moving

The Coriolis Effect

The **Coriolis effect** was named after G. G. de Coriolis, the French mathematician who discovered the effect in the 19th century. It results from the passage of air across the rotating earth's surface.

Imagine a parcel of air that is stationary over Point A on the equator, as shown in Figure 15-4. It is in fact moving with Point A as the earth rotates on its axis from west to east. Now, suppose that a pressure gradient exists, with a high pressure at Point A and a low pressure at Point B, directly north of A. The parcel of air at A starts moving toward B, but still with its motion toward the east due to the earth's rotation.

The further away from the equator a position is, the less the easterly motion of the earth's surface. Consequently, the further away from the equator it is, the more it will lag behind the easterly motion of the parcel of air. In the figure, Point B will have only moved to B, but the parcel of air will have moved to A. To an observer standing on the earth's surface, the parcel of air will *appear* to have turned to the right.

If the parcel of air was being accelerated (by a pressure-gradient force) in a southerly direction from a high-pressure area toward a low-pressure area near the equator, the earth's rotation toward the east would "get away from it" and so the air movement, or wind, would appear to turn right also—Point A having moved to A, but the air flow only reaching B to the west.

The faster the air flow, the greater the Coriolis effect—if there is no air movement, then there is no Coriolis effect. The effect is also greater in regions near the poles, where changes in latitude cause more significant changes in the speed at which each point on the earth is moving toward the east.

In the Northern Hemisphere, the Coriolis effect causes the wind to curve to the *right;* in the Southern Hemisphere, the situation is reversed and it deflects the wind to the *left.*

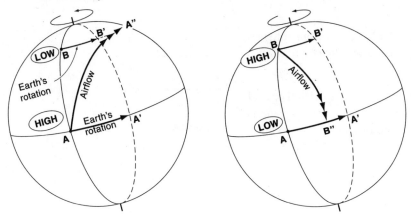

Figure 15-4. The Coriolis effect acts toward the right in the Northern Hemisphere

Note: Throughout the rest of this chapter, the discussion will only consider the Northern Hemisphere. The effects will be reversed in the Southern Hemisphere.

The Geostrophic Wind

The two influences on a moving airstream are:
- the pressure-gradient force (the *initiating* force); and
- the Coriolis effect (the *deviating* influence).

The pressure-gradient force starts the air moving and the Coriolis effect turns it right (in the Northern Hemisphere). This curving of the airflow over the earth continues until the pressure-gradient force is counterbalanced by the Coriolis effect, resulting in a wind flow that is steady and blowing in a direction parallel to the isobars. This balanced flow is called the **geostrophic wind.**

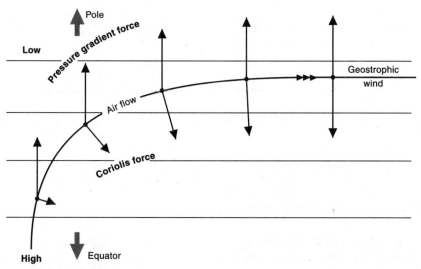

Figure 15-5. Balanced flow occurs parallel to the isobars—the geostrophic wind

The geostrophic wind is important to a weather forecaster because it flows in a direction parallel with the isobars, with the low pressure on its left, at a speed that is directly proportional to the spacing of the isobars (that is, proportional to the pressure gradient). This enables a reasonable estimate of wind direction and strength—the closer the isobars, the stronger the wind.

It is the Coriolis effect that causes the air movement created by the pressure gradient to not flow directly from a high to a low pressure area.

Buys Ballot's Law

Buys Ballot was a Dutchman who noticed that (in the Northern Hemisphere): *If you stand with your back to the wind the low pressure will be on your left.*

Flying from High to Low

If an airplane in the Northern Hemisphere is experiencing **right drift,** the wind is from the left and therefore, according to Buys Ballot's law, the airplane is flying toward an area of lower pressure. Low pressure often has poor weather associated with it, such as low cloud, rain and poor visibility in showers.

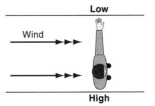

Figure 15-6. Buys Ballot's law

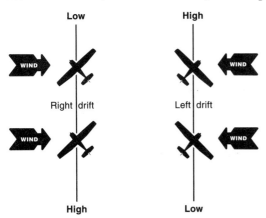

Figure 15-7. Pressure areas can be identified by the direction of wind drift

When flying towards an area of lower pressure the altimeter will over-read unless the pilot periodically resets the lower altimeter settings in the pressure window. This is not a healthy situation—beware below.

Flying from Low to High

If an airplane is experiencing **left drift,** the wind is from the right and so, according to Buys Ballot's Law, it is flying toward an area of higher pressure. High pressure often indicates a more stable atmosphere and generally better weather (although fog or poor visibility may occur).

The Gradient Wind

Isobars (the lines joining places of equal pressure) are usually curved. For the wind to flow parallel to these isobars, the airflow must be accelerated toward the center of the pressure pattern to cause it to deviate from its straight path. In the same manner as a stone when being swung on a string is pulled into the turn by a force, a curving air flow must have a resultant (or net) force acting on it to pull it into the turn. The resultant wind flow around the *curved* isobars is called the **gradient wind.**

In the Northern Hemisphere, the gradient wind flows clockwise around high-pressure areas (known as *anticyclonic motion*) and counterclockwise around low pressure areas (known as *cyclonic motion*).

For a wind that is blowing around a low (in the Northern Hemisphere), the net force results from the pressure-gradient force being greater than the Coriolis effect, thereby pulling the airflow in toward the low. For a wind that is blowing around a high, the net force results from the Coriolis effect being greater than the pressure-gradient force.

Since the Coriolis effect increases with speed, it follows that, with equally spaced isobars, the wind speed around a high will be greater than around a low.

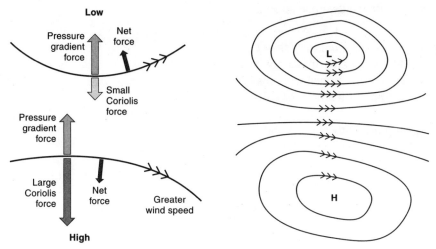

Figure 15-8. Wind flow is clockwise around a *high* and counterclockwise around a *low* in the Northern Hemisphere

The Surface Wind

The surface wind is important to pilots because of the effect it has on takeoff and landing. The surface wind is measured at 30 feet above level and open ground—where windsocks and other wind indicators are usually situated.

In the **friction layer** up to about 2,000 feet AGL, surface friction slows the wind down—a lower wind speed means less Coriolis effect and less deviation of the wind, so that the surface wind will tend to cross the isobars and flow out from a high and in to a low. The rougher the surface is, the greater the slowing-down. Friction forces will be least over oceans and flat desert areas, and greatest over hilly or city areas with many obstructions.

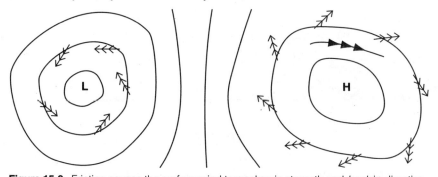

Figure 15-9. Friction causes the surface wind to weaken in strength and *back* in direction

A reduced wind speed results in a reduced Coriolis effect (since the Coriolis effect depends on speed). So, the pressure-gradient force will have a more pronounced effect in the lower levels, causing the wind to flow *in* toward low-pressure areas and *out* from high-pressure areas, rather than parallel to the isobars. In other words, the surface wind tends to "back" counterclockwise compared with the gradient wind.

For example, a strong southwesterly gradient wind at 5,000 feet AGL *backs* (change direction counterclockwise) to become a less-strong southerly wind at the surface, caused by friction between the wind and the surface causing the air movement to slow down, thereby reducing the Coriolis effect.

In the Northern Hemisphere:

- surface winds associated with **low-pressure** areas flow inward at an angle to the isobars in a *counterclockwise* manner.
- surface winds associated with **high-pressure** areas flow outward at an angle to the isobars in a *clockwise* manner.

Since there is less surface friction over oceans, the surface wind may slow to about two-thirds of the gradient wind strength and the backing may only be about 10°. Over land surfaces, where friction is greater, the surface wind may slow to just one-third of the gradient wind strength, with its direction some 30° back from the gradient flow at altitude.

Friction due to the earth's surface decreases rapidly with altitude and is almost negligible above 2,000 feet AGL. The turbulence due to wind flow over rough ground also fades out at about the same level.

Daily Variation

During the day, heating of the earth's surface by the rays of the sun, and the consequent heating of the air in contact with it, will cause *vertical* motion in the lower levels of the atmosphere. This promotes mixing of the various layers of air and consequently the effect of the gradient wind at altitude will be brought *closer* to the earth's surface.

The surface wind by day will resemble the gradient wind more closely than the surface wind by night—that is, the day surface wind will be seen as a stronger wind that has veered clockwise compared with the night surface wind.

Day—veer and increase.
Night—slack and back.

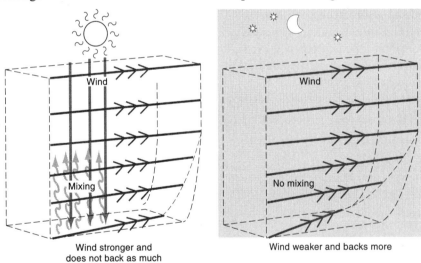

Wind stronger and does not back as much

Wind weaker and backs more

Figure 15-10. The daily variation of wind

During the night, mixing of the layers decreases. The gradient wind will continue to blow at altitude, but its effects will not be mixed with the airflow at the surface to such an extent as during the day. The night wind at surface level will drop in strength and the Coriolis effect will weaken—that is, compared with the day wind, the night wind will drop in strength and back counterclockwise in direction (Figure 15-10).

Wind in the Tropics

In tropical areas, pressure gradients are generally fairly weak and so will not cause the air to flow at high speeds. Local effects, such as land and sea breezes, may have a stronger influence than the pressure gradient.

The Coriolis effect that causes the air to flow parallel to the isobars is very weak in the tropics since the distance from the earth's axis remains fairly constant. The pressure gradient force, even though relatively weak, will dominate and so the air will tend to flow more from the high-pressure areas to the low-pressure areas across the isobars, rather than parallel to them.

Instead of using isobars (that join places of equal pressure) on tropical weather charts, it is more common to use:

- **streamlines** to indicate wind direction, which will be outdrafts from high-pressure areas and indrafts to low-pressure areas; in combination with:

- **isotachs,** which are dotted lines joining places of equal wind strength.

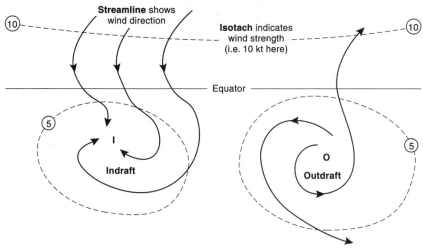

Figure 15-11. Streamline/isotach analysis chart

✍ Now complete **Review 15** on page 319.

For Aspiring Commercial Pilots

High-Level Weather

The Tropopause

High-level weather applies near to and above the **tropopause,** which is the border between the troposphere and the stratosphere. The tropopause varies in altitude from about 20,000 feet over the poles to 55,000–65,000 feet over the equator. In mid-latitudes, it is approximately 36,000 feet, which is its assumed level in the standard atmosphere.

Temperatures and winds vary significantly near the tropopause, with temperature above the tropopause no longer decreasing with altitude. Knowledge of these can assist you in achieving an efficient and comfortable flight.

The tropopause is characterized by a sudden change in the temperature lapse rate.

Jetstreams

A **jet stream** is a strong narrow current of air with horizontal motion, typically located in the upper troposphere or in the stratosphere. A jet stream looks similar to the shape of a ruler, with dimensions typically 1 nm deep, 100 nm wide, and 1,200 nm long. To be called a jet stream, the wind speeds must exceed 60 knots.

We have seen that the tropopause is not one continuous sheet, but descends from the equator to the poles in a number of steps. These steps in the tropopause are like horizontal line breaks and coincide with the *Hadley cells* found in the general circulation pattern. Each step has an intense temperature (thermal) gradient that will in turn mean there is a strong thermal wind component. As a consequence the upper winds will become very strong. These tubes of strong wind between the tropopause steps are called jet streams and are associated with narrow bands of windshear and severe turbulence.

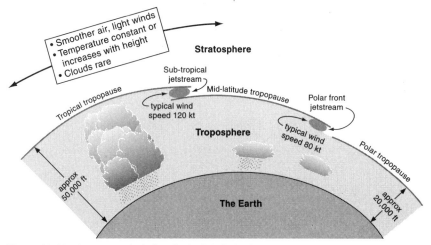

Figure 15-12. Jetstream winds flow in the breaks in the tropopause

In the winter months in the Northern Hemisphere the general circulation pattern moves further south (along with the sun), and the jetstreams increase in strength. The position of the jetstream over North America varies, but it is (in general terms) further south and stronger in winter, and moves further north in summer and is somewhat weaker.

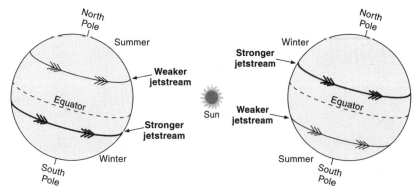

Figure 15-13. The position of jetstreams varies with the season

The position of the jetstream and its associated clear air turbulence can sometimes be visually identified by long streaks of high-level cirrus clouds (*see* next chapter). A jetstream is typically, 5,000 feet thick and associated with a deep low-pressure trough situated in the upper atmosphere near the tropopause. It may run in a curved path for thousands of miles around the earth at high altitude basically from west to east, but its path may meander quite a bit. By definition, the wind strength in a jetstream is **60 knots** or greater, with the strongest winds existing in the core of the jetstream tube. It is possible sometimes for a second and third jetstream to form.

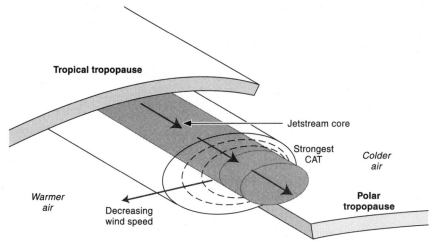

Figure 15-14. A jetstream

High-flying jets often take advantage of the strong winds in the core of the jetstream when they are flying from west to east, perhaps giving a tailwind of 100 knots or more (and avoid the jetstream when flying from east to west).

Note: Flying conditions near jetstreams are covered in Chapter 18.

How a Jetstream Forms

Wind velocity changes with altitude because of uneven temperatures in the horizontal. A warm air mass alongside a cold air mass (as is the case at the polar front) will be less dense and have relatively expanded pressure levels. Even though the pressures may be the same at ground level in the two air masses (in other words, with no pressure gradient), the pressure at altitude in the warm air mass will be greater than that at the same level in the cold air mass. A pressure-gradient force will exist and a wind will be initiated. In general, the higher the altitude in the troposphere, the steeper the pressure gradient and the stronger the wind.

Once the jetstream starts to flow, the Coriolis effect turns it to the right (in the Northern Hemisphere). In the situation illustrated, the wind will flow "out" of the page (that is, from west to east—as a westerly wind), and will be stronger at higher altitudes in the troposphere. If you look at weather charts and winds-aloft forecasts, you will often see westerlies that increase with altitude.

At the tropopause temperature stops decreasing. Since the polar tropopause is lower than the mid-latitude tropopause, temperature above it will stop decreasing with altitude, whereas temperature will continue decreasing in the "warm" air mass until its tropopause is reached, by which time it may be significantly colder than the "cold" air mass at the same level.

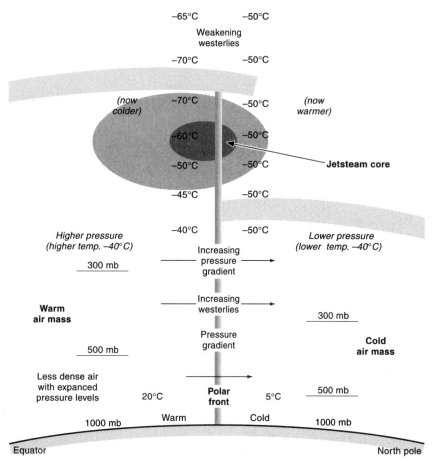

Figure 15-15. The polar front brings cold air down from polar regions

As well as the temperature gradient reversing with altitude, the pressure gradient will also start to reverse, and so the westerlies will start to weaken with increasing altitude above the tropopause, and may even become easterlies at great altitudes.

The westerly winds reach their maximum intensity in the break between the two tropopause sheets, often blowing in a narrow jetstream tube at speeds well in excess of 100 knots.

Clear Air Turbulence

Turbulence can also be expected at high altitudes in the vicinity of any jetstream. Turbulence above 15,000 feet AGL that is not associated with cumuliform clouds is known as **clear air turbulence (CAT).** If there is a change in wind strength of more than about *6 knots per 1,000 feet* of altitude change, then moderate or stronger clear air turbulence is probable.

✍ Commercial students complete **Review 15, Commercial** on page 319.

✍ Review 15

1. Wind is caused by differences in _____ .
➤ pressure

2. The driving force that initiates a wind is the (pressure gradient/Coriolis) force.
➤ pressure gradient

3. The pressure gradient force acts (parallel/perpendicular) to the isobars.
➤ perpendicular

4. The stronger the pressure gradient, the (weaker/stronger) the wind.
➤ stronger

5. A wind will initially tend to flow from a (high/low) pressure area to a (high/low) pressure area, before it is turned by the _____ force.
➤ high, low, Coriolis

6. In the Northern Hemisphere, the wind is deflected to the:
   (a) right by Coriolis force.
   (b) right by surface friction.
   (c) left by Coriolis force.
➤ (a)

7. Why does the wind have a tendency to flow parallel to the isobars above the friction level?
   (a) The Coriolis force tends to counterbalance the horizontal pressure gradient.
   (b) The Coriolis force acts perpendicular to a line connecting the highs and lows.
   (c) The friction of the air with the earth deflects the air perpendicular to the pressure gradient.
➤ (a)

8. Air tends to flow (clockwise/counterclockwise) around a low-pressure system in the Northern Hemisphere because of the _____ force.
➤ counterclockwise, Coriolis

9. The surface winds are usually (stronger/weaker) than the winds at 2,000 feet AGL because of _____ .
➤ weaker, friction

10. The surface winds associated with a high-pressure area in the Northern Hemisphere flow (inward/outward) in a (clockwise/counterclockwise) manner.
➤ outward, clockwise

11. Compared with the gradient wind that flows parallel to the isobars, the surface wind tends to (veer clockwise/back counterclockwise).
➤ back counterclockwise

12. The wind at 5,000 feet AGL is southwesterly while the surface wind is southerly. This difference in direction is primarily due to:
    (a) stronger pressure gradient at higher altitudes.
    (b) friction between the wind and the surface.
    (c) stronger Coriolis force at the surface.
➤ (b)

Commercial Review

1. The surface wind tends to flow across the isobars towards the lower pressure because of (the Coriolis force/the reduced Coriolis force caused by friction).
➤ the reduced Coriolis force caused by friction

2. When the isobars are close together, the pressure gradient force is (greater/smaller) and wind velocities are (stronger/weaker).
➤ greater, stronger

3. What causes air to flow counterclockwise around a low-pressure area in the Northern Hemisphere?
   (a) Coriolis force.
   (b) Surface friction.
   (c) Pressure gradient.
➤ (a)

4. A jetstream is defined as a wind of _____ knots or greater.
➤ 60 knots

5. The average altitude of the tropopause in mid-latitudes is _____ feet.
➤ 36,000 feet

6. Jetstreams are usually found (above/below/near) breaks in the tropopause.
➤ near

7. Upper-level jetstreams are often associated with (troughs/ridges) of (low/high) pressure in the upper atmosphere.
➤ troughs, low

8. The jetstream is generally (stronger/weaker) and further (north/south) in the summer compared with in the winter.

➤ weaker and further north

9. During the winter months in the middle latitudes, the jetstream shifts toward the:
   (a) north and speed decreases.
   (b) south and speed increases.
   (c) north and speed increases.

➤ (b)

10. You can expect greater turbulence in a (curving/straight) jetstream.

➤ curving

11. A strong windshear can be expected:
   (a) in the jetstream front above a core having a speed of 60 to 90 knots.
   (b) if the 5°C isotherms are spaced between 7° and 10° of latitude.
   (c) on the low-pressure side of a jetstream core where the speed at the core is stronger than 110 knots.

➤ (c)

12. A common location of clear air turbulence is:
   (a) in an upper trough on the polar side of a jetstream.
   (b) near a ridge aloft on the equatorial side of a high-pressure flow.
   (c) south of an east/west oriented high-pressure ridge in its dissipating stage.

➤ (a)

13. The jetstream and associated clear air turbulence can sometimes be visually identified in flight by:
   (a) dust or haze at flight level.
   (b) long streaks of cirrus clouds.
   (c) a constant outside air temperature.

➤ (b)

Clouds and Thunderstorms 16

Clouds

Clouds and thunderstorms present some of the biggest challenges to pilots of all levels. Do you fly through them? Do you fly around them? That all depends on what kind of clouds you've encountered.

A cloud is a visible aggregate of minute particles of water and/or ice in free air. The effect of clouds on aviation, particularly on flight, makes them an important topic in training as the VFR pilot is required to plan for and fly in visual meteorological conditions (VMC).

Low *stratus* clouds formed in stable atmospheric conditions can sit low over the ground, possibly even on the ground as fog, and cause an instrument-rated pilot to divert to an alternate destination. Towering cumulus clouds form in unstable conditions which allows moist air to rise and cool, and these can develop into one of the greatest hazards to an airplane, cumulonimbus clouds and thunderstorms.

The Naming of Clouds

Clouds may take on numerous different forms, many of which continually change. They are classified into four families according to height and named individually according to their nature. It is important to understand cloud classification because meteorological forecasts and reports use this system to give you a picture of the weather.

Clouds belong to one of four families depending on height. They are:

1. **High-level clouds** with a base above approximately 20,000 feet, and composed mainly of ice crystals in the below-freezing upper atmosphere (cirrus, cirrocumulus, cirrostratus).

2. **Middle-level clouds** with a base above approximately 6,500 feet (altocumulus, altostratus, nimbostratus).

3. **Low-level clouds** with a base below approximately 6,500 feet (stratocumulus, stratus, fair weather cumulus, nimbostratus).

4. **Clouds with extensive vertical development** (towering cumulus, cumulonimbus).

Clouds are named according to the following types:

- **cirriform** (or fibrous)—consisting mainly of ice crystals;
- **cumuliform** (or heaped)—formed by unstable air rising and cooling;
- **stratiform** (or layered)—formed by the cooling of a stable layer;
- **nimbus** (or rain-bearing), and **fractus** (fragmented);
- **castellanus** (common base with separate vertical development, often in lines); and
- **lenticularis** (lens-shaped, often formed in strong winds over mountains).

Nimbostratus, for example, means stratified clouds from which rain is falling. Altocumulus is middle-level heaped clouds. Cumulus fractus is fragmentary cumulus clouds. Cirrostratus is high-level stratified clouds consisting of ice crystals. Standing lenticular altocumulus clouds are lens-shaped, middle-level clouds standing in the one position, usually over a mountain range in strong winds. Nimbostratus is a hybrid cloud in terms of classification since its base can be low level or middle level, and it can have great vertical depth. Sometimes nimbostratus is 10,000 or even 15,000 feet thick, making it very dark when seen from underneath and capable of causing heavy rain for many hours.

Flying in clouds presents the qualified instrument-rated pilot with considerations such as poor visibility and the risk of icing—not a great risk in the high-level cirriform clouds consisting of ice crystals, but very great in clouds of extensive vertical development which may contain large supercooled water drops that will freeze on contact with a cold airplane.

Moisture in the Atmosphere

Clouds are formed when water vapor in the atmosphere condenses into water droplets or, in below freezing temperatures, into ice crystals. Water vapor is taken up into the atmosphere mainly by **evaporation** from the oceans and other bodies where water is present, or by **sublimation** directly from solid ice when the air overlies a frozen surface.

The Three States of Water

Water in its vapor state is not visible, but when the water vapor condenses to form water droplets we see it as cloud, fog, mist, rain or dew. Frozen water is also visible as high-level clouds, snow, hail, ice or frost. Water exists in three states—gas (vapor), liquid (water) and solid (ice).

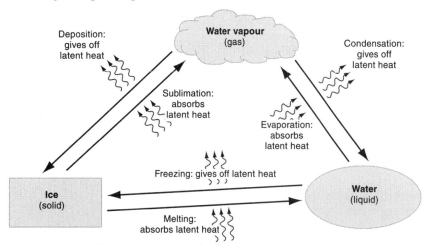

Figure 16-1. The three states of water

Under certain conditions water can change from one state to another, *absorbing* heat energy if it moves to a higher energy state (from ice to water to vapor) and *giving off* heat energy if it moves to a lower energy state (vapor to water to ice). This heat energy is known as **latent heat** and is a vital part of any change of state. The absorption or emission of latent heat is important in meteorological processes such as cloud formation, and evaporation of rain (virga).

The three states of water, the names of the various transfer processes and the absorption or giving-off of latent heat are shown in Figure 16-1.

Relative Humidity

The amount of water vapor present in the air depends on the amount of evaporation, which will be greater over wet surfaces such as oceans and flooded ground than over a desert or continent. The actual amount of water vapor in the air, known as humidity, is not as important as whether the air can support that water vapor or not. When a parcel of air is supporting as much water vapor as it can, it is said to be **saturated** and have a **relative humidity of 100%.**

Air supporting less than its full capacity of water vapor is said to be *unsaturated,* and will have a relative humidity of less than 100%. In clouds and fog, the relative humidity is 100% and the air is saturated; over a desert, relative humidity might be only 20%.

Dewpoint Temperature

Clouds are formed when air is cooled to its **dewpoint** temperature, and the excess water vapor condenses as liquid water or ice crystals, depending on temperature. The cooling of a parcel of air can occur by various means, such as:

- rising air cooling adiabatically as it expands; or
- air flowing over, or lying over, a cooling surface.

How much water vapor a particular parcel of air can support depends on the air temperature—warm air is able to support more water vapor than cold air. If the temperature of the air falls, it is capable of holding less water vapor, and so will move closer to being saturated—its relative humidity will rise. The relative humidity increases greatly with a decrease in temperature.

The temperature at which the relative humidity reaches 100%, and the excess water vapor starts to condense into water droplets, is known as the **dewpoint temperature.** Condensation may be delayed if there are insufficient condensation nuclei in the air, or conversely, certain types of condensation nuclei may induce condensation shortly before 100% relative humidity is reached. Typical condensation nuclei are small particles of hygroscopic (water-soluble) dust, salt, and so on. Clouds form when the water vapor actually condenses.

A parcel of air that has a temperature higher than its dewpoint is unsaturated. This means its relative humidity is less than 100%, since it is capable of holding more moisture at its current temperature. The closer the actual temperature of the air to its dewpoint, the closer it is to being saturated. In other words, as the temperature/dewpoint spread reduces with a fall in air temperature, the relative humidity increases.

At its dewpoint, the air will be fully saturated—its relative humidity will be 100%. If it becomes cooler than its dewpoint, then the excess water vapor will condense as visible water droplets (or, in sub-freezing temperatures below the frost point, deposit as ice crystals). The actual value of the dewpoint temperature for a particular parcel of air varies, depending on the amount of water vapor it contains. If the air is moist (for instance over a tropical ocean), the dewpoint temperature may be quite high, say +25°C; if the air is dry, the dewpoint temperature may be quite low.

If the air temperature falls to a dewpoint temperature which is above freezing, the water vapor will condense as liquid water droplets and become visible as clouds, fog or dew; if the dewpoint is below freezing, the excess water vapor may change to ice crystals (for example, high-level cirriform clouds, or frost on the ground on a below freezing night).

If the air in which clouds form is unable to support the water droplets (if they become too large and heavy), then the drops will fall as precipitation (rain, hail or snow).

Adiabatic Processes

The **temperature** of a gas depends on the number and energy of its molecules striking the measuring surface of a thermometer. In **adiabatic** processes, temperature can change as a result of pressure changes, even though heat energy is neither added to nor taken from the system. Expanding a gas and decreasing its pressure causes a lowering of temperature, because fewer molecules will collide with the measuring surface.

Conversely, compressing a gas and increasing its pressure will raise its temperature because more molecules will collide with the measuring surface. Placing your finger over the outlet of a bicycle pump illustrates that compressing air increases its temperature. Also, air that has been compressed and stored at room temperature will cool when it is released to the atmosphere and allowed to expand.

A common adiabatic process that involves the expansion of a gas and its cooling is when a parcel of air rises in the atmosphere. This can be initiated by the heating of the parcel of air over warm ground, causing it to expand and become less dense than the surrounding air, hence it will rise. A parcel of air can also be forced aloft as it blows over a mountain range, or as it is lifted over a front.

Unsaturated air will cool adiabatically at about 3°C/1,000 feet as it rises and expands. This is known as the **dry adiabatic lapse rate (DALR).** Air that is 12°C at ground level will cool adiabatically to 9°C if it is forced up to 1,000 feet AGL, and to 6°C at 2,000 feet AGL, and so on, provided it does not reach saturation point.

Cooler air can support less water vapor, so, as the parcel of air rises and cools, its relative humidity will increase. At the altitude where its temperature is reduced to the dewpoint temperature (that is, relative humidity reaches 100%), water will start to condense and form cloud.

Above this altitude, the now-saturated air will continue to cool as it rises but, because latent heat will be given off as the water vapor condenses into the lower energy liquid state, the cooling will not be as great. The rate at which saturated air cools as it rises is known as the **saturated adiabatic lapse rate (SALR)** and may be assumed to have a value of approximately half the DALR (1.5°C/1,000 feet). Air that is say 5°C inside a cloud will, if it is forced 1,000 feet higher, cool adiabatically to 3.5°C.

Note: At higher levels in the cloud where there is less water vapor to condense into water (since most of this has already occurred), there will be less latent heat given off and so SALR will increase.

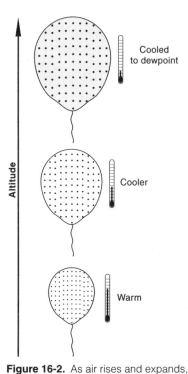

Figure 16-2. As air rises and expands, it cools adiabatically

The Formation of Clouds

Which Cloud Type Forms?

The structure or type of cloud that forms depends mainly on the **stability** of the air before lifting occurs. **Moist air** that is unstable will continue rising, forming cumulus-type cloud with significant vertical development and turbulence, whereas moist air that is stable has no tendency to continue rising and so will form stratus-type clouds with little vertical development and little or no turbulence. Some stratiform clouds, such as nimbostratus, can however form in a very thick layer. **Dry air** that is forced to rise, but does not cool to its dewpoint temperature, will not form clouds.

The type of cloud which forms depends on stability of the air.

Unstable air
could form cumulus
or cumulonimbus

Stable air
could form lenticularis,
stratus or stratocumulus

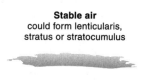

Figure 16-3. Cumuliform clouds form in unstable conditions

Stratiform clouds form in stable conditions

As long as a parcel of air given vertical movement is **warmer** than its surroundings, it will continue to rise. This is known as an **unstable** parcel of air. Its characteristics are:

- turbulence in the rising air;
- the formation of cumuliform clouds (heaped clouds);
- showery rain from these clouds, if there is precipitation; and
- good visibility between the showers (caused by the rising air carrying any obscuring particles away).

If the rising parcel of air is cooler than the ambient air around it, then it will stop rising because its density will be greater than the surroundings. An atmosphere in which air tends to remain at the one level, or to sink, is called a stable atmosphere.

Characteristics of stable air are:

- the formation of **stratiform** clouds (layer-type) with little vertical development and steady, if any, precipitation;
- poor visibility if there are any obscuring particles; and
- possibly smooth flying conditions with little or no turbulence.

The rate of temperature change as altitude is gained in the surrounding atmosphere (that is, in the air that is not rising) is called the **environmental lapse rate (ELR),** the **ambient lapse rate** or the **actual lapse rate.** Its relationship to DALR and SALR is the main factor in determining the levels of the bases and tops of the clouds that form. A great decrease in ambient air temperature with altitude (that is, a high ELR) encourages warm air to keep rising (that is, an unstable situation) and form clouds of great vertical development. A lesser ELR may indicate a stable situation. The actual environmental lapse rate varies from time-to-time and from place-to-place.

The stability in the atmosphere depends on the ambient lapse rate.

Clouds Formed by Convection due to Heating

Cold air moving over or lying over a warm surface will be warmed from below, and so become less stable. It will tend to rise, causing turbulence and good visibility. If the air is moist and unstable, cumuliform clouds will develop as the air ascends and cools adiabatically to its dewpoint temperature.

The ascending unsaturated air will cool at the dry adiabatic lapse rate of 3°C/1,000 feet. The closer the air temperature is to the dewpoint, the lesser height it has to rise before condensing to form clouds. The dewpoint decreases at about 0.5°C/1,000 feet, which means that the air temperature/dewpoint spread will decrease at approximately 2.5°C/1,000 feet in rising unstable air.

For working in degrees Fahrenheit, the DALR for unsaturated air is 5.4°F and the dewpoint lapse rate is approximately 1°F, so they converge at approximately 4.4°F/1,000 feet (which is the same as 2.5°C/1,000 feet).

$$\text{Cloud base in thousands of feet} = \frac{\text{air temperature} - \text{dewpoint}}{4.4°\text{F (or 2.5°C)}}$$

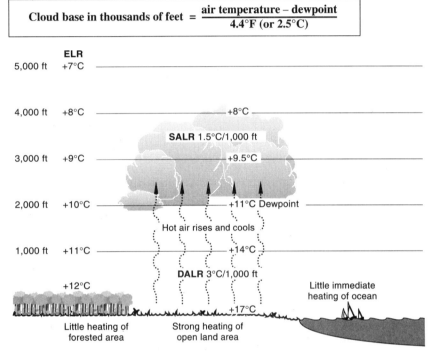

Figure 16-4. The temperature processes involved in the formation of a cumulus cloud

If the temperature at a given level is 17°C and the dewpoint is 12°C—a temperature/dewpoint spread of 5°C, then as the air rises this spread will decrease by approximately 2.5°C/1,000 feet. The temperature and dewpoint will have the same value at an altitude approximately ($^5/_{2.5}$ = 2) 2,000 feet higher.

The cloud base of the air in the above example will form at a level 2,000 feet higher than the given level, and if the air is still unstable, it will continue to rise and form a cumuliform cloud. Because the air is now saturated, latent heat will be given off as more water vapor condenses into liquid water droplets. This reduces the rate at which the rising saturated air cools to the saturated adiabatic lapse rate of approximately 1.5°C/1,000 feet.

Example 1. What is the approximate base MSL of clouds if the temperature at 3,000 feet MSL is 68°F and the dewpoint is 46°F?

$$\text{Cloud base in thousands of feet} = \frac{68 - 46}{4.4} = \frac{22}{4.4} = 5$$

$$\text{therefore the cloud base MSL} = 3,000 \text{ ft MSL} + 5,000 \text{ ft}$$

$$= 8,000 \text{ ft MSL}$$

Clouds Formed by Orographic Uplift

Air flowing over mountains rises and is cooled adiabatically. If it cools to below its **dewpoint temperature,** then the water vapor will condense and clouds will form.

Descending on the other side of the mountains, however, the airflow will warm adiabatically and, once its temperature exceeds the dewpoint for that parcel of air, the water vapor will no longer condense. The liquid water drops will now start to vaporize, and the clouds will cease to exist below this level.

The altitude at which the cloud base forms depends on the moisture content of the parcel of air and its dewpoint. The cloud base may be below the mountain tops, or well above them, depending on the situation. Having started to form, the clouds may sit low over the mountain as stratiform clouds (in stable air), or (if the air is unstable) may rise to high levels as cumulus clouds.

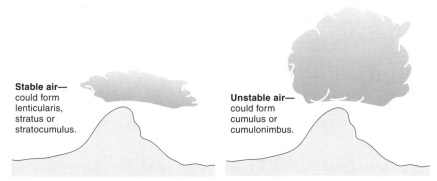

Stable air—
could form lenticularis, stratus or stratocumulus.

Unstable air—
could form cumulus or cumulonimbus.

Figure 16-5. Orographic uplift can lead to cloud formation

An almond or lens-shaped cloud that forms as a *cap* over a mountain is known as a lenticular cloud. It will remain more or less stationary while the air flows through it, possibly at speeds of 50 knots or more. Mount Shasta in northern California invariably has a lenticular cap cloud.

Sometimes, when an airstream flows over a mountain range and there is a stable layer of air above, standing waves occur. Clouds may form in the crest of the lee waves, and a rotor or roll cloud may form at a low altitude. The presence of standing lenticular altocumulus clouds is a good indicator that strong **turbulence** exists.

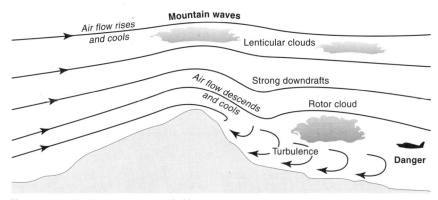

Figure 16-6. Lenticular cloud cap (left), and mountain waves

The Foehn (or Chinook) wind effect. If the air rising up a mountain range is moist enough to have a high dewpoint temperature and is cooled down to it before reaching the top of the mountain, then cloud will form on the windward side. If any precipitation occurs, moisture will be removed from the airflow and, as it descends on the lee side of the mountain, it will therefore be drier. The dewpoint temperature will be less and so the cloud base will be higher on the lee side of the mountain.

As the dry air beneath the cloud descends, it will warm at the dry adiabatic lapse rate of 3°C/1,000 feet, which is at a greater rate than the rising air cooled inside the cloud (saturated adiabatic lapse rate: 1.5°C/1,000 feet). The result is a **warmer** and **drier wind** on the lee side of the mountains. This very noticeable effect is seen in many parts of the world, for example the *foehn* (pronounced "fern") wind in Switzerland and southern Germany, from which this effect gets its name, the *chinook* wind which blows down the eastern slope of the Rocky Mountains, and the *Santa Ana* wind which blows from the east or northeast in southern California.

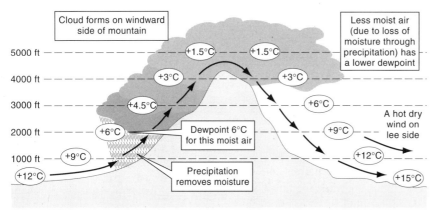

Figure 16-7. The foehn wind effect

Clouds Formed by Turbulence and Mixing

As air flows over the surface of the earth, frictional effects cause variations in local wind strength and direction. Eddies are set up which cause the lower levels of air to mix—the stronger the wind and the rougher the earth's surface, the larger the eddies and the stronger the mixing. The air in the rising currents will cool and, if the turbulence extends to a sufficient height, it may cool to the dewpoint temperature, water vapor will condense to form liquid water droplets and clouds will form.

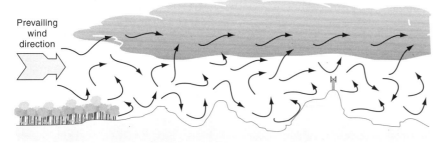

Figure 16-8. Formation of turbulence clouds

The descending air currents in the turbulent cloud layer will warm and, if the air's dewpoint temperature is exceeded, the liquid water droplets that make up the clouds will return to the water vapor state. The air will dry out and clouds will not exist below this altitude. With turbulent mixing, stratiform clouds may form over quite a large area, possibly with an undulating base. They may be continuous stratus or broken stratocumulus.

Clouds Formed by Widespread Ascent

When two large masses of air of differing temperatures meet, the warmer and less dense air will flow over (or be undercut by) the cooler air. As the warmer air mass is forced aloft it will cool and, if the dewpoint temperature is reached, clouds will form. The boundary layer between two air masses is called a **front.**

Widespread lifting can also result from latitudinal pinching of an air mass as it moves to higher latitudes and has to crowd into a smaller area.

Clouds can be formed by the widespread ascent of an air mass.

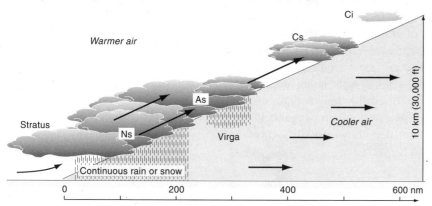

Figure 16-9. Cloud formation resulting from widespread ascent

Precipitation from Clouds

Precipitation refers to falling water that finally reaches the ground, including:

- *rain* consisting of liquid water drops;
- *drizzle* consisting of fine water droplets;
- *snow* consisting of branched and star-shaped ice crystals;
- *hail* consisting of small balls of ice;
- *freezing rain or drizzle*—liquid drops or droplets which freeze on contact with a cold surface (such as the ground or an aircraft in flight); and
- *dew, frost* or *ice.*

Intermittent or continuous precipitation (which often starts and finishes gradually, perhaps over a long period) is usually associated with stratiform clouds—for example, fine drizzle or snow from stratus and stratocumulus, heavy continuous rain or snow from nimbostratus, and steady rain from altostratus.

Rain or snow showers are associated with cumuliform clouds, and very heavy rain may fall from cumulonimbus storm clouds. The strong updrafts in these clouds carry the water droplets up to cooler levels where the condensation process continues and the drops grow in size and weight before they fall.

It is possible to use precipitation as a means of identifying the cloud type— rain or snow showers generally fall from cumuliform clouds, and nonshowery precipitation such as steady rain, light snow or drizzle falls from stratiform clouds, mainly altostratus and nimbostratus.

Figure 16-10. Rain showers fall from cumuliform clouds

For precipitation reported to be of light or greater intensity, the cloud will usually have to be at least 4,000 feet thick.

Rain (and snow) that falls from the base of clouds but evaporates before reaching the ground (hence is not really precipitation) is called **virga.** This can occur in areas of low humidity, often over deserts. One extremely important consequence of virga is that the evaporation of the rain absorbs latent heat from the air, creating a very cool and invisible parcel of air that may sink, or even plummet, quite rapidly toward the ground. This can sometimes result in a **microburst** or **downburst,** which are forms of downflow, usually beneath thunderstorms, that have brought many aircraft to grief.

Figure 16-11. Nonshowery (steady) precipitation falls from stratiform clouds

Figure 16-12. Virga

Sometimes the only indications of a microburst are high-level virga and a ring of dust blown up on the ground. Examine the microburst sequence which is included in the color section in this chapter. Microbursts are covered later in this chapter.

✐ Now complete **Review 16, Part (a)** on page 346.

High-Level Clouds

Cloud Type	Definition	Formation Processes	Composition
Cirrus (Ci)	Detached clouds in the form of white, delicate filaments, or white or mostly white patches or narrow bands. These clouds have a fibrous (hair-like) appearance, or a silky sheen, or both.	Widespread lifting	Ice crystals
Cirrostratus (Cs)	Transparent, whitish cloud veil of fibrous (hair-like) or smooth appearance, totally or partly covering the sky, and generally producing halo phenomena.	Widespread lifting	Ice crystals
Cirro-cumulus (Cc)	Thin, white patch, sheet or layer of clouds without shading, composed of very small elements usually in the form of grains and/or ripples, merged or separate, and more or less regularly arranged. Most of the elements have an apparent width of less than one degree.	Turbulence or perturbations in Ci or Cs	Ice crystals

Figure C-1. Fibrous cirrus

Figure C-2. Dense cirrus with a silky sheen

Figure C-3. Cirrus with hooks caused by jetstream wind

Figure C-4. Cirrostratus (halo is clearly visible)

Figure C-5. Cirrocumulus in grains (halo indicates ice crystals)

Figure C-6. Cirrocumulus formed in ripples

Middle-Level Clouds

Cloud Type	Definition	Formation Processes	Composition
Altostratus (As)	Grayish or bluish cloud sheet or layer of striated, fibrous or uniform appearance, totally or partly covering the sky, and having parts thin enough to reveal the sun at least vaguely, as if through ground glass. Altostratus does not show halo phenomena.	Widespread lifting	Likely to contain supercooled water
Altocumulus (Ac)	White or gray, or both white and gray patch, sheet or layer of cloud, generally with shading, composed of laminae (like fish scales), rounded masses and/or rolls, which are sometimes partly fibrous or diffuse, and which may or may not be merged. Most of the regularly arranged small elements usually have an apparent width of between one and five degrees.	Turbulence perturbations; thermal convection; orographic lifting; spreading of Cu	Supercooled water

Figure C-7. Thin altostratus (sun visible as if viewed through a ground-glass screen)

Figure C-8. Thick, opaque altostratus (bluish-gray in color, giving light rain)

Figure C-9. A broken layer of altocumulus (in rounded elements, formed by turbulence)

Figure C-10. A sheet of altocumulus in rolls (formed in the shear between wind layers)

Figure C-11. Lenticular altocumulus (formed in the crest of mountain waves)—***Note:*** Strong winds and turbulence are likely.

Figure C-12. Altocumulus resulting from the spreading out of cumulus tops under a stable layer

Figure C-13. Altocumulus floccus (Ac in "wool tufts")

Figure C-14. Altocumulus castellanus ("castles in the air")

Note: Both floccus and castellanus Ac indicate instability and moisture in the middle troposphere, with the possibility of thunderstorms forming.

Low-Level Clouds

Cloud Type	Definition	Formation Processes	Composition
Stratocumulus (Sc)	Gray or whitish, or both gray and whitish, patch, sheet or layer of cloud which almost always has dark parts composed of tessellations (like a mosaic), rounded masses and/or rolls, which are non-fibrous (except for virga), and which may or may not be merged. Most of the regularly arranged small elements have an apparent width of more than five degrees.	Turbulence perturbations; orographic lifting; spreading of Cu	Water droplets
Stratus (St)	Generally gray cloud layer with a fairly uniform base, which may give drizzle, ice prisms or snow grains. When the sun is visible through the cloud, its outline is clearly discernible. Stratus does not show halo phenomena, except possibly at very low temperatures. It sometimes appears in the form of ragged patches.	Radiation cooling coupled with turbulence; orographic lifting	Water droplets, supercooled drops and droplets above the freezing level
(Continued)			

Figure C-15. Stratocumulus in a continuous layer, base around 2,000 feet AGL

Figure C-16. Stratocumulus in a broken layer, base around 4,000 feet AGL

Figure C-17. Stratus with a low base

Figure C-18. A stratus sheet, base about 300 feet AGL

Cloud Type	Definition	Formation Processes	Composition
Nimbostratus (Ns)	Gray cloud layer, often dark, the appearance of which is rendered diffuse by more or less continuously falling rain or snow, which in most cases reaches the ground. Nimbostratus is thick enough to blot out the sun.	Widespread lifting	Water drops and droplets; supercooled drops and droplets above the freezing level
Cumulus (Cu)	Detached clouds, generally dense and with sharp outlines, developing vertically in the form of rising mounds, domes or towers, of which the bulging upper part often resembles a cauliflower. The sunlit parts of these clouds are mostly brilliant white. Their base is relatively dark and nearly horizontal. Sometimes cumulus is ragged.	Thermal convection	Water drops and droplets; supercooled water drops and droplets above the freezing level
Cumulonimbus (Cb)	A heavy and dense cloud, with a considerable vertical extent, in the form of a mountain or huge towers. At least part of its upper portion is usually smooth, fibrous or striated, and nearly always flattened. This part often spreads out in the shape of an anvil or vast plume. (Thunderstorms emanate from cumulonimbus clouds.)	Extreme thermal convection	Water drops and droplets below the freezing level; supercooled water drops and droplets above freezing level; ice crystals at the top

Figure C-19. Broken stratus (stratus fractus), formed in the break-up of a stratus layer

Figure C-20. Nimbostratus

Figure C-21. Cumulus of medium development

Figure C-22. Congested towering cumulus

Figure C-23. A cumulonimbus cloud in the early mature stage, starting to flatten at the top

Figure C-24. A line of cold-stream thunderstorms

Figure C-25. A fully developed thunderstorm

Figure C-26. Mature Cb clouds, entering the dissipating stage

Figure C-27. A rapidly rotating low-level roll cloud at the leading edge of a cold front, with very heavy rain at left from a cumulonimbus cloud

Figure C-28. A heavy rain shower from a storm cell within a cumulonimbus cloud accompanying a cold front

Figure C-29. Lightning from an evening thunderstorm

Figure C-30. A tornado

Figure C-31. Avoid tornados!

Frontal Activity

Figure C-32. Weather associated with the passage of a cold front

Figure C-33. Altostratus and altocumulus in the warm air above an approaching warm front

Orographic Clouds

Figure C-34. A cloud formed by lifting of moist, stable air

Figure C-35. Stationary caps on the peaks

Fog

Figure C-36. Valley fog forming at dusk—Swiss Alps, Europe

Figure C-37. Fog formed over the Pacific Ocean moving onshore by advection—Monterey Bay, California

Inversion Effects

Figure C-38. Sign of an inversion in the early morning

Figure C-39. A smog layer held down by an inversion

Microbursts and Virga

Figures C-40–43. Photo sequence showing the development of a potentially destructive microburst

Figure C-44. A wet microburst emanating from the base of a cumulonimbus cloud

Figure C-45. Virga—dry microbursts are possible beneath virga.

Computerized Weather Displays

Throughout the United States and many other parts of the world, weather presentations are becoming increasingly sophisticated and useful, thanks to the advent of high-quality data from weather satellites and the use of computer-enhancement techniques.

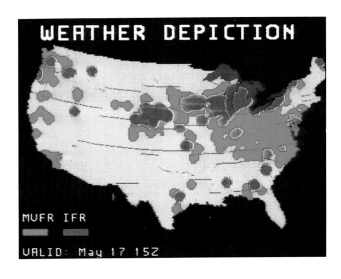

Figures C-46–50. Examples of color weather displays produced by private weather-data companies using National Weather Service information

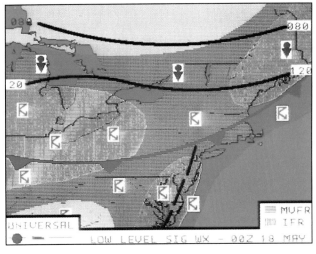

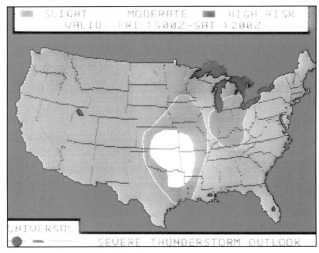

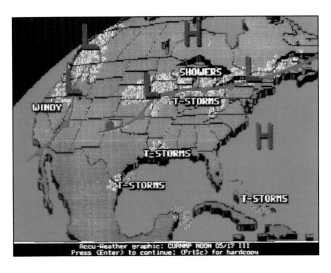

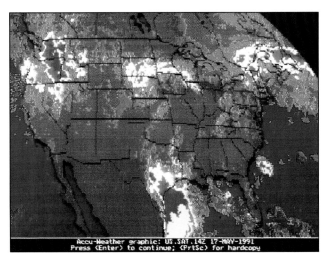

Thunderstorms

A **thunderstorm** is one or more cumulonimbus clouds accompanied by sudden electrical discharges known as **lightning,** which cause a sharp rumbling sound known as **thunder.** Thunderstorms generate spectacular weather which may be accompanied by lightning, thunder, heavy rain showers, and sometimes hail, squalls and tornados.

Thunderstorms are *only* associated with cumulonimbus clouds, and there may be several thunderstorm cells within the one cloud mass. Thunderstorms constitute a **severe hazard** to the aviator and must be avoided.

Lightning and Thunder

Lightning is simply a discharge of *static electricity* that has built up in the cloud. The air along the path that the lightning follows experiences intense heating, causing it to expand violently. The speed of this "expansion" is faster than the local speed of sound, which produces the familiar clap of thunder. By definition, all thunderstorms have lightning—since it is the lightning which causes the thunder.

The Three Necessary Conditions

Three conditions are necessary for a thunderstorm to develop, and they are:

- **deep instability** in the atmosphere, so that once the air starts to rise it will continue to rise (for example, a steep unstable lapse rate with warm air in the lower levels of the atmosphere and cold air in the upper levels);
- a **high moisture** content, so that clouds can readily form; and
- a **trigger action** (or catalyst or lifting force) to start the air rising, possibly caused by:
  - a front forcing the air aloft;
  - a mountain or other terrain forcing the air aloft (orographic ascent);
  - convective ascent from strong heating of air in contact with the surface;
  - heating of the lower layers of a cold polar air mass as it moves by advection to warmer latitudes, causing convective ascent and known as a *cold stream* thunderstorm;
  - advection of upper cold air over warm air beneath, which will then rise;
  - less-dense moist air (for example, from the Gulf of Mexico) moving up and over drier and denser continental air; or
  - cooling of the tops of large clouds at night by radiation which will cause the lower warmer air to rise (for example, thunderstorms in tropical areas at night or in the early mornings).

The Life Cycle of a Thunderstorm

The Cumulus Stage

When moist air rises, it is cooled until its dewpoint temperature is reached. Then the water vapor starts to condense out as liquid droplets, forming clouds. Latent heat is given off in the condensation process, and so the rising air cools at a lesser rate, with the release of large amounts of latent heat energy driving along the formation of the storm cloud. At this early cumulus stage in the formation of a thunderstorm, there are strong, warm **updrafts** over a diameter of one or two miles, with no significant downdrafts.

Air is drawn horizontally into the cell at all levels and causes the updraft to become stronger with altitude. The temperature inside the cloud is higher than the outside environment (because of the release of latent heat during the condensation), and the cloud continues to build to greater and greater heights.

For a thunderstorm to develop there must be deep instability, high moisture content and a trigger action.

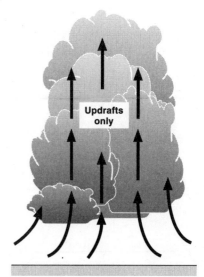

Figure 16-13. The cumulus stage in the development of a thunderstorm.

This growth often occurs at such a rate that an airplane cannot out-climb the growing cloud.

The strong, warm updrafts carry the water droplets higher and higher, to levels often much higher than the freezing level, where they may freeze or continue to exist as liquid water droplets in a supercooled state. Water condensation occurs, and the liquid droplets coalesce to form larger and larger drops.

The cumulus stage as a thunderstorm forms typically lasts 10 to 20 minutes and is characterized by continuous updrafts. If the cumulus cloud develops into a towering cumulus 25,000 feet high in only 10 minutes, then the average updraft strength exceeds 2,000 fpm.

The Mature Stage

The water drops eventually become too large and too heavy to be supported by the updrafts, even though the updrafts maybe in excess of 6,000 fpm, and so start to fall. As the drops fall in great numbers inside the cloud, they drag air along with them causing strong downdrafts. Often the first lightning flashes and the first rain from the cloud base will occur at this stage.

Rain commencing to fall from the base of a cumulonimbus cloud to the surface is an indication that the thunderstorm has entered the mature stage, and it is in this stage that the thunderstorm reaches its greatest intensity.

The descending air warms adiabatically, but the cold drops of water slow down the rate at which this occurs, resulting in **cool downdrafts** in contrast to the **warm updrafts** which are also present. Heavy rain or hail may fall from the base of the cloud at this stage; falls are generally heaviest for the first five minutes. The strong wind currents associated with the thunderstorm may throw **hailstones** well out from the core of the storm, possibly several miles, where they may fall in clear air.

The top of a mature storm cloud may reach as far up as the tropopause, which is perhaps 30,000 feet MSL in temperate latitudes and 50,000 feet MSL in the tropics. The storm cloud may now have the typical shape of a cumulonimbus, with the top spreading out in an *anvil* shape in the direction that the upper winds are blowing. Extremely large cumulonimbus with strong vertical development can sometimes push through the tropopause and into the stratosphere. Over the Midwestern plains, some thunderstorms reach well over 50,000 feet MSL.

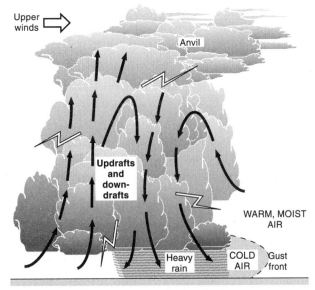

Figure 16-14. The mature stage of a thunderstorm

The violent updrafts and downdrafts (which are very close to each other in a mature thunderstorm) cause extremely strong windshear and turbulence, which can result in structural failure of the airframe. The rapidly changing direction from which the airflow strikes the wings could also cause a stall, so intentionally flying into a mature cumulonimbus cloud is very foolhardy.

As the cold downdrafts flow out of the base of the cloud at a great rate, they change direction and begin to flow horizontally as the ground is approached. Strong windshear and turbulence occur—causing the demise of many aircraft, large and small. The outflowing cold air will undercut the inflowing warmer air and, like a mini cold front, a gusty wind and a sudden drop in temperature may precede the actual storm.

Squalls may occur at the surface—a squall is defined as a sudden increase in wind speed of at least 15 knots that lasts more than one minute, with a peak of at least 20 knots. A *gust* is less dramatic than a squall and is defined as a brief increase in wind speed of at least 10 knots. A *roll cloud* may also develop at the base of the main cloud where the cold downdrafts and warm updrafts pass, indicating possible extreme turbulence.

The mature stage of a thunderstorm typically lasts between 20 and 40 minutes, and is characterized by updrafts and downdrafts, and by precipitation. There is so much water falling through the cloud toward the end of the mature stage that it starts to wash out the updrafts.

The Dissipating Stage
The cold downdrafts gradually cause the warm updrafts to weaken, thereby reducing the supply of warm, moist air to the upper levels of the cloud. The cool downdrafts continue (since they are colder than the ambient air surrounding the cloud) and spread out over the whole cloud, which starts to collapse from above. The dissipating stage of a thunderstorm is characterized by **downdrafts** only.

Eventually the temperature inside the cloud warms to reach that of the environment, and what was once a towering cumulonimbus cloud may collapse into stratiform cloud.

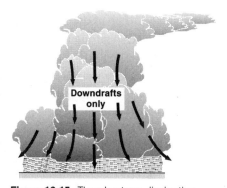

Figure 16-15. Thunderstorm dissipating

Severe Thunderstorms
Sometimes severe thunderstorms develop; these contain more than one storm cell, and have a prolonged mature stage of updrafts and downdrafts, with very strong windshears resulting. The cells within the one large storm may be at different stages in their life cycle. Strong winds aloft may cause the updrafts to slope. The rain and resulting downdrafts will be well-separated from the sloping updrafts, and so will not affect the updrafts and the moisture they are carrying up to the upper levels of the clouds. This can lead to the development of very large cumulonimbus clouds and *supercell* thunderstorms.

The strong downdrafts, on approaching the ground, tend to spread out in all directions, with the forward edge in front of the cloud forming a gust front. As the gust front advances, air is forced aloft and new storm cells can form.

Embedded Thunderstorms
Sometimes cumulonimbus clouds are embedded in a general cloud layer and, unlike many isolated and scattered thunderstorms, may not be detected by a pilot flying visually below the clouds or by an instrument-rated pilot flying without weather radar.

Figure 16-16. Embedded thunderstorms can be a hazard to aviation

The presence of embedded thunderstorms might be indicated to a pilot flying visually beneath the cloud base by heavy rain showers. In general, however, you should not fly into or under a cloud mass containing embedded thunderstorms unless you have airborne weather radar.

The Danger of Thunderstorms

Thunderstorms are hazardous to aviation. Their danger to aviation does not exist just inside or under the storm cloud, but for up to 10 or 20 miles or more.

Most jet transport aircraft and advanced aircraft are equipped with **weather radar** to enable the pilots to identify the position of storm cells and to divert around them by an appropriate distance. Visual pilots without weather radar have to use their eyes and common sense. This may be difficult if the storms are embedded and rising out of a general cloud base or out of layers of clouds that obscure the storm clouds. Frequent lightning from within a cumulonimbus cloud, the presence of rain clouds, and the presence of a roll cloud indicate a severe thunderstorm. **SIGMETs** are issued whenever possible to warn pilots of known or forecast thunderstorms and other weather hazards.

Some obvious dangers to airplanes from thunderstorms include:
- severe windshear (which may cause large flight path deviations and handling problems, loss of airspeed, and possibly structural damage);
- severe turbulence (causing loss of control and possible structural damage);
- severe icing (possibly the very dangerous clear ice that forms from large supercooled water drops striking a below-freezing surface);
- damage from hail (to the airframe and to the cockpit windows);
- reduced visibility;
- damage from lightning strikes, including electrical damage; and
- interference to radio communications and radio navigation instruments.

The most severe flying conditions, such as heavy hail and destructive winds, may be produced in a **squall line,** which is a nonfrontal band of very active thunderstorms, possibly in a long line that requires a large detour to fly around. This line of thunderstorms (sometimes more than one line) can form in the relatively warm air ahead of a cold front, and can be quite fast moving. A squall line may contain a number of severe steady-state thunderstorms, destructive winds, heavy hail and tornados. It can present a most intense hazard to aircraft.

Icing
The most critical icing levels for airplanes inside a cumulonimbus cloud is from the freezing level (0°C) up to an altitude where the temperature is –15°C, the range where it is most likely to encounter supercooled water drops (freezing rain). If possible, avoid this temperature band inside clouds.

Hailstones
Large hailstones often form inside cumulonimbus clouds as water adheres to already formed hailstones and then freezes, leading to even larger hailstones. In certain conditions hailstones can grow to the size of an orange. Heavy hail can damage the skin of an airplane and damage its windshield.

Almost all cumulonimbus clouds contain hail, with most of it melting before reaching the ground where it falls as rain. Strong air currents can sometimes throw hailstones out of the storm for a distance of several miles. On cold days, with freezing level at or near ground level, hail will fall from the cloud and reach the ground before melting.

Lightning Strikes

Lightning strikes can cause damage to electrical equipment in the airplane and to the airplane skin and antennas. It can also temporarily blind pilots, especially if flying at night in a darkened cockpit with their eyes adjusted to the darkness. A good precaution against this is to turn up the cockpit lights when in the vicinity of thunderstorms.

Lightning strikes seem to be most likely when flying in or near to cumulonimbus clouds at altitudes near the freezing level (plus or minus 5°C—that is, within about 2,500 feet of the freezing level).

Turbulence

Turbulence in the vicinity of a thunderstorm that causes large changes in attitude, altitude and airspeed, with the aircraft occasionally out of control for a moment, and causing you to experience severe pulling from the seat belt for about three quarters of the time, would be described as *continuous severe turbulence.*

Downbursts and Microbursts

Strong downdrafts that spread out near the ground are known as **downbursts.** A very strong downburst not exceeding two nautical miles in diameter is called a **microburst.**

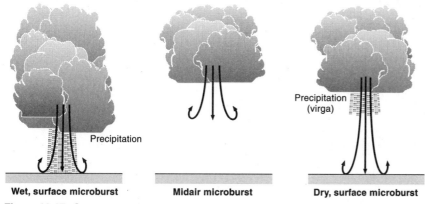

Figure 16-17. Some types of microbursts

Most aircraft do not have the performance capability or the structural strength to combat the extremely strong downdrafts, turbulence and windshear in downbursts and microbursts, and can be destroyed. Avoid downbursts and microbursts at all costs.

Downbursts and microbursts are mainly associated with cumulonimbus (thunderstorm) clouds, but they may also occur with smaller clouds, such as cumulus, or with clouds from which *virga* is falling.

Virga is rain that falls from high clouds and evaporates before it reaches the surface. In the process of evaporating, latent heat is absorbed from the surrounding air and a cold parcel of air is formed beneath the cloud; this may plummet earthward as a downburst or a microburst. It can sometimes be detected by eye as a ring of dust blown up where the microburst hits the ground and spreads out, or by sudden reversals of direction on a windsock. In extreme cases, microbursts have been known to blow hundreds of trees down in a radial pattern, and to blow trains off the rails.

Microbursts and downbursts may appear very suddenly and may or may not last very long. A typical life cycle lasts about 15 minutes from when the very strong shaft of downdrafts first strikes the ground. The wind spreads out horizontally in all directions, usually with the horizontal winds increasing in strength for the first 5 minutes and peak wind strength lasting 2–4 minutes.

Even though one airplane might make an approach satisfactorily underneath a large cloud, a following aircraft may not. There are a number of accidents to illustrate this. Always be on the lookout for large clouds with a bulging undersurface, for virga, or for any other indication of downbursts or microbursts.

Note: Operational factors relating to thunderstorms and microbursts are covered in Chapter 18.

Tornados and Water Spouts

A strongly growing large cumuliform cloud may "suck" air into it as an updraft. These strong updrafts may commence from just beneath the base of the cloud, or they may commence well below the cloud base from near the ground, from where they may raise objects or, if over a water surface, cause a water spout.

Tornados and water spouts are rotating funnels of air of small diameter. The central pressure will be much lower than in the surrounding air, creating a vortex of wind with speeds possibly exceeding 150 knots.

Figure 16-18. A tornado. Tornados and water spouts are a great hazard to aviation. Avoid them at all costs!

✍ Now complete **Review 16, Part (b)** on page 348.

For Aspiring Commercial Pilots

Lifted Index

The **lifted index** of a parcel of air is a measure of its stability. The lifted index is calculated by:

(a) theoretically lifting the parcel of air from the surface to the 500-millibar pressure level, and calculating its temperature based on cooling adiabatically by expansion; then

(b) subtracting this calculated value from the *actual* temperature of the air already at the 500 millibar pressure level.

Lifted index =	air temperature at 500 mb level	–	theoretical temperature at 500 mb level if the surface air is raised

If the "lifted" parcel of air has a temperature less than that existing in the actual air at the 500 mb pressure level, then the parcel would have no tendency to keep rising, and the lifted index would have a positive value—a *positive* lifted index indicates *stable* air.

If the lifted air is warmer than the environmental air, then it will tend to keep on rising, and the lifted index would have a negative value—a *negative* lifted index indicates *unstable* air.

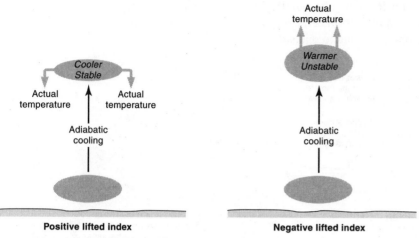

Figure 16-19. Positive lifted index (left) and negative lifted index (right)

Clouds at High Levels

The high-altitude **cirriform** clouds (cirrus, cirrostratus and cirrocumulus) which form in the very cold air at high levels usually consist of ice crystals, and so generally do not create a significant icing hazard, although you may experience continuous turbulence. Streaks of cirrus clouds may be associated with a jetstream. It is possible, also, for strong thunderstorms to punch their way up to very high levels, even above the tropopause, and these can create the usual cumulonimbus problems for high-flying pilots.

Haze layers sometimes exist at high levels near the tropopause, consisting of cirrus clouds with a very low density of ice crystals. They may not be visible from the ground but, when flying in them, your visibility might be greatly restricted and the ride may not be smooth. Sometimes both the visibility and smoothness of the ride can be improved by climbing above the haze, or by descending beneath it.

Water vapor from the exhausts of high-flying jets sometimes condenses in the cold air at high altitudes to form *exhaust condensation trails,* known as **contrails.**

Airborne Weather Radar

Airborne weather radar installed in sophisticated aircraft is a type of primary radar that can detect **water drops.** It *cannot* detect air currents, turbulence, windshear, hail, or the fact that instrument-flying conditions exist, but it can warn you of the possibility of these phenomena, since they are associated with cumulonimbus clouds, which do contain large water drops.

Large water drops reflect the radar beam transmitted from the airplane, and this reflected signal is shown on the radarscope in the cockpit as a **radar echo.** While the presence of strong windshear, turbulence and/or a microburst cannot be detected directly by most airborne weather radar equipment, their presence can be suspected if there is a return from an overlying cumulonimbus.

The radar display can be either monochrome or color, depending on the equipment installed. Color weather radar displays are extremely effective in portraying the weather, with a number of strong colors representing the intensity of the returns—usually graded from *green* for light rain, through *yellow* and *red,* to *magenta* for severe rain showers. Monochrome displays rely on *gray-scales* to display gradations of echo intensity.

Not all storm cells containing large drops of water will be detected initially, since nearer cells may mask the presence of more-distant cells.

Any storm cells strong enough to cause a radar echo should be avoided by at least 20 miles. To achieve this separation between two storm cells, they must be at least 40 miles apart. If not you should consider flying to one side of the pair.

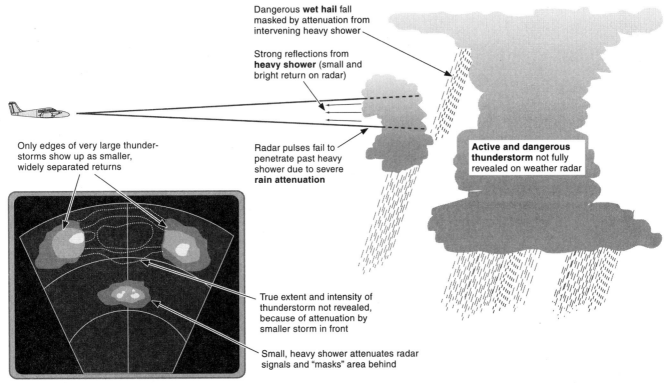

Dangerous **wet hail** fall masked by attenuation from intervening heavy shower

Strong reflections from **heavy shower** (small and bright return on radar)

Active and dangerous thunderstorm not fully revealed on weather radar

Only edges of very large thunderstorms show up as smaller, widely separated returns

Radar pulses fail to penetrate past heavy shower due to severe **rain attenuation**

True extent and intensity of thunderstorm not revealed, because of attenuation by smaller storm in front

Small, heavy shower attenuates radar signals and "masks" area behind

Figure 16-20. Storm cells appearing as echoes on a weather radarscope.

✍ Commercial students complete **Review 16, Commercial** on page 349.

✍ Review 16

Clouds and Thunderstorms

Part (a)

1. Clouds, fog or dew form when water vapor (is present/ condenses).
➤ condenses

2. Clouds arc divided into four families according to their (shape/height range/composition).
➤ height range

3. Name the four families of clouds.
➤ High-, middle-, low-level clouds, and those with extensive vertical development

4. Clouds with a base below approximately 6,500 feet are known as _____ clouds.
➤ low-level

5. The suffix *nimbus* and the prefix *nimbo,* means that the clouds are _____-bearing.
➤ rain-bearing

6. Clouds broken into fragments are often identified by the suffix (nimbus/cirrus/fractus).
➤ fractus

7. What are the processes by which moisture is added to unsaturated air?
   (a) Evaporation and sublimation.
   (b) Heating and condensation.
   (c) Supersaturation and evaporation.
➤ (a)

8. The process of liquid water altering its state to water vapor is known as _____ .
➤ evaporation

9. The process of solid ice altering its state to water vapor is known as _____ .
    ➤ sublimation

10. The amount of water vapor which air can hold largely depends on its (dewpoint/temperature/stability).
    ➤ temperature

11. What is meant by the term dewpoint? The temperature:
    (a) at which condensation and evaporation are equal.
    (b) at which dew will always form.
    (c) to which air must be cooled to become saturated.
    ➤ (c)

12. As a parcel of air is cooled, its relative humidity (increases/decreases/remains unchanged).
    ➤ increases

13. As a parcel of air is cooled to its dewpoint, its relative humidity will rise to _____%.
    ➤ 100%

14. Clouds, fog, or dew will always form when:
    (a) water vapor condenses.
    (b) water vapor is present.
    (c) relative humidity reaches 100 percent.
    ➤ (a)

15. If air in contact with the ground cools to its dewpoint temperature, which is above freezing, the excess water vapor will condense and form (frost/dew/ice).
    ➤ dew

16. For frost to form, the dewpoint (must/need not) be below freezing, and the collecting surface (must/need not) be below freezing.
    ➤ must, must

17. The process of excess water condensing out of the air to form cloud or fog may be delayed if there are insufficient _____ nuclei in the air.
    ➤ condensation

18. The presence of cumuliform cloud indicates moist (stable/unstable) air.
    ➤ unstable

19. Moist, stable air flowing upslope can be expected to:
    (a) produce stratus type clouds.
    (b) cause showers and thunderstorms.
    (c) develop convective turbulence.
    ➤ (a)

20. Turbulence, good visibility, cumuliform clouds and showery precipitation indicate moist (stable/unstable) air.
    ➤ unstable

21. An air mass being warmed from below will become (more/less) stable.
    ➤ less

22. Smooth flying conditions are more likely in (stable/unstable) air.
    ➤ stable

23. Turbulence and good visibility are more likely in (stable/unstable) air.
    ➤ unstable

24. Steady precipitation and little or no turbulence is a characteristic of (cumuliform/stratiform) cloud that is formed in (stable/unstable) air.
    ➤ stratiform, stable

25. Poor visibility, stratiform clouds and steady precipitation are more likely when the ambient lapse rate is (high/low), which indicates (stable/unstable) air.
    ➤ low, stable

26. Convective turbulence is indicated by (cirrus/nimbostratus/towering cumulus) clouds.
    ➤ towering cumulus

27. Stability can be determined from the value of the (ambient/dry adiabatic/saturated adiabatic) lapse rate.
    ➤ ambient

28. Unsaturated air being forced aloft will cool at a rate of _____ °C per 1,000 feet.
    ➤ 3°C per 1,000 feet

29. Saturated air being forced aloft will cool at a rate of _____ °C per 1,000 feet.
    ➤ 1.5°C per 1,000 feet

30. The ambient lapse rate in the *standard atmosphere* for air that is not rising or sinking is assumed to be _____ °C per 1,000 feet. It (can/will not) vary significantly from this value in an actual atmosphere.
    ➤ 2°C/1,000 feet, can

31. If a stable airmass is forced to ascend a mountain slope, the type of cloud most likely to develop is (cumuliform/stratiform) with (little/extensive) vertical development.
    ➤ stratiform, little

32. If an unstable air mass is forced upward, what type of clouds can be expected?
    (a) Stratus clouds with little vertical development.
    (b) Stratus clouds with considerable associated turbulence.
    (c) Clouds with considerable vertical development and associated turbulence.
➤ (c)

33. Flying conditions in or under cumulus-type clouds are usually (more/less) turbulent than for stratus-type clouds.
➤ more

34. An unstable cold air mass moving over a warm surface may give rise to (cumuliform/stratiform) clouds, (turbulent/smooth) flying conditions, and (good/poor) visibility.
➤ cumuliform, turbulent, good

35. The clouds with the greatest turbulence are (cumulus/cumulonimbus/nimbostratus/stratus) clouds.
➤ cumulonimbus

36. High-level clouds are composed mainly of (water vapor/water droplets/ice crystals).
➤ ice crystals

37. Flying conditions at and below the level of fair weather cumulus clouds are often (smoother/more turbulent).
➤ more turbulent

38. Flying conditions above fair weather cumulus clouds, compared with below them, are often (smoother/rougher).
➤ smoother

39. An almond or lens-shaped cloud which appears stationary, but may contain winds of 50 knots or more, is referred to as a _____ cloud.
➤ lenticular

40. Drizzle or steady rain is more likely from (stratiform/cumuliform) clouds.
➤ stratiform

41. Showers are more likely from (stratiform/cumuliform) clouds.
➤ cumuliform

42. The growth rate of raindrops is enhanced by (updrafts/no vertical movement), which is most likely in (cumulonimbus/cirrus) clouds.
➤ updrafts, cumulonimbus

43. Rain which evaporates before it reaches the ground is called _____ .
➤ virga

44. Evaporating rain will cause the air temperature to (increase/decrease).
➤ decrease

45. There (may/will not) be very strong downdrafts beneath virga.
➤ may

46. A very dangerous and localized downflow of air that may be quite narrow in extent is known as a _____ .
➤ microburst

47. On average, temperature and dewpoint in rising unsaturated air converge by about _____ °F or _____ °C for each 1,000 feet of height gained.
➤ 4.4°F, 2.5°C

48. What is the approximate cloud base of cumulus clouds if the temperature at 1,000 feet MSL is 70°F and the dewpoint is 48°F?
➤ 6,000 feet MSL
$$\left(\frac{70-48}{4.4} = \frac{22}{4.4} = 5, \text{ cloud base} = 1{,}000 \text{ ft MSL} + 5{,}000 \text{ ft}\right)$$

49. The surface air temperature at an airport is 82°F and the dewpoint is 38°F. What is the cloud base AGL if the air is unstable and convective cumuliform cloud develops? If the airport has an elevation 1,500 feet MSL, what is the approximate cloud base MSL?
➤ 10,000 ft AGL, 11,500 ft MSL $\left(\frac{82-38}{4.4} = \frac{44}{4.4} = 10\right)$

Part (b)

1. Thunderstorms are associated with (stratus/cirrus/stratocumulus/cumulonimbus) clouds.
➤ cumulonimbus clouds

2. All thunderstorms have (lightning/rain/hail).
➤ lightning

3. What three conditions are necessary for the formation of thunderstorms?
➤ high humidity, lifting force, and unstable conditions

4. An "unstable" lapse rate means that the lapse rate is (high/low) and that rising air will tend to keep rising.
➤ high

5. Name the three stages of a typical thunderstorm.
➤ cumulus stage, mature stage, dissipating stage

6. The cumulus stage of a thunderstorm is characterized by (updrafts/downdrafts/updrafts and downdrafts).

➤ updrafts

7. The mature stage of a thunderstorm is characterized by (updrafts/downdrafts/updrafts and downdrafts).

➤ updrafts and downdrafts

8. The dissipating stage of a thunderstorm is characterized by (updrafts/downdrafts/updrafts and downdrafts).

➤ downdrafts

9. Rain falling from the base of a storm cloud is an indication that (updrafts/downdrafts) have developed, and that the _____ stage in its life cycle has started.

➤ downdrafts, mature

10. Thunderstorms reach their greatest intensity in the _____ stage.

➤ mature

11. Thunderstorms that grow out of a massive cloud layer that possibly obscures them are known as _____ thunderstorms.

➤ embedded thunderstorms

12. The most hazardous flying conditions associated with a thunderstorm are due to (lightning/static electricity/ windshear and turbulence/hail/reduced visibility).

➤ windshear and turbulence

13. A nonfrontal narrow band of active thunderstorms that often develop ahead of a cold front is known as a _____ .

➤ squall line

Commercial Review

1. As the temperature/dewpoint spread reduces, the relative humidity (increases/decreases/stays the same) and the air becomes (more/less) saturated.

➤ increases, more

2. Relative humidity will increase as the spread between the actual temperature of a parcel of air and its dewpoint (increases/decreases).

➤ decreases

3. What is the approximate base of cumulus clouds if the temperature at 2,000 feet MSL is 70°F and the dewpoint is 52°F?

➤ 6,000 feet MSL

4. What height AGL would you expect the bases of convective-type cumuliform cloud to form if the surface weather report for the airport indicates temperature 89°F and dewpoint 45°F?

➤ 10,000 ft AGL $\left(\frac{89 - 45}{4.4} = \frac{44}{4.4} = 10 \right)$

5. A parcel of air that is warmer than the environmental air surrounding it will tend to (rise/sink). This is said to be (stable/unstable) air.

➤ rise, unstable

6. When an air mass is stable, which of these conditions are most likely to exist?
(a) Towering cumulus and cumulonimbus clouds.
(b) Moderate to severe turbulence at the lower levels.
(c) Smoke and/or dust are concentrated at the lower levels with resulting poor visibility.

➤ (c)

7. What determines the structure or type of clouds formed as a result of air being forced to ascend?
(a) The method by which the air is lifted.
(b) The stability of the air before lifting occurs.
(c) The relative humidity of the air after lifting occurs.

➤ (b)

8. A negative lifted index indicates (stable/unstable) air.

➤ unstable

9. When conditionally unstable air with high-moisture content and very warm surface temperature is forecast, one can expect what type of weather?
(a) Continuous precipitation.
(b) Fog and low stratus clouds.
(c) Strong updrafts and cumulonimbus clouds.

➤ (c)

10. Hail is most likely to be associated with _____ clouds?

➤ cumulonimbus

11. Which combination of weather-producing variables would likely result in cumuliform-type clouds, good visibility, and showery rain?
(a) Stable, moist air and orographic lifting.
(b) Unstable, moist air and orographic lifting.
(c) Unstable, moist air and no lifting mechanism.

➤ (b)

12. Hailstones (can/will not) be thrown outward from a storm cloud for several miles.

➤ can

13. Airborne weather radar identifies areas of possible turbulence by detecting (turbulence/windshear/water drops/lightning).

➤ water drops

14. If airborne weather radar is indicating an extremely intense thunderstorm echo, this thunderstorm should be avoided by a distance of at least (20/25/30) miles.

➤ 20 miles

15. The minimum distance that should exist between two storms causing intense weather radar echoes, before any attempt is made to fly between these thunderstorms is _____ miles, so that you can avoid each storm by at least _____ miles.

➤ 40 miles, 20 miles

16. If there are no echoes showing on an airborne weather radarscope, you (are/are not) guaranteed that good flying conditions exist.

➤ are not

17. The formation of predominantly stratiform or predominantly cumuliform clouds is dependent on the:
    (a) source of lift.
    (b) stability of the air being lifted.
    (c) temperature of the air being lifted.

➤ (b)

18. From which measurement of the atmosphere can stability be determined?

➤ the ambient lapse rate

19. The most hazardous condition associated with thunderstorms is (lightning/intense rain/windshear and turbulence).

➤ windshear and turbulence

20. What visible signs indicate extreme turbulence in thunderstorms?
    (a) Base of the clouds near the surface, heavy rain, and hail.
    (b) Low ceiling and visibility, hail and precipitation static.
    (c) Cumulonimbus clouds, very frequent lightning, and roll clouds.

➤ (c)

21. The most severe weather conditions, such as destructive winds, heavy hail, and tornados, are generally associated with:
    (a) fast-moving warm fronts.
    (b) slow moving warm fronts.
    (c) squall lines and steady-state thunderstorms.

➤ (c)

22. What minimum distance should exist between intense radar echoes before any attempt is made to fly between these thunderstorms?
    (a) 20 miles.
    (b) 30 miles.
    (c) 40 miles.

➤ (c)

Air Masses and Frontal Weather 17

Air Masses

An air mass is a large parcel of air with fairly consistent properties (such as temperature and moisture content) throughout. It is usual to classify an air mass according to:

• its origin;
• its path over the earth's surface; and
• whether the air is diverging or converging.

Origin and Path

A **polar** air mass originating in the polar regions will, of course, be very cold. A **tropical** air mass originating from near the equator will be very warm.

Maritime air flowing over an ocean will absorb moisture and tend to become saturated in its lower levels; **continental air** flowing over a land mass will remain reasonably dry since little water is available for evaporation.

Polar air flowing toward the lower latitudes will be warmed from below and so become unstable. Conversely, tropical air flowing to higher latitudes will be cooled from below and so become more stable (Figure 17-1 & Figure 17-1).

Note: Air masses in the polar and tropical regions usually overlie a surface long enough to take on its properties (heat and moisture), whereas air masses in the mid-latitude areas are constantly being disturbed by weather and so do not have such definite characteristics.

Divergence or Convergence

An upper air mass influenced by the **divergence** of air flowing out of a high-pressure system at the earth's surface will slowly sink (known as subsidence) and become warmer, drier and more stable.

An upper air mass influenced by **convergence** as air flows into a low-pressure system at the surface will be forced to rise slowly, becoming cooler, moister and less stable.

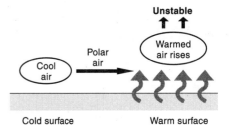

Figure 17-1. Polar air warms and becomes unstable

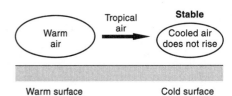

Figure 17-2. Tropical air cools and becomes stable

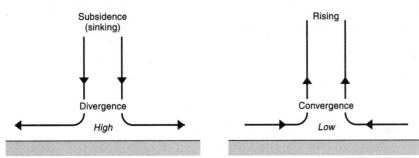

Figure 17-3. Subsiding air, resulting from divergence, is stable

Rising air, resulting from convergence, is unstable

The sources of most air masses that affect North America are shown below, classified by temperature and moisture level.

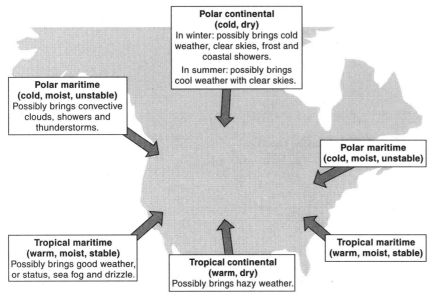

Figure 17-4. Air masses that affect North America

Note: The polar continental air mass from Canada can be modified by the addition of moisture over the Great Lakes.

Frontal Weather

Air masses have different characteristics, depending on their origin and the type of surface over which they have been passing. Because of these differences there is usually a distinct division between adjacent air masses. The boundary between two adjacent air masses is called a **front,** and there are two basic types—cold fronts and warm fronts.

Frontal activity describes the interaction between the air masses, as one mass replaces the other. When a front passes a point on the earth, or when you fly through a front, there is always a wind change and a temperature change (which may be large or small). The term *frontal zone* refers to the area affected by the front.

The Warm Front

If two air masses meet so that the warmer air replaces the cooler air at the surface, a **warm front** is said to exist. The boundary at the earth's surface between the two air masses is represented on a weather chart by a line with semicircles pointed in the direction of movement.

The slope formed in a warm front, as the warm air slides up over the cold air, is fairly shallow and so the cloud that forms in the (usually quite stable) rising warm air is likely to be stratiform. In a warm front the frontal air at altitude is actually well ahead of the frontal line shown at ground level on the weather chart. The cirrus clouds could be some 600 miles ahead of the surface front, and rain could be falling up to approximately 200 miles ahead of it. The slope of the warm front is typically 1 in 150, much flatter than a cold front, and has been exaggerated in Figure 17-6.

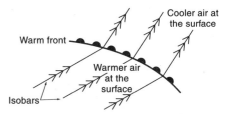

Figure 17-5. Depiction of a warm front on a weather chart

Rain falling into the cooler air beneath the surface of the warm front may cause precipitation-induced fog. If the air beneath the front is below freezing, freezing rain from the warmer air above may cause severe icing on an airplane.

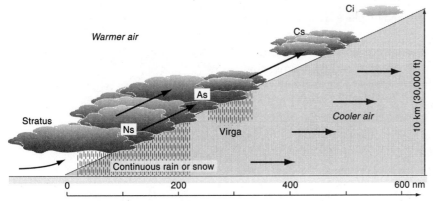

Figure 17-6. Cross section of a warm front

Observation from the Ground

As a warm front gradually passes, an observer on the ground may first see high cirrus clouds, which will slowly be followed by a lowering base of cirrostratus, altostratus and nimbostratus.

Rain may be falling from the altostratus and possibly evaporating before it reaches the ground (virga) and from the nimbostratus. The rain from the nimbostratus may be continuous until the warm front passes and may, by adding moisture to the cold air beneath the front, cause fog. Visibility may be quite poor.

The **atmospheric** (or barometric) **pressure** will normally fall continuously as the warm front approaches, and, as it passes, either stop falling or fall at a lower rate. The **air temperature** will rise as the warm air moves in over the surface. The warm air will hold more moisture than the cold air, and the dewpoint temperature in the warmer air will be higher. Relative humidity will decrease, and any frontal fog may dissipate.

There is always a wind change as a front passes. In the Northern Hemisphere, the **wind direction** will **veer** (a clockwise change of direction) as the warm front passes. Behind the warm front, and after it passes, there is likely to be stratus clouds; the visibility may still be poor. Weather associated with a warm front may extend over several hundred miles.

The general characteristics of a warm front are:

• lowering stratiform clouds;
• increasing rain, with the possibility of poor visibility and fog;
• possible low-level windshear before the warm front passes;
• falling atmospheric pressure that slows down or stops;
• winds veering (clockwise change of direction); and
• rising air temperature.

Observation from the Air

What a pilot sees, and in which order, will depend on the direction of flight. You may see a gradually lowering cloud base if in the cold sector underneath the warm air and flying toward the warm front, with steady rain falling.

If the airplane is at subzero temperatures, the rain may freeze and form ice on the wings, thereby decreasing their aerodynamic qualities. The clouds may be as low as ground level (that is, hill fog) and sometimes the lower layers of stratiform clouds can conceal cumulonimbus and thunderstorm activity. Visibility may be quite poor.

There will be a wind change either side of the front and a change of the airplane's heading may be required to maintain course.

The Cold Front

If a cooler air mass undercuts a mass of warm air and displaces it at the surface, a **cold front** is said to occur. The slope between the two air masses in a well-developed cold front is much steeper than a warm front, and typically about 1 in 50. This is due to surface friction tending to slow down the fast-moving cold air near ground level, and the frontal weather may occupy a band of only 30 to 50 miles.

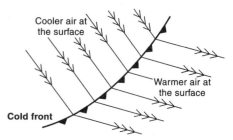

Figure 17-7. Depiction of a cold front on a weather chart

The boundary between the two air masses at the surface is shown on weather charts as a line with barbs pointing in the direction of travel of the front. The cold front moves quite rapidly, with the cooler frontal air at altitude lagging behind that at the surface.

The air that is forced to rise with the passage of a cold front is *unstable* and so the clouds that form are cumuliform in nature—for example, cumulus and cumulonimbus. Severe weather hazardous to aviation, such as thunderstorm activity, squall lines, severe turbulence and windshear, may accompany the passage of a cold front. Low-level windshear and turbulence is possible at an airport at or just after a cold front passes.

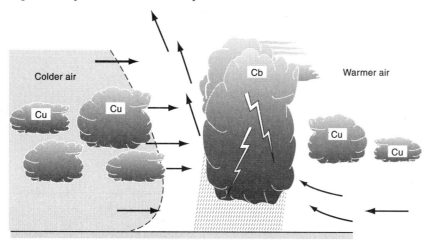

Figure 17-8. Cross section of a cold front

Observation from the Ground

The atmospheric pressure will fall as a cold front approaches and the change in weather with its passage may be quite pronounced. Prior to the cold front arriving, there may be middle-level altostratus or altocumulus present. Accompanying the front, there may be cumulus and possibly cumulonimbus clouds with heavy rain showers, thunderstorm activity and squalls, with a sudden drop in temperature and a veering wind direction as the front passes.

The cooler air mass will contain less moisture than the warm air, and so the dewpoint temperature after the cold front has passed will be lower. Once the cold front has passed, the pressure may rise rapidly.

The general characteristics of a cold front are:

- cumuliform cloud—cumulus, cumulonimbus;
- often a sudden drop in temperature, and a lower dewpoint temperature;
- possible low-level windshear as or just after the front passes;
- a veering of the wind direction (same as for a warm front); and
- a falling pressure that rises once the front is past.

Observation from the Air

Flying through a cold front may require diversions to avoid weather. There may be thunderstorm activity, violent winds (both horizontal and vertical) from cumulonimbus clouds, squall lines, windshear, heavy showers of rain or hail, and severe turbulence. Icing could be a problem. Visibility away from the showers and the clouds may be quite good, but it is still a good idea for a pilot to consider avoiding the strong weather activity that accompanies many cold fronts. A squall line may form ahead of the front.

The Occluded Front

Because cold fronts usually travel much faster than warm fronts, it often happens that a cold front overtakes a warm front, creating an **occlusion** (or occluded front). This may happen in the final stages of a frontal depression (which is discussed shortly). Three air masses are involved and their vertical passage, one to the other, will depend on their relative temperatures.

Because the air circulating around the northern side of a low is closer to the pole, it is more likely to be modified to a lower temperature than the more-southerly air. Therefore, it is common for a cold front to occur in the southwest sector of a low (and a warm front in the eastern sector). The occluded front is depicted on charts by a line with alternating barbs and semicircles pointing in the direction of motion of the front.

The clouds that are associated with an occluded front will depend on what clouds are associated with the individual cold and warm fronts. It is not unusual to have cumuliform clouds from the cold front as well as stratiform clouds from the warm front. Sometimes the stratiform clouds can conceal thunderstorm activity, a situation known as embedded thunderstorms.

Severe weather can occur in the early stages of an occlusion as unstable air is forced upward, but this period is often short.

Flight through an occluded front may involve encountering intense weather, as both a cold front and a warm front are involved, with a warm air mass being squeezed up between them. The wind direction will be different either side of the front.

The Stationary Front

A front that is not moving—or moving very slowly at, say, less than 5 knots—is called a **stationary front;** it may influence the weather in that area for a period of days.

Winds may be blowing behind each side of the front (perhaps in opposite directions) and within the frontal zone, and the weather may be a mixture of both cold front and warm front weather, although any thunderstorm activity will probably be less than in a fast-moving cold front.

A stationary front is depicted on weather charts by a line with barbs on one side and semicircles on the other.

Figure 17-11. Depiction of a stationary front

The Development and Decay of Fronts

The development of a front as one air mass overtakes or confronts another, or when strong temperature differences develop within an air mass, is called **frontogenesis.** The decay or dissipation of a front, as the frontal energy is expended and the temperature and pressure differences diminish, is called **frontolysis.**

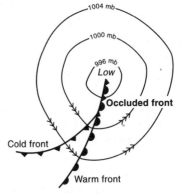

Figure 17-9. Depiction of an occluded front on a weather map

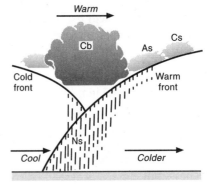

Warm front occlusion

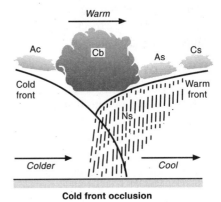

Cold front occlusion

Figure 17-10. Cross sections of occluded fronts

Depressions— Areas of Low Pressure

A **depression** or **low** is a region of low pressure at the surface, the pressure rising as you move away from its center. A low is depicted on a weather chart by a series of concentric isobars joining places of equal sea level pressure, with the lowest pressure in the center.

In the northern hemisphere, winds circulate counterclockwise around a low. Flying toward a low, an airplane will experience right drift.

Depressions generally are more intense than highs, being spread over a smaller area and with a stronger pressure gradient (change of pressure with distance). The more intense the depression, the "deeper" it is said to be. Lows move faster across the face of the earth than highs and do not last as long.

Because the pressure at the surface in the center of a depression is lower than in the surrounding areas, there will be an inflow of air, known as **convergence,** with the wind strength increasing toward the center of the low. The air above the depression will rise and flow outward.

The three-dimensional pattern of airflow near a depression is:

- convergence (inflow) in the lower layers in a counterclockwise direction;
- rising air above; and
- divergence (outflow) in the upper layers.

A depression at the surface may in fact be caused by divergence aloft removing air faster than it can be replaced by convergence at the surface.

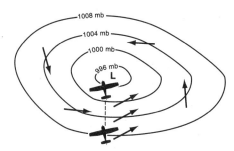

Figure 17-12. A depression or low-pressure system

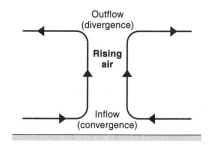

Figure 17-13. The three dimensional flow of air near a low

Weather Associated with a Depression

In a depression, the rising air will be cooling and so clouds will tend to form. Instability in the rising air may lead to quite large vertical development of cumuliform clouds accompanied by rain showers. Good visibility (except in the showers), may be expected since the vertical motion will tend to carry away all the particles suspended in the air. Some turbulence can be expected.

Troughs of Low Pressure

A V-shaped extension of isobars from a region of low pressure is called a **trough.** Air will flow into it at the surface (convergence) and rise. If the air is unstable, weather similar to that in a depression or a cold front will occur—for example, cumuliform cloud, possibly with cumulonimbus and thunderstorm activity.

The trough may in fact be associated with a front. Less prominent troughs, possibly more U-shaped than V-shaped, will generally have less severe weather.

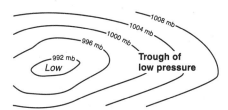

Figure 17-14. A trough

The Wave or Frontal Depression

The boundary between two air masses moving (relative to one another) side by side is often distorted by the warmer air bulging into the cold air mass, with the bulge moving along like a wave. This is known as a **frontal wave.**

The leading edge of the bulge of warm air is a warm front and its rear edge is a cold front.

The pressure near the tip of the wave falls sharply and so a depression forms, along with a warm front, a cold front, and possibly an occlusion. It is usual for the cold front to move faster across the surface than the warm front, but even then, the cold front moves only relatively slowly. Frontal waves can also form on a stationary front.

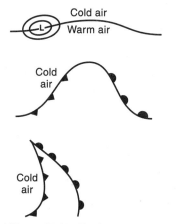

Figure 17-15. The frontal depression

The Hurricane or Tropical Revolving Storm

Hurricanes are intense cyclonic depressions that can be both violent and destructive. They originate over warm tropical oceans at about 10°–20° latitude during certain periods of the year, but often move into the mid-latitudes, especially in the eastern United States, which is threatened by such storms from the Atlantic, the Gulf of Mexico and the Caribbean. Hurricanes also form in the Pacific off the west coast of Mexico, but rarely threaten the mainland United States or Hawaii. They do sometimes, however, bring heavy clouds and rain to the southwestern United States.

Occasionally, weak troughs in these tropical areas develop into intense depressions. Air converges in the lower levels, flows into the depression and then rises—the warm, moist air forming large cumulus and cumulonimbus clouds. The very deep depression may be only quite small (200–300 miles in diameter) compared to the typical depression in temperate latitudes, but its central pressure can be extremely low.

Winds in hurricanes can exceed 100 knots, with heavy showers and thunderstorm activity becoming increasingly frequent as the center of the storm approaches. Despite the strong winds, hurricanes move quite slowly and usually only dissipate after encountering a land mass, which gradually weakens the depression through surface friction. They are then usually classified as tropical storms.

The *eye* of a hurricane is often only some 10 nm in diameter, with light winds and broken cloud. It is characterized by very warm subsiding air. Once the eye has passed, a very strong wind from the opposite direction will occur. In the northern hemisphere, if an aircraft is experiencing pronounced right drift due to a strong wind from the left, the eye of the hurricane is ahead.

In addition to the term hurricane, the tropical revolving storm is also known by other names in different parts of the world, such as *tropical cyclone* in Australia and the South Pacific, and *typhoon* in the South China Sea.

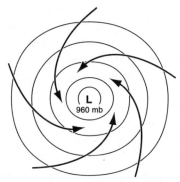

Figure 17-16. A hurricane or tropical revolving storm

Tropical revolving storms are best avoided by all aircraft.

Anticyclones— Areas of High Pressure

An **anticyclone** or **high** is an area of high pressure at the surface surrounded by roughly concentric isobars. Highs are generally greater in extent than lows, but with a weaker pressure gradient and slower moving, although they are more persistent than lows and last longer.

In the Northern Hemisphere, the wind circulates clockwise around the center of a high. Flying toward a high an aircraft will experience left drift.

The **three-dimensional flow** of air associated with an anticyclone is:

- an outflow of air from the high-pressure area in the lower layer of the atmosphere (divergence) in a clockwise direction; with
- slow subsidence of air over a wide area from above; and
- an inflow of air in the upper layers (convergence).

The high-pressure area at the surface originates when the convergence in the upper layers adds air faster than the divergence in the lower layers removes it.

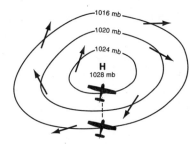

Figure 17-17. The anticyclone or high

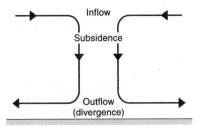

Figure 17-18. The three-dimensional flow of air near a high

Weather Associated with a High

The subsiding air in a high-pressure system will be warming as it descends. Cloud will tend to disperse as the dewpoint temperature is exceeded and the relative humidity decreases.

It is possible that the subsiding air may warm sufficiently to create an **inversion,** with the upper air that is descending warming to a temperature higher than that of air beneath it, and possibly causing stratiform clouds to form (stratocumulus, stratus) and/or trapping smoke, haze and dust beneath it. This can happen in winter in some parts of the country, leading to rather gloomy days with poor flight visibility. In summer, heating by the sun may disperse the clouds, leading to a fine but hazy day.

Subsidence inversions associated with an area of high pressure can be very strong indeed, causing phenomena such as the smog and gloom common in Los Angeles.

If the sky remains clear at night, which is often the case with high-pressure systems, greater cooling of the earth's surface by radiation heat-loss may lead to the formation of radiation fog. If the high pressure is situated entirely over land, the weather may be dry and cloudless but, with any air flowing in from the sea, extensive stratiform clouds in the lower levels can occur, possibly leading to steady precipitation. In stable air, there is usually little or no turbulence.

Subsiding air is very stable.

A Ridge of High Pressure

Isobars which extend out from a high-pressure system in a U-shape indicate a ridge of high pressure (like a ridge extending from a mountain). Weather conditions associated with a ridge are, in general, similar to the weather found with anticyclones.

A Col

The area of almost constant pressure (and therefore indicated by a few very widely spaced isobars) that exists between two highs and two lows is called a col. It is like a saddle on a mountain ridge.

Light winds are often associated with cols, with fog a possibility in winter and high temperatures in summer possibly leading to showers or thunderstorms.

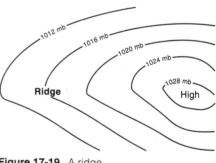

Figure 17-19. A ridge

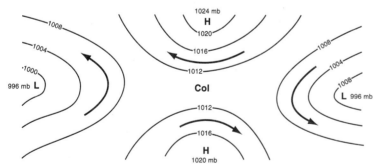

Figure 17-20. A col

✐ Now complete **Review 17** on page 359.

✐ Commercial students complete **Review 17, Commercial** on page 359.

✎ Review 17

Air Masses and Frontal Weather

1. An extensive body of air with fairly uniform temperature and moisture content horizontally is known as an _____ .
➤ air mass

2. A polar maritime air mass will be (cold/warm) and (dry/moist).
➤ cold, moist

3. A polar air mass moving toward the warmer mid-latitudes will tend to warm from below and so become more (stable/unstable).
➤ unstable

4. Unstable air tends to (rise/sink) and, if it contains sufficient moisture, (cumuliform/stratiform) clouds will form, with flying conditions likely to be (smooth/turbulent).
➤ rise, cumuliform, turbulent

5. A polar continental air mass will be (cold/warm) and (dry/moist).
➤ cold, dry

6. A tropical continental air mass will be (cold/warm) and (dry/moist).
➤ warm, dry

7. A tropical maritime air mass will be (cold/warm) and (dry/moist).
➤ warm, moist

8. A polar continental air mass moving down from Canada (may/will not) have its moisture content modified by the Great Lakes.
➤ may

9. The boundary layer between two different air masses is referred to as a:
   (a) frontolysis.
   (b) frontogenesis.
   (c) front.
➤ (c)

10. One weather phenomenon that will always occur when flying across a front is a change in the:
   (a) wind direction.
   (b) type of precipitation.
   (c) stability of the airmass.
➤ (a)

11. Steady precipitation preceding a front is an indication of:
   (a) stratiform clouds with moderate turbulence.
   (b) cumuliform clouds with little or no turbulence.
   (c) stratiform clouds with little or no turbulence.
➤ (c)

12. Whenever a front passes, a (temperature/precipitation/stability) change will usually occur.
➤ temperature

13. Warm air replacing cold air at the surface is known as a (warm/cold) front; the warm air will tend to slide (over/under) the cold air.
➤ warm, over

14. Cold air replacing warm air at the surface is known as a (warm/cold) front.
➤ cold front

15. The cold air will (undercut/flow over) the warm air.
➤ undercut

16. A cold front is usually (steeper/shallower) than a warm front, and (faster/slower) moving.
➤ steeper, faster

17. As a cold front forces warm air aloft, (cumuliform/stratiform) clouds are likely to develop, with (turbulent/smooth) flying conditions.
➤ cumuliform, turbulent

18. If a cold front overtakes a warm front, an _____ front occurs.
➤ occluded

19. A front that has little or no movement is called a _____ front.
➤ stationary

Commercial Review

1. A high-pressure area or ridge is an area of (descending/ascending) air, i.e. (stable/unstable) air.
➤ descending, stable

2. A low-pressure area or trough is an area of (descending/ascending) air, i.e. (stable/unstable) air.
➤ ascending, unstable

3. The general circulation of air associated with a high-pressure area in the Northern Hemisphere is (inward/outward) at the surface in a (clockwise/counterclockwise) fashion and (upward/downward).

➤ outward, clockwise, downward

4. Which is true with respect to a high or low-pressure system?
   (a) A high-pressure area or ridge is an area of rising air.
   (b) A low-pressure area or trough is an area of descending air.
   (c) A high-pressure area or ridge is an area of descending air.

➤ (c)

5. The general circulation of air associated with a high-pressure area in the Northern Hemisphere is:
   (a) outward, downward, and clockwise.
   (b) outward, upward, and counterclockwise.
   (c) inward, downward, and counterclockwise.

➤ (a)

6. When flying into a low-pressure area in the Northern Hemisphere, the wind direction and velocity will be from the:
   (a) left and decreasing.
   (b) left and increasing.
   (c) right and decreasing.

➤ (b)

7. Which is true regarding a cold front occlusion?
   (a) The air ahead of the warm front is colder than the air behind the overtaking cold front.
   (b) The air ahead of the warm front is warmer than the air behind the overtaking cold front.
   (c) The air ahead of the warm front has the same temperature as the air behind the overtaking cold front.

➤ (b)

8. Which in-flight hazard is most commonly associated with warm fronts?
   (a) Advection fog.
   (b) Radiation fog.
   (c) Precipitation-induced fog.

➤ (c)

9. Ice pellets encountered during flight are normally evidence that:
   (a) a warm front has passed.
   (b) there are thunderstorms in the area.
   (c) there exists a layer of warmer air above.

➤ (c)

10. In a cold front occlusion, the air ahead of the warm front is (warmer than/colder than/the same temperature as) the air behind the overtaking cold front.

➤ warmer than

11. Flying into a low-pressure area in the Northern Hemisphere, the wind direction will be from the (left/right), causing (left/right) drift, and the wind speed will be (increasing/decreasing).

➤ left, right, increasing

12. A weather chart shows a particular front as a line with barbs on one side and semicircles on the other. It is a _____ front.

➤ stationary

13. Squall lines often develop ahead of a (cold/warm) front.

➤ cold

14. Frontal waves normally form on (fast/slow) moving cold fronts or stationary fronts.

➤ slow

15. With a cold front, the most critical period for low-level windshear above an airport is as or just (after/before) the cold front passes.

➤ as or just after

Operational Weather Factors 18

Icing

Ice accretion on an airplane structure or within the engine induction system can significantly reduce flight safety by causing:

Icing can be hazardous to aviation.

- **Adverse aerodynamic effects**—ice build-up on the airframe structure can modify the airflow pattern around airfoils (wings and propeller blades), leading to a serious loss of lift and an increase in drag; ice/snow or frost has a thickness and/or roughness similar to medium or coarse sandpaper, and on the leading edge and upper surface of a wing it can reduce lift by as much as 50%, and increase drag also by as much as 50%.

- A **loss of engine power,** or complete stoppage, if ice blocks the engine air intake (in subzero temperatures) or carburetor ice forms (in moist air up to +25°C or +80°F).

- A **weight increase** and a **change in the CG position** of the airplane, as well as unbalancing of the various control surfaces and the propeller, perhaps causing severe vibration and/or control difficulties.

- Blockage of the pitot tube and/or static vent, producing **errors** in the cockpit **pressure instruments** (airspeed indicator, altimeter, vertical speed indicator).

- **Degradation in radio communications** and **radio navigation** (if ice forms on the antennas).

- **Loss of visibility** (if ice forms on the windshield).

The possibility of icing conditions can be determined from weather forecasts and prognostic (forecast) charts, but the most accurate information on icing conditions, both current and forecast, can be obtained from PIREPs (pilot reports), SIGMETs (weather advisories which warn of conditions that could be dangerous to all aircraft) and AIRMETs (which warn of hazards primarily for small aircraft). As a VFR (Visual Flight Rules) pilot, you will only be flying in VMC (Visual Meteorological Conditions), however the following section is provided for your general information. It will be important later during your instrument flight training.

Structural Icing

For ice to form on the aircraft structure, two conditions must be satisfied:

- there must be **visible moisture (clouds);** and
- the temperature must be **at or below freezing** (0°C or +32°F).

Aerodynamic cooling can lower the temperature of the airplane structure below that of the surrounding air by a few degrees. This makes it possible for ice to form on the structure even though the ambient air temperature is still a few degrees above freezing—so be on the watch for structural icing when the air temperature is below about +5°C (+41°F) and you are flying in visible moisture.

The ambient temperature usually decreases in the atmosphere as you climb. The altitude where the temperature has fallen to 0°C (+32°F) is known as the **freezing level,** and it is possible to estimate this level, at least approximately.

The rate at which temperature falls with altitude (the lapse rate) depends on a number of variables, but the standard (average) lapse rate is a temperature decrease of approximately 2°C for every 1,000 feet of altitude gained. For instance, if the air temperature is +8°C at 5,000 feet MSL, then you would need to climb approximately 4,000 feet for the temperature to fall to 0°C, and so the freezing level in this case is at 9,000 feet MSL.

In general terms, the worst continuous icing conditions are usually found near the freezing level in heavy stratified clouds or in rain, with icing possible up to 5,000 feet higher, but rarely above this where the droplets in the clouds are already frozen. In cumuliform clouds with strong updrafts, however, large water droplets may be carried to high altitudes making structural icing a possibility up to very high altitudes.

Clear Ice

Clear ice is the most dangerous form of structural icing. It is also called rain ice. It is most likely to form when you are flying through *freezing rain,* which consists of raindrops that spread out and freeze on contact with the cold airplane.

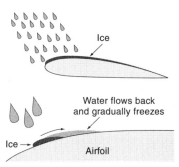

Figure 18-1. Clear ice formed from large, supercooled water drops

It is possible for liquid water drops to exist in the atmosphere at temperatures well below the normal freezing point of water 0°C (+32°F), possibly at –20°C (–4°F) or even lower. These are known as *supercooled* drops, and can occur when rain falls from air warmer than 0°C into a subzero layer of air beneath. Supercooled drops are in an unstable state, and will freeze on contact with a subzero surface such as the skin of an airplane, or the propeller blades.

Each drop will freeze gradually because of the latent heat released in the freezing process, which allows part of the water drop to spread backward before it freezes. The slower the freezing process, the greater the spread-back of the water before it freezes. The spread-back is greatest at temperatures just below freezing. The result is a sheet of solid, clear, glazed ice with very little air enclosed.

Clear ice can alter the aerodynamic shape of airfoils quite dramatically and reduce or destroy their effectiveness. Along with the increased weight, this creates a major hazard to flight safety.

Clear ice is a major hazard to flight safety.

The surface of clear ice is smooth, usually with undulations and lumps. It is very tenacious but, if it does break off, it could be in large chunks capable of doing damage.

A good indication to a pilot that **freezing rain** may exist at higher altitudes is the presence of ice pellets, formed by rain falling from warmer air and freezing on the way down through colder air. Wet snow, however, indicates subzero temperatures at some higher altitude, and warmer air at your level. The snow which formed in the subzero air above is now melting to form wet snow as it passes through your level.

Rime Ice

Rime ice occurs when tiny, supercooled liquid water droplets freeze on contact with a surface whose temperature is below-freezing. Because the drops are small, the amount of water remaining after the initial freezing is insufficient to coalesce into a continuous sheet before freezing. The result is a mixture of tiny ice particles and trapped air, giving a rough, opaque, crystalline deposit that is fairly brittle.

Rime ice is the most usual form of icing.

Rime ice often forms on leading edges and can affect the aerodynamic qualities of an airfoil or the airflow into the engine intake. It does cause a significant increase in weight.

Mixed Ice

Rain falling from clouds may consist of drops of many sizes. A mixture of clear ice (from large drops) and rime ice (from small drops) may result. This is known as *mixed ice*.

Frost

Frost occurs when moist air comes in contact with a subzero surface. The water vapor, rather than condensing to form liquid water, changes directly to ice in the form of frost. This is a white crystalline coating that can usually be brushed off.

Frost can form in clear air when the airplane is parked in subzero temperatures or when the airplane flies from below-freezing temperatures into warmer moist air—for example, on descent, or when climbing through a temperature inversion (where temperature increases with altitude).

Although frost is not as dangerous as clear ice, it can obscure vision through a cockpit window and can possibly affect the lifting characteristics of the wings, which can be extremely serious. Although frost does not alter the basic aerodynamic shape of the wing (like clear ice does), frost can disrupt the smooth airflow over the wing, causing early separation of the airflow from the upper surface of the wing and a consequent loss of lift.

Frost on the wings during takeoff may disturb the airflow sufficiently to prevent the airplane from becoming airborne at its normal takeoff speed, or prevent it from becoming airborne at all.

Frost remaining on the wings is dangerous, especially during takeoff.

Structural Icing and Cloud Type

Cumulus-type clouds nearly always consist predominantly of liquid water droplets at temperatures down to about –20°C (–4°F), below which either liquid-drops or ice-crystals may predominate. Newly formed parts of the clouds will tend to contain more liquid drops than in mature parts. The risk of airframe icing is severe in these clouds in the range 0°C to –20°C (+32°F to –4°F), and moderate to severe in the range –20° to –40°C (–4°F to –40°F), with only a small chance of structural icing below –40°C.

Since there is a lot of vertical motion in convective clouds, the composition of the clouds may vary considerably at the one level, and the risk of icing may exist throughout a wide altitude band in (and under) the clouds. Updrafts will tend to carry the water droplets higher and increase their size. If significant structural icing does occur, it may be necessary to descend into warmer air.

Stratiform clouds usually consist entirely or predominantly of liquid water drops down to about –15°C (+5°F), with a risk of structural icing. If significant icing is a possibility, it may be advisable to fly at a lower level where the temperature is above 0°C, or at a higher level where the temperature is colder than –15°C. In certain conditions, such as stratiform clouds associated with an active front or with orographic uplift, the risk of icing is increased at temperatures lower than usual; continuous upward motion of air generally means a greater retention of liquid water in the clouds.

Raindrops and drizzle from any type of clouds will freeze if they meet an airplane whose surface is below 0°C, with a severe risk of clear ice forming the bigger the water droplets are. You need to be cautious when flying in rain at freezing temperatures. This could occur for instance when flying in the cool sector underlying the warmer air of a warm front from which rain is falling.

High-level clouds, such as cirrus, with their bases above 20,000 feet, are usually composed of ice crystals which will not freeze onto the airplane, and so the risk of structural icing is only slight in these clouds.

Structural icing is most likely to accumulate rapidly on an airplane in conditions of **freezing rain,** for instance when flying in below-freezing air underneath the surface of a warm front from which rain is falling.

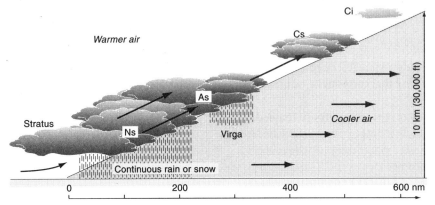

Figure 18-2. Danger area beneath a warm front

Induction Icing

Carburetor Icing

Ice can form in the carburetor and induction system of an engine in moist air with outside air temperatures as high as +25°C (+80°F). It will disturb or prevent the flow of air and fuel into the engine, causing it to lose power, run roughly and perhaps even stop.

> When the air is moist carburetor ice can form in air temperatures as high as 25°C!

Most airplanes whose engines have carburetors are fitted with a carburetor heat control that can direct hot air from around the engine into the carburetor, instead of the ambient air. The hot air can melt the ice and prevent further ice from forming. The correct method of using carburetor heat for your airplane will be found in the Pilot's Operating Handbook. Carburetor ice is covered in more detail in Chapter 5.

Engine Intake Icing

Structural icing near the engine air intake at subzero temperatures can restrict the airflow into the induction system and cause problems. Some aircraft have an *alternate air system* in case this occurs.

Instrument Icing

Icing of the pitot-static system can affect the readings of the pressure-operated flight instruments (the airspeed indicator, altimeter, and VSI). If the airplane has a pitot heater, then use it when appropriate.

Warning!

Ice of any type on the airframe or propeller, or in the carburetor and induction system, deserves your immediate attention. Wings contaminated by ice prior to takeoff will lengthen the takeoff run because of the higher speed needed to fly—a dangerous situation! Ice or frost on the leading edge and upper forward area of the wings (where the majority of the lift is generated) is especially dangerous. Flight into known icing conditions is not authorized and extremely hazardous if the aircraft is not certified for flight into known icing.

> An ice-laden airplane may be incapable of flight.

Cold Weather Operations

In extreme cold-weather conditions you should check the engine crankcase breathing lines, to ensure that vapors from the crankcase have not frozen and blocked the breathing lines with ice.

You should also consider preheating the cockpit and the engine to ensure that the electronic instruments and the engine are at normal temperatures before start-up. On start-up the time for the oil pressure to rise will be longer. The engine should be shut down if the oil pressure has not risen within 60 seconds.

After takeoff from a slushy runway in below-freezing conditions, you should consider cycling the gear up and down several times shortly after takeoff to ensure that any ice formed is broken off and blown away, and not freezing the landing gear in the up position.

✍ Now complete **Review 18, Part (a)** on page 377.

Visibility

Visibility is the greatest distance you can see and identify objects—it is a measure of how transparent the atmosphere is to the human eye.

The actual visibility is very important to a pilot, and strict visibility requirements are specified for visual flight operations.

Slant visibility may be quite different from horizontal visibility. A runway clearly visible through stratus, fog or smog from directly overhead an airport might be impossible to see when you are trying to join final approach.

It is essential that you conduct your VFR flight only in Visual Meteorological conditions (VMC). Instrument flight training will introduce you to reduced visibility operations.

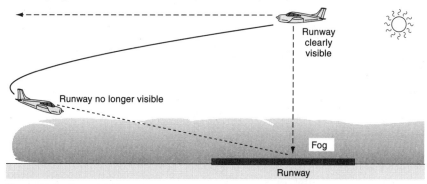

Figure 18-3. Slant visibility may be severely reduced by fog, smog or stratus

Particles in the Air

On a perfectly clear day visibility can exceed 100 miles, however this is rarely the case since there are always some particles suspended in the air, preventing all of the light from a distant object reaching your eyes.

Visibility can be reduced by particles suspended in the air.

Rising air (unstable air) may carry these particles up and blow them away, leading to good visibility; stable air that is *not* rising, however, will keep the particles in the lower levels, which may result in poor visibility.

Particles that restrict visibility include:
- minute particles so small that even very light winds can support them;
  - dust or smoke, causing haze;
  - liquid water or ice, producing mist, fog or clouds;
- larger particles of sand, dust or sea spray which require stronger winds and turbulence for the air to hold them in suspension; and
- precipitation (rain, snow, hail), the worst visibility being associated with very heavy rain or with large numbers of small particles—for example, thick drizzle or heavy, fine snow.

Unstable air that is rising may cause cumuliform clouds to form, with poor visibility in the showers falling from them, but good visibility otherwise, since the rising unstable air will carry the obscuring particles away. As well as causing good visibility, the rising unstable air may cause bumpy flying conditions.

Rain or snow will of course reduce the distance that you can see, as well as possibly obscuring the horizon and making it more difficult for you to keep the wings level or hold a steady bank angle in a turn. Poor visibility over a large area may occur in mist, fog, smog, stratus, drizzle or rain. As well as restricting visibility through the atmosphere, heavy rain may collect on the windshield and further restrict your vision, especially if the airplane is flying fast. If freezing occurs on the windshield, either as ice or frost, vision may be further impaired.

Strong winds can raise dust or sand from the surface and, in some parts of the world, visibility may be reduced to just a few feet in **dust** and **sandstorms**.

Sea spray often evaporates after being blown into the atmosphere, leaving small salt particles suspended in the air that can act as condensation nuclei. The salt particles attract water and can cause condensation at relative humidities as low as 70%, restricting visibility much sooner than would otherwise be the case. Haze produced by sea salt often has a whitish appearance, and may often be seen along ocean coastlines.

The position of the sun can also have a significant effect on visibility. Flying with the sun behind you where you can see the sunlit side of objects, visibility may be much greater than when flying into the sun. As well as reducing visibility, flying into the sun may also cause *glare*. If landing into the sun is necessary due to strong surface winds or other reasons, consideration should be given to altering the time of arrival.

Remember that the onset of **darkness** is earlier on the ground than at altitude and, even though visibility at higher altitudes might be good, flying low in the traffic pattern and approaching to land on a darkening field may cause problems.

Inversions and Reduced Visibility

An inversion occurs when the air temperature increases with altitude (rather than decreases, which is the usual situation).

A temperature inversion can act as a blanket, stopping vertical convection currents—air that starts to rise meets warmer air and so ceases rising. In other words, temperature inversions are associated with a **stable** layer of air. Particles suspended in the lower layers will be trapped there causing a rather dirty layer of smoke, dust, or pollution, particularly in industrial areas. These small particles may act as condensation particles or nuclei, and encourage the formation of fog if the relative humidity is high, the combination of smoke and fog being known as *smog*. There is usually an abundance of condensation nuclei in industrial areas as a result of the combustion process (factory smoke, car exhausts, and so on)—hence the poor visibility often found over these areas.

Similar poor visibility effects below inversions can be seen in rural areas if there is a lot of pollen, dust or other matter in the air.

Inversions can occur by cooling of the air in contact with the earth's surface overnight, or by subsidence associated with a high pressure system as descending air warms. The most common type of ground-based inversion is produced by terrestrial radiation on a clear, relatively still, night. This often leads to poor visibility in the lower levels the following morning caused by fog, smoke or smog.

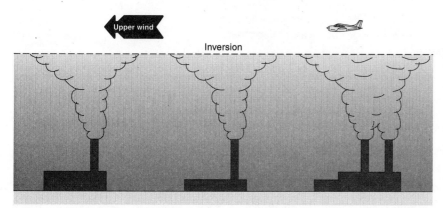

Figure 18-4. Reduced visibility and smooth flying conditions will usually be encountered beneath an inversion, and possible windshear passing through it

Flying conditions beneath a low-level inversion layer are typically smooth air (because the air is stable and not rising), with poor visibility, haze, fog, smog or low clouds. Because there is little or no mixing of the air above and below an inversion, the effect of any upper winds may not be carried down beneath the inversion. This may cause a quite sharp **windshear** as an airplane climbs or descends through the inversion.

Condensation

Visibility for a pilot can be dramatically reduced when invisible water vapor in the air condenses as visible water droplets and forms clouds or fog (fog simply being a cloud layer reaching ground level).

The amount of water vapor which a parcel of air can hold depends on its temperature—warm air being able to carry more water vapor than cold air. Warm air passing over a water surface, such as an ocean or a lake, is capable of absorbing much more water vapor than cooler air.

If the moist air is then cooled, say by being forced aloft and expanding or by passing over or lying over a cooling surface, it eventually reaches a point where it can no longer carry all of its invisible water vapor and is said to be saturated. The temperature at which **saturation** occurs is called the **dewpoint temperature** (or simply *dewpoint)* of that parcel of air. Any further cooling will most likely lead to the excess water vapor condensing out as visible water droplets and forming **fog** or **clouds,** a process encouraged by the presence of dust or other condensation nuclei in the air. If the air is extremely clean, with very few condensation nuclei, the actual condensation process may be delayed until the temperature falls some degrees below the dewpoint.

Air carrying a lot of water vapor, for instance warm air after passing over an ocean or large lake, will have a high dewpoint temperature compared with the relatively dry air over an arid desert. Moist air may only have to cool to a dewpoint of +25°C (+77°F) before becoming saturated, whereas less moist air may have to cool to +5°C (+41°F) before reaching saturation point. Extremely dry air may have to cool to a dewpoint temperature of –5°C (+23°F) before becoming saturated.

The closeness of the actual air temperature to the dewpoint of the air—often contained in surface aviation weather reports—is a good indication of how close the air is to saturation and the possible formation of clouds or fog.

If the water vapor condenses on contact with a surface such as the ground or an airplane that is below the dewpoint of the surrounding air, then it will form **dew** (or **frost,** if the temperature of the collecting surface is below freezing).

Clouds or fog form when the invisible water vapor condenses in the air as visible water droplets.

The reverse process to condensation may occur in the air if its temperature rises above the dewpoint, causing the water droplets to evaporate into water vapor and, consequently, the fog or clouds to disperse.

Fog

Fog is of major concern to pilots because it severely restricts vision near the ground. The condensation process that causes fog is usually associated with cooling of the air either by:

- an underlying cold ground or water surface (causing *radiation* or *advection fog);*
- interaction of two air masses (causing *frontal fog);*
- adiabatic cooling of a moist air mass moving up a slope (causing *upslope fog);* or
- very cold air overlying a warm water surface (causing *steam fog).*

The closer the temperature/dewpoint spread, and the faster the temperature is falling, the sooner fog will form. For instance, an airport with an actual air temperature of +6°C early on a calm, clear night, and a dewpoint of +4°C (a temperature/dewpoint spread of 2°C) is likely to experience fog when the temperature falls 2°C or more from its current +6°C.

Radiation Fog

Radiation fog forms when air is cooled to below its dewpoint temperature by losing heat energy as a result of radiation. Conditions suitable for the formation of radiation fog are:

- a **cloudless night,** allowing the land to lose heat by radiation to the atmosphere and thereby cool, also causing the air in contact with the ground to lose heat (possibly leading to a temperature inversion);
- **moist air** and a **small temperature/dewpoint spread** (a high relative humidity) that only requires a little cooling for the air to reach its dewpoint temperature, causing the water vapor to condense onto small condensation nuclei in the air and form visible water; and
- **light winds** (5–7 knots) to promote mixing of the air at low level, thereby thickening the fog layer.

These conditions are commonly found with a high-pressure system.

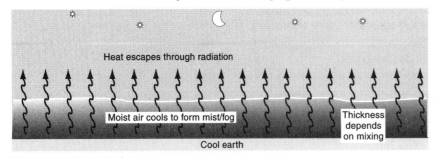

Figure 18-5. Radiation fog

Air is a poor conductor of heat, so that if the wind is absolutely calm, only the thin layer of air 1–2 inches thick actually in contact with the surface will lose heat to it. This will cause dew or frost to form on the surface itself, instead of fog forming in the air above it. **Dew** will form at temperatures above freezing, and **frost** will form at below freezing temperatures. This may inhibit the formation of radiation fog by removing moisture from the air. After dawn, however, the dew may evaporate and fog may form.

If the wind is stronger than about 7 knots, the extra turbulence may cause too much mixing and, instead of radiation fog right down to the ground, a layer of stratus may form above the surface.

Figure 18-6. The wind strength will affect the formation of dew/frost, mist/fog, or stratus

The temperature of the sea remains fairly constant throughout the year, unlike that of the land, which warms and cools quite quickly on a diurnal (daily) basis. Radiation fog is therefore much more likely to form over land, which cools more quickly at night, than over the sea.

The **dispersal** of radiation fog depends on the heating of the air. As the earth's surface begins to warm up again some time after sunrise, the air in contact with it will also warm, causing the fog to gradually dissipate. It is common for this to occur by early or mid-morning. Possibly the fog may rise to form a low layer of stratus before the sky fully clears.

If the fog that has formed overnight is thick, however, it may act as a blanket, shutting out the sun and impeding the heating of the earth's surface after the sun has risen. As a consequence, the air in which the fog exists will *not* be warmed from below and the radiation fog may last throughout the day.

An increasing wind speed could create sufficient turbulence to drag warmer and drier air down into the fog layer, causing it to dissipate.

Note: Haze caused by particles of dust or pollen in the air cannot, of course, be dissipated by the air warming—haze needs to be blown away by a wind.

Advection Fog

A warm, moist air mass moving across a colder surface will be cooled from below. If its temperature is reduced to the dewpoint temperature, then fog will form. Since the term advection means the horizontal flow of air, fog formed in this manner is known as **advection fog,** and can occur quite suddenly, day or night, if the right conditions exist, and can be more persistent than radiation fog.

For instance, a warm, moist maritime airflow over a cold land surface can lead to advection fog forming over the land. In winter, moist air from the Gulf of Mexico moving north over cold ground often causes advection fog extending well into the south-central and eastern United States.

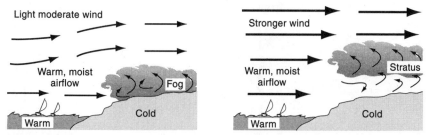

Figure 18-7. Fog or stratus caused by advection

Advection fog depends on a wind to move the relatively warm and moist air mass over a cooler surface. Unlike radiation fog, the formation of advection fog is *not* affected by overhead cloud layers, and can form with or without clouds obscuring the sky. Light to moderate winds will encourage mixing in the lower levels to give a thicker layer of fog, but winds stronger than about 15 knots may cause stratus clouds rather than fog. Advection fog can persist in much stronger winds than radiation fog.

Sea fog is a type of advection fog, and may be caused by:

- tropical maritime air moving toward the pole over a colder ocean or meeting a colder air mass; or by
- an airflow off a warm land surface moving over a cooler sea, affecting airports in coastal areas. Advection fog is common in coastal regions of California during summer.

Upslope Fog

Moist air moving up a slope will cool adiabatically and, if it cools to below its dewpoint temperature, fog will form. This is known as **upslope fog.** It may form whether there is cloud above or not. If the wind stops, the upslope fog will dissipate. Upslope fog is common on the eastern slopes of the Rockies and the Appalachian mountains.

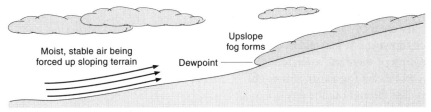

Figure 18-8. Upslope fog

Both upslope fog and advection fog need wind (but radiation fog does not).

Frontal Fog

Frontal fog forms from the interaction of two air masses in one of two ways.

- Clouds that extend down to the surface during the passage of a weather front (forming mainly over hills and consequently called *hill fog).*
- Air that becomes saturated by the evaporation from rain that has fallen— known as *precipitation-induced fog.*

These conditions may develop in the cold air ahead of a warm front (or an occluded front), the prefrontal fog possibly being very widespread. Rain or drizzle falling from relatively warm air into cooler air may saturate it, forming precipitation-induced fog which may be thick and long-lasting over wide areas. Precipitation-induced fog is most likely to be associated with a warm front, but it can also be associated with a stationary front or a slow-moving cold front.

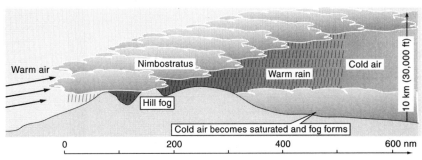

Figure 18-9. Fog associated with a warm front

Steam Fog

Steam fog can form when cool air blows over a warm, moist surface (a warm sea or wet land), cooling the water vapor rising from the moist surface to below its dewpoint temperature. Steam fog over polar oceans is sometimes called *arctic sea smoke*. It forms in air more than 10°C (20°F) colder than water, and can be very thick and widespread, causing serious visibility problems for shipping.

Low-level turbulence and the risk of severe icing can be present in steam fog.

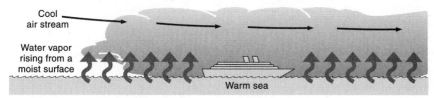

Figure 18-10. Steam fog

✍ Now complete **Review 18, Part (b)** on page 379.

Turbulence

Localized Friction Effects

The surface wind may bear no resemblance to the gradient wind at 2,000 feet AGL and above if it has to blow over and around obstacles such as hills, trees, and buildings. The wind will form turbulent eddies, the size of which will depend on both the size of the obstructions and the wind strength. This is known as *frictional turbulence* or *mechanical turbulence.*

Figure 18-11. Friction and obstacles affect the surface wind

Winds Associated with Mountains

Winds that flow over a mountain and down the lee side can be hazardous to aviation, not only because the air may be turbulent, but also because an airplane flying toward the mountain from the downwind or lee side will have to "climb" into the downflowing winds even to maintain altitude. For this reason, you should maintain a vertical clearance of several thousand feet above mountainous areas in strong wind conditions. Weather phenomena associated with mountains are known as **orographic effects.**

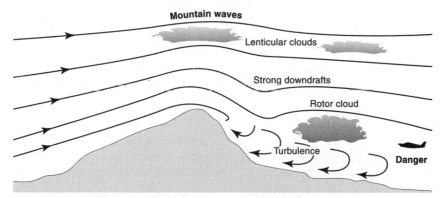

Figure 18-12. Avoid flying near mountains in strong winds

There may also be local wind effects near mountains, such as valley winds and the katabatic winds that flow down cool slopes at night and in the morning (as explained in Chapter 14).

Large mountains or mountain ranges cause an effect on the wind that may extend well above ground level resulting in **mountain waves,** possibly with associated *lenticular clouds.* These clouds are continuously forming and dissipating as they stand over the mountain, and do not appear to move. This may lead you to think that there is little or no wind present—definitely *not* the case.

The up-currents and down-currents associated with mountain waves can be quite strong, and can extend for 30 or 40 miles downwind of the mountains.

Flying in Turbulence

Some degree of turbulence is almost always present in the atmosphere and pilots quickly become accustomed to slight turbulence. Moderate or severe turbulence, however, is uncomfortable and can even overstress the airplane.

Vertical gusts increase the wing's angle-of-attack, causing an increase in the lift generated at that particular airspeed and therefore an increased load factor. Of course, if the angle-of-attack is increased beyond the critical angle, the wing will stall; this can occur at a speed well above the published 1g stall speed (known as an accelerated stall).

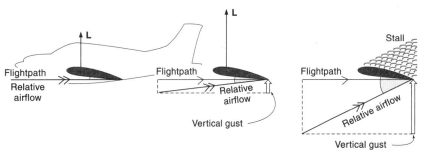

Figure 18-13. Vertical gusts increase the angle-of-attack, and will increase the load factor and/or stall the wings

The load factor (or g-force) is a measure of the stress on the airplane and each category of airplane is built to take only certain load factors. It is important that these load factors are not exceeded. One means of achieving this is to fly the airplane at the turbulence penetration speed (V_B) which is usually slower by some 10–20% than normal cruise speed, but not so slow as to allow the airplane to stall, remembering that in turbulence the airplane may stall at a higher indicated airspeed than that published.

Flight in Turbulence

When encountering turbulence:

- Fasten the seat belts.
- Maintain the level flight attitude for the desired flight phase (climb, cruise or descent), using whatever aileron movements are needed to retain lateral control, but be fairly gentle on the elevator to avoid over-stressing the airframe structurally through large changes in angle-of-attack and lift, and be prepared to accept variations in altitude.
- Use power to maintain speed, aiming to have the airspeed fluctuate around the selected turbulence penetration speed, which may require reducing power; the airspeed indicator will probably be fluctuating and so will be less useful than normal.

Turbulence Avoidance

It is obviously better to avoid turbulence, and to some extent this is possible.

- Avoid flying underneath, in or near thunderstorms where changes to airflow can be enormous.

- Avoid flying under large cumulus clouds because of the large updrafts that cause them.
- Avoid flying in the lee of hills when strong winds are blowing, since they will tumble over the ridges and possibly be quite turbulent as well as flowing down and into valleys at a rate which your airplane may not be able to out-climb.
- Avoid flying at a low level over rough ground when strong winds are blowing.

Clear Air Turbulence

Turbulence can also be expected at high altitudes in the vicinity of any **jetstreams** (tubes of strong wind flowing for many hundreds or thousands of miles, usually from west to east). Turbulence above 15,000 feet AGL that is not associated with cumuliform clouds is known as clear air turbulence (CAT). If there is a change in wind strength of more than about *6 knots per 1,000 feet* of altitude change, then moderate or stronger clear air turbulence is likely to exist.

Flying Conditions near Jetstreams

Flying conditions can be smooth *in* a jetstream, but turbulence can be expected on its edges where it meets with slower moving air—so **clear air turbulence (CAT)** is always a possibility near a jetstream.

CAT is likely to be greatest on the edges of the jetstream core, especially on the cold polar side of the jetstream where there may be strong windshear, strong curvature in the airflow, and cold air moving in by advection associated with sharply curving strong upper-level troughs. A strong windshear can be expected on the low-pressure side of a jetstream core if speed at the core is greater than 110 knots.

A curving jetstream associated with a deep upper-level trough will create the greatest turbulence, especially during the winter months when the jetstream wind speeds are greater.

If encountering CAT associated with a jetstream at high altitude, it is good airmanship to report it, and also to determine from other pilot reports (PIREPs) if smooth flight is being achieved at other levels. You might fly out of the CAT by climbing or descending several thousand feet, or by moving some miles laterally from the jetstream.

The Classification of Turbulence

So that pilots and FSS can communicate efficiently regarding turbulence, certain classifications are used and should be generally understood.

- **Light** turbulence causes slight, erratic changes in attitude and/or altitude. A pilot may feel a slight pull from the seat belt.
- **Moderate** turbulence causes some changes in attitude and/or altitude, and possibly in airspeed, but the aircraft stays in positive control at all times. A pilot will feel more pronounced pulls from the seat belt.
- **Severe** turbulence causes large changes in attitude and/or altitude, probably large changes in airspeed, and the aircraft may occasionally be momentarily out of control. You will experience severe pulling from the seat belt.
- **Extreme** turbulence causes violent changes in attitude and/or altitude and airspeed, with possible structural damage.

The *duration* of the turbulence can be described by:

- **occasional**—less than one-third of the time;
- **intermittent**—one to two-thirds of the time; and
- **continuous**—more than two-thirds of the time.

Windshear, Thunderstorms and Microbursts

A theoretical discussion of windshear, thunderstorms and microbursts is covered in Chapter 16. This section deals with the operational effects these potentially dangerous phenomenon can cause.

Windshear

A windshear is defined as a change in wind direction and/or speed in space. A windshear is a **changing** wind. This can mean a wind whose *speed* alters as you climb or descend to a different level. It can mean a wind whose *direction* changes from place to place or it can mean an updraft or a downdraft that an airplane has to fly through. Windshear is generally understood to mean a wind change within a short distance or a short space of time.

Windshear affects the flight path and the airspeed of an airplane and can be a hazard to aviation. It can be present at any level in the atmosphere, and can exist in both a horizontal and vertical direction.

Windshear is commonly experienced at high altitudes near a jetstream as clear air turbulence (CAT), near frontal zones, and at low levels associated with low-level temperature inversions, in or near thunderstorms or showers.

Windshear is a change in wind speed and/or direction within a short vertical or horizontal distance in the atmosphere.

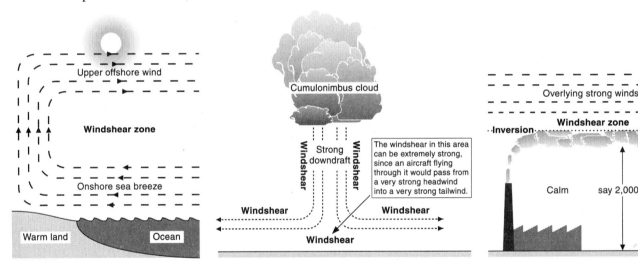

Figure 18-14. Windshear is a change of wind speed and/or direction between places

Some windshear is usually present to some extent as an airplane approaches the ground for a landing, because of the different speed and direction of the surface wind compared to the wind at altitude. Low-level windshear can be more pronounced at night or in the early morning when there is little mixing of the lower layers—for instance, when a temperature inversion exists with calm winds on and near the ground and overlying winds of 25 knots or greater.

When climbing or descending through a windshear zone, you should be alert for sudden airspeed changes. Flying into a suddenly decreasing headwind on approach, for instance, would cause a sudden loss of airspeed. You would counter this with appropriate changes of power and attitude. This is covered in Chapter 10.

Windshear can also be expected when a sea breeze or a land breeze is blowing, or when you are flying in the vicinity of a thunderstorm or a front.

Cumulonimbus clouds have enormous updrafts and downdrafts associated with them, and the effects can be felt up to 10 or 20 miles away from the actual cloud. These downdrafts can be so strong as to be classified as microbursts.

Windshear and turbulence associated with a thunderstorm can destroy an airplane.

Thunderstorms

Do *not* land or take off if there is an active thunderstorm approaching the airport. Sudden wind changes, severe turbulence and windshear are possible.

Avoid thunderstorms in flight by at least 10 miles and, in severe situations, by 20 miles. If you are passing downwind of them, you should perhaps increase this distance even further. Use your weather radar, if available, otherwise detour visually, making use of heavy rain showers, towering clouds, lightning and roll clouds as indicators of where mature storm cells are likely to be.

Remember that embedded thunderstorms may be obscured from sight by the general cloud layers, so avoid areas where embedded cumulonimbus clouds are forecast, unless you are equipped with a serviceable weather radar. Also avoid areas with six-tenths or more of thunderstorm coverage. Any thunderstorm with tops of 35,000 feet or higher should be regarded as extremely hazardous.

When flying in the area of thunderstorms:

- Fasten the seat belts and shoulder harnesses, and secure any loose objects.
- Turn up the cockpit lights at night to lessen the danger of temporary blindness from nearby lightning.
- Do not fly under thunderstorms, because you may experience severe turbulence, strong downdrafts, microbursts, heavy hail and windshear.

If you cannot avoid flying through or near a thunderstorm:

- Plan a course that will take minimum time through the hazardous area.
- Establish a power setting for the recommended turbulence penetration speed.
- Turn on pitot heat (to avoid loss of airspeed indication), carburetor heat or jet-engine anti-ice (to avoid power loss) and other anti-icing equipment (to avoid airframe icing). The most critical icing band within a cloud is from the freezing level (0°C) up to an altitude where the temperature is about –15°C, which is the temperature band where supercooled water drops may exist. Avoid this temperature band in large clouds if possible.
- Maintain your heading by keeping the wings level with ailerons, and do not make sudden changes in pitch attitude with the elevators because sudden changes in pitch attitude may overstress the airplane structure. It may be advisable to disconnect the autopilot, or at least its altitude-hold and speed-hold functions, to avoid the autopilot making sudden changes in pitch attitude (causing additional structural stress) and sudden changes in power (increasing the risk of a power loss).
- Avoid turns if possible, as this increases g-loading—continue heading straight ahead and avoid turning back once you have penetrated the storm, as a turn will increase stress on the airframe and also increase the stall speed. Maintaining the heading will most likely get you through the storm in minimum time.
- Allow the airspeed to fluctuate in the turbulence, avoiding rapid power changes.
- Monitor the flight and engine instruments, avoiding looking out of the cockpit too much to reduce the risk of temporary blindness from lightning.
- Use the weather radar effectively, occasionally tilting the antenna up or down to allow detection of thunderstorm activity at other levels.

Note: You may sometimes experience *St. Elmo's fire,* a spectacular static electricity discharge across the windshield, or from sharp edges or points on the airplane's structure, especially at night. St. Elmo's fire is not dangerous.

Microbursts

An aircraft entering the area of a microburst within 1,000–3,000 feet AGL will first encounter an increasing headwind. The aircraft will initially maintain its inertial speed over the ground (its groundspeed) and the increased headwind will cause it to have a higher airspeed, therefore increased performance. It will tend to fly above the original flight path. Then the aircraft will enter the downburst shaft and will be carried earthward in the strong downward air current—a dramatic loss of performance.

As the aircraft flies out of the downburst shaft (hopefully), the situation is not greatly improved. It will fly into an area of increasing tailwind. As the aircraft will tend to maintain its inertial groundspeed initially, the increasing tailwind will cause the airspeed to decay—a reduced airspeed, resulting in reduced aircraft performance.

Even with the addition of full power and suitable adjustments to pitch attitude by the pilot, the airplane may struggle to maintain a safe airspeed and flight path. Traversing some small, strong microbursts safely may be beyond the performance capabilities of any aircraft.

Figures 18-15 and 18-16 depict the likely effect on an aircraft encountering a microburst under a thunderstorm on approach and after takeoff.

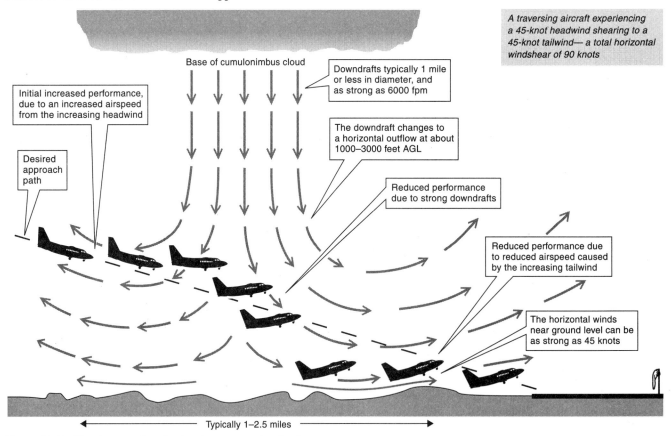

Figure 18-15. The dangers of a microburst on approach to land

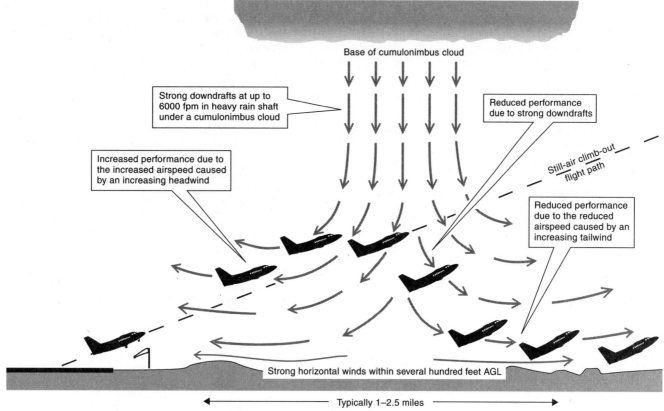

Figure 18-16. The dangers of a microburst after takeoff

✍ Now complete **Review 18, Part (c)** on page 380.

✍ Commercial students complete **Review 18, Commercial** on page 381.

✍ Review 18

Part (a)

1. What two conditions must be met for structural icing to occur on an airplane?

➤ visible moisture, temperature at or below freezing

2. How does frost affect the lifting surfaces of an airplane on takeoff?

(a) Frost may prevent the airplane from becoming airborne at normal takeoff speed.

(b) Frost will change the camber of the wing, increasing lift during takeoff.

(c) Frost may cause the airplane to become airborne at a lower angle-of-attack at a lower indicated airspeed.

➤ (a)

Operational Weather Factors

3. Large supercooled droplets striking a below freezing airplane are likely to form (clear ice/rime ice/frost).

➤ clear ice

4. Small supercooled droplets striking a below freezing airplane are likely to form (clear ice/rime ice/frost).

➤ rime ice

5. Structural icing is most likely to have the highest accumulation rate in conditions of (freezing rain/ freezing drizzle/snow/cumulous clouds).

➤ freezing rain

6. If the air temperature is +6°C at 1,500 feet MSL, and a standard temperature lapse rate exists, the freezing level will be approximately _____ feet MSL.

➤ 4,500 feet MSL

---

7. One in-flight condition necessary for structural icing to form is:
   (a) small temperature/dewpoint spread.
   (b) stratiform clouds.
   (c) visible moisture.
➤ (c)

8. Freezing rain consists of (supercooled water drops/ice pellets/warm water drops).
➤ supercooled water drops

9. The presence of ice pellets at the surface is evidence that there:
   (a) are thunderstorms in the area.
   (b) has been cold front passage.
   (c) is freezing rain at a higher altitude.
➤ (c)

10. Freezing rain can result when rain falls into a layer of air that is (above/below) 0°C.
➤ below

11. If you fly through rain which freezes on impact, then you know that temperatures at some higher altitude are (above/below) the freezing temperature of 0°C.
➤ above

12. If you fly through wet snow, then you know that temperatures at some higher altitude are (above/below) the freezing temperature of 0°C, and the temperature at your altitude is (above/below) 0°C.
➤ below, above

13. Clear ice (can/will not) alter the basic aerodynamic shape of the wing.
➤ can

14. Frost (can/will not) cause a loss of lift from the wings.
➤ can

15. You (should/need not) remove frost, ice or any other contaminant from the wings prior to flight.
➤ should

16. The risk of clear ice forming on the airplane structure is greater when flying in (cumuliform/cirrus) clouds.
➤ cumuliform

17. The family of clouds least likely to contribute to structural icing on an airplane is (low-/middle-/high-) level clouds.
➤ high-level

18. Why is frost considered hazardous to flight?
   (a) Frost changes the basic aerodynamic shape of the airfoils, thereby increasing lift.
   (b) Frost slows the airflow over the airfoils, thereby decreasing control effectiveness.
   (c) Frost spoils the smooth flow of air over the wings, thereby decreasing lifting capability.
➤ (c)

19. For carburetor icing to occur, the outside air temperature (must/need not) be below freezing.
➤ need not

20. Ice can form in the carburetor when the ambient air temperature is (below freezing only/above or below freezing).
➤ above or below freezing

21. The air entering the carburetor and induction system (cools/warms) as it expands through the venturi.
➤ cools

22. The control in the cockpit used to protect you against carburetor icing is called the _____ control.
➤ carburetor heat

23. Carburetor ice (may/will not) form when you are flying in moist air at +10°C.
➤ may

24. If ice forms over the pitot tube, the instrument(s) likely to give faulty indications is/are the _____ .
➤ airspeed indicator

25. If ice forms over the static vents, the instrument(s) likely to give faulty indications is/are the _____ .
➤ airspeed indicator, altimeter, vertical speed indicator

26. Which is true regarding preheating an aircraft during cold weather operations?
   (a) The cabin area as well as the engine should be preheated.
   (b) The cabin area should not be preheated with portable heaters.
   (c) Hot air should be blown directly at the engine through the air intakes.
➤ (a)

27. If necessary to take off from a slushy runway, the freezing of landing gear mechanisms can be minimized by:
    (a) recycling the gear.
    (b) delaying gear retraction.
    (c) increasing the airspeed to V_{LE} before retraction.
    ➤ (a)

28. During preflight in cold weather, crankcase breather lines should receive special attention because they are susceptible to being clogged by:
    (a) congealed oil from the crankcase.
    (b) moisture from the outside air which has frozen.
    (c) ice from crankcase vapors that have condensed and subsequently frozen.
    ➤ (c)

Part (b)

1. Poor visibility is more likely to result with (stable/unstable) air.
   ➤ stable

2. For an inversion to exist, temperature must (increase/decrease) with altitude.
   ➤ increase

3. The presence of an inversion (increases/decreases) the risk of poor visibility.
   ➤ increases

4. Flying conditions beneath a low-level temperature inversion are typically (smooth/turbulent) air and (good/poor) visibility.
   ➤ smooth, poor

5. Fog is formed when the air is cooled to its _____ temperature.
   ➤ dewpoint

6. The possibility of fog in industrial areas is increased because of the prevalence of _____ nuclei as a result of the combustion process.
   ➤ condensation nuclei

7. Which situation is most conducive to the formation of radiation fog?
   (a) Warm, moist air over low, flat land areas on clear, calm nights.
   (b) Moist, tropical air moving over cold, offshore water.
   (c) The movement of cold air over much warmer water.
   ➤ (a)

8. If the temperature/dewpoint spread is small and decreasing, and the temperature is 62°F, what type of weather is most likely to develop?
   (a) Freezing precipitation.
   (b) Thunderstorms.
   (c) Fog or low clouds.
   ➤ (c)

9. A mixture of smoke and fog is known as _____ .
   ➤ smog

10. In which situation is advection fog most likely to form?
    (a) A warm, moist air mass on the windward side of mountains.
    (b) An air mass moving inland from the coast in winter.
    (c) A light breeze blowing colder air out to sea.
    ➤ (b)

11. In order for advection fog to form, there (must/need not) be a wind.
    ➤ must

12. Advection fog is formed as (dry/moist) air is carried over a (warmer/cooler) surface.
    ➤ moist, cooler

13. Advection fog caused by a warm, moist airflow over a cold land surface is most likely in (inland/coastal) areas in (summer/winter).
    ➤ coastal, winter

14. Moist air moving up a slope will (cool/warm) adiabatically and may form _____ fog if its temperature reaches the _____ temperature.
    ➤ cool, upslope, dewpoint

15. Low-level turbulence can occur and icing can become hazardous in which type of fog?
    (a) Rain-induced fog.
    (b) Upslope fog.
    (c) Steam fog.
    ➤ (c)

16. What types of fog depend on wind in order to exist?
    (a) Radiation fog and ice fog.
    (b) Steam fog and ground fog.
    (c) Advection fog and upslope fog.
    ➤ (c)

Part (c)

1. When turbulence causes changes in altitude and/or attitude but aircraft control remains positive, that should be reported as:
   - (a) light.
   - (b) severe.
   - (c) moderate.
   ➤ (c)

2. Turbulence that is encountered above 15,000 feet AGL not associated with cumuliform cloudiness, including thunderstorms, should be reported as:
   - (a) severe turbulence.
   - (b) clear air turbulence.
   - (c) convective turbulence.
   ➤ (b)

3. The minimum vertical windshear value critical for probable moderate or greater turbulence is (4/6/8) knots per 1,000 feet.
   ➤ 6 knots/1,000 feet

4. What is an important characteristic of windshear?
   - (a) It exists in a horizontal direction only, and is normally found near a jetstream.
   - (b) It occurs primarily at the lower levels and is usually associated with mountain waves.
   - (c) It can be present at any level and can exist in both a horizontal and vertical direction.
   ➤ (c)

5. One of the most dangerous features of mountain waves is the turbulent areas in and:
   - (a) below rotor clouds.
   - (b) above rotor clouds.
   - (c) below lenticular clouds.
   ➤ (a)

6. When flying low over hilly terrain, ridges, or mountain ranges the greatest potential danger from turbulent air currents will usually be encountered on the:
   - (a) leeward side when flying with the wind.
   - (b) leeward side when flying into the wind.
   - (c) windward side when flying into the wind.
   ➤ (b)

7. The presence of standing lenticular altocumulus clouds is a good indication of:
   - (a) an approaching storm.
   - (b) very strong turbulence.
   - (c) heavy icing conditions.
   ➤ (b)

8. The wind at 5,000 feet AGL is southwesterly while the surface wind is southerly. This difference in direction is primarily due to:
   - (a) stronger pressure gradient at higher altitudes.
   - (b) friction between the wind and the surface.
   - (c) stronger Coriolis force at the surface.
   ➤ (b)

9. A pilot can expect a windshear zone in a temperature inversion whenever the wind speed at 2,000 to 4,000 feet above the surface is at least:
   - (a) 10 knots.
   - (b) 15 knots.
   - (c) 25 knots.
   ➤ (c)

10. Windshear can be associated with a change in wind (speed/direction/speed or direction) at any level in the atmosphere.
    ➤ speed or direction

11. There is a likelihood of (weak/strong) windshear within and near a thunderstorm.
    ➤ strong

12. With a warm front, the most critical period for low-level windshear above an airport is (before/after) the warm front has passed.
    ➤ before

13. Hazardous windshear is commonly encountered near the ground during periods:
    - (a) when the wind velocity is stronger than 35 knots.
    - (b) of strong low-level temperature inversion.
    - (c) following frontal passage.
    ➤ (b)

14. Possible mountain wave turbulence could be anticipated when winds of 40 knots or greater blow:
    - (a) across a mountain ridge, and the air is stable.
    - (b) down a mountain valley, and the air is unstable.
    - (c) parallel to the mountain peak, and the air is stable.
    ➤ (a)

Commercial Review

1. What is indicated if ice pellets are encountered at 8,000 feet?
   (a) Freezing rain at higher altitude.
   (b) You are approaching an area of thunderstorms.
   (c) You will encounter hail if you continue your flight.
   ➤ (a)

2. Radiation fog is most likely over (inland/coastal/oceanic) areas.
   ➤ inland

3. Advection fog is most likely over (inland/coastal/oceanic) areas.
   ➤ coastal

4. Which situation would most likely result in freezing precipitation?
   (a) Rain falling from air which has a temperature of 32°F or less into air having a temperature of more than 32°F.
   (b) Rain falling from air which has a temperature of 0°C or less into air having a temperature of 0°C or more.
   (c) Rain falling from air which has a temperature of more than 32°F into air having a temperature of 32°F or less.
   ➤ (c)

5. Steam fog is most likely over (dry inland/warm sea) areas.
   ➤ warm sea

6. Advection fog (can/will not) form suddenly during day or night, and is (more/less) persistent than radiation fog.
   ➤ can, more

7. Advection fog that has drifted over a coastal airport during the day may dissipate or be lifted to become low stratus clouds by winds _____ knots or stronger.
   ➤ 15 knots

8. Precipitation-induced fog is most commonly associated with (warm/cold/stationary) fronts.
   ➤ warm

9. Which conditions are favorable for the formation of a surface based temperature inversion?
   (a) Clear, cool nights with calm or light wind.
   (b) Area of unstable air rapidly transferring heat from the surface.
   (c) Broad areas of cumulus clouds with smooth, level bases at the same altitude.
   ➤ (a)

10. In what ways do advection fog, radiation fog, and steam fog differ in their formation or location?
    (a) Radiation fog is restricted to land areas; advection fog is most common along coastal areas; steam fog forms over a water surface.
    (b) Advection fog deepens as wind speed increases up to 20 knots; steam fog requires calm or very light wind; radiation fog forms when the ground or water cools the air by radiation.
    (c) Steam fog forms from moist air moving over a colder surface; advection fog requires cold air over a warmer surface; radiation fog is produced by radiational cooling of the ground.
    ➤ (a)

11. Fog produced by frontal activity is a result of saturation due to:
    (a) nocturnal cooling.
    (b) adiabatic cooling.
    (c) evaporation of precipitation.
    ➤ (c)

12. A situation most conducive to the formation of advection fog is:
    (a) a light breeze moving colder air over a water surface.
    (b) an airmass moving inland from the coastline during the winter.
    (c) a warm, moist airmass settling over a cool surface under no-wind conditions.
    ➤ (b)

13. Advection fog has drifted over a coastal airport during the day. What may tend to dissipate or lift this fog into low stratus clouds?
    (a) Night time cooling.
    (b) Surface radiation.
    (c) Wind 15 knots or stronger.
    ➤ (c)

14. With respect to advection fog, which statement is true?
    (a) It is slow to develop, and dissipates quite rapidly.
    (b) It forms almost exclusively at night or near daybreak.
    (c) It can appear suddenly during day or night, and it is more persistent than radiation fog.

➤ (c)

15. Which in-flight hazard is most commonly associated with warm fronts?
    (a) Advection fog.
    (b) Radiation fog.
    (c) Precipitation-induced fog.

➤ (c)

16. Ice pellets encountered during flight at any altitude are normally evidence of (snow/freezing rain/a thunderstorm) at a higher altitude.

➤ freezing rain

17. Ice pellets encountered during flight normally mean there is a layer of (warmer/colder) air above.

➤ warmer

18. The most likely form of structural ice resulting from flying through a large cumulus cloud at a temperature of −3°C is (frost/rime ice/clear ice).

➤ clear ice

<h1>Weather Reports and Forecasts</h1>

19

Introduction to Aviation Weather

Weather conditions vary from place-to-place and from time-to-time. It is good airmanship to make yourself aware of the weather that you are likely to encounter en route. You can do this by making your own observations and, for flights away from the local airport, you should obtain weather reports and forecasts.

Weather that has actually been observed is contained in weather reports. Weather that is expected to occur at some time in the future is contained in weather **forecasts** or shown graphically on **prognostic charts.**

Aviation weather reports and forecasts are produced by the National Weather Service (NWS) and made available for preflight from Flight Service Stations (FSS) and other offices by telephone, in person and sometimes by facsimile or computer modem. The data is available via personal computer through various private companies such as DUATS, Jepp-Link and Pan Am weather services. When you are airborne, reports and forecasts are available from the nearest FSS, and from: the en route flight advisory service (EFAS) on 122.0 MHz (callsign "Flight Watch") at the lower altitudes; the hazardous in-flight weather advisory service (HIWAS); transcribed weather broadcasts (TWEB); the automatic terminal information service (ATIS) and the automated weather observing systems: AWOS and ASOS.

Computer presentation of weather data

Obtaining a Weather Briefing

Obtaining Weather from Flight Service Stations

In the United States, the primary method of obtaining the most current aviation weather information is by calling a **Flight Service Station (FSS).** In most parts of the country, you can receive a briefing by dialing 1-800 WX BRIEF (1-800-992-7433), or you can look up the telephone number of an FSS under United States Government, Department of Transportation, Federal Aviation Administration, in a telephone book. The FAA's Airport/Facility Directory (A/FD) contains telephone numbers for weather briefings for all public-use airports. Pilots may also call a **National Weather Service Office (WSO)** or a **National Weather Service Forecast Office (WSFO)** for briefings.

Pilots can also obtain aviation weather information, up-to-the-minute satellite images and radar images via an internet connection with the World Wide Web.

Sometimes it is possible to visit a Flight Service Station or National Weather Service office for a briefing. Where available, a walk-in briefing is best because it allows you to examine charts and data yourself, and not depend only on what the briefer says.

When you call for a briefing, you can usually listen to recorded messages providing local conditions and forecasts, and then talk to a briefer to obtain additional information. Times are given in coordinated universal time (abbreviated to UTC or Z). Any reports or forecasts not routinely available at your particular FSS, WSO or WSFO can be obtained using the **request/reply service.**

Times in forecasts are given in UTC, also known as Zulu time, "Z." Converting between Z and local times is explained on page 523.

Obtaining Weather by Computer and Fax

An increasing number of pilots are obtaining weather information using personal computers and facsimile equipment, either at home or at a fixed-base operator at an airport. These methods are fast becoming common ways of obtaining preflight weather information.

Any certificated pilot may obtain a basic weather briefing via modem to a personal computer under the FAA-funded DUATS **(Direct User Access Terminal Service)** system. These free briefings are in code, similar to NWS data. DUATS has a toll-free number that you can call for assistance, and an explanatory booklet. Other companies also providing weather information for use on personal computers are JeppLink and Pan Am weather. On-demand facsimile weather services such as JeppFax and ZFX are also offered by private companies for a fee.

Pilot Responsibility

The growing use of recorded and computer briefings means that pilots must assume more responsibility for obtaining needed weather data. It also means you are less likely than in the past to be able to talk face-to-face or by telephone with a meteorologist who can help you understand the reports and forecasts.

You must learn how to read and understand coded forecasts and the various weather charts of reports and forecasts. The key to all American weather reports and forecasts is FAA Advisory Circular AC 00-45, *Aviation Weather Services,* available from the Federal Government Printing Office and fixed-base operators and pilot-supply shops.

The pilot is responsible for obtaining needed weather data.

TV and Newspapers

Before obtaining a specific briefing for a flight, you can get a good idea of general weather trends—the big picture—from newspaper weather forecasts and television weather programs. The Weather Channel, which is available on cable TV networks, broadcasts only weather reports and forecasts, including aviation segments, 24 hours. Local TV stations give detailed reports and forecasts for their viewing areas on news shows. These usually include satellite pictures and maps that give a good idea of the national picture for the coming day. Many of these local weather shows are presented by knowledgeable weathercasters who are using sophisticated graphics and live weather radar images—watching them is a good way to further your weather education.

TV and newspaper weather information can provide you with an overall "big picture."

Specific Weather Briefings

No matter how good the information you receive from a newspaper or television weather program, both common sense and the regulations require that you obtain a specific briefing for a flight to a destination away from your takeoff point. Use your chosen service: DUATS, Jepp-Link, PanAm or a Flight Service Station (FSS).

When you call or visit Flight Service, tell the briefer that you want a "flight weather briefing" and give the following information:

- that you are a pilot;
- whether the flight will be VFR or IFR;
- the aircraft's N-number and aircraft type;
- your departure point;
- your proposed route and destination;
- the altitude(s) you plan to fly at; and
- your estimated departure time, and estimated time en route.

This information will enable the briefer to give you the information you need.

Specific aviation weather briefings provide more specific weather information.

The **standard briefing** should follow the items specified in the FAA's *Flight Service Handbook.* If the briefer follows the standard format, you will receive all the needed information, but there is always a slight chance that the briefer might not give you a complete briefing. Also, if using a personal computer to gather weather information, you need some way to ensure that you receive all the needed data. For these reasons, have a form like Figure 19-1 ready to fill in. If you complete the *Pilot's Weather "Go or No-Go" Checklist,* you will be assured of getting a complete briefing every time.

A "standard briefing" is a full briefing.

PILOT'S WEATHER "GO OR NO-GO" CHECKLIST		
Synopsis and Area Forecast	Destination WX forecast	Temperature/dewpoint spread
Adverse WX data, inc. any: SIGMETs/AIRMETs; Center weather advisories; VNR (VFR not recommended)	Winds and temperatures aloft forecast	Better WX area forecast
Current en route WX	PIREPs, including top levels	Alternate airport WX forecast
Forecast en route WX	Freezing levels	NOTAMs

Figure 19-1. The weather "Go or No-Go" checklist

A good weather briefing should include at least the following:

- **Weather synopsis**—a brief statement explaining the causes of the weather. This should include the locations and movements of highs, lows, and fronts.
- **Adverse conditions**—information about any conditions that could be a hazard to your flight, such as thunderstorms, low ceilings, poor visibility, icing (AIRMETs—advising of conditions hazardous to small aircraft; SIGMETs—advising of conditions hazardous to all aircraft; convective SIGMETs—advising of weather associated with thunderstorms).
- **Current weather**—if you are leaving within two hours, reports of the current weather along your route should be included.
- **En route forecast**—the briefer should summarize the expected en route conditions in a logical order (departure, climb-out, cruise and arrival).
- **Destination terminal forecast**—this will be the forecast for one hour before your expected arrival time until an hour later.
- **Winds aloft**—a summary of the forecast winds aloft at and near your planned cruise level. The briefer can also supply the expected temperatures.
- **Notices to Airmen (NOTAMs)**—current NOTAMs for your route will be provided, but ask for information about military training routes and any NOTAMs that have been published. Only FSSs, and not NWS offices, can supply NOTAMs.

Other Types of Briefing

In addition to standard briefings, an FSS can offer two other kinds of briefings. When your planned departure is six or more hours away you should ask for an **outlook briefing.** It will include general information about expected weather trends that should help your planning. You need to ask for a more complete briefing later on, closer to your takeoff. When needing to update a previous briefing or to supplement mass-disseminated or recorded data, ask for an **abbreviated briefing.** Tell the briefer the type of previous information you received and when you received it.

An "outlook briefing" is useful 6 or more hours before the flight.

An "abbreviated briefing" is an update of, or supplement to, information you already have.

Updating your Weather Information in Flight

When airborne you can update weather information by contacting the en route flight advisory service (EFAS)—callsign *"Flight Watch"*—on 122.0 MHz.

This FSS frequency, the same all over the United Sates, is solely for the exchange of weather information. The data should flow two ways—in addition to receiving updated information, you should give pilot weather reports (PIREPs), an important source of information for the Weather Service on what is going on between stations. They provide other pilots' information which meteorologists usually cannot obtain from satellite photos and other sources—such as how turbulent the air is. You can also tune in to certain VORs which broadcast the **hazardous in-flight weather advisory service** (HIWAS) or **transcribed weather broadcasts (TWEB),** continuous recorded messages.

✍ Now complete **Review 19, Part (a)** on page 415.

Weather information can be updated in flight using Flight Watch (122.0 MHz), HIWAS, and/or TWEB.

Weather Reports

You should start your briefing by finding out what the current weather is along your planned route and what it has been doing the last few hours. When you have a good idea of the **current conditions,** you are ready to look at **forecasts** of what the weather is expected to be doing at the time of your flight.

Weather Depiction Charts

If you are obtaining a walk-in briefing or if you have a personal computer with graphics capability, the **weather depiction chart** is a good place to begin. The chart gives a broad-brush snapshot of the actual weather, showing fronts and areas of clouds and precipitation. It is a good chart for determining general weather conditions (IFR or VFR) on which to base your flight planning.

Weather depiction charts are prepared from surface aviation (METAR) reports. They give a broad overview of flying conditions at the validity time of the chart, allowing you to determine general weather conditions quite readily, and so provide a good starting point when flight planning. More specific information, however, does need to be obtained from forecasts, prognoses, and the latest pilot, radar and surface weather reports, to augment the general information shown on weather depiction charts.

Weather depiction charts show:
- the position of fronts;
- sky cover, cloud height or ceiling, weather (including types of precipitation or obstructions to vision) and reduced visibilities as observed at various stations;
- areas of IFR, marginal VFR (MVFR), and VFR conditions, as determined by cloud base and visibility:
  - **IFR** conditions are shown by a shaded area—ceiling less than 1,000 feet AGL and/or visibility less than 3 miles.
  - **MVFR** areas are shown by contoured areas without shading—cloud ceiling 1,000–3,000 feet AGL and/or visibility 3–5 miles.
  - **VFR** areas are shown by no contours at all—ceiling above 3,000 feet AGL and visibility greater than 5 miles.

At each station:
- sky cover is shown in the station circle (with "M" indicating missing data);
- cloud height or ceiling above ground level (AGL) is shown under the station circle in hundreds of feet (when the total sky cover is few or scattered, the height shown on the weather depiction chart is the base of the lowest layer);

Symbol	Total sky cover
◯	Sky clear
◔	Less than $\frac{1}{10}$ (Few)
◑	$\frac{1}{10}$ to $\frac{5}{10}$ inclusive (Scattered)
◕	$\frac{6}{10}$ to $\frac{9}{10}$ inclusive (Broken)
◕	$\frac{10}{10}$ with breaks (BINOVC)
●	$\frac{10}{10}$ (Overcast)
⊗	Sky obscured or partially obscured

Figure 19-2. Sky cover symbols

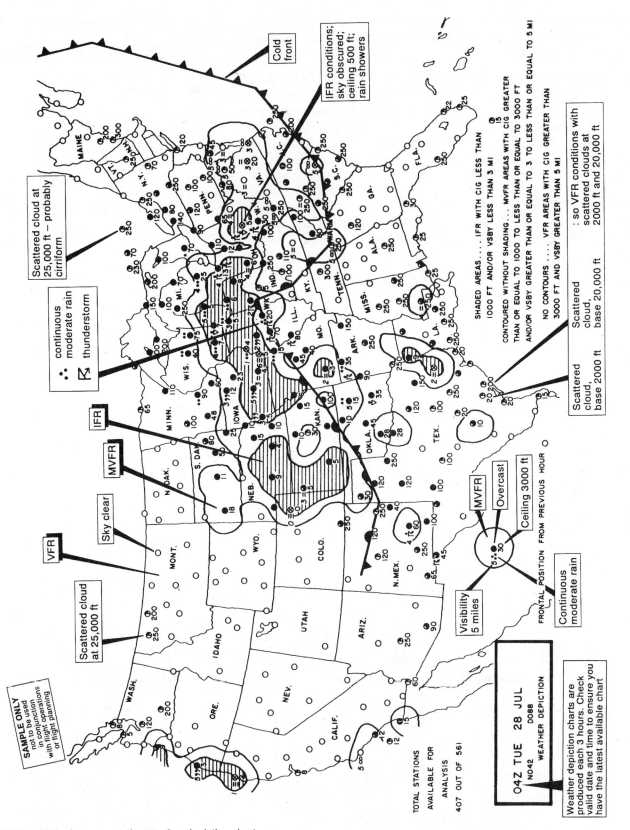

Figure 19-3. A representative weather depiction chart

- weather and obstructions to vision symbols are shown left of the station circle;
- visibility (if 6 miles or less) is shown to the left of the symbols for weather and obstructions to vision.

For example, rain is indicated by small black dots to the left of the station circle—a single dot representing intermittent rain, two dots side-by-side representing continuous rain, and three dots arranged in a triangle representing continuous moderate rain. Fog is indicated by two or three horizontal lines, arranged one above the other—three lines: visibility is less than one-quarter mile; two lines it is one-quarter mile or greater (and a visibility value would usually be added to the left of the fog symbol).

Surface Analysis Charts

The *surface analysis* chart, also known as the *surface weather* chart, provides an overview of the observed weather situation at the surface (ground level), and allows you to:

- locate the position of pressure systems and fronts at ground level; and
- overview surface winds, temperatures, dewpoints, visibility problems and total sky cover at chart time.

Note: The surface analysis chart does *not* show cloud heights or tops (even though it shows total sky cover in the small station model circle), nor does it show the expected movement of weather pressure systems (even though it shows their position at chart time).

The National Weather Service (NWS) prepares these charts from observations taken at many weather stations, and the validity time of the chart in coordinated universal time (UTC, also abbreviated as Z, which is pronounced as Zulu) corresponds to the time of observation. When using surface analysis charts, you should remember that weather moves and conditions change, so what is portrayed on the chart at its validity time may have changed.

Plotted	Interpreted
☽₈	Few clouds, base 800 feet, visibility more than 6
▽ ●₁₂	Broken sky cover, ceiling 1,200 feet, rain shower
5∞ ◐	Thin overcast with breaks, visibility 5 in haze
▲ ◑₃₀	Scattered at 3,000 feet, clouds topping ridges
2 ≡ ○	Sky clear, visibility 2, ground fog or fog
½ + ⊗	Sky partially obscured, visibility ½, blowing snow
¼ * ⊗₅	Sky obscured, ceiling 500, visibility ¼, snow
1 ⚡●₁₂	Overcast, ceiling 1,200 feet, thunderstorm, rain, visibility 1

Figure 19-4. Typical station plots

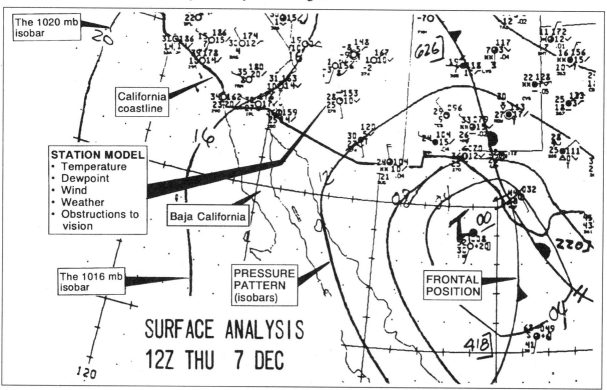

Figure 19-5. Extracted from a typical surface analysis chart

The actual chart may appear to be a bit jumbled, but the main features are shown below. The information for each station is set out in standard format, known as a **station model.** Detailed decoding information is available at Flight Service Stations and in FAA weather publications.

The closer the isobars are, the stronger the pressure gradient. If the pressure gradient is weak, sometimes dashed isobars are inserted at 2 millibar (mb) intervals (instead of the usual 4 mb).

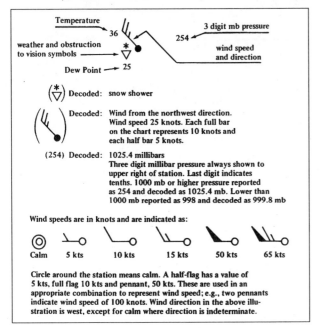

Figure 19-6a. A station model

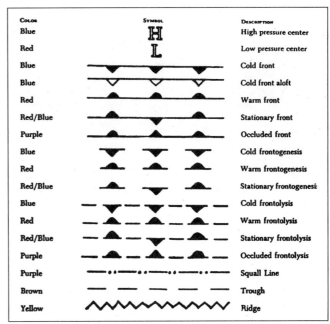

Figure 19-6b. Symbols on surface analysis charts

Radar Summary Charts

A radar summary chart shows areas of heavy precipitation detected by various radar stations around the country, and predicts their direction of movement. You should use the radar summary chart at the preflight planning stage, in conjunction with other charts, reports and forecasts. For instance, used in conjunction with a weather depiction chart, it can help provide a three-dimensional picture of clouds and precipitation. *Severe weather watch* areas (thunderstorms and tornados) are normally enclosed by boxes.

Heavy precipitation is often associated with thunderstorms and accompanied by the usual thunderstorm hazards, so is best avoided. Lines and cells of potentially dangerous thunderstorms, not shown on other charts, are shown on radar summary charts. Fog and clouds containing only small droplets are not depicted.

Radar echoes may be:

• individual cells—with individual movement indicated by an arrow with speed;

• an area of cells—shown as a contoured area that is shaded, with movement of the area indicated by a shaft to show direction, and barbs to show speed;

• a line of cells such as in a squall line—shown as a line with the direction of movement indicated.

The **intensity of the radar echoes** is shown by contours, one within the other if necessary:

- first contour—weak to moderate (radar levels 1 and 2);
- second contour—strong to very strong (levels 3 and 4); and
- third contour—intense and extreme (levels 5 and 6).

Be aware that radar summary charts can show where thunderstorms were, and where they were headed at the chart's validity time, but not where they are now.

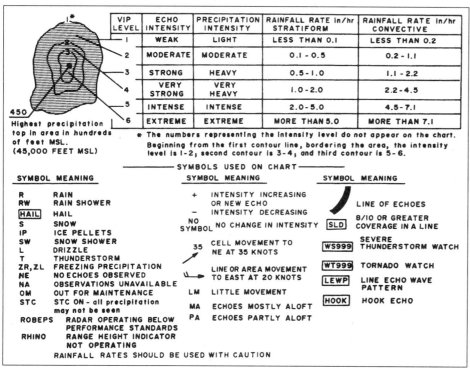

VIP LEVEL	ECHO INTENSITY	PRECIPITATION INTENSITY	RAINFALL RATE In/hr STRATIFORM	RAINFALL RATE In/hr CONVECTIVE
1	WEAK	LIGHT	LESS THAN 0.1	LESS THAN 0.2
2	MODERATE	MODERATE	0.1 - 0.5	0.2 - 1.1
3	STRONG	HEAVY	0.5 - 1.0	1.1 - 2.2
4	VERY STRONG	VERY HEAVY	1.0 - 2.0	2.2 - 4.5
5	INTENSE	INTENSE	2.0 - 5.0	4.5 - 7.1
6	EXTREME	EXTREME	MORE THAN 5.0	MORE THAN 7.1

450
Highest precipitation top in area in hundreds of feet MSL.
(45,000 FEET MSL)

✱ The numbers representing the intensity level do not appear on the chart. Beginning from the first contour line, bordering the area, the intensity level is 1-2; second contour is 3-4; and third contour is 5-6.

——— SYMBOLS USED ON CHART ———

SYMBOL	MEANING
R	RAIN
RW	RAIN SHOWER
HAIL	HAIL
S	SNOW
IP	ICE PELLETS
SW	SNOW SHOWER
L	DRIZZLE
T	THUNDERSTORM
ZR, ZL	FREEZING PRECIPITATION
NE	NO ECHOES OBSERVED
NA	OBSERVATIONS UNAVAILABLE
OM	OUT FOR MAINTENANCE
STC	STC ON - all precipitation may not be seen
ROBEPS	RADAR OPERATING BELOW PERFORMANCE STANDARDS
RHINO	RANGE HEIGHT INDICATOR NOT OPERATING

SYMBOL	MEANING
+	INTENSITY INCREASING OR NEW ECHO
−	INTENSITY DECREASING
NO SYMBOL	NO CHANGE IN INTENSITY
35	CELL MOVEMENT TO NE AT 35 KNOTS
	LINE OR AREA MOVEMENT TO EAST AT 20 KNOTS
LM	LITTLE MOVEMENT
MA	ECHOES MOSTLY ALOFT
PA	ECHOES PARTLY ALOFT

SYMBOL	MEANING
	LINE OF ECHOES
SLD	8/10 OR GREATER COVERAGE IN A LINE
WS999	SEVERE THUNDERSTORM WATCH
WT999	TORNADO WATCH
LEWP	LINE ECHO WAVE PATTERN
HOOK	HOOK ECHO

RAINFALL RATES SHOULD BE USED WITH CAUTION

Figure 19-7. Key to radar summary charts

The height of the tops and bases of the precipitation echoes is shown in hundreds of feet above and below a horizontal line (no number below the line indicates no reported echo base). The trend of liquid precipitation is indicated by "+" for increasing, and "−" for decreasing. For instance, "RW−" means decreasing rain showers, "TRW+" means increasing thunderstorms and rain showers. Be aware that radar can detect only precipitation—it cannot detect clouds, fog or icing conditions.

Severe weather watch areas are outlined on the radar summary chart by heavy dashed lines, usually in the shape of a rectangle, labeled something like "WS821", which is severe thunderstorm watch number 821, or "WT184", which is tornado watch number 184.

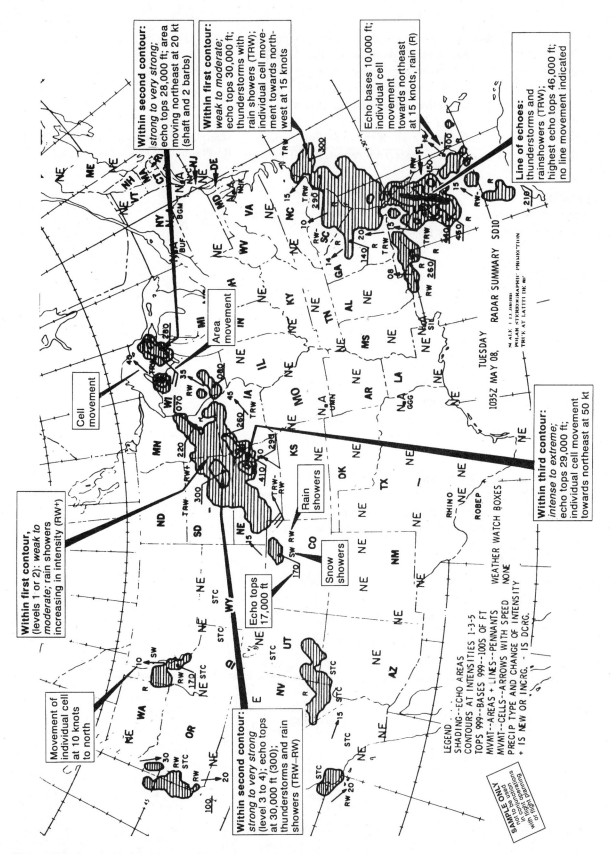

Figure 19-8. A typical radar summary chart

☞ Now complete **Review 19, Part (b)** on page 415.

METARS

Your best source of information about the current weather or past weather at a particular airport is the hourly **METAR report (Aviation Routine Weather Report).** At weather stations all over the world, observers note the weather about five or ten minutes before the end of each hour and transmit their observations. The coded reports follow a format that makes them relatively easy to translate once you understand the system.

A METAR observation will contain some or all of the following elements in the order given. If an element is missing in a METAR report, it will simply be skipped over.

If an element is missing in a METAR report, it will simply be skipped over.

Station Designator

The station designator is the standard 4-letter or combination letter and number code for the station. For example, KLAX for Los Angeles, KMDW for Chicago Midway.

Type and Time of Report

- **METAR** is for a scheduled hourly observation.
- **SPECI** is an unscheduled special observation showing a significant weather change.
- The day of the month is given (but not the month) and the time, in Zulu (UTC) the report was taken (2-digit date, 4-digit time).
- **AUTO** will be listed if the reports are generated by an ASOS/AWOS automated surface observing system. You may also find A01 or A02 in the remarks section, denoting what kind of automated system generated the report (A01 cannot tell the difference between types of precipitation, while A02 can).

Wind Direction, Speed and Character

Wind Direction, Speed and Character follow the date and time of the report. The wind direction and speed is given together, the first three digits representing the direction *from* which the wind is blowing in tens of degrees referenced to *true* north, and the following digits representing speed. Winds are listed in degrees (i.e. 220) or as V or VRB (variable).

- **12015KT** means wind from 120 degrees true (°T) at 15 knots; and
- **19008KT** means a wind from 190°T at 8 knots.
- **VRB04KT** means a wind from variable directions of four knots.

Further information about the wind's character is then added if necessary:

- **32020G32KT** means wind from 320°T at 20 knots gusting (G) to 32 knots;
- **18024PK WND39KT** means wind 180°T/24 knots with peak speed to 39 knots;
- **16020G32KT** means wind from 160°T/20 knots gusting to 32 knots.

Key to Aerodrome Forecast (TAF) and Aviation Routine Weather Report (METAR)

TAF KPIT 091730Z 091818 15005KT 5SM HZ FEW020 WS010/31022KT
   FM1930 30015G25KT 3SM SHRA OVC015 TEMPO 2022 1/2SM +TSRA
   OVC008CB
   FM0100 27008KT 5SM SHRA BKN020 OVC040 PROB40 0407 1SM -RA BR
   FM1015 18005KT 6SM -SHRA OVC020 BECMG 1315 P6SM NSW SKC

METAR KPIT 091955Z COR 22015G25KT 3/4SM R28L/2600FT TSRA OVC010CB
18/16 A2992 RMK SLP045 T01820159

Forecast	Explanation	Report
TAF	Message type: TAF-routine or TAF AMD-amended forecast, METAR-hourly, SPECI-special or TESTM-non-commissioned ASOS report	METAR
KPIT	ICAO location indicator	KPIT
091730Z	Issuance time: ALL times in UTC "Z", 2-digit date, 4-digit time	091955Z
091818	Valid period: 2-digit date, 2-digit beginning, 2-digit ending times. In U.S. METAR: CORrected ob; or AUTOmated ob for automated report with no human intervention; omitted when observer logs on	COR
15005KT	Wind: 3 digit true-north direction, nearest 10 degrees (or VaRiaBle); next 2-3 digits for speed and unit, KT (KMH or MPS); as needed, Gust and maximum speed; 00000KT for calm; for METAR, if direction varies 60 degrees or more, Variability appended, e.g. 180V260	22015G25KT
5SM	Prevailing visibility: in U.S., Statute Miles & fractions; above 6 miles in TAF Plus6SM. (Or, 4-digit minimum visibility in meters and as required, lowest value with direction)	3/4SM
	Runway Visual Range: R; 2-digit runway designator Left, Center, or Right as needed; "/"; Minus or Plus in U.S., 4-digit value, FeeT in U.S., (usually meters elsewhere); 4-digit value Variability 4-digit value (and tendency Down, Up or No change)	R28L/2600FT
HZ	Significant present, forecast and recent weather: see table (on back)	TSRA
FEW020	Cloud amount, height and type: SKy Clear 0/8, FEW >0/8-2/8, SCaTtered 3/8-4/8, BroKeN 5/8-7/8, OVerCast 8/8; 3-digit height in hundreds of ft; Towering CUmulus or CumulonimBus in METAR; in TAF, only CB. Vertical Visibility for obscured sky and height "VV004". More than 1 layer may be reported or forecast. In automated METAR reports only, CLeaR for "clear below 12,000 feet"	OVC010CB
18/16	Temperature: degrees Celsius; first 2 digits, temperature "/" last 2 digits, dew-point temperature; Minus for below zero, e.g., M06	18/16
A2992	Altimeter setting: indicator and 4 digits; in U.S., A-inches and hundredths; (Q-hectoPascals, e.g., Q1013)	A2992
		Continued

Key to Aerodrome Forecast (TAF) and Aviation Routine Weather Report (METAR) *Continued*

Forecast	Explanation	Report
WS010/3 1022KT	In U.S. TAF, non-convective low-level (≤ 2,000 ft) Wind Shear; 3-digit height (hundreds of ft); "/"; 3-digit wind direction and 2-3 digit wind speed above the indicated height, and unit, KT	
	In METAR, ReMarK indicator & remarks. For example: Sea-Level Pressure in hectoPascals & tenths, as shown: 1004.5 hPa; Temp/dew-point in tenths °C, as shown: temp. 18.2°C, dew-point 15.9°C	RMK SLP045 T01820159
FM1930	FroM and 2-digit hour and 2-digit minute beginning time: indicates significant change. Each FM starts on new line, indented 5 spaces.	
TEMPO 2022	TEMPOrary: changes expected for < 1 hour and in total, < half of 2-digit hour beginning and 2-digit hour ending time period	
PROB40 0407	PROBability and 2-digit percent (30 or 40): probable condition during 2-digit hour beginning and 2-digit hour ending time period	
BECMG 1315	BECoMinG: change expected during 2-digit hour beginning and 2-digit hour ending time period	

Table of Significant Present, Forecast and Recent Weather – Grouped in categories and used in the order listed below; or as needed in TAF, No Significant Weather.

QUALIFIER

Intensity or Proximity

\- Light   "no sign" Moderate   + Heavy

VC Vicinity: but not at aerodrome; in U.S. METAR, between 5 and 10SM of the point(s) of observation; in U.S. TAF, 5 to 10SM from center of runway complex (elsewhere within 8000m)

Descriptor

MI Shallow	BC Patches	PR Partial	TS Thunderstorm
BL Blowing	SH Showers	DR Drifting	FZ Freezing

WEATHER PHENOMENA

Precipitation

DZ Drizzle	RA Rain	SN Snow	SG Snow grains
IC Ice crystals	PE Ice pellets	GR Hail	GS Small hail/snow pellets
UP Unknown precipitation in automated observations			

Obscuration

BR Mist (≥ 5/8SM)	FG Fog (< 5/8SM)	FU Smoke	VA Volcanic ash
SA Sand	HZ Haze	PY Spray	DU Widespread dust

Other

SQ Squall	SS Sandstorm	DS Duststorm	PO Well developed dust/sand whirls
FC Funnel cloud	+FC Tornado/waterspout		

- Explanation in parentheses "( )" indicate different worldwide practices.
- Ceiling is not specified; defined as the lowest broken or overcast layer, or the vertical visibility.
- NWS TAFs exclude turbulence, icing & temperature forecasts; NWS METARs exclude trend fcsts
- Although not used in U.S., Ceiling And Visibility OK replaces visibility, weather and clouds if: visibility ≥ 10 km; no cloud below 5000 ft (1500 m) or below the highest minimum sector altitude, whichever is greater and no CB; and no precipitation, TS, DS, SS, MIFG, DRDU, DRSA or DRSN.

March 1996   UNITED STATES DEPARTMENT OF COMMERCE
NOAA/PA 96052   National Oceanic and Atmospheric Administration – National Weather Service

Figure 19-9. ASA's METAR/TAF decoder table

Visibility

The visibility is given next. Visibility is listed in statute miles, or quarters of statute miles (i.e. 3/4SM). **Runway visibility** is the horizontal distance a pilot can expect to see along a runway from a specific point on that runway. Runway visual ranges are listed as R23/3000FT (RVR runway 23 is 3,000 ft).

Visibility is the greatest distance, in statute miles or fractions thereof, at which objects can be seen and identified through at least 180 degrees of the horizon.

- 8 means visibility 8 statute miles.
- 1/2 means visibility $\frac{1}{2}$ statute mile.
- 11/2 means visibility $1\frac{1}{2}$ statute miles.

Significant Weather, Sky Condition and Ceiling

Any thunderstorms or other significant weather is listed here, followed by the sky condition and any ceiling. The weather is reported in a specific order:

- Intensity
- Proximity
- Descriptor
- Precipitation
- Obstruction to visibility
- Other

Some **weather symbols,** which are used regardless of visibility, are as follows:

TS	Thunderstorm	PE	Ice pellets
+TS	Severe thunderstorm	PESH	Ice pellet shower
RA	Rain	SN	Snow
SH	Rain shower	SNSH	Snow shower
DZ	Drizzle	SP	Snow pellets
FZRA	Freezing rain	SG	Snow grains
FZDZ	Freezing drizzle	IC	Ice crystals
GR	Hail		

Note: Precipitation is measured as light (–), moderate (no sign) and heavy (+).

Some **obstructions to vision symbols** are as follows:

DS	Dust storm	FG	Fog
SS	Sand storm	BR	Mist
BLSN	Blowing snow	HZ	Haze
BLPY	Blowing spray	VA	Volcanic ash
DZ	Drizzle	SG	Snow grains

Note: If there is no weather and no obstructions to vision, then no entries will appear in the report.

- **RA+FG** means heavy rain (RA+) as weather and fog (FG) as an obstruction to vision.

Clouds are listed as:

- Amount;
- Height;
- (Type); or
- Vertical Visibility

Scattered layers of clouds are listed if the sky is covered by 3/8 to 4/8 (octas) of clouds. A broken layer is 5/8 to 7/8 coverage. Heights of clouds AGL are reported in hundreds of feet; add two zeros to read the height. The height AGL of the base of the layer preceding the sky-cover designator is also shown.

- **SCT140** means a scattered layer with the base at 14,000 feet AGL.
- **SCT006 SCT15CU** means two layers, a scattered layer at 600 feet AGL and a second higher layer of cumulous clouds at 1,500 feet AGL with the *total* sky cover of that layer and all layers beneath it not exceeding SCT;
- **SKC** means sky clear with, of course, no base being reported. In an automated report this will be CLR.
- **OVC008** means a ceiling 800 feet AGL overcast.
- **BKN070 OVC150** means a ceiling 7,000 feet AGL of broken cloud and another layer base 15,000 feet AGL with it and all layers beneath it adding up to overcast.
- **VV005** means indefinite ceiling 500 feet AGL and sky obscured; *ceiling* is the height AGL of the lowest layer of clouds or obscuring phenomena aloft that is reported as BKN or OVC and not classified as thin, or the vertical visibility into surface-based obscuring phenomena that hides all the sky.

Temperature and Dewpoint

Temperature and dewpoint are given in degrees *Celsius,* separated from each other by a slash (/).

- **23/20** means a temperature of 23°C and dewpoint 20°C;
- **7/M09** means temperature 7°C and dewpoint minus 9°C.

Altimeter Setting

Following the temperature and dewpoint spread is the altimeter setting in inches of mercury. Only the last three digits are transmitted and the decimal point is omitted; the pilot must add a 2 or a 3 to bring it close to 30 inches (normal sea level pressures are in the range 28.00 to 31.00 inches of mercury).

- **A2995** means an altimeter setting of 29.95 inches;
- **A3013** means an altimeter setting of 30.13 inches.

Remarks and Coded Data

If included, the Remarks and Coded Data follow the altimeter group.

- The remarks in SLP013 means the Sea Level Pressure in hectopascals (1001.3, in this case);
- The remarks in T01760158 breaks down the temperature and the dewpoint spread at this station to the nearest $\frac{1}{10}$ degree Celsius; T for temperature, 0 for positive (1 if negative), 17.6 degrees Celsius temperature, 15.8 degrees Celsius dewpoint.

Example 1. Decode the following METAR weather report:

METAR KSAV 271853Z 28006 10SM OVC007 11/09 A2976 RMK A02 SLP075 T01060094

This breaks down into:

1	2	3	4	5	6	7	8	9	10	11	12
METAR	KSAV	271853Z	28006	10SM	OVC007	11/09	A2976	RMK	A02	SLP075	T01060094

- METAR stands for Aviation Routine Weather Report.
- KSAV is Savannah International Airport, Savannah, Georgia.
- 271853Z indicates it was a regular hourly observation taken on the 27th of the month at 1853Z (UTC).
- 28006 indicates a wind from 280 degrees blowing at 6 knots.
- The visibility is 10 statute miles and no weather or obstruction to vision are reported.
- The ceiling is overcast (8/8 coverage) at 700 AGL.
- The temperature is 11°C and the dewpoint is 9°C.
- The altimeter setting is 29.76 inches Hg.
- The remarks section follows.
- A02 means that the observation was taken from an automated system that can discern precipitation types (it must have been manned, or the word AUTO would have preceded the report).
- SLP075 indicates a Sea Level Pressure of 1007.5 hectopascals.
- T01060094 indicates that the temperature was a positive 10.6°C and the dewpoint was a positive 09.4°C.

Example 2. Another typical aviation routine weather report is:

METAR KLAX 201856Z 34005 11/2 RA+FG VV007 OVC 18/16 A2980 RMK RAB16

Los Angeles surface aviation weather report on the 20th of the month at 1856Z, wind 340°T/5 knots, visibility 1.5 statute miles, heavy rain and fog, sky indefinite, ceiling 700 feet AGL, overcast, temperature 18°C, dewpoint 16°C, altimeter 29.80 in. Hg, remarks: rain began at 16 minutes past the hour (that is, at 1816Z).

Pilot Weather Reports (PIREPs)

Pilot reports can be your best source—sometimes the only source—of information about what is going on *between* weather stations. Since the reports are voluntary, PIREPs may not be available to you on every flight, but you should still ask for them.

Pilot reports, identified by **UA** or by **UUA** if urgent, are often appended to surface aviation weather reports.

The form of a PIREP is UA followed by the mandatory items:

- /OV (over location);
- /TM (time);
- /FL (altitude or flight level);
- /TP (aircraft type);

and then by the optional items:

- /SK (sky cover);
- /WX (flight visibility and weather);
- /TA (temperature in degrees Celsius);
- /WV (wind velocity °M/kt);
- /TB (turbulence);
- /IC (icing);
- /RM (remarks).

Example 3. A typical PIREP, decoded below, is:

UA/OV 12 NW MDB/TM 1540/FL 120/TP BE55/SK 026 BKN 034/044 BKN-OVC/TA –11/IC MDT RIME 060-080/RM R TURBC INCRS WWD MH 270 TAS 185

This is a PIREP from a position 12 nautical miles northwest of MDB at time 1540Z; altitude, 12,000 feet MSL; aircraft type, Beech Baron; sky cover is first cloud layer, base 2,600 feet MSL broken, with tops at 3,400 feet MSL; and second cloud layer, base 4,400 feet MSL broken, occasionally overcast, with no reported tops; temperature, minus 11 degrees Celsius; icing, moderate rime between 6,000 and 8,000 feet MSL; remarks are: turbulence increasing westward, magnetic heading 270, true airspeed 185 knots.

You can generally interpret the abbreviations without too much trouble. For example:

- FL080/SK INTMTLY BL means sky cover is reported as the "airplane flying at 8,000 feet MSL is intermittently between layers".
- /TB MDT means turbulence moderate.
- /TP B757 means type Boeing 757.
- /SK OVC 075/085 OVC 150 means sky cover is an overcast layer with tops 7,500 feet MSL and no reported base, plus a second overcast layer, base 8,500 and tops 15,000 feet MSL.

If the METAR at the place where the UA PIREP containing those last cloud details also contained M9 OVC, then it is possible to calculate the thickness of the lower cloud layer. If the station elevation is, say, 2,300 feet MSL, then the cloud base is 3,200 feet MSL (elevation 2,300 feet MSL + ceiling 900 feet AGL). Since the pilot reported the tops of the lower layer at 7,500 feet MSL, the thickness of this layer is 4,300 feet (7,500 – 3,200).

Example 4.

PIREP AHN UA/OV AHN/RM 2038/FL DURGD/TP CE152/SK 055 SCT-BKN 080/TB MDT BLO 040

The report is from Athens, GA, and the aircraft was over the Athens VOR at 2038Z. The DURGD under FL means the pilot reported during descent. ("During climb is written DURGC".) Aircraft type, Cessna 152. The pilot encountered a scattered to broken layer of clouds with bases at 5,500 feet and tops at 8,000 feet. Note that all heights in PIREPs are referenced to mean sea level (MSL), since the pilot will be making estimates of height with reference to the altimeter. The pilot also reported moderate turbulence below 4,000 feet.

Note: When reporting turbulence, use the standard criteria given on page 373 so that other pilots derive correct information from your PIREP.

✍ Now complete **Review 19, Part (c)** on page 419.

Weather Forecasts

If you visit a FSS or Weather Service Office and check over the charts and reports described above, and also look at satellite photos, you should have a good idea of what the weather was doing at the time the information was gathered. Knowing what the weather is doing now, and what it has been doing in the last few hours, makes it easier to understand the forecasts of what it should be doing later on during your flight.

You need to develop a three-dimensional picture of the current weather, and then judge how this picture will change with time. Having studied the recently observed weather, it is now time for you to study the intelligent forecasts of meteorologists as to what the weather will do in the hours ahead.

Low-Level Significant Weather Prognostic Charts

Prognostic charts are *forecasts*, rather than observations, and are the only charts that can give you a good overall view of the weather that is expected to occur. The low-level significant weather prog is a four-panel chart that shows the general conditions that are forecast to occur from the surface to 24,000 feet MSL (the 400-mb pressure level) at the valid time (VT) of the chart, the two left hand panels for 12 hours from the issuance time, and the two right hand panels for 24 hours from the issuance time. Prognostic charts are usually issued four times daily. See Figure 19-12.

DEPICTION	MEANING
	SHOWERY PRECIPITATION (e.g. THUNDERSTORMS/RAIN SHOWERS) COVERING HALF OR MORE OF THE AREA
	CONTINUOUS OR INTERMITTENT PRECIPITATION (e.g. RAIN) COVERING HALF OR MORE OF THE AREA
	SHOWERY PRECIPITATION (e.g. SNOW SHOWERS) COVERING LESS THAN HALF OF THE AREA
	CONTINUOUS OR INTERMITTENT PRECIPITATION (e.g. DRIZZLE) COVERING LESS THAN HALF OF THE AREA

Figure 19-10. Some significant weather prognostic symbols

The upper panels show the **significant weather** prognosis (forecast) from the surface up to 24,000 feet, and include:

- forecast IFR weather—enclosed by smooth lines;
- forecast MVFR weather—enclosed by scalloped lines;
- forecast VFR areas—not outlined;
- forecast moderate, or stronger, turbulence—enclosed by long-dashed lines, with the upper and lower limits of the forecast turbulence given in hundreds of feet above and below a line, and the intensity of the turbulence represented by a symbol;
- forecast freezing level—short dashed lines at 4,000-foot intervals (dots when freezing level is at the surface)

The lower panels show the surface prognosis (weather forecast at the surface):

- forecast position and movement of pressure systems (highs, lows, fronts);
- forecast areas of precipitation and/or thunderstorms.

Note: The method of outlining the IFR and MVFR areas differs from that on the weather depiction charts.

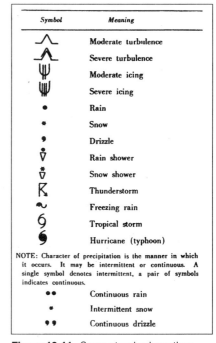

Symbol	Meaning
⋀	Moderate turbulence
⋀	Severe turbulence
ⱷ	Moderate icing
ⱷ	Severe icing
•	Rain
⁎	Snow
⸲	Drizzle
▽	Rain shower
▽	Snow shower
R	Thunderstorm
∿	Freezing rain
6	Tropical storm
6	Hurricane (typhoon)

NOTE: Character of precipitation is the manner in which it occurs. It may be intermittent or continuous. A single symbol denotes intermittent, a pair of symbols indicates continuous.

••	Continuous rain
⁎	Intermittent snow
⸲⸲	Continuous drizzle

Figure 19-11. Some standard weather symbols

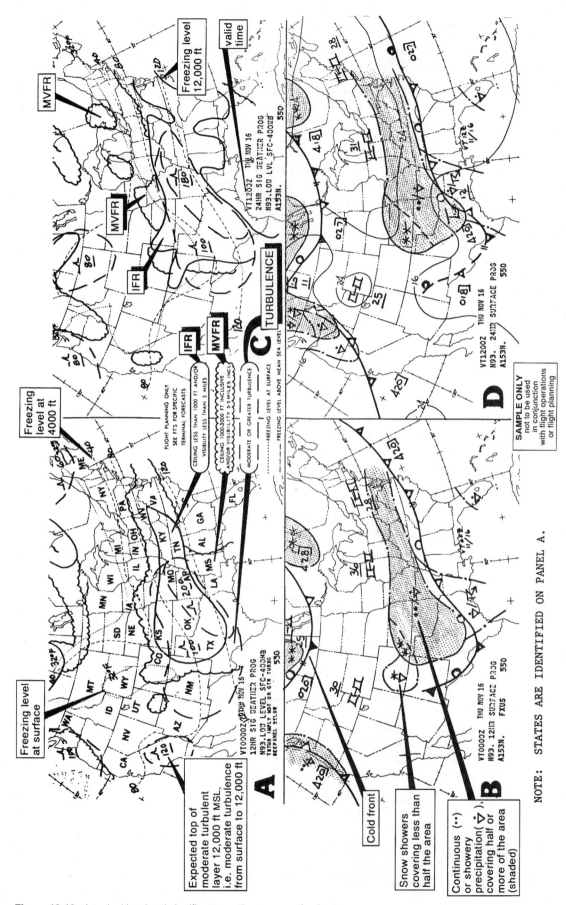

Figure 19-12. A typical low-level significant weather prognostic chart

The low-level significant weather prognostic chart (shown in Figure 19-12) can be used to determine which areas to avoid—that is, those with non-VFR weather, turbulence, and the possibility of icing above the freezing level.

Note: There is also a *high-level* significant weather chart covering the airspace from 24,000 feet (400 mb) to 63,000 feet (70 mb); small scalloped lines are used to show areas of cumulonimbus clouds.

Aerodrome Forecasts (TAF)

As the name indicates, aerodrome forecasts are for the weather at particular airports. They are issued three times a day and are valid for a 24-hour period. If the weather changes significantly between scheduled forecasts, amendments are issued. If the TAF is amended, it may not be valid for the entire 24 hours (abbreviated as TAF AMD). TAFs are issued in the following format:

Aerodrome forecasts (TAF) are the ones most used by pilots.

- Type
- Location
- Issuance Time
- Valid Time
- Forecast

The forecast is for cloud heights and amounts, visibility, weather and wind that would affect flying within **five to 10 miles** of the airport's center. If the forecast uses the term VC, (vicinity) it is referring to weather expected in the area of the airport (but not necessarily at the airport) that could affect flying there.

A code, much like that used for aviation routine weather reports (METAR), is used for the forecasts. The code used in the United States is much the same as that used in most other countries. If you fly overseas, you will have to learn a few of the slightly different International Civil Aviation Organization (ICAO) codes.

The format of the aerodrome forecast is essentially that of the METAR, but a few examples will illustrate the differences. There will be a date-time group, such as 261010, which means that the forecast is valid beginning on the 26th day of the month at 1000Z until 1000Z the following day; 23025G40KT means wind from 230°T/25 knots gusting to 40 knots; visibility is specified normally, for example 1/2 means $\frac{1}{2}$ statute mile, or is preceded with a "P" if the visibility is more than 6 statute miles; OVC006 means ceiling 600 feet AGL, TEMPO 1012 VV00 means temporarily, from 1000Z to 1200Z there will be a vertical visibility of zero; BECMG 1214 BKN020 3SM SN means that from1200Z to 1400Z there is an expected change to ceiling 2,000 feet AGL with a broken sky cover and a visibility of 3 statute miles in snow; PROB40 means "the probability of this occurring is 40%."

Example 5. An aerodrome forecast for Sacramento Executive airport in CA:

TAF KSAC 181919Z 34010KT SCT 011 OVC015 TEMPO 2022 BKN011 3SM – SHRAPROB40 VRB20G30KT VV005 1SM TSRA BECMG 2206 32010KT SCT020 BKN045 PROB40 BKN015 3SM -RA BECMG 0612Z 33025KT SCT060 PROB40 BKN030 -RA FM 1219Z 36020KT SKC.

Forecasts are given in UTC (Zulu time), but you can translate them into local times if it makes it easier for you. Pacific Daylight Time (PDT) is found by subtracting 7 hours from the UTC time.

TAF KSAC 181919 shows that it is an aerodrome forecast issued on the 18th day of the month beginning at 1900Z and running until 1900Z the next day. This means that the forecast begins at 1200 (noon) PDT. It reads:

"By 1200 PDT expect wind from 340 degrees at 10 knots, a scattered layer of clouds at 1100 ft, with an overcast layer at 1500 ft, temporary changes can be expected between 1300 and 1500 PDT of broken clouds at 1100 ft, three miles visibility and light rain showers. There is a 40 percent probability of variable winds at 20 gusting to 30 knots, an indefinite ceiling with a vertical visibility of 500 ft, one mile visibility in thunderstorms and rain, becoming, from 1500 PDT to 2300 PDT, wind from 320 degrees at 10 knots, a 2000 ft scattered layer of clouds with a higher broken layer at 4500 ft, there is a 40 percent probability of broken clouds at 1500 ft, three miles visibility in light rain, becoming, between 2300 PDT and 0500 PDT, wind from 330 at 25 knots, a scattered layer of clouds at 6000 ft, with a 40 percent probability of a broken layer of clouds at 3000 ft and light rain, from 0500 to 1200 PDT, wind from 360 degrees at 20 knots and sky clear."

✍ Now complete **Review 19, Part (d)** on page 420.

Area Forecasts (FA) and TWEB Route Forecasts

While terminal forecasts provide detailed predictions for airports, they do not tell you what to expect *between* airports. When obtaining a weather briefing, it is a good idea to look at the forecasts for airports along and near your route for an indication of what to expect. Two other kinds of forecasts are available to help you see the en route weather picture—area forecasts and TWEBs.

Area Forecasts (coded "FA") are issued three times a day (every eight hours) for six different areas of the 48 contiguous States and separately for Alaska and Hawaii. They are valid for 12 hours plus a 6-hour outlook period. The outlook, as with terminal forecasts, gives a generalized forecast.

Area forecasts are supplied in one section, containing:

• a **synopsis**—a brief summary of the location and movement of weather fronts, pressure systems and circulation patterns for the 18-hour period; plus

• a statement of **significant clouds and weather**—a 12-hour forecast, in broad terms, of clouds and weather significant to VFR flights, giving a summary of the sky condition, cloud heights, visibility, weather and/or obstructions to visibility, and surface winds of 30 knots or more. It concludes with a categorical **outlook** valid for 6 hours.

Transcribed Weather Broadcast (TWEB) Route Forecasts provide information similar to an area forecast, except that they are in a *route* format covering weather 25 miles either side of particular routes. TWEB can be monitored by calling selected locations (TEL-TWEB numbers are in the A/FD) and, in flight, by tuning to suitable navigational facilities (shown on Sectionals and IFR charts).

```
SFOC FA 101145
SYNOPSIS AND VFR CLDS/WX
SYNOPSIS VALID UNTIL 110600...CLDS/WX VALID UNTIL 110000
OTLK VALID 110000-110600   WA OR CA AND CSTL WTRS
```

> **AREA FORECAST (FA)**
> **VALIDITY & COVERAGE**

The data originated from the San Francisco weather center, and it is an Area Forecast (FA) for the 10th of the month, effective from 1145Z (UTC). It contains a synopsis, and clouds and weather appropriate to VFR operations. The synopsis is valid until 0600Z on the 11th; the significant clouds and weather group is valid until 0000Z on the 11th.

Outlooks (in the forecasts) are valid from 0000Z, and cover a six-hour period (to 0600Z). The forecast and attached Airmets cover Washington State, Oregon, California and coastal waters.

Note: We mainly show the information for a part of Oregon in this example.

```
SEE AIRMET SIERRA FOR IFR CONDS AND MTN OBSCN.
TSTMS IMPLY SVR OR GTR TURBC SVR ICG LLWS AND IFR CONDS.
NON MSL HGTS NOTED BY AGL OR CIG
```

> **REFERENCE TO**
> **IMPORTANT WEATHER**

Refer to Airmet Sierra (later in the briefing data) for details of IFR (Instrument Flight Rules) weather conditions and any mountain obscuration. Where thunderstorms are mentioned, this implies severe or greater turbulence, severe icing, low-level windshear and IFR conditions.

Non-mean sea level heights are appended with the terms *AGL* (above ground level) or *CIG* (ceiling).

```
SYNOPSIS...WEAK HIGH LVL TROF OVER THE SFO FA AREA. TROF XPCD
TO DRFT EWD THRU 06Z. RDG ALF BLDG ACRS THE ERN PAC.
```

> **THE SYNOPSIS**

Synopsis of the weather situation:

There is a weak high-level trough over the San Francisco area-forecast area. The trough is expected to drift eastward through 0600Z.

A ridge (of high pressure) aloft is building across the eastern Pacific Ocean area.

```
OR CASCDS WWD
CSTL SXNS...10-20 BKN 40 BKN 100. VSBYS 3-5L-F. 18Z-20Z BCMG 15
SCT-BKN 35 BKN 80 BKN. WDLY SCT RW-. OTLK...VFR.
WILLAMETTE VLY-NRN CASCDS...15 SCT-BKN 40 BKN 100. OCNL VSBYS 3-
5L-F. 19Z-21Z BCMG 30-50 BKN 80 BKN. WDLY SCT RW-. OTLK...VFR.
```

> **SIGNIFICANT CLOUDS**
> **AND WEATHER**

Significant clouds and weather for Oregon, Cascades westward (includes the slopes of the Cascades):

Coastal sections—broken clouds (5–7 oktas—that is, 5 to 7 eighths of the sky covered), base 1,000 to 2,000 feet MSL; broken clouds, base 4,000 feet MSL up to 10,000 feet MSL. Visibility 3 to 5 miles in light drizzle *(the hyphen after the L means that the drizzle is light)* and fog.

Between 1800Z and 2000Z, clouds becoming scattered (1–4 oktas) to broken, base 1,500 feet MSL; broken clouds, base 3,500 feet MSL; and again at base 8,000 feet MSL. Widely scattered light rain showers. The outlook for this region is for the weather conditions to become suitable for VFR operations.

For the Willamette valley to the northern *Cascades*—scattered to broken clouds, base 1,500 feet MSL; broken clouds, base 4,000 feet MSL up to 10,000 feet MSL. Occasionally, the visibility will be between 3 to 5 miles in light drizzle and fog.

Then, between 1900Z and 2100Z, the clouds will lift to become broken, base between 3,000 and 5,000 feet MSL; and also broken, base 8,000 feet MSL. Widely scattered light rain showers are forecast. The outlook for this region is also for VFR conditions.

Figure 19-13. A typical Area Forecast and group of AIRMETs (with decode explanation)

Weather Advisories

AIRMETs (WA)

AIRMETs warn of hazards primarily to small aircraft; they cover a **6-hour period** and are **issued four times a day.**

AIRMETs are primarily for small aircraft

- AIRMET Tango—**Turbulence (and low-level windshear)**—a forecast of non-thunderstorm-related turbulence of moderate or greater intensity, and low-level windshear, valid until the stated time.
- AIRMET Sierra—**IFR Weather and Mountain Obscuration**—a forecast that identifies aviation weather hazards that meet in-flight advisory criteria.
- AIRMET Zulu—**Icing**—a forecast of non-thunderstorm-related icing of light or greater intensity, often using VOR points to outline the area of icing (it sometimes extends beyond the FA boundary).

Pilots often have more trouble deciphering area forecasts and AIRMETs because of the many contractions used, and also because they describe the location of areas of turbulence and icing by referring to VORs, often outside the forecast area. Practice, with a list of the common contractions, is the best way to learn to read this data. When checking the AIRMETs, look for VORs along or within 100 miles or so either side of your planned route. If you find such a VOR listed, then you can look closer to see if your flight is likely to be affected.

Note: Be aware that *hyphens* in weather data can be used for three purposes:
- to indicate a range—for example VSBY 3-5, "visibility 3 to 5 miles";
- for spacing—VSBY 3-F, "visibility 3 miles in fog";
- to condition a phenomenon as *lighter*—RW-, "light rain showers".

An example of a typical area forecast and group of AIRMETs, with explanatory expansion, is shown in Figure 19-13.

SIGMETs (WS) and Convective SIGMETs (WST)

*S*IGMETs warn of conditions that could be dangerous to all aircraft (severe icing, and severe/extreme turbulence). *Convective* SIGMETs are observations and/or forecasts that warn of conditions associated with thunderstorms that could be dangerous to all aircraft—tornados, large hail, embedded thunderstorms, large Cb areas (and with severe icing, severe turbulence and low-level windshear implied). They are issued when necessary to alert pilots of these conditions.

SIGMETs are for all aircraft

Center Weather Advisories (CWA)

Advice of the sudden development in the weather situation will often first be issued in the form of a Center Weather Advisory, for conditions beginning within 2 hours. This may be used to supplement an area forecast or prior to the issue of the appropriate AIRMET or SIGMET.

VFR Not Recommended (VNR)

When VFR flight operations are considered inadvisable, Flight Service will include a "VNR" statement in standard briefings.

Convective Outlook (AC)

The AC takes the form of a coded message which forecasts the possibility for general, as well as severe, thunderstorm activity during the following 24 hours.

Winds and Temperatures Aloft Forecasts (FD)

Winds and temperatures aloft forecasts contain forecast upper winds in degrees true and knots, and forecast upper temperatures in degrees Celsius.

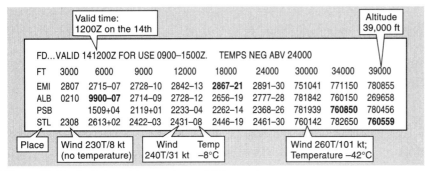

Figure 19-14. A winds and temperatures aloft forecast

2867 – 21 at 18,000 feet MSL decodes as a wind from 280°T (by adding a 0 after the first two digits) at 67 knots and temperature –21°C (+/– precedes temperature up to 24,000 feet, above this all temperatures will be below zero and so no signs need be given); at 30,000 feet. 9900 decodes as winds light-and-variable (that is, less than 5 knots).

Then, for winds aloft in the 100–199 knots range, to overcome the problem that only two digits are available for wind speed the forecaster adds 50 to the direction and subtracts 100 from the speed; you need to reverse this when decoding. At 39,000 feet, at STL 760559 decodes as a wind from 260°M (76 – 50 = 26) at 105 knots and –59°C. **Interpolate** to estimate the winds and temperatures at intermediate levels.

Example 6. If the winds and temperatures aloft forecast shows:

24000	30000
2367–26	781938

You can estimate the conditions at FL270 by interpolating as follows:

FL240 is wind 230° at   67 knots and temperature –26°C
FL300 is wind 280° at 119 knots and temperature –38°C
Differences: 50°   52 knots   and   12°C

Interpolating for FL270 (halfway between) gives differences of 25° in direction, 26 knots in speed, and 6°C in temperature. So, the estimated values are: wind from 255°T (230 + 25) at 93 knots (67 + 26) and temperature –32°C (–26 – 6).

Temperatures may be asked for in the written test in °C, or as a deviation from the ISA standard (+15°C at MSL, decreasing at 2°C per 1,000 feet, and remaining constant at –57°C above approximately 36,000 feet). At 24,000 feet, ISA = 15 – (2 × 24) = 15 – 48 = – 33°C; a temperature here of, say, –35°C (2°C cooler) is ISA – 2. A temperature of –26°C, which is 7°C warmer, is ISA+7.

Severe Weather Outlook Charts (AC)

The severe weather outlook chart is issued each morning and provides a **preliminary 24-hour outlook** for thunderstorm activity, tornados and watch areas. It is presented in two panels, the first for the time period 0000Z–1200Z, and the second for the period 1200Z–2400Z, and is used for advanced planning.

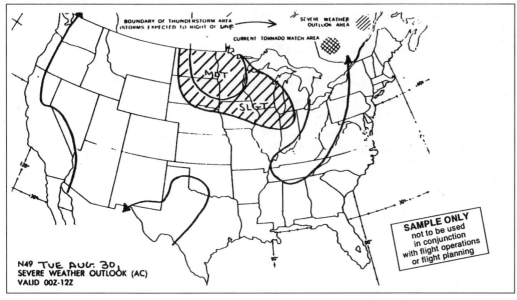

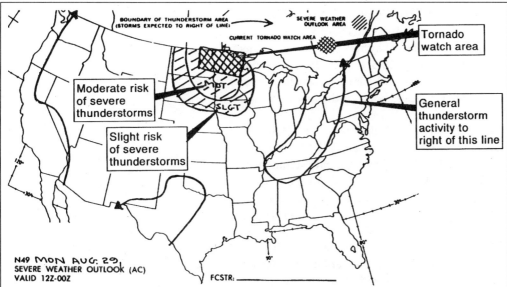

Figure 19-15. Example of a severe weather outlook chart

An area of forecast **general thunderstorm activity** is represented by a line with an arrowhead—when you face in the direction of the arrowhead, thunderstorm activity is expected to the right of that line.

Forecast **severe thunderstorms** are shown by a single-hatched area, which may be labeled SLGT (slight risk) or MDT (moderate risk). Any **tornado watches** in effect at chart time are shown by crosshatched areas.

Staying Informed in the Air

After receiving a briefing and taking off, you should remain aware that weather forecasts are just that—forecasts. They are scientific *estimates* of what the weather will be like at various times in the future. Forecasts can and do go wrong. Stay alert to what you see as you fly. There is no real excuse for being caught by unforecast weather changes.

If the weather shows any signs of turning out to be worse than you and your airplane are prepared to deal with, then you must devise an alternative plan of action. You may have to land short of your destination or divert to an alternate airport and wait out the weather.

The **en route flight advisory service (EFAS)** on 122.0 MHz—callsign "Flight Watch"—is the best source of weather information en route. Call Flight Watch (between 0600 and 2200 local time) with your aircraft identification and the name of the nearest VOR. This puts you in contact with someone at a Flight Service Station with immediate access to the latest weather, including "live" weather radar. You can normally expect to receive actual weather and thunderstorm activity along your proposed route from Flight Watch, but not complete weather briefings. Actual destination weather and the terminal forecast will be provided on request.

Flight Watch—122.0 MHz (0600–2200 local time)

To assist the EFAS specialists and other pilots, you are encouraged to report good as well as bad weather, and to confirm forecast conditions as well as unexpected conditions. Flight Watch is an information exchange frequency for pilots and weather briefers. FSSs that provide EFAS are listed on the inside rear cover of Airport/Facility Directory (A/FD) books.

Also, the NWS and FAA broadcast SIGMETs, **Convective SIGMETs,** and AIRMETs on navigation and air traffic control frequencies to warn pilots of weather that may not have been forecast when they received their weather briefings. Flight Service Stations broadcast SIGMETs and AIRMETs upon receipt, and at periodic intervals thereafter (see AIM para 7-9, which states at 15 minutes past the hour and 45 minutes past the hour for the first hour after issuance).

Continuous in-flight weather advisories are broadcast by HIWAS—the hazardous in-flight weather advisory service—on certain VORs (shown on aeronautical charts and in the A/FD). HIWAS messages include summarized SIGMETs, AIRMETs and PIREPs. A HIWAS *alert* (advice to monitor the actual HIWAS message on the VOR frequency) will be broadcast on all communications frequencies in the area, except emergency frequencies (such as 121.5 MHz).

Transcribed Weather Broadcasts (TWEB)—continuous broadcasts of tape-recorded weather and NOTAM information on certain NDBs and VORs—is generally oriented toward a particular route. FSS will transcribe any important new data onto the tape periodically, making TWEB a very useful source of current data. Stations carrying TWEB are specified on aeronautical charts. Some TWEB broadcasts are also accessible by telephone, with the telephone numbers (TEL-TWEB) listed in the A/FD. TWEBs are made available for preflight and in-flight planning, but are not substitutes for specialist-provided preflight briefings.

Airport Weather Broadcasts

- The **automatic terminal information service (ATIS)** is a continuous broadcast of recorded noncontrol information at certain airports containing weather information, runway in use and other pertinent remarks. ATIS broadcasts are updated upon the receipt of any official weather, regardless of content change and reported value. The ATIS may be broadcast on a discrete VHF frequency (requiring you to listen using a VHF-COM radio). ATIS frequencies are published on instrument charts and in the A/FD, which also includes their hours of operation. For example, Yakima Air Terminal ATIS operates between 1400–0600Z‡. Time conversion is GMT –8 (–7 DT), making the hours 0600–2200 local standard time.

Note: The ‡ symbol indicates that the same local times apply when daylight saving time (DT) is in effect—that is, still 0600–2200 local time.

Weather at many airports is reported by automated weather observing equipment:

- **AWOS** (automated weather observing system) which transmits data over a COM or navaid frequency at the airport (see A/FD);
   - AWOS-A reports altimeter setting;
   - AWOS-1 reports altimeter setting, wind data and usually temperature, dewpoint and density altitude;
   - AWOS-2 reports the same as AWOS-1 plus visibility;
   - AWOS-3 reports the same as AWOS-1 plus visibility and cloud/ceiling data.

- **ASOS** (automated surface observing system) which reports the same as AWOS-3 plus precipitation (type and intensity) and freezing rain occurrence (a future enhancement); ASOS is a more sophisticated and newer system than AWOS and as well as being transmitted on radio frequencies, the observations feed into the weather observation system, METAR reports, which are appended with *A02A* (facility attended) and *A02* (facility unattended) immediately after the report time, as well as the ATIS at the airport.

Note: Automated observing equipment has fixed sampling paths, and unlike a human observer who can take into account variations that are evident, the automated equipment may observe readings of, say, cloud base and visibility which are significantly different (better or worse) than what an arriving pilot may encounter at the end of an instrument approach to the airfield.

✍ Now complete **Review 19, Part (e)** on page 422.

For Aspiring Commercial Pilots

Constant Pressure Analysis Charts

A constant pressure analysis chart shows weather data at a particular *pressure level* in the atmosphere, rather than at a particular *altitude*. They are useful for determining **winds** and **temperatures** aloft. The upper air measurements are usually taken by radiosonde instruments carried aloft by balloon, with the information then radioed back to the ground station.

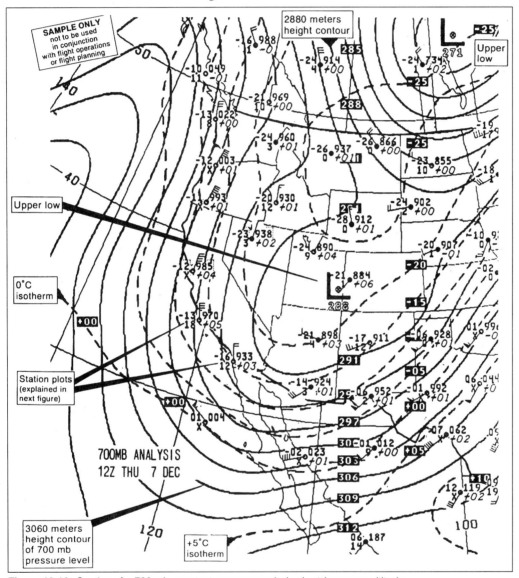

Figure 19-16. Section of a 700 mb constant pressure analysis chart (pressure altitude 10,000 feet)

In contrast to constant pressure charts, **surface charts,** with which you are already familiar, are based on a constant altitude, with pressure variations being plotted. They show *isobars,* lines joining points of equal pressure, and allow you to estimate the wind direction and strength near that level, based on the weather pattern (highs and lows) and the closeness of the isobars. The wind flows clockwise around a high pressure system in the Northern Hemisphere, above the friction layer (more than about 2,000 feet AGL), and counterclockwise around a low pressure system. The closer the isobars, the stronger the wind.

At *upper* levels in the atmosphere, however, the lower air density causes the relationship between the isobars and the wind to alter, and *constant pressure* charts become more useful than *constant altitude* charts. They are just a different means of plotting the same data to better describe the same weather situation. The pressure systems in the upper levels may differ from those shown on surface charts, and often they have more bearing on the actual flying weather.

The various constant pressure charts relate to approximate altitudes MSL:
- 850 mb and 5,000 feet MSL—this chart is good for forecasting poor weather which often occurs in the lower levels, such as heavy clouds, thunderstorms, rain, snow, overcast, and fronts;
- 700 mb and 10,000 feet MSL;
- 500 mb and 18,000 feet MSL;
- 300 mb and 30,000 feet MSL;
- 200 mb and 39,000 feet MSL.

If you plan to cruise at 10,000 feet MSL, you should look at the 700 mb chart. The 700 millibar pressure level, which is equivalent to about 10,000 feet pressure altitude in the standard atmosphere, will vary in its MSL height in any real atmosphere. By plotting contour lines showing the altitudes at which the specified pressure level is found, 700 mb in this case, an upper air picture of pressure distribution is formed, in exactly the same way that variations in *height* are shown by contours on a land-survey map.

Plotted at each reporting station, at the level of the specified pressure, are:
- the height of that pressure surface (in meters);
- changes in this height over the past 12 hours;
- temperature;
- temperature/dewpoint spread (useful in determining cloud formation); and
- wind direction and speed.

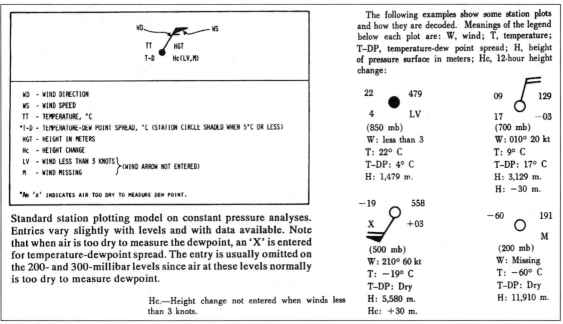

Figure 19-17. A station model

Height contours—join places where the pressure level is at equal heights MSL, and these *height pattern contours* depict highs, lows, troughs and ridges in the upper atmosphere in a similar way to isobars on the surface charts. A *high height center* on a 700 mb constant pressure chart is analogous to a *high pressure center* at about 10,000 feet. Winds will parallel the contours, flowing clockwise around a *high* height center in the northern hemisphere and counter-clockwise around a *low*. Fronts, if they reach as high as the specified pressure level, are depicted in the normal manner.

Isotherms—dashed lines joining places of equal temperature—allow you to determine if you are flying toward warmer or cooler air. Temperatures near to and below freezing, and a temperature/dewpoint spread of 5°C or less, indicate a risk of structural icing.

Isotachs—lines joining places of equal wind strength, are shown as short, dashed lines—with strong wind areas indicated by *hatching*. Areas with winds of 70–110 knots are hatched; this area may include a clear area of stronger winds from 110–150 knots, and perhaps containing another hatched area of even stronger winds.

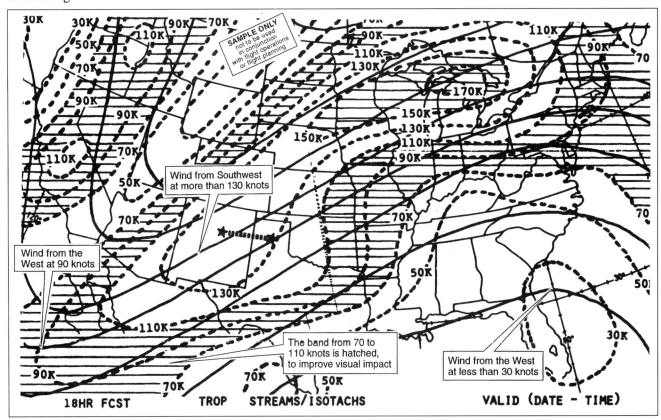

Figure 19-18. Extract from a chart showing isotachs (tropopause wind prog chart)

If the constant pressure surface is high, then it has warm air beneath it. A consequence of this is that a parcel of warm air will not tend to rise through the already warm air, and so the weather in the vicinity of a *warm upper high* is likely to be typical of a high pressure system—good, although with a possibility of restricted visibility.

Conversely, if the constant pressure surface is low, then it has cool air beneath it. A parcel of warm air that starts to rise from the surface will tend to keep rising through the cooler air, an unstable situation, and so a *cold upper low* is an indicator of possible unstable conditions and poor flying weather.

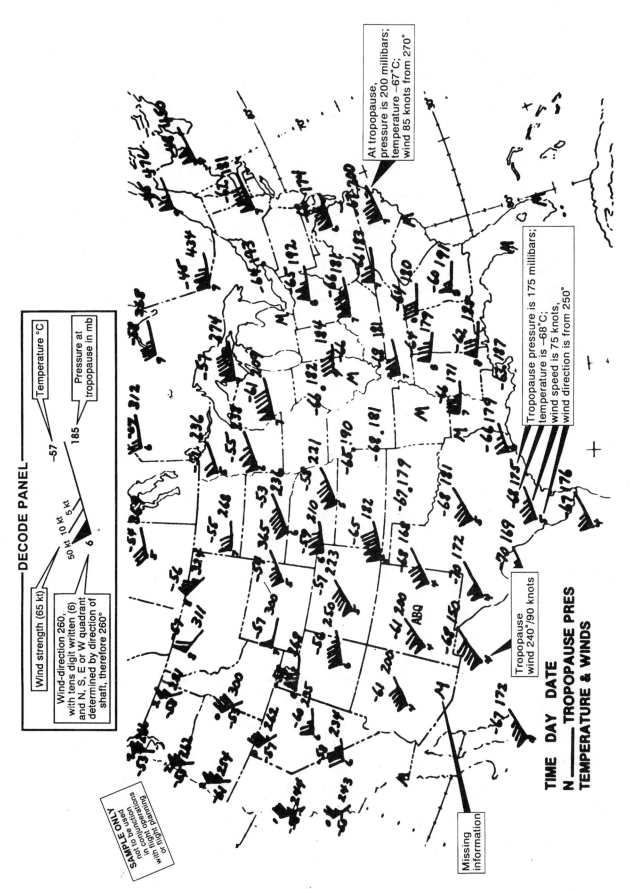

Figure 19-19. Extract of observed tropopause pressure, temperature and winds panel

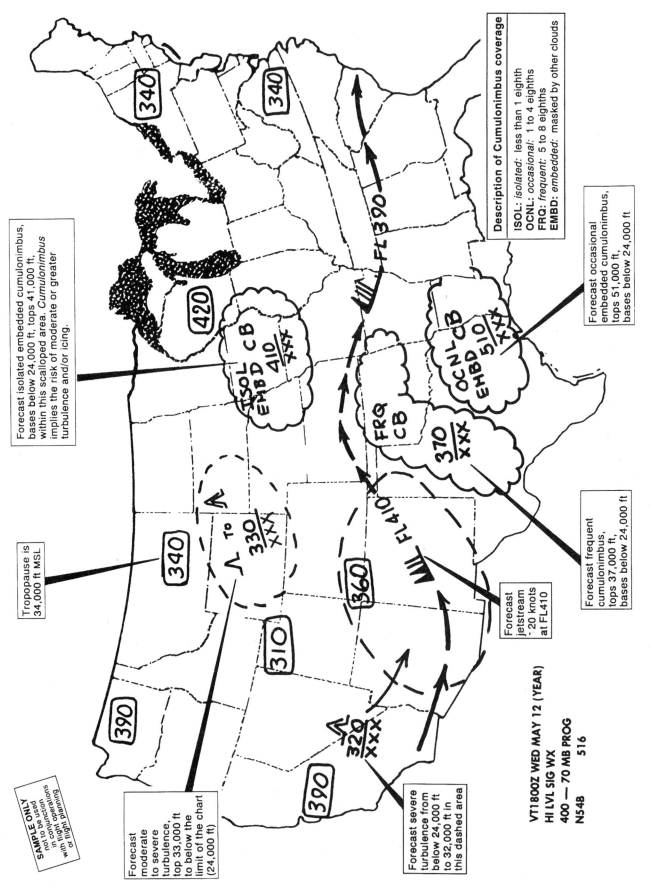

Figure 19-20. Example of a high-level significant weather prognosis chart

The following labels appear within the figure:

Forecast isolated embedded cumulonimbus, bases below 24,000 ft, tops 41,000 ft, within this scalloped area. *Cumulonimbus* implies the risk of moderate or greater turbulence and/or icing.

Tropopause is 34,000 ft MSL

SAMPLE ONLY not to be used in conjunction with flight planning

Forecast moderate to severe turbulence, top 33,000 ft to below the limit of the chart (24,000 ft)

Forecast severe turbulence from below 24,000 ft to 32,000 ft in this dashed area

Forecast jetstream – 20 knots at FL410

Forecast frequent cumulonimbus, tops 37,000 ft, bases below 24,000 ft

Forecast occasional embedded cumulonimbus, tops 51,000 ft, bases below 24,000 ft

Description of Cumulonimbus coverage

ISOL: *isolated:* less than 1 eighth
OCNL: *occasional:* 1 to 4 eighths
FRQ: *frequent:* 5 to 8 eighths
EMBD: *embedded:* masked by other clouds

VT1800Z WED MAY 12 (YEAR)
HI LVL SIG WX
400 — 70 MB PROG
N54B   516

Chart values: 340, 340, 420, ISOL CB EMBD 410/XXX, FL390, OCNL CB EMBD 510/XXX, FRQ CB 370/XXX, 340, A TO 330/XXX, FL410, 360, 310, 320/XXX, 390, 390

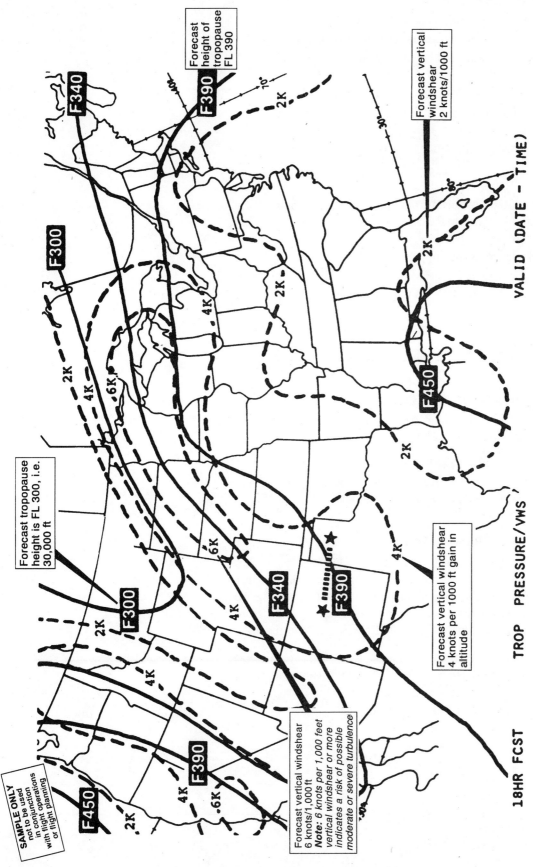

Figure 19-21. Extract of tropopause height/vertical windshear prognosis panel

Tropopause Data Charts

The tropopause data chart has various panels which show:

- the observed winds, pressures and temperatures at the tropopause;
- a prognosis (forecast) for high-level significant weather and maximum winds;
- a prognosis for *tropopause height/vertical windshear;* and
- observed winds aloft for 34,000 feet (250 mb).

Other Weather Information

RADAT

Sometimes **freezing level data,** obtained from upper air (rawinsonde) observation stations and codified by the term RADAT**,** is provided in surface aviation weather reports. It includes:

- relative humidity at the freezing level in percent; and
- the height (in hundreds of feet above mean sea level) at which the upper air sounding passed through the 0°C isotherm (the freezing level).

Example 7.

RADAT 86 0 55

This decodes as: relative humidity 86% at the freezing level, and the freezing level was passed at 5,500 feet MSL.

Composite Moisture Stability Chart

The composite moisture stability chart has one panel which is an analysis of observed freezing level data from upper air observations.

Radar Weather Reports (SD)

Sometimes radar weather reports are available indicating the position and intensity of thunderstorm cells detected by a radar station.

Example 8.

DFW 1735 LN 7TRW++/+ 75/30 160/50 170/110 12W C2520 MT470 AT 140/45

This decodes as: Dallas–Fort Worth at 1735Z, a line of very heavy thunderstorms, increasing in intensity and covering $7/10$ of the sky, in the area defined by the 075° bearing, 30 nautical miles (nm); the 160° bearing, 50 nm; the 170° bearing, 110 nm; a 12 nm wide band of cells moving from 250° at 20 knots; maximum tops (MT) 47,000 feet located on the 140° bearing at 45 nm.

✍ Commercial students complete **Review 19, Commercial** on page 426.

✍ Review 19

Part (a)

1. Weather reports and forecasts are usually obtained from a _____ , but may also be obtained from a _____ office.

➤ Flight Service Station (FSS), National Weather Service Office (WSO)

2. The number to call for a telephone weather briefing in most of the United States is _____ .

➤ 1 800 WX BRIEF

3. Weather reports and forecasts may be obtained by personal computer. (True/False)?

➤ true

4. The government book with information about weather reports and forecasts is _____ .

➤ Aviation Weather Services (FAA Advisory Circular AC 00-45)

5. A brief statement explaining the causes of the weather is called a _____ .

➤ synopsis

6. A weather briefing that is provided when the information requested is 6 or more hours in advance of the proposed departure time is:
   (a) an outlook briefing.
   (b) a forecast briefing.
   (c) a prognostic briefing.

➤ (a)

7. When you are in the air, you may receive weather updates by calling _____ on frequency _____ .

➤ Flight Watch, 122.0 MHz

Weather Reports and Forecasts

8. What information should you give a weather briefer?

➤ The fact that you are a pilot; VFR or IFR; N-number of aircraft; aircraft type; departure point; the route; destinations; en route altitude; time of departure; time en route

9. Which type weather briefing should a pilot request, when departing within the hour, if no preliminary weather information has been received?
   (a) An outlook briefing.
   (b) An abbreviated briefing.
   (c) A standard briefing.

➤ (c)

10. Which type of weather briefing should a pilot request to supplement mass disseminated data?
    (a) An outlook briefing.
    (b) A supplemental briefing.
    (c) An abbreviated briefing.

➤ (c)

Part (b)

1. The weather depiction chart is a weather (report/forecast).

➤ report

2. Of what value is the Weather Depiction Chart to the pilot?
   (a) For determining general weather conditions on which to base flight planning.
   (b) For a forecast of cloud coverage, visibilities, and frontal activity.
   (c) For determining frontal trends and air mass characteristics.

➤ (a)

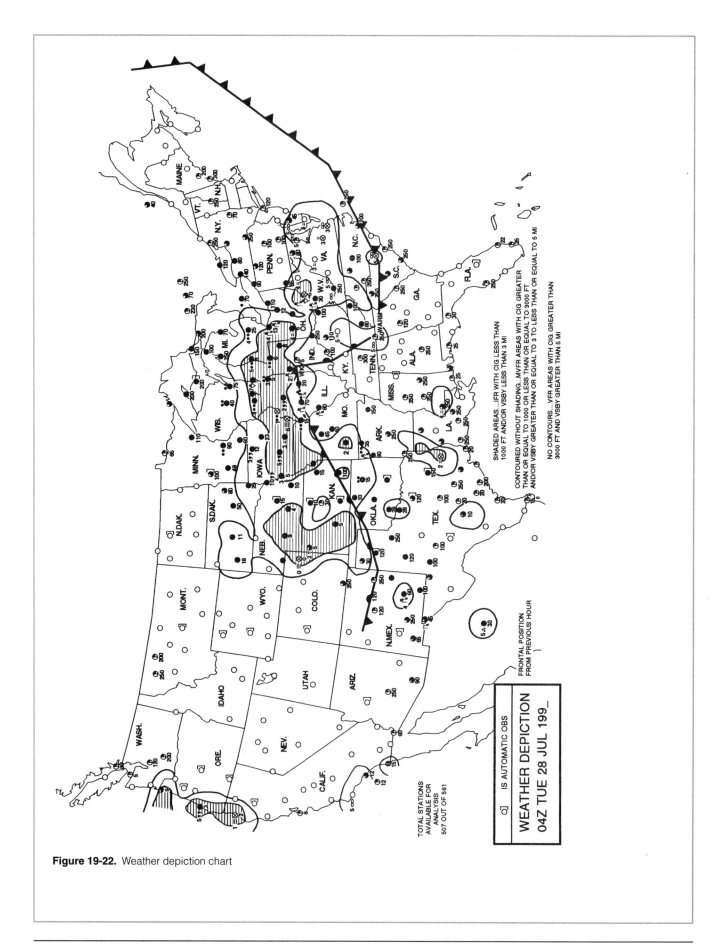

Figure 19-22. Weather depiction chart

For Questions 3–7 refer to Figure 19-22.

3. The ceiling in southeast New Mexico in the contoured area without shading is _____ feet and the sky (is/is not) overcast. There (are/are not) thunderstorms, and the visibility is _____ miles. Conditions are (IFR/MVFR/VFR).

➤ 6,000 feet, is, are, 4, MVFR

4. The front extending from New Mexico to Indiana is a (stationary/warm/cold/occluded) front.

➤ stationary

5. The IFR weather in eastern Texas is due to:
   (a) intermittent rain.
   (b) fog.
   (c) dust devils.

➤ (b)

6. The IFR conditions along the coast of Oregon and California is caused by low ceilings of _____ feet with _____ and _____ .

➤ 300 feet, fog and drizzle

7. The weather for a flight from Arkansas to southeast Alabama will have broken to scattered clouds at _____ feet.

➤ 25,000 feet

8. The surface weather chart shows the position of pressure systems and fronts at (ground level/10,000 feet/30,000 feet) at (chart valid time/some specific time in the future).

➤ ground level, chart valid time

9. The surface weather chart is also known as the _____. Which of the following does it show? Surface winds; temperatures; dewpoints; obstructions to vision; the position of fronts; the movement of fronts; total sky cover; cloud ceilings and tops.

➤ surface analysis chart, it shows all except the *movement* of fronts and cloud ceilings and tops

10. The radar summary chart is:
    (a) a forecast of thunderstorm location.
    (b) a report of where precipitation was located at the chart's valid time.
    (c) a report of areas of heavy air traffic.

➤ (b)

11. The radar summary chart is a good source of information on areas of fog and low clouds (true/false)?

➤ false

12. Radar can detect (precipitation/clouds/ice).

➤ precipitation

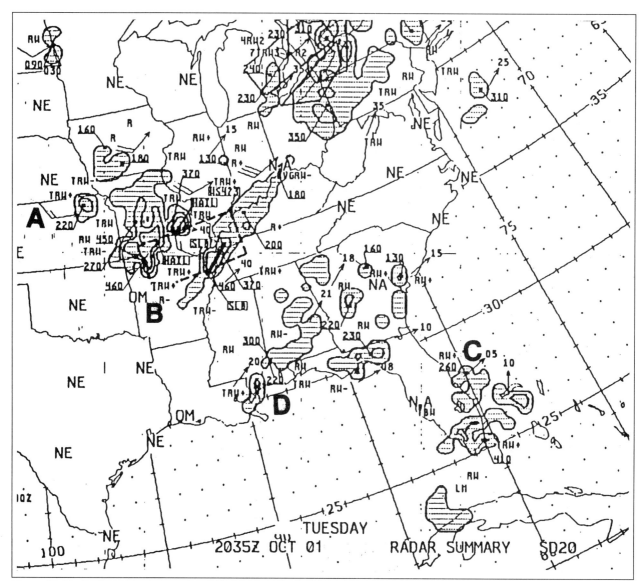

Figure 19-23. Radar summary chart

For Questions 13–17 refer to Figure 19-23.

13. What is the direction and speed or movement of the radar return at Area D?

    (a) Southeast at 30 knots.

    (b) Northeast at 20 knots.

    (c) West at 30 knots.

➤   (b)

14. What is the direction and speed of movement of the radar return at Area A?

    (a) 020° at 20 knots.

    (b) East at 15 knots.

    (c) Northeast at 22 knots.

➤   (b) (one barb partially obscured by the A)

15. What does the dashed line at Area B enclose?

    (a) Areas of heavy rain.

    (b) Severe weather watch area.

    (c) Areas of hail ¼ inch in diameter.

➤   (b)

16. In Area C, the symbol 'RW+' indicates _____ .

➤   rain showers increasing in intensity

17. The highest cloud tops in the vicinity of Area D are at_____ feet.

➤   30,000 feet

Part (c)

1. A normal scheduled hourly weather observation that forms a surface aviation weather report is symbolized by the letters (METAR/SA/SP/SR/RS).

   ➤ METAR

2. A special unscheduled weather observation that forms a surface aviation weather report, and shows a significant weather change, is symbolized by the letters _____ .

   ➤ SPECI

3. Routine aviation weather reports are (observations/forecasts) that are normally made _____ (how often).

   ➤ observations, hourly

4. Translate this routine aviation report from Great Falls, Montana (KGFT):
   SPECI KGFT 251750Z 28004 4SM BKN010 OVC015 10/09 A2989 RMKS VIRGA VC

   ➤ Record special on the 25th day of the month at 1750Z; winds from 280 degrees true at 4 knots; 4 miles visibility; 1,000 feet broken clouds; an overcast layer at 1,500 feet; 10°C temperature, 09°C dewpoint; altimeter setting 29.89; virga (precipitation that evaporates before reaching the ground) seen in the vicinity.

For Questions 5–8 refer to Figure 19-24.

5. The turbulence reported by the pilot in this PIREP is of _____ intensity from _____ feet MSL to _____ feet MSL.

   ➤ moderate, 5,500 feet MSL to 7,200 feet MSL

6. Describe the report of icing in this PIREP in terms of intensity, type and altitude band.

   ➤ light to moderate, clear ice, from 7,200 feet MSL to 8,900 feet MSL

7. This PIREP was made at what time and altitude, and from what type of aircraft? What wind did the pilot report at that altitude, and what temperature?

   ➤ 1800Z, 12,000 feet, BE 90, 090°T/21 knots, –9°C

8. If the terrain elevation is 1,295 feet MSL, what is the height above ground level of the base of the ceiling?
   (a) 505 feet AGL.
   (b) 1,295 feet AGL.
   (c) 6,586 feet AGL.

   ➤ (a)

UA /OV OKC–TUL /TM 1800 /FL 120 /TP BE90 /SK 018 BKN 055 / /072 OVC 089 /CLR ABV /TA –9/WV 0921/TB MDT 055–072 /IC LGT–MDT CLR 072–089.

Figure 19-24.

```
INK SA 1854 CLR 15 106/77/63/1112G18/000
BOI SA 1854 150 SCT 30 181/62/42/1304/015
LAX SA 1852 7 SCT 250 SCT 6HK 129/60/59/2504/991
MDW RS 1856 –X M7 OVC 11/2R+F 990/63/61/3205/980/RF2 RB12
JFK RS 1853 W5 X 1/2F 180/68/64/1804/006/R04RVR22V30 TWR VSBY 1/4
```

Figure 19-25. Surface aviation weather report

9. Decode the METAR report for Boise, Indiana (KBOI). "METAR KBOI 041854Z 13004 30SM SCT150 16/09 A3015 RMK SLP181." Are the conditions VFR or IFR?

➤ METAR for KBOI, taken on the 4th day of the month at 1854Z, wind 130°T/4 knots, visibility 30 miles, 15,000 feet base of scattered clouds, temperature 16°C, dewpoint 09°C, altimeter setting 30.15 in. Hg, Remarks: sea level pressure 1018.1 hectopascals. Definitely VFR conditions.

10. Decode the METAR report for Amarillo, Texas (KAMA). "METAR KAMA 041453Z 14007KT M1/4SM FZFG OVC001 M03/M03 A2998 RMK A02 SLP164 T10281033." Are the conditions VFR or IFR?

➤ Aviation routine weather report for Amarillo, the 4th day of the month at 1453Z. Wind from 140 degrees at 7 knots. Visibility measured one-quarter mile in freezing fog, ceiling of clouds 100 feet overcast. Temperature minus 03 degrees Celsius, dewpoint minus 03 degrees Celsius. Altimeter 29.98 in. Hg. Remarks: Automated system with precipitation detection, sea level pressure 1001.64 hectopascals, temperature 2.8 degrees Celsius, dewpoint 3.3 degrees Celsius. Conditions are definitely IFR.

11. The remarks section in a METAR has "RAB12" listed. This means:
    (a) Rain and fog have reduced visibility to 2 miles and rain began at 1812Z.
    (b) rain began at 12 minutes past the hour.
    (c) the barometer has risen 12 in. Hg.

➤ (b)

12. What are the current conditions depicted for Chicago Midway Airport (KMDW)?
    (a) Sky partially obscured, measured ceiling 700 overcast, visibility 1½, heavy rain, fog.
    (b) Thin overcast, measured 700 ceiling overcast, visibility 1½, heavy rain, fog.
    (c) Sky partially obscured, measured ceiling 700 overcast, visibility 11, occasionally 2, with rain and heavy fog.

➤ (a)

13. Altitudes for clouds in pilot reports are (MSL/AGL).
➤ MSL

14. Ceiling is defined as the height above the Earth's surface of the:
    (a) lower reported obscuration and the highest layer of clouds reported as overcast.
    (b) lowest layer of clouds or obscuring phenomena reported as broken, overcast, and not classified as thin or partial.
    (c) lowest layer of clouds reported as scattered, broken, or thin.

➤ (b)

15. Translate the following pilot report from Blythe, California (BLH):
    BLH UA /OV BLH080035/TM 2117/FL085/TP C172/ SK 050 SCT 090/TA 05/TB VERY LGT BLO 050

➤ PIREP at position BLH radial 080 and 35 DME at time 2117Z, 8,500 feet MSL, Cessna 172, scattered clouds bases 5,000 feet MSL and tops 9,000 feet MSL, temperature +5°C, very light turbulence below 5,000 feet MSL

Part (d)

1. A forecast of future weather is often called a (report/prog).
➤ prog

2. The chart that gives you an overall view of the weather forecast for particular times in the future is called the _____ .
➤ low-level significant weather prog chart

3. How are Significant Weather Prognostic Charts best used by a pilot?
    (a) For overall planning at all altitudes.
    (b) For determining areas to avoid (freezing levels and turbulence).
    (c) For analyzing current frontal activity and cloud coverage.

➤ (b)

4. How do you know what time the forecast shown in a particular panel of a low-level significant weather prog chart is for?
➤ VT—valid time—in the lower left corner of the chart

For Questions 5–10 refer to Figure 19-26.

```
OK FT 011447

GAG FT 011515 100 SCT 250 SCT 2610. 16Z 60 SCT C100 BKN 3315G22 CHC C50 BKN
   5TRW. 01Z 250 SCT 3515G25. 09Z VFR WIND..

HBR FT 011515 C120 BKN 250 BKN 3010. 17Z 100 SCT C250 BKN 3215G25 CHC C30 BKN
   3TRW. 00Z 250 SCT 3515G25. 09Z VFR WIND..

MLC FT 011515 C20 BKN 1815 BKN OCNL SCT. 20Z C30 BKN 1815G22 CHC C20 BKN
   1TRW. 03Z C30 BKN 2015 CHC C7 X 1/2TRW+G40. 09Z MVFR CIG TRW..

OKC FT 011515 C12 BKN 140 BKN 1815G28 LWR BKN V SCT. 18Z C30 BKN 250 BKN
   2315G25 LWR BKN OCNL SCT CHC C7 X 1/2TRW+G40. 21Z CFP 100 SCT C250 BKN
   3315G25 CHC C30 BKN 5TRW–. 02Z 100 SCT 250 SCT 3515G25. 09Z VFR WIND..

PNC FT 011515 C100 BKN 250 BKN 1810. 16Z CFP 20 SCT C100 BKN 3115 SCT V BKN. 00Z
   250 SCT 3515G25. 09Z VFR WIND..

TUL FT 011515 C20 BKN 1915G22. 19Z C30 BKN 1815G25 CHC 3TRW. 23Z CFP C100 BKN
   250 BKN 3215G25 CHC C30 BKN 5TRW. 09Z VFR WIND..
```

Figure 19-26.

5. Interpret the TAF forecast for KGAG: TAF KGAG 041135Z 041212 06008KT P6SM 0VC003 FM1500 08008KT P6SM 0VC006 BECMG 1618 BKN010 FM1900 10010KT P6SM BKN012 0VC250 TEMPO 2024 SCT012 0VC250 FM0000 11008KT P6SM BKN012 BKN100 PROB30 0412 5SM -RA 0VC010

➤   KGAG aerodrome forecast valid on 4th day of month from 1200Z until 1200Z the following day.
    Initial time period from 1200Z: wind from 60 degrees at 8 knots; visibility better than six miles; 300 ft. overcast cloud layer. From 1500Z: wind from 80 degrees at 8 knots; better than six miles visibility; ceiling of 600 ft. overcast clouds, becoming from 1600Z to 1800Z: broken clouds at 1000 ft. From 1900Z the wind shifts to 100 degrees at 10 knots, visibility better than six miles, with a ceiling of broken clouds at 1200 ft. and another overcast layer of clouds at 25,000 ft. Temporary conditions from 2000Z to 2400Z are a scattered layer of clouds at 1200 ft., an overcast layer of clouds at 25,000 ft. From 0000Z expect winds from 110 degrees at 8 knots and visibility better than six miles with broken clouds at 1200 ft. and 10,000 ft., with a probability of 30% that between 0400Z and 1200Z there will be 5 miles visibility in light rain with overcast clouds at 1000 ft.

6. What are the conditions for KTUL from 0200Z to 0000Z? FM0200 04025G35KT SKC

➤   VFR and windy

7. What are the weather conditions at KMLC expected to be from 1200Z to 1500Z? FM 1215 18010KT 3SM +TSRA OVC010 BKN030
    (a) Ceilings 2,000 to 3,000 feet with southerly winds.
    (b) Ceiling 700 feet, sky obscured, visibility ½ mile in thundershowers.
    (c) Ceilings 1,000 and 3,000 feet with thunderstorms and rain showers.

➤   (c)

8. According to the TAF for KOKC, the cold front should pass through: TAF KOKC 041135Z 041212 12008KT P6SM OVC008 TEMPO 1215 4SM BR OVC005 FM1500 23015G25KT 4SM RA OVC010 BKN100 PROB40 1SM TSRA FM2000 35020G35KT P6SM BKN250 FM0500 01010KT P6SM SKC.
    (a) between 1800Z and 2100Z.
    (b) by 2000Z.
    (c) after 0500Z.

➤   (b)

9. What wind conditions are expected at KOKC at 1600Z (see TAF in question 8)?

➤   230°T/15 knots gusting to 25 knots

10. What type conditions are forecast at KOKC from 1500Z to 2000Z (see TAF in question 8)?
    (a) MVFR and VFR.
    (b) MVFR, with chance of IFR.
    (c) VFR and IFR.

➤   (b) (ceiling 1,000 ft overcast with 4 miles visibility and rain, so MVFR; with a 40% probability of one mile visibility and thunderstorms with rain, so a chance of IFR)

For Questions 11–13 refer to the following forecast.

TAF KHVR 181818Z SCT003 BKN012 OVC030 –RA
BECMG 0306Z PROB40 OVC003 –RA. BECMG 2000Z
35008 BKN015 OVC030 OCNL –RA. BECMG OO03Z
32008 SCT015 BKN035 PROB40 –RA. 0310Z SCT035
TEMPO BKN035. BECMG 1012Z SCT010 1SM FG. BCMG
1215Z VV005 FG. FM 1500Z SKC.

11. You plan to arrive at Havre at noon MST on the first day of the forecast. What time in UTC is this? What is the ceiling forecast to be? Could it be lower?

➤ 1900Z; 1,200 feet; yes—300 feet (see page 523 for MST)

12. What time is fog forecast to form? When is it forecast to clear? Give both UTC and MST times.

➤ 1000 UTC or 3 a.m. MST to form; 1500 UTC or 8 a.m. MST to clear

13. What is the ceiling forecast to be at 3 p.m. MST on the forecast's first day? What is the wind forecast for this time? Is there a chance of rain forecast?

➤ 1500 broken; 350°T/8 knots; yes, 40 percent probability of light rain

For Questions 14–17 refer to Figure 19-27.

14. Interpret the weather symbol depicted in the southern California area on the 12-hr significant weather prognostic chart.

➤ moderate turbulence from the surface to 18,000 feet

15. The band of weather associated with the cold front in the western states is expected to move in a direction toward the _____ at a speed of _____ knots.

➤ east, 30 knots

16. What weather is forecast for the Gulf Coast area just ahead of the cold front during the first 12 hours?

➤ Marginal VFR (outlined by scalloped lines) with some areas of IFR (outlined by smooth lines) as shown in upper chart, and some associated thunderstorms and showers shown in lower chart.

17. At what altitude is the freezing level over northeastern Oklahoma, on the 24-hour Significant Weather Prognostic Chart?
   (a)   4,000 feet.
   (b)   8,000 feet.
   (c)   10,000 feet.

➤ (b)

18. What area around an airfield is a TAF forecast for?
   (a)   Only the area within the airport boundary.
   (b)   Within five miles of the airport center.
   (c)   Within 25 miles of the airport center.

➤ (b)

19. What ceiling and/or visibility would you expect if you saw MVFR in the outlook section of an area forecast?

➤ ceiling from 1000 to 3000 feet, visibility 3 to 5 miles

20. Altitudes given for ceilings in weather reports and forecasts are height above ground level (AGL) or height above mean sea level (MSL)?

➤ AGL

21. A forecast or report not routinely available at your FSS, WSO, or WSFO can be obtained using the _____ / _____ service.

➤ request/reply

22. An aerodrome forecast, symbolized by the letters _____ , is a forecast of weather expected within a radius of _____ miles of the airport center. If the term 'VC', which means _____ , is used, then the area referred to is from _____ miles to _____ miles from the airport.

➤ TAF, 5 miles, vicinity, 5 miles to 25 miles

23. Aerodrome forecasts are normally issued _____ times daily in the contiguous United States and are valid for _____ hours.

➤ 3 times daily, 24 hours

Part (e)

1. To best determine general forecast weather conditions over several states, the pilot should refer to:
   (a) area forecasts.
   (b) weather depiction charts.
   (c) satellite maps.

➤ (a)

2. What amount of time is covered in the main part of an area forecast? How much additional time is covered in the outlook part?

➤ 12 hours, 6 hours

3. Freezing levels and areas of probable icing aloft (are/are not) found in area forecasts.

➤ are

4. If your destination does not have a terminal forecast, a general idea of the weather can be obtained from the current _____ forecast.

➤ area forecast

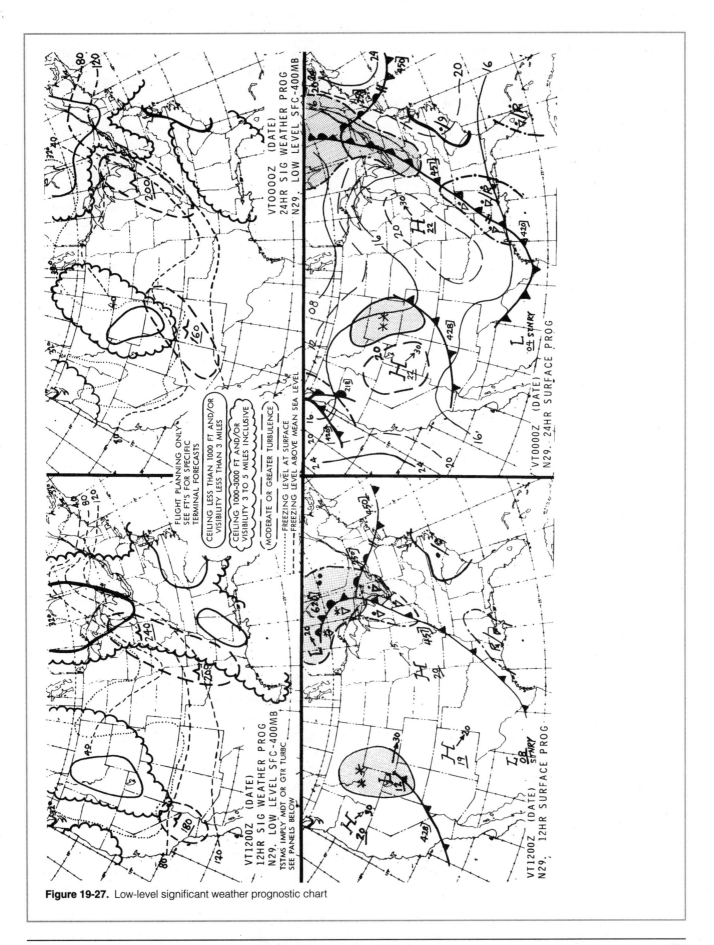

Figure 19-27. Low-level significant weather prognostic chart

For Questions 5–11 refer to Figure 19-28.

5. What hazards are forecast in the Area Forecast for TN, AL, and the coastal waters?
   (a) Thunderstorms with severe or greater turbulence, severe icing, and low-level wind shear.
   (b) Moderate rime icing above the freezing level to 10,000 feet.
   (c) Moderate turbulence from 25,000 to 38,000 feet due to the jetstream.

   ➤ (c)

6. What sky conditions and obstructions to vision are forecast for all of the area except Tennessee (TN) from 1040Z until 2300Z?

   ➤ 8,000 feet scattered to clear, except visibility below 3 miles in fog until 1500Z over south-central Texas

7. What is the forecast ceiling and visibility for Tennessee from 2300Z through 0500Z?
   (a) 500 feet to less than 1,000 feet, and 1 mile to less than 3 miles.
   (b) 1,000 to 3,000 feet, and 3 to 5 miles.
   (c) 3,000 feet or greater, and 5 miles or greater.

   ➤ (c) (since outlook is VFR)

8. A forecast similar to an area forecast but with the information contained in a route format is a (FA/METAR/TWEB/FT)

   ➤ TWEB (transcribed weather broadcast)

9. TWEBs may be broadcast on certain (FSS/NDB/NDB and VOR) frequencies.

   ➤ NDB and VOR

10. TWEBs are (continuous/periodic) broadcasts of tape-recorded w_____ and N_____ information.

   ➤ continuous, weather, NOTAM

11. How wide a corridor are TWEB forecasts valid for?

   ➤ 25 miles on either side of the route

For Questions 12–16 refer to Figure 19-29.

12. What wind and temperature aloft is forecast for KSTL at 18,000 feet?

   ➤ 230°T/56 knots, –16°C

13. What wind and temperature aloft is forecast for KDEN at 30,000 feet?

   ➤ 230°T/53 knots, –47°C

14. What wind and temperature aloft is forecast for KMKC at 3,000 feet?

   ➤ 050°T/7 knots, no temperatures forecast for 3,000 feet MSL or within 2,500 feet AGL

15. The winds and temperatures aloft forecast indicates that, although not indicated in the tabulated values, temperatures above _____ feet MSL are negative.

   ➤ 24,000 feet

16. The coded group for light and variable winds less than _____ knots in winds aloft forecast is _____ .

   ➤ 5 knots, 9900

17. AIRMETs are issued as a warning of weather conditions particularly hazardous to which aircraft?
   (a) Small single-engine aircraft.
   (b) Large multi-engine aircraft.
   (c) All aircraft.

   ➤ (a)

18. What information is contained in a convective SIGMET?
   (a) Tornados, embedded thunderstorms, and hail ¾ inch or greater in diameter.
   (b) Severe icing, severe turbulence, or widespread dust storms lowering visibility to less than 3 miles.
   (c) Surface winds greater than 40 knots or thunderstorms equal to or greater than video integrator processor (VIP) level 4.

   ➤ (a)

19. What is indicated when a current convective SIGMET forecasts thunderstorms?
   (a) Moderate thunderstorms covering 30 percent of the area.
   (b) Moderate or severe turbulence.
   (c) Thunderstorms obscured by massive cloud layers.

   ➤ (c)

20. A SIGMET warns of weather that could be dangerous to any aircraft. (true/false)?

   ➤ true

21. Flight Watch is an FSS weather advisory service that may be contacted on frequency _____ MHz for information regarding actual weather and thunderstorm activity along the proposed route.

   ➤ 122.0 MHz

```
DFWH FA Ø41Ø4Ø
HAZARDS VALID UNTIL Ø423ØØ
OK TX AR LA TN MS AL AND CSTL WTRS
FLT PRCTNS. . .TURBC. . .TN AL AND CSTL WTRS
                . . .ICG. . .TN
                . . .IFR. . .TX
TSTMS IMPLY PSBL SVR OR GTR TURBC SVR ICG AND LLWS
NON MSL HGTS NOTED BY AGL OR CIG
THIS FA ISSUANCE INCORPORATES THE FOLLOWING AIRMETS STILL IN
EFFECT. . .NONE.

DFWS FA Ø41Ø4Ø
SYNOPSIS VALID UNTIL Ø5Ø5ØØ
AT 11Z RDG OF HI PRES ERN TX NWWD TO CNTRL CO WITH HI CNTR
OVR ERN TX.  BY Ø5Z HI CNTR MOVS TO CNTRL LA.

DFWI FA Ø41Ø4Ø
ICING AND FRZLVL VALID UNTIL Ø423ØØ
TN
FROM SLK TO HAT TO MEM TO ORD TO SLK
OCNL MDT RIME ICGIC ABV FRZLVL TO 1ØØ. CONDS ENDING BY 17Z.
FRZLVL 8Ø CHA SGF LINE SLPG TO 12Ø S OF A IAH MAF LINE.

DFWT FA Ø41Ø4Ø
TURBC VALID UNTIL Ø423ØØ
TN AL AND CSTL WTRS
FROM SLK TO FLO TO 9ØS MOB TO MEI TO BUF TO SLK
OCNL MDT TURBC 25Ø-38Ø DUE TO JTSTR. CONDS MOVG SLOLY EWD
AND CONTG BYD 23Z.

DFWC FA O41Ø4Ø
SGFNT CLOUD AND WX VALID UNTIL Ø423ØØ. . . OTLK Ø423ØØ-Ø5Ø5ØØ
IFR. . .TX
FROM SAT TO PSX TO BRO TO MOB TO SAT
VSBY BLO 3F TIL 15Z.
OK AR TX LA MS AL AND CSTL WTRS
8Ø SCT TO CLR EXCP VSBY BLO 3F TIL 15Z OVR PTNS S CNTRL TX.
OTLK. . .VFR.
TN
CIGS 3Ø-5Ø BKN 1ØØ VSBYS OCNLY 3-5F BCMG AGL 4Ø-5Ø SCT TO
CLR BY 19Z. OTLK. . .VFR.
```

Figure 19-28. Area forecast (old style)

```
FD WBC 151745
BASED ON 151200Z DATA
VALID 1600Z FOR USE 1800-0300Z.  TEMPS NEG ABV 24000
```

FT	3000	6000	9000	12000	18000	24000	30000	34000	39000
ALS			2420	2635–08	2535–18	2444–30	245945	246755	246862
AMA		2714	2725+00	2625–04	2531–15	2542–27	265842	256352	256762
DEN			2321–04	2532–08	2434–19	2441–31	235347	236056	236262
HLC		1707–01	2113–03	2219–07	2330–17	2435–30	244145	244854	245561
MKC	0507	2006+03	2215–01	2322–06	2338–17	2348–29	236143	237252	238160
STL	2113	2325+07	2332+02	2339–04	2356–16	2373–27	239440	730649	731960

Figure 19-29.

Commercial Review

1. In area forecasts (FA) what method is used to describe the location of each icing phenomenon?
   (a) VOR points outline the affected area(s) within the designated FA boundary, but not beyond the FA boundary.
   (b) State names and portions of states, such as northwest and south central, are used to outline each affected area.
   (c) VOR points are used to outline the area of icing, including VOR points outside the designated FA boundary, if necessary.

   ➤ (c)

2. Area forecasts are prepared _____ times a day, and consist of a _____-hour forecast period followed by a _____-hour outlook.

   ➤ 3, 12, 6

3. What reference available in flight contains information similar to an area forecast, except that it is presented in a route format?

   ➤ TWEB

4. What is the upper limit of the Low Level Significant Weather Prognostic Chart?
   (a) 30,000 feet.
   (b) 24,000 feet.
   (c) 18,000 feet.

   ➤ (b)

5. Hachuring (hatching) on a Constant Pressure Analysis Chart indicates:
   (a) a hurricane eye.
   (b) wind speed 70 knots to 110 knots.
   (c) wind speed 110 knots to 150 knots.

   ➤ (b)

6. Can you derive winds and temperatures aloft from a constant pressure chart?

   ➤ yes

7. What weather is implied on a 'HI LVL SIG WX PROG' chart in an area enclosed by small scalloped lines?

   ➤ cumulonimbus clouds, and the associated icing and moderate or greater turbulence

8. The chart that provides a ready means of locating observed frontal positions and pressure centers is the _____ chart.

   ➤ surface analysis chart

9. On a Surface Analysis Chart, the solid lines that depict sea level pressure patterns are called:
   (a) isobars.
   (b) isogonals.
   (c) millibars.

   ➤ (a)

10. The station originating the following METAR report has a field elevation of 3,500 feet MSL. If the sky cover is one continuous layer, what is its thickness?
    OVC005 OVC075 1/2SM HZ 15/14 A3000

    ➤ 3,500 feet thick
    (base MSL = elev. 3,500 + ceiling 500 = 4,000 ft MSL tops MSL = 7,500 ft MSL; therefore thickness = tops 7,500 ft MSL—base 4,000 ft MSL = 3,500 ft)

11. Describe the cloud coverage reported by a pilot in the following UA:
    UA/OV15NW MOB 1355/SK OVC 025/045 OVC 090

    ➤ The pilot reports the sky as overcast with the top of the lower overcast layer at 2,500 feet MSL, and a second overcast layer with base at 4,500 feet MSL and tops at 9,000 feet MSL.

12. The best means of determining observed weather conditions between weather reporting stations is (PIREPs/AIRMETs/FAs/TAF).

    ➤ PIREPs

13. The visibility entry of P6SM in a TAF specifically implies that the surface visibility is expected to be more than _____ miles.

    ➤ 6 miles

14. Aerodrome forecasts are issued _____ times daily, and are valid for _____ hours.

    ➤ 3 times daily, 24 hours

15. What does 'MT 460 AT 140/55' mean in a RAREP (radar weather report)?

    ➤ maximum tops of thunderstorm cells is 46,000 feet, located on a bearing of 140°M from the station at 55 nm

16. The remarks section of the hourly aviation weather report contains the following coded information: 'RADAT 87045'.
    What is the meaning of this information?
    (a) Radar echoes with tops at 45,000 feet were observed on the 087 radial of the VORTAC.
    (b) A pilot reported thunderstorms 87 DME miles distance on the 045 radial of the VORTAC.
    (c) Relative humidity was 87% and the freezing level (0°C) was at 4,500 feet MSL.

    ➤ (c)

Flight Operations Section Five

Regulations 20

Introduction

The Code of Federal Regulations 14 (14 CFR) is designed to regulate aviation and to keep flying safe and efficient. This chapter is a sample of paraphrased and abbreviated regulations relevant to private and commercial pilots. As a responsible pilot you should have in your personal library a copy of the current 14 CFR and the Aeronautical Information Manual (AIM), obtainable from the FAA and most pilot shops. These are the official documents on which aviation is based and they are updated continuously. Study these documents in conjunction with this chapter.

You can tackle the review questions piece-by-piece as you work your way through this chapter but, just prior to taking the FAA Knowledge Exam, it is a good idea to complete the review once more from start to finish.

Definitions and Abbreviations

To ensure that all aviators speak the same technical language it is necessary to define certain terms, such as aircraft, night and operator. Part 1.1 is the place to find the legal definitions of aviation terminology.

Many commonly used aviation terms, such as *above ground level,* or *instrument landing system,* are abbreviated. Part 1.2 defines these abbreviations.

Some useful definitions from Part 1.1 include:

- **Night** is the time from the end of evening civil twilight through the hours of darkness until the beginning of morning civil twilight. As you know, darkness does not descend immediately at sunset, but rather after it following a period of twilight. Similarly, there is a period of twilight in the morning before the sun can actually be seen.

- An **Air traffic clearance** means an authorization by Air Traffic Control (ATC), for the purpose of preventing collision between known aircraft, to proceed under specified traffic conditions in Class A, B, C, D or E airspace.

Some other definitions (not necessarily found in Part 1.1) include:

- An **Authorized Instructor** is an instructor who has a valid ground instructor certificate or current flight instructor certificate with appropriate ratings issued by the Administrator, or any other person authorized by the Administrator to give instruction.

- An **airplane flight simulator** is a device that is a full-sized airplane cockpit replica of a specific type of airplane, or make, model, and series of airplane. It includes the hardware and software necessary to represent the airplane in ground and flight operations, including a force cueing system (motion sensations) and a visual cueing system. The simulator must be evaluated, qualified and approved by the Administrator.

- A **flight training device** is a full-sized replica of instruments, equipment, panels and controls of an airplane or rotorcraft in an open flight deck area or an enclosed cockpit. It includes the hardware and software necessary to simulate the airplane or rotorcraft in ground and flight operations, but it does not have a force cueing system or a visual cueing system. It must be evaluated, qualified and approved by the Administrator.

- A **PCATD** is a flight training device that combines a personal computer and flight simulation software, along with appropriate hardware necessary to simulate an airplane in ground and flight operations. Some visual cues may be available, although no force cues are necessary. PCATDs may be used in lieu of, and for not more than, 10 hours of time that ordinarily may be acquired in a flight simulator or flight training device authorized for use under Part 61 or Part 141 towards an initial instrument rating. However, the FAA has not authorized the use of PCATDs for conducting practical tests nor for accomplishing recency of experience requirements. The device must be approved by the Administrator.

If you intend to log simulator or flight training device time as part of the time required for a certificate or rating, or as time required for maintaining your currency and proficiency, be sure you do so on a piece of equipment that has been approved by the Administrator.

Pilot Qualifications

Category and *class* are two terms that you will often hear, but they have different meanings depending on whether they are being used in reference to airmen (pilot certificates, ratings, privileges, and limitations), or in reference to the certification of aircraft.

Category, when used for *pilot* qualification purposes (certification of airmen), is a broad classification of aircraft into families such as:

- airplane (fixed-wing and heavier-than-air);
- rotorcraft (heavier-than-air and supported by rotor-generated lift—for example, helicopters and gyroplanes);
- glider (heavier-than-air and not depending on an engine);
- lighter-than-air (airships and balloons supported by a gas weighing less than air); and
- powered-lift (such as a tilt rotor).

Class, when used for *pilot* qualification purposes, is a further classification of aircraft within a category having similar operating characteristics. Examples of *airplane* class ratings (Part 61.5) that may be earned and placed on a pilot certificate are:

- single-engine land (SEL);
- multi-engine land (MEL);
- single-engine sea (SES); and
- multi-engine sea (MES).

Your pilot qualifications will be
- **category—airplane**
- **class—single-engine land (SEL).**

Aircraft Certification

Category, when used for *aircraft* certification purposes, is a grouping of aircraft based on **intended use** or **operating limitations,** such as:

- transport;
- normal (all maneuvers except aerobatics and spins—Part 23);
- utility (normal category maneuvers plus limited aerobatics, including spins);
- acrobatic;
- limited;
- restricted; and
- provisional.

For an airplane to be flown, it must have a current Airworthiness Certificate (except in certain abnormal situations). An Airworthiness Certificate, once issued, remains in force as long as any maintenance or alteration of the aircraft is performed as required by the Regulations (Part 21). An airplane should only be flown in the permitted maneuvers. For instance, a *utility category* airplane may fly all normal maneuvers plus limited acrobatics, including spins, but may not fly acrobatic maneuvers such as loops and rolls (Part 23).

Class, when used for *aircraft* certification purposes, is a broad grouping of aircraft having similar characteristics of propulsion, flight, or landing, such as:

- airplane;
- balloon;
- rotorcraft;
- land plane;
- glider; or
- seaplane; or
- powered-lift.

Abbreviations and Symbols

There are various airspeeds that are important when flying, some of which are target airspeeds to provide best performance, and others which are limit airspeeds to protect the structural integrity of the airplane. Many of these airspeeds are symbolized as **V-speeds,** and these are found in Part 1.2. Examples are:

- V_S—the stall speed or minimum steady flight speed at which the airplane is controllable.
- V_{SO}—the stall speed or minimum steady flight speed in the landing configuration. (An easy way to remember this is to think of the "0" as "flaps Out").
- V_{S1}—the stall speed or minimum steady flight speed in a specific configuration (for instance, flaps up and landing gear retracted).
- V_{NO}—the maximum structural cruise speed (marked by intersection of green and yellow arcs on airspeed indicator).
- V_{NE}—the never-exceed speed (red line on airspeed indicator).
- V_{FE}—the maximum flap extended speed (high-speed end of the white arc on airspeed indicator).
- V_F—the design flap speed.
- V_{LO}—the maximum landing-gear operating speed.
- V_{LE}—the maximum landing-gear extended speed (faster than V_{LO} in some airplanes because of the greater structural strength once the gear is lowered).
- V_X—the speed for best angle of climb (used to clear obstacles by achieving the steepest possible climb-out gradient).
- V_Y—the speed for best rate of climb (used to gain altitude as quickly as possible).

✍ Now complete **Review 20, Part (a)** on page 453.

Part 61—Pilot Certification

Requirement to Carry Pilot Certificate and Medical Certificate

To act as pilot-in-command (or as a required pilot flight crewmember), you must have in your personal possession or readily accessible in the aircraft a current pilot certificate issued under Part 61 and a current medical certificate issued under Part 67.

You are required to present your pilot or flight instructor certificate and medical certificate for inspection on the request of the FAA Administrator or his representative, an authorized representative of the Safety Board (NTSB), or a law enforcement officer.

Certificates and Ratings

Pilot certificates that may be issued include:

- student pilot;
- recreational pilot;
- private pilot;
- commercial pilot; and
- airline transport pilot.

A **flight instructor** and **ground instructor certificate** may also be issued.

Ratings may be placed on pilot and flight instructor certificates as:

- an aircraft category rating (airplane, rotorcraft, glider, lighter-than-air, powered-lift);
- an airplane class rating (SEL, MEL, SES, MES); a rotorcraft class rating; or a lighter-than-air class rating;
- an aircraft type rating for advanced and/or large aircraft—examples: a B757 (Boeing 757) type rating; a CE500 (Cessna Citation) type rating; and
- an instrument rating.

Duration of Pilot and Flight Instructor Certificates

The student pilot certificate and flight instructor certificate both expire at the end of the 24th month after the month in which they were issued or renewed. All other pilot certificates do not have a specific expiration date.

> The student pilot certificate is valid for 2 years to the end of the month.

Duration of Medical Certificates

A third-class (or higher) medical certificate, which is required for operations requiring a private, recreational, or student pilot certificate expires at the end of the 36th month after the month of the date of examination shown on the certificate if the holder is less than 40 years old on the date of the examination. If the pilot is 40 years old or older on the date of the examination, the certificate is only valid for 24 months.

> The medical certificate for a Private Pilot Certificate lasts for 3 years to the end of the month for pilots less than 40 years old.

A second-class (or higher) medical certificate, which is required for operations requiring a commercial pilot certificate, expires at the end of the 12th month after the month of the date of examination shown on the certificate. A first-class medical certificate, which is required of Airline Transport Pilots, expires at the end of the sixth month after the month of the examination shown on the certificate.

General Limitations

Unless you hold a **category and class rating** for that aircraft, you may not act as pilot-in-command of an aircraft that is carrying another person or is operated for compensation or hire. An exception is when you are taking a practical test with an examiner or when you hold a logbook or certificate endorsement for solo operations in training for a rating and you are supervised by an authorized instructor.

No person may act as pilot-in-command of a **tailwheel airplane** unless that person has received and logged flight training from an authorized instructor in a tailwheel airplane and received an endorsement in the person's logbook from an authorized instructor who found the person proficient in the operation of a tailwheel airplane. The flight training must include at least the following the maneuvers and procedures:

- Normal and crosswind takeoffs and landings;
- Wheel landings (unless the manufacturer has recommended against such landings); and
- Go-around procedures.

If you hold a private or commercial pilot certificate then, to act as pilot-in-command of a **high performance airplane,** you must receive and log ground and flight training from an authorized flight instructor who then certifies (endorses) in your logbook that you are proficient to fly airplanes with more than 200 horsepower.

To act as pilot-in-command of a **complex airplane**, you must receive and log ground and flight training from an authorized flight instructor who then certifies in your logbook that you are proficient to fly airplanes with retractable landing gear, flaps, and a controllable propeller.

To act as pilot-in-command of a **pressurized airplane**, you must receive and log flight training from an authorized flight instructor in normal cruise flight operations while operating above 25,000 feet MSL; proper emergency procedures for simulated rapid decompression without actually depressurizing the aircraft; and emergency descent procedures. The ground training must include at least the following subjects:

- High-altitude aerodynamics and meteorology;
- Respiration;
- Effects, symptoms, and causes of hypoxia and any other high-altitude sickness;
- Duration of consciousness without supplemental oxygen;
- Effects of prolonged usage of supplemental oxygen;
- Causes and effects of gas cxpansion and gas bubble formation;
- Preventive measures for eliminating gas expansion, gas bubble formation, and high-altitude sickness;
- Physical phenomena and incidents of decompression; and
- Any other physiological aspects of high-altitude flight.

You must hold a specific **type rating** to act as pilot-in-command of:

- a large aircraft (more than 12,500 pounds certificated takeoff weight, other than lighter-than-air);
- a helicopter for operations requiring an airline transport pilot certificate; or
- a turbojet-powered airplane.

Equipment Required For Practical Tests

You must supply an aircraft appropriate and qualified for the practical test you are about to take. If the test is for a multiengine rating, for example, you must supply a multiengine airplane for the test. If the test is for a commercial rating, the airplane used must be complex. If you are taking the test for an instrument rating, be sure to arrive with a view limiting device. Required equipment for each practical test is listed in the *Practical Test Standards* for that rating or certificate.

Pilot Logbooks

Part 61 of the Regulations tells pilots how to log flight time. Flight time begins when an aircraft moves under its own power for the purpose of flight and ends when the aircraft comes to rest after landing.

The aeronautical training and experience used to meet the requirements for a certificate or rating, or the recent flight experience requirements must be logged. The **pilot-in-command** has final authority and responsibility for the operation and safety of the flight; has been designated as pilot-in-command before or during the flight; and holds the appropriate category, class, and type rating, if appropriate, for the conduct of the flight.

You may log as **pilot-in-command** only that flight time during which you are:

- the sole manipulator of the controls of an aircraft on which you are rated;

- flying solo; or

- when acting as pilot-in-command of an aircraft requiring more than one pilot.

You may log as **second-in-command** time all flight time during which you act as second-in-command of an aircraft requiring more than one pilot. You may log **solo time** only when you are the sole occupant of the aircraft.

All time logged as instructional must be certified by the authorized instructor from whom it was received.

All instrument approaches logged must include the place and type of approach completed, whether conditions were simulated or actual, and, in the case of simulated conditions, the name of the safety pilot. When a flight simulator or flight training device is used, the type of device should be logged.

Flight Review

To act as pilot-in-command, you must have, since the beginning of the 24th month prior to this flight, successfully completed, and had endorsed in your logbook, either:

Flight reviews and proficiency checks are valid for 2 years to the end of the month.

- a (biennial) flight review (consisting of at least 1 hour of flight instruction and 1 hour of ground instruction); or

- a proficiency check for a pilot certificate or rating.

The flight review lasts for 2 years to the end of the month. Instrument proficiency checks are valid for six months, after which the pilot must meet currency requirements or receive another instrument proficiency check.

A flight simulator or flight training device may be used to meet the flight review or proficiency check requirements if:

- it has been approved for that purpose by the Administrator.

- it is being used in accordance with an approved course conducted by a training center that operates under Part 142 of the Regulations.

- it represents an aircraft or set of aircraft for which the pilot is rated.

Recent Flight Experience: Pilot-in-Command

To carry passengers by day, you must have made three takeoffs and three land-ings within the preceding 90 days in an aircraft of the same *category* and *class* (or *type* if a type rating is required). For tailwheel airplanes, the landings must be to a full stop (because steering "taildraggers" on the ground is more difficult compared with steering nosewheel aircraft).

To carry passengers **at night,** you must have made three takeoffs and three landings to a full stop in the hours between 1 hour after sunset to 1 hour before sunrise within the preceding 90 days in an aircraft of the same category, class, and, if required, type. Note that for *recency of experience* the definition of night is different to that in Part 1.1 of the Regulations. The requirement for three *full-stop* landings at night applies to both nosewheel and tailwheel airplanes. The takeoffs and landings may be performed in an approved simulator at a Part 142 training facility.

To carry passengers, you must have made three takeoffs and three landings within the preceding 90 days.

Change of Address

Unless you notify the FAA Airman Certification Branch in Oklahoma City in writing of any change in your permanent mailing address, you may not exercise the privileges of your pilot certificate after 30 days from the date you moved.

Glider Towing

To act as pilot-in-command of an aircraft towing a glider, you must:

You must be properly qualified to tow gliders.

- hold a private pilot certificate or higher with a powered aircraft category rating;
- have an endorsement in your logbook from an authorized instructor certify-ing that you:
  - have received ground and flight instruction in gliders; and
  - are proficient in the techniques and procedures essential to the safe towing of gliders;
- have logged at least three flights as the sole manipulator of the controls of an aircraft towing a glider or simulating glider-towing flight procedures while accompanied by a suitably qualified pilot;
- have logged at least 100 hours of pilot-in-command time in the aircraft cate-gory, class, and type, if required, that the pilot is using to tow a glider; and
- within the preceding 12 months made at least 3 actual or simulated glider tows while being accompanied by a suitably qualified pilot, or made at least 3 flights as pilot-in-command of a glider towed by an aircraft.

Private Pilot Privileges and Limitations

A private pilot may not act as pilot-in-command of an aircraft that is carrying passengers or property for compensation or hire, nor may he be hired or compensated to act as pilot-in-command of any aircraft.

But a private pilot may share operating expenses with a passenger, although he may not pay less than the *pro rata* share of the operating expenses of the flight. The expenses shared may involve only fuel, oil, airport expenditures, or rental fees. A private pilot can carry passengers on business trips if the flight is only incidental to that business or employment. A private pilot who is an aircraft salesman and who has at least 200 hours of logged flight time may demonstrate an aircraft in flight to a prospective buyer.

Under certain strict constraints, including FAA notification and a donation to the charitable organization concerned, a private pilot who has logged at least 200 hours may carry paying passengers on an airlift for a charitable organization.

✍ Now complete **Review 20, Part (b)** on page 453.

Part 91—General Operating and Flight Rules

Responsibility and Authority of the Pilot-in-Command

The pilot-in-command of an aircraft is directly responsible for, and is the final authority as to, the operation of that aircraft.

In the event of an in-flight emergency requiring immediate action, the pilot-in-command may deviate from the Regulations to the extent required to meet that emergency. On the request of the Administrator (of the FAA), a written report of the deviation should be sent to the FAA.

The pilot is responsible for the operation of the aircraft.

Aircraft Airworthiness

The pilot-in-command is responsible for determining whether that aircraft is in condition for safe flight. The pilot-in-command shall discontinue the flight when unairworthy mechanical, electrical or structural conditions occur.

Flight Manual, Marking, and Placard Requirements

You must operate within the limitations specified in the approved Flight Manual, on markings and placards, or as otherwise prescribed. Within the aircraft, there should be an FAA-approved Flight Manual or Pilot's Operating Handbook (which should include weight-and-balance information).

Operate within the limitations of your aircraft.

Note: The required documents on board an aircraft can be remembered using the mnemonic AROW:

A Airworthiness Certificate;

R Registration Certificate;

O Operating limitations (Flight Manual, POH, placards, etc.);

W Weight and balance information (in the Flight Manual, POH, or separate).

Dropping Objects

No object should be dropped from an aircraft in flight that creates a hazard to persons or property. You may drop an object if reasonable precautions are taken to avoid injury or damage to persons or property.

Alcohol and Drugs

Alcohol and other drugs are not compatible with flying.

No person may act, or attempt to act, as a crewmember:

- within 8 hours after the consumption of any alcoholic beverage;
- while under the influence of alcohol;
- while using any drug that affects their faculties in any way contrary to safety; or
- while having 0.04% by weight or more of alcohol in the blood.

You may be asked by a law enforcement officer or by the Administrator to submit to a blood alcohol test if they suspect you are intoxicated. Except in an emergency, a pilot may not allow an intoxicated person, or one under the influence of drugs (other than a medical patient under proper care) to be carried on that aircraft.

Preflight Action

Each pilot-in-command shall, before beginning a flight, become familiar with all available information concerning that flight. This information must include:

- for all flights:
  - runway lengths at the airports of intended use; and
  - the airplane's takeoff and landing distance data; and
- for any flight not in the vicinity of an airport:
  - weather reports and forecasts;
  - fuel requirements;
  - alternatives available if the planned flight cannot be completed; and
  - any known traffic delays.

Prepare thoroughly for a flight.

Flight Crewmembers at Stations

During takeoff and landing, and while en route, each required flight crewmember shall be at their station with the safety belt fastened. The shoulder harness should be fastened during takeoff and landing, but is not required en route.

Crewmembers are permitted to leave their stations to attend to other duties in connection with the operation of the aircraft, or because of physiological needs.

When at your flight station, wear your safety belt.

Use of Safety Belts, Shoulder Harnesses and Child Restraint Systems

The pilot must ensure that all persons on board are:

- briefed on how to fasten and unfasten their safety belt, and shoulder harness if fitted;
- notified that they must wear their safety belt, and shoulder harness if fitted, during taxi, takeoff and landing;
- wearing their safety belt, and shoulder harness if fitted, during taxi, takeoff and landing (except for infants under 2 years of age held on an adult's lap, parachutists sitting on the floor or someone aiding in floatplane operations on the water); and
- children under 2 not held by an adult should be occupying an approved child restraint system (such restraint system are placarded as approved for aircraft use) and must be accompanied during the flight by a designated guardian adult.

Operating Near Other Aircraft

You must not operate an aircraft so close to another as to create a collision hazard.

You must not operate an aircraft in formation flight except by arrangement with the pilot-in-command of each aircraft in the formation, and you must not carry passengers for hire when flying in formation.

Keep clear of other aircraft.

Right-of-Way

Each person operating an aircraft should be vigilant so as to see and avoid other aircraft. If a rule gives another aircraft right-of-way, then you should give way to that aircraft, and not pass over, under, or ahead of it unless well clear.

- An aircraft in distress has right-of-way.
- When aircraft are approaching head-on, or nearly so, each shall turn right.
- When two aircraft of different categories are converging at approximately the same altitude, the more maneuverable aircraft must give way to the less-maneuverable in this order: airplanes or rotorcraft, airships, gliders, balloons.

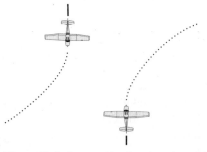

Figure 20-1. Approaching head-on, turn right

For instance, an airplane must give way to an airship, glider, or balloon. A glider must give way to a balloon, but has right-of-way over a powered airplane.

- When two aircraft of the same category are converging, the aircraft to the other's right has right-of-way. Airplanes and rotorcraft (for example, helicopters) are considered to be equally maneuverable, and so have equal rights. However, an aircraft that is towing or refueling other aircraft has the right-of-way over all other engine-driven aircraft.

- An airplane being overtaken has right-of-way, and the overtaking airplane shall alter course to the right to pass well clear.

- An aircraft landing, or on final approach to land, has right-of-way over aircraft in flight or operating on the surface, but it should not take advantage of this rule to force an aircraft that has just landed off the runway. If two aircraft are approaching an airport for the purpose of landing, the lower aircraft has right-of-way, but it shall not take advantage of this rule to cut in front of another aircraft on final approach to land or to overtake that aircraft.

Similar right-of-way rules apply to **water operations,** with seaplanes and vessels on crossing courses giving way to the right.

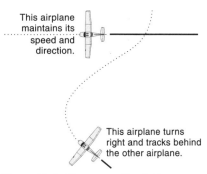

Figure 20-2. Give way to the right

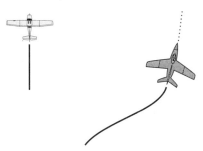

Figure 20-3. Overtaking, keep right

Aircraft Speed

Maximum indicated airspeed below 10,000 feet MSL is 250 KIAS, or 288 mph (unless otherwise authorized). This speed also applies in Class B airspace.

Maximum indicated airspeed at or below 2,500 feet AGL within 4 nautical miles of the primary airport of a Class C or Class D airspace area is 200 KIAS, or 230 mph (unless otherwise authorized or required by ATC, or unless the operation is within Class B airspace, in which case 250 KIAS applies). A maximum indicated airspeed limit of 200 KIAS also applies to the airspace underlying Class B airspace, or in a VFR corridor through Class B airspace.

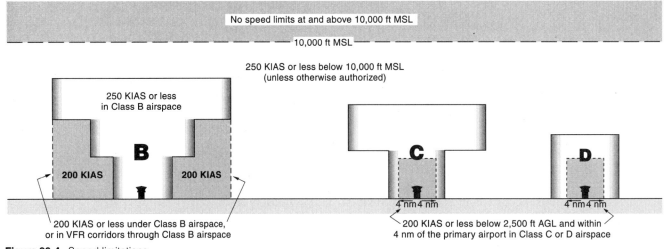

Figure 20-4. Speed limitations

If minimum safe airspeed for your airplane exceeds these speeds, ATC should be notified and the aircraft should be operated at the minimum safe speed.

Minimum Safe Altitudes

Except when taking off or landing, no person may operate an airplane below the following altitudes:

- **Anywhere**—an altitude allowing, if an engine fails, an emergency landing without undue hazard to persons or property on the surface.

- **Over congested areas**—over any congested area of a city, town, or settlement, or over an open-air assembly of persons, an altitude of 1,000 feet above the highest obstacle within a horizontal distance of 2,000 feet of the aircraft.
- **Over other than congested areas**—an altitude of 500 feet above the surface, except over open water or sparsely populated areas. In those cases, the aircraft may not be operated closer than 500 feet to any person, vessel, vehicle, or structure.

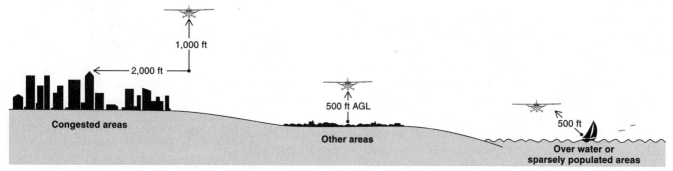

Figure 20-5. Minimum safe altitudes

Altimeter Settings

Cruise altitude below 18,000 feet MSL should be maintained with reference to an altimeter that has its pressure window set to the current reported altimeter setting of a station along the route and within 100 nautical miles of the aircraft (or, if not available, an appropriate available station). In a no-radio aircraft, you should set the altimeter to the departure airport elevation prior to takeoff, or set an appropriate altimeter setting available before departure in the pressure window.

Compliance with ATC Clearances and Instructions

You shall not deviate from an ATC clearance except in an emergency or if the deviation is in response to a traffic alert and collision avoidance system resolution advisory. If you do deviate from an ATC clearance in an emergency, then you shall notify ATC of that deviation as soon as possible.

If you are given priority by ATC in an emergency (even though you may not have deviated from any rules), you shall, on request, submit a detailed report of that emergency to the manager of that ATC facility within 48 hours.

ATC Light Signals

If you experience radio communications failure, ATC may use light signals originating in the control tower to communicate basic commands.

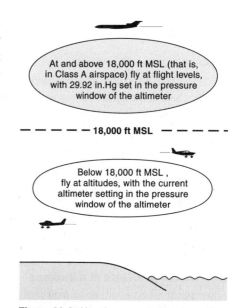

At and above 18,000 ft MSL (that is, in Class A airspace) fly at flight levels, with 29.92 in.Hg set in the pressure window of the altimeter

— — — — — 18,000 ft MSL — — — — —

Below 18,000 ft MSL , fly at altitudes, with the current altimeter setting in the pressure window of the altimeter

Figure 20-6. Use the current altimeter setting when flying below 18,000 feet MSL

Color and Type of Signal	Meaning with respect to Aircraft on the Surface	Meaning with respect to Aircraft in Flight
Steady Green	Cleared for takeoff	Cleared to land
Flashing Green	Cleared to taxi	Return for a landing (followed by a steady green at the proper time to indicate cleared to land)
Steady Red	Stop	Give way to other aircraft and continue circling
Flashing Red	Taxi clear of runway in use	Airport unsafe—do not land
Flashing White	Return to starting point on airport	Not applicable
Alternating Red and Green	Exercise extreme caution	Exercise extreme caution

Figure 20-7. ATC light signals

✍ Now complete **Review 20, Part (c)** on page 455.

Operating on or in the Vicinity of an Airport in Class G Airspace

When approaching to land at an airport in Class G airspace, make all turns to the left, unless there are approved light signals or visual markings indicating that turns should be made to the right.

Operating on or in the Vicinity of an Airport in Class E Airspace

As for Class G (above), when approaching to land, and when departing, comply with any traffic patterns established by the FAA for that airport. Two-way radio communications must be established prior to 4 nautical miles from the airport, up to and including 2,500 feet AGL. If the aircraft radio fails in flight, the pilot-in-command may operate that aircraft and land if weather conditions are at or above basic VFR weather minimums, visual contact with the tower is maintained, and a clearance to land is received.

Class E airspace also includes **Federal airways** that exist between radio navigation facilities and/or intersections. Federal airways extend laterally 4 nautical miles either side of the centerline and extend from 1,200 feet AGL, or the floor of the Class E airspace if lower, up to but not including 18,000 feet MSL (but with no upper limit in Hawaii).

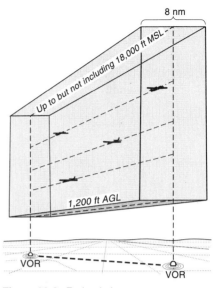

Figure 20-8. Federal airways

Operating on or in the Vicinity of an Airport in Class D Airspace

To operate in Class D airspace:

- Two-way radio communications must be established with ATC before entering the Class D airspace. Two-way radio communications must be established before taxiing at the primary airport on departure, and as soon as possible after departure from a satellite airport without an operating control tower.
- ATC clearances are required to taxi, take off, or land.
- Comply with other applicable Regulations unless otherwise authorized by ATC.

Class D airspace generally exists around smaller controlled airports (one or more primary airports, or satellite airports).

Operations in Class C Airspace

To operate in Class C airspace, you must:

- comply with the Regulations above; and
- use an altitude-encoding transponder.

Class C airspace exists around certain large and busy airports. (Part 71)

Operations in Class B Airspace

To operate in Class B airspace, you must:

- comply with Regulations above (for all other airspace);
- obtain an ATC clearance to operate in the Class B airspace;
- use an altitude-encoding altimeter in the Class B airspace and within 30 nautical miles of the primary airport for the Class B airspace area;
- have VOR available if operating IFR (not required for VFR); and
- satisfy certain pilot rating requirements:
    (a) have a private pilot certificate or higher; or
    (b) be a solo student pilot or recreational pilot seeking private pilot certification who has:
    – received both ground and flight instruction for that specific Class B airspace or airport;
    – logbook endorsement by an instructor within the previous 90 days for conducting solo flight in that specific Class B airspace or airport.

Class B airspace exists around certain large and busy airports. (Part 71)

Student pilots may not take off or land at certain major airports (listed in Part 91).

Restricted and Prohibited Areas

Flight is not permitted in restricted or prohibited areas without the permission of the using or controlling agency (shown on Sectional charts). More information about restricted and prohibited areas is found in Part 73.

Operations in Class A Airspace (at and above 18,000 feet MSL)

VFR flights are not permitted in Class A (controlled) airspace—only IFR flights with an ATC clearance.

Class A airspace exists at and above 18,000 feet MSL.

Fuel Requirements for Flight in VFR Conditions

After considering wind and forecast weather conditions, you must ensure that there is enough fuel to fly:

Always carry sufficient fuel.

- to the first point of intended landing; plus
- sufficient reserve fuel to fly for an additional 30 minutes by day, or 45 minutes at night, at normal cruise speed.

Basic VFR Weather Minimums

The basic weather minimums required for you to fly VFR are stated in terms of flight visibility and distance from clouds (horizontally and vertically). For VFR operations within Class B, C, D and E surface areas around airports with an operating control tower, you require:

- cloud ceiling at least 1,000 feet AGL; and
- ground visibility at least 3 statute miles (usually measured by ATC but, if not available, flight visibility at least 3 statute miles as estimated by the pilot).

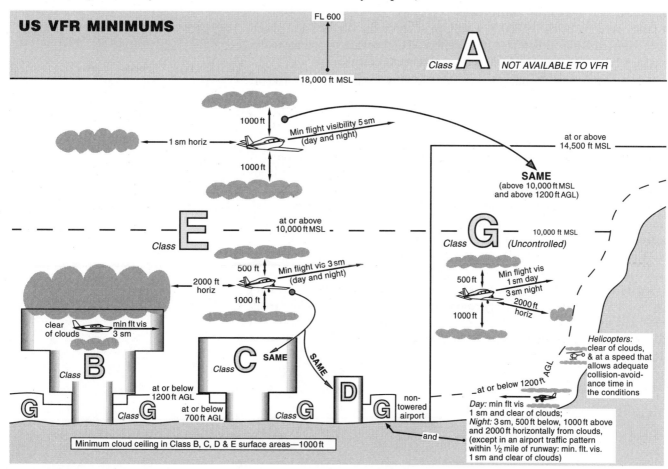

Figure 20-9a. VFR weather minimums

	Class A Airspace	Class B Airspace	Class C Airspace	Class D Airspace	Class E Airspace	Class G Airspace
VFR minimum visibility ...	Not applicable (IFR only)	3 statute miles	3 statute miles	3 statute miles	*3 statute miles	**1 statute mile
VFR minimum distance from clouds ...	Not applicable (IFR only)	Clear of clouds	500 feet below; 1,000 feet above; and 2,000 feet horizontal	500 feet below; 1,000 feet above; and 2,000 feet horizontal	*500 feet below; 1,000 feet above; and 2,000 feet horizontal	**500 feet below; 1,000 feet above; and 2,000 feet horizontal

*Different visibility minimums and distance from cloud requirements exist for operations above 10,000 feet MSL in Class E airspace.

**Different visibility minimums and distance from cloud requirements exist for night operations, operations above 10,000 feet MSL, and operations below 1,200 feet AGL in Class G airspace.

Figure 20-9b. VFR weather minimums

The requirements are slightly less restrictive in Class G airspace, with a less-restrictive daytime visibility below 10,000 feet MSL (1 statute mile only) and, below 1,200 feet AGL by day a less-restrictive separation from clouds (clear of clouds, with no distance-from-cloud requirements). In Class B airspace aircraft are required to remain clear of clouds. In Class C, D, E and at night, Class G airspace, aircraft are required to maintain a minimum distance of 1,000 feet above, 500 feet below and 2,000 feet horizontal from clouds. Also, in Class G airspace, when the visibility is less than 3 statute miles but not less than 1 statute mile during night hours, an airplane may be operated clear of clouds if operated in an airport traffic pattern within one-half mile of the runway.

Special VFR Weather Minimums

A pilot operating below 10,000 feet MSL in or above the airspace designated on the surface for an airport may be issued an ATC clearance to operate under special VFR, which reduces the normal requirements down to:

- flight visibility 1 statute mile (and ground visibility 1 statute mile for takeoff and landing); and
- clear of clouds.

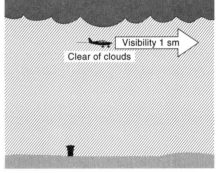

Figure 20-10. ATC may issue a special VFR clearance

To take off or land at any airport in Class B, C, D and E airspace under special VFR, the ground visibility at the airport must be at least 1 statute mile. If ground visibility is not reported, then the flight visibility during takeoff or landing must be at least 1 statute mile.

A noninstrument-rated pilot may be issued a special VFR clearance by day but, to operate under special VFR *at night,* you must be instrument-rated, instrument-current and flying in an IFR-equipped airplane.

Airports in Class B, C or D airspace have a control tower from which you can request a special-VFR clearance. Airports in Class E airspace do not have a control tower, but your request for special VFR can be relayed via Flight Service Station to the ATC facility responsible for that Class E airspace (only ATC, and not a Flight Service Station, can issue an ATC clearance, although a Flight Service Station may relay it to you). Special VFR is prohibited at some airports (see 14 CFR, Part 91).

VFR Cruise Altitude or Flight Level

VFR cruise altitudes or flight levels, when more than 3,000 feet AGL, are:

- on a magnetic course of magnetic north to magnetic 179: **odds+500 feet**— for example, 3,500 feet MSL, 15,500 feet MSL; and

- on a magnetic course of magnetic 180 to magnetic 359: **evens+500 feet**— for example, 4,500 feet MSL, 16,500 feet MSL.

(You can memorize this as "West Evens, East Odds, plus 500 feet," or "WEEO+500.")

Civil Aircraft: Certifications Required

The aircraft should carry within it:

- the current Airworthiness Certificate clearly displayed;

- the Registration Certificate.

Emergency Locator Transmitters

The batteries in an emergency locator transmitter (ELT) must be replaced, or recharged, when the ELT has been used for more than 1 cumulative hour or 50% of the battery's useful life.

ELTs transmit an audible tone on the emergency frequencies 121.5 MHz and 243.0 MHz. A short ELT ground test should be conducted only in the first 5 minutes after any hour, and then for only 3 cycles. To check that an ELT has not been inadvertently activated, say by a hard landing, you should monitor the emergency frequency 121.5 MHz (see AIM for details). It is good airmanship to do this before normal engine shutdown at the conclusion of each flight.

Aircraft Lights

An aircraft operating on the ground or in flight between sunset and sunrise should have lighted **position lights** (sometimes called navigation lights). In Alaska, where twilight hours in summer can be long and bright, the lighting requirements are different.

U.S.-registered civil aircraft must have an approved aviation red or aviation white anticollision light system. If the anticollision light system fails you may continue to a location where repairs or replacement can be made. The anticollision lights need not be lighted when the pilot-in-command determines that, because of operating conditions, it would be in the interest of safety to turn the lights off.

Supplemental Oxygen

Crew oxygen requirements for operations under Part 91 Regulations:

- Crew members are not required to use oxygen up to a cabin pressure altitude of 12,500 feet MSL.

- At cabin pressure altitudes above 12,500 feet up to and including 14,000 feet, the required minimum flight crew may fly without supplemental oxygen for up to 30 minutes. Supplemental oxygen must be provided and used for at least the time in excess of 30 minutes at these cabin pressure altitudes.

- At cabin pressure altitudes above 14,000 feet, the required minimum flight crew must be provided with and use supplemental oxygen during the entire time at those cabin altitudes.

Passenger oxygen requirements:

- At cabin pressure altitudes above 15,000 feet, each occupant (flight crew and passengers) must be provided with supplemental oxygen.

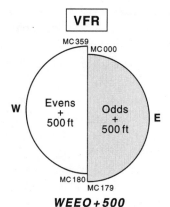

Figure 20-11. VFR cruise altitudes and flight levels above 3,000 feet AGL

Most aircraft are required to carry emergency locator transmitters. Refer to the regulation for exceptions and placarding rules.

Turn position lights on between sunset and sunrise.

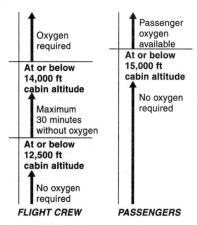

Figure 20-12. Oxygen requirements

ATC Transponder and Altitude Reporting Equipment, and Use

A Mode C (Mode 3/A 4096 code capability, or the newer and more advanced Mode S) transponder is required to be turned on in all aircraft operating:

- in Class A airspace (at and above 18,000 feet MSL);
- in all airspace of the 48 contiguous states and the District of Columbia at and above 10,000 feet MSL, except at and below 2,500 feet AGL;
- in Class B airspace, and within 30 nautical miles of any airport listed in Part 91, Appendix D, Section 1, from the surface up to 10,000 feet MSL (this list contains most major US airports—Class B airspace primary airports such as: Atlanta, Denver, Los Angeles, Miami, Minneapolis, both New York airports, San Francisco, St Louis, and both Washington airports);
- in Class C airspace, and above it to 10,000 feet MSL;
- from the surface to 10,000 feet MSL within a 10 nm radius of any airport listed in Part 91, Appendix D, Section 2, except the airspace below 1,200 feet AGL that is outside the lateral boundaries of the surface area of the airspace designated for that airport.

A functioning Mode C or Mode S transponder is not required in Class D, E or G airspace, unless one of the above applies—for example, operating within 30 nautical miles of San Francisco International but outside of the Class B and C airspace areas. Exceptions to this transponder-equipment regulation are also listed in Part 91—these include aircraft without original electrical systems, balloons and gliders in certain circumstances.

If your transponder fails in flight, and you are, or will be, operating in airspace where it is required equipment, you should notify ATC immediately. ATC may authorize deviation from the requirement to have an operating transponder to allow you to continue to the airport of your ultimate destination, including any intermediate stops, or to proceed to a place where suitable repairs can be made, or both. For a continuing waiver you should make a request to ATC at least one hour before the proposed flight.

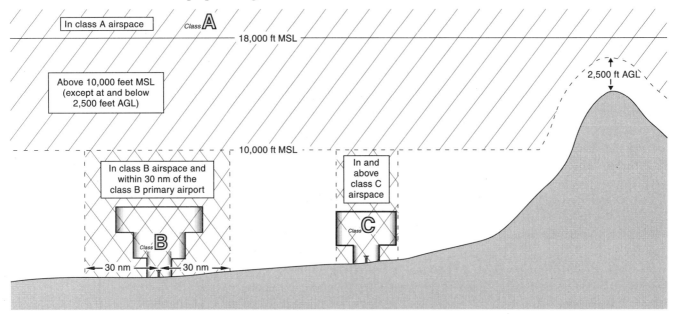

Figure 20-13. A transponder is required in the shaded airspace.

Aerobatic Flight

Aerobatic flight means intentional maneuvers involving an abrupt change in aircraft attitude, an abnormal attitude, or abnormal acceleration, that is not necessary for normal flight. You may not perform aerobatics:

- over any congested area of a city, town, or settlement;
- over an open air assembly of persons;
- within or above the lateral boundaries of the surface areas of Class B, C, D or E airspace designated for an airport;
- within 4 nautical miles of the centerline of any Federal airway;
- below an altitude of 1,500 feet AGL; or
- when the flight visibility is less than 3 statute miles.

Parachutes and Parachuting

Each occupant of an aircraft must wear a parachute for maneuvers that exceed 60° bank angle, or 30° nose-up or nose-down. Parachutes are not required for spin training with a flight instructor, designated examiner or Airline Transport pilot.

Modern parachutes (including chair-types) carried for emergency use must have been packed by a certificated and appropriately rated parachute rigger within the preceding 120 days.

Restricted Category Civil Aircraft: Operating Limitations

You may not operate a restricted category civil aircraft:

- for other than the special purpose for which it is certificated (for example, crop dusting, seeding, banner towing, and so on);
- to carry persons or property for compensation or hire;
- over a densely populated area;
- in a congested airway; or
- near a busy airport used by passengers.

You may not ride in a restricted category aircraft unless you are a required crewmember or crewmember trainee, or your skills are specially required for that flight. Other limitations may also apply (see Part 91).

Aircraft Having Experimental Certificates: Operating Limitations

You may not operate an aircraft that has an experimental certificate:

- for other than the purpose for which the certificate was issued;
- to carry persons or property for compensation or hire;
- over a densely populated area, or in a congested airway, unless authorized by the Administrator.

Pilots must advise their passengers via clearly displayed placarding that they are riding in an experimental aircraft. Other limitations may also apply (see Part 91).

Primary Category Aircraft: Operating limitations.

No person may operate a primary category aircraft carrying persons or property for compensation or hire. You may not operate a primary category aircraft that is maintained by the pilot-owner under an approved special inspection and maintenance program unless you are the pilot-owner or a designee of the pilot-owner.

Maintenance, Preventive Maintenance, and Alterations (General)

The owner or operator of an aircraft is primarily responsible for maintaining that aircraft in an airworthy condition. Part 43 of the Regulations details what maintenance pilots may perform on their own aircraft.

Maintenance Required

Each owner or operator of an aircraft shall ensure that prescribed inspections and maintenance are carried out, and that maintenance personnel make appropriate entries in the aircraft maintenance records indicating that the aircraft has been approved for return to service.

Operations after Maintenance, Preventive Maintenance, Rebuilding or Alteration

After an aircraft has undergone maintenance, preventive maintenance, rebuilding or alteration, then for the Airworthiness Certificate to remain valid:

- applicable maintenance record entries in the aircraft logbooks must be made;
- the aircraft should not be operated until it has been approved for return to service by an authorized person;
- if the flight characteristics or operation in flight have been altered appreciably, passengers may not be carried until the aircraft is test flown satisfactorily by an appropriately rated pilot with at least a private pilot certificate.

Inspections

You may not operate an aircraft unless within the preceding 12 calendar months it has had either:

Aircraft must be properly maintained and regularly inspected.

1. an annual inspection; or
2. an inspection for the issuance of an Airworthiness Certificate.

As a general rule, you may not operate an aircraft carrying persons for hire, or give flight instruction for hire, unless within the preceding 100 hours the aircraft has received:

1. an annual inspection; or
2. an inspection for the issuance of an Airworthiness Certificate; or
3. a 100-hour inspection.

The **annual inspection** is a requirement, and is the normal inspection that is done during the life of the airplane following the initial airworthiness inspection. The annual inspection is more thorough than the 100-hour inspection and can replace it (but not vice versa). With FAA approval, a series of progressive checks through the year may replace the annual/100-hour inspections. People who own their own airplanes and operate them privately, and not for hire, typically do not have 100-hour inspections done.

An annual inspection is more thorough than a 100-hour inspection, and so can replace it.

   Rental aircraft and those used for **flight instruction** require annual inspections and 100-hour inspections. The 100-hour limitation may be exceeded by not more than 10 hours while en route to reach a place where the inspection can be done, but this excess time must be included in computing the next 100 hours of service.

For example, if a 100-hour inspection is due when the tachometer reads 1395.3, the next inspection is due at 1495.3 hours. If the actual inspection is done at 1497.3 hours (that is, 2 hours later than the due time) because of a 3-hour flight to the place where the inspection was done, the next 100-hour inspection will still be due at 1595.3 hours (that is, the 2 hours overdue forms part of the next 100 hours, and the next 100-hour inspection is due 100 hours from the prior due time).

Annual inspections occur every 12 calendar months, so an aircraft that had an annual inspection performed on July 9 this year is due for another annual inspection no later than July 31 next year.

Annual inspections are valid for 1 year to the end of the month.

Normally an Airworthiness Certificate remains in effect as long as the maintenance, preventive maintenance, and alterations are performed in accordance with the Regulations and are entered correctly in the maintenance records.

ATC Transponder Tests and Inspections

To be used, a transponder must have been tested and inspected satisfactorily within the preceding 24 calendar months. For example, if this is carried out on any day in November, it is valid until the last day of November, 24 months hence—that is, 2 years to the end of the month.

Transponder tests and inspections are valid for 2 years to the end of the month.

Maintenance Records

The owner or operator of an aircraft shall keep records of:

The owner or operator must keep detailed maintenance records.

- maintenance, preventive maintenance, alteration;
- 100-hour inspections, annual inspections, progressive inspections; and
- any other required or approved inspections.

Preventive maintenance is defined in Part 1.1 as simple or minor preservation operations and the replacement of small standard parts not involving complex assembly operations. Preventive maintenance items that the *pilot* may perform are found in Part 43, and include such items such as oil changes, replenishing hydraulic fluid, and servicing the landing gear wheel bearings. It does not include structural work on the airframe, or major adjustments to the engine.

Maintenance records apply to each aircraft (including airframe), each engine, each propeller, rotor, and each appliance of the aircraft. The records must include:

- a description of the work performed and the date of completion;
- the signature, and certificate number of the person approving the aircraft for return to service;
- total time in service of the airframe, engine and propeller;
- current status of life-limited parts;
- time since last overhaul of all items requiring overhaul on a specified time basis;
- current inspection status including time since the last inspection required;
- current status of applicable Airworthiness Directives (ADs), which must be complied with for the aircraft to remain airworthy; and
- copies of the forms prescribed by Part 43 for each major alteration.

Rebuilt Engine Maintenance Records

An aircraft engine rebuilt by the manufacturer or its agent may have a new maintenance record (that is, zero hours) without previous operating history, but it should specify date of rebuilding, and each change as required by Airworthiness Directives (ADs) and specified Service Bulletins.

A rebuilt engine can be returned to "zero time."

National Transportation Safety Board—NTSB

The NTSB is the United States National Transportation Safety Board, which is charged with investigating aircraft accidents and incidents. The procedures that a pilot should use to report such matters are specified in document 49 CFR Part 830.

Document NTSB 830 refers to accidents and incidents.

49 CFR Part 830

NTSB Part 830 covers rules pertaining to the notification and reporting of aircraft accidents or incidents and overdue aircraft, and preservation of aircraft wreckage, mail, cargo, and records.

An **accident** involves the death or serious injury of a person, or substantial damage to an aircraft, between the time any person boards the aircraft with the intention of flight and the time they disembark.

An **incident** is an occurrence other than an accident, associated with the operation of an aircraft, which affects or could affect the safety of operations.

An accident must be reported immediately to the nearest NTSB field office, followed by a written report within 10 days.

The following serious incidents must also be reported immediately, but a written report is only required on request from the NTSB:

Report *accidents* immediately, followed by a written report to the NTSB within 10 days. Report *serious incidents* immediately, followed by a written report to the NTSB if requested.

- a flight control system malfunction or failure;
- the inability of a required flight crewmember to perform normal flight duties as a result of injury or illness;
- failure of a turbine (jet) engine;
- an in-flight fire;
- an aircraft collision in flight;
- significant damage to other property by the aircraft operation;
- an overdue airplane believed to have been involved in an accident—(a written report is required after 7 days if an overdue airplane is still missing).

Prior to the time the NTSB (or its authorized representative) takes custody of aircraft wreckage, mail, cargo and records, it must not be disturbed or moved except to the extent necessary to remove persons injured or trapped, to protect the wreckage from further damage, or to protect the public from injury.

Only disturb aircraft wreckage and contents for good reasons.

✍ Now complete **Review 20, Part (d)** on page 457.

Regulations for Commercial Pilots

In addition to the knowledge contained earlier in this chapter, as an aspiring Commercial Pilot you are also required to be familiar with the following Regulations. Commercial pilots need to understand that the Regulations are set up to overlap each other. Depending on the type of operation you are participating in, you may be governed by several levels of Regulations, beginning with the most lenient, Part 91, and progressing through Parts 135, 125 and, if you become a pilot for a scheduled commercial operator, even Part 121.

Definitions—the Operation of Aircraft

To operate an aircraft is to use an aircraft, to cause to use an aircraft, or to authorize to use an aircraft. Therefore, the term **operator** is primarily applied both to the pilot and to the person who authorizes the pilot's use of the aircraft, but could also be applied solely to the pilot.

A **commercial operator** is a person, who for compensation or hire, engages in air commerce by the carriage of persons or property in an aircraft (other than as an air carrier).

Operational control is the exercise of authority over initiating, conducting, or terminating a flight.

Part 61

Airplane Rating: Aeronautical Experience

The aeronautical experience requirements to obtain a commercial pilot certificate are found in this Regulation. A commercial pilot without an instrument rating may not carry passengers for hire on cross-country flights of more than 50 nautical miles, or at night.

Part 91

Portable Electronic Devices

Portable electronic devices which may cause interference with the navigation or communication system may not be operated on aircraft being flown in commercial operations. Items excluded from this include portable voice recorders, hearing aids, heart pacemakers, and electric shavers.

Truth in Leasing

A copy of a lease for a large civil US aircraft must be mailed to the FAA, Oklahoma City, within 24 hours of its execution.

Fuel Requirements for Flight in IFR Conditions

For an IFR flight by an instrument-rated pilot, after considering wind and forecast weather conditions, the pilot must ensure that there is enough fuel to fly:

- to the first point of intended landing; plus
- from that airport to any required alternate airport; plus
- sufficient reserve fuel to fly for an additional 45 minutes at normal cruise speed.

Minimum Altitudes for IFR Operations

Except when necessary for takeoff and landing, you may not operate an aircraft IFR:

- below the prescribed minimum IFR altitudes; or (if none are prescribed)
- below 2,000 feet above the highest obstacle in mountainous terrain within 4 nautical miles of the course to be flown, and 1,000 feet above non-mountainous terrain.

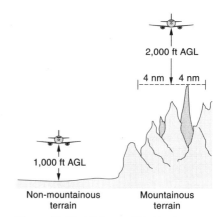

Figure 20-14. Minimum IFR altitudes

IFR Cruise Altitude or Flight Level

In **Class A, B, C, D, or E airspace,** maintain the altitude or level assigned by ATC. However, you should *flight plan* at an appropriate cruise level as outlined below.

When in **Class G airspace,** an IFR flight should cruise at:

- on a magnetic course of north to MC179: **odds**—for example, 5,000 feet MSL, 15,000 feet MSL, FL190, FL230; and
- on a magnetic course of MC180 to MC359: **evens**—for example, 4,000 feet MSL, 16,000 feet MSL, FL180, FL280.

This regulation applies up to FL290. (WEEO: West evens; East odds.) Above FL290, the vertical spacing changes from 2,000 to 4,000 feet.

If ATC assigns you a **VFR-on-top** clearance, you should maintain a VFR altitude or flight level (WEEO+500).

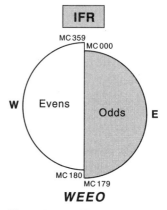

Figure 20-15. IFR cruise altitudes and flight levels

Instrument and Equipment Requirements for Aircraft in the US Standard Category

For **VFR flight by day,** a *standard category* aircraft requires:

- an airspeed indicator;
- an altimeter;
- a magnetic direction indicator;
- a tachometer (rpm) for each engine;
- a fuel gauge;
- shoulder harnesses (for relatively new model aircraft);
- an emergency locator transmitter (ELT) (if required by Part 91.207); and
- flotation gear and a pyrotechnic signal device(s) if beyond the power-off gliding distance from shore.

Additional items for **VFR flight by night** are:

- approved position (navigation) lights;
- an approved aviation red or white anticollision light;
- at least one electric landing light if the aircraft is operated for hire;
- an adequate source of electrical energy; and
- spare fuses that are accessible.

Other items are required for certain aircraft—for instance, those with altitude engines, or retractable landing gear.

Towing: Other than Gliders

To tow anything other than a glider (for example, a banner) requires a **Certificate of Waiver** issued by the Administrator of the FAA.

Limited Category Civil Aircraft: Operating Limitations

You may not operate a limited category civil aircraft to carry persons or property for compensation or hire.

Part 119

Certification: Air Carriers and Commercial Operators

Part 119 governs aircraft in commercial operations when common carriage is not involved, in operations of U.S.-registered civil airplanes with a seat configuration of 20 or more passengers, or a maximum payload capacity of 6,000 pounds or more. This part prescribes the types of air operator certificates issued by the Federal Aviation Administration, including:

- air carrier certificates and operating certificates;
- the certification requirements an operator must meet in order to obtain and hold a certificate authorizing operations under Part 121, 125, or 135 of this chapter and operations specifications for each kind of operation to be conducted and each class and size of aircraft to be operated under Part 121 or 135 of this chapter;
- the requirements an operator must meet to conduct operations under Part 121, 125, or 135 of this chapter and in operating each class and size of aircraft authorized in its operations specifications;
- requirements affecting wet leasing of aircraft and other arrangements for transportation by air;
- requirements for obtaining deviation authority to perform operations under a military contract and obtaining deviation authority to perform an emergency operation; and
- requirements for management personnel for operations conducted under Part 121 or Part 135 of this chapter.

Persons subject to this part must comply with the other requirements of this chapter, except where those requirements are modified by or where additional requirements are imposed by Part 119, 121, 125, or 135 of this chapter.

Part 125

Certification and Operations: Airplanes having a seating capacity of 20 or more passengers or a maximum payload capacity of 6,000 pounds or more.

Part 125 refers to aircraft operations where common carriage (such as scheduled operations or advertising or using agents—that is, *holding out* to furnish air transportation)—is not involved. Operating under Part 125 requires that you also operate under Part 91. A Part 125 certificate holder must display a true copy of the Part 125 in each aircraft.

Part 125 operations include *nonscheduled* operations (that is, *not* an air carrier) using an aircraft with 20 or more passenger seats or with a maximum payload of 6,000 pounds or more.

A person authorized to operate airplanes under any **air carrier operating certificate** (such as, Part 121 for Air Carriers, Part 129 or Part 135) is not eligible to operate under Part 125.

The pilot-in-command of a Part 125 operation (nonscheduled) must hold at least a commercial pilot certificate, an appropriate category, class, and type rating, and an instrument rating and has had at least 1,200 hours of flight time as a pilot, including 500 hours of cross-country flight time, 100 hours of night flight time, including at least 10 night takeoffs and landings, and 75 hours of actual or simulated instrument flight time, at least 50 hours of which were actual flight.

The second-in-command must hold at least a commercial pilot certificate with appropriate category and class ratings, and a current instrument rating. Recent experience requirements can be met in the airplane, or by doing three takeoffs and three landings within the preceding 90 days in the type of airplane or in an approved visual simulator.

Part 135—Commuter and On-Demand Operators

Applicability of Part 135 to Air Taxi and Commercial Operators

Part 135 prescribes the rules governing:

- some commuter air taxi operations;
- the transportation of mail by aircraft under a postal services contract;
- the carriage of persons or property for compensation or hire as a commercial operator (not an air carrier) in aircraft having:
    - a maximum seating capacity of less than 20 passengers; or
    - a maximum payload capacity of less than 6,000 pounds; or
    - if within any one state of the US, 30 seats or less, or payload 7,500 pounds or less.

Some commuter and even some sightseeing operations (such as those operating in the Grand Canyon area) must also operate under Part 119 and Part 121 rules.

Part 135 does *not* apply to:

- student instruction;
- nonstop sightseeing flights within 25 statute miles (sm) of the airport;
- ferry or training flights;
- aerial work operations (including crop dusting, banner towing, aerial photography or survey, fire fighting, and others).

Pilot-in-Command Qualifications

A pilot-in-command during Part 135 IFR operations must:

- hold at least a commercial pilot certificate with appropriate category and class ratings (and type rating if required);
- have at least 1,200 hours of flight time as a pilot, including 500 hours cross-country flight time, 100 hours night flight time, and 75 hours of actual or simulated instrument flight time (at least 50 of which were in actual flight); and
- for an airplane, hold an instrument rating, or an airline transport pilot certificate with an airplane category rating.

✍ Commercial students complete **Review 20, Commercial** on page 459.

✍ Review 20

Part (a)

1. Night is defined as starting at _____ and ending at _____ .

   ➤ the end of evening civil twilight, the beginning of morning civil twilight

2. With respect to the certification of airmen, which is a class of aircraft?
   (a) Airplane, rotorcraft, glider, lighter-than-air.
   (b) Single-engine land and sea, multiengine land and sea.
   (c) Lighter-than-air, airship, hot air balloon, gas balloon.

   ➤ (b)

3. With respect to the certification of aircraft, which is a class of aircraft?
   (a) Airplane, helicopter, glider, hot air balloon.
   (b) Normal, utility, aerobatic, limited.
   (c) Transport, restricted, provisional.

   ➤ (a)

4. An ATC clearance provides:
   (a) priority over all other traffic.
   (b) adequate separation from all traffic.
   (c) authorization to proceed under specified traffic conditions in Class A, B, C, D and E airspace.

   ➤ (c)

5. With respect to the certification of aircraft, *utility* is a (category/class) of aircraft.

   ➤ category

6. With respect to the certification of aircraft, *airplane* is a (category/class) of aircraft.

   ➤ class

7. An Airworthiness Certificate remains valid (permanently/provided the aircraft is maintained and operated according to the Regulations).

   ➤ provided the aircraft is maintained and operated according to the Regulations

8. Where can you find the legal definitions of *Air Traffic Control* and *Air Traffic Clearance?*

   ➤ Part 1.1

Regulations

9. To achieve the greatest gain in altitude in the shortest distance, you should fly at (V_X/V_Y/V_{LE}).

   ➤ V_X

10. To achieve the greatest gain in altitude in the shortest time, you should fly at (V_X/V_Y/V_{LE}).

    ➤ V_Y

11. Maximum landing gear extended speed is symbolized by _____ .

    ➤ V_{LE}

12. Maximum flap extended speed is symbolized by _____ .

    ➤ V_{FE}

13. Maximum structural cruise speed is symbolized by _____ .

    ➤ V_{NO}

14. V_{S0} is defined as the:
    (a) stalling speed or minimum steady flight speed in the landing configuration.
    (b) stalling speed or minimum steady flight speed in a specified configuration.
    (c) stalling speed or minimum takeoff safety speed.

    ➤ (a)

Part (b)

1. Name two documents that must be in your possession any time you fly as pilot-in-command.

   ➤ (1) a current pilot certificate and (2) a current medical certificate

2. When must a current pilot certificate be in the pilot's personal possession or readily accessible in the aircraft?
   (a) When acting as a crew chief during launch and recovery of a glider.
   (b) Only when passengers are carried.
   (c) Anytime when acting as pilot-in-command or as a required crewmember.

   ➤ (c)

3. A private pilot certificate (has/does not have) a specific expiration date.

   ➤ does not have

4. For private pilot operations, a Third-Class or Second-Class medical certificate issued on July 15, this year is valid until midnight on:
   (a) July 15, 2 years later.
   (b) July 31, 1 year later.
   (c) July 31, 3 years later, if the pilot was younger than 40 on the date of the examination.

   ➤ (c)

5. For private pilot operations, a First-Class Medical Certificate issued on October 21, this year, will expire at midnight on:
   (a) October 21, 2 years later.
   (b) October 31, next year.
   (c) October 31, 2 years later, if the pilot was 40 or older on the date of the examination.

   ➤ (c)

6. You are required to hold a type rating to act as pilot-in-command of an aircraft having a maximum certificated takeoff weight of more than _____ pounds.

   ➤ 12,500

7. In order to act as pilot-in-command of a high-performance, complex airplane, a pilot must have:
   (a) made three solo takeoffs and landings in a high-performance airplane.
   (b) received and logged flight training in an airplane that has more than 200 horsepower, and/or retractable landing gear, flaps, and a controllable propeller.
   (c) passed a flight test in a high-performance airplane.

   ➤ (b)

8. To carry passengers, you must have made _____ takeoffs and _____ landings within the preceding _____ days in an aircraft of the same category and class, or type. For tailwheel airplanes, the landings (must/need not) be to a full stop.

   ➤ 3, 3, 90, must

9. The three takeoffs and landings that are required to act as pilot-in-command at night must be done during the time period from:
   (a) sunset to sunrise.
   (b) 1 hour after sunset to 1 hour before sunrise.
   (c) the end of evening civil twilight to the beginning of morning civil twilight.

   ➤ (b)

10. If recency of experience requirements for night flight are not met and official sunset is 1830, the latest time passengers may be carried is:
    (a) 1829.
    (b) 1859.
    (c) 1929.

    ➤ (c)

11. Unless you notify the FAA Airman Certification Branch in _____ City in writing of any change in your permanent mailing address, you may not exercise the privileges of your pilot certificate after _____ days from the date of moving.

    ➤ Oklahoma, 30

12. A certificated private pilot may not act as pilot-in-command of an aircraft towing a glider unless there is entered in the pilot's logbook a minimum of:
    (a) 100 hours of pilot flight time in any aircraft.
    (b) 100 hours of pilot flight time in powered aircraft.
    (c) 200 hours of pilot flight time in powered aircraft.

    ➤ (b)

13. As one requirement to act as pilot-in-command of an aircraft towing a glider, you must have made at least _____ actual or simulated glider tows while accompanied by a suitably qualified pilot within the previous _____ months.

    ➤ 3, 12

14. In regard to general privileges and limitations, a private pilot may:
    (a) act as pilot-in-command of an aircraft carrying a passenger for compensation if the flight is in connection with a business or employment.
    (b) not pay less than the pro rata share of the operating expenses of a flight with passengers, provided the expense involve only fuel, oil, airport expenditure, or rental fees
    (c) not be paid in any manner for the operating expenses of a flight.

    ➤ (b)

15. What is the exception to the rule that a private pilot may not act as pilot-in-command of an aircraft carrying passengers or property for compensation or hire?

    ➤ during an airlift for a charitable organization, when the FAA has been notified and a donation made to the charitable organization

Part (c)

1. The final authority as to the operation of an airplane is the (FAA/pilot-in-command/owner).

   ➤ pilot-in-command

2. Who is responsible for determining if an aircraft is in condition for safe flight?
   (a) A certificated aircraft mechanic.
   (b) The pilot-in-command.
   (c) The owner or operator.

   ➤ (b)

3. In an in-flight emergency requiring immediate action, the pilot-in-command (may/must not) deviate from the Regulations to the extent required to meet that emergency. A written report of the deviation should be sent to the FAA (on request/immediately/within 7 days/within 24 hours).

   ➤ may, on request

4. Where may an aircraft's operating limitations be found?
   (a) On the Airworthiness Certificate.
   (b) In the current, FAA-approved flight manual, approved manual material, markings, and placards, or any combination thereof.
   (c) In the aircraft airframe and engine logbooks.

   ➤ (b)

5. In addition to a valid Airworthiness Certificate, which documents should also be carried onboard an aircraft? What is a useful acronym to help you remember these?

   ➤ AROW

6. You (may/may not) drop an object from an aircraft in flight provided you have taken reasonable precautions to avoid injury or damage to persons or property.

   ➤ may

7. To act as a crewmember, a person must not have consumed alcohol in the preceding _____ hours.

   ➤ 8

8. What is the blood alcohol limit for a person to act as a crewmember even if they have not consumed alcohol in the previous 8 hours?

   ➤ 0.04% by weight

9. May a medical patient under the influence of drugs be carried on an aircraft? What about other people under the influence of drugs or alcohol?

   ➤ yes, no

10. Which preflight action is specifically required of the pilot prior to each flight?
    (a) Check the aircraft logbooks for appropriate entries.
    (b) Become familiar with all available information concerning the flight.
    (c) Review wake turbulence avoidance procedures.

    ➤ (b)

11. Preflight action, as required for all flights away from the vicinity of an airport, shall include:
    (a) the designation of an alternate airport.
    (b) a study of arrival procedures at airports/heliports of intended use.
    (c) an alternate course of action if the flight cannot be completed as planned.

    ➤ (c)

12. Prior to (all/cross-country) flights, you should consider runway lengths and takeoff/landing distances required.

    ➤ all

13. The pilot's seat belt (is/is not) required to be worn en route.

    ➤ is

14. Flight crewmembers are required by the Regulations to keep their seat belts and shoulder harnesses fastened during _____ .

    ➤ takeoffs and landings

15. The pilot (is/is not) required by the Regulations to brief passengers on how to fasten and unfasten their safety belt.

    ➤ is

16. With certain exceptions, safety belts are required to be secured about passengers during:
    (a) taxi, takeoffs, and landings.
    (b) all flight conditions.
    (c) flight in turbulent air.

    ➤ (a)

17. No person may operate an aircraft in formation flight:
    (a) over a densely populated area.
    (b) in Class D airspace under special VFR.
    (c) except by prior arrangement with the pilot-in-command of each aircraft.

    ➤ (c)

18. Which category of aircraft must give right-of-way to all others in normal circumstances: (airplane/balloon/glider/airship)?

    ➤ airplane

19. Which aircraft has the right-of-way over all other air traffic?
   (a) A balloon.
   (b) An aircraft in distress.
   (c) An aircraft on final approach to land.
   ➤ (b)

20. An airplane refueling another (has/does not have) right-of-way over a glider.
   ➤ does not have (it only has right-of-way over other engine-driven aircraft)

21. What action is required when two aircraft of the same category converge, but not head-on?
   (a) The faster aircraft shall give way.
   (b) The aircraft on the left shall give way.
   (c) Each aircraft shall give way to the right.
   ➤ (b)

22. An airplane is converging at an angle with a helicopter on its left. Which one has right-of-way?
   ➤ the airplane

23. A glider and an airplane are on a head-on collision course. What action should be taken?
   ➤ both should turn right

24. An airship and an airplane are converging, with the airship left of the airplane's position. Which aircraft has the right-of-way?
   ➤ the airship

25. When two or more aircraft are approaching an airport for the purpose of landing, the right-of-way belongs to the aircraft:
   (a) that has the other to its right.
   (b) that is the least maneuverable.
   (c) at the lower altitude, but it shall not take advantage of this rule to cut in front of or to overtake another.
   ➤ (c)

26. In an overtaking situation, the aircraft being overtaken (has/does not have) right-of-way.
   ➤ has

27. An aircraft being overtaken should expect to be passed on the (right/left).
   ➤ right

28. Maximum speed below 10,000 feet MSL is _____ KIAS for all aircraft.
   ➤ 250 KIAS

29. Maximum speed in Class B airspace is _____ KIAS for all aircraft.
   ➤ 250 KIAS

30. Maximum speed in Class C or D airspace within 4 nautical miles of the primary airport is _____ KIAS for all aircraft.
   ➤ 200 KIAS

31. Except when necessary for takeoff or landing, an aircraft may not be operated closer than what distance from any person, vessel, vehicle, or structure?
   (a) 500 feet.
   (b) 700 feet.
   (c) 1,000 feet.
   ➤ (a)

32. Except when necessary for takeoff and landing, the minimum safe altitude for a pilot to operate over congested areas is an altitude of _____ feet above the highest obstacle within a horizontal radius of _____ feet.
   ➤ 1,000 feet, 2,000 feet

33. Except when necessary for takeoff or landing, what is the minimum safe altitude for a pilot to operate an aircraft anywhere?
   (a) An altitude allowing, if a power unit fails, an emergency landing without undue hazard to persons or property on the surface.
   (b) An altitude of 500 feet above the surface and no closer than 500 feet to any person, vessel, vehicle, or structure.
   (c) An altitude of 500 feet above the highest obstacle within a horizontal radius of 1,000 feet.
   ➤ (a)

34. Prior to takeoff, you should set in the pressure window of the altimeter (the current reported altimeter setting/29.92).
   ➤ the current reported altimeter setting

35. When cruising below 18,000 feet MSL, you should set in the pressure window of the altimeter (the current reported altimeter setting/29.92).
   ➤ the current reported altimeter setting

36. When would a pilot be required to submit a detailed report of an emergency which caused the pilot to deviate from an ATC clearance?
   (a) When requested by ATC.
   (b) Immediately.
   (c) Within 7 days.
   ➤ (a)

37. If the control tower uses a light signal to direct a pilot to give way to other aircraft and continue circling, the light will be:
   (a) flashing red.
   (b) steady red.
   (c) alternating red and green.
➤ (b)

38. A steady green light directed from the control tower to an aircraft in flight means _____ .
➤ cleared to land

39. An alternating red and green light signal directed from the control tower to an aircraft in flight is a signal to:
   (a) hold position.
   (b) exercise extreme caution.
   (c) not land; the airport is unsafe.
➤ (b)

40. A flashing white light directed from the control tower to an aircraft on the ground means _____ .
➤ return to the starting point on the airport

41. While on final approach for landing, the control tower directs an alternating red and green light at you, followed by a flashing red light. What actions should you take?
➤ exercise extreme caution, then on seeing flashing red (only) abandon the approach because the airport is unsafe and the ATC message is *"do not land"*

Part (d)

1. Approaching to land at an airport in Class G airspace, if not otherwise indicated all turns should be made to the (right/left).
➤ left

2. When departing an airport located in Class E airspace, you should make all turns to the (left/comply with any FAA traffic pattern established at that airport).
➤ comply with any FAA traffic pattern established for that airport

3. Operating from a satellite airport located in Class D airspace, two-way radio communications must be established with ATC (prior to takeoff/as soon as possible after departure).
➤ as soon as possible after departure

4. An ATC clearance (is/is not) required to operate at an airport located in Class D airspace.
➤ is

5. What minimum radio equipment is required to operate in Class C airspace?
➤ two-way radio communications, and an altitude-encoding transponder

6. An encoding altimeter is required in _____ airspace.
➤ Class B and C

7. What fuel is required for a VFR flight by day?
➤ flight fuel plus 30 minutes at normal cruise speed

8. What fuel is required for a VFR flight at night?
➤ flight fuel plus 45 minutes at normal cruise speed

9. In what airspace may a special VFR clearance be issued by ATC?
➤ Class B, C, D or E surface areas, except at the airports listed in Part 91, Appendix D, Section 3

10. The visibility and distance-from-clouds requirements of a special VFR clearance are _____ .
➤ visibility 1 sm, and clear of clouds

11. May a non-instrument-rated pilot fly special VFR at night?
➤ no

12. VFR cruise altitudes are required to be maintained when flying more than _____ feet AGL, based on (true/magnetic) (course/heading).
➤ 3,000 feet AGL, magnetic course

13. What is the next higher appropriate cruise altitude or flight level to 5,000 feet MSL for a VFR flight along an airway whose magnetic course is MC 180?
➤ 6,500 feet MSL

14. The batteries in an emergency locator transmitter (ELT) must be replaced, or recharged, when the ELT has been used for more than (1/2/3/5) cumulative hour(s), or (100/70/50/10)% of the battery's useful life.
➤ 1 hour, 50%

15. When may you conduct a ground test of an ELT?
➤ during the first 5 minutes after any hour

16. Except in Alaska, you should display position lights during the period from _____ until _____ .
➤ sunset to sunrise

17. When flying above a cabin altitude of _____ feet MSL, a pilot operating under Part 91 Rules is required to use supplemental oxygen continuously.

➤ 14,000

18. When operating an aircraft at cabin pressure altitudes above 12,500 feet MSL up to and including 14,000 feet MSL, supplemental oxygen shall be used during:
    (a) the entire flight time at those altitudes.
    (b) that flight time in excess of 10 minutes at those altitudes.
    (c) that flight time in excess of 30 minutes at those altitudes.

➤ (c)

19. An operable 4096-code transponder with an encoding altimeter is required in which airspace?
    (a) Class A, Class B (and within 30 miles of the Class B primary airport), and Class C.
    (b) Class D and Class E (below 10,000 feet MSL).
    (c) Class D and Class G (below 10,000 feet MSL).

➤ (a)

20. The minimum altitude for aerobatic flight is _____ .

➤ 1,500 feet AGL

21. The minimum flight visibility for aerobatic flight is _____ .

➤ 3 statute miles

22. In which airspace is acrobatic flight prohibited?
    (a) Class D airspace, Class E airspace designated for Federal Airways.
    (b) All Class E airspace below 1,500 feet AGL.
    (c) All Class G airspace.

➤ (a)

23. A chair-type parachute must have been packed by a certificated and appropriately rated parachute rigger within the preceding:
    (a) 60 days.
    (b) 90 days.
    (c) 120 days.

➤ (c)

24. An annual inspection was due at 1259.6 hours, but was actually done at 1261.2 hours. When is the next 100-hour inspection due?
    (a) 1349.6 hours.
    (b) 1359.6 hours.
    (c) 1361.2 hours.

➤ (b)

25. Rental aircraft and those used for flight instruction require (annual/100-hour/both annual and 100-hour) inspections.

➤ both annual and 100-hour

26. The annual inspection (can/cannot) replace a 100-hour inspection. The reverse (does/does not) apply.

➤ can, does not

27. An aircraft which had an annual inspection on August 3 this year is due for another annual inspection no later than _____ next year.

➤ August 31

28. No person may use an ATC transponder unless it has been tested and inspected within at least the preceding:
    (a) 6 calendar months.
    (b) 12 calendar months.
    (c) 24 calendar months.

➤ (c)

29. The expiration date of the last annual aircraft inspection is found on the (Airworthiness Certificate/Registration Certificate/maintenance records).

➤ maintenance records

30. An accident must be reported to the NTSB (immediately/within 10 days).

➤ immediately

31. May aircraft wreckage be moved prior to the time the NTSB takes custody?
    (a) Yes, but only if moved by a federal, state, or local law enforcement officer.
    (b) Yes, but only to protect the wreckage from further damage.
    (c) No, it may not be moved under any circumstances.

➤ (b)

32. A forced landing because of piston-engine failure (must/need not) be notified immediately to the nearest NTSB field office.

➤ need not

33. An in-flight fire (must/need not) be notified immediately to the nearest NTSB field office.

➤ must

34. The operator of an aircraft that has been involved in an accident is required to file an accident report within how many days?
   (a) 5.
   (b) 7.
   (c) 10.
   ➤ (c)

35. An overdue aircraft believed to have been involved in an accident (must/need not) be notified immediately to the nearest NTSB field office.
   ➤ must

Commercial Review

1. A person, who for compensation or hire, engages in air commerce by the carriage of persons or property in an aircraft, other than as an *air carrier,* is known as (an operator/a commercial operator).
   ➤ a commercial operator

2. The exercise of authority over initiating, conducting, or terminating a flight is known as _____ .
   ➤ operational control

3. Regulations which refer to an operator relate to that person who:
   (a) acts as pilot-in-command of the aircraft.
   (b) is the sole manipulator of the aircraft controls.
   (c) causes the aircraft to be used or authorizes its use.
   ➤ (c)

4. A normal category aircraft (may/may not) perform spins.
   ➤ may not

5. Which is the correct symbol for the stalling speed or the minimum steady flight speed in a specified configuration?
   (a) V_S.
   (b) V_{S1}.
   (c) V_{S0}.
   ➤ (b)

6. Design flap speed is symbolized by _____.
   ➤ V_F

7. For commercial pilot operations, a first or second-class medical certificate on April 5 this year is valid until midnight on _____ (1/2/3) years later.
   ➤ April 30, 1

8. You are required to have a category and class rating appropriate to the aircraft being flown prior to a (test flight/solo flight/flight for compensation or hire).
   ➤ flight for compensation or hire

9. To act as pilot-in-command of an aircraft under Part 91, a commercial pilot must have satisfactorily accomplished a flight review or completed a proficiency check within the preceding:
   (a) 6 months.
   (b) 12 months.
   (c) 24 months.
   ➤ (c)

10. If a pilot does not meet the recency of experience requirements for night flight and official sunset is 1800 CST, the latest time passengers should be carried is:
   (a) 1759 CST.
   (b) 1829 CST.
   (c) 1859 CST.
   ➤ (c)

11. A commercial pilot without an instrument rating may not carry passengers for hire on cross-country flights of more than _____ nm. Carrying passengers at night (is/is not) prohibited for this pilot.
   ➤ 50, is

12. If a large civil US aircraft is leased, then a copy of the lease must be mailed to the FAA in _____ City within a period of _____.
   ➤ Oklahoma, 24 hours

13. Portable electronic devices which may cause interference with the navigation or communications system may not be operated on aircraft being flown:
   (a) along Federal airways.
   (b) within the US.
   (c) in commercial operations.
   ➤ (c)

14. The required preflight action relative to alternatives available, if the planned flight cannot be completed, is applicable to:
   (a) IFR flights only.
   (b) any flight not in the vicinity of an airport.
   (c) any flight conducted for hire or compensation.
   ➤ (b)

15. In addition to other preflight actions for IFR flight, regulations require that you, as pilot-in-command, become familiar with all available information concerning that flight, including runway lengths and takeoff and landing distance data for your aircraft. For IFR flights, or any flight not in the vicinity of an airport, four other items are specifically mentioned in the Regulations. What are they?

➤ (1) weather reports and forecasts; (2) fuel requirements; (3) alternatives available if the planned flight cannot be completed; (4) any known traffic delays

16. At night, the pilot of aircraft A sees only the green light of aircraft B, which is converging from the (left/right). Therefore aircraft (A/B) has right-of-way.

➤ left, A

17. If weather conditions at the destination require an alternate airport to be designated on your flight plan, what minimum fuel is required?

➤ flight fuel from departure airport to destination airport, plus flight fuel from destination airport to alternate airport, plus 45 minutes reserve at normal cruise speed

18. Normal day VFR reserve fuel is _____ minutes, whereas night VFR reserve fuel and IFR reserve fuel, day or night, is _____ minutes.

➤ 30, 45

19. If no IFR minimum altitude is prescribed, the minimum IFR altitude for a route in designated mountainous terrain is _____ feet above the highest obstacle within _____ nautical miles of the route; and the clearance required above non-mountainous terrain is _____ feet.

➤ 2,000, 4, 1,000

20. An IFR flight on a westerly course should be planned at (odd/odd+500/even/even+500) altitudes or flight levels, as appropriate.

➤ even

21. Which is required equipment for powered aircraft during VFR night flights?
    (a) Anticollision light system.
    (b) Gyroscopic direction indicator.
    (c) Gyroscopic bank-and-pitch indicator.

➤ (a)

22. A transponder must be tested and inspected within _____ calendar months. If not, it (may/may not) be used.

➤ 24, may not

23. A pilot operating a flight under Part 125 may find that he or she must also comply with rules set down in Part 119 (true/false).

➤ true

24. Part 135 applies to carriage of persons and property for compensation or hire in aircraft with less than _____ passenger seats or a maximum payload capacity of less than _____ pounds.

➤ 20 seats, 6,000 pounds;

25. By day, you should fly VFR no lower than _____ feet AGL and at least _____ feet horizontally from any obstacle.

➤ 500, 500

26. By night over terrain not designated as mountainous, you should fly VFR at an altitude of at least _____ feet above the highest obstacle within a horizontal distance of _____ from the intended course.

➤ 1,000, 5 miles

27. By night over designated mountainous terrain, you should fly VFR at an altitude of at least _____ feet above the highest obstacle within a horizontal distance of _____ from the intended course.

➤ 2,000, 5 miles

Charts and Airspace 21

Aeronautical Charts

If you want to navigate an airplane efficiently from one place to another over long distances or in poor visibility, you need to refer to some representation of the earth. This representation must be smaller in size than the earth portraying a picture of a "reduced earth."

The simplest and most accurate reduced representation of earth is a globe, which retains the spherical shape of the earth and displays the various oceans, continents, cities, and so on. A cumbersome globe is not the ideal navigation tool to have in a cockpit or to carry in a navigation bag, especially if detailed information is required, hence the need for maps or charts that can be folded and stowed away. The task of the "map-maker" or cartographer is to project a picture of a reduced-earth globe onto a flat surface and make a map or chart from this.

Maps represent the earth's surface, or parts thereof, on a flat surface; **charts** are maps which show additional information or special conditions, sometimes using only an outline of geographical features such as the coastline. Since most maps that pilots use show specific aeronautical and navigational data, they are referred to as charts. Since most maps that pilots use show specific aeronautical and navigational data, they are referred to as charts.

The Form or Shape of the Earth

The exact shape of the earth's surface is constantly changing. Volcanoes erupt and grow, new islands form and others disappear, landslides and earthquakes cause large land movements, the ocean surface continually changes in height with the tides, and, on a very long-term basis, the continents gradually move.

The regular geometric shape that the earth resembles most is a sphere, but even when all the surface bumps are ironed out, the earth is still not a perfect sphere. It is slightly flat at the North and South Poles, forming a flattened (oblate) spheroid, the polar diameter being approximately 23 nautical miles (nm) less than the equatorial diameter (6,865 nm as against 6,888 nm). For the purposes of practical navigation, however, the earth can be treated as a sphere.

The earth rotates on its own axis as well as moving in an orbit about the sun. This axis of rotation is called the geographic **polar axis,** and the two points where it meets the surface of the sphere are called:

- the northern geographic pole or **true north;** and
- the southern geographic pole or **true south.**

If you stand anywhere on earth and face toward the northern geographic pole, then you are facing true north.

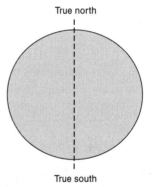

Figure 21-1. The earth is a slightly flattened (oblate) sphere

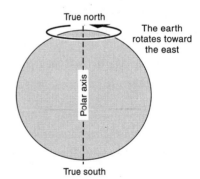

Figure 21-2. The earth rotates about its own axis

Imaginary Lines on the Earth's Surface

A **great circle** drawn on the earth's surface is one whose plane passes through the center of the earth. Great circles have some significant properties, including those below.

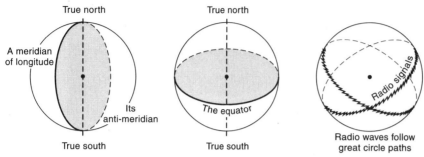

Figure 21-3. A great circle has the center of the earth as its axis

- A great circle is the largest circle that can be drawn on the surface of the earth or on any sphere.
- The shortest distance between any two points on the surface of a sphere is the arc of a great circle.
- Only one great circle can be drawn between two points on the surface of a sphere (unless the two points are diametrically opposed, as are the geographic poles).

Some examples of great circles are: meridians of longitude, the equator, and the paths that radio waves follow.

A **small circle** is any circle on the surface of a sphere that is not a great circle and therefore the center of a small circle is not at the center of the earth. Parallels of latitude (other than the equator) are small circles.

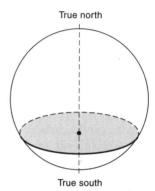

Figure 21-4. The plane of a small circle does not pass through the center of a sphere

Latitude and Longitude

A convenient way of specifying the position of any point on earth is to relate it to the imaginary lines that form the **latitude** and **longitude** grid on the surface of the earth.

Latitude. The reference for latitude is the plane of the **equator,** the great circle whose plane is perpendicular (at right angles, or 90 degrees) to the polar axis.

- The **latitude** of a place is its angular distance in degrees from the equator, measured at the center of the earth and designated either north or south. For instance, Detroit, Michigan is at 42°N latitude.
- A **parallel of latitude** joins all points of the same latitude and (except for the equator) is a small circle. Detroit, Boston, Barcelona in Spain, Rome in Italy, Istanbul in Turkey, Tashkent in Uzbekistan and Shenyang in China are all about 42° north of the equator, and therefore the line joining them is called the 42°N parallel of latitude.
- Parallels of latitude are parallel to the equator and to each other.
- The longest parallel of latitude is the equator (latitude 0°). The other parallels, as you move away from the equator toward the higher latitudes, progressively decrease in size until the 90° parallels of latitude become just points at the north and south geographic poles.

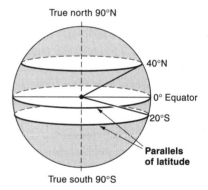

Figure 21-5. Latitude

Longitude. The basic reference for longitude is the **Greenwich meridian,** which is also known as the **prime meridian.** It is that half of the great circle which contains the polar axis (about which the earth rotates), and passes through the Greenwich Observatory situated near London, England, as well as

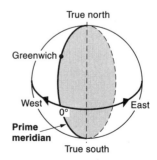

Figure 21-6. The prime meridian

the north and south geographic poles. The prime meridian is designated as *longitude 0°*.

The other half of the same great circle that makes up the prime meridian is on the other side of the earth from Greenwich. It passes down the western side of the Pacific Ocean and is known as *longitude 180°*. It can be reached by traveling 180 degrees either east or west from the prime meridian. Therefore longitude 180° can be called either 180°E or 180°W. It is also called the **anti-meridian** of Greenwich.

- All of the great circles containing the polar axis (and therefore the north and south geographic poles) are called **meridians of longitude.**

- Meridians of longitude are specified by their angular difference in degrees east or west from the prime meridian.

Specifying Position

The parallels of latitude and meridians of longitude form an imaginary grid over the surface of the earth. Position of any point on the earth can be specified by:

- its **latitude**—the angular position N or S of the plane of the equator; together with

- its **longitude**—the angular position E or W of the prime meridian.

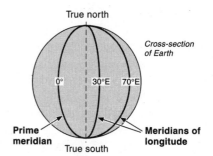

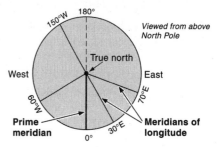

Figure 21-7. The longitude of a place is the angle between its meridian of longitude and the prime (Greenwich) meridian, measured east or west from the prime meridian

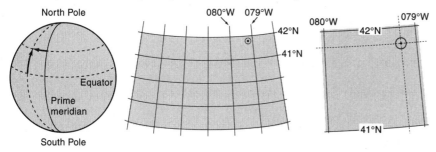

Figure 21-8. The position of Warren in Pennsylvania is 41°50′N, 79°08′W

It is usually sufficiently accurate to specify the latitude and longitude of a place in degrees and minutes (one minute is $\frac{1}{60}$ of one degree). For more accuracy, each minute is divided into 60 seconds of arc. The symbols used are degrees (°), minutes (″), and seconds (′). For example, the position of Warren in Pennsylvania is N41°50′, W079°08′, accurate to the nearest minute.

Modern electronic navigation systems are very accurate, requiring latitude and longitude to be expressed to an accuracy of 0.1 of arc (6 seconds of arc is the same as 0.1′ of arc). To cater for these systems, aeronautical charts and documents such as the Airport/Facility Directory would show position N522°0'36, W105°25′6 as N52°20.6′, W105°25.1′.

Latitude and longitude are the normal means to indicate a particular position on earth. They are most commonly used at the flight planning stage when preparing the charts and flight plan. Once in flight, however, there are other means of specifying the position of the aircraft, such as:

- by position over or abeam a landmark or radio beacon—for instance, *"Over Tuscaloosa, Abeam Mansfield, Over Casa Grande VOR,"* or

- by range (distance) and bearing from a landmark or radio beacon—for instance, *"10 nm on a bearing of 290°T from Ocean City."*

Note: The use of place names needs to be confined to places that are likely to be known to the recipient of the message, and that are shown on the commonly used aeronautical charts. In the United States, place names are frequently duplicated and can be misleading.

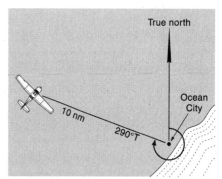

Figure 21-9. Specifying position on the earth by range and bearing

Distances

The standard unit of distance in navigation is the **nautical mile (nm),** which is the length of 1 minute of the arc of any great circle on earth. There are 360 degrees in a circle and 60 minutes in a degree, making $60 \times 360 = 21{,}600$ minutes of arc in a circle. The circumference of the earth is therefore $60 \times 360 = 21{,}600$ minutes of arc, which is 21,600 nm.

Latitude (the angular distance north or south of the equator) is measured up and down a meridian of longitude (which is a great circle) and therefore:

- 1 minute of latitude at any point on earth = 1 nautical mile;
- 1 degree of latitude at any point on earth = 60 nautical miles.

This is very useful for measuring distances on a chart, although the usual means of measuring distance is to use the scale line or a plotter.

Longitude is measured around the parallels of latitude (all small circles, except for the equator), and so 1 minute of longitude varies in length, depending on where it is on the earth's surface.

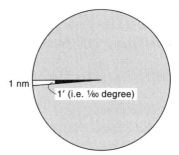

Figure 21-10. 1 nm is the length of 1 minute of arc of a great circle on the earth

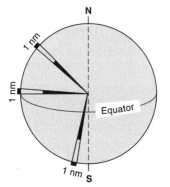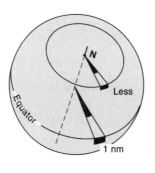

Figure 21-11. 1 minute of latitude = 1 nm; 1 minute of longitude varies in length

The only place where 1 minute of longitude is equal to 1 nm is around the equator—the higher the latitude, the further away from the equator the place is, and the shorter the length of 1 minute of longitude in that region.

Angles

The most fundamental reference from which angles are measured is that of true north, from 000°T, through 090°T, 180°T, 270°T, to 360°T. As Figure 21-12 shows, if an airplane follows a long-range great circle course, the course direction will gradually change. A great circle route will therefore cross successive meridians at a gradually changing angle.

Sometimes it is convenient to fly a course whose direction remains constant when referred to true north, so that the course crosses all meridians of longitude at the same angle. This is known as a **rhumb line.**

The rhumb line and great circle between two places coincide only if the two places lie on either the same meridian of longitude (which is a great circle) or on the equator which is also a great circle. In practical terms, the great circle direction and the rhumb line direction may be considered to be the same over short distances of less than 200 nm.

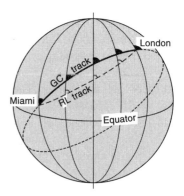

Figure 21-12. The great circle and the rhumb line tracks between two places

Direction is the angular position of one point to another without reference to the distance between them. It is expressed as the angular difference from a specified reference direction. In air navigation this reference direction is either:

- north (for *true* or *magnetic* bearings); or
- the heading (or the nose) of the aircraft (for *relative* bearings).

You must always be very clear as to whether you are referring direction to true north or to magnetic north, the difference between the two being the magnetic variation. In this chapter, we are referring direction to true north.

A true course of 085°T (85° measured clockwise from true north) may be written as TC 085. A magnetic course of 130°M (130° measured clockwise from magnetic north) may be written as MC 130.

It is usual to refer to direction as a three-figure group to prevent any misunderstanding. For example, north is referred to as 360 or 000, east is referred to as 090, south-west as 225.

Direction is usually specified as a three-figure group.

Representing the Spherical Earth on Flat Charts

The latitude–longitude grid is translated onto maps and charts by cartographers whose major task is to represent the spherical surface of the earth on a flat sheet of paper. The process consists of:

- scaling the earth down to a reduced earth; and then
- projecting the reduced earth's surface onto a flat piece of paper.

The process always leads to some distortion of areas, distances, angles or shapes. By using certain mathematical techniques when projecting the spherical earth onto a flat chart, the cartographer can preserve some properties, but not all. Some property will always be distorted to a greater or lesser extent depending on how the points on the surface of the reduced spherical earth are transferred onto the flat chart.

Unlike a sphere, certain other curved surfaces (such as a cylinder or a cone) can be cut and laid out flat. By projecting points on the surface of the reduced earth onto either a conical or cylindrical surface (which can then be flattened out to form a sheet), less distortion occurs and a better chart results, compared with a projection onto an already flat sheet like that illustrated in Figure 21-13.

A simplified view of chart-making is to think of a light projecting the shadows of the latitude–longitude grid of the reduced sphere onto a cone (Lambert conical projection) or onto a cylinder (Mercator cylindrical projection). The cone or cylinder is then laid out flat to form a chart.

Charts based on conic and cylindrical projections are widely used in aviation, mainly because they:

- **preserve shapes** (or at least minimize distortions);
- **preserve angular relationships** (in mathematical terminology, charts that exhibit this important property are said to be *conformal* or *orthomorphic);* and
- have a reasonably **constant scale** over the whole chart.

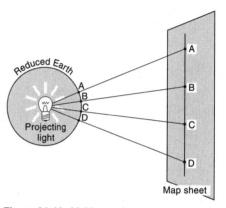

Figure 21-13. Making a chart

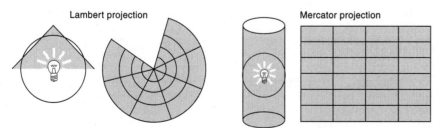

Figure 21-14. A conical projection (Lambert) and a cylindrical projection (Mercator)

Scale

There are various ways of describing just how much the earth is scaled down on a particular chart. Scale is defined as the ratio of the chart length compared to the earth distance that it represents.

$$\text{Scale} = \frac{\text{chart length}}{\text{chart distance}} \quad \text{(with both items in the same unit)}$$

The greater the chart length for a given earth distance, the *larger* the scale and the more detail that can be shown. A large-scale chart covers a small area in detail. For example, a 1:250,000 (one to one-quarter million) chart has a larger scale and can show more detail than a 1:500,000 (one to one-half million) aeronautical chart.

Large scale charts cover small areas in detail.

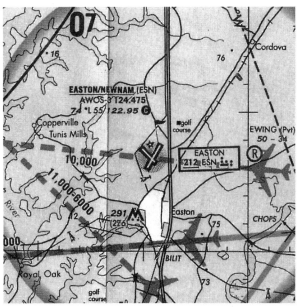 

Figure 21-15. Sample excerpts from 1:250,000 Terminal Area (left) and 1:500,000 Sectional VFR charts covering the same physical area

Scale can be expressed in various ways:

- As a **representative fraction.** For instance, sectionals are 1:500,000 charts (one to one-half million), where 1 inch on the chart represents 500,000 inches (7 nautical miles) on the earth, or where 1 nm on earth is represented by 1 half-millionth of a nautical mile on the chart.

- As a **graduated scale line,** situated at the bottom of the chart. A graduated scale line allows you to measure off the distance between two points on the chart and match it against the scale line. Make sure that you use the correct scale line (usually nautical miles), since there may be various ones so that nautical miles, statute miles or kilometers can be measured.

- In **words**—for instance, "1 inch equals 5 nm," which means that 5 nm on the earth's surface is represented by 1 inch on the chart.

Figure 21-16. Scale lines from a 1:250,000 chart (top) and a 1:500,000 chart

✐ Now complete **Review 21, Part (a)** on page 487.

Town of Leakesville

Highway 45

Maximum Elevation Figure (MEF) 900 ft MSL; (highest known feature, including terrain and obstacles, in this latitude–longitude quadrangle)

Railroad

Military training route IR31 (IFR), 10 nm wide

Military training route VR1021 (VFR, no segments above 1,500 ft AGL)

SPECIAL MILITARY ACTIVITY CONTACT MOBILE FSS ON 122.1R 116.8T FOR ACTIVITY STATUS

State border between Mississippi & Alabama

Power transmission line

31° North parallel of latitude

Group of unlit obstructions 672 ft MSL, 420 ft AGL (see Item ❶ on facing page)

088° West meridian of longitude

Single, unlit obstruction 591 ft MSL, 321 ft AGL (therefore the ground elevation is 270 ft MSL)

ARRIVING VFR AIRCRAFT SHOULD CONTACT MOBILE APPROACH CONTROL WITHIN 20 NM ON 118.5 269.3

Class C airspace band and boundary (see Item ❸ on facing page)

Class C airspace within 5-nm circle (see Item ❷ on facing page)

Boundary of Military Operations Area (MOA)

Not to be used for Navigation

Class D airspace (see Item ❹ on facing page)

Airspace extension (magenta, so Class E)

Class E airspace boundary (see Item ❺ on facing page)

Horn Island visual check point

Boundary of Warning Area W-453

A-292 CAUTION HIGH VOLUME OF ROTARY AND FIXED WING TRAINING SURFACE TO 17,500

BON SECOUR NATIONAL WILDLIFE REFUGE

R-2908

Restricted Area R-2908

1°E isogonic line (magnetic variation 1°E)

WARNING W-453

SECTIONAL CHART
NEW ORLEANS
(Excerpt) SCALE 1:500,000
Part (A)—Airspace, Miscellaneous,
Obstructions & Topographic Data

Sectional Chart Excerpt No. 1

467

LEGEND

Airports having <u>Control Towers</u> are shown in <u>Blue</u>, all others in <u>Magenta</u>. Consult Airport/Facility Directory (A/FD) for details involving airport lighting, navigation aids, and services.

AIRPORTS

 Other than hard-surfaced runways   ⚓ Seaplane Base

Hard-surfaced runways 1500 ft. to 8069 ft. in length

Hard-surfaced runways greater than 8069 ft. or some multiple runways less than 8069 ft.

All recognizable hard-surfaced runways, including those closed, are shown for visual identification.

ADDITIONAL AIRPORT INFORMATION

Ⓡ Private "(Pvt)" – Non-public use having emergency or landmark value

Military – Other than hard-surfaced. All military airports are identified by abbreviations AFB, NAS, AAF, etc. For complete airport information consult DOD FLIP.

Ⓗ Heliport-Selected Public   Ⓤ Unverified   ⊗ Abandoned – paved, having landmark value, 3000 ft. or greater   Ⓕ Ultralight Flight Park Selected

Services – fuel available and field tended during normal working hours depicted by use of ticks around basic airport symbol. (Normal working hours are Mon thru Fri 10:00 A.M. to 4:00 P.M. local time.) Consult A/FD for service availability at airports with hard-surfaced runways greater than 8069 ft.

☆ Rotating airport beacon in operation Sunset to Sunrise.

AIRPORT DATA

FSS – Flight Service Station
RFSS – Remote Flight Service Station(Canada)
NO SVFR – Fixed-wing special VFR flight is prohibited.
CT – 118.3 – Control Tower (CT) – primary frequency
NFCT – Non-Federal Control Tower
★ – Star indicates operation part-time (see tower frequencies tabulation for hours of operation).
Ⓒ – Indicates Common Traffic Advisory Frequencies (CTAF)
ATIS 123.8 – Automatic Terminal Information Service
AWOS-3 135.425 – Automated Weather Observing System
UNICOM – Aeronautical advisory station
VFR Advsy – VFR Advisory Service shown where ATIS not available and frequency is other than primary CT frequency
285 – Elevation in feet
L – Lighting in operation Sunset to Sunrise
*L – Lighting limitations exist, refer to Airport/Facility Directory.
72 – Length of longest runway in hundreds of feet; usable length may be less.

When facility or information is lacking, the respective character is replaced by a dash. All lighting codes refer to runway lights. Lighted runway may not be the longest or lighted full length. All times are local.

RADIO AIDS TO NAVIGATION AND COMMUNICATION BOXES

⬡ VHF OMNI RANGE (VOR)
⬡ VORTAC
⊡ VOR-DME

Non-Directional Radiobeacon

RBn
POINT LOMA
302 ▬▬
H+00 & ev 6m

Marine Radiobeacon

○ Other facilities, i.e., Commercial Broadcast Stations, FSS Outlets-RCO, etc.

OAKDALE
362 *116.8 OAK ▬▬ Ⓣ

Underline indicates no voice on this freq
* – Operates less than continuous or On-Request.
Ⓣ – TWEB   ■ – HIWAS
R – Receive only

CHICAGO CHI

Heavy line box indicates Flight Service Station (FSS). Freqs. 121.5, 122.2, 243.0, and 255.4 (Canada – 121.5, 126.7 and 243.0) are normally available at all FSSs and are not shown above boxes. All other freqs. are shown.

For Local Airport Advisory use FSS freq. 123.6.

In Canada, all available RFSS frequencies are shown.

Frequencies above thin line box are remoted to NAVAID site. Other freqs. at controlling FSS may be available as determined by altitude and terrain. Consult Airport/Facility Directory for complete information.

122.1R
MIAMI
Controlling FSS

AIRPORT TRAFFIC SERVICE AND AIRSPACE INFORMATION

Only the controlled and reserved airspace effective below 18,000 ft. MSL are shown on this chart. All times are local.

▨ Class B Airspace
▨ Class C Airspace (Mode C See F.A.R. 91.215/AIM.)
- - - Class D Airspace

40 Ceiling of Class D Airspace in hundreds of feet (A minus ceiling value indicates surface up to but not including that value.)

—— Class E Airspace

Class E Airspace with floor 700 ft. above surface
Class E Airspace with floor 1200 ft. or greater above surface that abuts Class G Airspace.

2400 MSL Differentiates floors of Class E
4500 MSL Airspace greater than 700 ft. above surface

Class E Airspace low altitude Federal Airways are indicated by center line.

 V 3 ←270°
Intersection – Arrows are directed towards facilities which establish intersection

Prohibited, Restricted, Warning and Alert Areas Canadian Advisory and Restricted Areas

MOA – Military Operations Area

Special Airport Traffic Areas (See F.A.R. Part 93 for details.)

MODE C
(See F.A.R. 91.215/AIM.)

National Security Area

Terminal Radar Service Area (TRSA)

←IR21 MTR – Military Training Routes

OBSTRUCTIONS

⋏ 1000 ft. and higher AGL
⋏ below 1000 ft. AGL
or Group Obstruction
Obstruction with high-intensity lights May operate part-time
2049 ← Elevation of the top above mean sea level
(1149) ← Height above ground
UC ← Under construction or reported: position and elevation unverified

NOTICE: Guy wires may extend outward from structures.

MISCELLANEOUS

—1°E— Isogonic Line (1990 VALUE)
✈ Ultralight Activity   Fl ☆ Flashing Light
Hang Glider Activity   ● Marine Light
Glider Operations
NAME (Magenta, Blue, or Black)
▼ Visual Check Point
⚐ Parachute Jumping Area (See Airport/Facility Directory.)

TOPOGRAPHIC INFORMATION

—— Roads
95 40 Road Markers
Railroad
Bridges And Viaducts
⊥ ⊥ Power Transmission Line
■- - -■ Aerial Cable
■ Landmark Feature – stadium, factory, school, golf course, etc.
♈ Outdoor Theatre
⊙ Lookout Tower P-17 (Site Number) 618 (Elevation Base of Tower)
♦ CG Coast Guard Station
⬭ Race Track
● Tank-water, oil or gas
○ Oil Well   ● Water Well
⚒ Mines And Quarries
Mountain Pass
11823 (Elevation of Pass)

Rocks
Pier   Dams

Perennial Lake

Non-Perennial Lake

Left margin

MILITARY TRAINING ROUTES (MTRs)

All IR and VR MTRs are shown, and may extend from the surface upwards. Only the route centerline, direction of flight along the route and the route designator are depicted – route widths and altitudes are not shown.

Since these routes are subject to change every 56 days, and the charts are reissued every 6 months, you are cautioned and advised to contact the nearest FSS for route dimensions and current status for those routes affecting your flight.

Routes with a change in the alignment of the charted route centerline will be indicated in the Aeronautical Chart Bulletin of the Airport/Facility Directory.

Military Pilots refer to Area Planning AP/1B Military Training Route North and South America for current routes.

53 RD EDITION December 9, 1993

Includes airspace amendments effective November 11, 1993 and all other aeronautical data received by October 14, 1993 Consult appropriate NOTAM's and Flight Information Publications for supplemental data and current information.

This chart will become OBSOLETE FOR USE IN NAVIGATION upon publication of the next edition scheduled for JUNE 23, 1994.

CONTOUR INTERVAL 500 feet
Intermediate contour 250 feet
Auxiliary contours 100 foot intervals

HIGHEST TERRAIN elevation is 720 feet located at 32°11'N – 84°42'W

Critical elevation .... •4254
Approximate elevation x3200
Doubtful locations are indicated by omission of the point locator (dot or "x")

12799
12000
9000
7000
5000
3000
2000
1000
Sea Level

(ASA NOTE: THIS CONTOUR-SHADES BOX IS FROM THE GREAT FALLS SECTIONAL CHART; HIGHEST ELEV'N 12,799 FT MSL)

SECTIONAL CHART NEW ORLEANS (Excerpt) SCALE 1:500,000 — Part (B)—Airport Data & Navigation Facilities

Sectional Chart Excerpt No. 2

469

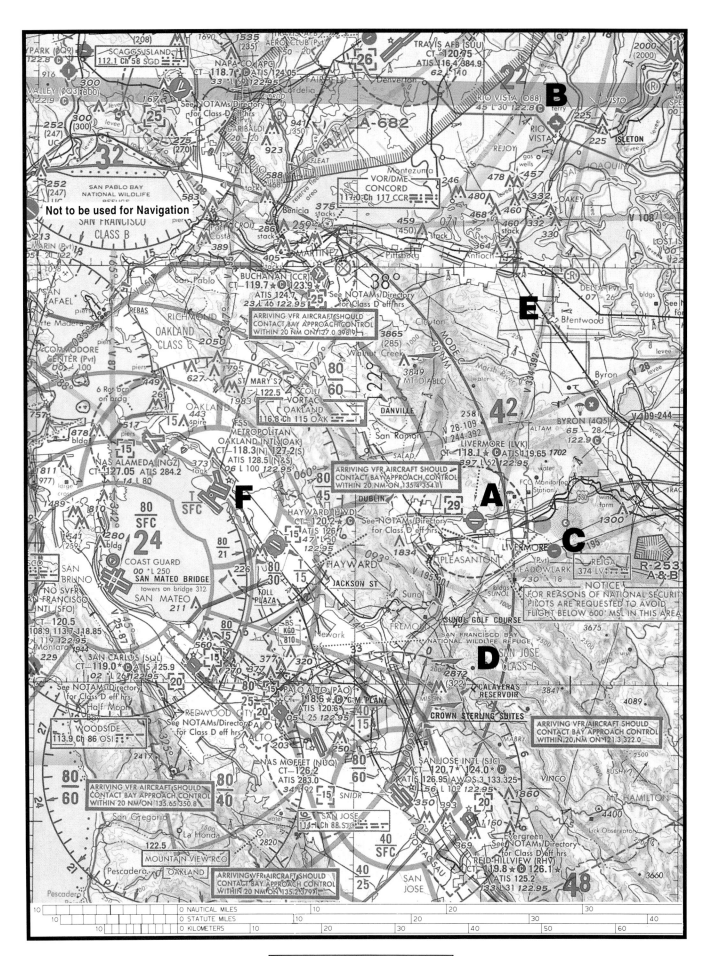

Not to be used for Navigation

Sectional Chart Excerpt No. 3

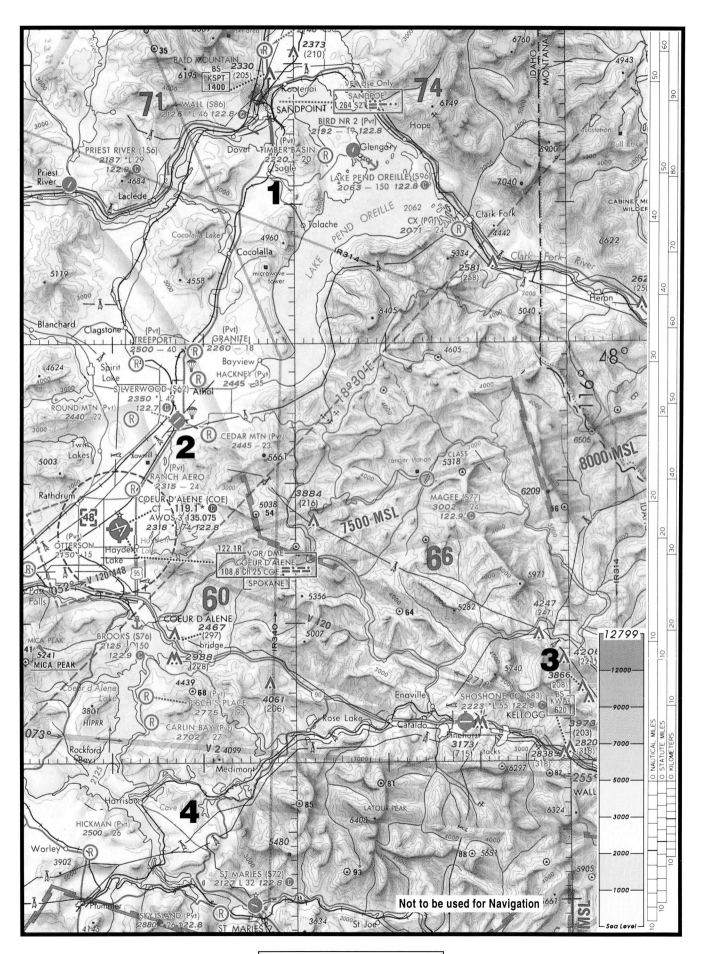

Not to be used for Navigation

Sectional Chart Excerpt No. 4

CG-21
WORLD AERONAUTICAL CHART
(Excerpt) SCALE 1:1,000,000
Lambert Conformal Conic Projection Standard Parallels 33°20' and 38°40'
Horizontal Datum: North American Datum of 1983
Topographic data corrected to March 1993

Not to be used for Navigation

Important Note

Longitude 79°W

Boundary of *Evers* Military Operations Area (MOA)

3000 ft MSL contour

4980 ft MSL spot height

Longitude 80°W

VOR with HIWAS; controlling FSS is *Elkins*

Maximum Elevation Figure (MEF) 5200 ft MSL in this lat-long quadrangle

1000 ft MSL contour

The 39th parallel of latitude (39°N)

Braxton County airport, elev 1270 ft

Scale: 10' of lat. =10nm

Longitude 81°W

Spot height 1500 ft MSL

Terrain between 1000 ft MSL and 2000 ft MSL

Important Note for flights at or below 5000 ft MSL

Class C Airspace area (Mode C)

Latitude 38°N

VFR TERMINAL AREA CHART
SAN FRANCISCO
(Excerpt) SCALE 1:250,000

30-mile radius of *SFO*: Mode C (altitude-encoding) transponder required

Livermore Class D surface area; up to 2900 ft MSL

Two railroads

Populated area (City of Livermore)

IFR Arrival Route

Hang gliding in this area

Area of *San Jose* Class C airspace: from 1500 ft MSL to 4000 ft MSL

Danville visual check point

Communications instructions

ARRIVING VFR AIRCRAFT SHOULD CONTACT BAY APPROACH CONTROL WITHIN 20 NM ON 135.4 354.1

Maximum Elevation Figure (MEF) 3400 ft MSL in this latitude–longitude quadrangle

Victor airways 195 and 301 (Class E)

Meridian of longitude (122°00'W, marked on chart)

Isogonic line; var'n 15°45'E

Unlit obstruction, elev'n 2245 ft MSL (220 ft AGL)

Oakland Class C airspace area; from surface to, but not including, floor of overlying Class B airspace

SFO Class B altitude in *Area F*: from 2100 ft MSL to 8000 ft MSL

San Carlos Class D airspace area: from surface to, but not including, 1500 ft MSL in NE area *(minus 15* means up to, but not including, 1500); from surface to 2000 ft MSL in SW area *(no minus,* so ceiling is *inclusive)*

Palo Alto airport; part-time Tower on freq. 118.6 MHz (is a CTAF when tower closed; refer NOTAMs for hrs); ATIS on 120.6; elev 50ft; rwy lights; longest rwy 2500 ft; UNICOM 122.95

Oakland VORTAC and compass rose, aligned with magnetic north (variation approx 16°E)

Not to be used for Navigation

Boundary of *San Francisco* International airport Class B surface area; labeled *Area A:* from surface to 8000 ft MSL

Power line

Parallel of latitude (37°30'N, marked at side of chart)

Freeway

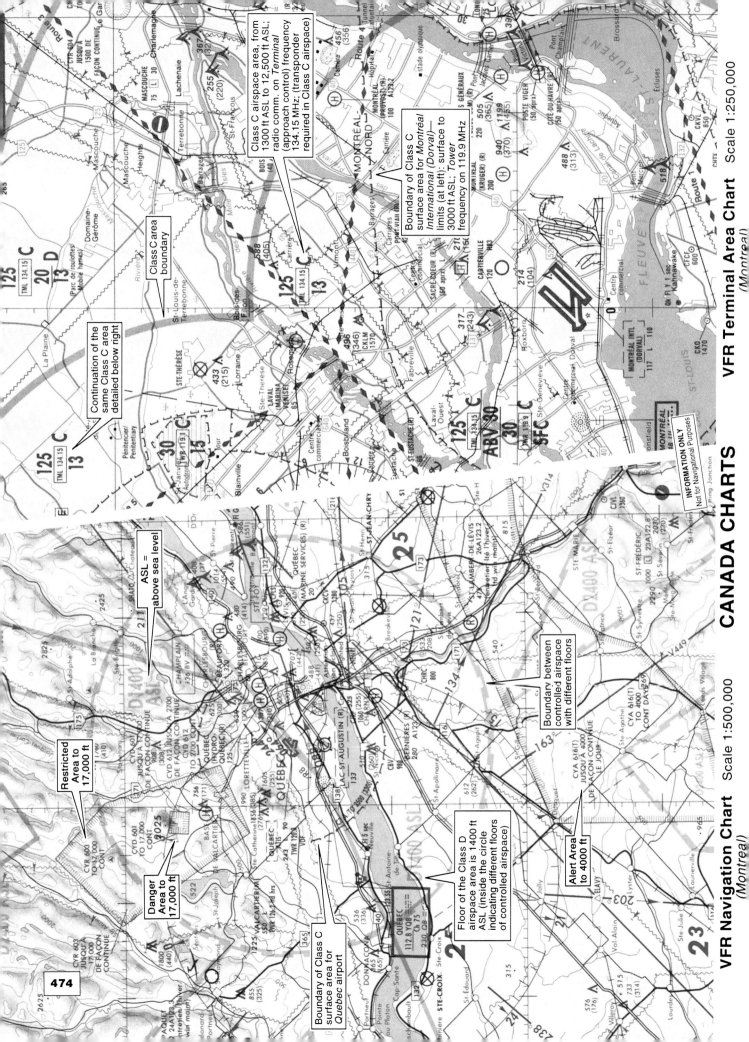

Class C airspace area, from 1300 ft ASL to 12,500 ft ASL; radio comm. on *Terminal* (approach control) frequency 134.15 MHz; (transponder required in Class C airspace)

Boundary of Class C surface area for *Montréal International (Dorval)*—limits (at left); surface to 3000 ft ASL; *Tower* frequency on 119.9 MHz

Class C area boundary

Continuation of the same Class C area detailed below right

ASL = above sea level

Boundary between controlled airspace with different floors

Restricted Area to 17,000 ft

Danger Area to 17,000 ft

Boundary of Class C surface area for *Quebec* airport

Floor of the Class D airspace area is 1400 ft ASL (inside the circle indicating different floors of controlled airspace)

Alert Area to 4000 ft

INFORMATION ONLY
Not for Navigational Purposes

CANADA CHARTS

VFR Terminal Area Chart   Scale 1:250,000
(Montreal)

VFR Navigation Chart   Scale 1:500,000
(Montreal)

474

VFR Charts

When navigating by visual reference to the ground, the pilot refers to land features. A **topographical** chart showing the surface features of the area in detail is therefore of great value. There are various topographical charts available for visual navigation in the United States, including (in order of importance):

- **Sectional Charts,** which are the most common charts used for visual navigation; their scale is 1:500,000 (half-million);
- **VFR Terminal Area Charts,** scale 1:250,000 (quarter-million), showing more detail around busy airports; and
- **1:1,000,000 Navigation Charts,** which have a small scale and are sometimes used for long-distance visual navigation.

Most aviation charts are based on the Lambert conformal conic projection. The chart sheet is formed from a cone that cuts the sphere representing the reduced earth at two standard parallels of latitude. Just which two parallels of latitude are chosen by the cartographer depends on which part of the earth, and how much of it, he wants to represent on that particular chart.

The standard parallels are usually mentioned on the title section of the chart—for example, on the Seattle Sectional the standard parallels are stated to be 41°20 and 46°40. The scale at the standard parallels is correct. Between them it contracts, and outside of them it expands. For practical purposes however, you can assume a constant scale over the whole chart.

SEATTLE
SECTIONAL AERONAUTICAL CHART
SCALE 1:500,000
Lambert Conformal Conic Projection Standard Parallels 41° 20´ and 46° 40´
Horizontal Datum: North American Datum of 1983
Topographic data corrected to October 1993

VFR TERMINAL AREA CHART
SEATTLE
SCALE 1:250,000
Lambert Conformal Conic Projection Standard Parallels 33° and 45°
Horizontal Datum: North American Datum of 1983
Topographic data corrected to April 1993

Figure 21-17. Most charts are based on the Lambert conformal conic projection

The Sectional and VFR Terminal Area charts have the following properties:

- they are conformal—angles and bearings are accurate;
- constant scale over the whole chart in practical terms;
- shapes are preserved in practical terms; and
- the true course between two places is a straight line.

Sectional Charts

Sectionals are colorful charts that show significant ground details, such as height of terrain, position of rivers and lakes, cities, railroads, roads, and so on, as well as aeronautical details in the airspace above, including federal airways and airspace boundaries and altitudes. The aeronautical information also includes ground features such as airports, which are sometimes easy to see from an airplane and sometimes not, as well as the position of radio navigation aids.

Ground Features

Topographical information shown on sectionals is that considered to be of most value to visual navigation. Features shown on the chart will be evident on the ground. It is impossible to show everything. For example, an isolated rocky outcrop may not be considered significant by the cartographer and therefore will not be shown. You might spot it on the ground, yet not find it depicted on the chart.

Ground features may change with changing seasons.

If, however, there is an isolated rock shown on the chart, it will certainly exist on the ground. The same thing may be said about cultural features depicted on charts, such as radomes and golf courses. If they are shown on the chart, then they may be suitable as landmarks for visual navigation.

Drainage and Water Features. Drainage and water features (hydrographic features) are usually depicted in blue. Hydrographic features include creeks, streams, rivers, canals, lakes, reservoirs, swamps, marshes, shorelines, tidal flats, and so on. Just how they are depicted on the chart is explained by the chart legend, but bear in mind that after a flood, for instance, what might be shown as a small stream on the chart may have become a raging torrent.

Relief. There are various ways of bringing ground contours into relief so that an impression of hills, mountains, valleys, and so on, is obtained when you look at the chart. Sectionals charts show **contours**—lines joining places of equal elevation above mean sea level—to depict relief. The closer that the contour lines are together on the chart, the steeper the terrain.

The basic contour interval on sectionals is in 500-foot vertical steps, with 250-foot contour intervals in gently rolling areas—for example, 250 feet MSL, 500 feet MSL, 750 feet MSL.

Color or layer tinting in 1,000-foot steps up to 2,000 feet MSL, then in 2,000-foot steps, is used in conjunction with the contour lines to give even more relief. The colors or tints used for the various ground elevations are shown on a table on the chart legend. The shades of color start with light green for low land just above sea level, then go through shades of brown, gradually darkening as the ground becomes higher. Remember that a particular color may indicate ground elevation up to the level of the next contour above it.

Refer to the legend and chart excerpts on pages 467 to 474.

Hill Shading. Hill shading is used to give a three-dimensional effect on some aeronautical charts. Hill shading shows darkened areas on the low side of high ground where you would expect to see shadows with the light coming from the northwest (a graphic standard).

Spot Elevations. Spot elevations (or spot heights) are shown using a black spot with an adjacent number to indicate the elevation (height MSL—above mean sea level) in feet. These elevations are generally accurate (unless amended by NOTAM), or unless shown on the chart by an **x** instead of a •. Doubtful locations are indicated by omission of the • or **x**.

Spot elevations are normally used to show local peaks and other critical elevations that are significantly higher than the surrounding terrain. The spot heights may not be higher than all other terrain in the general area, so you should always check hypsometric tints as well as spot heights. The highest point on each chart has its elevation printed slightly larger than the rest. It also rates a mention on the color-tint table, and its position in latitude and longitude is specified there.

Obstructions. Obstructions are shown on sectionals using their own symbols, differing slightly for obstructions 1,000 feet above ground level (AGL) and higher, and for those below 1,000 feet AGL. A bold number gives the elevation MSL of the highest point on the obstruction, and a lighter number in parentheses gives its height AGL. Be aware that guy wires may extend outward from some structures. You can determine the elevation of the terrain at the base of the obstruction by subtracting the obstruction height AGL from its elevation MSL. Lighted obstructions have flash lines radiating from the top of their symbols.

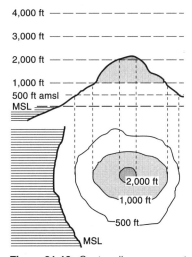

Figure 21-18. Contour lines represent changes in height MSL

Maximum Elevation Figures. Maximum elevation figures (MEFs) for specified areas are shown on sectionals. Thousands of feet are shown as a large number, with the hundreds shown as a smaller number beside it—for example, **3^1** (3,100 feet MSL), and **5^6** (5,600 feet MSL). MEFs concern the highest known feature lying within the specified latitude–longitude quadrangle, and include terrain and obstructions. Elevations are rounded up to the next 100 feet, or higher if thought appropriate.

MEFs concern the highest known feature including terrain and obstructions.

If you fly 500 feet higher than the MEF, you will clear all terrain and obstacles in that quadrangle by 500 feet vertically, which is normal minimum VFR clearance when flying over open terrain. Over congested areas, you are required by Part 91 of the regulations to have a clearance of 1,000 feet vertically, in which case you would add 1,000 feet or more to the MEF.

Hazards to Aviation. Hazards to aviation information are also depicted. These include certain aerial activities such as parachuting and hang-gliding, as well as permanent obstructions such as radio masts and elevated cables.

Cultural Features

Cultural features are of great help in visual navigation. It is not possible to show every town or house on the chart, so a choice is made to show what is significant. A group of, say, 100 houses is obviously of little significance if it lies in the middle of a city the size of Los Angeles, and so will not be specifically depicted on the chart, yet in the western desert areas it may be extremely significant and will be shown.

Roads and railroads can be of great assistance for visual air navigation. Those that are most significant will be clearly shown on the chart. Distinctive patterns such as curves, roads running parallel to and crossing railroad lines, road or railroad junctions, forks, overpasses and tunnels, are especially useful.

Many other easily seen cultural features, such as isolated golf courses, hospitals, factories, microwave stations, ranches, sawmills, and so on, may also be shown. Pilots are requested to fly no lower than 2,000 feet AGL over national wildlife refuges, where there may be a lot of bird activity, and where a certain amount of tranquillity might be appreciated. Examine the chart legend carefully and become familiar with the symbols.

Pilots are requested to fly no lower than 2,000 feet AGL over national wildlife refuges.

Aeronautical Information on Sectionals

Most people are familiar with topographical and cultural information, since these are surface features which are shown on a road map and in an atlas. A pilot, however, operates in a three-dimensional environment and therefore requires information on the airspace above the surface of the earth as well.

Aeronautical information is vital information for a pilot, showing not only the position of airports on the ground, but also the division of airspace, the location on the ground of radio navigation aids such as VORs and NDBs, and of course other information such as special use airspace.

Sectional chart legends explain this information clearly and thoroughly, although sometimes you have to search for the information in the legend and its associated notes. It is a good idea to memorize the most commonly used symbols for airports, airspace, obstructions, and so on. If in doubt, check the legend.

Use the legend to explain chart information.

Airports. Airports are shown on sectionals as:
- circles, for airports with runways that are not hard-surfaced;
- shaded circles, showing hard-surfaced runways 1,500–8,000 feet long; or
- shaded runways, for hard-surfaced runways longer than 8,000 feet.

Blue indicates airports equipped with control towers. **Magenta** is used for all other airports. If fuel is available and the airport is attended in normal working hours, four small ticks are shown around the basic airport symbol. A star K near the airport symbol indicates a rotating beacon from sunset to sunrise. Further information regarding airport lighting, navigation aids, and services may be found in the Airport/Facility Directory (A/FD).

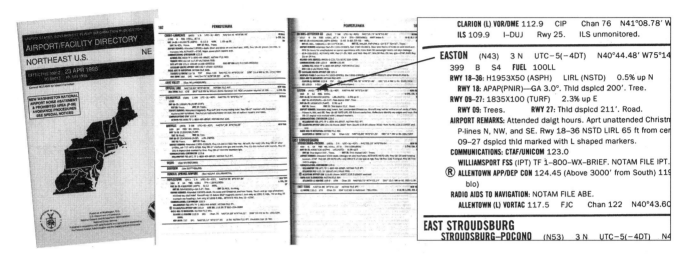

Figure 21-19. The Airport/Facility Directory (A/FD)

The identifier for each airport shown on the Sectional chart will have, where appropriate:

- the airport name—for example, Seattle Tacoma International (Intl), Boeing Field, King County Intl, Renton, McChord Air Force Base (AFB);
- the control tower frequency, for example, **CT 120.1** (a star ★ indicates part-time, NFCT indicates a Non-Federal Control Tower, a **C** indicates the Common Traffic Advisory Frequency—CTAF);
- the ATIS frequency—for example, ATIS **134.85**
- field elevation, lighting, longest runway, UNICOM frequency—for example, **313L 115 122.95,** which means: field elevation 313 feet MSL, lighting in operation sunset to sunrise (★**L** if on-request, part-time, or pilot-controlled), longest runway 11,500 feet, and UNICOM frequency 122.95 MHz;
- FSS above the airport name, where a Flight Service Station is at the airport (with advisory services available on 123.6 MHz if no tower in operation).

Radio Frequencies. Communications boxes shown on sectional charts indicate frequencies to be used. At airports *with* operating control towers, you should use the control tower frequency. At airports *without* operating control towers, you should use the common traffic advisory frequency (CTAF), which may be:

- the FSS advisory frequency at airports without control towers but with FSS;
- the control tower frequency if there is a control tower, but it is not attended (in which case there may be no wind or runway-in-use information available, and you would have to use the UNICOM to obtain this information);
- the UNICOM frequency if there is no tower or FSS (UNICOM is a nongovernment frequency);
- MULTICOM 122.9 MHz if there is no tower, FSS or UNICOM.

When inbound to or outbound from an airport *without* an operating control tower, you should communicate your position and monitor traffic on the CTAF within a 10-mile radius of the airport.

When the control tower is operating, use tower frequency.

Use CTAF frequency at airports without operating control towers.

Navigation Facilities. Navigation facilities shown on sectionals include VORs, VORTACs, VOR/DMEs, and NDBs.

- NDBs are surrounded by a small circle lightly shaded with magenta-colored dots.

- VORs, VORTACs and VOR/DMEs are shown in blue, and have a large compass rose aligned with *magnetic* north centered on them to help in plotting radials where necessary.

The direction of true north is indicated by the meridians of longitude, and the angle between this and magnetic north on the VOR compass rose depends on the magnetic variation in that area.

Information on each radio facility is shown nearby in a radio navaid information box. The Hazardous Inflight Weather Advisory Service (HIWAS) is available on navaid frequencies whose information box has a small solid square ■ inside its lower right corner; Transcribed En route Weather Broadcasts (TWEB) are available if a white **T** in a solid-circle symbol appears in the upper right-hand corner of the information box.

Position Information on Sectionals

The latitude/longitude grid is clearly marked on sectional charts. True bearings are measured from a meridian of longitude, which is the direction of true north.

The east/west **parallels of latitude** indicate degrees north or south of the equator (north in the United States of course). They are labeled at either side of the 1:500,000 sectional chart in one-degree (1°) intervals, which are also 60 nm intervals. Each degree is divided into 60 minutes (′), with marks each 1′ and 10′, and a full line across the chart at 30′. In the northern hemisphere, latitude is measured up from the bottom of the chart (from the equator toward the pole).

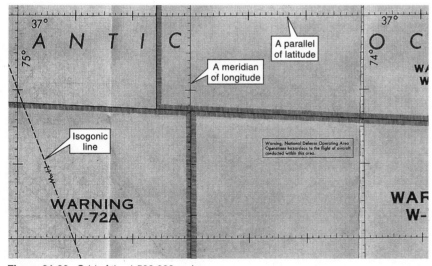

Figure 21-20. Grid of the 1:500,000 series

The north–south **meridians of longitude** are labeled at the top and/or bottom of the chart in degrees east or west of the prime meridian. Each degree is divided into 60 minutes, with marks each 1′ and 10′, and a full line up the chart at 30′.

Magnetic Information

Isogonic lines, or *isogonals,* join places of equal magnetic variation. They are indicated on sectional charts by dashed magenta lines. Magnetic bearings can be found by applying the magnetic variation to the true bearing.

Isogonals are lines on a chart joining places of equal variation.

The **agonic line** (where true north and magnetic north are the same direction, and variation is zero) lies in between the areas experiencing west variation and those experiencing east variation. The agonic line passes through the eastern side of the United States.

Because the earth's magnetic poles are gradually moving, the amount of magnetic variation at a particular place will also gradually change over a period of years. Every year the isogonic information on the charts is updated.

Compass roses aligned with *magnetic* north are shown around VORs, since VOR radials are magnetic courses away from a VOR.

VOR radials are magnetic courses away from a VOR.

VFR Terminal Area Charts

VFR Terminal Area Charts have a larger scale (1:250,000, or quarter-million) than Sectionals (1:500,000) and are used to show more detail around busy terminal areas. They look similar to sectional charts in that they also display both topographical and aeronautical information.

On the rear face of many VFR Terminal Area Charts are **VFR Flyway Planning Charts,** which show suggested VFR flyways and altitudes designed to help VFR pilots avoid major controlled traffic flows in busy terminal areas. These charts are not to be used as your primary navigation chart. Ground references shown on the VFR Flyway Planning Charts only provide a guide for improved visual navigation.

A sample excerpt of a VFR Terminal Area Chart is shown on page 473.

1:1,000,000 Navigation Charts

As you can imagine, charts having a scale of one to one million cover quite a lot of territory compared to the quarter-and half-million charts. This scale is often used when large distances are involved, to provide pilots mainly with topographical information (mountains, lakes, rivers, deserts, coastlines, and so on) and cultural information (cities, towns, highways, country roads, railroads, and so on). Aeronautical information is shown, but it is not as detailed as that shown on Sectionals or VFR Terminal Area Charts.

There are two major series of 1:1,000,000 aeronautical charts:
• the Operational Navigation Chart (ONC) series; and
• the ICAO World Aeronautical Chart (WAC) series.

Both series use much the same symbols and are based on the same projection as the half-million charts, the Lambert conformal conic projection.

Detail such as isogonic lines, restricted airspace, obstructions, irrigation channels, railroads and road systems change from time to time, and so the charts are reprinted regularly—about every two years for busy areas and every five or six years for more remote parts of the world. As with all aeronautical charts, ensure that you use only the latest edition and study the legend carefully prior to flight.

The **ONC** series originates from military sources but is available to civil pilots for most areas of the world.

The **ICAO World Aeronautical Chart (WAC)** series originates from civil aeronautical sources. It is widely used in those parts of the world where the 1:1,000,000 scale is better suited to en route navigation, such as the Far East, South-East Asia and Australia, because of the large distances involved. Each country producing charts in the WAC series does so according to the ICAO standards.

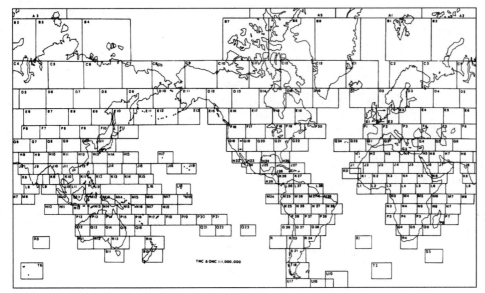

Figure 21-21. ONC world coverage

NOTAM amendments are sometimes issued for WACs; these corrections are added by hand on the appropriate chart (known as manuscript amendments).

As some areas of the world have not been charted accurately, there is a small reliability diagram at the bottom left hand corner of each WAC that will alert you to the reliability of the chart information.

A sample WAC excerpt is shown on page 472.

✍ Now complete **Review 21, Part (b)** on page 487.

TOPOGRAPHIC BASE
RELIABILITY DIAGRAM

A. Compiled from accurate topographic maps and surveys.

B. Compiled from other available topographic information. Liable to vertical error.

Figure 21-22. A WAC reliability panel

Airspace

United States airspace is organized into six classes (A, B, C, D, E and G), in line with the International Civil Aviation Organization (ICAO) airspace classification system. Airspace Classes A through E are allocated to controlled airspace where Class A is the most restrictive and Class E the least restrictive, being allocated to general controlled airspace. Uncontrolled airspace is Class G. (Class F, although available in the ICAO system, has not been allocated in the United States.) The airspace classification system links various parameters to each class, including:

- entry requirements (for example, radio contact for all aircraft in Class C airspace; ATC clearance for IFR flights in controlled airspace, and so on);
- minimum pilot qualifications;
- two-way communication and transponder equipment requirements;
- VFR weather minimums (where VFR is available); and
- aircraft separation, conflict resolution and traffic advisory services.

AIRSPACE FEATURES	CLASS A AIRSPACE	CLASS B AIRSPACE	CLASS C AIRSPACE	CLASS D AIRSPACE	CLASS E AIRSPACE	CLASS G AIRSPACE
Flight Operations Permitted	IFR	IFR and VFR	IFR and VFR	IFR and VFR	IFR and VFR	IFR and VFR
Entry Prerequisites	ATC clearance	ATC clearance	IFR clearance/ VFR radio contact	IFR clearance/ VFR radio contact	Clearance/radio for IFR	None
Minimum Pilot Qualifications	Instrument Rating	Private Plot Certificate/ *endorsed student	Student Certificate	Student Certificate	Student Certificate	Student Certificate
Two-Way Radio Communications	Yes	Yes	Yes	Yes	IFR	No
VFR Minimum Visibility	*not applicable*	3 statue miles	3 statue miles	3 statue miles	**3 statue miles	***1 statue miles
Aircraft Separation	All	All	IFR, SVFR and rwy operations	IFR, SVFR and rwy operations	IFR, SVFR	None
Conflict Resol'n (collision avoidance)	*not applicable*	*not applicable*	Between IFR an d VFR flights	No	No	No
Traffic Advisories	*not applicable*	*not applicable*	Yes	Workload permitting	Workload permitting	Workload permitting
Safety Advisories	Yes	Yes	Yes	Yes	Yes	Yes

*Operations at some class B airports requires a minimum of a Private Pilot Certificate—*see* Part 91 of the regulations

**Visibility and cloud clearance requirements increase above 10,000 feet MSL.

***Visibility and cloud clearance requirements decrease below 1,200 feet AGL; increase above 10,000 feet MSL, and at night—*see* Part 91 of the regulations or the AIM.

Figure 21-23. Summary of the United States airspace classification system

Subdivision of Airspace

Class A Airspace

Class A airspace generally extends from 18,000 feet MSL up to and including FL600. Class A airspace is only available to aircraft operating on an IFR flight plan.

Class B Airspace

Class B airspace generally extends from the surface to 10,000 feet MSL surrounding the nation's major airports. The configuration of each Class B airspace is individually tailored and consists of a surface area with two or more larger radius layers above. Class B airspace is shown on sectional charts with a **thick blue solid line.**

To fly within Class B airspace the **minimum pilot qualification** is a private pilot certificate or an endorsed student pilot certificate for Class B airspace at a specific airport (*see* Part 61 of the regulations). The minimum required **airplane equipment** includes a two-way radio communication and a 4096-code transponder with Mode C capability (altitude reporting). IFR aircraft are required to carry VOR or TACAN equipment. VFR requirements are 3 sm visibility and clear of clouds.

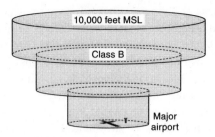

Figure 21-24. Class B Airspace

Class B airspace **operating rules** include:

• ATC clearance must be obtained before entering or departing the airspace.

• Fly on published VFR Transition Routes found on the back of VFR Terminal Area Charts.

• Contact ATC at geographical fixes shown on the sectional charts by small flags to obtain a clearance prior to entering Class B airspace.

If possible avoid Class B airspace by using VFR corridors, Terminal Area VFR Routes, or by flying above or below the Class B airspace.

Class C Airspace

Class C airspace generally extends from the surface to 4,000 feet AGL around a busy airport which has:

• an operational control tower;

• a radar approach control; and

• a certain number of IFR operations or passenger enplanements.

Class C airspace areas are depicted by **solid magenta lines** on sectional charts. The configuration of each Class C airspace is individually tailored, usually with two tiers. The vertical limits of Class C airspace are indicated on the chart with the circle and are expressed in hundreds of feet MSL. The upper limit is shown above the straight line and the bottom limit (which may be SFC for surface area altitude) beneath the line. For example, refer to Sectional Chart Excerpt No. 1 (page 467) and the Class C airspace around Mobile Regional Airport. The limits in the surface area are "$\frac{42}{SFC}$" which means that Class C airspace extends from the surface to 4,200 feet MSL. The limits for the outer area are 42/15 which means that the C Class airspace extends from 1,500 to 4,200 feet MSL.

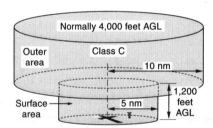

Figure 21-25. Class C airspace

To fly in Class C airspace no specific **pilot certification** is required and the minimum **airplane equipment** includes two-way communication and a 4096 transponder with Mode C (altitude reporting). Class C **operating rules** require the establishment of two-way radio communications with approach control before entering Class C airspace. In addition, unless otherwise authorized or required by ATC, airplanes below 2,500 feet AGL and within 4 nm of the primary airport must not exceed an indicated airspeed of 200 knots. Class C radar services are usually provided beyond Class C airspace out to 20 nm from the primary airport.

The minimum **VFR weather requirements** for Class C airspace are shown in Figure 21-26.

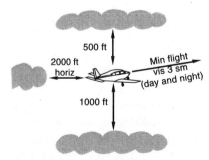

Figure 21-26. VFR requirements

Class D Airspace

Class D airspace surrounds airports which have an operational control tower but are not associated with Class B or C airspace. Class D airspace generally extends from the surface to 2,500 feet AGL and is cylindrical in shape, plus extensions up to 2 nm necessary to include instrument approach and departure paths. On sectional charts Class D airspace is shown as a dashed or **segmented blue line,** with a blue segmented box showing the top of the Class D airspace in hundreds of feet MSL. For example on Sectional Excerpt No. 4 (page 471), Coeur D'Alene is surrounded by Class D airspace with an upper limit of 4,800 feet MSL.

To fly in Class D airspace no specific **pilot certification** is required, and the minimum **airplane equipment** is an operational two-way radio. Class D **operating rules** include establishing two-way radio contact before entering Class D airspace and maintaining two-way radio contact while in Class D airspace. In addition, airplanes within 4 nm of the primary airport in the Class D airspace and at or below 2,500 feet AGL must not exceed 200 KIAS. The VFR minimums are the same as those for Class C airspace. When the control tower is not operating, the Class D airspace reverts to Class E.

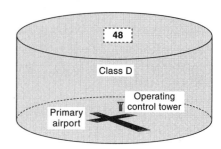

Figure 21-27. Class D airspace

Class E Airspace

Class E airspace is controlled airspace that is not Class A, B, C or D. Class E airspace includes airspace around airports without control towers, airspace used to transit between terminal or en route environments, Federal Airways including Victor airways (*see* Note 3), plus unallocated airspace over the United States from 14,500 feet MSL up to Class A airspace beginning at 18,000 feet MSL, or any overlying Class B, C or D airspace. Class E airspace lower limits are:

- the surface around airports marked by **segmented magenta lines;**
- 700 feet AGL in areas marked by **light magenta shading;**
- 1,200 feet AGL in areas marked by **light blue shading;**
- as depicted numerically by a **blue staggered line** as shown on Sectional Excerpt No. 4 just north of area 3 (page 471); and
- 14,500 feet MSL if none of the others apply.

To fly in Class E airspace, no specific pilot certification is required and there are no specific equipment or operating requirements. The minimum VFR requirements are the same as for Class C and D if operating below 10,000 feet MSL. At or above 10,000 feet MSL, VFR conditions are increased to flight visibility 5 sm, with 1,000 feet vertical separation from clouds and 1 sm horizontal separation from clouds. An ATC clearance is required to fly IFR in Class E airspace.

Class G Airspace

Class G airspace is the remaining airspace other than special use or restricted airspace.

The minimum VFR requirements in Class G airspace depend on day or night and altitude above the surface. At or below 1,200 feet AGL by day, the minimum visibility is 1 statute mile (sm) and the airplane must remain clear of clouds. By day above 1,200 feet AGL but below 10,000 feet MSL, the minimum visibility is 1 sm and the airplane must remain at least 2,000 feet horizontally from, 500 feet below and 1,000 feet above clouds. For night VFR minimums, *see* Part 91. You do not need an ATC clearance to fly IFR in Class G airspace.

Note 1: Refer to Part 71 of the regulations for more detail on the airspace classes. Also, airspeed rules are contained in Part 91 (*see* Chapter 20).

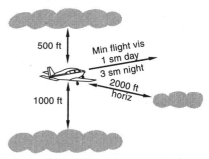

Figure 21-28. VFR minimum requirements below 10,000 feet MSL, but above 1,200 feet AGL, by day

Note 2: Some airports offer optional radar advisory services in airspace known as **Terminal Radar Service Areas (TRSAs).** The primary airport of a TRSA is Class D. The boundaries are marked on sectionals with thick dark-gray lines. Pilots can choose whether or not to participate with ATC by squawking 1200 or an ATC assigned code while flying in TRSA airspace. There are very few TRSAs.

Note 3: **Victor Airways** are low-altitude federal airways connecting VORs along specified radials, and are for use by both IFR and VFR aircraft. They are shown on sectionals by straight blue lines containing the airway designator and its magnetic direction, for example, *V31–348°.* Any **intersections** fixed by radio navaids are indicated by fine blue arrows directed toward the relevant facilities. Victor airways are normally 8 nm wide, and extend vertically from 1,200 feet AGL up to but not including 18,000 feet MSL. Unusually high floors will be marked. You should normally cruise at an appropriate altitude along Victor airways which, for VFR aircraft, is "odds+500 feet" on easterly routes, and "evens+500 feet" on westerly routes.

Note 4: **Special Visual Flight Rules (SVFR).** If the weather is *below* VFR minimum requirements, a SVFR clearance must be obtained before entering surface areas in Class B, C, D and E airspace. Special VFR conditions will only be allowed if the IFR traffic is not heavy and providing the SVFR flight will not delay IFR operations. All SVFR aircraft must remain clear of cloud and the visibility must be in excess of 1 statute mile. SVFR operations by fixed-wing aircraft are *prohibited* in some Class B and C surface areas because of the volume of IFR traffic. A list of these areas is contained in Part 93 of the regulations. They are also depicted on sectional charts by the words NO SVFR near the airport symbol.

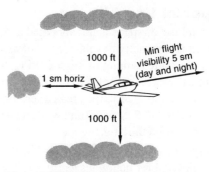

Figure 21-29. VFR minimum requirements above 10,000 feet MSL

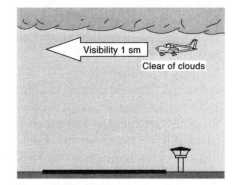

Figure 21-30. SVFR minimum requirements

Summary of Basic VFR Weather Minimums

Airspace	Flight Visibility	Distance from Clouds	Airspace	Flight Visibility	Distance from Clouds
Class A	Not applicable	Not applicable	*Class G* **1,200 ft or less** above the surface (regardless of MSL or altitude)		
Class B	3 sm	Clear of clouds	**Day**, except as provided in Part 91	1 sm	Clear of clouds
			Night, except as provided in Part 91	3 sm	500 ft below 1,000 ft above 2,000 ft horiz.
Class C	3 sm	500 ft below 1,000 ft above 2,000 ft horiz.	**More than 1,200 ft** above the surface but less than 10,000 ft MSL		
Class D	3 sm	500 ft below 1,000 ft above 2,000 ft horiz.	**Day**	1 sm	500 ft below 1,000 ft above 2,000 ft horiz.
Class E Less than 10,000 ft MSL	3 sm	500 ft below 1,000 ft above 2,000 ft horiz.	**Night**	3 sm	500 ft below 1,000 ft above 2,000 ft horiz.
At or above 10,000 ft MSL	5 sm	1,000 ft below 1,000 ft above 1 sm horiz.	**More than 1,200 ft above the surface and at or above 10,000 ft MSL**		1,000 ft below 1,000 ft above 1 sm horiz.

Figure 21-31. Part 91 summary of basic VFR weather minimums

Special Use Airspace

Special use airspace is not allocated a class. It consists of that airspace within which certain activities must be confined because of their nature such as military aerobatic training or missile firing. Special use airspace is shown on aeronautical charts (except for controlled firing areas where activity ceases when aircraft are spotted in the area either visually or by radar).

Prohibited, Restricted and Warning Areas are outlined on sectionals by **blue lines with hachuring.**

- **Prohibited Areas** contain airspace within which the flight of aircraft is prohibited for national security or other reasons.

- **Restricted Areas** contain airspace within which the flight of aircraft is subject to restrictions, but is not totally prohibited, because of hazards such as artillery firing, aerial gunnery or guided missiles. Penetrating Restricted Areas without authorization from the using or controlling authority may be extremely hazardous.

- **Warning Areas** are similar to restricted areas, except that they are beyond the 3-mile limit from the United States coastline and are therefore in international airspace.

- **Military Operations Areas (MOAs)** consist of airspace of defined vertical and lateral limits established to separate military training activities (usually involving aerobatic or abrupt flight maneuvers) from civil Instrument Flight Rules (IFR) traffic. Any FSS within 100 miles of the MOA should be able to advise if it is active or not and, if it is active, you should contact the controlling agency for traffic advisories. VFR pilots should exercise extreme caution when flying in an active MOA. **MOAs** are outlined on sectionals by **magenta lines with hachuring.**

- **Alert Areas** depicted on sectional charts by **blue boxes** show airspace within which there may be a lot of pilot training or unusual aerial activity.

Other Airspace

- **Military Training Routes (MTRs)** are for military low-altitude high-speed training and may be flown by military aircraft either under the Instrument Flight Rules (indicated on the chart by IR), or under the Visual Flight Rules (VR). Military training routes are depicted with a **thin gray line.**

    - MTRs at or below 1,500 feet AGL (with no segment above 1,500 feet AGL) are identified by 4-digit numbers, for instance, IR 1006, and VR 1007.

    - MTRs above 1,500 feet AGL (with some segments possibly below 1,500 feet AGL) are identified by 3-digit numbers, for instance, IR 008, and VR 009.

    - Alternate IR/VR military training routes are identified normally, but with a final letter suffix, such as IR 008A, or VR 009B.

- **Airspace not defined** on aeronautical charts may be restricted temporarily by NOTAM (Notice to Airmen) for purposes such as disaster relief, and temporarily prohibited for space flights, presidential flights, and so on. Airport Advisory Areas exist within 10 statute miles of any airport where a control tower is not operating but where a FSS provides an advisory service to arriving and departing aircraft. It is not mandatory to participate in the airport advisory service program, but it is strongly recommended.

✍ Now complete **Review 21, Part (c)** on page 489.

✍ Review 21

Part (a)

1. The plane of a great circle on the earth (passes/does not pass) through the center of the earth.
   ➤ passes

2. A parallel of latitude joins all points of the same latitude and is a (small/great) circle except for the _____ .
   ➤ small, equator

3. Parallels of latitude (are/are not) parallel to the equator and to each other.
   ➤ are

4. The basic reference for longitude is the _____ that passes through the _____ Observatory just outside London, England.
   ➤ prime meridian, Greenwich

5. Meridians of longitude all pass through the north and south geographic poles and are (small/great) circles.
   ➤ great

6. Longitude is angular position _____ or _____ of the prime meridian.
   ➤ east or west

7. The length of one minute of arc of a great circle on the earth's surface is _____ nm.
   ➤ 1 nm

8. 1 degree of latitude is _____ nm.
   ➤ 60 nm

9. Scale is the ratio of _____ .
   ➤ chart length to earth distance

10. A large scale map can show (more/less) detail than a small scale map.
    ➤ more

Part (b)

For Question 1 refer to Sectional Chart Excerpt No. 2 on page 469.

1. What is the minimum altitude required to clear the single obstacle 6 nm to the SE of Mobile Regional Airport?
   ➤ 1,434 feet (434 + 1,000 because of being in a congested area)

Charts and Airspace

For Questions 2 onward refer to the Sectional Chart Excerpt No. 4 (page 471) and Figure 21-32 when required.

2. The obstacle 4 nm northeast from Wall Airport near Sandpoint is _____ feet AGL, which is _____ feet MSL. What minimum altitude is necessary to clear it by 500 feet?
   ➤ 210 feet AGL, 2,373 feet MSL, 2,873 feet MSL

3. If Coeur d'Alene Tower is not in operation, which frequency should be used as a Common Traffic Advisory Frequency (CTAF) to monitor airport traffic?
   ➤ 119.1 MHz (the tower frequency, even though the tower is unattended, *see* AIM Chapter 4 Section 1)

4. If Coeur d'Alene Tower is not in operation, which frequency should be used as a Common Traffic Advisory Frequency (CTAF) to self-announce positions and intentions?
   (a) 119.1 MHz.
   (b) 122.1/108.8 MHz.
   (c) 122.8 MHz.
   ➤ (a)

5. What is the correct UNICOM frequency to be used at Coeur d'Alene Tower to request fuel?
   (a) 119.1 MHz.
   (b) 122.1/108.8 MHz.
   (c) 122.8 MHz.
   ➤ (c)

6. For information about parachute jumping and glider operations at Silverwood Airport, you should refer to the _____ .
   ➤ Airport/Facility Directory (check A/FD contents)

7. The vertical limits of that portion of the Class E airspace over Magee Airport are _____ to _____ .
   ➤ 7,500 feet MSL up to but not including 18,000 feet MSL (floor is normally 1,200 feet AGL unless otherwise specified, as is the case here)

8. Silverwood airport (area 2), compared with Shoshone County Airport (area 3), is further (north/south) and so has a (higher/lower) northerly latitude, and is further (west/east) and so has a more (westerly/easterly) longitude.
   ➤ north, higher, west, westerly

```
COEUR D'ALENE
§  COEUR D'ALENE AIR TERM   (COE)   9 NW   UTC-8(-7DT)   47°46'27"N 116°49'11"W          GREAT FALLS
     2318   B   S4   FUEL 80, 100, JET A   OX 1,2                                          H-1B, L-9A
     RWY 05-23: H7400X140 (ASPH)      S-57, D-95, DT-165   HIRL   0.7%up NE                IAP
     RWY 05: MALSR.      RWY 23: REIL. VASI(V4L)—GA 3.0°TCH 39'.
     RWY 01-19: H5400X75 (ASPH)      S-50, D-83, DT-150
     RWY 01: Rgt tfc.
     AIRPORT REMARKS: Attended Mon–Fri 1400–0300Z‡. Rwy 23 REIL's out of service indefinitely. ACTIVATE HIRL
       Rwy 05-23; MALSR Rwy 05—122.8. Rwy 19 is designated calm wind rwy. Control Zone effective Mon-Fri.
       1400–0300Z‡.
     COMMUNICATIONS: CTAF 119.1      UNICOM 122.8
       SPOKANE FSS (SFF) TF 1–800–527–3960. NOTAM FILE COE.
       RCO 122.1R 108.8T (SPOKANE FSS)
     ® SPOKANE APP/DEP CON 125.8
       TOWER 119.1 (1700-2300Z‡ Sat–Sun ocassional Mon–Fri).      GND CON 121.8
     RADIO AIDS TO NAVIGATION: NOTAM FILE GEG.
       SPOKANE (H) VORTAC 115.5     GEG     Chan 102     47°33'54"N 117°37'33"W     048° 35 NM to fld.
       2760/21E.
       (T) VOR/DME 108.8     COE     Chan 25     47°46'26"N 116°49'11"W     at fld. 2290/19E. NOTAM FILE COE.
       LEENY NDB (LOM) 347     CO     47°44'35"N 116°57'36"W     053° 6.0 NM to fld.
       ILS 110.7 I-COE Rwy 05 LOM LEENY NDB.
```

Figure 21-32. Coeur d'Alene A/FD excerpt

9. What is the latitude and longitude of Shoshone County Airport (area 3)? Its elevation is _____ feet MSL. It has (some/no) lighting, and (soft/hard)-surfaced runways the longest of length _____ feet. The color (blue/magenta) indicates that this airport (has/does not have) a control tower. The CTAF is on _____ MHz, which you could select on your (VHF-NAV/VHF-COM) radio.

➤ N47°33′ W116°12′, 2,223 feet MSL, some, hard-surfaced, 5,500 feet, magenta, does not have, 122.8 MHz, VHF-COM.

10. What is the latitude and longitude of Silverwood airport (area 2)? Its elevation is _____ feet MSL. It has (some/no) lighting, and (soft/hard)-surfaced runways the longest of length _____ feet. The CTAF is on _____ MHz. What aeronautical activity, apart from aircraft, can you expect in the vicinity? Which official document would you refer to for further information about this activity? Silverwood airport is (southeast/northwest/northeast/southwest) of Shoshone County airport.

➤ N47°54 W116°43′, 2,350 feet MSL, some, hard-surfaced, 4,200 feet, 122.7 MHz, parachuting, A/FD (airport/facility directory), northwest

11. Which airport is located at approximately N48°18′ W116°34′? The airport lies (north/south/east/west) of the town. Is fuel available? Is there an FSS located on the airport? What radio navigation aid is situated near the airport, what is its frequency, on which equipment could you select it in the aircraft, and how could you identify that you have selected it correctly?

➤ Wall, north, yes, no, SANDPOE NDB, frequency 264 kHz, automatic direction finder (ADF), Morse code ident SZT (dit-dit-dit dah-dit-dit-dit dah)

12. What is the latitude and longitude of Coeur d'Alene airport? The airport lies (north/south/east/west) of the town. The color (blue/magenta) indicates that this airport (has/does not have) a control tower. The elevation is _____ feet MSL. It has (some/no) lighting, and (soft/hard)-surfaced runways—the longest runway having a length of _____ feet. The control tower operates (full/part)-time on frequency _____ MHz. When the tower is not functioning, the CTAF is (the same/a different) frequency _____ MHz. These frequencies can be selected on your _____ radio. Automatic weather information is available on frequency _____ MHz, which you can select on your _____ radio. UNICOM is available on frequency _____ MHz, which you can select on your _____ radio. The airport is surrounded by Class _____ airspace which extends from the surface (up to/up to and including) _____ feet MSL, which is _____ feet above the level of the airport. To clear the highest obstacle in the latitude-longitude quadrangle surrounding Coeur d'Alene airport by 500 feet, you would need to fly at an altitude of _____ feet MSL.

➤ N47°47′ W116°49′, north, blue, has, 2,318 feet MSL, some, hard-surfaced, 7,400 feet, part-time, 119.1 MHz, the same, 119.1 MHz, VHF-COM, 135.075 MHz, VHF-COM, UNICOM 122.8 MHz, VHF-COM, Class D, up to and including 4,800 feet MSL, 2,500 feet AGL, 6,500 feet MSL

13. What is the magnetic course and distance from Shoshone County airport to Silverwood airport?

➤ 298°M (316°T – 18°E variation), 30 nm

14. The flag symbol at Mica Peak to the SW of Coeur d'Alene airport is:
    (a) a compulsory IFR checkpoint.
    (b) a visual checkpoint to identify position for initial call up.
    (c) that Coeur d'Alene airport has special traffic patterns.
    ➤ (b)

15. Which statement is true relating to the blue and magenta colors used to depict airports on Sectional Aeronautical Charts.
    (a) Airports having control towers are shown in blue; all others in magenta.
    (b) Airports having runways capable of handling large aircraft are shown in blue; all others in magenta.
    ➤ (a)

Part (c)

1. Class B airspace surrounds the nation's (major/minor) airports.
   ➤ major

2. Class B airspace extends in tiers from the surface up to _____ feet MSL. It is shown on Sectional charts by a (blue/magenta) (segmented/solid) line surrounding the primary airport.
   ➤ 10,000 feet MSL, blue solid

3. What minimum pilot certification is required for operation within Class B airspace?
   (a) Private pilot certificate or student pilot certificate with appropriate logbook endorsements.
   (b) Commercial pilot certificate.
   (c) Private pilot certificate with an instrument rating.
   ➤ (a)

4. There is (a high degree of/little) radar control available in Class B airspace, and VFR minimum weather requirements are reduced to visibility of _____ and _____ .
   ➤ high degree, 3 sm, clear of clouds

5. Class C airspace surrounds (busy IFR/small VFR only) airports. Class C airspace is indicated on Sectional charts by thick (magenta/blue) (segmented/solid) lines. The primary airport in Class C airspace (will/will not) have an operating control tower, and (will/will/not) have a radar approach control.
   ➤ busy IFR, magenta, solid line, will, will

6. Sketch a typical Class C airspace. The surface area typically extends out to _____ nm and up to _____ feet (AGL/MSL). The outer area of the Class C airspace typically extends out to _____ nm and up to approximately _____ feet AGL which is shown in the chart as feet (AGL/MSL).
   ➤ for diagram see Figure 21-25 on page 483, 5 nm and 4,000 feet AGL, 10 nm and 4,000 feet AGL, MSL

7. What is minimum radio equipment required for operation within Class C airspace?
   (a) two-way radio communication equipment and a 4096 transponder.
   (b) two-way radio communications equipment and a 4096-code transponder and a DME.
   (c) two-way radio communications equipment and a 4096-code transponder with an encoding altimeter (mode C).
   ➤ (c)

8. Before entering Class C airspace you should make radio contact with _____ on the published frequency.
   ➤ approach control

9. Speed limit is _____ KIAS when below _____ feet AGL and within _____ nm of the primary airport in the Class C surface area.
   ➤ 200 KIAS, 2,500 feet AGL, 4 nm

10. Basic VFR minimum weather conditions in Class C airspace are visibility _____ sm, and a distance from clouds of _____ feet below clouds, _____ feet above clouds, and _____ feet horizontally from clouds.
    ➤ 3 sm, 500 feet below, 1,000 feet above, 2,000 feet horizontally

11. Two-way radio contact (is/is not) required in Class D airspace. An altitude reporting altimeter (is/is not) required in Class D airspace. Radar control (is always/may) be available in Class D airspace.
    ➤ is, is not, may

12. Class D Airspace around an airport with a control tower reverts to Class _____ airspace when the tower is not operating.
    ➤ E

13. Basic VFR weather minimums in Class D airspace are visibility _____ , and distance from clouds _____ .
    ➤ 3 sm, 500 feet below clouds, 1,000 feet above clouds, 2,000 feet horizontally from clouds

14. A Special VFR clearance given ATC in Class B, C, D or E airspace permits you to operate in weather conditions of _____ and _____ .

➤ visibility 1 sm, clear of clouds (*see* Part 91)

15. The lower limit of Class E airspace is generally 14,500 feet MSL but is often designated lower. On sectional charts magenta shading indicates a Class E lower limit of _____ feet AGL, and blue shading indicates a Class E lower limit of _____ feet AGL.

➤ 700 feet AGL, 1,200 feet AGL

16. The upper limit of Class E airspace is at the floor of any overlying Class A, B, C or D airspace. (True/False?)

➤ True

17. A minor airport with a part-time control tower will be surrounded by Class _____ airspace when the tower is operating, and by Class _____ airspace when the tower is not operating. This airspace starts (at/several thousand feet above) the surface.

➤ D, E, at

For questions 18 to 23 refer to Sectional Chart Excerpt No. 4 on page 471.

18. What are the visibility and cloud requirements required by the regulations to operate at Wall Airport near Sandpoint below 1,200 feet AGL?

➤ visibility 1 mile and clear of clouds (since the airspace around the airport is Class G airspace and you are below 1,200 feet)

19. Identify the airspace over Wall Airport near Sandpoint that exists from the surface up to 14,500 feet MSL.

➤ Class G airspace (it lies outside any shaded areas)

20. Identify the airspace over Shoshone County airport that exists from the surface up to 14,500 feet MSL.

➤ Class G airspace from surface up to 1,200 feet AGL, then Class E (federal airway) with floor at 1,200 feet AGL (shaded blue band) extending upward

21. The vertical limits of Class E airspace designated as a Federal Airway over Magee Airport are;
   (a) 1,200 feet AGL to 10,000 feet MSL.
   (b) 7,500 feet MSL to 12,500 feet MSL.
   (c) 7,500 feet MSL to 17,999 feet MSL.

➤ (c)

22. Identify the airspace over Coeur d'Alene airport that exists from the surface up to 14,500 feet MSL.

➤ Class D airspace up to and including 4,800 feet MSL, then Class E (federal airway) above this (shaded blue band)

23. What type of military operations would you expect along IR314 crossing Lake Pend Oreille?

➤ low altitude high-speed military training, under IFR, above 1,500 feet AGL but with some sectors possibly below 1,500 feet AGL

For questions 24 onward refer to Sectional Chart Excerpt No. 3 on page 470.

24. San Francisco International airport is a (major/minor) airport. The airspace surrounding San Francisco International airport is Class _____ airspace. Directly overhead the airport this airspace extends from the surface to a ceiling of _____ feet MSL.

➤ major, Class B, 8,000 feet MSL

25. The airspace surrounding San Jose International airport is Class _____ airspace. Directly overhead the airport this airspace extends from the surface to a ceiling of _____ feet MSL.

➤ Class C, 4,000 feet MSL

26. Class C airspace typically has a ceiling of _____ feet (AGL/MSL). The elevation of San Jose International airport is _____ feet MSL.

➤ 4,000 feet AGL, 56 feet MSL

27. What is the meaning of the flag symbol shown at Crown Sterling Suites (area D)?

➤ visual checkpoint for initial radio call prior to entering the San Jose Class C airspace

28. The requirement for a Mode C transponder is within _____ nm of San Francisco International airport.

➤ 30 nm (*see* 30 nm arc and Part 91)

29. Is Special VFR (SVFR) flight permitted in the airspace surrounding San Francisco International airport? This is indicated on the chart by the words _____ .

➤ no, NO SVFR

30. The airspace surrounding Palo Alto airport is Class _____ , extending from the surface to a ceiling of _____ .

➤ Class D, 2,000 feet MSL

31. What class airspace surrounds Rio Vista airport (*see* area B), and what airspace lies above it?

➤ Class G airspace up to 700 feet AGL, with Class E airspace above indicated by the magenta shading (floor of the Class E airspace is at 700 feet AGL, so at 700 feet AGL the rules of the more restricting airspace—in this case Class E apply)

32. What class airspace surrounds Livermore airport (*see* area A), and what airspace lies above it? Is a Mode C transponder required to operate at this airport? Is fuel available? Is there an airport beacon? Is there a control tower? Is there an ATIS? Is there a UNICOM frequency? The light green shading around Livermore airport indicates that the elevation of the terrain is _____ . The darker green shading to the north indicates that the elevation of the terrain is _____ . The spot elevation in the tan area is _____ feet MSL. The maximum elevation figure in this latitude-longitude quadrangle is _____ .

➢ Class D uncontrolled airspace up to 2,900 feet MSL, with Class E airspace above, yes (since its within the 30 nm radius of San Francisco International airport); yes, yes, yes—part-time on 118.1 MHz; yes—on 119.65 MHz; yes—on 122.95 MHz; below 1,000 feet MSL; 1,000 to 2,000 feet MSL; 2,581 feet MSL; 4,200 feet MSL

33. VFR flights in Class B airspace must operate with a minimum flight visibility of _____ and remain _____ .

➢ 3 sm and clear of clouds

34. The VFR minimums for flight in Class C airspace, day or night, are: flight visibility _____ ; distance from clouds: _____ below, _____ above, _____ horizontal. This (is/is not) the same as in Class D airspace.

➢ 3 sm; 500 feet below, 1,000 feet above and 2,000 feet horizontal; is

35. The VFR minimums for flight in Class E airspace at or above 10,000 feet MSL are: flight visibility _____; distance from clouds: _____ below, _____ above, _____ horizontal.

➢ 5 sm; 1,000 feet below, 1,000 feet above, 1 sm horizontal

36. The VFR minimums for flight in Class E airspace below 10,000 feet MSL, day or night, are: flight visibility _____ ; distance from clouds: _____ below, _____ above, _____ horizontal.

➢ 3 sm; 500 feet below, 1,000 feet above, 2,000 feet horizontal

37. The VFR minimums for flight in Class G airspace 1,200 feet or less AGL (regardless of MSL altitude) by day are: flight visibility _____ ; distance from clouds: _____ .

➢ 1 sm; clear of clouds

38. The VFR minimums for flight in Class G airspace below 10,000 feet, but higher than 1,200 feet AGL (regardless of MSL altitude) by day are: flight visibility _____ ; distance from clouds: _____ below, _____ above, _____ horizontal.

➢ 1 sm; 500 feet below, 1,000 feet above, 2,000 feet horizontal

39. The VFR minimums for flight in Class G airspace at or above 10,000 feet and more than 1,200 feet AGL (regardless of MSL altitude), day or night, are: flight visibility _____ ; distance from clouds: _____ below, _____ above, _____ horizontal.

➢ 5 sm; 1,000 feet below, 1,000 feet above, 1 sm horizontal

40. The VFR minimums for flight in Class G airspace more than 1,200 feet above the surface (regardless of MSL altitude) by night are: flight visibility _____ ; distance from clouds: _____ below, _____ above, _____ horizontal.

➢ 3 sm; 500 feet below, 1,000 feet above, 2,000 feet horizontal

41. An airplane may be operated at night, in the traffic pattern of an airport in Class G airspace, in a flight visibility of _____ and _____ of clouds, if flown within _____ mile of the runway.

➢ 1 sm, clear of clouds, ½ mile

42. Pilots flying over a national wildlife refuge are requested to fly no lower than:
   (a) 1,000 feet AGL.
   (b) 2,000 feet AGL.
   (c) 3,000 feet AGL.

➢ (b)

43. Military Operations Areas are outlined on sectional charts by _____ .

➢ magenta lines with hachuring

44. What action should a pilot take when operating under VFR in a Military Operations Area (MOA)?
   (a) Obtain a clearance from the controlling agency prior to entering the MOA.
   (b) Operate only on the airways that transverse the MOA.
   (c) Exercise extreme caution when military activity is being conducted.

➢ (c)

Airports and Airport Operations 22

Airports

Airports come in all shapes and sizes. Some have long, hard-surfaced runways, others have short, grass runways, some have operating control towers to regulate the flow of traffic in the airspace around the airport as well as on the ground (known as *controlled* airports, *towered* airports or *tower-controlled* airports), and others have no active control tower (known as *uncontrolled* airports or *nontowered* airports), where the traffic is self-regulating according to specified FAA procedures.

An **ATC clearance** is authorization for a VFR aircraft to proceed under specified conditions in Class B, C or D airspace. An ATC clearance to takeoff at a controlled airport should be obtained from the control tower if it is in operation. Time references will be in UTC (Coordinated Universal Time).

A very good source of information for correct procedures is the **Aeronautical Information Manual (AIM),** which contains an entire chapter on airport operations.

An ATC clearance is required for you to operate in Class B, C or D controlled airspace.

Taxiway and Runway Markings

Study the airport chart prior to taxiing at an unfamiliar airport so that your taxi route from the parking area to the takeoff holding point follows the shortest and most expeditious route. The same applies when taxiing back to the parking area after landing.

Study the airport chart before operating at an unfamiliar airport.

Further airport information may be found in the Airport/Facility Directory (A/FD). A full explanation of all terms is found at the front of the A/FD.

Runways are named according to their magnetic direction, rounded-off to the nearest 10°. For instance, a runway whose direction is 274°M is named Rwy 27. When used in the opposite direction (094°M), it is named Rwy 9.

Runway directions are rounded-off to the nearest 10°.

Taxiway Markings

Taxiway markings are **yellow.** The taxiway **centerline** may be marked with a continuous yellow line, and the **edges** of the taxiway may be marked by two continuous yellow lines 6 inches apart. Airplanes should taxi with their nose-wheel on the yellow centerline.

Taxiway markings are yellow.

Taxiway **holding lines,** across the width of the taxiway, consist of two continuous and two dashed yellow lines, spaced 6 inches between dashes. The two continuous lines are on the side from which an aircraft will approach a runway when taxiing, and if you are instructed to hold short of the runway or if you are not cleared onto the runway, you should stop with no part of the aircraft extending beyond the holding line.

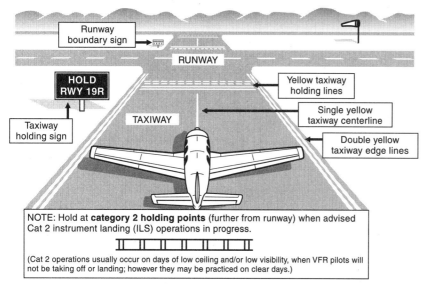

Figure 22-1. Taxiway markings are in yellow

Taxiway and Runway Signs

Next to the holding line at the edge of the taxiway there may be **runway holding position signs** with white characters on a red background.

There may also be a **runway boundary sign** that faces the runway and is visible to pilots exiting the runway. It will also be adjacent to the holding position marked on the pavement and may even be painted on the rear face of the holding sign. The sign has black markings on a yellow background. After landing, you will be clear of the runway when your aircraft is completely past this sign and the holding lines on the pavement. A **no-entry sign** (red and white) prohibits the entry of an aircraft.

Figure 22-2. Runway holding position sign

Figure 22-3. Runway boundary sign

Figure 22-4. No-entry sign

Runway Markings

Runway markings vary in complexity according to the operations likely to occur on that particular runway. To assist pilots landing and stopping at the conclusion of a successful precision instrument approach, some precision instrument runways have very specific markings, as shown below.

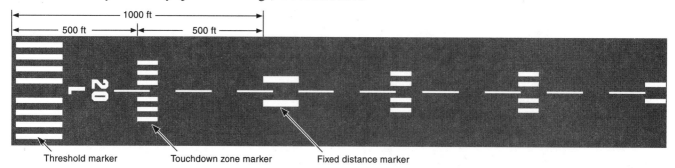

Figure 22-5. Markings on a precision instrument runway

Ensure that you know whether the full length of the runway is available for landing or not. A **displaced threshold** showing the start of the landing portion of the runway will be indicated by white arrows pointing to a thick white solid line across the runway, or by yellow chevrons. If arrows are used, that part of the runway may be available for takeoff, but not for landing. If chevrons, rather than arrows are used, then that part of the runway is only suitable for use during an aborted takeoff (as a stopway). If the whole runway is totally unusable, it will have a large cross (×) at each end.

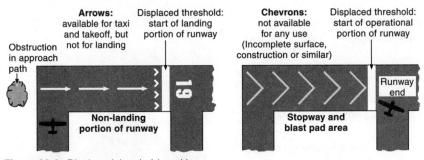

Figure 22-6. Displaced threshold markings

Figure 22-7. Closed runway (or taxiway)

Airport Lighting

The main aeronautical lighting provided at an airport to assist pilots to maneuver their airplanes at night consists of:

- taxiway lighting;
- runway lighting;
- an airport beacon;
- approach lighting;
- visual approach slope indicators (VASI); and
- red warning lights on significant obstacles.

The approach lights and runway lights at an airport are controlled by:

- the control tower personnel (when the tower is active);
- the FSS, at some locations where no control tower is active; or
- the pilot (at certain airports).

The pilot may request ATC or FSS to turn the lights on (or off), or to vary their intensity if required. On a hazy day with restricted visibility, but with a lot of glare, maximum brightness might be necessary; on a clear dark night, a significantly lower brightness level will be required.

Taxiway Lights

Taxiways are lit in one of two ways for the guidance of pilots, with either:

- two lines of taxiway **blue edge** lights; or
- one line of **centerline green** taxiway lights.

At some airports, there is a mixture of the two types, centerline green on some taxiways, and blue edge on others. Taxiway lights are omnidirectional, which means they shine in all directions, since a taxiing aircraft may be coming from any direction.

Taxiway lights are either centerline green or blue edge.

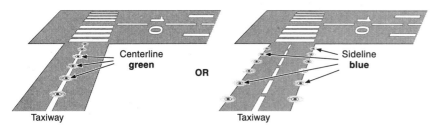

Figure 22-8. Taxiway lighting

At certain points on the taxiway, there may be **red stop-bars** installed, to indicate the position where an airplane should hold position, for instance before entering or crossing an active runway.

Runway Lighting

Runway lighting defines the boundaries of the actual landing area. Some advanced systems on precision instrument approach runways also provide you with distance-down-the-runway information.

Runway edge lights are white, and outline the edges of runways during periods of darkness or restricted visibility.

The **runway end lights** each have two colors, showing green at the near end to aircraft on approach, and red to airplanes stopping at the far end.

Note: Runway lighting is the extent of the airport lighting at basic airports.

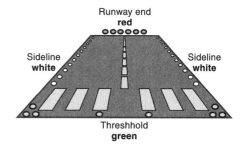

Figure 22-9. Basic runway lighting at night

Advanced runway edge lights are classified according to the intensity or brightness they are capable of producing:

• HIRL—high intensity runway lights;

• MIRL—medium intensity runway lights;

• LIRL—low intensity runway lights.

Runway edge lights are white, except on instrument runways where amber replaces white for the last 2,000 feet (or last-half on runways shorter than 4,000 feet) to form a *caution* zone for landings in restricted visibility.

Runway end identifier lights (REIL) consist of a pair of synchronized white flashing lights located each side of the runway threshold at the approach end. They serve to:

• identify a runway end surrounded by many other lights;

• identify a runway end which lacks contrast with the surrounding terrain; and

• identify a runway end in poor visibility.

In-runway lighting is embedded in the runway surface of some precision approach runways. It consists of:

• **Touchdown zone lighting (TDZL)**—bright white lights either side of the runway centerline in the touchdown zone (from 100 feet in from the landing threshold to 3,000 feet or the half-way point, whichever is the lower).

• **Runway centerline lighting (RCLS)**—flush centerline lighting at 50 feet intervals, starting 75 feet in from the landing threshold to within 75 feet of the stopping end. RCLS also includes **runway-remaining lighting,** where the centerline lighting seen by a stopping airplane is:

  – initially all white;

  – alternating red and white from 3,000 feet-to-go point to 1,000 feet-to-go;

  – all red for the last 1,000 feet.

• **Taxiway turn-off lights**—a series of green in-runway lights spaced at 50 feet intervals defining a curved path from the runway centerline onto the taxiway.

Pilot-Controlled Lighting Systems

At selected airports, when ATC and/or FSS facilities are not manned, *airborne* control of the lights is possible using the VHF-COM. The Airport Facilities Directory (A/FD) specifies the type of lighting available, and the VHF-COM frequency used to activate the system.

To use an FAA-approved **pilot-activated** lighting system, simply select the appropriate VHF frequency on the VHF-COM, and depress the microphone switch a number of times. Key the mike 7 times within 5 seconds, to activate the lights at maximum intensity, and then key it a further 5 or 3 times, for medium or low intensity lights respectively, if desired.

All lighting is activated for 15 minutes from the time of the most recent transmission. If pilot-activated lights are already on as you commence an approach, it is good airmanship to reactivate them and thereby ensure good lighting throughout the approach and landing.

For pilot-controlled lights at maximum intensity, select the frequency and key the mike seven times within five seconds. Activation lasts 15 minutes.

Approach Light Systems (ALS)

At many airports, an approach lighting system (ALS) extends out from the approach end of the runway to well beyond the physical boundaries of the airport, possibly into forested or built-up areas.

Approach lights do *not* mark the boundaries of a suitable landing area—they simply act as a lead-in to a runway for a pilot on approach to land.

ALS lighting is a standardized arrangement of white and red lights, consisting basically of extended centerline lighting, with crossbars sited at specific intervals back along the approach path from the threshold before the runway is reached.

Visual Approach Slope Indicators (VASI)

In conditions of poor visibility and at night, when the runway environment and the natural horizon may not be clearly visible, it is often difficult for a pilot to judge the correct approach slope of the airplane toward the touchdown zone of the runway. A number of very effective visual approach slope indicators provide visual slope guidance to a pilot on approach.

Lateral guidance is provided by the runway, the runway lights or the approach light system. The slope guidance provided by a **visual approach slope indicator (VASI)** is to the touchdown zone, which will probably be some 1,000 feet in from the runway threshold. The VASI slope is typically 3°.

The typical **2-bar VASI** has two pairs of wingbars alongside the runway, usually at 500 feet and 1,000 feet from the approach threshold. It is sometimes known as the *red-on-white* system, since these two colors are used to indicate to the pilot whether the airplane is on slope, too high or too low. The pilot will see:

- all bars white if high on approach;
- the near bars white and the far bars red if right on slope; and
- all bars red if low on slope.

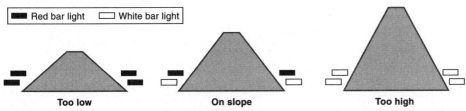

Figure 22-10. Perspectives on approach using a 2-bar VASI—fly "red-on-white"

During the approach, the airplane should be maintained on a slope within the *white* sector of the near bars and the *red* sector of the far bars. If the airplane flies above or below the correct slope, the lights will change color from white to pink, to red, or visa versa.

The plane of the VASI approach slope only provides guaranteed obstacle clearance in an arc 10° left or right of the extended centerline out to a distance of 4 nautical miles (nm) from the runway threshold, even though the VASI may be visible in good conditions out to 5 nm by day and 20 nm by night.

There are other operational considerations when using the *red-on-white* VASI. At maximum range, the white bars may become visible before the red bars, because of the nature of red and white light. In haze or smog, or in certain other conditions, the white lights may have a yellowish tinge about them. In addition, if water collects in or on the light lens false indications may occur.

When extremely low on slope, the two wingbars (all lights red) may appear to merge into one red bar—at close range to the threshold this would indicate a critical situation with respect to obstacle clearance, and the pilot must take urgent action.

Some VASI systems use a reduced number of lights, in which case they may be known as an **abbreviated VASI** or **AVASI.**

The **3-bar VASI** has an additional wingbar at the far end, intended to assist the pilots of large passenger airliners. Pilots of such airplanes will use the second and third wingbars, and ignore the first to allow for the extra length of the airplane.

Pilots of smaller airplanes should refer only to the two nearer wingbars, and ignore the further "long-bodied" wingbar. On slope, the indications should be (top bar red and ignored), middle bar red and lower bar white.

The **precision approach path indicator (PAPI)** is a development of the VASI, and also uses red/white light signals for guidance in maintaining the correct approach angle, but the lights are arranged differently and their indications must be interpreted differently. PAPI has a single wingbar, which will consist of four light units on one or both sides of the runway adjacent to the touchdown point. There is no pink transition stage as the lights change from red to white.

If the airplane is on slope, the two outer lights of each unit are white and the two inner lights are red. Above slope, the number of white lights increase, and below slope the number of red lights increase.

A **pulsating visual approach slope indicator (PVASI)** consists of a single light unit, positioned on the left side of a runway adjacent to the touchdown point, which projects three or four different "bands" of light at different vertical angles, only one of which can be seen by a pilot on approach at any one time.

The indications provided by a typical PVASI are:

- pulsing white—above glide slope;
- steady white—on glide slope (alternating red/white on some systems); and
- pulsing red—below glide slope.

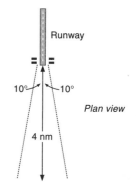

Figure 22-11. The extent of useful VASI information

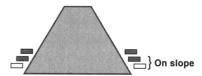

Figure 22-12. Correct view for the pilot of a smaller airplane using the 3-bar VASI

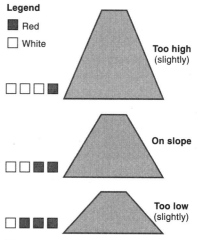

Figure 22-13. Slope guidance using PAPI

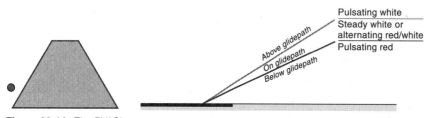

Figure 22-14. The PVASI

The **tri-color VASI** is a short-range visual slope aid ($\frac{1}{2}$ mile by day, 5 miles by night), and consists of a single-light unit that indicates:

- amber if above slope;
- green if on slope; and
- red if below slope.

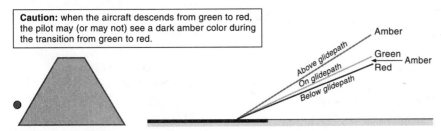

Caution: when the aircraft descends from green to red, the pilot may (or may not) see a dark amber color during the transition from green to red.

Figure 22-15. The tri-color VASI

The **T-VASI** is a system that has a horizontal bar of white lights either side of the runway aiming point. If the airplane is right on slope, you will see the horizontal bar only. If you are high on slope, single lights will appear above this bar, forming an inverted-T, and indicating fly down. If you are low on slope, single lights will appear below the bar, forming a T, and indicating fly up. The number of vertical lights give an indication of how far off slope you are. If extremely low, the lights turn red.

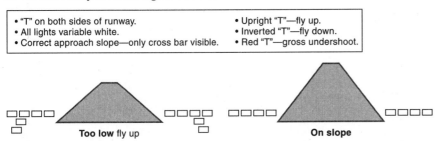

- "T" on both sides of runway.
- All lights variable white.
- Correct approach slope—only cross bar visible.
- Upright "T"—fly up.
- Inverted "T"—fly down.
- Red "T"—gross undershoot.

Too low fly up   **On slope**   **Too high** fly down

Figure 22-16. T-VASI

Airport Beacon

The airport beacon is designed to help the pilot visually locate the airport from some distance away. Some airport beacons rotate, others transmit pulses of light, the effect being the same—flashes of one or two alternating colors, which are:

- green/white/green/white—at **civil land airports;**
- green/white-white/green/white-white—at **military land airports;**
- green/yellow/white—at **lighted heliports;** and
- white/yellow—at **lighted water ports.**

An airport rotating beacon that is operating during daylight hours indicates that weather in the Class B, C or D airspace around that airport, which will have an operating control tower, is below basic VFR weather minimums (ground visibility less than 3 miles and/or ceiling less than 1,000 feet). This is a good warning for VFR pilots.

✐ Now complete **Review 22, Part (a)** on page 509.

Airport Operations

Listening to the ATIS

The ATIS (automatic terminal information service) is a prerecorded continuous broadcast containing weather information including wind and altimeter setting, possibly runway information (for example, "Runway two three left in use, Runway five closed"), tower frequency, and other essential but routine information. The ATIS will not, however, contain control information such as ATC clearances to specific aircraft.

As the ATIS is updated throughout the day, its designation will also change — from *Information Alfa* to *Information Bravo* to *Information Charlie,* and so on. It is good airmanship to listen to the ATIS before taxiing, and then on initial contact with ground control to advise "Information Delta," or as appropriate, to avoid them passing the information to you again. You should also listen to the ATIS about 25 miles from the airport at which you intend to land.

If possible, listen to the ATIS before operating at an airport.

Before Taxiing

At airports **with an operating control tower,** you should obtain a clearance to taxi to the takeoff runway. Your request for a taxi clearance should include:

Obtain a taxi clearance at an airport with an operating control tower.

- the station called (for example, Hagerstown Ground Control);
- your callsign;
- your location on the airport;
- the ATIS code (if received);
- a request for taxi instructions (if necessary);
- type of operation planned (VFR or IFR); and
- destination or direction of flight.

You should start your callsign with the make or model of your aircraft followed by its registration. (The November for N, to designate United States-registered aircraft, may be dropped). For example: "Cessna Eight Niner Hotel Foxtrot"; "Warrior Five Two Mike India." Each digit should be stated individually and each letter should be expressed in the phonetic alphabet. Ground Control should be addressed as "… Ground Control," and the tower as "… Tower."

Some typical taxi calls to the tower follow:

> *Pilot:* Hagerstown Ground Control
> Beechcraft Three Eight Seven Four Alfa
> at city ramp
> ready to taxi
> departing VFR northwest bound

> *Tower:* Beechcraft Seven Four Alfa
> Hagerstown Ground Control
> wind calm, altimeter two nine point nine five
> taxi Runway Zero Two
> contact tower one two zero point three when ready for departure

Some typical taxi clearances provided by ATC at other airports with operating control towers are:

> *Tower:* Runway One Eight
> taxi via Taxiway Echo

This clearance permits you to taxi along the designated taxi route to the assigned runway. You may cross other runways that intersect the taxi route, but you may not cross or enter the assigned runway.

Tower: Runway One Eight
taxi via Taxiway Echo
hold short of Runway Two Seven

This clearance permits you to taxi along the designated taxi route toward the assigned takeoff runway, which is Runway 18, but only as far as the holding point prior to Runway 27. A further taxi clearance is required to proceed. It may take the form of something like: *"Cross Runway Two Seven without delay."*

At airports **without an operating control tower,** a clearance to taxi is not required, and you should advise your taxi intentions on the appropriate frequency (for example, the FSS at McAlester, addressed as *"McAlester Radio,"* and the UNICOM at Frederick, addressed as *"Frederick UNICOM"*). For example:

Pilot: London Radio
Cessna Five One Three Six Delta
ready to taxi
VFR departing to the southeast
request Airport Advisory

The key to communications at airports *without* an operating control tower is to use the **Common Traffic Advisory Frequency (CTAF).** The CTAF may be a UNICOM, MULTICOM, FSS or tower frequency (even though the tower is not operating). The CTAF for any particular airport may be obtained from aeronautical charts, the A/FD, or by contacting any FSS. If the FSS is physically located on the airport it can provide a **local airport advisory service** and give weather and traffic information (this is not an ATC control service).

The Standard Traffic Pattern

To maintain some form of safe and orderly flow of traffic at an airport, and to allow easy and safe access to the active runway, aircraft are flown in a standard traffic pattern. For good operational reasons, the preferred direction of takeoff and landing is into the wind, therefore the same direction will generally be used by aircraft both taking off and landing.

At airports without an operating control tower, *advise* your taxi intentions to others.

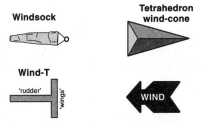

Figure 22-17. Wind and landing direction indicators

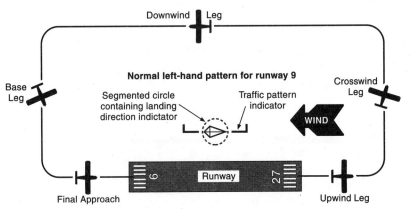

Figure 22-18. The traffic pattern is rectangular

The traffic pattern is a rectangular ground path based on the runway in use. The **standard pattern** is to the left of the runway with all turns being made to the left. At some airports and on some particular runways, however, the patterns are right-hand to avoid built-up areas, high terrain or restricted airspace.

At tower-controlled airports takeoff and landing directions will be advised from the tower or on the ATIS.

The standard traffic pattern is left hand.

The tower will advise takeoff and landing direction.

At airports *without* an operating control tower, make use of any **segmented circle** with its associated wind indicator and traffic pattern indicators to assist you in determining which runway to use and the direction of the traffic pattern. You should comply with any FAA traffic pattern established for a particular airport (*see* A/FD).

Some airports have **parallel runways,** with a left traffic pattern off Runway Left, and a right traffic pattern off Runway Right, and with a "no transgression zone" between the two patterns.

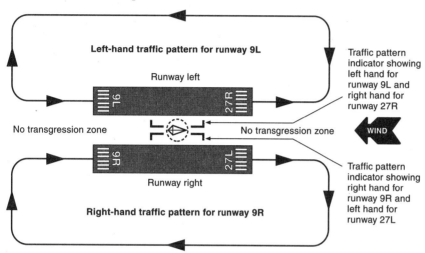

Figure 22-19. Left and right traffic patterns for parallel runways

The traffic pattern is referenced to the runway on which it is based, for example, "left traffic for Runway 36" refers to the pattern based on Runway 36. The 36 indicates that the runway heading is somewhere in the range 355°–360°–005°.

The Legs of a Traffic Pattern

Following takeoff, climb straight ahead on the **upwind leg** until beyond the departure end of the runway and within 300 feet of pattern altitude. The upwind leg of the traffic pattern is an extension of the runway in the direction of take off and landing.

Within 300 feet of pattern altitude and beyond the end of the runway, begin a turn to the **crosswind leg.** The crosswind leg of the traffic pattern is a flight path at right angles to the runway in use and beyond its departure end. Continue the climb to pattern altitude and then level off. With the correct setting in the pressure window of the altimeter, pattern altitude is indicated when the altimeter shows the pattern height above the airport added to the airport's elevation. Pattern altitudes at some airports may be different for various reasons (to avoid high terrain or remain beneath certain airspace), but will almost certainly lie in the range of 800–1,200 feet above the airport.

At pattern altitude, a turn is made to **downwind leg,** which is a flight path parallel to the runway in the opposite direction to takeoffs and landings. On the downwind leg, the airplane is flown at traffic pattern altitude parallel to the runway. A downwind radio call is often made to alert other aircraft and Air Traffic Control of your position. Descent for landing may be commenced at any convenient point after passing abeam your intended touchdown point on the runway.

At a suitable point at the end of downwind leg, a turn to **base leg** is made, and the descent continued or started. The base leg of a traffic pattern is a flight path at right angles to the landing runway, and off its approach end, extending from downwind leg to the intersection of the extended runway centerline.

Ideally, a turn from base leg onto **final approach** should be completed by 400 feet above airport elevation.

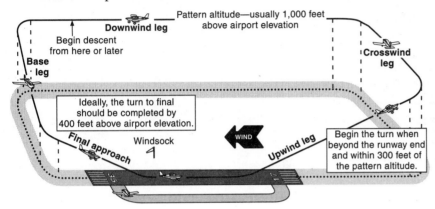

Figure 22-20. The normal traffic pattern

Allow for Wind Effect in the Traffic Pattern

While flying in the pattern, a pilot should aim to fly a rectangular path over the ground. This means that, on any leg where there is a crosswind component, drift should be allowed for and a wind correction angle (WCA) applied to compensate for the wind effect. Select a reference point on the ground well ahead of the airplane, and make sure that the airplane tracks directly toward it to keep your pattern rectangular.

Departing the Traffic Pattern

At an airport *with* an operating control tower, follow any instructions given by ATC, and make any necessary radio calls. Follow any special procedures applicable to your airport.

If the tower is *not* active at your field, then you should plan a traffic pattern departure that will not conflict with other aircraft that are in the pattern or entering it. The recommended procedure for departing where there is a nonoperational control tower is to either:

• extend the upwind leg as you climb out after takeoff and then, when clear of other pattern traffic, maneuver to achieve your desired course heading; or

• continue climbing out on the upwind leg and then, when at or above pattern altitude, turn 45° left and depart the pattern. (In a right-hand pattern, the turn would be 45° right.)

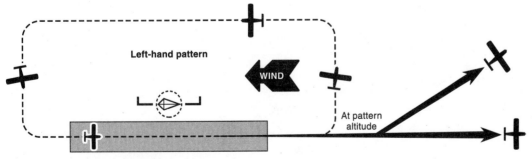

Figure 22-21. Departing the traffic pattern

Ensure that the current altimeter setting is set in the pressure window, so that the altimeter will read altitude above mean sea level (MSL). This enables you to accurately determine when you have reached pattern altitude. If the airport has an elevation of 890 feet, and the pattern is to be flown 1,000 feet above this, then traffic pattern altitude is reached when the altimeter indicates (890 + 1,000) = 1,890 feet MSL.

Radio Calls Departing from Airports Without an Operating Control Tower

When you are departing from an airport that does *not* have an active control tower, you should make **advisory radio calls** to a UNICOM, MULTICOM, or FSS. You may or may not receive a response, but your calls are important since they alert other traffic to your position. These advisory calls should be made:

- before taxiing from the parking position; and
- before taxiing onto the runway for departure.

Some typical advisory calls from a pilot departing an airport without an operating control tower are:

> *Pilot:* Ocean City traffic
> Queen Air 7155 Bravo at hangar two
> taxiing to runway two six
> Ocean City

> *Pilot:* Ocean City traffic
> Queen Air 7155 Bravo
> departing runway two six
> departing the pattern to the southwest
> climbing to six thousand
> Ocean City

Radio Calls Departing from Airports With an Operating Control Tower

When you are departing from an airport with an operating control tower, say in Class D airspace, you should:

- listen to the **ATIS** if available;
- contact **ground control** before taxi—transmit your aircraft identification, position on field, request a taxi clearance, and specify your flight status (VFR or IFR), direction of flight or destination, and ATIS identifier (if received);
- contact **tower** before takeoff—transmit your aircraft identification, ready for departure, your runway, and direction of flight.

Some typical radio calls between a pilot about to taxi for departure and the tower controllers are:

> *Pilot:* Hagerstown ground control
> Cessna 5345 Alfa at city ramp ready to taxi
> departing VFR southeast bound

> *Ground:* Cessna 5345 Alfa
> Hagerstown ground control, wind calm
> altimeter 30.05, taxi runway zero two
> contact tower 120.3 when ready for departure

> *Pilot:* Cessna 5345 Alfa

After the pilot has taxied to a point near the runway and completed his runup, he changes frequency and calls the tower:

    Pilot: Hagerstown tower
              Cessna 5345 Alfa ready for departure runway two
              VFR southeast bound
    Tower: Cessna 5345 Alfa
              Hagerstown tower
              Runway zero two, clear for takeoff
    Pilot: Cessna 5345 Alfa

After takeoff, you should continue to monitor the tower frequency, and keep a good lookout for other traffic until well clear of the Class D airspace.

If you are operating from a satellite airport inside the Class D airspace, but it does not have an operating control tower, then you should contact the appropriate ATC facility as soon as possible after takeoff.

Entering the Traffic Pattern

You should always know the elevation of the airport you intend to use, so that you can fly toward it at an appropriate altitude. Ensure that the altimeter pressure window is set to current altimeter setting, so that the altimeter reads altitude above mean sea level (MSL).

If you are returning to an airport that has an ATIS broadcast on a specific VHF frequency, then it is good airmanship to listen to it some 25 nm out.

When entering the traffic pattern at an airport *with* an operating control tower, follow any ATC instructions that are given to you.

At airports *without* operating control towers, follow the standard recommended procedures that will avoid conflict with other aircraft. The segmented circle provides a visual indication to pilots flying overhead as to the runway in use and the direction, left or right, of the pattern. Enter on a 45° angle to the downwind leg at traffic pattern altitude.

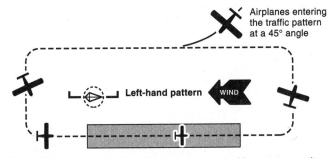

Figure 22-22. Entering the pattern at an airport without an operating control tower

Radio Calls Arriving at Airports Without an Operating Control Tower

When you are in flight and approaching an airport *without* an operating control tower, you should make advisory radio calls on the **Common Traffic Advisory Frequency (CTAF):**

- 10 miles out;
- on the 45° entry to the downward leg;
- entering downwind leg;
- on base leg;
- on final; and
- on leaving the runway after you have landed.

Some typical advisory calls from a pilot inbound to an airport without an operating control tower are:

    Pilot: Ocean City traffic
            Apache 225 Zulu, 10 miles south descending through three thousand
            on the 45° angle to enter downwind
            runway one seven at Ocean City

    Pilot: Ocean City traffic
            Apache 225 Zulu
            entering downwind runway one seven at Ocean City

    Pilot: Ocean City traffic
            Apache 225 Zulu
            turning base runway one seven at Ocean City

    Pilot: Ocean City traffic
            Apache 225 Zulu
            final runway one seven full stop at Ocean City

    Pilot: Ocean City traffic
            Apache 225 Zulu
            clear of runway one seven at Ocean City

Note: If the CTAF is a Flight Service Station (FSS) frequency, you could also "request airport advisory" in your initial call to obtain takeoff and landing information. You may also request airport advisory on CTAF at airports without FSS, but you are not as likely to receive it. Also, when expressing altitudes, use full hundreds, for example, "four thousand five hundred" for 4,500 feet MSL; "one six thousand" for 16,000 feet MSL.

Radio Calls Arriving at Airports With an Operating Control Tower

When you are in flight and approaching an airport *with* an operating control tower, you should:

• at 25 miles out, listen to the **ATIS;**

• before entering Class B, C or D airspace, contact the ATC facility providing services in that airspace with aircraft identification, position, altitude, and intentions—then respond to any instructions.

Obtain an ATC clearance to land (which will come in the form "Cessna 45 Alfa, cleared to land") before landing.

    After landing and taxiing clear of the runway, you should contact **ground control** when directed, and advise "clear of runway." If you are unfamiliar with the airport, you should also request taxiing instructions.

Some typical radio calls between an inbound pilot and a tower controller are:

At 15 miles out:

    Pilot: Hagerstown tower
            Cessna 5345 Alfa
            fifteen miles southeast at two thousand five hundred
            landing Hagerstown

    Tower: Cessna 5345 Alfa
            Hagerstown tower
            runway two in use
            wind calm
            altimeter 30.04
            enter left downwind
            report turning left base

The pilot enters the downwind leg of a left traffic pattern, and then calls when turning onto base leg as instructed:

Pilot: Hagerstown tower
         Cessna 5345 Alfa turning left base runway two

Tower: Cessna 45 Alfa
         cleared to land

Pilot: Cessna 45 Alfa

The pilot lands, and then taxis straight ahead on the runway to the first safe taxiway to clear the active runway. He taxis clear of the runway, then changes frequency and calls ground control when directed.

Pilot: Hagerstown ground control
         Cessna 5345 Alfa clear of runway two
           request taxi instructions to city ramp
           unfamiliar with airport

Ground: Cessna 45 Alfa taxi to city ramp
         continue straight ahead
         turn right at the first intersection

Pilot: Cessna 45 Alfa

Airport Radar Services

Radar has greatly simplified ATC procedures by enabling the controller to see a picture on the radar screen of the air traffic in his area of responsibility. The transponder carried in the aircraft can provide the radar controller with further information on the screen, such as aircraft identification and altitude. Unless otherwise authorized, VFR aircraft should squawk transponder **code 1200.**

When passing traffic information to you, the radar controller will often use the clock system to specify the other aircraft's position relative to your track, and also give its distance in miles, direction of flight, and altitude. The controller sees your *track,* rather than your heading, and so you will have to allow for any wind drift angle when you look out the window and search for other traffic. Note that, even in a radar environment, the pilot has the ultimate responsibility to see and avoid other traffic.

Various levels of radar service are available, depending on the particular airspace, the nature of the operation (IFR/VFR), and the controller's workload.

If you ever experience **radio failure,** you should squawk **7600** on your transponder. This will alert the tower controller to your radio communications failure. You should observe the traffic flow, enter the traffic pattern keeping a particularly good lookout, and watch for light signals from the tower (*see* Figure 22-24). If the radio failure occurs on the ground, you would normally not takeoff but taxi back to a parking position for repairs or clarification.

Normal transponder code for VFR is 1200.

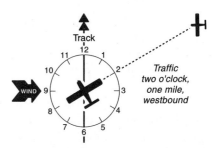

Figure 22-23. Radar traffic information service

Following radio communications failure, keep a good lookout, squawk code 7600, observe the traffic flow, enter the traffic pattern, and watch for light signals from the tower.

Color and Type of Signal	Meaning with respect to Aircraft on the Surface	Meaning with respect to Aircraft in Flight
Steady Green	Cleared for takeoff	Cleared to land
Flashing Green	Cleared to taxi	Return for a landing (followed by a steady green at the proper time to indicate cleared to land)
Steady Red	Stop	give way to other aircraft and continue circling
Flashing Red	Taxi clear of runway in use	airport unsafe—do not land
Flashing White	Return to starting point on airport	Not applicable
Alternating Red and Green	Exercise extreme caution	Exercise extreme caution

Figure 22-24. Light signals used by control tower

TRSA Radar Service

Terminal Radar Service Areas (TRSA) around a few airports are a leftover from earlier airspace arrangements, and normally include the Class D airspace surrounding the primary airport (shown on Sectional Charts as a blue segmented line) and the airspace used transitioning between the terminal and en route environments (shown on Sectional Charts with solid black lines and altitudes for each segment). Aircraft participation in TRSA services is optional.

Basic Radar Service

Basic radar service can provide traffic advisories and limited radar vectoring on a workload-permitting basis to VFR aircraft arriving at Class D airports and occasionally at airports in Class E or G airspace. Basic radar service exists primarily to aid tower controllers sequencing arriving and departing traffic.

Traffic Sequencing for Pilots

Basic service with traffic sequencing is provided to adjust the flow of arriving VFR and IFR aircraft into the traffic pattern and to provide traffic information to departing VFR aircraft. VFR aircraft may be assigned specific headings to fly (vectors), as well as specific altitudes, to aid controllers in facilitating traffic separation.

Full Radar Services

Full service provides sequencing and separation for all participating VFR and IFR aircraft, and is typically encountered in and around busy Class B, C, and D airspace. IFR traffic is always accorded the highest level of radar service during all segments of flight.

In a radar environment, pilots of **arriving aircraft** should contact approach control on the published frequency, usually at approximately 25 miles, and give callsign, aircraft type, position, altitude, transponder code, destination, ATIS information received, and request traffic information. Approach control will issue wind and runway, except when the pilot states *"have numbers"* or *"have ATIS information."* Traffic information will be advised on a workload-permitting basis. Radar service is automatically terminated when approach control advises the pilot to contact the control tower for further landing instructions.

Pilots of **departing** aircraft are encouraged, on initial contact with ground control, to request radar traffic information in the proposed direction of flight, for example:

San Carlos ground control, Mike seven three two, Cessna one seventy two, ready to taxi, VFR southbound at two thousand five hundred feet, have information Charlie, request radar traffic information.

After receiving a takeoff clearance from the tower and becoming airborne, the tower will advise when to contact departure control.

When departing and being advised that the radar service is being terminated, you should set the **normal VFR code 1200** in your transponder. Be careful not to pass through any of the emergency codes when selecting 1200: 7500—unlawful interference, 7600—radio failure, or 7700—emergency.

✍ Now complete **Review 22, Part (b)** on page 510.

Review 22
Airports and Airport Operations

Part (a)

1. The numbers 9 and 27 on a runway indicate that the runway is oriented approximately:
   (a) 009° and 027° true.
   (b) 090° and 270° true.
   (c) 090° and 270° magnetic.

   ➤ (c)

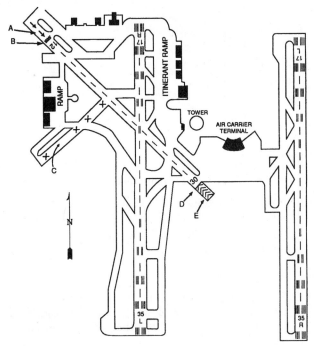

Figure 22-25. Airport diagram

For questions 2 to 4 refer to Figure 22-25.

2. Area C on the airport depicted is classified as a:
   (a) stabilized area.
   (b) multiple heliport.
   (c) closed runway.

   ➤ (c)

3. For runway 12, landing may be commenced at position (A/B/D/E).

   ➤ B

4. That portion of runway 12 identified by the letter A may be used for:
   (a) landing.
   (b) taxiing and takeoff.
   (c) taxiing and landing.

   ➤ (b)

Figure 22-26.

Figure 22-27.

5. The sign in Figure 22-26 in red-and-white indicates _____ .

   ➤ no entry

6. The sign shown in Figure 22-27 in black-on-yellow indicates _____ .

   ➤ runway boundary

7. An airport's rotating beacon operated during daylight hours indicates that the weather in the control zone is below (basic VFR/special VFR/IFR) minimums, which are visibility less than _____ miles and/or ceiling less than _____ feet.

   ➤ basic VFR, 3, 1,000

8. The color pattern emitted by the rotating beacon at a civil airport is _____ followed by _____ followed by _____ .

   ➤ green, white, green

9. The color pattern emitted by the rotating beacon at a lighted heliport is _____ followed by _____ followed by _____ .

   ➤ green, yellow, white

10. A military air station can be identified by a rotating beacon that emits:
    (a) white and green alternating flashes.
    (b) two, quick, white flashes between green flashes.
    (c) green, yellow, and white flashes.

    ➤ (b)

11. Pilot-activated lighting can be activated at maximum intensity by clicking the VHF-COM microphone _____ times within 5 seconds. Medium intensity may be obtained by clicking the microphone a further _____ times.

    ➤ 7, 5

12. Airport taxiway edge lights are identified at night by:
    (a) white directional lights.
    (b) blue omnidirectional lights.
    (c) alternate red and green lights.

    ➤ (b)

13. Taxiway centerline lights are colored _____ .

   ➤ green

14. When using a precision approach path indicator (PAPI), three white lights and one red light indicates (high/slightly high/on/slightly low/low) on glide slope.

   ➤ slightly high

15. A red light signal from a tri-color VASI indicates (above/on/ below) glide slope.

   ➤ below

16. An amber light signal from a tri-color VASI indicates (above/on/below) glide slope.

   ➤ above

17. A below glide slope indication from a pulsating approach slope indicator is a:
   (a) pulsating white light
   (b) steady white light.
   (c) pulsating red light.

   ➤ (c)

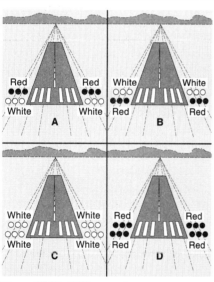

Figure 22-28. VASI examples

For questions 18 and 19 refer to Figure 22-28.

18. Illustration A indicates that the aircraft is (above/on/below) the glide slope.

   ➤ on

19. VASI lights as shown by illustration C indicate that the airplane is:
   (a) off course to the left
   (b) above the glide slope.
   (c) below the glide slope.

   ➤ (b)

Part (b)

1. An FSS physically located on an airport without an operating control tower can provide a _____ .

   ➤ local airport advisory service

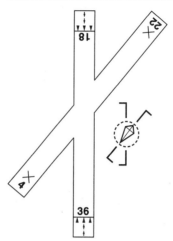

Figure 22-29.

For questions 2 to 5 refer to Figure 22-29.

2. Select the proper traffic pattern and runway for landing:
   (a) left-hand traffic and Runway 18.
   (b) right-hand traffic and Runway 18.
   (c) left-hand traffic and Runway 22.

   ➤ (b)

3. The segmented circle indicates that the traffic patterns are (left/right)-hand for Runway 22, and (left/right)-hand for Runway 4. Runway 22 and Runway 4 (are/are not) available for use.

   ➤ left, right, are not

4. The traffic patterns indicated in the segmented circle have been arranged to avoid flights over an area to the:
   (a) south of the airport.
   (b) north of the airport.
   (c) north-northeast of the airport.

   ➤ (c)

5. A landing on Runway 18 would be with a (left/right)-quartering (head/tail)-wind.

   ➤ right headwind

6. If two-way radio communication fails at an airport with a tower and cannot be restored, the recommended procedure is to observe the _____ flow, enter the _____ , and look for a _____ from the tower. Squawk transponder code _____ .

   ➤ traffic, traffic pattern, light signal, 7600

7. A steady green light signal directed from the control tower to an aircraft in flight is a signal that the pilot:
   (a) is cleared to land.
   (b) should give way to other aircraft and continue circling.
   (c) should return for landing.
   ➤ (a)

8. An alternating red and green light directed from the control tower to you in flight indicates that _____ .
   ➤ you should exercise extreme caution

9. A flashing red light signal directed from the control tower to you in flight indicates that _____ .
   ➤ the airport is not safe and you should not land there

10. A steady red light signal directed from the control tower to you in flight indicates that _____ .
    ➤ you should give way to other aircraft and continue circling

11. A flashing white light signal from the control tower to a taxiing aircraft is an indication to:
    (a) taxi at a faster speed.
    (b) taxi only on taxiways and not cross runways.
    (c) return to the starting point on the airport.
    ➤ (c)

12. A steady green light signal directed from the control tower to you while on the ground indicates that you are _____ .
    ➤ cleared for takeoff

For questions 13 to 21 refer to Figure 22-30. You may refer to the legend of any A/FD to help you (the legend will be provided in the Knowledge Exam).

13. The 3-letter identifying code for Lincoln Municipal Airport is _____ .
    ➤ LNK

14. The elevation of Lincoln Municipal Airport is _____ feet MSL.
    ➤ 1,214 feet MSL

15. Traffic pattern altitude (TPA) at Lincoln Municipal Airport is _____ feet MSL, which is _____ feet AGL.
    ➤ 3,414 feet MSL, 2,200 feet AGL

16. Runway 17 Right at Lincoln Municipal Airport is (soft/hard)-surfaced, and is _____ feet long and _____ feet wide.
    ➤ hard-surfaced, 12,901 feet long 200 feet wide

§ **LINCOLN MUNI** (LNK) 4 NW UTC-6(-5DT) 40°51'03"N 96°45'32"W   OMAHA
 1214 B S4 FUEL 100LL, JET A TPA—3414 (2200) ARFF Index C   H-1E, 3A, 4F, L-11B
 RWY 17R-35L: H12901X200 (ASPH-CONC-AFSC) S-100, D-200, DT-400 HIRL   IAP
   RWY 17R: MALSR. VASI(V4L)—GA 3.0° TCH 55'. Rgt tfc. Arrest device.
   RWY 35L: MALSR. VASI(V4L)—GA 3.0° TCH 55'. Arrest device.
 RWY 14-32: H8620X150 (ASPH-CONC-GRVD) S-80, D-170, DT-280 MIRL
   RWY 14: REIL. VASI(4VL)—GA 3.0°TCH 48'.
   RWY 32: VASI(4VL)—GA 3.0°TCH 53'. Thld dsplcd 431'. Pole.
 RWY 17L-35R: H5500X100 (ASPH-CONC-AFSC) S-49, D-60 HIRL .8% up N
   RWY 17L: VASI(V4L)—GA 3.0°TCH 33'. RWY 35R: VASI(V4L)—GA 3.0°TCH 35'. Light standard. Rgt tfc.
 AIRPORT REMARKS: Attended continuously. Arresting barrier located 2200' in from thld 17R and 1500' in from
   thld 35L. Arresting barrier in place departure end Rwy 17R-35L during military operations and approach
   end during emergencies. Airport manager advise 43000 lbs GWT single wheel Rwy 17L-35R. For MALSR
   Rwy 17R and 35L ctc Twr.; When Twr clsd MALSR Rwy 17R and 35L preset to Med intst.
 WEATHER DATA SOURCES: LLWAS
 COMMUNICATIONS: CTAF 118.5 ATIS 118.05 UNICOM 122.95
   COLUMBUS FSS (OLU) TF 1-800-WX-BRIEF. NOTAM FILE LNK.
   RCO 122.65 (COLUMBUS FSS)
 Ⓡ APP/DEP CON 124.0 (170°-349°) 124.8 (350°-169°) (1200-0600Z‡)
 Ⓡ MINNEAPOLIS CENTER APP/DEP CON 128.75 (0600-1200Z‡)
   TOWER 118.5 125.7 (1200-0600Z‡) GND CON 121.9 CLNC DEL 120.7
 ARSA ctc APP CON
 RADIO AIDS TO NAVIGATION: NOTAM FILE LNK. VHF/DF ctc COLUMBUS FSS
   (H) VORTACW 116.1 LNK Chan 108 40°55'26"N 96°44'30"W 185° 3.8 NM to fld. 1370/9E
   LEMMS NDB (MHW/LOM) 385 LN 40°44'50"N 96°45'44"W 354° 4.8 NM to fld. Unmonitored.
   ILS 111.1 I-OCZ Rwy 17R
   ILS 109.9 I-LNK Rwy 35L LOM LEMMS NDB.
 COMM/NAVAID REMARKS: Freq 121.5 not available at tower.

SAMPLE ONLY not to be used in conjunction with flight operations or flight planning

Figure 22-30.

17. The Common Traffic Advisory Frequency (CTAF) at Lincoln Municipal Airport is _____ MHz, which (is/is not) the same as the control tower frequency.

➤ 118.5 MHz, is

18. The ATIS at Lincoln Municipal Airport is on frequency _____ MHz.

➤ 118.05 MHz

19. The recommended communications procedure for landing at Lincoln Municipal Airport during the hours when the tower is not in operation is to monitor the airport traffic, and announce your position and intentions on frequency _____ MHz, which is the _____ frequency.

➤ 118.5 MHz, Common Traffic Advisory Frequency

20. You are approaching Lincoln Municipal Airport from the west at noon local time, which is _____ UTC (or Z). Lincoln Municipal Approach Control is active from _____ UTC to _____ UTC, which means you (should/cannot) contact it on frequency _____ MHz. Aircraft approaching from the east would use _____ MHz.

➤ 1800Z (1200 local + 6 hours), 1200Z to 0600Z, should, 124.0 MHz, 124.8 MHz

21. Traffic patterns in effect at Lincoln Municipal are:
    (a) to the right on 17L and 35L; to the left on 17R and 35R.
    (b) to the left on 17L and 35L; to the right on 17R and 35R.
    (c) to the right on runways 14 and 32.

➤ (b)

22. If you require radar service when departing a primary airport in Class D airspace, you should request it (on initial contact with ground control/from the tower immediately after takeoff).

➤ on initial contact with ground control

23. You are on a heading MH 090 and the ATC radar facility issues you the advisory "Traffic 3 o'clock, 2 miles, westbound". You should look (left/right/ahead), which will be to the (north/south/east/west).

➤ right, south

24. An ATC radar facility issues the following advisory to a pilot flying north in a calm wind:
    "Traffic 9 o'clock, 2 miles, southbound ......"
    Where should the pilot look for this traffic?
    (a) South.
    (b) North.
    (c) West.

➤ (c)

25. At airports without operating control towers, ATC clearances to taxi, takeoff and land (are/are not) required.

➤ are not

26. At airports with operating control towers, ATC clearances to taxi, takeoff and land (are/are not) required regardless of weather conditions.

➤ are

27. Ground control at San Carlos airport should be addressed as _____ .

➤ San Carlos Ground

28. The control tower at San Carlos airport should be addressed as _____ .

➤ San Carlos Tower

29. Automatic Terminal Information Service (ATIS) is the continuous broadcast of recorded information concerning:
    (a) pilots of radar-identified aircraft whose aircraft is in dangerous proximity to terrain or to an obstruction.
    (b) nonessential information to reduce frequency congestion.
    (c) noncontrol information in selected high-activity terminal areas.

➤ (c)

30. A clearance to taxi to the active runway at an airport with an operating control tower permits you to taxi via the taxiways, (to cross/not to cross) intersecting nonactive runways, and (to enter/not to enter) the active runway.

➤ to cross, not to enter

31. After landing at a tower-controlled airport, when should the pilot contact ground control?
    (a) When advised to do so by the tower.
    (b) Prior to turning off the runway.
    (c) After reaching a taxiway that leads directly to the parking area.

➤ (a)

Visual Navigation Fundamentals **23**

Air Navigation

Air navigation involves basic principles that apply to all airplanes, from the simplest trainers to the most sophisticated passenger jets.

Our objective in *The Pilot's Manual* is to show you navigation techniques that will not increase your workload in the cockpit to an unacceptable degree, and still allow time to fix your position and navigate the airplane safely to your desired destination.

We make the assumption that you already know how to fly the airplane; the objective here is to add the basic principles of air navigation to these flying skills. Other aspects that have a bearing on the conduct of a cross-country flight are covered in the chapters to follow.

This chapter concentrates on accurate navigation of a light aircraft, flown by a single pilot in VFR conditions. When flying cross-country you are the pilot, the navigator and the radio operator. You must:

- primarily fly the airplane safely and accurately;
- navigate correctly;
- attend to the radio and other aspects of your duty in the cockpit.

In short, you must, **"Aviate, navigate and communicate."**

To conduct a cross-country flight efficiently, the navigation tasks must be coordinated with (and not interfere with) the smooth flying of the airplane. It is most important that you, as pilot/navigator, clearly understand the basic principles underlying navigation so that correct techniques and practices can be applied quickly and accurately without causing too much distraction or apprehension.

> Remember the key words: "aviate, navigate, communicate" in that order.

Navigating an airplane, unlike a car or ship, is **three-dimensional**—you must think of *altitude* (vertical navigation) as well as *direction* (horizontal navigation). Also, you must think of *time*.

Horizontal Navigation

Types of Navigation

Visual Navigation
The basic method of visual navigation is map-reading, commonly referred to as **pilotage.** Map-reading requires more or less continuous visual reference to the ground, and the ability to map-read is restricted in poor visibility or with partial cloud cover, and at night. Map-reading involves comparing the map to the ground features and determining your actual position relative to the planned course.

> *Pilotage* is map-reading.

As a back-up to pilotage you can use deduced reckoning, commonly known as **dead reckoning** or **DR.** This allows you to apply current conditions of speed, direction and wind to your latest known position *(a fix)* and thus deduce where you should be at a certain time.

> *Dead reckoning* is calculating headings, distances and times.

Radio Navigation

Radio navigation uses radio equipment installed in the airplane and tuned to ground-based radio beacons. This enables the instrument-rated pilot to fly along radio position lines, without visual reference to the ground. Typical radio navigation systems are VOR, NDB, and DME, with the more advanced area navigation systems of LORAN C, RNAV and GPS. The VFR pilot may also use these radio navigation aids to assist in visual navigation.

Radio navigation **uses electronic aids.**

Before Flight

Being properly prepared is essential if a cross-country flight is to be successful. Always **flight plan** carefully and meticulously. This sets up an accurate base against which you can measure your in-flight navigation performance.

Flight plan carefully.

Preflight consideration should be given to the following items:

- Serviceability of your watch or aircraft clock. *Time* is vital to accurate navigation.
- Contents of your "nav bag" pencils, flight computer, protractor and scale (or a plotter), suitable aeronautical charts, and relevant flight information publications.
- Preparation of the appropriate maps and charts.
- Desired route.
- Terrain en route.
- Airspace en route (Class B, C, D, E, G, special use).
- Suitability of the destination airport and any alternate airports.
- *Forecast* weather en route and at the destination and alternate airports (plus any reports of *actual* weather that might be available).
- Calculation of accurate headings, groundspeeds and estimated time intervals.
- Consideration of fuel consumption, and accurate fuel planning.

It sounds like a lot, but each item considered individually is very simple to understand.

In Flight

Since you spent considerable time preparing an accurate flight plan, it is important to fly the plan accurately. Once the airplane is in flight, flying a reasonably accurate **heading** (which involves reference to both the heading indicator and outside cues) is essential if the airplane is to track toward the desired destination. Maintaining **cruise airspeed,** and comparing your progress and actual **times of arrival** at various fixes with those estimated at the flight planning stage will normally ensure a pleasant and drama-free journey.

Fly accurate headings, check times, and keep a flight log.

Speed

Speed is the rate at which distance is covered, or more precisely, *distance per unit time.* The standard unit for speed is the knot, (abbreviated *kt*). 1 knot equals 1 nautical mile per hour.

The speed of the airplane through the air is its **true airspeed (TAS),** which may have to calculated from the indicated airspeed (IAS) using a flight computer, or obtained from tabulated values in the Pilot's Operating Handbook (POH). TAS is the actual speed of the airplane relative to the air mass.

Because of the design of the airspeed indicator in the airplane, the airspeed that it indicates is usually *less* than the true airspeed because of the lower air density at altitude. The flight computer can be used to convert the indicated airspeed that you read in the cockpit into a true airspeed. Some airspeed indicators have a correction scale incorporated in their design.

Direction and Speed Combined

An airplane flies in the medium of air. Its motion relative to the air mass is specified by its direction (known as **heading**) and its speed through the air mass (**true airspeed**).

When considered together HDG/TAS constitute what is known as a **vector** quantity, which requires both **magnitude** (in this case *TAS)* and **direction** (here *HDG)* to be completely specified. HDG/TAS is the *velocity* (direction and speed) of the airplane through the air.

HDG/TAS is symbolized by a single-headed arrow ——————>——; the direction of the arrow indicates the direction of movement along the vector line.

Altitude 7,000 ft
Temp +10°C

IAS 131 knots,
TAS 147 knots

Figure 23-1. IAS and TAS indicator

The HDG/TAS vector fully describes the motion of the airplane relative to the air mass.

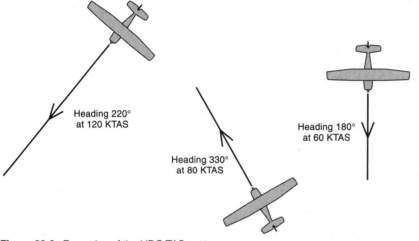

Heading 220°
at 120 KTAS

Heading 330°
at 80 KTAS

Heading 180°
at 60 KTAS

Figure 23-2. Examples of the HDG/TAS vector

The Effect of Wind

The general movement of air relative to the ground is called **wind velocity** and is abbreviated to **W/V.** Like HDG/TAS, W/V is a *vector* quantity because both direction and magnitude are specified. By convention, the wind direction is expressed as the direction *from* which it is blowing. For example, a northerly wind blows from the north toward the south. W/V is symbolized by a triple-headed arrow ——————>>>——.

The W/V vector fully describes the horizontal motion of the air mass relative to the earth's surface.

A westerly wind
of 30 knots,
i.e. 270/30

A wind blowing
from 030° at 10 knots,
i.e. 030/10

A wind blowing
from 210° at 20 knots,
i.e. 210/20

Figure 23-3. Examples of the W/V vector

With a W/V of 230/20, the air mass will be moving relative to the earth's surface from a direction of 230 degrees at a rate of 20 nm per hour. In a 6 minute period, for example, the air mass will have moved 2 nm (6 min = $^{1}/_{10}$ hour; $^{1}/_{10}$ of 20 nm = 2 nm) from a direction of 230 degrees (and therefore toward 230 – 180 = 050 degrees).

Wind is the air mass moving over the ground.

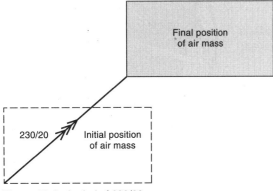

Figure 23-4. A wind of 230/20

The motion of the airplane relative to the surface of the earth is made up of two velocities: the airplane moving relative to the air mass (HDG/TAS); and the air mass moving relative to the surface of the earth (W/V).

The airplane flies through the air mass, and the wind moves the air mass over the ground.

Adding these two together gives the resultant vector of the airplane moving relative to the surface of the earth. This is the track and groundspeed (TR/GS), which is symbolized by a double headed arrow ———≫———.

The angle between the HDG and the actual ground track (TR) is called the **drift angle.**

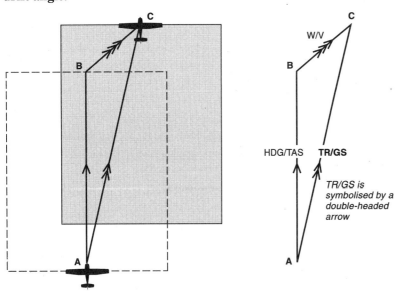

Figure 23-5. HDG/TAS + W/V = TR/GS—the triangle of velocities

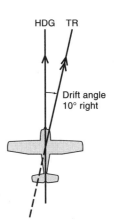

Figure 23-6. Drift is the angle between heading and ground track

An airplane flying through an air mass is in a similar situation to a swimmer crossing a fast-flowing river. If you dive in at position A and head off through the water in the direction of B, the current will carry you downstream toward C. To an observer sitting overhead in the branch of a tree, you will appear to be swimming a little bit sideways as you get swept downstream, even though in fact you are swimming straight through the water.

In the same way, it is quite common to look up and see an airplane flying somewhat sideways in strong-wind situations. Of course the airplane is not actually flying sideways through the air, rather it is flying straight ahead relative to the air mass and it is the wind velocity (W/V) which, when added to the airplane's motion through the air (HDG/TAS), gives it the resultant motion over the ground (TR/GS).

These three vectors form what is known as **the triangle of velocities**. It is a pictorial representation of the vector addition: HDG/TAS + W/V = TR/GS.

Achieving the Desired Course (CRS)

Your objective during visual navigation is to steer a heading so that the **track** made good over the ground exactly overlies the desired **course.**

At the flight planning stage you will know the desired course (also known as course required) and will have obtained a forecast wind velocity.

Using the planned true airspeed, you will be able to calculate the **heading** required to "make good" the desired course by applying a **wind correction angle (WCA)** into the wind to counteract drift. You will also be able to calculate the expected groundspeed.

Apply a wind correction angle (WCA) to counteract drift, and thereby achieve the desired course.

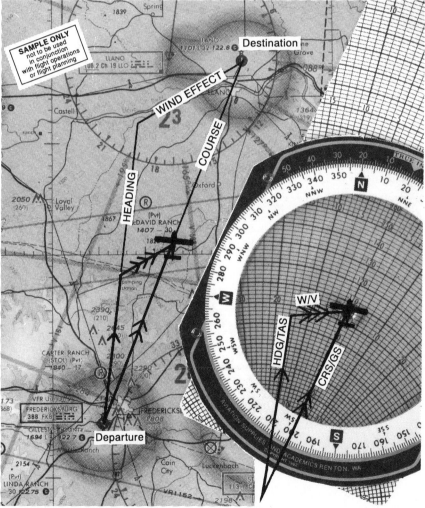

Figure 23-7. The triangle of velocities—calculating a heading to achieve the desired course

Later on during the flight you may find that, even though you have flown the HDG/TAS accurately, your *actual* ground track differs from the *desired* course; in other words there is a **tracking error.** This error could be specified as either distance off-course, or degrees off-course.

The tracking error is most likely caused by the *actual* wind being different from the *forecast* wind that you used at the flight planning stage. You will then have to make adjustments to the HDG in order to achieve your desired course.

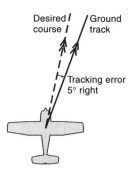

Figure 23-8. Tracking error is the angle between desired course and actual track

Vertical Navigation

Introduction

Navigating an airplane requires three-dimensional awareness. Correct vertical navigation using the altimeter is important for three basic reasons:

- For **terrain clearance,** to ensure that you will not collide with terrain or fixed obstacles on the ground.
- For **traffic separation,** to allow you to cruise at an altitude different from that of nearby aircraft, and so to ensure safe vertical separation.
- To calculate the **performance capabilities** of the aircraft and its engine, so as to operate safely and efficiently.

For aviation purposes, the standard unit of altitude is the *foot* in the United States and the western world. In other parts of the world, such as Eastern Europe and some of Asia, the unit used is the *meter.*

On maps and charts in the United States the altitude of terrain is given as altitude in feet above mean sea level (MSL). It is therefore essential that you know the aircraft's altitude above mean sea level so that you can compare this with the altitude of any terrain or obstructions and determine if there is sufficient vertical separation. Normally you would plan on at least 500 feet vertical separation when flying over open country, and at least 1,000 feet over congested areas. Most cross-country flights occur much higher than this.

Terrain elevation is given as altitude in feet above mean sea level (MSL).

Mean sea level pressure varies from place-to-place, from day-to-day, and indeed from hour-to-hour, as the various high and low pressure systems move across the surface of the earth. This will require you to periodically adjust the pressure window in your altimeter.

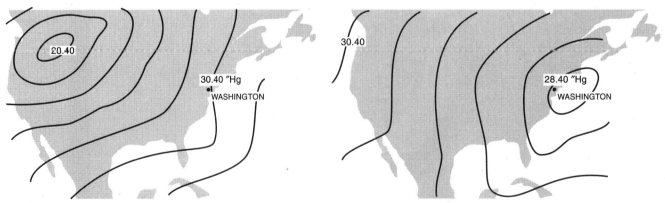

Figure 23-9. Two different synoptic situations

Flying cross-country below 18,000 feet MSL in the United States, we need to periodically update the altimeter setting so that the altimeter continues to indicate altitude based on the *current* sea level pressure in that area. You should use a current reported altimeter setting of a station along your route and within 100 nm of your position (Part 91 of the regulations).

Periodically update the altimeter setting.

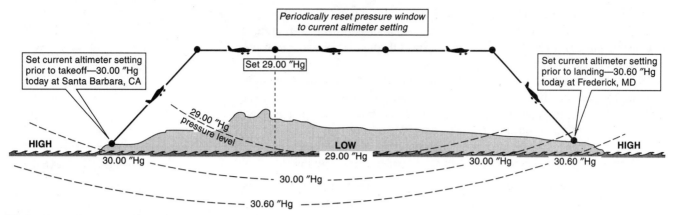

Figure 23-10. Periodically reset current reported altimeter setting

Flying higher than 18,000 feet MSL, separation from terrain is not a problem in the United States. All aircraft above 18,000 feet should be operating on standard pressure (29.92 in. Hg) so that their altimeters are all measuring altitude above the same datum. This will ensure vertical separation from other high-flying aircraft. An indication of 23,000 feet on the altimeter with 29.92 in. Hg set is called **flight level** 230, abbreviated as FL230.

VFR Cruise Altitude

To separate different types of traffic, Part 91 specifies that aircraft flying higher than 3.000 feet above the surface (AGL) according to the Visual Flight Rules (VFR) should cruise at "full thousands plus 500 feet."

To vertically separate VFR aircraft flying in opposing directions, VFR cruise altitudes are specified according to the direction in which they are flying.

- On a magnetic course of magnetic north to MC179: **odds+500 feet**; for example 3,500 feet MSL, 5,500 feet MSL, 7,500 feet MSL.

- On a magnetic course of MC 180 to MC 359: **evens+500 feet**; for example 4,500 feet MSL, 6,500 feet MSL, 8,500 feet MSL.

Safety Altitude

Part 91 specifies **minimum safe altitudes** which you must comply with. They are a minimum of 500 feet above the surface in noncongested areas, 1,000 feet above the highest obstacle within a 2,000 feet radius in congested areas, and sufficient altitude to glide clear if an engine fails.

Where possible on cross-country operations, choose a suitable cruise level above these minimums that will ensure adequate terrain clearance and vertical separation from other aircraft. A suitable technique is to determine a **safety altitude** which will ensure adequate terrain clearance, then select an appropriate cruise level above this safety altitude according to your magnetic course.

Note: In certain circumstances it may not always be possible to cruise above the calculated safety altitude, for example due to overlying controlled airspace around a major airport. In such cases, extra care to avoid terrain and obstructions should be taken, particularly in minimum visibility, until it is possible to climb above the safety altitude.

There are no hard and fast rules as to how far either side of course you should consider, or how high above obstacles you should fly. Reasonable values are 1,000 feet or 1,500 feet above the highest obstacle within 5 nm or 10 nm either side of course. This allows for navigation errors. Over long distances or mountainous areas, 15 or 20 nm might be more appropriate.

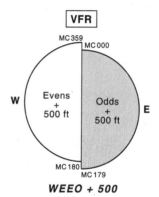

Figure 23-11. VFR cruise altitudes above 3,000 feet AGL

To determine a safety altitude determine the highest obstacle en route to a set amount either side of course, then add a safety clearance altitude above this.

To assist you in determining the highest obstacle, it is a good idea to mark in lines 5 nm (or 10 nm) either side of course. Another approach to finding a reasonable buffer is to add 10% to the elevation of the highest obstacle en route plus a further 1,500 feet.

If you remain above your calculated safety altitude, there should be sufficient buffer to absorb any indication errors in the altimeter (position, instrument and temperature errors) and to stay out of any turbulent areas near the ground, where a downdraft or windshear could be dangerous. In certain circumstances (such as in standing waves downwind of mountain ridges), it may be advisable to add more vertical clearance than usual to give sufficient safety margin.

Example 1. Elevation of the highest obstacle within 5 nm of course is 438 feet MSL. A reasonable safety altitude in good conditions would be 438 + 1,000 feet = 1,438 feet. If the highest obstacle within 10 nm of course is 798 feet, and you wish to be more conservative, then a reasonable safety altitude would be 798 + 1,000 = 1,798 feet. Because these are below 3,000 feet AGL, you do not need to apply the *WEEO + 500* rule.

Example 2. Calculate a conservative safety altitude above an obstacle 2,117 feet MSL.

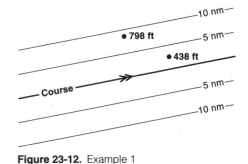

Figure 23-12. Example 1

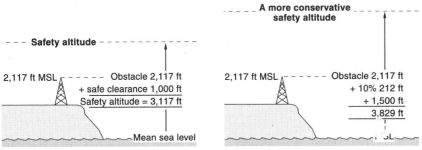

Figure 23-13. Example 2 using 1,000 feet clearance

Figure 23-14. Example 2 using 10% plus 1,500 feet

✍ Now complete **Review 23, Part (a)** on page 530.

Time

Time is of great importance to the air navigator, and the clock is one of the basic instruments used in the cockpit.
Time enables you to:
- regulate affairs on board your airplane;
- measure the progress of your flight;
- anticipate arrival time (ETA) at certain positions;
- calculate a safe endurance for flight;
- estimate when weather conditions at the destination are likely to improve; and
- measure rest periods between flights.

For flight planning and navigation purposes we usually do not refer to the year or the month, but only the **day** of the month as the **date,** followed by the **time** in **hours and minutes.** As most air navigation occurs within a few hours, and only rarely in excess of 30 hours, we can be reasonably confident of which year and month we are talking about, and so there is no need to specify them.

Seconds, which are $\frac{1}{60}$ of a minute, are usually too short a time interval for us to be concerned with in practical navigation. It is usual to express date/time as a six-figure date/time group.

In the six-figure date/time group:

- the **date** is a two-figure group for the day of the month from 00 to 31, and is followed by:
- the **time,** written as a four-figure group on a 24 hour clock—the first two figures representing the hours from 00 to 24, and the last two figures representing the minutes from 00 through to 59.

Example 3. Express September 13, 10:35 a.m. as a six-figure date/time group.

Date	Time	
13	10	35
day	hr	min

Answer: 131035

Example 4. Express 3:21 p.m. on March 17, as a six-figure date/time group.

$$3{:}21 \text{ p.m.} = 1200$$
$$+ \quad 321$$
$$\overline{1521} \text{ on the 24 hr clock}$$

Answer: 171521

In the eight-figure date/time group:

To specify the **month,** the six-figure date/time group is preceded by two figures representing the month, and so is expanded into an eight figure time-group. This is often used in NOTAMs (Notices to Airmen):

- the first two numbers refer to month;
- the second two numbers refer to the date; and
- the last four numbers refer to the time.

Example 5. 5:45 p.m. on September 30 may be written as:

SEP 30 17 45

or 09 30 17 45

or 09301745

The Relationship between Longitude and Time

In one day, the earth makes one complete rotation of 360° with respect to the chosen celestial body, which is the sun. The time of day is a measure of this rotation and indicates how much of that day has elapsed or, in other words, how much of a rotation has been completed.

As observers on the earth, we do not feel its rotation about its own axis, but rather we see the sun apparently move around the earth. In one mean solar day the sun will appear to have traveled the full 360° of longitude around the earth. 360° of longitude in 24 hours is equivalent to **15° per hour.**

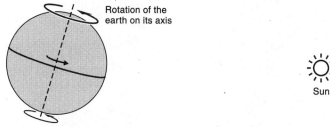

Rotation of the earth on its axis

Sun

Figure 23-15. The earth rotates at 15° of longitude per hour

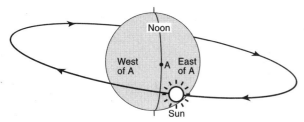

Figure 23-16. The *apparent* motion of the sun around the earth

Local Time

Time is a measure of the rotation of the earth, and any given time interval can be represented by a corresponding angle through which the earth turns. Suppose that the sun (the celestial reference point) is directly overhead at noon. For every point along that same meridian of longitude, the sun will be at its highest point in the sky for that day.

Meridians of longitude further east are ahead in local time; meridians of longitude further west are behind in local time.

Example 6. Place A is 45° of longitude west of Place B. How much earlier or later will noon occur at A compared to B?

Answer. At the rate of 15° per hour, 45° arc of longitude = 3 hours, and because A is to the west of B, noon will occur three hours later at A.

Coordinated Universal Time (UTC)

UTC is the local mean time at the meridian of longitude that runs through the observatory at Greenwich, England, and is known as the **prime meridian.** Until recently the international time standard was the well known *Greenwich mean time (GMT).* This term has now been replaced by **coordinated universal time (UTC),** which is also known as **Zulu (Z).** UTC is a universal time, and all aeronautical communications around the world are expressed in UTC. For this reason, you need to be able to convert quickly and accurately from local time to UTC, and vice versa.

*Longitude east—Universal least;
Longitude west—Universal best.*

Standard or Local Time

Standard times operate in a similar fashion to zone times in that all clocks in a given geographical area are set to the local mean time of a given standard meridian. This is known as **standard time** or **local time** for that area.

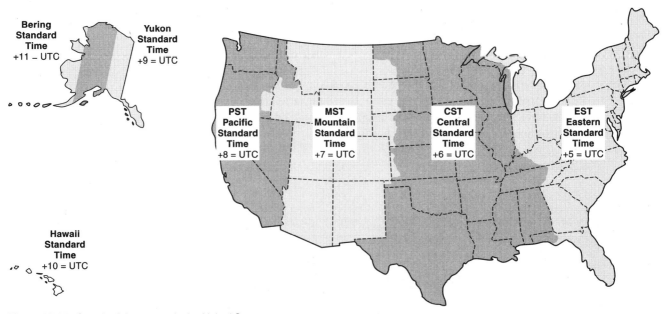

Figure 23-17. Standard time zones in the United States

To Change UTC Time to Local Time	TIME ZONE	To Change Local Time to UTC Time
Subtract 4 hours	**Eastern Daylight**	Add 4 hours
Subtract 5 hours	**Eastern Standard**	Add 5 hours
Subtract 5 hours	**Central Daylight**	Add 5 hours
Subtract 6 hours	**Central Standard**	Add 6 hours
Subtract 6 hours	**Mountain Daylight**	Add 6 hours
Subtract 7 hours	**Mountain Standard**	Add 7 hours
Subtract 7 hours	**Pacific Daylight**	Add 7 hours
Subtract 8 hours	**Pacific Standard**	Add 8 hours
Subtract 9 hours	**Yukon Standard**	Add 9 hours
Subtract 10 hours	**Alaska, Hawaii Standard**	Add 10 hours
Subtract 11 hours	**Bering Standard**	Add 11 hours

When involved in flights between different time zones, it is easiest to work entirely in UTC and convert the answer at the end.

Example 7. You depart New York, NY at 0945 Eastern Standard Time on a flight of 6 hours 10 minutes duration to Denver, Colorado. At what time should your friends meet you in Denver?

```
Depart NY        09 45  EST
                 +5
                 -----
                 14 45  UTC
Flight time       6 10
Arrive Denver    20 55  UTC
                 -7
                 -----
                 13 55  MST
```

Answer: 1355 Mountain Standard Time

Light from the Sun

The sun's rays strike different parts of the earth at different angles depending on latitude and season.

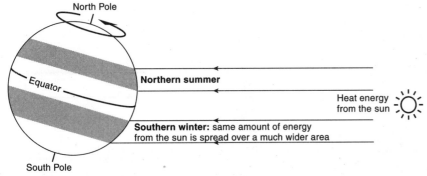

Figure 23-18. The sun does not shine evenly on the earth

Sunrise occurs when the upper limb of the sun (the first part visible) is on the visible horizon and **sunset** occurs when the upper limb of the sun (the last part visible) is just disappearing below the visible horizon. **Sunlight** occurs between sunrise and sunset.

As we have all observed when waking early, it starts to become light well before the sun actually rises, and it stays light until well after the sun has set. This period of incomplete light, or if you like, incomplete darkness, is called **twilight,** and the period from the start of morning twilight until the end of evening twilight is called **daylight.**

In the tropics the sun rises and sets at almost 90° to the horizon, which makes the period of twilight quite short, and the onset of daylight or night quite dramatically rapid.

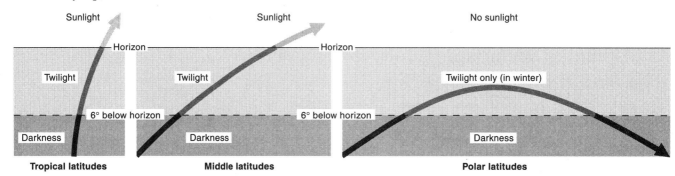

Figure 23-19. The higher the latitude, the longer the twilight

In the higher latitudes, toward the North and South Poles, the sun rises and sets at a more oblique angle to the horizon, consequently the period of twilight is much longer and the onset of daylight or darkness far more gradual than in the tropics.

At certain times of the year inside the Arctic and Antarctic Circles, the period of twilight occurs without the sun actually rising above the horizon at all during the day. This is the winter situation.

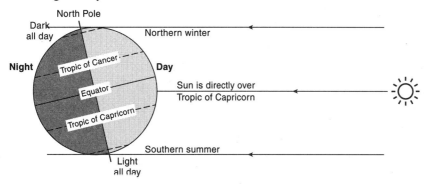

Figure 23-20. The sun does not shine evenly on the earth

While to an observer at sea level the sun may appear to have set and the earth is no longer bathed in sunlight, an airplane directly overhead may still have the sun shining on it. In other words, the time at which the sun rises or sets will depend on the altitude of the observer.

In fact it is possible to take off after sunset at ground level and climb to an altitude where the sun appears to rise again and shine a little longer on the airplane. This is especially noticeable in polar regions when the sun might be just below the horizon, as seen from sea level, for long periods of time (twilight).

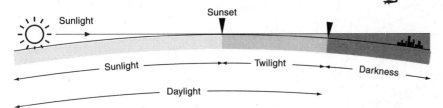

Figure 23-21. An airplane can be in sight of the sun after it has set on the earth below

It is easy to be deceived by brightness at altitude only to find a few minutes later after a descent to near ground level, and possibly under some cloud cover, that it has become very dark. High ground to the west of an airport will also reduce the amount of light from the sun reaching the vicinity of the airport as night approaches (an important point to remember when flying). Good airmanship may dictate using an earlier arrival time than the end of daylight when planning a flight, if, for example, the destination airport has high ground to the west, or the weather forecast indicates poor visibility or cloud cover approaching from the west, as in a cold front. Another important consideration related to sunset is that many smaller airports close at sunset. This may also apply to the alternate airport(s) chosen for a flight.

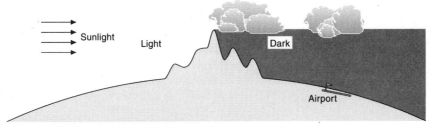

Figure 23-22. Local sunrise and sunset is affected by terrain

The times at which sunrise and sunset occur depend on two things:

- The **date:** In summer sunrise is earlier and sunset later, therefore the daylight hours are longer in summer. The reverse occurs in winter.

- The **latitude:** In the northern summer for instance, place B in the figure below is experiencing sunrise while place A is already well into the day, and it is still night at place C, yet all are on the same meridian of longitude. Because of this they all have the same local time, but are experiencing quite different conditions of daylight because they are on different latitudes.

Figure 23-23. Places A, B & C, although on the same meridian, experience different sunrise and sunset times because they are on different latitudes

The official source in the United States for times including sunrise, sunset, and beginning and end of daylight is the **American Air Almanac.**

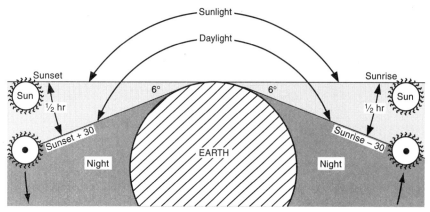

Figure 23-24. In the United States, official night commences at sunset +30 minutes and night ends at sunrise –30 minutes

Daylight Time

To take advantage of the longer daylight hours and the better weather in summer, the clocks in many countries are put forward in the spring, usually by one hour, to give a new standard time known as **daylight time.** For example, in New York, 1200 EST becomes 1300 Eastern Daylight Time.

Make allowances for these when planning a flight that may end near the onset of darkness. It is good airmanship to plan on arriving well before the end of daylight. Common sense would encourage you to increase this margin on long journeys or on flights where it is difficult to estimate accurately your time of arrival. Remember also that the further south you are in the United States the shorter the twilight time.

Spring, (clocks) forward.
Fall, (clocks) back.

The Dateline

Suppose that the time at the Greenwich meridian is 261200 (261200 UTC). Now, if you instantaneously travel *eastward* from Greenwich to the 180° east meridian, the local mean time there is 12 hours ahead of the local mean time at Greenwich, that is 262400 local mean time at 180°E, or midnight on the 26th local mean time at 180°E. If, however, you travel *westward* from Greenwich to the 180° west meridian, then the time there is 12 hours behind Greenwich, 260000 or, as it is usually written, 252400 at 180°W, midnight on the 25th. Note that the time is midnight in both cases but, on one side of the 180° meridian it is midnight on the 25th, and on the other side it is midnight on the 26th.

The 180°E and 180°W meridians are the one and the same meridian, the anti-meridian to Greenwich. In its vicinity, midnight occurs on different dates, depending on which side of the 180° meridian you are on. Making a complete trip around the world, you would lose a day traveling westward or gain a day traveling eastward.

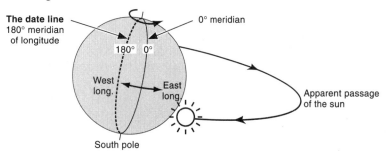

Figure 23-25. The dateline runs basically along the 180° meridian

To prevent the date being in error and to provide a starting point for each day, a **dateline** has been fixed by international agreement, and it basically follows the 180° meridian of longitude, with minor excursions to keep groups of islands together. Crossing the dateline, you alter the date by one day—in effect changing your time by 24 hours to compensate for the slow change during your journey around the world.

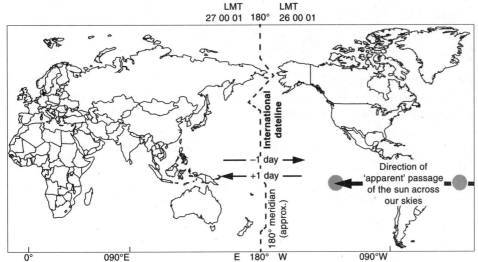

Figure 23-26. Crossing the dateline traveling eastward—subtract one day; traveling westward—add one day

✍ Now complete **Review 23, Part (b)** on page 531.

Summary of Terminology

Horizontal and Vertical Navigation

Heading/True Airspeed (HDG/TAS)

Heading (HDG) is the actual heading of the airplane in degrees. It may be related to true north, magnetic north or compass north.

True airspeed (TAS) is the actual speed of the airplane through the air. It will differ significantly from the airspeed indicated on the airspeed indicator (the indicated airspeed—IAS) because the air is less dense the higher the airplane flies.

You will need to do a small calculation on the flight computer to convert IAS to TAS when flying at altitude or in abnormally high temperatures. This can also be done directly on some airspeed indicators using a temperature/altitude scale.

The normal unit for airspeed is the knot. KIAS (knots indicated airspeed) is used in aerodynamics, but KTAS (knots true airspeed) is used in navigation. The normal unit of distance for navigation is the **nautical mile (nm)** and if it is distance relative to the air, we call it an **air nautical mile (anm)**.

Wind Velocity (W/V)

Wind velocity is the wind vector (magnitude and direction). Wind direction is expressed in degrees true or magnetic and is the direction from which the wind is blowing. Wind speed is in knots—1 knot equals 1 nm per hour.

Ground Track/Groundspeed (TR/GS)

Ground track (TR) is the *actual* path of the airplane over the surface of the earth, and is usually expressed in degrees true or magnetic. (Course is the *desired* or *intended* path over the ground).

Groundspeed (GS) is the actual speed of the airplane over the ground and is measured in knots. A GS of 120 knots means that 120 ground nautical miles would be covered in 1 hour at that GS.

Drift—Counteracted by Wind Correction Angle

Drift is the difference between the HDG and the actual ground track. It is wind that blows the airplane from its HDG/TAS through the air onto its TR/GS over the earth's surface.

Drift is measured *from* the **HDG** (the nose of the airplane) *to* the **TR,** and is specified in degrees left or right of HDG. A good pilot/navigator will calculate and apply a wind correction angle (WCA) to counteract the drift so that the actual ground track is indeed the desired course.

Tracking Error (TE)

The difference between the *actual* ground track and the *desired* course is called tracking error, and is specified in distance or degrees off-course.

Note: Do not confuse tracking error with drift.

Latitude

Latitude is the angular distance of a place north or south from the equator, measured in degrees, minutes, and seconds.

Longitude

Longitude is the angular distance of a place from the prime meridian, longitude 000° through Greenwich, also measured in degrees, minutes and seconds.

Nautical Mile
A nautical mile is the length of 1 minute of latitude measured down a meridian.

Knot
A knot is a unit of speed. 1 knot equals 1 nautical mile per hour.

Great Circle
A great circle is a circle on the earth's surface whose center is the center of the earth. It provides the shortest distance between two places on the surface of the earth.

Altitude
Altitude is the altitude in feet above a reference level, usually (MSL). Altitude MSL is used when cruising below 18,000 feet MSL in the United States.

Flight Level
A flight level is the altitude in hundreds of feet above the 29.92 in. Hg reference pressure level (FL230 = 23,000 feet). Flight levels are used when cruising above 18,000 feet MSL in the United States.

Time

Coordinated Universal Time (UTC)
Coordinated Universal Time is the universal time in all aeronautical communications around the world.

Standard or Local Time
Standard or local time is a specific time datum applied to all clocks in a given geographical area.

Daylight Time
Daylight time is standard time plus 1 hour. Applied in many countries to take advantage of longer daylight hours and better summer weather.

Dateline
The dateline is a line drawn approximately along the 180° meridian of longitude in order to provide a starting point for each day.

♙ Review 23

Part (a)

1. For most navigation purposes, distance is stated in _____ .

➤ nautical miles.

2. One nautical mile traveled over the ground or water is sometimes referred to as a _____ .

➤ ground nautical mile

3. One nautical mile traveled through an air mass is called an _____ .

➤ air nautical mile

4. The usual navigation unit for airspeed is the _____ , which is 1 _____ per hour.

➤ knot, nautical mile

5. The accepted unit of length for shorter distances such as runway length is the _____ .

➤ foot

6. The accepted unit for altitude is the _____ .

➤ foot

7. 1 nautical mile = _____ feet.

➤ 1 nm = 6,076 feet

8. As a simple method of expressing direction we divide a full circle into 360 degrees and number them from 000 through 090, 180, 270 to 360 in a (clockwise/counterclockwise) direction.

➤ clockwise

9. The speed of the airplane relative to the air mass is called its _____, which is abbreviated as _____ .

➤ true airspeed, TAS

10. To completely specify the motion of an airplane relative to an air mass we need to specify two things: its _____ and its _____ .

➤ heading, true airspeed

11. The *heading/true airspeed* vector is symbolized by a _____-headed arrow.

➤ single-headed arrow

12. The movement of an air mass relative to the ground is called _____ .

➤ wind

Visual Navigation Fundamentals

13. The wind direction, by convention, is the direction that the wind blows _____ .

➤ from

14. The speed of an airplane relative to the ground is called its _____ .

➤ groundspeed

15. The direction in which an airplane points is called its _____ .

➤ heading

16. The direction of travel over the ground is called an airplane's _____ .

➤ track

17. The angle between the direction an airplane is pointing (its heading) and the direction in which it is traveling over the ground (its ground track) is called the _____ angle.

➤ drift

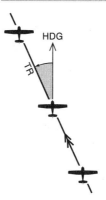

Figure 23-27.

18. Label the shaded angle shown in Figure 23-27.

➤ drift angle

19. Refer to Figure 23-27. Is this drift left or right?

➤ left drift

20. Sometimes the actual drift experienced in flight differs from that expected and the airplane makes good a track which is different to the desired course. The difference between desired course and the ground track is called the _____ .

➤ tracking error

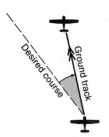

Figure 23-28.

21. Label the shaded angle in Figure 23-28.
➤ tracking error

22. Is this tracking error left or right?
➤ right

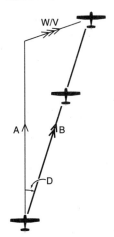

Figure 23-29.

23. In Figure 23-29, label the vectors A and B and the angle D with their appropriate navigation terms.
➤ A: HDG/TAS; B: TR/GS; D: drift

24. Which statement best fits the situation in Figure 23-29?
    (a) TAS exceeds GS.
    (b) GS exceeds TAS.
    (c) Drift is left.
➤ (b)

25. The earth rotates on its axis and the two points where this axis meets the earth's surface are called the physical _____ pole and the physical _____ pole. They are also referred to as _____ and _____ .

➤ north, south, true north, true south

Part (b)

Express the following dates and times as a six-figure date/time group:

1. November 29, 10:15 a.m.
➤ 291015

2. July 19, 3:17 p.m.
➤ 191517

3. April 1, 5 p.m.
➤ 011700

4. Express the dates and times above as an eight-figure date/time group.
➤ 11291015, 07191517, 04011700

Convert the following time intervals to arc units:

5. 1 hour
➤ 15 degrees

6. 9 hours 30 minutes
➤ 142.5 degrees (142°30')

For questions 7 and 8 refer to Figure 23-30.

7. An aircraft departs an airport in the central standard time zone at 0930 CST for a 2-hour flight to an airport located in the Mountain Standard Time zone. The landing should be at what time?
    (a) 0930 MST.
    (b) 1030 MST.
    (c) 1130 MST.
➤ (b)

8. An aircraft departs an airport in the eastern daylight time zone at 0945 EDT for a 2-hour flight to an airport located in the Central Daylight Time zone. The landing should be at what coordinated universal time?
    (a) 1345Z.
    (b) 1445Z.
    (c) 1545Z.
➤ (c)

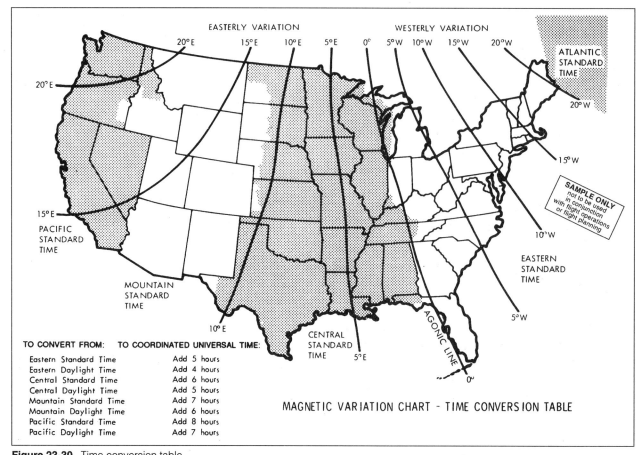

Figure 23-30. Time conversion table

9. Convert 150 degrees of arc to time.

➤ 10 hours

---

10. At 1200 Pacific Standard Time in Los Angeles, it will be _____ UTC, and _____ Eastern Standard Time in New York.

➤ 2000 UTC, 1500 EST

---

11. At 0500 Mountain Daylight Time in Denver, it will be _____ Zulu, and _____ Pacific Daylight Time in San Francisco.

➤ 1100Z, 0400 PDT

---

12. You depart Santa Barbara, California at 0600 Pacific Standard Time for a 5 hour 30 minute flight to Denver, Colorado, where you expect to arrive at _____ UTC, which is_____ MST.

➤ 1930 UTC, 1230 MST

---

13. Traveling eastward across the dateline from Hong Kong to Hawaii, you would expect to (lose/gain) 1 day.

➤ lose

---

14. The official source of sunrise and sunset times is the _____ (a publication not required by pilots).

➤ American Air Almanac

---

15. High ground to the west of an airport will cause the (earlier/later) onset of darkness.

➤ earlier

---

16. Sunrise and sunset times vary with the _____ and the _____ .

➤ latitude and date

---

17. For Daylight Time, clocks are (advanced/retarded) by _____ hour(s).

➤ advanced by 1 hour

Using the Flight Computer

General Description

The mechanical flight computer is a wonderful invention that vastly simplifies navigation tasks. It consists of two circular sheets of metal or card through the center of which passes a movable grid.

The flight computer has two sides:

A flight computer has a calculator side and a wind side.

- a **calculator side**—used for speed–distance–time–fuel computations (and many others); and

- a **wind side**—used to calculate headings to steer and groundspeeds resulting from the effect of any wind that is blowing.

The Calculator Side of the Flight Computer

The calculator side of the flight computer consists of two circular discs riveted together at the center so that the smaller top disc can rotate over the larger bottom disc. It may look complicated at first but you will soon become familiar with it.

The calculator side of a flight computer is used for simple math calculations.

The *outer* scale on the bottom disc and the *inner* scale on the top disc are used to represent speed, distance, fuel or other units. Although the scales are only numbered from 10 to 99, they can easily be used for any number. For example, "17" can stand for 0.17, 1.7, 17 or 170. In addition the spacing of the numbers is not equal. This causes you no problems except that you must be careful using the graduations. For example, the first graduations past 11, 30 and 70 are 11.1, 30.5 and 71 respectively.

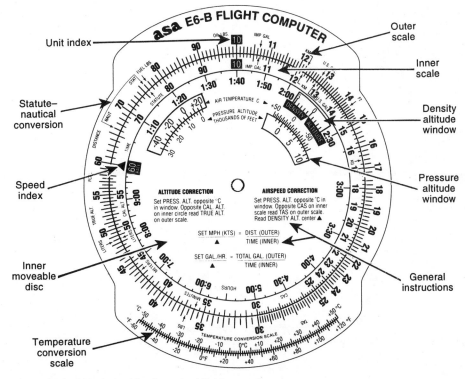

Figure 24-1. Calculator side of a typical flight computer

The Wind Side of the Flight Computer

The wind side of the flight computer allows you to handle navigation problems involving the *triangle of velocities* in a quick and accurate manner. Components of the wind side are:

The wind side of a flight computer is used for 'triangle of velocities' navigation calculations.

1. A circular, rotatable **compass rose** (or azimuth circle) set in a fixed frame which is marked with an **index** at the top.

2. A transparent plastic **plotting disc** attached to the rotatable compass rose, marked with a **grommet** in the center.

3. A **sliding grid** marked with radial lines which can be used to determine the *wind correction angle (WCA)*. This plate slides through the frame and compass rose assembly, hence the term "slide" flight computer which is often used to refer to this type.

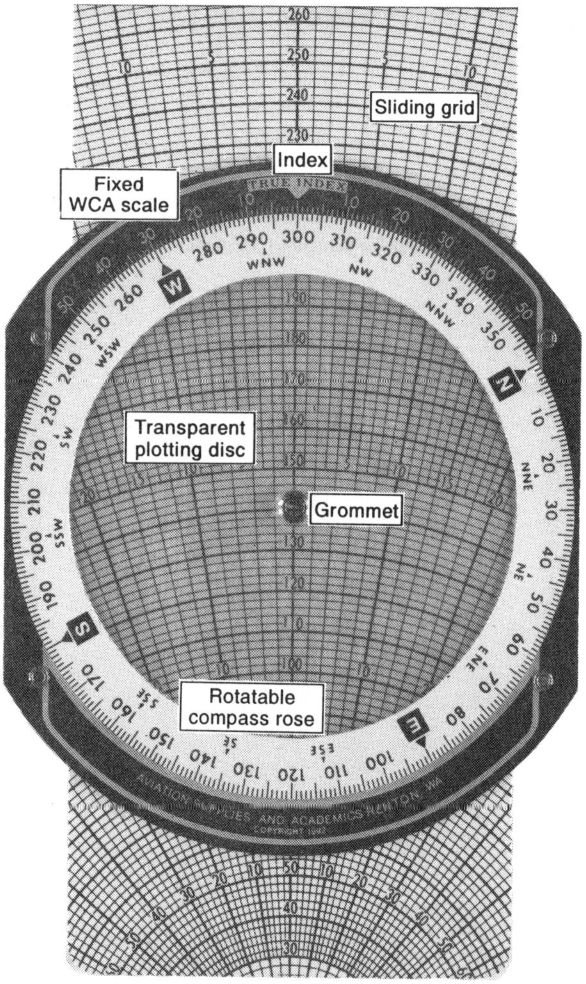

Figure 24-2. Wind side of the slide flight computer

Use of the Flight Computer

The main use of the flight computer is for **flight planning.** You will know:

• the **planned course** and **ground distance** from the chart;

• the planned **indicated airspeed (IAS)** and **cruising altitude;** and

• the **forecast wind** and forecast **temperature** at cruise altitude.

You will want to find (in order):

- the **true airspeed (TAS);**
- the **heading** required to "make good" the required course; and
- the expected **groundspeed,** so that you can calculate the **time** en route and **fuel** requirements.

The following pages explain and demonstrate how you will do this using examples. Starting on page 543 we show that the flight computer is also very useful for conversions, such as nautical miles to statute miles and °F to °C.

The Flight Computer for Flight Planning

The two scenarios that we will use through this part of the chapter are outlined below and will be referred to as Scenario A and Scenario B.

Scenario A		Scenario B	
Planned course	300°T	Planned course	172°T
Distance	88 nm	Distance	384 nm
Planned IAS	100 knots	Planned IAS	145 knots
Planned pressure altitude	6,500 feet	Planned pressure altitude	9,500 feet
Forecast temperature at cruise altitude	+20°C	Forecast temperature at cruise altitude	–5°C
Forecast wind	160°T/30	Forecast wind	300°T/40
Fuel flow	12 gph	Fuel flow	18 gph
Variation	9° West	Variation	11° East

Figure 24-3. Scenarios A and B

Finding TAS

When flying en route you will fly at a certain IAS which you can read directly off the airspeed indicator. However from Chapter 1 we know that IAS is related to dynamic pressure ($\frac{1}{2}\rho V^2$), which varies with both speed and air density. Therefore when an airplane climbs, to maintain the same IAS, while the air density reduces, the real speed or TAS must increase. TAS is important for navigation.

At higher altitudes, true airspeed (TAS) is greater than indicated airspeed (IAS).

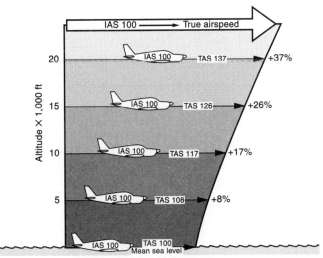

Figure 24-4. With IAS constant, TAS increases with increase in altitude

Although IAS is of aerodynamic importance, navigation requires a knowledge of the TAS. Provided you know your planned or actual IAS, your planned or actual pressure altitude, and the forecast or actual outside temperature, you can determine TAS quickly and easily using the flight computer. You can also find the TAS from your Pilot's Operating Handbook for specified conditions.

Example 1. Find the TAS in scenario A.

Step 1. Allow for variation in air density.

On the calculator side of your flight computer locate the pressure altitude window for airspeed correction shown in Figure 24-5. The numbers in the pressure altitude window represent pressure altitude in thousands of feet. The 5 therefore represents 5,000 feet pressure altitude, and the first gradu-ation to the right of the 5 represents 6,000 feet pressure altitude. Immedi-ately above the pressure altitude window is the air temperature scale which extends from +50°C on the left to –70°C on the right.

Rotate the inner disc to line up 6,500 feet against +20°C (the second long graduation to the left of the 0). This is shown in Figure 24-5. Once correctly aligned do not rotate the inner disc further because you will disturb the air density correction.

Step 2. Find TAS.

Using Figure 24-5 locate the *outer* scale which represents TAS and the *inner* scale which represents IAS. Unlike the scales in Figure 24-1 which are perfectly aligned (10 against 10, 11 against 11, and so on), the scales on your flight computer will be offset. This is because you have aligned 6,500 feet altitude against +20°C in Step 1, which has allowed for the reduced density at your cruise altitude.

Now find the 10 on the inner scale which represents 100 knots IAS. *See* Figure 24-5. Directly opposite the 10 on the inner scale is 11.4 on the outside scale which is used to represent TAS. The TAS is therefore 114 knots.

Answer. 114 KTAS.

Example 2. What is the expected TAS in scenario B?

First line up –5°C against 9,500 feet in the pressure altitude window. *See* Figure 24-6. Then locate 14.5 (for 145 knots) on the inner scale and read off 16.7 on the outer scale. The TAS is therefore 167 knots.

Answer. 167 KTAS.

Finding Heading and Groundspeed

At this stage of flight planning you already know:
- the intended course (CRS) in °T, measured on an aeronautical chart;
- the wind velocity (W/V) in °T/knots, obtained from the weather forecast; and
- the expected true airspeed obtained by converting IAS to TAS (or from the Pilot's Operating Handbook).

You can then calculate:
- the heading (HDG) to steer; and
- the groundspeed (GS) that should be achieved.

Scenario A	
Planned course	300°T
Distance	88 nm
Planned IAS	100 knots
Planned pressure altitude	6,500 feet
Forecast temperature at cruise altitude	+20°C
Forecast wind	160°T/30
Fuel flow	12 gph
Variation	9° West

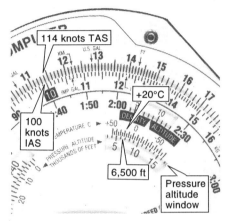

Figure 24-5. Example 1

Scenario B	
Planned course	172°T
Distance	384 nm
Planned IAS	145 knots
Planned pressure altitude	9,500 feet
Forecast temperature at cruise altitude	–5°C
Forecast wind	300°T/40
Fuel flow	18 gph
Variation	11° East

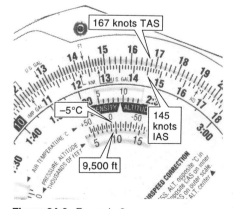

Figure 24-6. Example 2

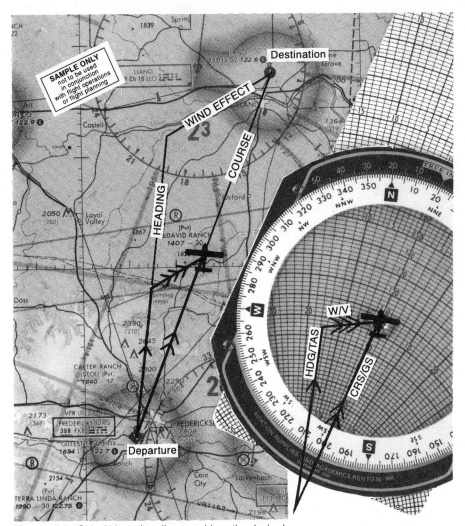

Figure 24-7. Calculating a heading to achieve the desired course

Example 3. Find the HDG and GS in scenario A.

Step 1. Place the W/V on the plotting disc (Figure 24-8a).

Rotate the compass rose until the wind direction 160°T is under the true index. Mark the start of the W/V vector 30 knots vertically *above* the grommet.

At this stage in your training, it is a good idea to mark in the full W/V, showing the three arrowheads of the W/V vector pointing down toward the grommet. This will give you a very clear picture as the whole triangle of velocities is developed on the plotting disc. When you become familiar with the use of the computer, drawing each vector becomes unnecessary, and just one single mark, known as the *wind dot* or *wind cross,* to illustrate the extent of the wind velocity is all that is needed.

Scenario A	
Planned course	300°T
Distance	88 nm
Planned IAS	100 knots
Planned pressure altitude	6,500 feet
Forecast temperature at cruise altitude	+20°C
Forecast wind	160°T/30
Fuel flow	12 gph
Variation	9° West

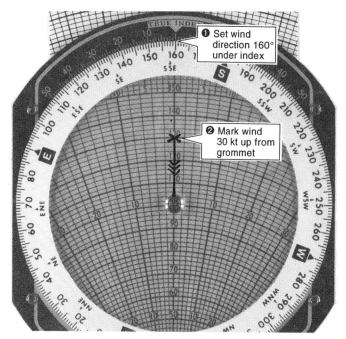

❶ Set wind direction 160° under index

❷ Mark wind 30 kt up from grommet

Figure 24-8a. Example 3, Step 1

❸ Set CRS 300° under index

Figure 24-8b. Example 3, Step 2

Step 2. Place the TR/GS vector on the plotting disc.

The desired course is known (having been measured on the chart); ground-speed is not known. Therefore, only one aspect of the TR/GS vector is known—its direction, but not its magnitude.

Rotate the compass rose until the required CRS of 300°T is under the index.

Step 3. Place the HDG/TAS vector on the plotting disc.

True airspeed is known, but the heading is not. In this case, only one aspect of the HDG/TAS vector is known—its magnitude.

Move the slide and place the TAS 114 (found in Example 1) knots speed arc under the wind dot (which is the starting point of the W/V vector). Note that the end of the HDG/TAS vector is where the W/V begins.

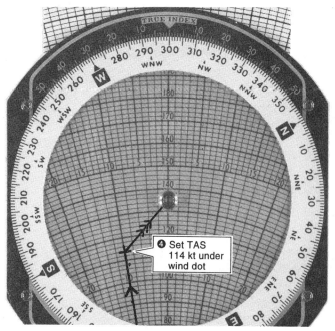

❹ Set TAS 114 kt under wind dot

Figure 24-8c. Example 3, Step 3

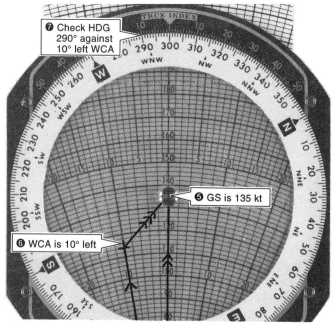

❼ Check HDG 290° against 10° left WCA

❺ GS is 135 kt

❻ WCA is 10° left

Figure 24-8d. Example 3, Step 4

Step 4. Read off the answers for HDG and GS.

The GS of 135 knots appears under the grommet. From the drift lines, the wind correction angle is 10° to the left of the course. This means to achieve CRS 300T, the airplane must be headed 10 into the wind and flown on a HDG of 290°T to allow for the 10° right drift.

Finally, to find the magnetic heading, apply the variation. If variation is 9W, then 290°T is 299°M (variation west, magnetic best).

Answer. Magnetic heading 299°M, groundspeed 135 knots.

Example 4. Find the HDG and GS in scenario B.

Steps 1 & 2.

Place the wind velocity vector on the disc by plotting the wind speed with the compass rose at 300°. Then rotate the compass rose until the required CRS of 172°T is under the index.

Scenario B	
Planned course	172°T
Distance	384 nm
Planned IAS	145 knots
Planned pressure altitude	9,500 feet
Forecast temperature at cruise altitude	–5°C
Forecast wind	300°T/40
Fuel flow	18 gph
Variation	11° East

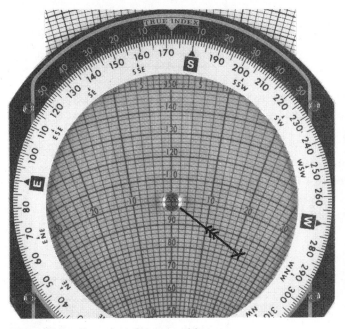

Figure 24-9a. Example 4, Steps 1 and 2

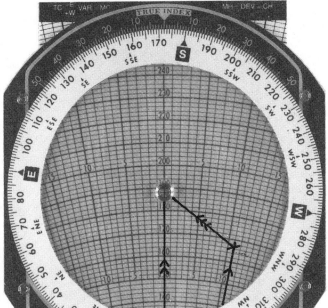

Figure 24-9b. Example 4, Steps 3 and 4

Steps 3 & 4.

Place the HDG/TAS vector on the plotting disc and read off the answers, which are GS 188 knots and WCA 11° right. (TAS of 167 knots was found in Example 2). HDG is 172°T + 11°WCA = 183°T. Finally find magnetic heading by allowing for magnetic variation (11°E).

Answer. Magnetic heading 183 – 11°E = 172°M (variation east, magnetic least), groundspeed 188 knots.

Finding the Time En Route and Fuel Requirements

The *time en route* and *fuel requirements* are found using the calculator side of the flight computer. The inner and outer scales, which you have already used to represent IAS and TAS respectively, can also be used for many other problems. When using the flight computer to solve *speed–time–distance* problems and *fuel calculations,* which are rate problems, the inner scale represents time and the outer scale represents distance or fuel.

In rate problems:

> **The inner scale represents time.**
> **The outer scale represents distance or fuel**

Speed–Time–Distance Problems

There are three basic problems:

1. How far will you travel at a given speed in a specified time?
2. How long will it take to fly a given distance at a known speed?
3. What is the groundspeed achieved knowing time and distance traveled?

You can solve these problems using the equations below with your electronic calculator, or by using your flight computer, as explained in the following examples.

$$\text{Speed} = \frac{\text{Distance}}{\text{Time}} \qquad \text{Time} = \frac{\text{Distance}}{\text{Speed}} \qquad \text{Distance} = \text{Time} \times \text{Speed}$$

Example 5. How long will the flight in scenario A take?

Rough calculation:

At 135 knots groundspeed (from Example 3), the airplane will cover 135 gnm in 1 hour. Therefore it will take about ⅔ of an hour (40 minutes) to cover 88 gnm.

Method:

In 1 hour you will cover 135 nm (135 knots), therefore place 60 (to represent 60 minutes) on the inner scale, against 13.5 (to represent 135 nm) on the outer distance scale. Now find 8.8 (88 nm) on the outer scale and read off the time it will take to cover this distance on the inner scale. *See* Figure 24-10.

Answer. 39 minutes.

Example 6. How long will the flight in scenario B take?

Rough calculation:

At 188 knots groundspeed (from Example 4), the airplane will cover 188 gnm in 1 hour, so it will take approximately 2 hours to cover 384 nm.

Method:

Place 60 (60 minutes) on the inner scale against 18.8 (188 nm) on the outer distance scale. Now find 38.4 (384 nm) and read off the time it will take to cover this distance on the inner scale. The answer is 122 minutes (12.2 on the inner scale) which is also shown in hours, just over 2 hours (2:00), on the inner fixed scale shown in Figure 24-11.

Answer. 122 minutes.

Scenario A	
Planned course	300°T
Distance	88 nm
Planned IAS	100 knots
Planned pressure altitude	6,500 feet
Forecast temperature at cruise altitude	+20°C
Forecast wind	160°T/30
Fuel flow	12 gph
Variation	9° West

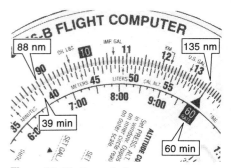

Figure 24-10. Example 5

Scenario B	
Planned course	172°T
Distance	384 nm
Planned IAS	145 knots
Planned pressure altitude	9,500 feet
Forecast temperature at cruise altitude	–5°C
Forecast wind	300°T/40
Fuel flow	18 gph
Variation	11° East

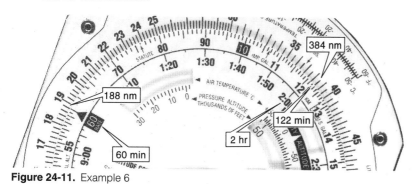

Figure 24-11. Example 6

Fuel Consumption Problems

Example 7. In scenario A, how much fuel would you expect to use during the flight?

Rough calculation:

At 12 gph, 12 gallons will be used in 60 minutes, therefore in 40 minutes you would use 8 gallons.

Method:

Place 60 minutes opposite to 12 gallons and then read off 7.8 gallons opposite 39 minutes. *See* Figure 24-12.

Answer. 7.8 gallons.

Figure 24-12. Example 7

Example 8. In scenario B, how much fuel would you expect to use during the flight?

Rough calculation:

122 minutes is just over 2 hours, therefore at 18 gph you would expect to use approximately 18 × 2 = 36 gallons.

Method:

In 1 hour you will use 18 gallons, therefore place 60 on the inner fuel scale against 18 on the outer fuel scale. Then look for 122 on the inner scale which is opposite 36.6, say 37 gallons. *See* Figure 24-13.

Answer. 37 gallons.

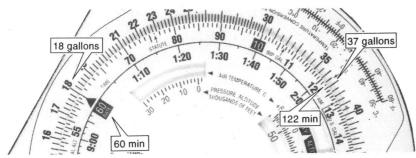

Figure 24-13. Example 8

Example 9. In flight you may be faced with other fuel consumption problems. If you have burned 3.5 gallons in 10 minutes, how much fuel will you burn in the next 35 minutes?

Rough calculation:

At 0.35 gal/min for 35 minutes is about (0.35 × 35) 12 gallons.

Method:

1. Set up 10 min on the inner time scale against 3.5 gallons on the outer scale.

2. Against 35 min on the inner time scale read off 12.25, say 12.3 gallons on the outer scale. *See* (a) in Figure 24-14.

Answer. 12.3 gallons (not 1.23 or 123).

The circular slide rule is now set up to answer many other problems relevant to this situation, such as:

What is the rate of fuel consumption in gallons/hr?

Answer. 21 gallons/hr. *See* (b) in Figure 24-14.

How long would it take to burn 28 gallons?

Answer. 80 min. *See* (c) in Figure 24-14.

✍ Now complete **Review 24, Part (a)** on page 548.

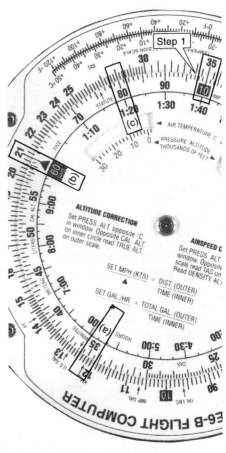

Figure 24-14. Example 9

Finding Wind Components

Quite often a wind needs to be broken down into its two components:

- the **headwind** or **tailwind** component; and
- the **crosswind** component.

This is especially the case when taking off and landing, because:

1. For **performance** reasons, you often need to know the headwind or tailwind component to determine the takeoff or landing distance required.
2. For reasons of **safe handling** of the airplane, you always need to know the approximate crosswind component on a particular runway that you intend using and not exceed the maximum crosswind specified in the Pilot's Operating Handbook.

Winds found on forecasts, and which are most likely to be used for flight planning purposes, are given in degrees true. The winds in takeoff and landing reports broadcast by Air Traffic Control however, are given in degrees magnetic, so that they can be easily related to runway direction, which is always in °M. This applies to the direction of the wind given to you by the control tower, or as broadcast on the automatic terminal information services (ATIS).

A runway whose centerline lies in the direction 074°M will be designated RWY 7 or RWY 07. A runway whose centerline lies in the direction 357°M will be designated RWY 36. A wind of 350°M/25 knots would favor RWY 36, which is almost directly into the wind. RWY 7 would experience a strong crosswind from the left; the pilot should determine just how strong the crosswind is before using this particular runway. Since both wind direction from the tower and runway direction are measured from the same datum (magnetic north), there is no need to convert into degrees true for this particular computer manipulation. When using your computer, work either totally in true or totally in magnetic.

When discussing takeoff and landing performance in Chapter 10, we determined wind components mentally and on a chart. Here we show you how to do it using the wind side of your flight computer. An alternative technique is to use the crosswind correction table on the back of the sliding card on some flight computers. *See* Figure 24-15.

Example 10. What crosswind and headwind components exist on Runway 18 if the wind broadcast by the Tower is 120°M/30? (Runway 18 means the runway direction is approximately 180°M.)

Step 1. Set up the W/V on the sliding grid (see Figure 24-16).

1. Set wind direction under index.
2. Mark the start of the W/V vector above the grommet.

Step 2. Draw in headwind and crosswind components.

1. Rotate the compass rose until the runway direction 180°M is under the index.
2. Run a horizontal line from the wind dot across to the centerline and make a mark.
3. Read off the headwind (or tailwind) component, in this case 15 knots headwind.

Step 3. Find the crosswind component.

1. Rotate the compass rose until the crosswind component is aligned with the grid.
2. Adjust the sliding grid (if necessary), and read off the crosswind component, in this case 26 knots crosswind from the left.

Answer. 15 knots headwind, 26 knots crosswind from the left.

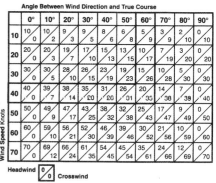

Figure 24-15. Crosswind correction table

Using a Crosswind Correction Table

To solve the problem in Example 10 using a conventional crosswind correction table, refer to Figure 24-15. Move vertically down the 60° column (the angle between wind direction and runway direction) until you meet the wind speed row of 30 knots. Directly read off 15 knots headwind and 26 knots crosswind.

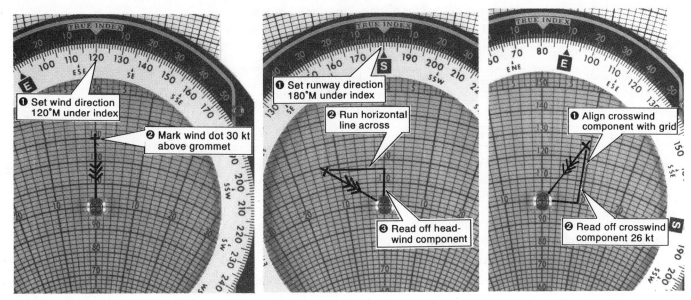

Figure 24-16. Example 10

Conversions on the Flight Computer

As a pilot you will often have to convert from one unit of measurement to another. Some of the common conversions are labeled on the scales of the circular slide rule to help you, but which ones and precisely how it is done varies from computer to computer, so we suggest that you refer to your computer handbook as well as to this manual.

Temperature Conversions

Most flight computers have a temperature conversion scale where conversions from **Fahrenheit** to **Celsius** and vice versa can be read directly.

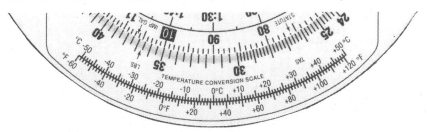

Figure 24-17. A typical temperature conversion scale

Example 11. What is +90°F in °C?
Answer. 32°C. *See* Figure 24-18.

Example 12. What is –10°C in °F?
Answer. 14°F. *See* Figure 24-19.

Distance Conversions

It is an unfortunate fact of life that we have to deal with the same physical distance being measured in different units. In day-to-day life in the United States, longer distances are measured in **statute miles,** which are smaller than nautical miles which are normally used in aviation navigation.

Nautical miles used in navigation are relevant because of their relationship to the *angular* measurement of latitude on the earth. One *minute* of latitude is equal to 1 nautical mile, and so 1 *degree* of latitude will equal 60 nm. We need to understand the relationship between these various units of distance and be able to convert from one to the other.

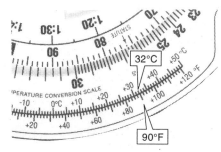

Figure 24-18. Example 11

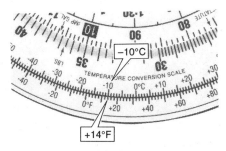

Figure 24-19. Example 12

One **meter** is $\frac{1}{10,000,000}$ (one ten millionth) of the distance from the equator to a pole, which makes one kilometer $\frac{1}{10,000}$ of the distance from the equator to a pole. Thus the average distance from the equator to a pole is 10,000 kilometers.

A **kilometer** is much shorter than a nautical mile. The kilometer is the standard unit of distance in most of Europe and many other parts of the world. The relationship between the navigation, statute and metric units is:

> **1 nm = 1.15 sm = 1.852 km (1,852 meters).**

Most flight computers can provide us with accurate conversions using indexes for nautical miles, statute miles and kilometers marked on the outer scale, making it quite straight forward to convert these units without having to remember the exact relationships.

How to Convert from One Unit to Another

- As with all computer calculations, carry out a rough mental check; then
- Set the known quantity on the inner scale of the computer against its index on the outer scale; then
- Against the index of the required unit on the outer scale, read off the answer on the inner scale.

Example 13. Convert 10 nautical miles to statute miles and kilometers.

Rough calculation:
1 nm is slightly over 1 sm and approximately equal to 2 km.
Therefore 10 nm is a little over 10 sm and approximately equal to 20 km.
Method:
See Figure 24-20.
Answer. 10 nm = 11.5 sm = 18.5 km.

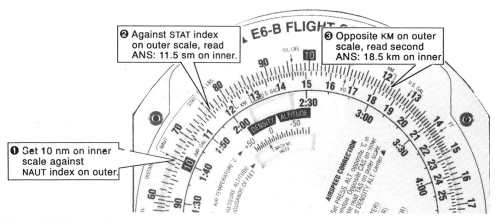

Figure 24-20. Example 13

The above method may also be used to convert speeds.

Example 14. Convert 231 kph to knots and mph.

Rough calculation:
1 km is about 0.5 nm and slightly over 0.5 sm.
Therefore 230 kph is about 115 knots and slightly over 115 mph.
Method:
See Figure 24-21.
Answers. 231 kph = 125 knots = 144 mph.

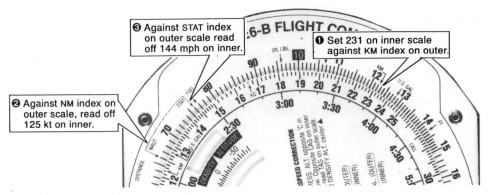

Figure 24-21. Example 14

Volume Conversions

In aviation worldwide we are faced with three different sorts of volumetric units—the **U.S. gallon,** the **imperial gallon,** and the **liter.** In most general aviation aircraft the fuel gauges are marked in U.S. gallons. However, you may find different units in other countries. There is a possibility of confusion here, so you must become very confident in converting fuel quantities and weights from one unit to another.

For rough calculations, the conversion factors are:

> **1 U.S. gallon = 0.8 imperial gallon = 4 liters**

This calculation is very simple on the flight computer, which has indexes marked on the outer scale for U.S. GAL, IMP GAL and LITERS.

1. Set the known quantity on the inner scale against its index on the outer scale.

2. Against the desired index on the outer scale read off the answer on the inner scale.

Note 1: Imperial gallons are rarely used in the United States, and in general, the "U.S." is dropped from U.S. gallons. Whenever "gallons" are mentioned, assume U.S. gallons, not imperial gallons.

Note 2: Flight computers normally have indexes for both U.S. gallons and imperial gallons, so make sure that you use the correct ones in your conversions.

Example 15. Convert 24 U.S. gallons to liters and imperial gallons. *See* Figure 24-22.

Rough calculation:
1 U.S. gallon is 4 liters and a little less than 1 imperial gallon.
Therefore 24 U.S. gallons is 24 × 4 = 96 liters and a little less than 24 imperial gallons.

Answer. 24 U.S. gallons = 91 liters = 20 imperial gallons.

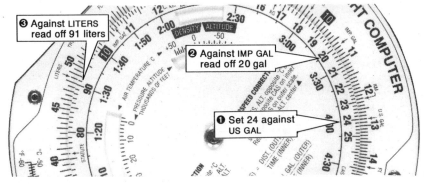

Figure 24-22. Example 15

Volume to Weight Conversions

Converting **U.S. gallons** to **pounds** is made easy by the FUEL LBS index on the outer scale. For rough calculations remember that 1 U.S. gallon of aviation gasoline weighs 6 pounds (lb).

Example 16. What does 8 U.S. gallons of aviation gasoline weigh? *See* Figure 24-23.

Rough calculation:
1 U.S. gallon weighs 6 pounds.
Therefore 8 U.S. gallons weigh 8 × 6 = 48 pounds.

Method:
Set 8 on inner scale against U.S. GAL on outer scale. Against FUEL LBS on outer scale, read off 48 on inner scale.

Answer. 8 U.S. gallons = 48 pounds.

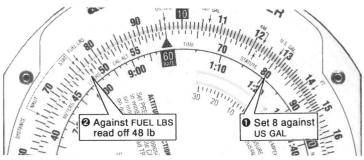

Figure 24-23. Example 16

Weight Conversions

Converting between **kilograms** and **pounds** is made easy by the LBS index on the outer scale and the KG index on the inner scale. For rough calculations remember that 1 kg is about 2 lb.

Example 17. Convert 83 lb to kg. *See* Figure 24-24.

Rough calculation:
1 lb is about 0.5 kg.
Therefore 83 lb is approximately 40 kg.

Method:
Align LBS on the outer scale against KG on the inner scale. Against 83 lb on the outer scale, read off 37.5 kg on the inner scale, which is the answer in kg.

Answer. 83 pounds = 37.5 kilograms.

Figure 24-24. Example 17

✍ Now complete **Review 24, Part (b)** on page 549.

For Aspiring Commercial Pilots

Calculating the Wind Velocity in Flight

After obtaining two position fixes en route, it is possible to determine the *actual* W/V, which can then be used in your further in-flight calculations rather than the less accurate forecast wind.

The two position fixes enable you to determine the actual ground track (TR) and the actual groundspeed achieved between the two positions, assuming you have maintained a reasonably steady heading and true airspeed.

This problem can be summarized as:

Known	Find
HDG/TAS and TR/GS	W/V

Remember that in the United States it is usual for visual pilots to work in true.

Example 18. Finding a W/V in flight.

Known:

– HDG 143°M

– Variation 5°W

– TAS 120 knots

– TR 146°T, GS 144 knots.

Find:

– W/V.

Step 1. Place the TR/GS vector under the grommet.

Rotate the compass rose and set track 146°T under the index. Set the GS 144 knots under the grommet. *See* Figure 24-25a.

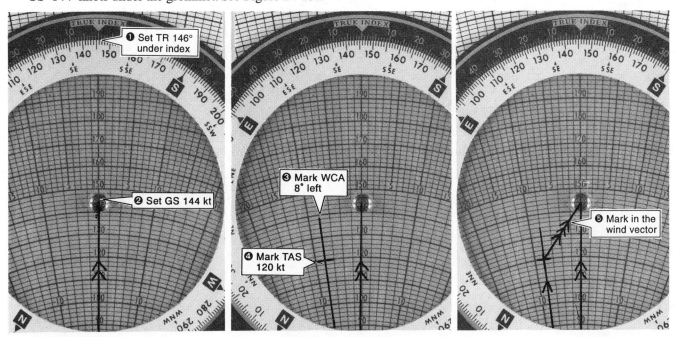

Figure 24-25a. Example 18   **Figure 24-25b.**   **Figure 24-25c.**

Step 2. Place the HDG/TAS vector on the plotting disc.

From HDG 138°T (143°M – 5°W) and TR 146°T, the drift is 8° right; the HDG is 8° left of TR (the wind correction angle is 8° left). Mark in the HDG direction as the 8° drift line to the left of track. Mark the TAS where the 120 knots speed arc intersects the drift line; this now indicates the HDG/TAS vector (Figure 24-25b). Mark in the wind vector (Figure 24-25c). Remember, the W/V blows the aircraft from HDG to TR.

Step 3. Step 3. Determine the W/V.

Rotate the compass rose until the wind dot is on the index line with the arrows pointing down toward the grommet. The direction from which it is blowing, 360°T, is now indicated under the index. Read off the wind strength 30 knots. (Setting a definite speed arc under the grommet, 100 knots in this case, makes the wind strength easier to read.) *See* Figure 24-25d.

Answer. W/V 360°T/30 knots.

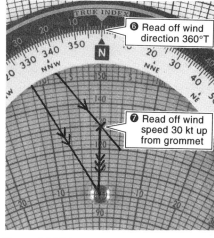

Figure 24-25d.

✎ Commercial students complete **Review 24, Commercial** on page 550.

✎ Review 24

Part (a)

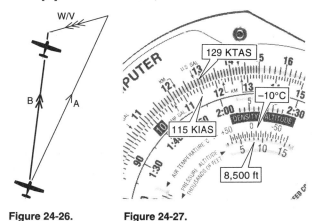

Figure 24-26.   Figure 24-27.

1. Label the sides marked A and B in Figure 24-26.

➤ A: HDG/TAS;   B: TR/GS

2. The wind blows an airplane from its _____ to its _____ .

➤ heading to its ground track

3. At the flight planning stage, we measure the direction of the desired _____ on our chart.

➤ course

4. Using the forecast wind velocity given in knots and true, and knowing the true airspeed that we can expect from our airplane at the selected altitude, we can calculate _____ and _____ .

➤ heading, groundspeed

Using the Flight Computer

5. What is the expected TAS at 8,500 feet if the temperature is –10°C and the IAS 115 knots?

➤ 129 KTAS (*see* Figure 24-27)

6. The planned course is 240°T and the forecast wind 140°T/30. If the expected TAS is 129 knots and the variation 8° East, what is the required magnetic HDG and expected GS?

➤ True heading 240 – 13 = 227°T
Magnetic heading 227 – 8 = 219°M
Groundspeed = 131 knots

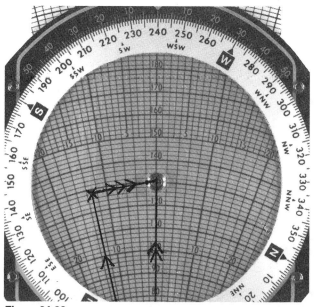

Figure 24-28.

7. How long will it take to fly 85 nm at a groundspeed of 131 knots?

➤ 39 minutes (Remember the rough check)

Figure 24-29.

8. How much fuel will you use in 39 minutes at a fuel flow of 15 gph?

Figure 24-30.

➤ approximately 10 gallons

9. Calculate the true heading and groundspeed for TAS 98 knots, W/V 280T/35 and course 072°T.

➤ HDG 062°T, GS 127 knots

10. To achieve a course of 300°T, calculate the magnetic heading and groundspeed if you plan to cruise at 10,000 feet where the forecast wind velocity and temperature is 280°T/25 and +6°C, at an indicated airspeed of 100 knots. Variation is 6°W.

➤ TAS 119 knots, HDG 296°T and 302°M, GS 95 knots

11. At a GS of 183 knots, how far will you travel in 17 minutes?

➤ 52 nm

12. At a GS of 120 knots, how far will you travel in 10 minutes?

➤ 20 nm

13. If we cover 23 nm over the ground in 9 minutes, what is our GS?

➤ 153 knots

14. If we cover 22 gnm in 10 minutes, what is our GS? How long will it take us to reach the next checkpoint which is 73 nm further on in the same direction?

➤ GS 132 knots, ETE 33 min

15. What is the time en route for the following flight? Distance 57 nm, true course 213°T, wind 090°T/16, TAS 90 knots. Add 2 minutes for the climb-out.
    (a) 33 minutes.
    (b) 37 minutes.
    (c) 41 minutes.

➤ (b)

16. Refer to Sectional Chart excerpt No. 4 on page 469. What is the estimated time en route from Sandpoint Airport (area 1) to St. Maries Airport (area 4)? The wind is 215°T/25 and the TAS is 125 knots.
    (a) 27 minutes.
    (b) 30 minutes.
    (c) 34 minutes.

➤ (c) 34 minutes (distance 59 nm, course 181°T, GS 104 knots)

17. Refer to Sectional Chart excerpt No. 4 on page 469. What is the estimated time en route from St. Maries Airport (area 4) to Priest River (area 1)? The wind is 300°T/14 and the true airspeed is 90 knots. Add 3 minutes for climb-out.
    (a) 38 minutes.
    (b) 43 minutes.
    (c) 48 minutes.

➤ (b) Total time including climb-out 43 minutes (distance 54 nm, course 346°T, GS 80 knots, time 40 minutes)

18. If you burn 5 gallons of fuel in 24 minutes, what is your rate of fuel consumption, and how long would it take to burn 8 gallons?

➤ 12.5 gallons/hour, 38 minutes

19. If full tanks is 26 gallons of usable fuel and the average consumption rate is 5.5 gal/hr, calculate the safe endurance for flight if you wish to retain 1 hour's fuel as reserve.

➤ 224 minutes or 3 hours 44 min (20.5 gal of flight fuel available)

Part (b)

1. Convert +32°F to °C.

➤ 0°C

2. Convert +20°C to °F.

➤ +68°F

3. Convert 55 nm to kilometers.

➤ 102 km

4. Convert 50 knots to km/hr (or kph).

➤ 92.5 km/hr

5. Convert 631 lb to kg.
➤ 287 kg

6. Convert 80 kg to lb.
➤ 176 lb

7. To refuel from 16 gal to 45 gal you should order _____ liters.
➤ 29 gal = 110 liters

8. What does 45 gallons of aviation gasoline weigh?
➤ 270 lb

Commercial Review

1. Given:
   True course .... 105°
   True heading .... 085°
   True airspeed .... 95 kt
   Groundspeed .... 87 kt
   Determine the wind direction and speed.
   (a) 020°T/32
   (b) 030°T/38
   (c) 200°T/32
➤ (a) Wind 020°T/32 (true heading 085° with 20° left WCA)

2. If fuel consumption is 80 pounds per hour and groundspeed is 180 knots, how much fuel is required for an airplane to travel 460 nm?
   (a) 205 pounds.
   (b) 212 pounds.
   (c) 460 pounds.
➤ (a) approximately 205 pounds (time 153 minutes)

3. If fuel consumption is 14.7 gallons per hour and groundspeed is 157 knots, how much fuel is required for an airplane to travel 612 nm?
   (a) 58 gallons.
   (b) 60 gallons.
   (c) 64 gallons.
➤ (a)

4. Given:
   Wind .... 175°T/20
   Distance .... 135 nm
   True course .... 075°
   True airspeed .... 80 kt
   Fuel consumption .... 105 lb/hr

Determine the time en route and fuel consumption.
   (a) 1 hour 28 minutes and 73.2 pounds.
   (b) 1 hour 38 minutes and 158 pounds.
   (c) 1 hour 40 minutes and 175 pounds.
➤ (c)

5. An airplane departs an airport under the following conditions:
   Airport elevation .... 1,000 ft
   Cruise altitude .... 9,500 ft
   Rate of climb .... 500 fpm
   Average true airspeed .... 135 kt
   True course .... 215°
   Average wind velocity .... 290°T/20
   Variation .... 3°W
   Deviation .... –2°
   Average fuel consumption .... 13 gal/hr
   Determine the approximate time, compass heading, distance, and fuel consumed during the climb.
   (a) 14 minutes, 234°, 26 nm, 3.9 gallons.
   (b) 17 minutes, 224°, 36 nm, 3.7 gallons.
   (c) 17 minutes, 242°, 31 nm, 3.5 gallons.
➤ (b) Climb 8,500 feet at 500 fpm will take 17 minutes. At 13 gal/hr, the fuel used is 3.7 gal. Use wind side of flight computer to calculate °T. Convert to °M, then allow for deviation. Use the groundspeed to find distance.

6. An airplane descends to an airport under the following conditions:
   Cruising altitude .... 7,500 ft
   Airport elevation .... 1,300 ft
   Descends to .... 800 ft AGL
   Rate of descent .... 300 ft/min
   Average true airspeed .... 120 kt
   True course .... 165°
   Average wind velocity .... 240°T/20
   Variation .... 4°E
   Deviation .... –2°
   Average fuel consumption .... 9.6 gal/hr
   Determine the approximate time, compass heading, distance, and fuel consumed during the descent.
   (a) 16 minutes, 168°, 30 nm, 2.9 gallons.
   (b) 18 minutes, 164°, 34 nm, 3.2 gallons.
   (c) 18 minutes, 168°, 34 nm, 2.9 gallons.
➤ (c) 5,400 feet descent at 300 fpm takes 18 minutes. At 9.6 gal/hr, the fuel used is 2.9 gallons. Use a flight computer to calculate °T. Convert to °M and allow for deviation. Use the groundspeed from the computer to find the distance.

Flight Planning 25

Flight Management

Cross-country flying is a significant step forward in your training. As the pilot-in-command of a cross-country flight, you have certain duties to perform, both on the ground and in flight. The main flight management tasks are to fly the airplane and to navigate it to the destination. This involves careful flight planning and accurate en route navigation.

Flight management applies to the planning stage on the ground as well as to the actual flight. You should train yourself to plan a VFR cross-country flight of a duration near the range of the airplane within **30 minutes**—this includes completing a flight log, preparing a fuel log, calculating weight and balance taking into account the expected loading, and filing a flight plan. Doing all this inside 30 minutes will take practice!

Train yourself to plan a flight within 30 minutes.

You have limited resources in the cockpit which need to be managed efficiently. For example, it is difficult to measure courses and distances on a chart in flight while trying to fly in rough air—it shows better management to do the chart work on the ground prior to flight. The better the flight planning prior to flight, the easier the en route navigation!

Personal Navigation Equipment

The two most vital instruments for visual navigation are the **magnetic compass** and the **clock.** Provided that the airplane's position has been positively fixed within the previous twenty minutes or so, and its speed is known (at least approximately), its position during flight can be deduced from the direction it has traveled and the time taken from the fix.

A **flight case,** satchel or nav bag that fits comfortably within reach in the cockpit should be used to hold your navigation equipment. A typical flight case should contain:

Check your flight case.

- relevant charts covering at least 50 nautical miles either side of your planned course;
- a flight computer;
- a scale rule and protractor (or a plotter);
- pens and pencils;
- relevant documents (such as the Airport/Facility Directory);
- spare flight log forms;
- a flashlight; and
- sunglasses.

Weather and Operational Considerations

You should obtain **weather information** and **notices to airmen (NOTAMs)** by the most convenient means available to you, which may be via a computer printout, a Flight Service Station, NWS briefing office (weather only) or by telephone.

Check weather and NOTAMs.

```
******** FDC NOTAMs ********
!FDC 7/5477 ZMA FL.. FI/T AIRWAY ZMA, V51 SHEDS INT, FL, MRA 3000.
!FDC 7/5432 ZMA FI/T AIRWAY ZMA V509 CROWD INT FL. TO ST.
PETERSBURG /PIE/ VORTAC FL. MOCA 2600.
```

Figure 25-1. A typical NOTAM

```
METAR KFPR 261148Z 00000KT 10SM FEW020 BKN080 A2998
METAR KVRB 261150Z VRB03KT 10SM - SHRA FEW009 SCT035 BKN070
BKN200
22/21 A2999 RMK TSE35 MOV E SLP156 60087 70156 10250 20217 51017
METAR KSRQ 261150Z 05006KT 10SM SKC 25/24 A3001
current hourly report not available for SPG
METAR KSPG 261050Z 05010KT 10SM SCT150 26/25 A3001

TAF KVRB 261120Z 261212 VRB04KT P6SM
SCT025 BKN050 TEMPO 1213 3SM
TSRA
BKN025CB
FM1300 02007KT P6SM SCT030
TEMPO 1318 5SM SHRA BKN025
FM1800 03010KT P6SM SCT030
TEMPO 1820 BKN025
TAF KSRQ 261130Z 261212 06005KT P6SM SKC
FM1400 06008KT P6SM SCT030 SCT250
FM1900 05009KT P6SM SCT040
SCT250 PROB30 1923 3SM TSRA BKN025CB
FM0200 VRB03KT P6SM FEW020 SCT250
```

Figure 25-2. Some typical weather information

Flight Service Stations (FSS) can provide three basic types of preflight briefing:

- a **standard briefing**—a full briefing including adverse conditions, VFR flight recommended or not, weather synopsis, current conditions, en route forecast, destination forecast, winds aloft, relevant NOTAMs, known ATC delays; or

- an **abbreviated briefing**—to supplement information you already have; or

- an **outlook briefing**—for advanced planning purposes (for a flight 6 or more hours from the time of briefing).

Flight Service Stations can provide a standard, abbreviated, or outlook briefing.

The Area Forecast will give cloud bases above mean sea level and the Aerodrome Forecast above ground level. From this information the most suitable cruising altitude can then be chosen. You should read and analyze the weather information so that you can make well-based judgments regarding your proposed flight, especially the "go/no-go" decision. Analyze the weather reports and forecasts, weather charts, pilot weather reports, SIGMETs, AIRMETs, NOTAMs, windshear reports, and whatever other relevant information is available. Don't forget to walk outside and have a look at the sky yourself! It sounds like a lot, but the information will be presented to you in a logical manner—and the more practiced you become in planning a flight, the easier it will seem.

From this information, and from your knowledge of your own experience and capabilities, you can now make a firm, positive and confident "go/no-go" decision. This is a command decision, possibly the most important decision of the whole flight.

Make a sensible "go/no-go" decision.

Pre-Flight Planning

Preparing the flight plan involves several steps. While your first few cross-country flights will take a long time to plan, you should aim, by practice, to speed up the process so that you can do this within 30 minutes from start to finish.

Select and use current and appropriate aeronautical charts which, for most VFR flights will be a *Sectional* chart, together with *Terminal* charts for any nearby Class B airspace.

Use only current charts, and check for terrain and airspace.

Select the route over which you want to fly. Note the nature of the terrain and the type of airspace along this route and to either side of it:

- **terrain:** check the height of any obstacles within (say) 10 miles either side of your proposed course;
- **airspace:** check the route for:
    - different classes of airspace;
    - prohibited areas, restricted areas or warning areas;
    - other airports.

It may be best to avoid particularly high or rugged terrain (especially if you are flying a single-engine airplane), areas of dense air traffic, and areas of bad weather such as coastal fog, low clouds, and thunderstorms.

Choose turning points and prominent checkpoints which will be easily identified in flight, and which cannot be confused with other nearby ground features. Remember you are sitting on the left-hand side of the airplane. Select appropriate en route radio navigation aids, and note the communications facilities. Allow for necessary fuel stops. Mark the route on your sectional chart, and **enter the checkpoints** on the flight log.

Choose prominent checkpoints.

Note any suitable **alternate airports** available on or adjacent to the route, in case an unscheduled landing becomes necessary. Information on airports is available in the A/FD.

Note any suitable en route alternate airports.

Altitude

It is good airmanship to calculate a **safety altitude** that provides adequate clearance above terrain and obstacles. A quick means of determining the height of the highest obstacle or terrain is to use the **maximum elevation figure (MEF)** published for each latitude–longitude quadrangle on Sectional charts. To be less restricted, you could instead find the highest terrain or obstacle within 5 nm or 10 nm either side of track. Then apply a safety buffer, say of 1,000 feet or whatever your flight instructor suggests, to obtain a safety altitude. Enter this figure on your flight log. This is not a requirement, but it provides a safe minimum altitude to fly at if, for instance, cloud forces you down.

Terrain awareness is vital.

Select a suitable **cruise altitude** for each leg and enter it in the flight log. Considerations should include:

- terrain;
- overlying airspace restrictions;
- the cloud base; and
- VFR cruise altitudes.

The **VFR cruise altitudes,** when more than 3,000 feet above the surface, are:

(a) on a magnetic course 000° to 179° magnetic—*odd* thousands plus 500 (for example 3,500, 5,500, 7,500 feet MSL);

(b) on a magnetic course 180° to 359° magnetic—*even* thousands plus 500 (for example 4,500, 6,500, 8,500 feet MSL);

Note: Cruise altitudes, as well as VOR radials, are based on *magnetic* course.

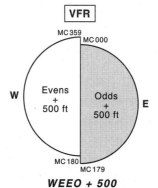

Figure 25-3. VFR cruise altitudes above 3,000 feet AGL

Courses and Distances

For each leg of the flight, mentally estimate the course direction and the distance in nautical miles before measuring it accurately (ensuring that you are using the correct scale). Insert the accurately measured figures on the flight log.

Estimating course and distance prior to actual measurement will avoid gross errors.

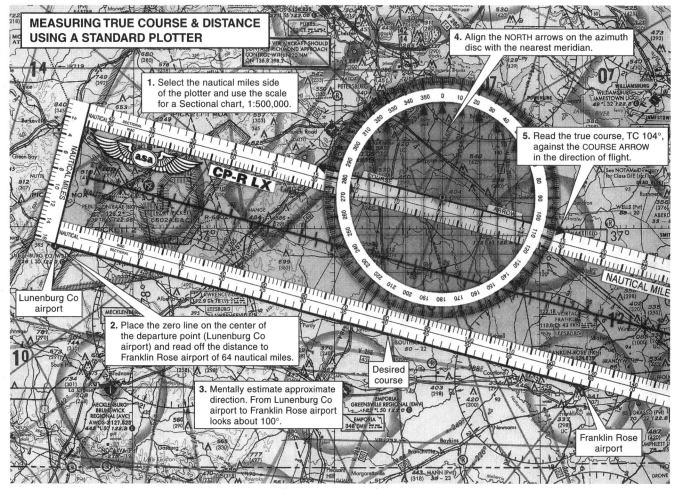

MEASURING TRUE COURSE & DISTANCE USING A STANDARD PLOTTER

1. Select the nautical miles side of the plotter and use the scale for a Sectional chart, 1:500,000.

2. Place the zero line on the center of the departure point (Lunenburg Co airport) and read off the distance to Franklin Rose airport of 64 nautical miles.

3. Mentally estimate approximate direction. From Lunenburg Co airport to Franklin Rose airport looks about 100°.

4. Align the NORTH arrows on the azimuth disc with the nearest meridian.

5. Read the true course, TC 104°, against the COURSE ARROW in the direction of flight.

Lunenburg Co airport

Desired course

Franklin Rose airport

Figure 25-4. Measuring true course and distance on a standard plotter

Remember to measure true course against a meridian of longitude at the approximate midpoint of each leg (to avoid errors caused by converging meridians). Apply *magnetic variation* to the measured true course to find the magnetic course.

Variation east, magnetic least; variation west, magnetic best.

Distance Markers or Time Markers

To assist you in flight, it is suggested that each leg be subdivided using small marks placed at regular intervals along the course lines drawn on the chart. These may be:

• distance markers each 10 nautical miles (nm); or
• distance markers at the ¼, ½ and ¾ points; or
• time markers each 10 minutes; or
• time markers at the ¼, ½ and ¾ points.

Time markers have to wait until you have calculated groundspeeds and time intervals. Once in flight, these may vary from the flight planned values, unlike the distance markers. Engraving a pencil with 10 nm marks (in the correct scale for the chart) will help you estimating distances, particularly in flight.

Figure 25-5. A pencil engraved (by yourself) with 10 nm nicks is very useful

Course Guides

To allow easier in-flight estimation of any deviation from the desired course, it is useful to draw in 5° or 10° guides either side of course emanating from each turning point. This avoids having to use a protractor or plotter in flight.

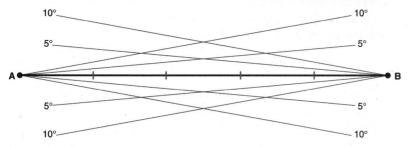

Figure 25-6. Course guides and distance markers

Speed, Time and Heading Calculations

Once the route has been selected and the courses and distances measured, the flight plan may be completed. Calculations of headings, groundspeeds, time intervals and fuel consumption must all be made. For a full explanation of how to perform these calculations, refer to Chapter 24 on the flight computer.

Completing the Flight Log

Insert the forecast winds, the selected cruise altitude, and the TAS for each leg onto the flight log. Remember that for a given indicated airspeed, the true airspeed will be greater at higher altitudes and temperatures because of the decreased air density. Converting IAS to TAS is easily done on the calculator side of the computer, but most Pilot's Operating Handbooks directly provide cruise TAS information in the published cruise tables.

On the wind side of the flight computer, use the forecast wind to set up the triangle of velocities and calculate wind correction angle, heading and groundspeed for each leg (*see* Chapter 24).

Note: It is most important when using the wind side of the computer that you work *completely* in degrees true (or *completely* in degrees magnetic).

Having measured the distance of each leg and calculated the expected groundspeed, determine the *estimated time interval* and insert it on the flight log. Then add all of the individual time intervals together and obtain the *total* time interval for the whole flight.

Since climb to altitude will be at a lower airspeed (and higher fuel consumption) than cruising flight, some pilots add a climb allowance, say 2 minutes and 0.5 gallon, to the cruise-only figures calculated for the first leg.

To check for gross errors, compare the total time en route with the total distance for the flight, considering the average GS expected.

Also, confirm that you will arrive with adequate daylight remaining. You should plan to arrive with at least 30 minutes of daylight remaining. Ask your flight instructor for guidance. If diversion to an alternate airport is a possibility, then you should plan for a departure time that will allow you to fly to the destination airport, then to the alternate airport and still arrive well before the end of daylight.

Fuel Calculations

The fuel consumption for various power settings is published in the Pilot's Operating Handbook. These figures assume **correct leaning** of the fuel/air mixture when cruising at 75% maximum continuous power or less. Leaning the mixture can decrease fuel consumption by up to 20%. From the estimated time interval for the whole flight and the published fuel consumption rate, calculate the expected flight fuel.

Reserve fuel should also be carried to allow for in-flight contingencies such as diversions, fuel consumption poorer than that published and unexpected headwinds en route. A **fixed reserve fuel** of 45 minutes by night and 30 minutes by day is required. This fixed reserve is only intended to be used in an emergency. Any fuel over and above the minimum fuel required is known as *margin fuel*. Insert the fuel calculations onto the flight log.

Always ensure sufficient fuel is carried.

Weight and Balance

At this stage of flight planning, when the fuel required and the passenger and baggage load is known, it is appropriate to consider weight and balance. For a flight to be legal, the airplane must not exceed any weight limitation, and must be loaded so that the center of gravity (CG) lies within the approved range throughout the flight. Complete a load sheet (if necessary) to verify that the requirements are met. *See* Chapter 12 for more on weight and balance.

Do not exceed weight and balance limitations.

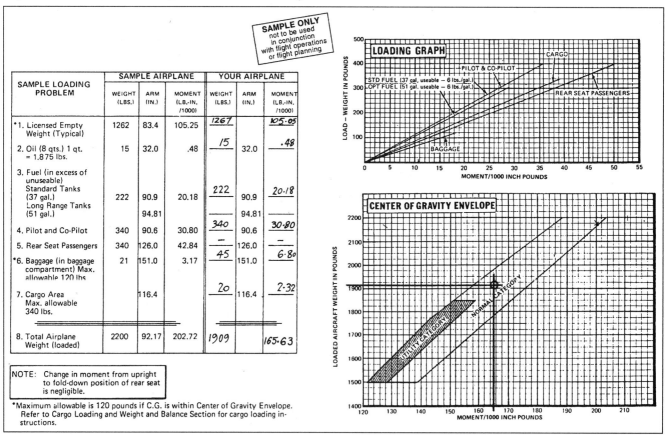

Figure 25-7. A typical load sheet

Takeoff and Landing Performance

Having considered weight and balance, you will know the expected takeoff weight and landing weight of the airplane. If any doubt exists regarding the suitability of the departure, destination and alternate airports, then reference should be made to the takeoff and landing **performance charts** in the Pilot's Operating Handbook. The official source of **airport data** is the Airport/Facility Directory. **Weather data** (wind and temperature) affecting the performance can be obtained from the forecast. *See* Chapter 10 for more on takeoff and landing performance.

TAKEOFF DISTANCE
SHORT FIELD

SAMPLE ONLY not to be used in conjunction with flight operations or flight planning

CONDITIONS:
Flaps 10°
Full Throttle Prior to Brake Release
Paved, Level, Dry Runway
Zero Wind

NOTES:
1. Short field technique as specified in Section 4.
2. Prior to takeoff from fields above 3000 feet elevation, the mixture should be leaned to give maximum RPM in a full throttle, static runup.
3. Decrease distances 10% for each 9 knots headwind. For operation with tailwinds up to 10 knots, increase distances by 10% for each 2 knots.
4. For operation on a dry, grass runway, increase distances by 15% of the "ground roll" figure.

WEIGHT LBS	TAKEOFF SPEED KIAS		PRESS ALT FT	0°C		10°C		20°C		30°C		40°C	
	LIFT OFF	AT 50 FT		GRND ROLL FT	TOTAL FT TO CLEAR 50 FT OBS	GRND ROLL FT	TOTAL FT TO CLEAR 50 FT OBS	GRND ROLL FT	TOTAL FT TO CLEAR 50 FT OBS	GRND ROLL FT	TOTAL FT TO CLEAR 50 FT OBS	GRND ROLL FT	TOTAL FT TO CLEAR 50 FT OBS
1670	50	54	S.L.	640	1190	695	1290	755	1390	810	1495	875	1605
			1000	705	1310	765	1420	825	1530	890	1645	960	1770
			2000	775	1445	840	1565	910	1690	980	1820	1055	1960
			3000	855	1600	925	1730	1000	1870	1080	2020	1165	2185

Figure 25-8. Excerpt from a Cessna 152 takeoff performance chart

LANDING DISTANCE
SHORT FIELD

SAMPLE ONLY not to be used in conjunction with flight operations or flight planning

CONDITIONS:
Flaps 30°
Power Off
Maximum Braking
Paved, Level, Dry Runway
Zero Wind

NOTES:
1. Short field technique as specified in Section 4.
2. Decrease distances 10% for each 9 knots headwind. For operation with tailwinds up to 10 knots, increase distances by 10% for each 2 knots.
3. For operation on a dry, grass runway, increase distances by 45% of the "ground roll" figure.
4. If a landing with flaps up is necessary, increase the approach speed by 7 KIAS and allow for 35% longer distances.

WEIGHT LBS	SPEED AT 50 FT KIAS	PRESS ALT FT	0°C		10°C		20°C		30°C		40°C	
			GRND ROLL FT	TOTAL FT TO CLEAR 50 FT OBS	GRND ROLL FT	TOTAL FT TO CLEAR 50 FT OBS	GRND ROLL FT	TOTAL FT TO CLEAR 50 FT OBS	GRND ROLL FT	TOTAL FT TO CLEAR 50 FT OBS	GRND ROLL FT	TOTAL FT TO CLEAR 50 FT OBS
1670	54	S.L.	450	1160	465	1185	485	1215	500	1240	515	1265
		1000	465	1185	485	1215	500	1240	520	1270	535	1295
		2000	485	1215	500	1240	520	1270	535	1300	555	1330
		3000	500	1240	520	1275	540	1305	560	1335	575	1360

Figure 25-9. Excerpt from a Cessna 152 landing performance chart

The Flight Plan Form

Fill out the flight plan form, and insert any relevant *emergency equipment* carried in the REMARKS section.

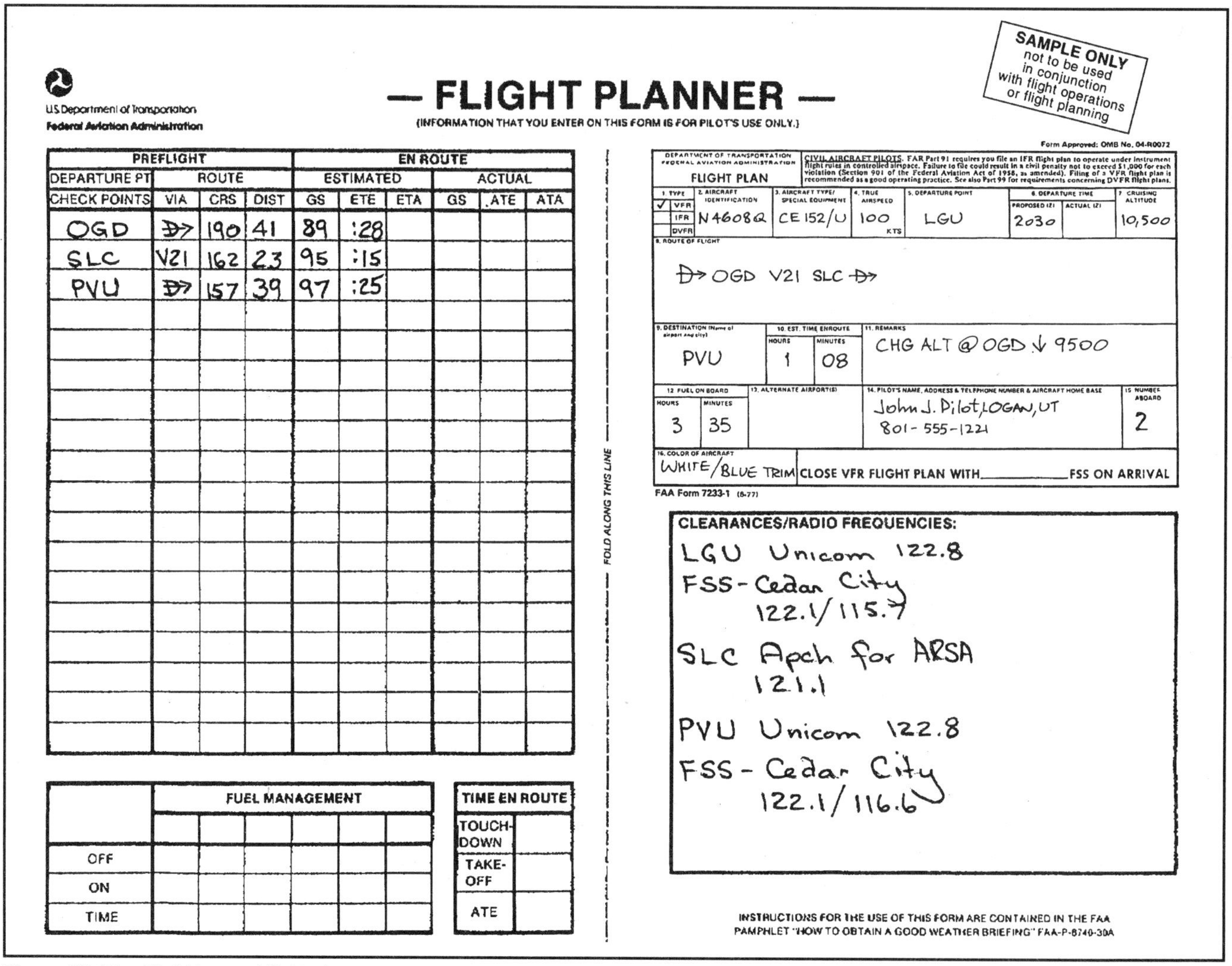

Figure 25-10a. Flight log and flight plan

In Block 2 of the flight plan form, the letter "U" indicates that you are equipped with a transponder with altitude encoding. In Block 7, you should insert your initial cruise altitude—other cruise altitudes may be requested from ATC en route. In Block 9, you should insert the final destination airport if no stopover at intermediate airports for more than 1 hour is anticipated. In Block 11, you should insert the amount of usable fuel on board expressed in time (total endurance).

Flight Notification
Prior to flight, contact the Flight Service Station (FSS) and file the flight plan.

SPECIAL EQUIPMENT SUFFIX LIST

VOR, TACAN, DME NAVIGATION SYSTEMS
/X no transponder.
/T transponder with no altitude encoding capability
/U transponder with altitude encoding capability.
/D DME, but no transponder.
/B DME and transponder, but with no altitude encoding capability.
/A DME and transponder with altitude encoding capability.

AREA NAVIGATION SYSTEMS
/R RNAV and transponder with altitude encoding capability.
/C RNAV and transponder, but with no altitude encoding capability.
/W RNAV but no transponder.
/G Global Positioning System (GPS)/Global Navigation Satellite System (GNSS) equipped aircraft with oceanic, en route, terminal, and GPS approach capability.

Figure 25-10b. Special equipment suffixes for flight plan form

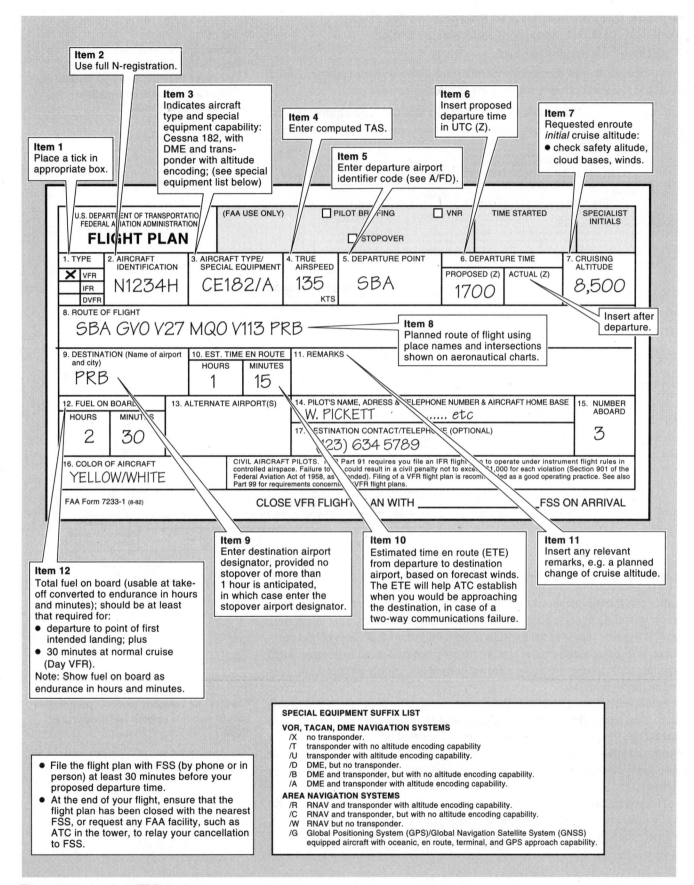

Item 1
Place a tick in appropriate box.

Item 2
Use full N-registration.

Item 3
Indicates aircraft type and special equipment capability: Cessna 182, with DME and transponder with altitude encoding; (see special equipment list below)

Item 4
Enter computed TAS.

Item 5
Enter departure airport identifier code (see A/FD).

Item 6
Insert proposed departure time in UTC (Z).

Item 7
Requested enroute *initial* cruise altitude:
● check safety altitude, cloud bases, winds.

| U.S. DEPARTMENT OF TRANSPORTATION FEDERAL AVIATION ADMINISTRATION **FLIGHT PLAN** | (FAA USE ONLY) | ☐ PILOT BRIEFING ☐STOPOVER | ☐ VNR | TIME STARTED | SPECIALIST INITIALS |

1. TYPE	2. AIRCRAFT IDENTIFICATION	3. AIRCRAFT TYPE/ SPECIAL EQUIPMENT	4. TRUE AIRSPEED	5. DEPARTURE POINT	6. DEPARTURE TIME		7. CRUISING ALTITUDE
☒ VFR ☐ IFR ☐ DVFR	N1234H	CE182/A	135 KTS	SBA	PROPOSED (Z) 1700	ACTUAL (Z)	8,500

8. ROUTE OF FLIGHT
SBA GVO V27 MQO V113 PRB

Item 8
Planned route of flight using place names and intersections shown on aeronautical charts.

Insert after departure.

9. DESTINATION (Name of airport and city) PRB	10. EST. TIME EN ROUTE HOURS 1 | MINUTES 15	11. REMARKS	
12. FUEL ON BOARD HOURS 2 | MINUTES 30	13. ALTERNATE AIRPORT(S)	14. PILOT'S NAME, ADDRESS & TELEPHONE NUMBER & AIRCRAFT HOME BASE W. PICKETT ...... etc 17. DESTINATION CONTACT/TELEPHONE (OPTIONAL) (123) 634 5789	15. NUMBER ABOARD 3
16. COLOR OF AIRCRAFT YELLOW/WHITE	CIVIL AIRCRAFT PILOTS. FAR Part 91 requires you file an IFR flight plan to operate under instrument flight rules in controlled airspace. Failure to file could result in a civil penalty not to exceed $1,000 for each violation (Section 901 of the Federal Aviation Act of 1958, as amended). Filing of a VFR flight plan is recommended as a good operating practice. See also Part 99 for requirements concerning DVFR flight plans.		

FAA Form 7233-1 (8-82)   CLOSE VFR FLIGHT PLAN WITH _____ FSS ON ARRIVAL

Item 9
Enter destination airport designator, provided no stopover of more than 1 hour is anticipated, in which case enter the stopover airport designator.

Item 10
Estimated time en route (ETE) from departure to destination airport, based on forecast winds. The ETE will help ATC establish when you would be approaching the destination, in case of a two-way communications failure.

Item 11
Insert any relevant remarks, e.g. a planned change of cruise altitude.

Item 12
Total fuel on board (usable at take-off converted to endurance in hours and minutes); should be at least that required for:
● departure to point of first intended landing; plus
● 30 minutes at normal cruise (Day VFR).
Note: Show fuel on board as endurance in hours and minutes.

● File the flight plan with FSS (by phone or in person) at least 30 minutes before your proposed departure time.
● At the end of your flight, ensure that the flight plan has been closed with the nearest FSS, or request any FAA facility, such as ATC in the tower, to relay your cancellation to FSS.

SPECIAL EQUIPMENT SUFFIX LIST

VOR, TACAN, DME NAVIGATION SYSTEMS
/X   no transponder.
/T   transponder with no altitude encoding capability
/U   transponder with altitude encoding capability.
/D   DME, but no transponder.
/B   DME and transponder, but with no altitude encoding capability.
/A   DME and transponder with altitude encoding capability.

AREA NAVIGATION SYSTEMS
/R   RNAV and transponder with altitude encoding capability.
/C   RNAV and transponder, but with no altitude encoding capability.
/W   RNAV but no transponder.
/G   Global Positioning System (GPS)/Global Navigation Satellite System (GNSS) equipped aircraft with oceanic, en route, terminal, and GPS approach capability.

Figure 25-11. A typical VFR flight plan

Airplane Documentation and Preparation for Flight

You should check that the required documents are carried:

- *"AROW"*—for the airplane; and
- pilot certificate and medical certificate (and logbook with endorsements if you are a student pilot)—for yourself as pilot-in-command.

You must be familiar with these airplane documents, any equipment list, weight and balance data, maintenance requirements and appropriate records.

"AROW"
• Airworthiness Certificate
• Registration Certificate
• Operating limitations (Flight Manual etc.)
• Weight and balance information
***See* page 436 for details.**

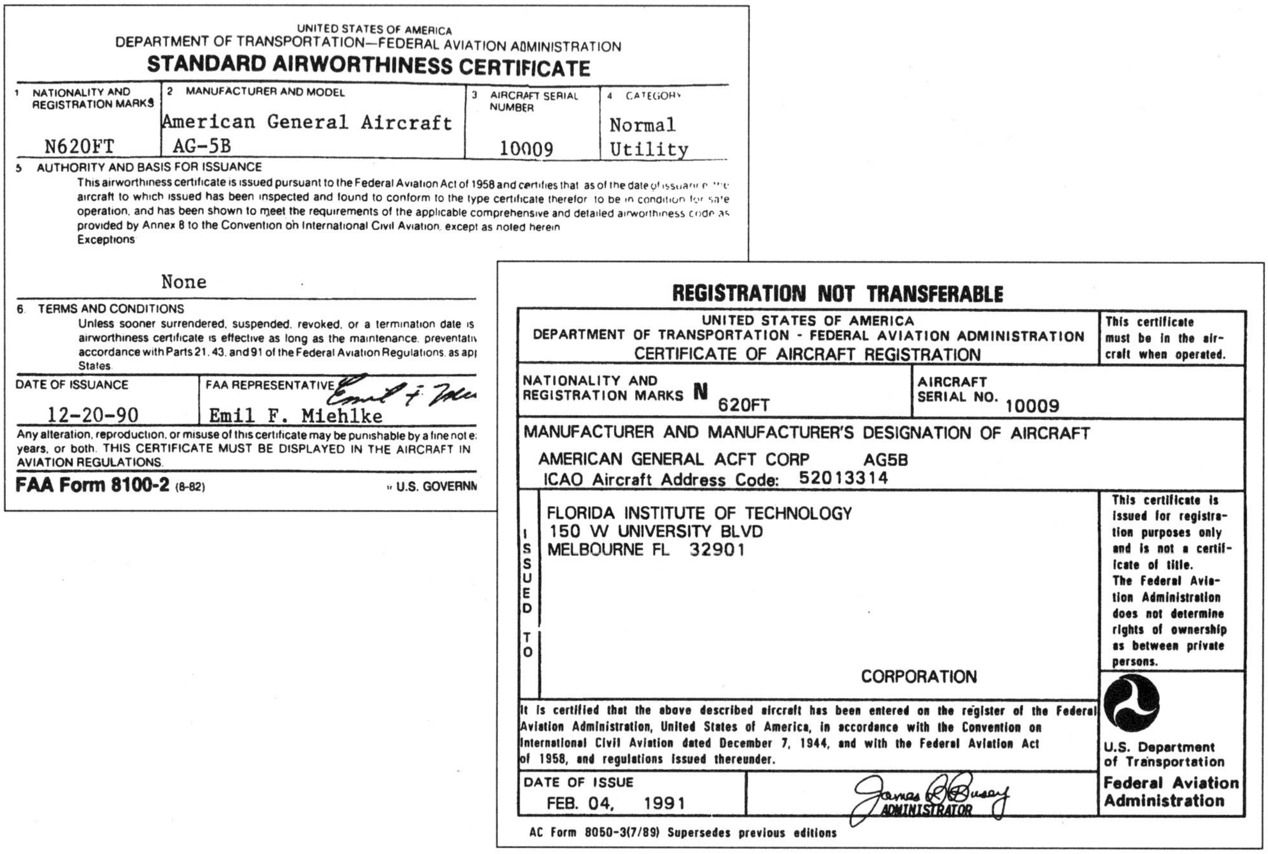
UNITED STATES OF AMERICA
DEPARTMENT OF TRANSPORTATION—FEDERAL AVIATION ADMINISTRATION
STANDARD AIRWORTHINESS CERTIFICATE

1 NATIONALITY AND REGISTRATION MARKS	2 MANUFACTURER AND MODEL	3 AIRCRAFT SERIAL NUMBER	4 CATEGORY
N620FT	American General Aircraft AG-5B	10009	Normal Utility

5 AUTHORITY AND BASIS FOR ISSUANCE
This airworthiness certificate is issued pursuant to the Federal Aviation Act of 1958 and certifies that as of the date of issuance the aircraft to which issued has been inspected and found to conform to the type certificate therefor to be in condition for safe operation, and has been shown to meet the requirements of the applicable comprehensive and detailed airworthiness code as provided by Annex 8 to the Convention on International Civil Aviation, except as noted herein
Exceptions

None

6 TERMS AND CONDITIONS
Unless sooner surrendered, suspended, revoked, or a termination date is airworthiness certificate is effective as long as the maintenance, preventati accordance with Parts 21, 43, and 91 of the Federal Aviation Regulations, as app States

DATE OF ISSUANCE	FAA REPRESENTATIVE
12-20-90	Emil F. Miehlke

Any alteration, reproduction, or misuse of this certificate may be punishable by a fine not e years, or both. THIS CERTIFICATE MUST BE DISPLAYED IN THE AIRCRAFT IN AVIATION REGULATIONS.
FAA Form 8100-2 (8-82) U.S. GOVERNM

REGISTRATION NOT TRANSFERABLE

UNITED STATES OF AMERICA
DEPARTMENT OF TRANSPORTATION - FEDERAL AVIATION ADMINISTRATION
CERTIFICATE OF AIRCRAFT REGISTRATION

This certificate must be in the aircraft when operated.

NATIONALITY AND REGISTRATION MARKS	AIRCRAFT SERIAL NO.
N 620FT	10009

MANUFACTURER AND MANUFACTURER'S DESIGNATION OF AIRCRAFT
AMERICAN GENERAL ACFT CORP AG5B
ICAO Aircraft Address Code: 52013314

ISSUED TO
FLORIDA INSTITUTE OF TECHNOLOGY
150 W UNIVERSITY BLVD
MELBOURNE FL 32901

CORPORATION

This certificate is issued for registration purposes only and is not a certificate of title. The Federal Aviation Administration does not determine rights of ownership as between private persons.

It is certified that the above described aircraft has been entered on the register of the Federal Aviation Administration, United States of America, in accordance with the Convention on International Civil Aviation dated December 7, 1944, and with the Federal Aviation Act of 1958, and regulations issued thereunder.

DATE OF ISSUE	
FEB. 04, 1991	ADMINISTRATOR

U.S. Department of Transportation
Federal Aviation Administration

AC Form 8050-3(7/89) Supersedes previous editions

Figure 25-12. Examples of airworthiness and registration certificates

Ensure that there is adequate fuel on board and complete your normal preflight duties, including the external (walk-around) inspection and internal inspection. Never hurry this aspect of the flight. It is most important that the preflight preparation is thorough and, even if you are running behind schedule because flight planning took longer than expected (a common reason), do not rush your normal preflight duties.

Correct and complete preflight preparation should ensure a smooth and trouble free flight.

Settle into the cockpit and place your navigation equipment and charts where they are readily accessible. Ensure that the charts are folded so that at least 20 nm either side of course is visible. Ensure that no metallic or magnetic objects are placed near the magnetic compass. Check on the comfort of your passengers (at this stage your flight instructor), and carry out any necessary briefing.

These final checks are worthwhile since, once the engine starts, the noise level will be higher, communication will be slightly more difficult, and you will be busier with the normal workload of manipulating the airplane.

Route segment	Safety Altitude	Altitude	Temp °C	TAS	Course			Wind °T	Heading						Speed/Distance/Time			
					TC (ref long)	Var	MC (VOR)		WCA	TH	Var	**MH**	Dev	CH	GS	Dist	ETE ATE	ETA ATA
Peter Creek R																		
Dermott	2800	5500	+10	107	062	4E	058	270/30	−9	053	4E	049	+1	050	132	65	30	
Kelly	1300	5500	+10	107	177	3E	174	270/30	+12	189	3E	186	+2	188	105	47	25	
															TOTAL	122	55	

Base your selection of cruise altitude on Magnetic Course (also use it when selecting VOR radials)

Calculate MH at flight planning stage, and apply any deviation in flight (found on compass card in aircraft)

DEVIATION CARD

FOR

N	30	60	E	120	150

STEER

001	031	060	089	118	149

FOR

S	210	240	W	300	330

STEER

181	213	242	271	301	330

ON ☒ RADIOS ☐ NO

Figure 25-13. Flight log for a flight from Peter Creek to Kelly, via Dermott

✍ Now complete **Review 25.**

✍ Review 25

1. When planning a VFR flight you should study _____ forecasts and _____ .
➤ meteorological forecasts, NOTAMs

2. Detailed information on airports is found in the _____ Directory.
➤ Airport/Facility Directory

3. You should normally plan a VFR flight to cruise at least _____ feet AGL over open country.
➤ 500 feet AGL

4. You should fly above mountainous terrain by at least _____ feet AGL, and you are requested to clear wildlife refuges by at least _____ feet AGL.
➤ 2,000 feet AGL, 2,000 feet AGL

5. When planning to fly more than 3,000 feet AGL, you should base your VFR cruise altitude on (true heading/magnetic heading/magnetic course/true course).
➤ magnetic course

6. VOR radials are based on (true/magnetic) north.
➤ magnetic

7. Cloud bases in Area Forecasts are given in feet (MSL/AGL).
➤ MSL

Flight Planning

8. Cloud bases in Terminal Aerodrome Forecasts are given in feet (MSL/AGL).
➤ AGL

9. What are suitable cruise altitudes at or above your safety altitude of 4,300 feet MSL if the cloud bases are at 7,000 feet MSL and your planned magnetic course is:
    (a) MC 060;
    (b) MC 250;
    (c) MC 179;
    (d) (d) MC 180.
➤ (a) 5,500 feet MSL; (b) 4,500 feet MSL or 6,500 feet MSL; (c) 5,500 feet MSL; (d) 4,500 feet MSL or 6,500 feet MSL

10. If you are planning a long VFR flight, you should show on the flight plan form communicated to FSS (all/the lowest/the highest/the initial) cruise altitude.
➤ the initial cruise altitude

11. Fuel information on a flight plan form submitted to FSS is expressed in (gallons/ hours and minutes).
➤ hours and minutes

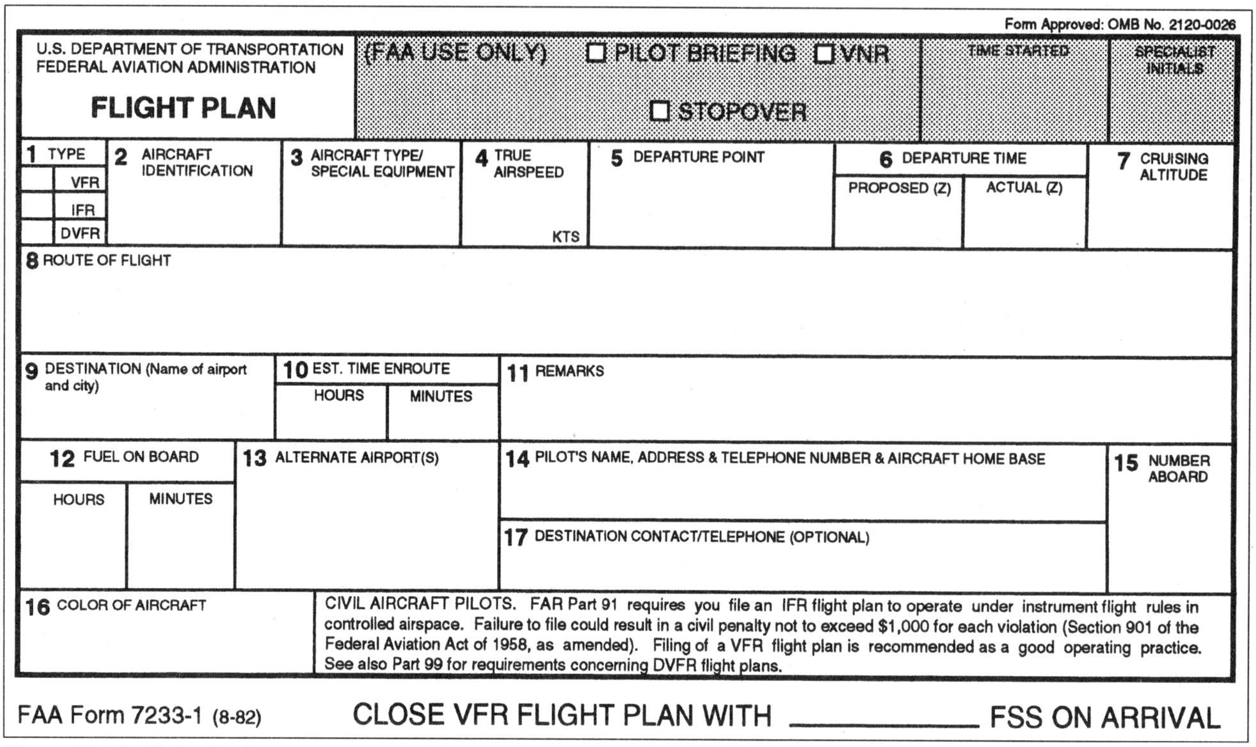
Form Approved: OMB No. 2120-0026
U.S. DEPARTMENT OF TRANSPORTATION
FEDERAL AVIATION ADMINISTRATION
FLIGHT PLAN
(FAA USE ONLY) ☐ PILOT BRIEFING ☐ VNR
☐ STOPOVER
TIME STARTED
SPECIALIST INITIALS
1 TYPE
VFR
IFR
DVFR
2 AIRCRAFT IDENTIFICATION
3 AIRCRAFT TYPE/ SPECIAL EQUIPMENT
4 TRUE AIRSPEED
KTS
5 DEPARTURE POINT
6 DEPARTURE TIME
PROPOSED (Z)
ACTUAL (Z)
7 CRUISING ALTITUDE
8 ROUTE OF FLIGHT
9 DESTINATION (Name of airport and city)
10 EST. TIME ENROUTE
HOURS
MINUTES
11 REMARKS
12 FUEL ON BOARD
HOURS
MINUTES
13 ALTERNATE AIRPORT(S)
14 PILOT'S NAME, ADDRESS & TELEPHONE NUMBER & AIRCRAFT HOME BASE
15 NUMBER ABOARD
17 DESTINATION CONTACT/TELEPHONE (OPTIONAL)
16 COLOR OF AIRCRAFT
CIVIL AIRCRAFT PILOTS. FAR Part 91 requires you file an IFR flight plan to operate under instrument flight rules in controlled airspace. Failure to file could result in a civil penalty not to exceed $1,000 for each violation (Section 901 of the Federal Aviation Act of 1958, as amended). Filing of a VFR flight plan is recommended as a good operating practice. See also Part 99 for requirements concerning DVFR flight plans.
FAA Form 7233-1 (8-82)
CLOSE VFR FLIGHT PLAN WITH ____________ FSS ON ARRIVAL

Figure 25-14. Flight plan form

For questions 12 to 14 refer to Figure 25-14.

12. If more than one cruising altitude is intended which should be entered in block 7 of the flight plan?
    (a) Initial cruising altitude.
    (b) Highest cruising altitude.
    (c) Lowest cruising altitude.

➤ (a)

13. What information should be entered in block 9 for a VFR day flight?
    (a) The name of the airport of first intended landing.
    (b) The name of destination airport if no stopover for more than 1 hour is anticipated.
    (c) The name of the airport where the aircraft is based.

➤ (b)

14. What information should be entered in block 12 for a VFR day flight?
    (a) The estimated time en route plus 30 minutes.
    (b) The estimated time en route plus 45 minutes.
    (c) The amount of usable fuel on board expressed in time.

➤ (c)

15. How should a VFR flight plan be closed at the completion of the flight at a controlled airport?
    (a) The tower will automatically close the flight plan when the aircraft turns off the runway.
    (b) The pilot must close the flight plan with the nearest FSS or other FAA facility on landing.
    (c) The tower will relay the instructions to the nearest FSS when the aircraft contacts the tower for landing.

➤ (b)

En Route Navigation 26

Introduction

As the pilot/navigator of a light airplane operating in visual conditions, you must be able to fly the airplane accurately and safely, and at the same time carry out the necessary navigation activities which will ensure that you arrive at your planned destination.

The basis of successful navigation is proper **preflight planning.** You must ensure that you measure the intended courses and distances accurately, and then apply the correct forecast wind velocities and planned TAS so as to derive the headings and groundspeeds. Once airborne, you must be able to confirm the actual track of the airplane over the ground and, if this turns out to be different from your planned course, know how to make proper estimates of the alteration to your heading so as to regain the planned course.

The aim of this chapter is to show you how to go about the business of pilot/navigation in an effective manner, and with the minimum interruption to the main task—flying the airplane safely. There are several components to successful pilot/navigation:

- **flight planning;**
- **chart-reading** (sometimes referred to as *pilotage*) which means determining your position over the ground by comparing the ground features with those marked on the chart;
- using **radio navigation aids** to assist and/or confirm your map-reading;
- **making corrections** to your flight path over the ground so as to regain your planned course and reach your destination; and
- using **deduced reckoning** to back up your other visual navigation methods.

As explained in Chapter 25, we need to work out a navigation plan for all flights. From this plan we will have established the headings, groundspeeds and time intervals between points on the route. We will also have preselected suitable ground features (or checkpoints) which we can use to assess the accuracy of our plan. To assist in the identification of these features we can note the estimated elapsed time between them, and if we have drawn tracking error lines, we will be able quickly to assess what alterations to heading we must make.

By flying your planned heading for an estimated time, you should arrive at or near the next checkpoint at the planned time. By comparing the chart to the ground, you will be able to *visually fix* your position without using radio navigation equipment.

Fixing the aircraft's position is not a continuous process second by second throughout the flight, but rather a regular process repeated every 10 or 15 minutes. (This may need to be reduced to a shorter interval in areas requiring very precise tracking like VFR Transition Routes through busy Class B airspace.)

A *fix* is the geographical position of an aircraft at a specific time determined by visual reference to the surface of the earth, or by radio navigation equipment.

A *pinpoint* is the ground position of an aircraft at a specific time determined by direct observation of the ground.

If you try to identify ground features to obtain a fix at shorter time intervals than this, then you may find yourself just flying from feature to feature without any time being available for the other important navigation tasks, such as planning ahead and monitoring the fuel situation.

For normal en route navigation you should fly the flight plan, fly accurately (by scanning the instruments and looking well ahead) and periodically identify landmarks.

Note: After each fix, it is a good idea to use the ground track and groundspeed achieved to mentally plan ahead to the next feature, so that you can anticipate it appearing in your view.

Compensating for Wind Effect

Most navigation calculations are to compensate for wind effect, so if the wind differs in either speed or direction from the forecast wind, then a **tracking error** will probably result.

If it is not possible to fix the position of the airplane, we can determine a DR position by plotting the calculated ground track and distance flown since the last fix, and mark this point on our chart.

At the flight planning stage, a forecast wind was used to calculate a HDG for the airplane to make good the desired course. This wind will almost certainly not be precisely the same as the actual wind experienced in flight.

Whether your ground track in flight is left or right of the desired course will depend on whether you have allowed a wind correction angle that is greater or lower than the actual drift.

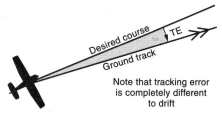

Figure 26-1. Tracking error is the angular difference between the desired course and the ground track

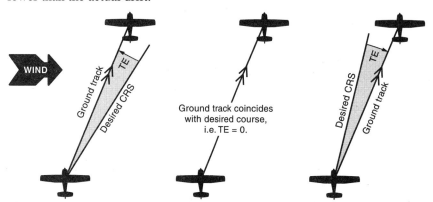

Figure 26-2. Tracking error results if WCA is greater or lesser than actual drift

If we find that we are not maintaining the planned course, then we can counteract a tracking error by modifying the heading and so regain the original course.

It is also usual to find that the actual in-flight groundspeed differs from that expected at the flight planning stage, when all we had at hand was the forecast winds. This means that the original **estimated times en route (ETEs)** to cover certain distances could be somewhat in error and may need to be modified once an accurate in-flight check of groundspeed is obtained. The **estimated time of arrival (ETA)** at any point can then be revised.

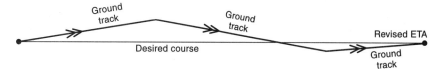

Figure 26-3. In-flight modification of HDGs and ETEs is usual in en route navigation

First and foremost, the most important way to keep in-flight navigation workload to a minimum is to be thorough in your preflight preparation. For in-flight navigation, concentrate on simple mental calculations and simple flight computer operations.

This will allow you to modify the headings and estimated times en route (ETEs) calculated at the flight planning stage without too much "head-down" work, and the methods that we discuss here will be adequate for most situations.

Airmanship

Airmanship is common sense. Fly the airplane accurately at all times (HDG ±5°; altitude ±100 feet; indicated airspeed ±5 knots). Even though you are looking out of the cockpit most of the time to monitor the attitude and heading of the airplane and to check for other traffic, you should periodically check the flight instruments to achieve precise heading, airspeed and altitude.

Fly accurately.

Setting the correct power and holding the attitude will result in the required performance in general terms but, to fly precisely, you will need to refer to the flight instruments and make suitable minor adjustments to the attitude and the power. This means take a quick look at the relevant flight instruments every 10 seconds or so throughout the flight. Strive to develop a rapid scan rate, which will assist accurate flying.

A rapid scan rate will assist accurate flying.

Ensure that the airplane is in trim, and can fly itself accurately "hands-off;" not that you will actually fly it hands-off, but correct trimming will considerably lighten your task of maintaining altitude and heading. Check that the IAS used in your preflight calculations is within 5 knots of that actually being flown, and that the altitude is within 100 feet; if not, do something about it by adjusting the power and the attitude.

Keep the airplane in trim.

Keep your paperwork in the cockpit neat and accessible. Do not work head-down for more than a few seconds at a time.

Keep a good lookout!

Continually **observe weather** conditions, not only ahead of you, but also to either side and behind (just in case you have to beat a hasty retreat). You must assess any deterioration in weather and modify your flight accordingly. Ask Flight Watch for an update on the weather en route and at your destination airport if you desire this information. Their function is to provide a service to you.

Be aware of the total weather picture.

Take appropriate action to **avoid hazardous conditions.** For instance, it is good airmanship to divert around thunderstorms instead of flying near or under them, and to avoid areas of fog and reduced visibility, as well as dense smoke from fires because the visibility will be reduced and the air turbulent.

Obtain a position fix every 10 or 15 minutes and update your headings and ETAs (more frequently in poor visibility and/or congested airspace).

Periodically fix your position.

Also, carry out **regular en route checks** of the magnetic compass and heading indicator alignment, engine instruments, and electrical and other systems. This en route check can be remembered by a convenient mnemonic such as "FREHA:"

Periodically check the operation of your airplane.

F ➤ Fuel ON and sufficient;
Fuel tank usage monitored;
Mixture, leaned as required for the cruise;
Fuel pump (if installed), as required.

R ➤ Radio frequency correctly selected, volume and squelch satisfactory, any required calls made.

E ➤ Engine: oil temperature and pressure within limits; carburetor heat if required; other systems checked, such as the electrical system, suction (if vacuum-driven gyroscopes are installed).

H ➤ Heading indicator (direction indicator or directional gyro) aligned with the magnetic compass, and your position checked on the chart.

A ➤ Altitude checked and the correct current altimeter setting in the pressure window.

Maintain a **time awareness,** so you always know how much fuel you have left and how much further (in terms of time) you can go before refueling.

Think of time.

The Flight Sequence

Departure from an Airport

On your initial exercises, the simplest method of departure may be to set your initial heading from directly over the top of the field at cruise speed and at the cruise altitude. The actual method of departing an airport will depend on the direction of the airport traffic pattern, and the nature of the airport and surrounding terrain.

Many airports have no restrictions placed on them, but this is not always the case. For instance, a number of airports lie within Class B, C, or D airspace, and have VFR Transition Routes which must be adhered to. Other airports may have local restrictions because of heavy traffic, high terrain or nearby built-up areas calling for special departure or arrival procedures. Refer to the Airport/Facility Directory, and to Terminal Area Charts.

If you depart by any means other than departing from over the top, then a simple calculation of **actual time of departure (ATD)** needs to be made. Your en route **estimated times of arrival (ETAs)** will be based on this (at least initially, until groundspeed checks allow you to update them).

We will consider *two* possible methods of departing on a course of, for example, 150°M from an airport where the appropriate runway to use is RWY 6 and the traffic pattern is left-handed. Assume airport elevation to be 1,200 feet MSL.

Since your compass will be experiencing acceleration and turning errors while setting course, ensure that the gyroscopic heading indicator is aligned with the magnetic compass prior to commencing your takeoff roll, and ensure that both the compass and the HI agree at least approximately with the runway direction.

Method 1. Turning in the Direction of the Traffic Pattern

After takeoff, climb out straight ahead and turn in the direction of the traffic pattern. Continue turns in the pattern direction and set course *overhead* the field at a suitable altitude above other aircraft in the traffic pattern. Log the actual time of departure (ATD) in the appropriate place on the flight log. The ATD will be your time of setting course overhead the airport.

Method 2. Climbing Straight Ahead until Well Clear of the Traffic Pattern before Turning to Take Up the Desired Heading

This second method can be used to *intercept* your desired course some distance from the airport, rather than setting course over the top. As you will not set course overhead the field, once on course you will need to estimate your actual time of departure (ATD) as if you had set course directly overhead. A GS of 120 knots is equivalent to 2 nm per minute, so if you set course at say 4 nm from the airport at time 1234 UTC and your estimated GS is about 120 knots, the ATD would be 2 minutes prior to this at 1232 UTC.

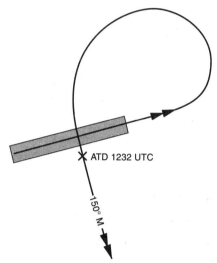

Figure 26-4. Method 1: Setting course overhead

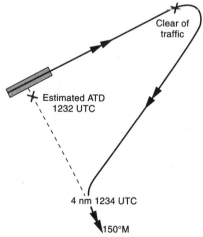

Figure 26-5. Method 2: Setting course en route and calculating ATD

If there is a laid down departure route via a specific point, then you can log your time of departure from that specific point. The main purpose is to have a starting point in time for your en route time calculations. Remember that fuel, however, is being burned from the moment the engine starts.

Immediately after setting course, you should log the actual time of departure (ATD) and insert your estimate overhead the first checkpoint, based on the ATD and the flight-planned ETE.

Rough Check of Departure Ground Track

On departure you should have in mind some ground feature en route which is within 10 or 15 nm of the airport, against which you can check that you are indeed tracking in approximately the right direction.

Example 1. After takeoff from a certain airport and taking up the calculated heading to achieve your desired course of say TC 150, you should pass slightly left of a large lake about 8 nm from the airport. To confirm that it is the correct lake, the chart shows a large hill with a radio mast on its northwest side, so you should use these to confirm your identification of it.

Within the first few minutes you should ensure that you are making good the correct course by obtaining a fix. Use your flight-planned groundspeed to calculate the ETA at the next checkpoint. If you are in any doubt, check the heading indicator against the magnetic compass. For accuracy, apply the deviation correction found on the card in the cockpit to amend degrees magnetic to degrees compass.

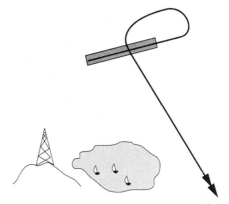

Figure 26-6. Check approximate course direction soon after departure

Cruise

On reaching the cruise level you should ensure that you have the correct local altimeter setting in the pressure window.

Establish cruise speed and cruise power and trim the airplane. Scan all the vital instruments and systems for correct operation. Verify that the gyroscopic HI is aligned with the magnetic compass. Now is a good time to do a full FREHA en route check.

It is good airmanship to check right away that you are achieving the desired heading and true airspeed (TAS) in cruise. This may be done very quickly by:

- noting a pre-planned ground "confidence feature" that lies on or close to the outbound track;
- setting the adjustable *temp/TAS* scale, if installed on your ASI, so that, as well as reading IAS on one scale, the other scale indicates TAS;
- using your flight computer (by setting pressure altitude against temperature, and reading off TAS on the outer scale against IAS on the inner); or
- approximation (at 5,000 feet TAS is about 8% greater than IAS, and at 10,000 feet TAS is about 17% greater than IAS);

If the achieved TAS is significantly different from that expected, then you should check:

- correct power set;
- correct airplane configuration—flaps up, and landing gear up and position of cowl flaps (if appropriate).

Check correct altimeter setting.

From two position fixes separated by about 20 to 30 nm, you should be able to establish an accurate groundspeed and determine if your heading is achieving the desired course or not. Naturally, if you are about to fly over featureless terrain or water where position fixing will be difficult, there is nothing to stop you using fixes obtained on the climb. Good airmanship is just a matter of common sense.

As soon as possible during the cruise obtain a groundspeed and heading check.

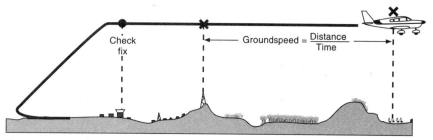

Figure 26-7. Obtain a check on GS and tracking early in the cruise

If the actual GS is significantly different from that calculated, then you will have to revise your ETAs. If your actual ground track differs significantly from the desired course, then you will have to make a HDG change. Make use of the best available information to estimate a suitable heading. Techniques of calculating the amount of HDG change are discussed later in this chapter.

To get good fixes you need to select good checkpoints and make use of your map-reading skills.

Chart-Reading in Flight

The success of map-reading depends on four basic factors:

- A knowledge of **direction.**
- A knowledge of **distance.**
- A knowledge of **groundspeed.**
- The selection and identification of **landmarks** and **checkpoints.**

Select good checkpoint features. Landmarks and checkpoints that can be easily identified, and which will be within your range of visibility when you pass by them, are best. Just how conspicuous a particular feature may be from the air depends on:

- the flight visibility;
- the dimensions of the feature;
- the relationship of your selected feature to other features; the angle of observation;
- the plan outline of the feature if you are flying high; and
- the elevation and side appearance of the feature if you are flying low.

Preferably the feature should be unique in that vicinity so that it cannot be confused with another nearby similar feature. A feature that is long in one dimension and quite sharply defined in another is often useful, because:

- if a long feature (such as a railroad, canal or road) runs *parallel* to your planned course, it can assist in maintaining accurate tracking; and
- if a long feature *crosses* the course it can be used as a position line to aid in determining an updated groundspeed (GS).

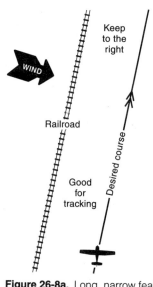

Figure 26-8a. Long, narrow features are particularly useful to parallel

The relationship between your selected feature and other nearby ground features is very important for a positive confirmation of your position. For example, there may be two small towns near each other, but you have chosen as a feature the one that has a single-track railroad to the west of the town and with a road that crosses a river on the north side of the town, whereas the other town has none of these features. This should make positive identification fairly easy.

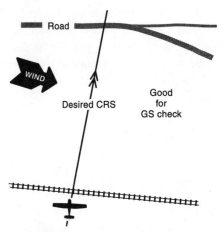

Figure 26-8b. Long, narrow features are particularly useful to cross perpendicular to, as well

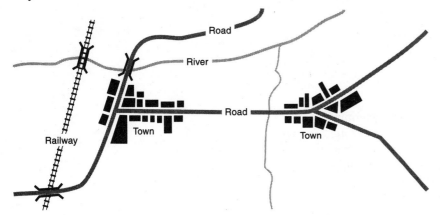

Figure 26-9. Confirm identification of your selected feature by its relationship with other features

Position Lines

A **position fix** is obtained when you can positively identify the position of the airplane relative to the ground. A **position line** is not as specific as a fix because you can only identify the position of the airplane as being somewhere along that line, and not actually fixed at a particular point.

You may see a position line referred to as a **PL line of position (LoP)**. Position lines can be obtained:

- from long narrow features such as railroads, roads, highways, and coastlines;
- from two features that line up as the airplane passes them (known as **transit bearings**);
- from magnetic bearings to (and from) a feature—this need not only be visual, it can also be a radio position line (a magnetic bearing from an NDB or VOR).

A position line is an extended straight line joining two points, somewhere along which the airplane was located at a particular time.

Figure 26-10. Each of these airplanes is on the same position line

It is normal to show a position line on your chart as a straight line with an arrowhead at either end, and with the time written in UTC at one end.

Figure 26-11. Marking a position line

Of course, if you can obtain two position lines that cut at a reasonable angle, then you can obtain a **good position fix.** For the airplane to be on both position lines at the one time, it must be at the point of intersection. For this reason, certain well-defined points along *Victor airways,* shown on aeronautical charts, are known as *intersections.*

Victor airways intersections are labeled at well-defined points.

Figure 26-12. Two position lines with a good cut can give you a fix

It is often possible to select two different VORs and determine which radials you are on. By marking these two radials (which are magnetic bearings from the VOR) on the chart using the compass roses centered on each of the VORs, the two position lines will intersect at your position. Radio navigation aids (such as VOR, NDB and DME) are discussed in detail in Chapter 28.

Feature Selection

Do not choose a multitude of landmarks and checkpoints. Just one good checkpoint every 10 or 15 minutes is sufficient. At a groundspeed (GS) of 120 knots, this puts them 20 to 30 nm apart. Using fixes any closer together than this can introduce significant errors in your calculations.

Knowing direction, distance and groundspeed, you can think ahead, and anticipate the appearance of a landmark.

Example 2. From a chart, the pilot chooses a small hill with a radio mast as a suitable checkpoint about 4 nm right of the desired course and about 20 nm ahead. If the groundspeed is 120 knots the pilot will expect to be abeam of this feature in 10 minutes. If the present time is 1529 UTC, the estimated time en route (ETE) of 10 minutes gives an estimate at, or abeam, the checkpoint at 1539 UTC. He will, of course, be keeping an eye out for it for some minutes prior to this.

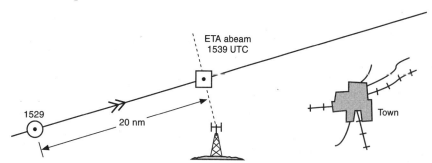

Figure 26-13. Look for a definite feature at a definite time

If, instead of passing 4 nm abeam of the feature as expected, the airplane passes directly overhead, the pilot recognizes from this fix that the airplane is off-course. It is appropriate to confirm that the feature is indeed the selected feature and not another nearby similar one. This can be done by checking the surrounding area for additional ground detail, say a small nearby town with a railroad junction. Strive to take in the whole picture.

Once certain of the position of the airplane at a particular time, the pilot can calculate a new heading to achieve the desired course. Two easy ways

Chart-reading is used to confirm your flight planning.

to do this are by using course guides (or *fan-lines*) already marked on the chart by you at the flight planning stage, or by using the "1-in-60 rule" (to be discussed shortly).

Chart Orientation in the Airplane

In flight, you should relate the land features and their relative bearing from the airplane to their representations on the chart. To do this it is best to place the chart so that your desired course runs from bottom to top.

If, according to the chart, a landmark is 30° off-course to the right from the present position of the airplane, then you should be able to spot it by looking out of the airplane window approximately 30° to the right of course. (Note: It may not be 30° to the right of the heading of the airplane because the heading may differ from the course, depending on the wind correction angle applied.)

With the chart oriented correctly in the cockpit, the features shown to the right of the course drawn on your chart will appear on the right of the airplane's ground track as you fly along. The only disadvantage is that it may be difficult to read what is printed on the chart, unless you happen to be flying north.

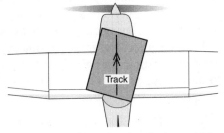

Figure 26-14. Orient the chart in the cockpit

Select a suitable feature on the chart 10 minutes or so ahead of your present position, calculate an ETA at, or abeam, it and then at the appropriate time (two or three minutes before the ETA) start looking for the actual feature on the ground. Do not expect the feature to be dead ahead. You should include a look-out 30° either side of the nose, and beneath the aircraft to several miles ahead. Your chosen landmark need not be in view at the time you choose it, but you should anticipate it coming into view at the appropriate time. If you have flown the plan accurately, and the weather forecast has been correct, then the feature should be where you expect it to be.

Log Keeping

The purpose of keeping an in-flight log is to record flight data. This enables you to determine your position at any time by DR and to have readily at hand the information required for position reporting by radio.

Keeping an in-flight log, however simple, helps in the methodical navigation sequence of:

- calculation of HDG to achieve a desired CRS;
- calculation of GS and ETE to determine ETA at the next checkpoint;
- anticipation and recognition of checkpoints; and
- recalculation of HDG, GS and ETEs if necessary.

An in-flight log need only be very basic. On a normal cross-country flight you should log:

- takeoff time on the flight log;
- actual time of departure (ATD) on the flight log;
- fixes (position and time) on the chart;
- ground track on the chart;
- changes of HDG (and airspeed), and time of making them;
- calculated GS;
- ETEs and revised ETAs at checkpoints; and
- altitudes.

This sounds like a lot, but it isn't. Indicating ground track and fixes on the chart simplifies things for you, as these cover the two fundamentals of your progress toward your destination.

Position Lines

Groundspeed Checks

You should continually update your groundspeed (GS) as the opportunities arise. *Time* is of vital importance in navigation and your time of arrival anywhere will depend on the GS that you achieve.

Position lines that are approximately at right angles to your course can assist in updating your GS. Noting the amount of time it takes to cover the distance between the two position lines allows you to calculate the GS.

Frequent groundspeed checks are important.

Example 3.

1351 UTC—Crossing a railroad perpendicular (at right angles) to course.

1359 UTC—Transit bearing of a radio mast and a bend in a river perpendicular to course 18 nm further on. 18 nm in 8 minutes = **GS 135 knots.**

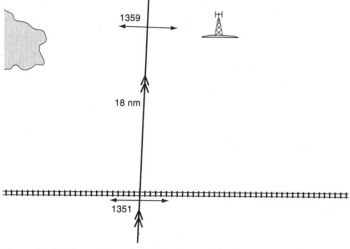

Figure 26-15. Groundspeed check using position lines perpendicular to track

These position lines need not only be visual. You could also make use of radio position lines from an abeam NDB or VOR radio navigation station.

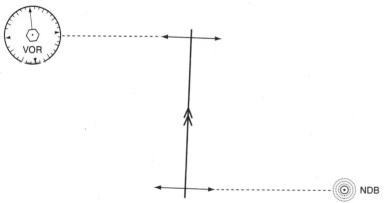

Figure 26-16. GS check using radio position lines from abeam radio navigation beacons (NDBs and VORs)

You can also carry out very simple GS checks using *distance measuring equipment (DME)* radio navaid stations directly on course, either ahead or behind. DMEs are discussed in detail in Chapter 28.

Example 4.

1325 UTC—DTY DME 67 nm and tracking directly toward the DME station.

1331 UTC—DTY DME 60 and tracking directly toward the DME station.

7 nm in 6 minutes = **GS 70** (which can now be used to revise ETAs).

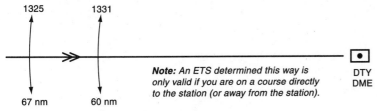

Figure 26-17. GS check using DME

Estimating Drift

If you have a position line roughly parallel to course you can use it to estimate the drift angle. Tracking directly overhead a long straight railroad makes a visual estimate of your drift angle quite easy, as does tracking along a radio position line to (or from) an NDB or VOR radio navaid station.

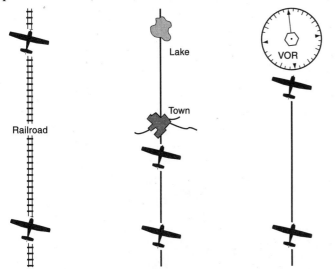

Figure 26-18. Determining drift angle from position lines parallel to track

✍ Now complete **Review 26, Part (a)** on page 590.

Off-Course Heading (HDG) Corrections

It is usual to find that the actual ground track differs from the desired course that you plotted on the chart at the flight planning stage. If this is the case, then you will have to make some precise corrections to the heading so that you can return to course at some point further on.

Since the in-flight workload for the pilot/navigator can be quite high, we will concentrate on quick methods of mentally calculating course corrections.

The angle between the ground track and the required course is called tracking error (TE).

The angle at which you want to close on your required course is known as the closing angle (CA). The size of the CA will depend on how much further down the ground track you wish to rejoin course. The sooner you want to rejoin the desired course the greater the CA will have to be.

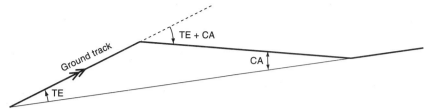

Figure 26-19. Tracking error and closing angle

Figure 26-19 shows that to rejoin the desired course at the chosen position will involve a *course change* equal to **TE + CA.** (This equation makes use of a theorem of geometry that says the external angle of a triangle equals the sum of the two interior opposite angles.)

It is at this point that we make an approximation that simplifies our in-flight calculations. We assume that a **course change** of, say, 15° can be achieved by a **heading change** of the same 15°. This is not perfectly accurate because the effect of the wind may cause a different drift angle after making a significant heading change, but within limits it is accurate enough for visual navigation.

The big advantage for pilot/navigators in doing this is that it allows us to make course corrections without having to calculate the actual wind velocity.

For angles up to about 15°, we can assume that a course change can be achieved by an equal heading change.

Correction Angle (Closing Angle)

With **course guides** (or fan-lines) already drawn on the chart at the flight planning stage and emanating from certain checkpoints along the route, the estimation of TE and CA to regain course at that next checkpoint is made very easy. After obtaining a fix, you can estimate TE and CA, which, when added together, will give you the required course change (and the required heading change) to close course at the next checkpoint.

An advantage is that you do not have to measure distance off-course, although this is in fact quite simple to do. A disadvantage is that you must have passed over the point from which the course guides emanate and you will rejoin course at the point ahead where the course guides close. Sometimes this is not the situation and other methods need to be employed.

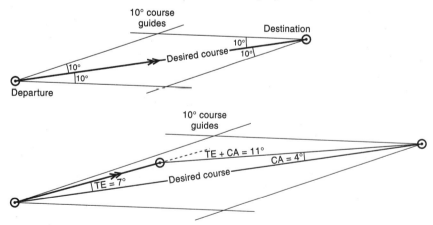

Figure 26-20. Track correction using course guides (or fan-lines)

If 5° and 10° course guides (10° is adequate if you are navigating a short stage) are drawn either side of the desired course on your chart, then estimation of tracking error in flight becomes easy.

The **1-in-60 rule** can be used to estimate correction angle. This is the most useful method of regaining course for the VFR pilot/navigator.

The 1-in-60 rule is based on the fact that: **1 nm subtends an angle of 1° at a distance of 60 nm.** This statement can be extended to say that:

- 5 nm subtends an angle of 5° at 60 nm;
- 10 nm subtends an angle of 10° at 60 nm; and
- 15 nm subtends an angle of 15° at 60 nm.

We cannot always wait until we have flown 60 nm to find our distance off-course, but that is of no concern because it is the *ratios* that we are interested in.

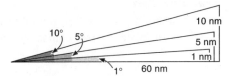

Figure 26-21. The 1-in-60 rule

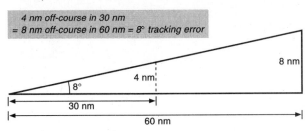

Figure 26-22. Example 5

Figure 26-23. The ratios set up on the calculator side

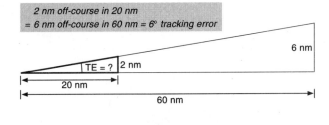

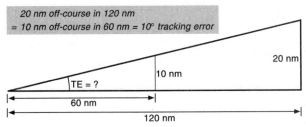

Figure 26-24. Determining tracking error using the 1-in-60 rule

Example 5. 4 nm off-course in 30 nm distance run is the same as:
    8 nm off-course in 60 nm, a **tracking error** of 8°.
We can do this calculation mentally or by computer.

✍ Now complete **Review 26, Part (b)** on page 590.

Tracking Error

If we change our TR by the amount of the calculated tracking error, we will simply *parallel* the desired course, and not reintercept it.

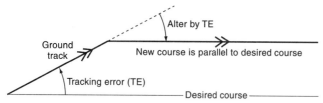

Figure 26-25. Paralleling course by altering HDG by the angle of TE

The same 1-in-60 rule can be applied to the CA once we have chosen the point at which we wish to rejoin course.

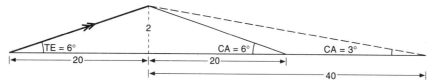

Figure 26-26. Calculating closing angle by the 1-in-60 rule

Now, knowing both TE and CA allows you to make a **heading change** (TE + CA) that should change your ground track by the same amount.

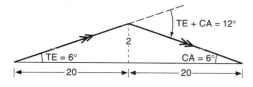

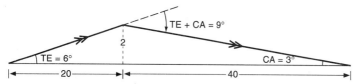

Figure 26-27. Changing HDG (and TR) by 'TE + CA' to rejoin desired course

Notice that **to regain course** at a distance ahead equal to the distance already traveled, you can simply change heading by **doubling the TE** so in this case the closing angle will equal the tracking error. If you had determined your tracking error at the halfway point, then this method would bring you back on-course at the next checkpoint.

This is also a convenient method of regaining course if you have to make a diversion, say around a thunderstorm en route. Turn a suitable angle off-course for so many minutes, and then turn back double that angle for the same number of minutes, and you should find yourself roughly back on course (depending on wind effect).

Example 6. After flying 25 nm on MH 085, you find yourself 4 nm left of course. What should be your new heading to regain course 25 nm further on?

    4 nm left of course in 25 nm = TE 10° left.

    To close 4 nm in a further 25 nm = CA 10°.

Therefore we need to **change heading 20° to the right,** to MH 105.

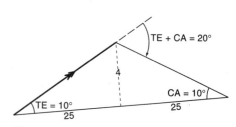

Figure 26-28. Example 6

Example 7. After 40 nm on MH 320 we find ourselves right of course by 4 nm. What heading should we steer to regain course in a further 20 nm?

4 nm in 40 = 6 in 60 = 6° TE to the right.

4 nm in 20 = 12 in 60 = 12° CA.

Therefore **change heading 18° to the left,** to MH 302.

✍ Now complete **Review 26, Part (c)** on page 590.

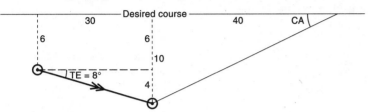

Figure 26-29. Example 7

Example 8. We obtain a fix 6 nm right of course, and 30 nm further on find ourselves 10 nm right of course after flying a steady heading of MH 065. Find the heading to steer to regain course 40 nm further on.

Figure 26-30. 1-in-60 rule, Example 8

We only have sufficient information to determine the ground track between the two fixes. To find the tracking error we will have to relate it, not to the desired course itself, but to a line *parallel* to the desired course.

TE =   4 nm in 30 = 8 in 60 = 8°.

CA = 10 nm in 40 nm = 15 in 60 = 15°.

Therefore to regain course 40 nm further on we need to **change heading by 23° to the left,** to MH 042.

Example 9. We obtain a fix 3 nm *left* of the desired course and take up heading MH 080 to rejoin course after 50 nm. 20 nm further on, we obtain a second fix 2 nm *right* of course and immediately change heading to rejoin course at the 50 nm point (now only 30 nm further on). Calculate the new heading.

Since we have no information regarding the tracking of the airplane prior to the first fix, we can only be sure of the ground track between the two fixes. The ground track, and therefore the heading, will have to change by an amount equal to TE + CA.

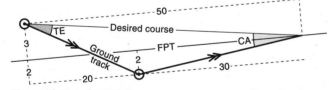

Figure 26-31a. Example 9

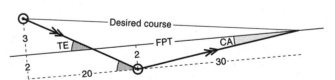

Figure 26-31b. Example 9

The CA shown in Figure 26-31a is the usual closing angle—in this case between desired course from the first fix and desired course from the second fix. The CA shown in Figure 26-31b is a different angle—between original course and desired course from the second fix.

The *sum* of TE + CA from Figure 26-31a is the same as the sum of TE + CA from Figure 26-31b. The latter method is used in this example (Figure 26-30b) because of its simplicity.

Working: TE = 5 nm in 20 = 15°. CA = 2 nm in 30 = 4°.

Therefore to rejoin course at the desired point we need to **alter heading by 19° to the left,** to MH 061.

✍ Now complete **Review 26, Part (d)** on page 591.

The Ratio Method

Course Corrections

The ratio method is an extension of the 1-in-60 rule.

If you wish to regain course in the *same* distance or time since you were last on-course, then change heading by double the TE because the CA will be equal to the TE.

If you wish to regain course in *double* the distance that it took you to get off-course, then the CA will be equal to only one-half the TE.

If you wish to regain course in only *half* the distance that it took you to get off-course, then the CA will be double the TE.

The following figures illustrate the ratio method of using the 1-in-60 rule.

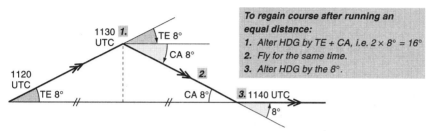

At point 1 (Figure 26-32) alter heading to *regain* course. At point 3, when back on course, alter heading to *maintain* course.

Figure 26-32. Example 10

Now we can regain course at *any* point we like. To do this we:

- alter HDG by the TE to approximately parallel the flight-planned CRS;
- alter HDG further by the CA (closing angle) to close on the CRS wherever we want; and then
- when CRS is regained, alter HDG back by the CA.

Now, so far we have only discussed how to regain the desired course. Once we do this, if we do not alter the heading we used to regain course we will fly straight through the desired course.

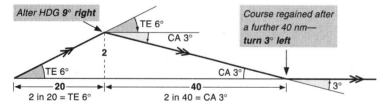

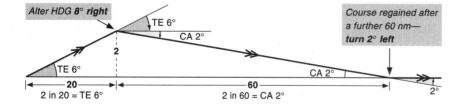

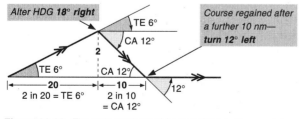

Figure 26-33. The ratio method of finding CA (closing angle)

Maintaining Desired Course

From the preceding diagrams it is clear that to remain on-course you will have to alter your latest ground track (the track flown over the ground as you returned to the desired course) by an amount equal to the chosen CA.

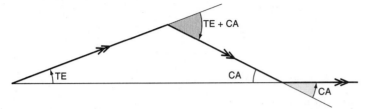

Figure 26-34. When back on-course, change heading by the chosen closing angle

The Inverse-Ratio Method

In some congested areas, it is difficult to fly direct routes over long distances because of the presence of different classes of airspace, and restricted and prohibited areas. Normally we have to fly a series of shorter legs with a number of turning points to avoid such areas. It is sound planning to select turning points that can be easily identified, such as prominent landmarks.

With short legs, the 1-in-60 rule can be simplified even further by concentrating on the CA to the next turning point and using what is known as the **inverse-ratio** method.

The inverse-ratio method is especially useful at the half-way point. Previously we saw that, to rejoin course in a distance equal to that already traveled since we were last on-course, TE = CA. We would then alter heading by this amount which (since TE = CA) is equal to 2 CA. This is the situation if we fix the position of the airplane at the half-way point along a straight course leg.

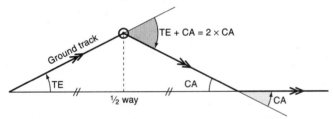

Figure 26-35. If "distance-to-go" = "distance-gone," then alter heading by '2 × CA'

The inverse-ratio method can also be used at other points en route. At any common fraction of the ground track gone then, to regain course, alter heading by *CA the inverse of the fraction of the distance gone.*

- At the half-way point, alter heading by CA 2, as we have just seen.
- At the third-way point, alter heading by CA × 3.
- At the quarter-way point, alter heading by CA × 4.
- At the fifth-way point, alter heading by CA × 5.

Example 10. A course leg is 45 nm. After traveling 15 nm, you are 2 nm to the left of course. You need to regain course at the next turning point.

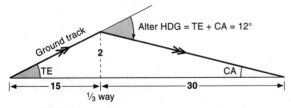

Figure 26-36. Example 10

Previous method:
TE is 2 nm in 15 nm = 8 nm in 60 nm = 8° TE.
CA is 2 nm in 30 nm = 4 nm in 60 nm = 4° CA.
Alter heading by TE + CA = 12°.

Inverse-ratio method:
$^1/_3$ of ground track gone.
Alter heading by CA $\times$ 3 = 4° $\times$ 3 = 12°.

Eyeballing and the Inverse-Ratio Method

Proper preparation of our chart can make in-flight course corrections easy. Mark 5° and 10° course guides either side of the desired course from the *end* of that course. Divide the course into quarters and mark these points. It is now easy to eyeball both closing angle and fraction of course gone for any fix that we obtain.

Example 11.

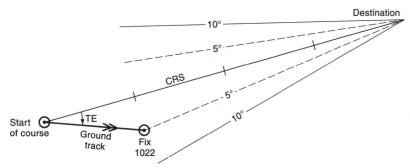

Figure 26-37. Example 11

By eyeball, CA = 5° and fraction gone is $^1/_4$.
Alter heading by 5° $\times$ 4 = **20° to the left.**

Note: The same inverse-ratio method can be used to revise the ETE.

Time gone from start to fix is 7 min,
therefore total time for leg = 7 $\times$ 4 = **28 min.**

A limitation of the inverse-ratio method is that it only allows for one alteration of heading per leg, and it only regains course at the next turning point. For short legs this is not a significant disadvantage and the method is more than adequate. Its simplicity greatly reduces the workload in the cockpit for just a little extra effort at the flight planning stage.

A Slightly Harder Application of the Inverse-Ratio Method

Some pilots have trouble accurately estimating the fraction of the distance gone. Eyeballing will not be perfect but, as long as your estimate is reasonable, a practical course correction can be made.

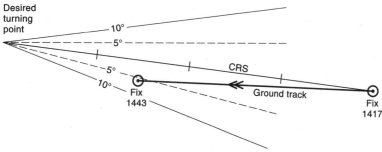

Figure 26-38. Example 12

Example 12. Calculating a heading alteration and a revised ETA.

By eyeball: fraction gone two thirds. CA = 6°.

Alter heading by "6° × one and a half" ($\frac{3}{2}$ being the inverse ratio of $\frac{2}{3}$) = 9° to the right.

Time gone = 26 min.
Revised total time = 26 × one and a half = 39 min.
Revised ETA = 1417 + 39 = 1456 UTC.

Answer. Alter heading by 9° right. Revised ETA 1456 UTC—no computer manipulations were necessary.

✍ Now complete **Review 26, Part (e)** on page 591.

Diversions

En Route Diversions

Occasionally, en route, you have the need to divert around a thunderstorm, a heavy rain shower, or a town. If there are suitable landmarks you can use these to assist you to divert around the "obstacle" and then to return to course.

If there are no suitable landmarks, then it is a good idea to follow a simple procedure such as:

• Divert 60° to one side of the desired course for a suitable time (and note the HDG and time flown).

• Parallel course for a suitable time (and note the time flown).

• Return at 60° for the same time to return to course.

• Take up a suitable HDG to maintain course.

Note: A 60° diversion is convenient because an equilateral (equal-sided) triangle's three angles are each 60°. However, depending on circumstance, a different angle can be flown.

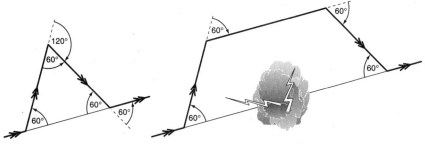

Figure 26-39. The angles of an equal-sided triangle are each 60°

With a 60° diversion followed immediately by a 60° return to course, the actual distance flown on the diversion is *double* the on-course distance. In nil-wind conditions this will take *double* the time.

If the initial 60° diversion HDG is flown for 2 minutes, and the "return to course leg" is flown for 2 minutes then the dogleg has therefore taken 4 minutes, which means the direct on-course time interval has been exceeded by 2 minutes. Our ETA at the next checkpoint will therefore be 2 minutes later than previously estimated. If we had flown 5 minute diversion legs, then it would add 5 minutes to our ETA. The length of the leg flown parallel to course will not affect the ETA.

Note: We have assumed no-wind conditions in this discussion. If a significant wind is blowing, then you have to make appropriate allowances for it.

Diversion to an Alternate Airport

Sometimes it may be necessary to divert from our planned destination. This may be because of deteriorating weather at the destination, the possibility of running out of daylight if you continue the flight to your original destination, or a suspected mechanical problem that suggests an early landing would be advisable. If the diversion entails a small change in HDG (say up to 15°), then using the 1-in-60 rule is adequate.

Example 13. You are tracking TC 320 to your destination airport which is 135 nm further on when you receive a weather report stating that a large thunderstorm is approaching the airport. Your HDG is MH 315 and your GS is 133 knots.

You decide to divert and land at a small airport which, from your present position, is located 10 nm to the right of course and 42 nm distant. Calculate an approximate HDG to steer and an approximate ETE.

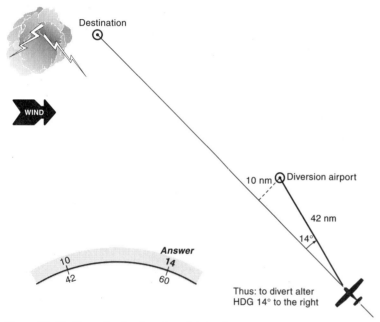

Figure 26-40. Example of a diversion slightly off the desired course using the 1-in-60 rule

10 nm in 42 nm = 14 in 60 = 14° to the right of your present ground track.

Because the change in direction is only 14°, a course change of 14° will be achieved reasonably accurately by a HDG change of 14°. (This is because the wind effect will not differ greatly between the two courses.) Similarly, we can assume the GS to be unaltered because of the similar winds on the two similar courses.

Therefore: Steer a HDG of (315 + 14) = **MH 329** to achieve a CRS of (320 + 14) = TC 334.

42 nm at a GS of 133 knots = **ETE 19 minutes.**

If a diversion requires a *significant change* of heading (and this is often the case), then the wind effect on the new course may differ significantly from that on the original course. The drift experienced may be quite different on the two different headings. In this case it will be necessary to use your computer to calculate the HDG and GS on the new CRS using the latest and most accurate W/V that you have.

Example 14. En route from ALFA to BRAVO. Approaching CHARLIE, you decide to divert to DELTA.

The best technique to use is to maintain HDG and original CRS to the next checkpoint (say CHARLIE) and carry out calculations to enable you to divert from that known position. (5 minutes should be more than enough to get yourself organized for an accurate diversion.)

Measure the **course and distance** from your diversion point to the diversion airport, and, using the known TAS and the most accurate (W/V) available, calculate the HDG to steer, and the expected GS, from which you can find an ETE and ETA overhead the airport.

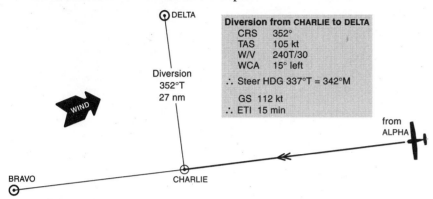

Figure 26-41. Example of a diversion involving a significant change of heading

Check your answers with quick mental approximations.

Calculations: CHARLIE to DELTA, TC 352, 27 nm, VAR 5°W.
TAS 105, W/V 240°T/30

By computer: WCA is 15° left, steer TH 337 **MH 342**
GS 112 knots, **ETE** (for 27 nm) **15 min.**

Some Practical Hints on Diversions

Diversions sometimes become necessary at the most inopportune moments, possibly when you have other problems on your hands. It therefore pays to have a few tricks up your sleeve to allow you to make quick and practical diversions without having to get your computer out and go "head-down" in the cockpit.

If you can estimate direction and distance by eyeballing, then your diversion will be easier. Once you have taken up an approximate diversion heading and settled into the diversion course, you can calculate an accurate heading, distance to go, groundspeed and ETE in a more relaxed atmosphere.

When established on your diversion, inform the nearest FSS and do not forget to **close your flight plan** when you arrive at the diversion airport. Pilots usually close flight plans after landing by telephoning the nearest FSS, or by requesting the controllers in the tower to relay the cancellation to FSS.

Eyeballing Course

Estimation of course is surprisingly easy and, with a bit of practice, you can achieve a ±5° accuracy. In fact, you should *always* estimate your course before measuring it with a protractor or plotter—this will avoid making 180° or 90° errors. Estimating before measuring will also help you develop faith in your ability to estimate to a practical degree of accuracy.

"Halving known angles" is the simplest means of estimating angles. Halving the angle between a quadrantal point and a cardinal point will give you an angle of 22.5°, say 22°, and halving this again will give you 11°. An accuracy of ±5° will be achieved with practice.

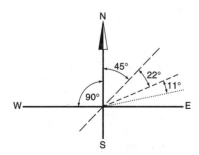

Figure 26-42. Halving angles as a means of estimating track

Estimating Distance

The average adult top thumb-joint will cover about 10 nm on a 1:500,000 Sectional chart (and 5 nm on 1:250,000 VFR Terminal Chart). Check yours!

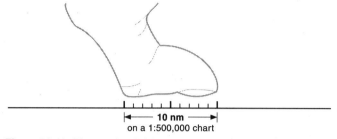

Figure 26-43. The top thumb-joint covers approx. 10 nm at 1:500,000

A full hand span might measure 60 nm on a 1:500,000 chart. Check yours!

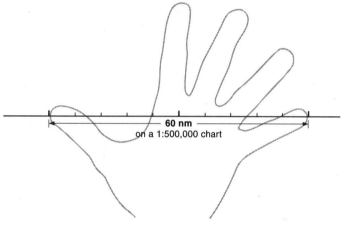

Figure 26-44. A full hand span is approx. 60 nm on a 1:500,000 chart

If you have a 60 nm span and a 10 nm top thumb-joint, then you have an built-in 1:60 measuring device, ideally designed to measure 10°.

10 nm in 60 nm = 10°, by the 1-in-60 rule.

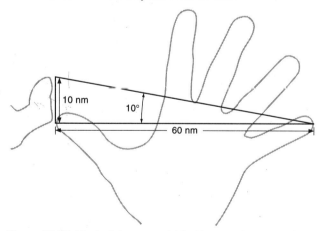

Figure 26-45. The built-in personal 1-in-60 measuring device for 10°

Navigation Operations

Visibility

As a VFR pilot, you should only conduct cross-country flights in visual meteorological weather conditions that are forecast to permit continual observations of the ground. You should generally be able to spot each check feature at an appropriate time prior to reaching or passing abeam it.

Poor Visibility

Poor visibility may be caused by smoke, haze, mist, rain, or smog. It makes the handling of the airplane more difficult since the lack of a natural horizon makes holding an attitude more difficult. Poor visibility also means that checkpoints may not come into view until you are almost upon them and, if the checkpoints are some distance off-course, you may not even see them.

Sooner or later you will be faced with reduced visibility. If you feel that VFR conditions cannot be maintained, or if the visibility (even if in excess of VFR minimum requirements) is not adequate for your particular flight and your particular experience, you should think about turning back or diverting to a destination with better weather.

Consideration should also be given to slowing down the airplane and even extending some flap in a precautionary configuration. A slower speed gives you more time to see things, as well as reducing your radius of turn if maneuvering is required.

If you are expecting poor visibility en route, select more en route checkpoints that are closer to your desired course. This will reduce the time between fixes and reduce the anxiety you feel if you do not spot one of the check features, but the next one comes up on time shortly thereafter. If several checkpoints fail to appear, you could have reason to feel uncertain of position.

Good visibility decreases the workload on the VFR pilot/navigator.

Poor visibility increases workload dramatically.

Uncertain of Position

If you have flown for some time without obtaining a fix (say 20 or 30 minutes), you may feel a little uncertain of your precise position. You will be able to calculate a DR position (using expected TR and GS), but you may feel a little anxious that you cannot back this up with a positive fix over or abeam some ground feature. Don't panic, you are not yet lost.

If a checkpoint does not come into view at the expected time, log HDG (compass and heading indicator readings) and time. If the heading indicator is incorrectly set, then you have the information needed to make a fair estimate of your actual position, so reset the HI and calculate a HDG and ETE to regain the desired course; or if the HI is aligned correctly with the compass, then the non-appearance of a landmark, while it will perhaps cause you some concern, need not indicate that you are grossly off-course. You may not have seen the landmark for some perfectly legitimate reason, such as bright sunlight obscuring your vision, poor visibility, a change in the ground features not reflected on the chart (such as removal of a TV mast or the emptying of a reservoir), or if you are navigating above even a small amount of cloud, the inconvenient positioning of some clouds may have obscured your check point.

If you consider the situation warrants it, make a radio call to FSS or ATC. They may be able to fix your position by radar or VHF/DF. If you obtain a fix, or if the next checkpoint comes up on time, the flight can continue and normal navigation procedures apply once again. If still unable to fix your position, follow the procedure below.

If uncertain of your position, consider a radio call to FSS or ATC.

Procedure when Lost

Becoming lost is usually the result of some human error. Being lost is totally different from being *temporarily uncertain* of your position, where you can determine a reasonably accurate DR position.

It is impossible to lay down a set of hard and fast rules on what to do, except to give you the advice that careful preflight planning and in-flight attention to the normal, simple en route navigation tasks will ensure that you will not get lost. Also, using radio navigation aids (discussed shortly) to back up your visual navigation will help to keep you oriented.

If you change your thinking from one of being *uncertain of position* to one of being *lost,* then make use of a nearby FSS or ATC and any radar or position-fixing service if available. If you are still lost, maintain HDG (if terrain, visibility and what you know of the proximity of controlled airspace permit) and carry out a **sequence of positive actions.** If a vital checkpoint is not in view at your ETA, then continue to fly for 10% of the time since your last positive fix. Decide what your last positive fix was, and **check the headings flown since that last fix,** ensuring that:

If lost, you must formulate a plan of action.

- the magnetic compass is not being affected by outside influences such as a camera, portable radio, headset or other magnetic material placed near it;
- the HI is aligned with the magnetic compass correctly;
- magnetic variation and drift have been correctly applied to obtain your HDGs flown;
- an estimate of course direction on the chart against that shown on the flight plan is correct.

Read from ground to chart. Look for **significant ground features** or combinations of features and try to determine their position on the chart. Establish a **"most probable area"** in which you think you are. There are several ways in which this can be done, and we recommend that you consult your flight instructor for his or her preferred method.

Two suggested methods for establishing a "most probable area" are:

Method 1. Estimate the distance flown since the last fix and apply this distance, plus or minus 10%, to an arc 30° either side of what you estimate the probable ground course to be.

Method 2. Estimate your "most probable position" and draw a circle around it of radius equal to 10% the distance flown since the last fix.

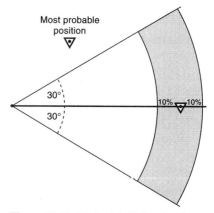

Figure 26-46. Method 1. Estimating the "most probable area" that you are in

Figure 26-47. Method 2 for estimating "most probable position"

- Establish a **safety altitude** at which to fly in order to ensure adequate clearance of all obstacles in what you consider the general area to be. Use MEF to determine the highest terrain or obstruction in the area as a basis from which to establish a safety altitude. Be especially careful in conditions of poor visibility or low clouds.

- Check **large features** within this area of the chart with what can be seen on the ground. Try to relate those features seen on the ground with those shown on the chart. Confirm the identification of any feature by closely observing secondary details around the feature. For instance, a small irregular lake may be confirmed by the position of a small town on a bend in the railroad as it turns from west to south. Double check any fix.

When you do positively establish a fix, recheck your HI and recommence normal navigation activity. Calculate the HDG, GS and ETE for the next check feature and set course for it.

If you are still unable to fix your position, you should consider taking one of the following actions:

- Inform ATC and request assistance.
- Increase the 'most probable area' by 10, 15 or even 20% of the distance flown from the last fix.
- Climb to a higher altitude to increase your range of vision.
- Turn toward a known prominent line feature, such as a coastline, large river, railroad or road, and then follow along it to the next town where you should be able to obtain a fix.
- Steer a reciprocal heading and attempt to return to your last fix.

Note the following important points of airmanship:

- If you want to cover as much ground as possible with the fuel you have available, you should fly the airplane for **best range.**
- Keep a **navigation log** going.
- Remain positively **aware of time.** Keep your eye on the fuel and on the time remaining until the end of daylight. If darkness is approaching, remember that it will be darker at ground level than at altitude, and that it becomes dark very quickly in the tropics.
- If you decide to carry out a precautionary search and landing (a forced landing with the use of power), allow sufficient time and fuel to do this on the assumption that two or three inspections might have to be made before finding a suitable landing area.

Why Did You Become Lost?

If at any stage you became lost, you should systematically try to determine the reason (either in flight or post flight) so that you can learn from the experience. Common reasons for becoming lost include:

- Incorrectly calculated HDGs, GSs, and ETEs (hence the need for you always to make *mental estimates* of approximate answers to these items).
- Incorrectly synchronized HI. Remember to check that the gyroscopic HI is aligned correctly with the magnetic compass every 10 or 15 minutes.
- A faulty compass reading (caused by transistor radios, cameras and other metal objects placed near the compass).
- Incorrectly applied variation (variation west, magnetic best; variation east, magnetic least).
- Incorrectly applied drift (compared with CRS, the HDG should be into the wind. Flying north with a westerly wind blowing would mean that the HDG should be to the left of course and into the wind.
- A wind velocity significantly different from that forecast, and not allowed for in flight by the pilot.
- A deterioration in weather, reduced visibility, increased cockpit workload.

- An incorrect fix, such as mis-identification of a check feature.
- A poorly planned diversion from the original desired course.
- Not paying attention to carrying out normal navigation tasks throughout the flight.

With regular checks of HI alignment with the magnetic compass, reasonably accurate flying of HDG, and with position fixes every 10 or 15 minutes, none of these errors should put you far off-course. It is only when you are slack and let things go a bit too far, that you become lost.

Mental Navigation Checks

If you develop the skill of carrying out mental navigation checks in flight, then it will be less likely that you will ever make a gross navigational error. Each time you are flying, not only on cross-countries but also out in the local training area, practice estimating tracks, distances and altitudes.

Develop the skill of making quick mental checks.

Wind Components

When flight planning and also en route, it is a good idea to keep a mental check on all your heading and GS calculations. Some formulae based on trigonometry can be memorized, but it is easier to remember the following:

- a headwind component reduces groundspeed to less than true airspeed;
- a tailwind component increases groundspeed to more than true airspeed;
- to achieve the desired course, the airplane must be headed somewhat into wind.

Example 15. Your desired course is west and the wind is from 220°. Having a headwind component, your GS should be less than TAS.

Your heading must be into the wind compared to desired course and so will be to the left of west, a heading less than 270°. With this in mind, you check that your flight plan and en route calculations reflect this, with GS less than TAS, and HDG less than the course in this case.

Estimating Distances

Keep in mind that a **sight-down** angle of 45° from the horizon gives an approximate horizontal distance equal to your altitude AGL—either ahead or to the side.

Example 16.

(a) If you are 7,000 feet above terrain which is 1,000 feet MSL, height above ground level is 6,000 feet AGL (approx. 1 nm), and so a sight-down angle of 45° gives a horizontal distance of 1 nm.

(b) At 12,000 feet AGL, a sight-down angle of 45° gives 2 nm.

(c) At 3,000 feet AGL, a sight-down angle of 45° gives 0.5 nm.

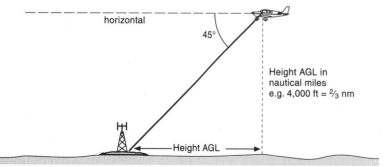

Figure 26-48. Estimating distances using sight-down angle 45° below the horizon

Low-Level Navigation

Low-level navigation means navigation at about 500 feet AGL. It is carried out in the same way as normal navigation at higher altitudes, with a few special considerations.

At a low level you will have a limited field of vision. You will also have to keep a constant lookout because of your close proximity to terrain. This means that at the preflight stage you should study your charts and choose suitable checkpoints, reasonably close to course and perhaps greater in number than for a similar flight at a higher altitude.

The elevation of nearby features above the general level of the surrounding terrain is more important for a low-level flight, because they will be seen side-on rather than from above.

Spot heights such as radio masts, factory chimneys, and church steeples are useful at low level, but may be almost invisible when flying at high altitudes. Railroads at the bottom of cuttings may be visible from altitude, but not visible from a low level unless you are directly over them.

The presence of unusually high and difficult-to-see obstructions and built-up areas must be anticipated and avoided.

Your limited field of vision means that you need to anticipate the sighting of check features and recognize them quickly (hence the need for careful study of your charts before commencing the low-level navigation exercise).

If a ground feature fails to appear at its ETA, there will be no time to be too concerned and search for it. Assume that it has been passed and concentrate on looking for the next check features, which should not be too far ahead. Only if you fail to spot several consecutive check features should you become "uncertain of your position". Mental DR in such a situation is invaluable in determining the probable position.

Log keeping on a low-level exercise will be restricted because of the greater concentration required on things outside the cockpit. Because of airplane handling considerations, and the need to keep a good lookout, it may at times be impossible to make any but the briefest log entries or marks on your chart.

Use check features with vertical extent for low level navigation.

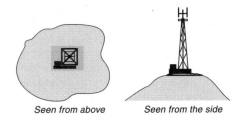

Seen from above   *Seen from the side*

Figure 26-49. The side elevation of check features is important in low-level navigation

Keep a good lookout and your head up at low level.

The Emergency Locator Transmitter (ELT)

In remote areas visual searches can be difficult. The emergency locator transmitter (ELT), if properly used, can allow the search area to be reduced quickly so that the visual search can be concentrated in a small area.

ELT is a generic (family) term covering devices known as crash locator beacons or emergency locator beacons. They all operate on both 121.5 and 243.0 MHz.

A few common sense points on the use of the ELT are:

- Know how to use the ELT and how to gain access to it if it is not remotely controlled. Review the operating instructions for your particular beacon prior to flight.

- Ensure that the battery is fully charged.

- Ensure that the ELT is capable of operating properly (tests are restricted so seek the advice of the authorities before activating a test as it may result in the commencement of unnecessary search and rescue action).

- If you are forced down, however, do not be reluctant to activate the ELT at an appropriate time.

✍ Now complete **Review 26, Part (f)** on page 591.

⬚ Review 26

Part (a)

1. The angle between the HDG and the ground track is called _____ .

➤ drift

---

2. The angle between the desired course and the ground track is called the _____ .

➤ tracking error

---

3. A known position of an airplane at a given time is called a _____ or a _____ .

➤ fix, pinpoint

---

4. Normal en route visual navigation should consist of flying accurate _____ and identifying _____ .

➤ headings, landmarks

---

5. You cross a small town at 0325 UTC followed by a railroad junction some 27 nm further on at 0340 UTC. What is your groundspeed?

➤ 108 knots

Part (b)

1. If you are 3 nm off-course to the right in 20 nm, what is your tracking error?

➤ 9° right

En Route Navigation

2. If you are 5 nm off-course to the right in 30 nm, your tracking error is _____ .

➤ 10° right

---

3. If you are 2 nm off-course to the left in 40 nm, tracking error is _____ .

➤ 3° left

Part (c)

1. You are 2 nm left of course after traveling 15 nm.
   (a) What is the tracking error?
   (b) To regain course in another 15 nm, what is the closing angle?
   (c) To regain course in another 30 nm, what is the closing angle?

➤ (a) 8° left; (b) 8°; (c) 4°

---

2. You are 4 nm right of course after traveling 20 nm. By how many degrees should you change heading to regain course in another 40 nm?

➤ TE = 12°, CA = 6°, so change heading by 18° left

---

3. You are on a long flight of 249 nm across featureless terrain. After flying a steady HDG for 96 nm you find yourself 13 nm right of course. By what amount should you alter your HDG by to regain course:
   (a) at the destination?
   (b) 50 nm before the destination?
   (c) 20 nm before the destination?

➤ (a)13° left; (b) 16° left; (c) 14° left; (*see* Figure 26-50)

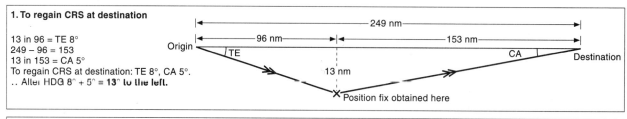

1. To regain CRS at destination

13 in 96 = TE 8°
249 – 96 = 153
13 in 153 = CA 5°
To regain CRS at destination: TE 8°, CA 5°.
∴ Alter HDG 8° + 5° = **13° to the left.**

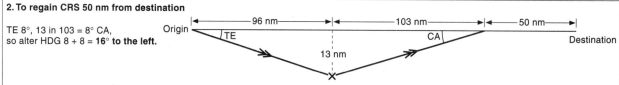

2. To regain CRS 50 nm from destination

TE 8°, 13 in 103 = 8° CA,
so alter HDG 8 + 8 = **16° to the left.**

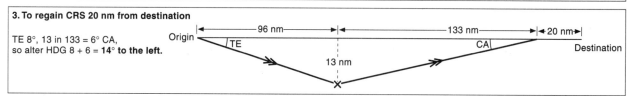

3. To regain CRS 20 nm from destination

TE 8°, 13 in 133 = 6° CA,
so alter HDG 8 + 6 = **14° to the left.**

Figure 26-50.

4. At 0315 UTC you are on course, MH 080. At 0325 UTC you are 3 nm left of course after traveling 20 nm. By what amount should you alter HDG to be back on course at 0335 UTC?

➤ TE = 3 in 20 = 9° left
   Note: We assume that in the following 10 minutes you will travel the same distance as in the previous 10 minutes, i.e. 20 nm; therefore CA = 3 in 20 = 9°. Alter HDG by 18° to the right, i.e. to MH 098.

Part (d)

1. We obtain a fix 5 nm left of course and make a HDG correction in an attempt to return to course. 20 nm further on we find that we are now 8 nm left of course.
   (a) What is the TE?
   (b) What is the closing angle (CA) if we want to return to course in another 60 nm?
   (c) By how much should we alter HDG to do this?

➤ (a) TE = 3 in 20 = 9°; (b) CA = 8 in 60 = 8°;
   (c) Alter HDG 17° to the right

2. You are 3 nm left of course and make a HDG change to regain course. 30 nm later you pinpoint your position as 3 nm right of course.
   (a) What is your TE?
   (b) What is the CA to regain course in another 15 nm?
   (c) If your HDG was MH 110, what will be your new HDG?

➤ (a) TE = 6 in 30 = 12°;
   (b) CA = 3 in 15 = 12°;
   (c) Alter HDG by 24° to the left, i.e. to MH 086.

Part (e)

1. Having maintained HDG MH 320 you fix your position 2 nm left of course in 15 nm and wish to regain course in another 30 nm.
   (a) What is your TE?
   (b) What is your CA?
   (c) What should you alter HDG to initially?
   (d) What should you alter HDG to on regaining course?

➤ (a) TE = 2 in 15 = 8°;
   (b) CA = 2 in 30 = 4°;
   (c) Alter HDG by TE + CA = 12° to the right, to MH 332;
   (d) Remove the CA by turning 4° left to MH 328.

2. MH 293 and 4 nm right of course after 34 nm.
   (a) What is the TE?
   (b) What is the CA to regain course in another 48 nm?
   (c) What HDG should you take up to regain course?
   (d) On course, what would you expect your HDG to be?

➤ (a) TE = 4 in 34 = 7 in 60 = 7° (by computer);
   (b) CA = 4 in 48 = 1 in 12 = 5 in 60 = 5°;
   (c) MH 281;
   (d) MH 286.

Part (f)

1. Navigation in remote areas requires very careful _____ planning.

➤ preflight

2. When navigating in remote areas especially, you should maintain _____ accurately and keep an in-flight _____ .

➤ HDGs, log

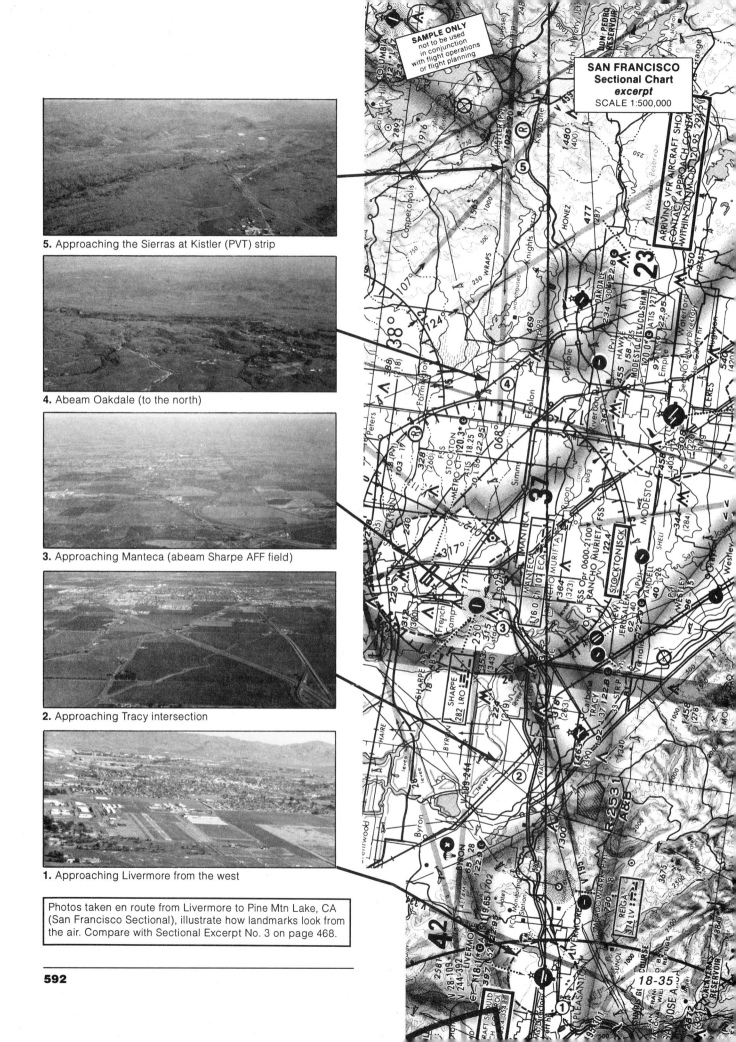

5. Approaching the Sierras at Kistler (PVT) strip

4. Abeam Oakdale (to the north)

3. Approaching Manteca (abeam Sharpe AFF field)

2. Approaching Tracy intersection

1. Approaching Livermore from the west

Photos taken en route from Livermore to Pine Mtn Lake, CA (San Francisco Sectional), illustrate how landmarks look from the air. Compare with Sectional Excerpt No. 3 on page 468.

SAN FRANCISCO Sectional Chart *excerpt* SCALE 1:500,000

SAMPLE ONLY not to be used in conjunction with flight operations or flight planning

592

Radio Navigation 1 **27**

The VOR

The VOR is a very high frequency (VHF) radio navigation aid that is extensively used in instrument flying. It is also extremely useful in assisting you during VFR navigation operations. Its full name is the **very high frequency omni-directional radio range,** commonly abbreviated to the VHF omni range, VOR, or omni.

Each VOR ground station transmits on a specific VHF frequency between 108.00 and 117.95 megahertz (MHz), which is immediately below the frequency range used for VHF communications. A separate VHF-NAV radio is required for navigation purposes, but is usually combined with the VHF-COM in a NAV/COM set.

A VOR ground station can be selected on the VHF-NAV radio set.

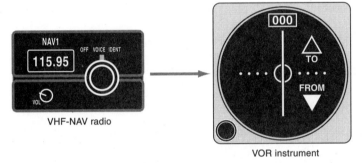

Figure 27-1. VOR equipment in the cockpit

The VOR was developed in the United States during the late 1940s, and was adopted by the International Civil Aviation Organization (ICAO) as the standard short-range radio navigation aid in 1960. When introduced, it offered principal advantages over the NDB, including:

- a reduced susceptibility to electrical and atmospheric interference (including thunderstorms);
- the elimination of *night effect,* since VHF signals are line-of-sight and not reflected by the ionosphere (as are NDB signals in the low and medium frequency band).

Many VORs are paired with distance measuring equipment (DME). Selection of the VOR on the VHF-NAV set in the cockpit also selects the paired DME, thereby providing both tracking and distance information.

VORs are often paired with a DME.

VOR Radials

As its name **omni** suggests, a VOR ground transmitter radiates signals in all directions. Its most important feature, however, is that the signal in any particular direction differs slightly from its neighbors. These individual directional signals can be thought of as courses or position lines radiating out from the VOR ground station, in much the same way as spokes from the hub of a wheel.

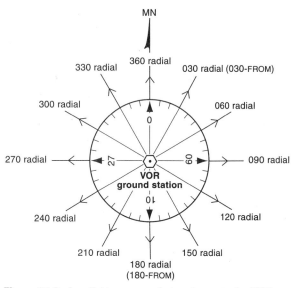

Figure 27-2. A radial is a magnetic bearing FROM the VOR

By convention, 360 different tracks away from the VOR are used, each separated from the next by 1°, and each with its direction related to magnetic north. Each of these 360 VOR courses or position lines is called a **radial**. The 075 radial may be written R-075.

An airplane tracking *outbound* on the 060 radial will diverge from an airplane tracking outbound on the 090 radial.

Conversely, if they both reverse direction and track *inbound* on the 060 radial *(240-TO* the VOR) and the 090 radial *(270-TO),* their tracks will converge.

When a VOR is operating normally, the radials are transmitted to an accuracy of ±2° or better.

A radial is the *magnetic* bearing outbound from a VOR.

How the VOR Works

The VOR ground station transmits two VHF radio signals:

- the **reference phase** signal, which is omni-directional (the same in all directions); and
- the **variable phase** signal, which rotates uniformly at a rate of 1,800 rpm, with its phase varying at a constant rate throughout the 360°.

The antenna of the VOR airborne receiver picks up the signals, whose **phase difference** (the difference between the wave peaks) is measured, this difference depending on the bearing of the airplane from the ground station. In this manner, the pilot can determine the **magnetic bearing** of the airplane from the VOR ground station.

Figure 27-3a. A VOR antenna

Figure 27-3b. A VOR ground station

The signals transmitted by the VOR ground station are:

- in-phase on magnetic north, which is the reference for VOR signals;
- 90° out of phase at magnetic east 090°M;
- 180° out of phase at magnetic south 180°M;
- 270° out of phase at magnetic west 270°M; and
- 360° out of phase (back in-phase) at magnetic north 360°M, or 000°M.

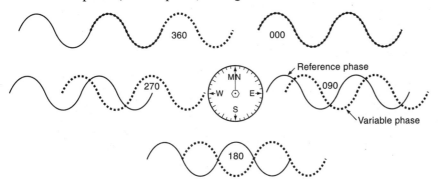

Figure 27-4. The VOR transmits two signals with a phase difference between them

To avoid confusion between various VORs and to ensure that you are using the correct beacon, each VOR transmits its own particular identification signal or ident in the form of a two-or three-lettered Morse code signal, which should be checked before using the VOR for navigation.

Check the Morse code ident before using a VOR.

These codes can be found in the navigation boxes on your flight charts. Any associated DME will have a coded identifier broadcast about every 30 seconds, modulated at 1350 Hz. This means that about one DME ident at a higher pitch tone is heard for every three or four VOR idents.

Some VORs may also carry **voice** transmissions either identifying them (for example *"Linden VOR,"* alternating with the coded identifier), or carrying a message such as a relevant ATIS or TWEB. The voice identifier of the VOR must have the word "VOR" or "VORTAC" stated after its name for the VOR to be considered identified.

Some VORs transmit voice messages.

If the VOR ground station is undergoing maintenance, the coded identifier is *not* transmitted, but it is possible that navigation signals will still be received. Sometimes a coded TEST signal *(dah dit dit-dit-dit dah)* is transmitted when maintenance is in progress. If this code is heard, do *not* use the selected station for navigation.

VOR Range

The VOR is a very high frequency aid, and has little interference from atmospheric noise in the operating band. Reception is line-of-sight, but may be affected by the terrain surrounding the ground station, the height of the VOR beacon, the altitude of the airplane and its distance from the station.

The VOR signal is line-of-sight.

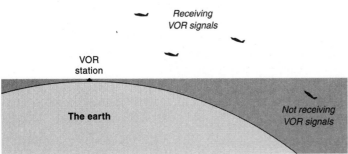

Figure 27-5. VHF line-of-sight signals

Different VORs may operate on the same frequency, but they will be well separated geographically so that there is no interference between their VHF line-of-sight signals. The higher the airplane's altitude, however, the greater the possibility of interference.

VORs on Aeronautical Charts

Most aeronautical charts show the position, frequency and Morse code ident of each VOR ground station. Information on a particular VOR may be found in the A/FD, and any changes in this information will be referred to in NOTAMs (to which you should refer prior to flight). You should take time to read the Directory Legend at the front of the A/FD regarding Radio Aids to Navigation.

VOR radials are based on magnetic north.

A VOR ground station may be represented in various ways on a chart; the common representations are shown in Figure 27-6. Since **magnetic** north is the reference direction for VOR radials, a magnetic north **arrowhead** usually emanates from the VOR symbol, with a compass rose heavily marked each 30° and the radials shown in 10° intervals. This is generally adequate for in-flight estimation of an off-airway course to an accuracy of ±2°, however, when flight planning prior to flight, you should measure precisely.

Victor airways, which will be of use to the VFR pilot, are published on Sectional charts, with the courses marked in degrees magnetic, thereby making it easy for you to plan without having to use a protractor or plotter. If, for some reason, you measure the course in degrees true using a protractor, then variation needs to be applied to convert to magnetic.

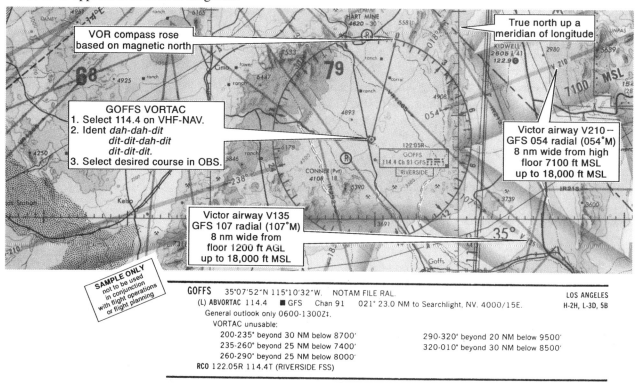

Figure 27-6. A VOR and its radials represented on a Sectional chart, and in the A/FD

The Victor airways between VORs shown on the charts are marked at either end with the radial out of that VOR. These radials are not always exact reciprocals of each other, especially on east-west tracks, because great circles (which the airways are) cross the north-south meridians of longitude at different angles and magnetic variation changes slightly across the country (and this affects the calculation of the *magnetic* course, which a radial is, from the *true* course).

VOR/DME, TACAN and VORTAC

Most civil VORs have an associated DME, hence providing both azimuth and distance information, and are known as **VOR/DMEs.** The VOR operates in the VHF range, but the DME, even though *automatically* selected along with the VOR selection, operates in the UHF range.

The military has developed a different navigation system, called TACAN (Tactical Air Navigation), that operates in the UHF band, and also provides both azimuth and distance information. It requires special airborne equipment (installed only in military aircraft) for the azimuth information to be received, however civil aircraft can receive the TACAN distance information using the DME.

A civil pilot can use only DME information from a TACAN.

When a TACAN ground station has been integrated with a VOR/DME ground station, the combined facility is known as a VORTAC. The end result for a civil pilot using a VORTAC is the same as using a VOR/DME—he has both VOR and DME information available.

VOR Cockpit Instruments

VOR cockpit displays vary in type, but they are all reasonably similar in terms of operation. The VOR cockpit display, VOR indicator, or omni bearing indicator (OBI), displays the omni bearing selected by the pilot on the course card using the **omni bearing selector (OBS)**, a small knob which is geared to the card. The omni bearing selector is also known as the course selector.

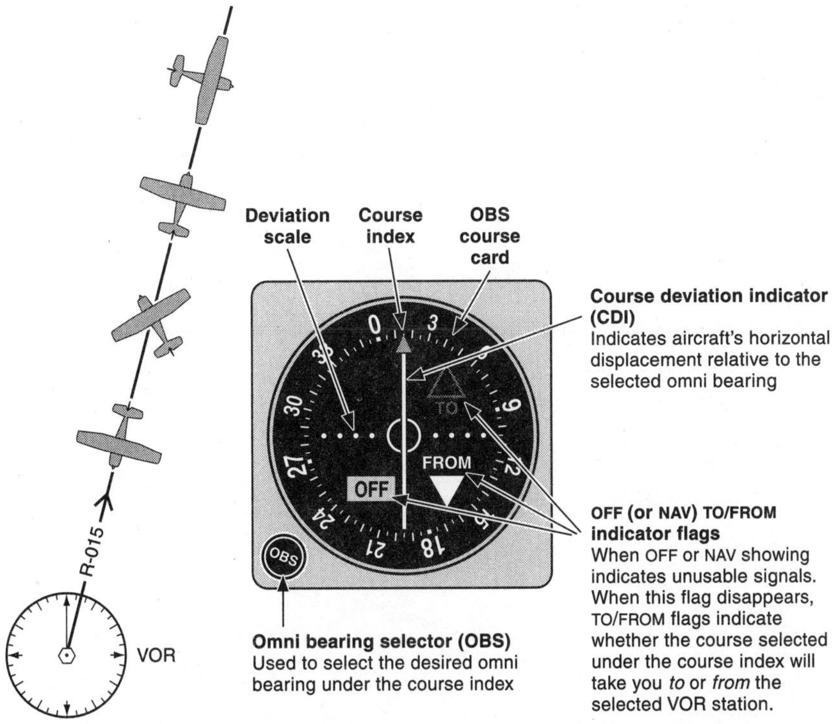

Figure 27-7. The VOR cockpit display (OBI) for airplanes on the 015 radial

The VOR cockpit instrument is able to display the aircraft orientation relative to the selected OBS course by noting the position of a **course deviation indicator (CDI)** and a TO/FROM flag. The TO/FROM may be a solid arrowhead ▼. There are various other presentations of the VOR cockpit indicator with which you should be familiar. These are usually in the form of an RMI or a HSI.

VOR Indicator

Course Deviation Indicator

If the airplane is *on* the selected radial, then the VOR needle, known as the **course deviation indicator (CDI),** is centered. If the airplane is *not* on the selected course, then the CDI will *not* be centered.

The CDI in the VOR cockpit instrument indicates off-course deviation in terms of *angular deviation from the selected course*. At all times, the reference when using the VOR is the *selected* course under the course index.

The amount of *angular* deviation from the selected course is referred to in terms of *dots*; there are 5 dots either side of the central position. The inner dot on both sides is often represented by a circle passing through them.

Each dot on the VOR is equivalent to 2° course deviation.

- If the airplane is on the selected course, the CDI is centered.
- If the airplane is 2° off the selected course, the CDI is displaced 1 dot from the center (on the circumference of the inner circle).
- If the airplane is 4° off the selected course, the CDI is displaced 2 dots.
- If the airplane is 10° or more off the selected course, the CDI is fully deflected at 5 dots.

Full-scale deflection of the CDI at 5 dots indicates a course deviation of 10° or more

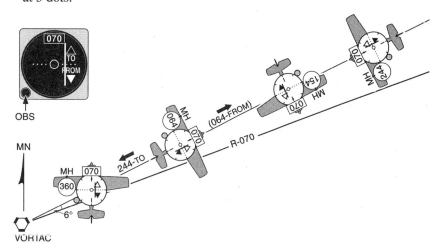

Figure 27-8. Each of these airplanes is displaced 6° from the 070 radial

Since the CDI indicates *angular* deviation, the actual *distance* off-course for a given CDI indication will be smaller the closer the airplane is to the ground station. In a manner of speaking, airplanes tracking inbound are funneled in toward the VOR ground station.

You should be especially vigilant in the vicinity of a VOR which is being used for navigation on VFR flights, as there may be a number of aircraft converging on the VOR from other directions.

The TO or FROM Arrow

The 090 radial, which is a magnetic bearing of 090 away FROM the station, is the same position line as 270-TO the station. If an airplane is on this position line, then the CDI will be centered when either 090 or 270 is selected with the OBS. Any ambiguity in your mind regarding the position of the airplane relative to the VOR ground station is resolved with the TO/FROM indicator.

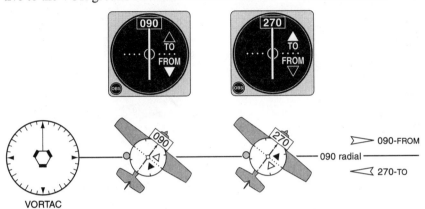

Figure 27-9. Using the TO/FROM flag

The TO or FROM flags or arrows indicate whether the selected omni bearing will take you *to* the VOR ground station, or away *from* it.

The Radio Magnetic Indicator (RMI)

The radio magnetic indicator (RMI) is a remote indicating compass with one or two ADF/VOR needles. In some aircraft, it is also possible to use an RMI needle to point to the VOR ground station as if it were an NDB. This can, on occasions, be very useful.

The RMI combines a remote indicating compass and a relative bearing indicator into the one instrument.

The RMI compass card is automatically aligned so that it indicates the aircraft magnetic heading, and the RMI needles point at the ground stations to which they are tuned. These ground stations, on many RMIs, may be either an NDB or a VOR; the selection of either ADF or VOR is made with small switches at the base of the RMI.

In Figure 27-10, the pilot has selected RMI needle 1 to the ADF, hence:

- the head of needle 1 indicates magnetic bearing TO the NDB; and
- the tail of needle 1 indicates magnetic bearing FROM the NDB.

RMI needle 2 has been selected to the VOR, hence:

- the head of needle 2 indicates magnetic bearing TO the VOR; and
- the tail of needle 2 indicates magnetic bearing FROM the VOR **(radial).**

Using the RMI with one needle selected to a VOR allows the VOR to be used as if it were an NDB for orientation and tracking purposes. For more information refer to Chapter 28 on the RMI and the NDB.

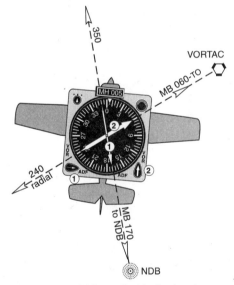

Figure 27-10. RMI needle 1 indicating the NDB; RMI needle 2 indicating the VOR

The Horizontal Situation Indicator (HSI)

The horizontal situation indicator (HSI) is a remote indicating compass with a VOR indicator superimposed on it. It provides you with an easily understood pictorial display and is one of the most popular navigation instruments ever devised. It shows the magnetic heading and the position of the airplane relative to the selected course. *See* Figure 27-11a.

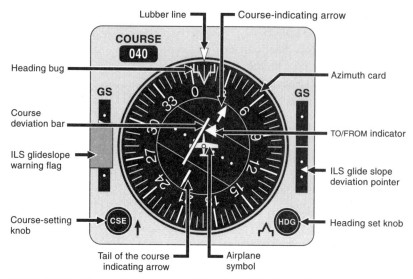

Lubber line — Course-indicating arrow

COURSE
040

Heading bug

GS

Course deviation bar

ILS glideslope warning flag

Course-setting knob — CSE

Tail of the course indicating arrow

Airplane symbol

Azimuth card

TO/FROM indicator

GS

ILS glide slope deviation pointer

Heading set knob — HDG

Figure 27-11a. The airplane on magnetic heading 010, about to intercept 040-TO the VOR, flying an intercept angle of 30° in zero wind

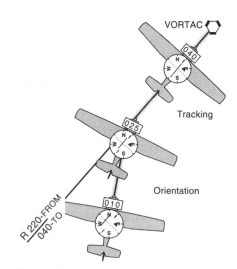

VORTAC

Tracking

Orientation

R 220-FROM
040-TO

Figure 27-11b.

A wonderful feature of the HSI over the traditional VOR indicator is that the HSI is always a **command instrument.** If the airplane turns, the remote indicating compass card turns, carrying the VOR display with it, and so the HSI will always show the CDI deflection *toward* the selected course. In Figure 27-11a, the selected course is out to the left. If the airplane turns 180°, to MH 190, the HSI will show the selected course 040 out to the right of the airplane, as indeed it is. An HSI exhibits no reverse sensing.

✍ Now complete **Review 27, Part (a)** on page 611.

Operational Use of the VOR

Preparing the VOR Equipment for Use

A radio navigation aid is of little value if you do not use it correctly. Prior to using the VOR, you must:

- ensure that the VOR has been checked as suitably accurate for radio navigation;
- ensure electrical power is available, and switch the VHF-NAV ON;
- select the desired frequency;
- identify the VOR; and
- check that the OFF flag is not showing.

Always select, tune and identify the VOR before use.

The VOR Receiver Check

There are five ways in which the VOR receiver may be checked for accuracy prior to flight (specified in AIM Chapter 1, para 4).

- **VOT** (FAA VOR test facility), or a radiated test signal from an appropriately-rated radio repair station (usually on 108.0 MHz). These are test signals which allow the VOR to be tested for accuracy *on the ground.* To use the VOT service:
  - (a) Tune the VOT frequency (found in the A/FD or on the A/G Communications panel of the Enroute Low Altitude Chart).
  - (b) Center the CDI by turning the OBS, which should read *360-FROM* or *180-TO,* with an acceptable accuracy of ±4°. Should the VOR operate an RMI, its needle should point to 180°±4° with any OBS setting.

- **FAA Certified Ground Checkpoint** (specified in the A/FD). This is a **certified radial** that should be received at specific points on the airport surface.

    (a) Position the airplane on the ground checkpoint at the airport.

    (b) Tune the VOR and select the designated radial with the OBS. The CDI must be within ±**4°** of the radial, with the *FROM* flag showing (since it is a *radial),* for the accuracy of the VOR receiver to be acceptable.

- **FAA Certified Airborne Checkpoint** (specified in the A/FD). This is a certified radial that should be received over specific *landmarks* while airborne in the immediate vicinity of the airport.

    (a) Tune the VOR and select the designated radial with the OBS.

    (b) Visually position the airplane over the landmark, and center the CDI with the OBS. The course reading on the omni bearing indicator must be within ±**6°** of the designated radial for the accuracy of the VOR receiver to be acceptable.

- **Dual System VOR Check.** If a *dual* system VOR (units independent of each other except for the antenna) is installed in the aircraft, one system may be checked against the other.

    (a) Tune both systems to the same VOR ground facility and center the CDI on each indicator using the OBS.

    (b) The maximum permissible variation between the two indicated bearings is **4°**, and this applies to tests carried out both *on the ground* and *in the air.*

- **Course Sensitivity Check.** This is *not* a required check.

    (a) Center the CDI and note the indicated bearing.

    (b) Turn the OBS until the CDI lies over the last (5th) dot which, ideally, indicates a bearing difference of 10°. Between 10° and 12° is acceptable sensitivity.

ORIENTATION:

Using a Single VOR Position Line

Orientation is a term that means to determine an airplane's approximate position. The first step in orientation is to establish a *position line* along which the airplane is known to be at a particular moment.

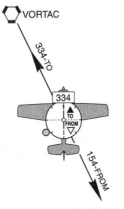

Figure 27-12. On the 154 radial

To obtain a position line using the VOR, you should:

- rotate the OBS until the CDI is centered; and
- note whether the TO or FROM flag is showing.

Example 1. The pilot rotates the OBS until the CDI is centered, which occurs with *334* under the course index and the TO flag showing. Could another reading be obtained with the CDI centered?

In this location, the CDI will be centered with either:

– *334-TO; or*

– *154-FROM.*

Using Two Position Lines to Fix Position

One position line alone does *not* allow you to *positively* fix the position of the airplane; it only provides a line somewhere along which the airplane lies. It requires *two or more* position lines to positively fix the position of an airplane. To be of any real value for position fixing, the two position lines need to cut, or intersect, at an angle of at least 45°; any cut less than this decreases the accuracy of the fix.

Radio position lines can be provided by any convenient radio navigation aids, including VORs, NDBs and DMEs. Positions defined on charts by this means are known as **intersections.**

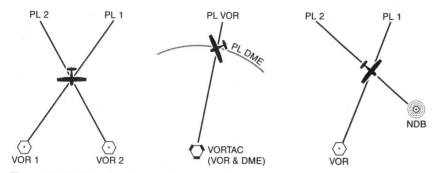

Figure 27-13. Fixing position requires two position lines with a good intersection

Two VORs

Many airplanes are fitted with *two* independent VHF-NAV systems, enabling two different VORs to be tuned at the same time. Two position lines from two different VOR ground stations can then be obtained simultaneously. In an airplane with only *one* VHF-NAV set, you can obtain two position lines using the one VHF-NAV by retuning it from one VOR to another.

Example 2. An airplane fitted with two VHF-NAVs is tracking MC 134-TO to VOR-A. The pilot obtains the following indications:

> **VOR 1:** VOR-A 115.2 is selected, the *tracking* VOR, and the CDI centers with *134-TO.*

> **VOR 2:** VOR-B 113.8 is selected, the *crossing* VOR, and the CDI centers with *220-FROM.*

> The two VOR position lines intersect at a good angle, and the pilot has a fairly positive indication of where the airplane is.

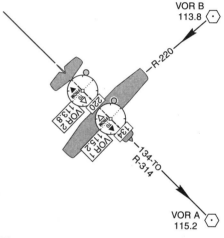

Figure 27-14. Fixing position using two VORs

VOR and a DME

A common form of en route position fixing between aids is the VOR/DME fix, based on a ground station where the DME is co-located with the VOR ground station. This is also the case with a VORTAC.

The VOR can provide a straight position line showing the **radial** that the airplane is on, and the DME can provide a circular position line showing the **distance** that the airplane is from the ground station. The intersection of the lines is the position of the airplane.

Example 3. An airplane tracking north from Squaw Valley (SWR 113.2) has the cockpit indications of:

> SWR VOR *002-FROM;* and
> SWR DME 16 nm.

> Where is the airplane?

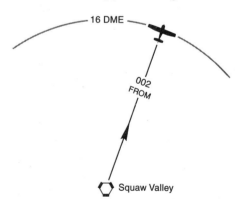

Figure 27-15. Example 3—Fixing position using a co-located VOR/DME (or VORTAC)

Over a VOR

As an airplane approaches a VOR, the CDI will become more and more sensitive as the ±10° funnel either side of course becomes narrower and narrower.

As the airplane passes through the **zone of confusion** over the VOR ground station, the CDI may flick from side to side, before settling down again as the airplane moves away from the VOR. The flag will also change from *TO* to *FROM* (or vice versa), and the red OFF flag may flicker in and out of view because of the unusable signal.

The zone of confusion can extend in an arc of 70° over the station, so it may take a minute or so for the airplane to pass through it before the CDI and the FROM flag settle down, and the OFF flag totally disappears.

VOR **station passage** is indicated by the first positive complete reversal of the TO/FROM flag.

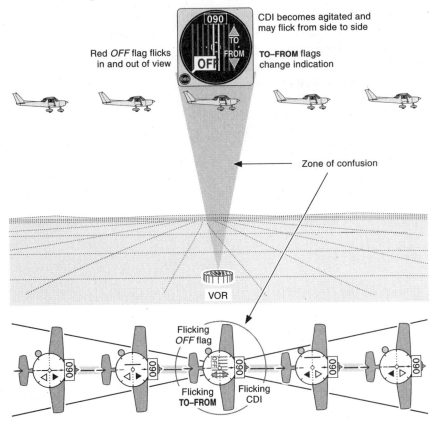

Figure 27-16. Fixing position over a VOR

Passing Abeam a VOR

A common means of checking flight progress is to note the time passing *abeam* (90° to the side of) a nearby VOR ground station. The most straightforward procedure is to select and identify the VOR, and under the course index, set the radial perpendicular (at 90°) to your course.

Example 4. An airplane is tracking MC350, and will pass approximately 20 nm abeam a VOR ground station out to its right.

The VOR radial perpendicular to course is the 260 radial, and so 260 should be set with the OBS.

The CDI will be fully deflected to one side if the airplane is well away from the abeam position, and will gradually move from full deflection one side to full deflection on the other side as the airplane passes through the ±10° arc either side of the selected radial. The airplane is at the abeam position when the CDI is centered.

It is suggested that you set the *radial* (the bearing FROM) the off-course VOR in the OBS, in which case the CDI will be on the **same side as the VOR** until you have passed the radial. In Figure 27-17, the VOR is off-course to the right, and *before* passing abeam the ground station, the CDI will be out to the right. It will center to indicate the abeam position, and then move to the other side.

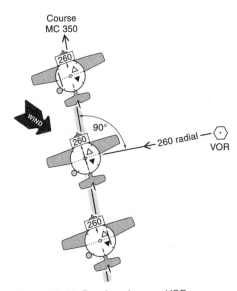

Figure 27-17. Passing abeam a VOR

The abeam position can also be identified by setting the bearing TO the VOR under the course index (rather than the radial *from* the VOR), in which case the movement of the CDI will be from the opposite side. It is better practice to standardize on a method, and we suggest setting the radial *from*.

The VOR Display

The VOR indicates the position of the airplane with respect to the *selected* VOR course, and the actual VOR display in the cockpit will be the same regardless of the airplane's heading. If the airplane could turn in a circle on-the-spot, the VOR indications would remain the same, and the CDI would not move. Each of the airplanes shown in Figure 27-18 will have the same VOR display, provided the same course is set under the course index with the OBS.

The CDI position will *not* change as the airplane changes heading.

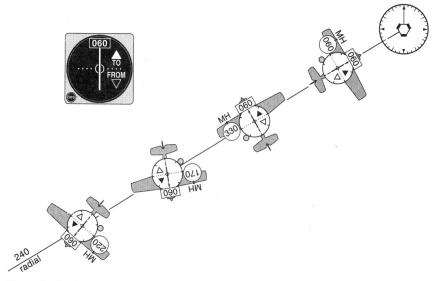

Figure 27-18. The VOR cockpit display is *not* heading sensitive

Orientation Without Altering the OBS

It is possible, without altering the omni bearing selector, to determine which quadrant the airplane is in with respect to the selected course. In Figure 27-19, the selected omni bearing is 340.

- The CDI is deflected left, which indicates that, when looking in direction 340, the airplane is out to the right (of the line 340–160); and

- The *FROM* flag indicates that tracking 340 would take the airplane *from* the VOR ground station. Therefore the airplane is ahead of the line 250–070 when looking in the direction 340.

This puts the airplane in the quadrant:

- away from the CDI; and

- away from the TO/FROM flag.

Therefore the airplane is between 340 and 070 radials (omni bearings *from* the VOR ground station).

Note: No information is available from the VOR cockpit display regarding airplane heading. Heading information in degrees magnetic must be obtained from the heading indicator.

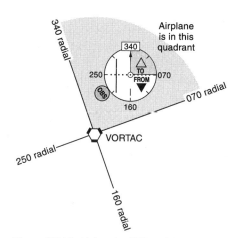

Figure 27-19. Using the CDI and the TO/FROM flag for orientation without moving the omni bearing selector. The airplane is in the quadrant away from the CDI and TO/FROM flag

Orientation with a VOR using the RMI

Orientation using an RMI-equipped airplane is considerably easier than when using the OBS presentation.

The single needle tuned to the selected VOR station makes orientation with the VOR very easy, and it does not involve altering the OBS (omni bearing selector).

In Figure 27-20, RMI needle 2 indicates that the magnetic bearing *TO* the VOR is MB 043 (hence the airplane is on the 223 radial). Note that there is no need to alter the OBS to determine this, as would be necessary if an RMI were not installed. Without an RMI, the pilot would have had to alter the OBS until the CDI centered at either *043-TO or 223-FROM*.

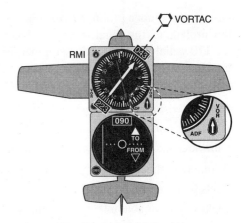

Figure 27-20. The RMI indicates 043 TO the VOR

Intercepting Course

Orientation

To orient your airplane you need to ask the questions: "Where am I? Where do I want to go? How do I get there?"

The easiest method of orienting the airplane using the VOR is to rotate the OBS until the CDI centers. This can occur on one of two headings (reciprocals of each other); choose the one with the omni bearing that most resembles the airplane's magnetic heading. If the airplane is heading *toward* the VOR ground station, then the TO flag will show; if it is heading *away from* the VOR, then the FROM flag will show.

Select the desired course in degrees magnetic using the omni bearing selector (OBS). Determine which way to turn to intercept the course, and then take up a suitable intercept heading.

Intercepting an Outbound Course

Example 5. An airplane is tracking inbound on the 170 radial to a VOR *(350-TO)*. ATC instructs the pilot to take up a heading to intercept the 090 radial outbound *(090-FROM)*.

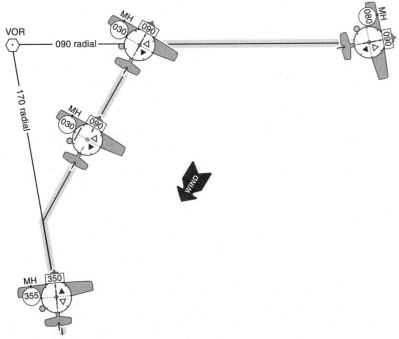

Figure 27-21. Intercepting a course outbound from a VOR

Orientation is not a problem in Example 5 since the pilot already knows where the airplane is (the usual situation). The better method **tracking inbound** on the 170 radial is to have 350 set under the course index, since the airplane is tracking *350-TO the VOR*. This ensures that the VOR indicator is a command instrument (fly *toward* the CDI needle to regain course).

The pilot visualizes the situation:

- tracking northward toward the VOR;
- the course, *090-FROM,* lying ahead to the right.

To intercept the *090-FROM* course, the pilot:

- sets 090 under the course index;
- takes up a suitable intercept heading (MH 030 for a 60° intercept); and
- maintains MH 030 until the CDI moves from full-scale deflection toward the center. To avoid overshooting the course, the pilot would anticipate the interception, and *lead-in* by commencing a turn just prior to intercepting course with the CDI centered. A 60° intercept will require a 60° turn which, at standard-rate of 3°/second, will take 20 seconds.

Intercepting an Inbound Course

Example 6. ATC instructs a pilot to track inbound on the 010 radial to a particular VOR. The pilot:

- selects and identifies the VOR; then
- orients himself with respect to the VOR (perhaps by centering the CDI suitably);
- sets the desired course under the course index; inbound on the 010 radial, *190-TO;* and determines the relative position of this course;
- takes up a suitable intercept heading, and waits for the CDI to center.

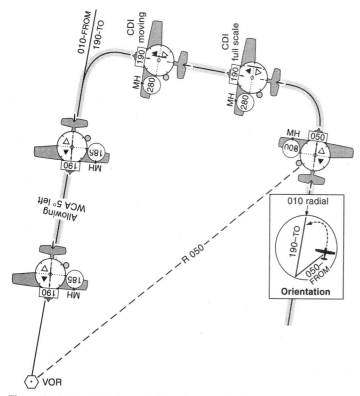

Figure 27-22. Intercepting an inbound course to a VOR

In the case illustrated in Figure 27-22:

- the CDI centers on *050-FROM* (it would also center on *230-TO*);
- the pilot has chosen a 90° intercept, steering MH 280 to intercept *190-TO;* and
- as the CDI starts to move (within 10° of the selected course), the pilot leads in to smoothly join course, and allows a wind correction angle of 5° to counter a wind from the east.

Intercepting Course with the RMI Selected to a VOR

If the pilot wishes to intercept the 090 inbound course to the VOR, then he would (since he has already oriented the airplane using the RMI):

- set 090 under the course index with the OBS (already done); and
- take up a suitable intercept heading.

If the pilot is uncertain of his orientation, he can use the ADF technique of imagining:

- the airplane on the *tail* of the needle in its current situation; and
- the airplane on the *tail* of the needle where he wants to go (*090-TO*).

On MH010, it would be an 80° intercept. If the pilot wanted a 60° intercept, he would turn to MH030. Tracking on MH030, the RMI needle will gradually fall toward 090. Once the airplane is within 10° of the selected course on the VOR cockpit display, the CDI will start to move.

At this stage, the pilot could shift his attention to the VOR indicator, and turn in to track on *090-TO*. In this case, he is tracking in on *090-TO* allowing a wind correction angle of 5° left to counteract the wind from the north by steering MH 085.

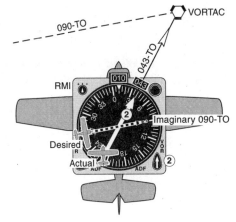

Figure 27-23. Determining "Where to go?" using the RMI

Tracking

Tracking to a VOR

To track *to* a VOR:

- select the VOR **frequency**;
- **identify** the station (*Morse code ident* as shown on the chart, or *voice ident* with VOR stated after the name);
- check that the red OFF warning flag is not displayed; and
- select the **omni bearing** of the desired course with the OBS.

Orient the airplane with respect to the desired course, and then take up a suitable intercept heading using the heading indicator (aligned with the magnetic compass). If the airplane is heading approximately in the direction of the desired course, the center circle will represent the airplane, and the CDI the desired course; to intercept course in this case, the pilot would turn toward the CDI.

This is using the VOR indicator as a **command instrument**. This *commands* you to turn *toward* the CDI to regain course. Be aware, however, that this only applies when the airplane's heading is in roughly the same direction as the selected omni bearing.

On intercepting the course, you should steer a suitable heading to maintain the course, allowing a suitable wind correction angle to counter any wind effect. Remaining on course is indicated by the CDI remaining centered.

Since you are flying toward the VOR, the "TO" flag should be displayed.

Example 7. In Figure 27-24, with the desired course 030 set under the course index, the CDI is out to the right.

Since the airplane's initial heading agrees approximately with the course of 030, the pilot concludes that the course is out to the right of the airplane.

The CDI out to the right **commands** him to turn right to regain track and center the CDI.

The pilot has taken up a heading of MH050 to intercept a course of *030-TO* the VOR, which will give him a 20° intercept. This shallow intercept is satisfactory if the airplane is close to the course.

If the airplane is well away from the course, then a 60° or 90° intercept might be more appropriate. This would be MH 090 or MH 120.

Determining Wind Correction Angle

When tracking inbound on *360-TO* a VOR with 360 set under the course index, MH 360 will allow the airplane to maintain course provided there is no cross-wind component.

If, however, there is a westerly wind blowing, then the airplane will be blown to the right of course unless a wind correction angle (WCA) is applied and the airplane steered on a heading slightly into wind. This is MH 352 in the center diagram of Figure 27-25.

If, on the other hand, there is an easterly wind blowing, the airplane will be blown to the left of course, unless a wind correction angle is applied and the airplane steered on a heading slightly into wind, such as MH 005 in the right diagram of Figure 27-25.

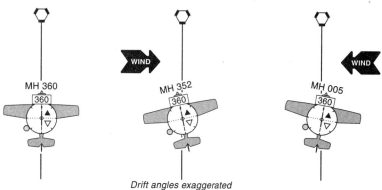

Drift angles exaggerated

Figure 27-25. Tracking inbound and allowing for drift

Just how great the WCA need be is determined in flight by trial and error (although any preflight calculations using the flight computer when flight planning may suggest a suitable starting figure for WCA).

If the chosen WCA is not correct, and the airplane gradually departs from course causing the CDI to move from its central position, then the heading should be altered to regain the course (CDI centered), and then a new magnetic heading flown with an improved estimate of WCA. This process of achieving a suitable WCA by trial and error is known as **bracketing.**

In the real world the wind frequently changes in both strength and direction, and so the magnetic heading required to maintain course will also change from time to time. This becomes obvious by gradual movements of the CDI away from its central position, which the pilot will notice in his regular scan of the radio navigation instruments, and which he will correct by changes in magnetic heading using the heading indicator.

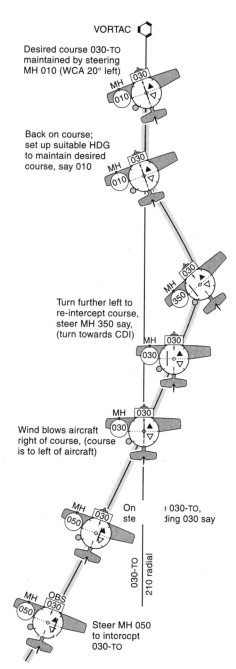

Figure 27-24. Using the CDI as a command instrument when tracking to a VOR

Tracking From a VOR

To track *FROM* a VOR (assuming the VOR has not already been selected and identified):

- select the VOR frequency;
- identify the station;
- check that the red *OFF* warning flag is *not* displayed; and
- select the omni bearing of the desired course with the OBS.

Orient the airplane with respect to the course, and then take up a suitable intercept heading using the heading indicator (aligned with the magnetic compass). If the airplane is heading approximately in the direction of the course, the center circle will represent the airplane, and the CDI will represent the course.

To intercept course in this case, the pilot would turn toward the CDI. This is using the CDI as a **command instrument.** Be aware, however, that this only applies when the heading is roughly in the same direction as the selected omni bearing.

On intercepting course, the pilot steers a suitable heading to maintain it, keeping in mind the wind direction and strength. If the course is maintained, the CDI will remain centered.

Since you are flying away from the VOR the *FROM* flag will be displayed.

Example 8. In Figure 27-26, with the course 140 set in the omni bearing selector (OBS), the CDI is out to the right. Since the airplane's initial heading agrees approximately with the course of 140, the pilot concludes that the course is out to the right of the airplane (or, in this case, straight ahead and to the right).

The pilot steers MH220 to intercept a course of *140-FROM* the VOR, which will give him an 80° intercept. This is satisfactory if the airplane is well away from the course. If the airplane is close to course, then a 60° or 30° intercept might be more appropriate which, in this case, would be MH 200 or MH170.

Using the CDI as a Command Instrument

Use the CDI as a **command instrument** whenever possible. With the course set in the OBI, and the airplane headed at least roughly in the same direction as the selected course, the CDI will act as a **command instrument.**

By flying toward the deflected CDI, the pilot can center it, and thereby regain course. *See* Figure 27-27.

- tracking *060-TO* the VOR, set 060 under the course index;
- tracking *030-FROM* the VOR, set 030 under the course index.

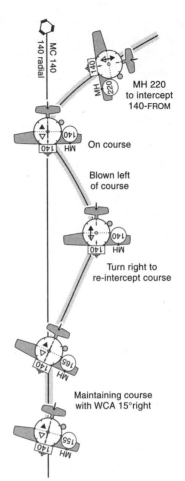

Figure 27-26. Using the CDI as a command instrument when tracking from a VOR

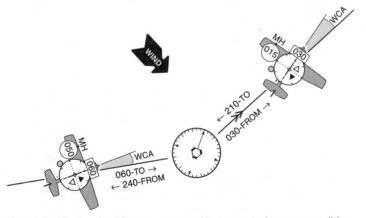

Figure 27-27. Use the CDI as a command instrument whenever possible

A minor complication can arise when the airplane is steered on a heading approximating the reciprocal of the course selected on the OBI. Under these circumstances, the CDI is *not* a command instrument. This situation is called *reverse sensing*.

Example 9. Suppose a pilot has been tracking *140-FROM* a VOR, with 140 selected in the OBI and by steering MH 140. The airplane has drifted left of course, and so the CDI will be deflected to the right of center. *See* Figure 27-28. To regain the 140-FROM course, the pilot must turn toward the needle, in this case toward the right. As the heading and OBI selection are similar, the CDI is used as a command instrument.

Suppose now that he wishes to return to the VOR ground station on the reciprocal track, which is *320-TO* the VOR, and so turns through approximately 180° to MH 320 without altering the 140 set under the course index. The VOR indicator, because it is not heading-sensitive, indicates exactly as it did before the turn, with the CDI as seen by the pilot out to the right of center.

To regain course on this reciprocal heading, the pilot would turn, not toward the CDI, but away from it. Turning toward the CDI on this reciprocal heading to the selected course would take the pilot further away from the selected course. In this case, the VOR indicator is no longer a command instrument.

This inconvenience can be easily removed, and the OBI used as a command instrument again, by selecting the new course under the course index, 320, which approximates the heading being flown. The immediate effect will be for:

• the *TO* flag to appear, replacing the FROM flag; and

• the CDI to swing across to the other side.

The CDI will now be out to the left, and a turn toward it will bring the airplane back toward the selected course. The VOR indicator is once again a command instrument, easier to understand, and easier to fly.

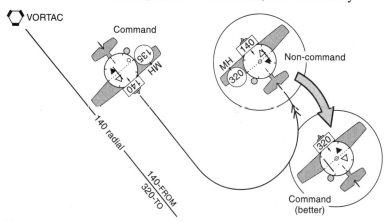

Figure 27-28. For ease of operation, use the CDI as a command instrument

✍ Now complete **Review 27, Part (b)** on page 611.

✍ Commercial students complete **Review 27, Commercial** on page 615.

Review 27

Part (a)

1. The VOR is a (VHF/LF/MF) radio navigation aid.
   ➤ VHF

2. Many VORs are coupled with a (ILS/DME/NDB).
   ➤ DME

3. A VOR ground station combined with a military TACAN ground station is known as a _____ . It (does/does not) provide both VOR and DME information.
   ➤ VORTAC, does

4. A radial is the (magnetic/true) bearing (to/from) a VOR ground station.
   ➤ magnetic bearing, from

5. You are instructed by ATC to track outbound on the 070 radial from a VOR. The more suitable heading is (070/250).
   ➤ MH 070

6. You are instructed to track inbound on the 050 radial. The more suitable heading is (050/230).
   ➤ MH 230

7. A particular VOR may be identified by its _____ .
   ➤ Morse code ident or voice ident

8. A VOR ground station should transmit to an accuracy of at least _____° accuracy.
   ➤ ±2° accuracy

9. VOR stands for _____ .
   ➤ VHF omni-directional radio range

10. The radio set in the cockpit used to select a VOR is the (VHF-COM/VHF-NAV/ADF).
    ➤ VHF-NAV

11. The needle in the VOR cockpit display is the CDI. CDI stands for _____ .
    ➤ course deviation indicator

12. Any one of 360 tracks may be selected in the VOR cockpit display using the OBS, which stands for _____ .
    ➤ omni bearing selector

Part (b)

1. A 1 dot deviation of the CDI on the VOR cockpit display indicates a displacement of _____° from the selected course.
   ➤ 2°

2. A 5 dot deviation of the CDI on the VOR cockpit display indicates a displacement of _____° from the selected course.
   ➤ 10° or more

3. If the CDI is centered with 090 selected in the OBS, and the *FROM* flag is showing, what radial is the airplane on?
   ➤ 090 radial

4. If the CDI is centered with 090 selected in the OBS, and the *TO* flag is showing, what radial is the airplane on?
   ➤ 270 radial

5. If the CDI is 2 dots right with 090 selected in the OBS, and the *TO* flag is showing, what radial is the airplane on?
   ➤ 274 radial (*094-TO*)

6. If the CDI is 1 dot left with 090 selected in the OBS, and the *FROM* flag is showing, what radial is the airplane on?
   ➤ 092 radial

7. You are flying MH 080, with the OBS selected to 080, CDI needle showing 2 dots right, and the *FROM* flag showing. Desired course is the 080 radial outbound. Is the desired course out to your left or right?
   ➤ right

8. You are flying MH 300, with the OBS selected to 300, the CDI needle showing 3 dots left, and the *TO* flag showing. Desired course is 300°M to the VOR. Is the desired course out to your left or right?
   ➤ left

9. You are flying MH 300, with the OBS selected to 300, the CDI needle showing 3 dots left, and the *TO* flag showing. If the airplane is now turned to the reciprocal heading of MH 120, would the indications in the VOR cockpit display change in any way (assuming the OBS is left unaltered).
   ➤ no (the VOR cockpit display is not heading sensitive)

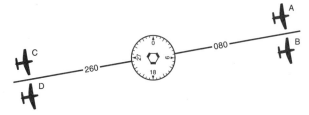

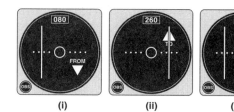

Figure 27-29.

10. Refer to Figure 27-29. VOR indication (i) applies to airplane (A/B/C/D). Repeat for VOR indications (ii) and (iii).

➤ (i) Airplane B; (ii) Airplane B; (iii) Airplane D.

11. The position of VOR receiver checkpoint(s) can be found in which document?

➤ Airport/Facility Directory

12. When the CDI needle is centered during an airborne VOR check using just one VOR receiver in the airplane, the omni bearing selector should read within (2°/4°/6°) of the selected radial.

➤ 6°

13. When making an airborne VOR check, what is the maximum allowable tolerance between the two indicators of a dual VOR system (two VOR units independent of each other except for the antenna)?

➤ 4° between the two indicated bearings to a VOR

14. For a VOR receiver check with the airplane located on the designated checkpoint on the airport, set the designated (radial/bearing) into the OBS. The CDI must be within _____ ° of the radial, and the flag should show (TO/OFF/FROM).

➤ radial, 4°, *FROM*

15. Refer to Figure 27-30. When checking a dual VOR system by use of a VOT, which illustration indicates that the VORs are satisfactory?

➤ (a)

16. Refer to Figure 27-31. Which illustration shows an acceptable operational check of dual VORs using one system against the other?

➤ (d)

17. The VOT frequency for a particular airport can be found in the _____ Directory and on the _____ panel of the Enroute Low Altitude Chart.

➤ Airport/Facility Directory, A/G Voice Communication panel

18. A VOR may be positively identified by either a _____ code identification or, in some cases, by a recorded _____ identification.

➤ Morse code, voice

19. If a VOR is undergoing maintenance, then its identification (is/is not) removed. It (may/will not) transmit navigation signals.

➤ is, may

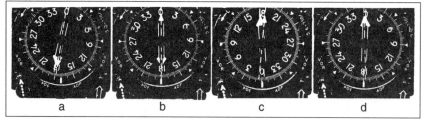

Figure 27-30.

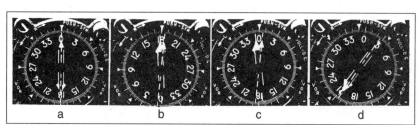

Figure 27-31.

20. A VOR identification signal is transmitted about once every _____ seconds.

➤ 10

21. If a single coded identification from a VORTAC is received only once approximately every 30 seconds, then the VOR (may/must not) be used for navigation, and the DME (may/must not) be used for navigation.

➤ must not, may

22. To check the sensitivity of a VOR receiver, changing the OBS to move the CDI from the center position to overhead the last dot should cause a bearing change of between _____° and _____°.

➤ 10° and 12°

23. VOR station passage is indicated by:
    (a) the first full-scale deflection of the CDI.
    (b) the first movement of the CDI as the airplane enters the zone of confusion.
    (c) the first positive, complete reversal of the TO-FROM indicator.

➤ (c)

24. After overflying a VOR ground station, you select the desired radial and fly a heading estimated to keep you on that course. If, however, there is a steady half-scale deflection of the CDI as you fly some miles away from the station, you will be (flying parallel to/diverging from) the radial.

➤ diverging from

25. The RMI combines the functions of a _____ and ADF/VOR needles.

➤ remote indicating compass

26. The HSI combines the functions of a _____ and a VOR indicator.

➤ remote indicating compass

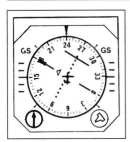

Figure 27-32.

27. Refer to Figure 27-32. The aircraft is located (northwest/northeast/southeast/southwest) of the VORTAC.

➤ northeast

28. Refer to Figure 27-33. No. 1 NAV is a (VOR/HSI).

➤ HSI

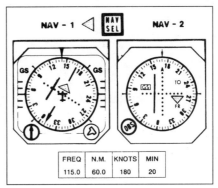

FREQ	N.M.	KNOTS	MIN
115.0	60.0	180	20

Figure 27-33.

29. Refer to Figure 27-33. No. 2 NAV is a (VOR/HSI).

➤ VOR

30. On which radial is the aircraft as indicated by the No. 1 NAV?

➤ R-345 (2.5 dots = 5° before reaching the selected R-350 FROM)

31. Which OBS selection on the No. 1 NAV would center the CDI and change the ambiguity indication to a TO?

➤ 165 (345-FROM to center the CDI = 165-TO)

32. The angular displacement from the desired radial on the No. 2 NAV is _____°.

➤ 4°

33. Which OBS selection on the No. 2 NAV would center the CDI?

➤ 174 (aircraft is 2 dots = 4° to the right of the selected R-170)

34. Which OBS selection on the No. 2 NAV would center the CDI and change the ambiguity indication to a TO?

➤ 354 (174-FROM to center the CDI = 354-TO)

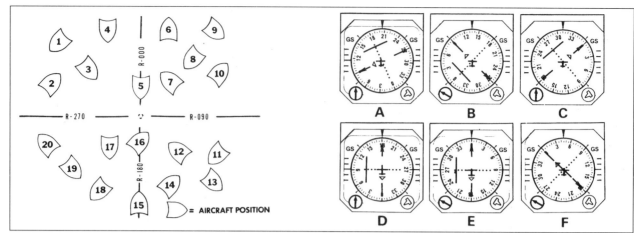

Figure 27-34.

For Questions 35 to 40 refer to Figure 27-34.

35. HSI presentation D corresponds to aircraft position (4/5/ 15/17).

➤ 17

36. HSI presentation E corresponds to aircraft position (5/6/ 15/17).

➤ 6

37. HSI presentation F corresponds to aircraft position (2/ 10/14/16).

➤ 16

38. HSI presentation A corresponds to aircraft position (1/8/ 11/18).

➤ 1

39. HSI presentation B corresponds to aircraft position (3/9/ 13/19).

➤ 19

40. HSI presentation C corresponds to aircraft position (6/7/ 12/20).

➤ 12

41. Flying a heading that is approximately the reciprocal of the VOR bearing selected on the OBS would result in (command/reverse) sensing.

➤ reverse

42. To track outbound on the 030 radial of a VOR station, the recommended procedure is to set (030/210) in the OBS and make heading corrections (toward/away from) the CDI. The *(TO/FROM)* flag would be in the window.

➤ 030, toward, FROM

43. To track inbound on the 030 radial of a VOR station, the recommended procedure is to set (030/210) in the OBS and make heading corrections (toward/away from) the CDI. The *(TO/FROM)* flag would be in the window.

➤ 210, toward, TO

Commercial Review

For Questions 1 to 6 refer to Figure 27-35.

1. Which illustration indicates that the airplane will intercept the 360 radial at a 60° angle inbound, if the present heading is maintained?

    (a) C.

    (b) D.

    (c) E.

    ➤ (a)

2. Which statement is true regarding illustration F, if the present heading is maintained?

    (a) The airplane will cross the 240 radial at a 60° angle.

    (b) The airplane will intercept the 240 radial at a 45° angle.

    (c) The airplane will intercept the 060 radial at a 60° angle.

    ➤ (c)

3. Which illustration indicates that the airplane will intercept the 060 radial at a 75° angle outbound, if the present heading is maintained?

    (a) D.

    (b) E.

    (c) F.

    ➤ (b)

4. Which illustration indicates that the airplane should be turned 150° left to intercept the 360 radial at a 60° angle inbound?

    (a) A.

    (b) B.

    (c) C.

    ➤ (a)

5. Which instrument shows the aircraft to be northwest of the VORTAC?

    (a) A.

    (b) B.

    (c) C.

    ➤ (b)

6. Which statement is true regarding illustration D if the present heading is maintained?

    (a) The airplane will cross the 060 radial at a 15° angle.

    (b) The airplane will intercept the 240 radial at a 30° angle.

    (c) The airplane will cross the 180 radial at a 75° angle.

    ➤ (a)

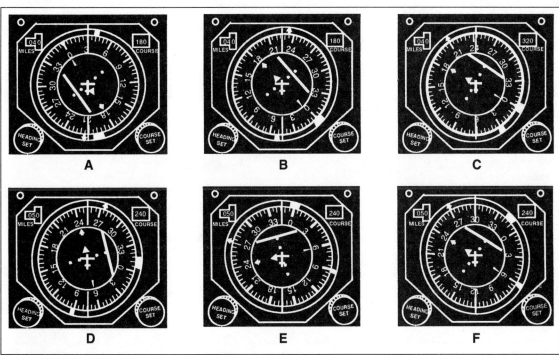

Figure 27-35.

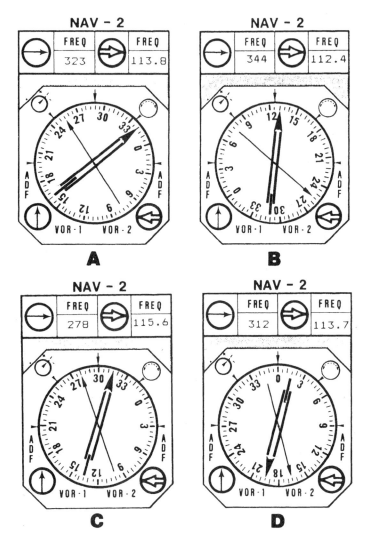

Figure 27-36.

For Questions 7 to 9 refer to Figure 27-36.

7. If an aircraft has the indications shown in instrument group C, then makes a 180° turn to the left and continues straight ahead, it will intercept which radial?

   (a) 135 radial.

   (b) 270 radial.

   (c) 360 radial.

➤ (a) (Note: The double-arrowed needle is selected to a VOR, hence "radial" refers to the tail of this needle.)

8. Which instrument shows the aircraft in a position where a straight course after a 90° left turn would result in intercepting the 180 radial?

   (a) B.

   (b) C.

   (c) D.

➤ (b) (refers to RMI 'C')

9. Which instrument shows the aircraft in a position where a 180° turn would result in the aircraft intercepting the 120 radial?

   (a) B.

   (b) C.

   (c) D.

➤ (c) (which refers to RMI 'D.' It would take some time on MH 180 to intercept the 120 radial, depending on how close you are to the VOR, but you would eventually intercept it off this heading.)

Radio Navigation 2 **28**

The NDB and the ADF

The **nondirectional beacon (NDB)** is the simplest form of radio navigation aid used by aircraft. It is a ground-based transmitter which transmits radio energy in all directions, hence its name—the nondirectional beacon.

The **ADF** or **automatic direction finder** installed in an airplane has a needle which indicates the direction from which the signals of the selected NDB ground station are being received. This is extremely useful information for pilots flying in instrument conditions and/or at night. It can also be of use to VFR pilots during visual navigation. Flying *to* an NDB in an airplane is similar to following a compass needle to the north pole—fly the airplane toward where the needle points, and eventually you will arrive overhead. Flying *away from* the north pole, however, with the magnetic compass needle pointing behind, could take the airplane in any one of 360 directions.

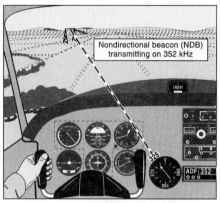

Figure 28-1. A correctly tuned ADF indicates the direction of the selected NDB from the aircraft

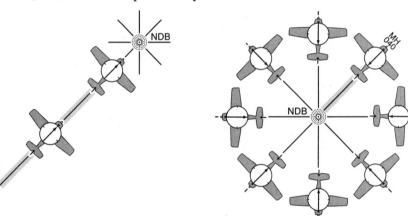

Figure 28-2. Flying to a station is straightforward

Figure 28-3. Flying away from a station requires further information

Similarly, flying away from an NDB using only the ADF needle will not lead the airplane to a particular point (unlike flying *to* an NDB). The airplane could end up anywhere! Further information is required.

The ADF and the Heading Indicator

The extra information required by the pilot, in addition to that supplied by the ADF needle, comes from the magnetic compass or, more commonly, from the heading indicator. Accurate navigation can be carried out using the aircraft **ADF needle** which points at an NDB ground station, and the airplane **heading indicator (HI)** which indicates the airplane's magnetic heading (MH).

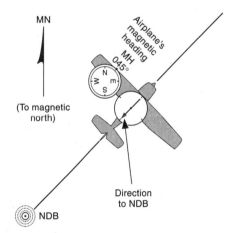

Figure 28-4. The ADF/NDB combination needs support from a magnetic compass (or from a heading indicator)

Note: Since a heading indicator will slowly drift out of alignment, it is vital to periodically realign it with the magnetic compass in straight flight at a steady speed, say every 10 minutes or so.

The ADF/NDB combination, in conjunction with the heading indicator, can be used to **track** to the NDB on any desired course, pass over the NDB, and track outbound on whatever course is desired, or to **fix** the airplane's position.

The ADF in the airplane should, whenever possible, be selected to an NDB relevant to the desired path of the airplane. If tracking en route between two NDBs, the changeover point from one NDB to the next would reasonably be the halfway point, depending of course on their relative ranges.

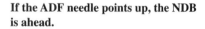

Figure 28-5. Periodically realign the HI with the magnetic compass in steady flight

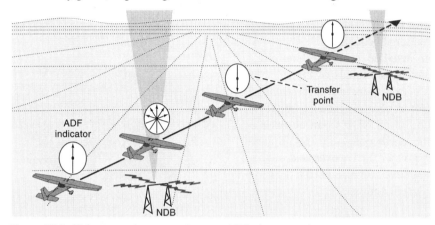

Figure 28-6. Flying towards, over, and past an NDB, then on to the next one

If the NDB is ahead, the ADF needle will point up the dial; if the NDB is behind, the ADF needle will point down the dial. As the airplane passes *over* the NDB, the ADF needle will become very sensitive and will swing from ahead to behind.

If the ADF needle points up, the NDB is ahead.

The NDB/ADF combination is the simplest form of radio navigation in theory, yet it requires a competent pilot to use it accurately in practice. Other advanced systems, such as the VOR, are more complicated in principle, but easier to use in practice.

If the ADF needle points down, the NDB is behind.

The NDB

The nondirectional beacon (NDB) is the ground-based part of the combination. It is referred to as *nondirectional* because no particular direction is favored in its transmissions; the NDB radiates identical electromagnetic energy in *all* directions.

The NDB is a ground-based transmitter.

Figure 28-7. Two types of NDB transmitting antennas

Each NDB transmits on a given frequency in the low-frequency or medium-frequency LF/MF band (somewhere between 200 and 1750 kHz).

To avoid confusion between various NDBs, and to ensure that the correct beacon is being used, each NDB transmits its own particular identification signal or **ident** in the form of a two- or three-lettered Morse code signal, which should be checked by the pilot before using the NDB for navigation. These codes can be found in the navigation boxes on your aeronautical charts.

Identify an NDB before using it for navigation.

The normal sources of NDB frequency and identification information are the charts, which you should be carrying in the cockpit. More detailed information on a particular NDB, or any other radio aid, is available in the A/FD.

NDB Range

For long range en route navigation where no other aids are available, a reasonably powerful NDB with a range of 100 nautical miles (nm) or more is usually required. Some NDBs used for long distance overwater tracking, for instance in the Pacific area, may have a range of 400 nm. In the United States, however, where route segments are relatively short and there are many aids, especially VORs, most NDBs have only a short range.

The range of an NDB depends on:

- the power of transmission (10–2,000 watts);
- the frequency of transmission;
- atmospheric conditions existing at the time—such as electrical storms, which can generate spurious signals, and periods of sunrise and sunset, which can distort or reflect the signals from an NDB; and
- the nature of the earth's surface over which the signals travel.

In the United States, NDBs are classified according to their range, or **standard service volume (SSV)** radius:

Class	Range	Class	Range
Compass locator	15 nm	H	50 nm
MH	25 nm	HH	75 nm

The distances above are the same at all altitudes. The classification (and range) for an individual NDB can be checked in the A/FD. The range of individual H-class NDB stations may be *less* than 50 nm; such restrictions will be published in NOTAMs, and in the A/FD.

NDB Accuracy

An ideal NDB signal received at an airplane may be accurate to ±2°, however various factors may reduce this accuracy considerably. These factors include:

- **Thunderstorm effect:** causing the ADF needle to be deflected toward a nearby electrical storm (cumulonimbus cloud) and away from the selected NDB.
- **Night effect**: at night, NDB signals can be refracted by the ionosphere and then return to earth as strong skywaves, causing interference with the normal NDB surface waves, and resulting in a fading signal and a wandering ADF needle (most pronounced at dawn and dusk).
- **Interference:** from other NDBs transmitting on similar frequencies (this can be particularly significant at night).
- **Mountain effect:** caused by reflections of the NDB signals from mountains.
- **Coastal effect:** caused by the NDB signal bending slightly toward the coastline when crossing it at an angle.

NDB Identification

Each NDB is identifiable by a two- or three-lettered Morse code identification signal which is transmitted along with its normal signal. This is known as its **ident.**

You *must* identify an NDB before using it for any navigational purposes within its operational range and, if using it for some length of time, then it should be periodically reidentified.

The lack of an ident may indicate that the NDB is out of service, even though it may still be transmitting (say for maintenance or test purposes), and it must *not* be used for navigation. When under test, the coded word **TEST** may sometimes be transmitted: *dah dit dit-dit-dit dah.* If this, or another incorrect ident is heard, then the selected NDB must not be used.

If a test or incorrect ident is heard, the NDB must not be used.

To identify most NDBs, select AUDIO on the ADF, listen to the Morse code signal confirming that the correct ident is being received. All NDBs in the U.S. can be identified with the ADF *mode selector* in the ADF position. In continental Europe and some of the Pacific Islands, however, there are still some NDBs that require selection of BFO (beat frequency oscillator) to enable identification. The BFO imposes a tone onto the NDB carrier wave to make it audible.

Figure 28-8. A typical NDB ident

It is also possible, in a situation where the communications radio (VHF COM) has failed, for ATC to transmit voice messages on the NDB frequency, and for a pilot to receive them on the ADF if AUDIO is selected. Those that do not have a voice capability will have a "no-voice" designator *W* included in their class designator in the A/FD, for example: HW.

Note: Broadcasting stations may also be received by an ADF, since they transmit in the LF/MF bands. It is not good airmanship, however, to use broadcasting stations as navigational aids, since they are difficult to identify precisely. Even if an announcer says, *"This is the Fort Worth Country and Western Hour,"* it is possible that the transmission is coming, not from the main transmitter, but from an alternative or emergency transmitter located elsewhere, or even a relay station miles away from the main transmitter.

The ADF

The airborne partner of the ground-based NDB is the **automatic direction finder,** usually referred to as the **ADF.** It operates on the **radio compass** principle whereby the ADF needle indicates the direction from which the signals are coming. Under ideal conditions, the ADF needle will point directly at the NDB antenna; under less-than-ideal conditions, the signals from the NDB antenna may not follow a straight path, and so the direction indicated by the ADF needle will be somewhat in error.

The ADF is an airborne receiver.

The automatic direction finder has three main components:

- The **ADF receiver,** installed in the cockpit radio panel, which the pilot tunes to the frequency of the desired NDB and verifies with the ident.
- The **antenna system,** comprising a loop antenna and a sense antenna (or their modern equivalent, a single combined unit) which together determine the signal direction.
- The **ADF cockpit display,** either a *fixed-card* or a *rotatable-compass-card,* with a pointer or needle indicating the signal direction. The top of the dial represents the nose of the airplane and the bottom of the dial represents its tail. Ideally, the ADF needle will point continually and automatically toward the NDB ground station.

Figure 28-9. The airborne ADF equipment

ADF antenna mounted under fuselage

ADF control panel

ADF card and pointer

ADF Control Panel

There are various types of ADF that may be fitted to an airplane and, prior to flight, you must be familiar with the set that you will use.

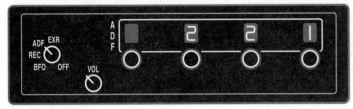

Figure 28-10. Typical ADF control panel

You must be able to select and positively identify the NDB that you wish to use, and then verify that the ADF needle is indeed responding to the signals from that NDB. The correct procedure, any time a new NDB is to be used, is to confirm:

- **selected;**
- **identified;** and
- **ADFing** (giving a sensible bearing to the NDB).

✍ Now complete **Review 28, Part (a)** on page 657.

The ADF Mode Selector or Function Switch

The mode selector has various positions that the pilot may elect to use:

OFF: to switch the ADF OFF.

ADF: the normal position when the pilot wants **bearing information** to be displayed automatically by the needle. Most NDBs can be identified with the mode selector in this position (with the volume knob adjusted accordingly).

> The ADF mode selector is usually selected to ADF.

ANT (sometimes REC): abbreviations for *antenna* or *receiver.* In this position, only the signal from the sense antenna is used, with no satisfactory directional information being available to the ADF needle. The reason for this function position is that it gives the best audio reception to allow easier identification, and better understanding of any voice messages. Never leave the mode selector in this position if you are navigating using the ADF—the ADF needle will remain stationary with no obvious indication that it is not responding! It is possible, however, to identify most NDBs with the mode selector in the ADF position (which is a safer position), and for the ANT position to be avoided.

BFO (sometimes CW): abbreviations for *beat frequency oscillator* or *continuous wave*. This position, rarely required in the United States, is selected when identifying the few NDBs that use A0/A1 or A1 transmissions, which are unmodulated carrier waves whose transmission is interrupted to provide the NDB's Morse code identification. Since no audio message is carried on an unmodulated carrier wave, the BFO (as part of the airborne equipment) imposes a tone onto the carrier wave signal to make it audible so that the NDB signal can be identified. Again, do not leave the mode selector switch in this position when navigating using the ADF.

TEST: Placing the mode selector into the TEST position will deflect the ADF needle from its current position. Switching the mode selector back to ADF should cause the needle to swing back and indicate the direction of the NDB. This function should be tested every time as part of the *selected, identified, ADFing* tuning procedure. Some ADF sets have a separate TEST button which only needs to be pressed to deflect the needle, and then released to check the return of the needle. You only have to deflect the needle approximately 30°, and watch the return, for the test to be satisfactory.

Note: On some ADF equipment, the TEST function is achieved using the ANT/REC position, which drives the needle to the 090 position. Returning the mode selector to ADF should see the needle start ADFing again.

VOL: The volume knob will probably be separate from the mode selector. With audio selected to the headset or cockpit speakers, the VOL knob should be adjusted so that the ident or any voice messages on the NDB or compass locator may be heard. If signal reception is poor in ADF mode, then try ANT/REC; if there is no signal reception, try BFO/CW. Remember to return the mode selector to ADF.

Frequency Knobs

NDBs transmit on frequencies in the range 200–1,750 kilohertz, the most common band being 200–400 kHz. To allow easier and accurate selection of any particular frequency, most modern ADFs have knobs that allow digital selection, in 100, 10 and 1 kHz steps. Some ADFs may have a band selector (200–400; 400–800; 800–1600 kHz), with either a tuning knob or digital selection for precise tuning.

ADF Cockpit Displays

The basic purpose of an automatic direction finder in an airplane is for its needle to point directly toward the selected NDB ground station. The ADF cockpit display is a *card* or *dial* placed vertically in the instrument panel so that:

Remember, with an ADF, the needle always points to the NDB station.

- if the ADF needle points up, the NDB is ahead;
- if the ADF needle points down, then the NDB is behind;
- if the ADF needle points to one side, then the NDB is located somewhere to that side of the fore-aft axis of the airplane.

To convey this information, various presentations are used, three of which we will consider:

- the **relative bearing indicator (RBI)**, also known as the **fixed-card ADF;**
- the **manually rotatable-card ADF**; and
- the **radio magnetic indicator (RMI).**

The Relative Bearing Indicator (RBI)

The **relative bearing indicator (RBI)** is also known as the **fixed-card ADF.** This display has an ADF needle that can rotate against the background of a fixed azimuth card of 360°, with 000 (360) at the top, 180 at the bottom, and so on. The RBI is common in older airplanes.

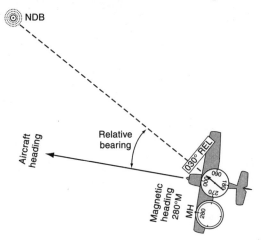

Figure 28-11. A fixed-card ADF is a relative bearing indicator

On the RBI, the ADF needle indicates the **relative bearing (RB)** of the NDB from the airplane.

The relative bearing of the NDB from the aircraft is the angle between the aircraft's heading and the direction of the NDB. Relative bearings are usually described clockwise from 000 to 360, however it is sometimes convenient to describe the bearing of the NDB relative to the nose or tail of the airplane.

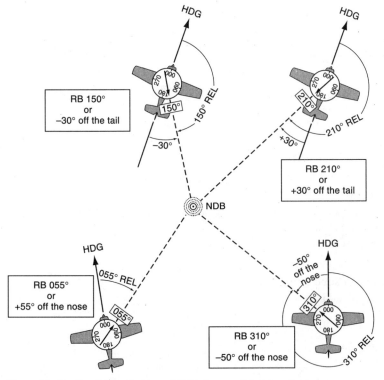

Figure 28-12. The RBI or fixed-card ADF shows relative bearings

Each time the airplane changes its magnetic heading, it will carry the fixed card with it, and so the ADF needle will indicate a different relative bearing.

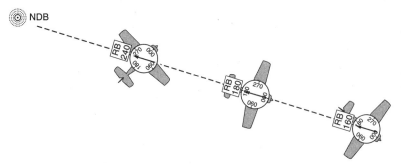

Figure 28-13. With each change of MH, the ADF needle will indicate a different RB

It is not the needle that moves, but rather the fixed-card—the needle continues to point at the station. The principle is easily understood if you stand, point at an object, and then turn and face another direction while continuing to point at the object. Your arm indicates the same direction to the object, but it makes a different angle with your body because you have changed your heading. The relative bearing of the object has changed because your heading has changed.

Orientation Using the RBI

The airplane can be oriented with respect to the NDB if you know the **MH** of the airplane (from the magnetic compass or HI) and the **relative bearing (RB)** of the NDB from the airplane.

In practice, magnetic heading is flown using the HI which should be realigned with the magnetic compass in steady flight every 10 minutes or so. Our illustrations will therefore display the heading indicator instead of the magnetic compass.

In Figure 28-14a, the airplane is flying MH 280, and the ADF indicates RB 030 to the NDB.

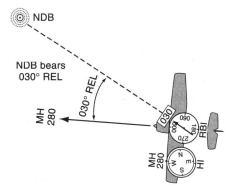

Figure 28-14a. Orientation: Where am I? using an RBI

MH 280	+	RB 030	=	MB 310 to NDB
Aircraft Magnetic Heading	+	Relative Bearing of NDB from aircraft	=	Magnetic Bearing of NDB from aircraft

The Magnetic Bearing To or From the NDB

A very useful and quick pictorial means of determining MB to an NDB, using a RBI and a HI, is to translate the ADF needle onto the HI, by paralleling a pencil (Figure 28-14b) or by using your imagination. MH + RB = MB to ground station.

The magnetic bearing of the aircraft *from* the NDB is the *reciprocal* of the magnetic bearing *to* the NDB. This is MB 130 *from* the NDB, which can be visualized as the *tail* of the pencil (or needle).

Note: An easier method of finding reciprocals than adding or subtracting 180°, is to either: add 200 and subtract 20; or subtract 200 and add 20.

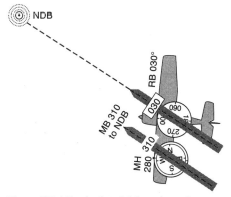

Figure 28-14b. A pictorial (but clumsy) method of finding MB

Example 1.

MB 310 to NDB	MB 270 to NDB	MB 085 to NDB
−200	−200	+200
+20	+20	−20
MB 130 from NDB	MB 090 from NDB	MB 265 from NDB

The Rotatable-Card ADF

The **rotatable-card ADF** is an improvement on the fixed-card ADF, because it allows the pilot to rotate the card so that the ADF needle indicates, not relative bearing, but magnetic bearing to the NDB. This is done by aligning the ADF card with the HI compass card each time the airplane's magnetic heading is changed.

To align a manually rotated ADF card:

• note magnetic heading on the HI; then
• rotate the ADF card, setting MH under the index.

When the ADF card is aligned with the HI, the ADF needle will indicate the MB *to* the NDB. This eliminates any need for mental arithmetic, which is advantageous. Note also that the tail of the needle, 180° removed from its head, indicates the magnetic bearing of the airplane *from* the NDB.

Any time the aircraft changes magnetic heading, you can then manually align the ADF card with the HI (after ensuring, of course, that the HI is aligned with the magnetic compass).

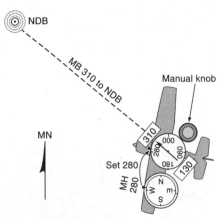

Figure 28-15. Using a rotatable-card ADF

Any time the aircraft changes magnetic heading, manually align the ADF card with the HI.

The Radio Magnetic Indicator (RMI)

The next step up from a rotatable-card ADF is an instrument whose card remains aligned automatically, called the **radio magnetic indicator,** or **RMI.** The RMI display has the ADF needle superimposed on a card that is continuously and automatically being aligned with magnetic north. It is, if you like, an automatic version of the rotatable-card ADF—an *automatic* combination of the HI and RBI.

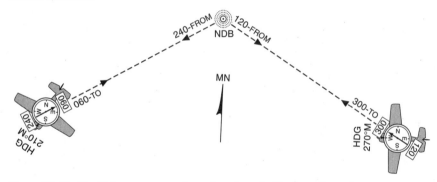

Figure 28-16. The RMI compass card remains aligned with magnetic north

The RMI is the best ADF presentation, and the easiest to use, but unfortunately the most expensive and usually only encountered in more sophisticated aircraft.

As an airplane turns and its MH alters, the RMI card (which automatically remains aligned with magnetic north) will appear to turn along with the ADF needle. In reality, of course, it is the compass card and the RMI needle that remain stationary, while the airplane turns about them. Before, during and after the turn, the RMI's needle will continue to indicate the current MB *to* the NDB.

The RMI needle will always indicate the MB *to* the NDB.

The tail of the RMI needle will indicate the MB *from* the NDB.

Gyro-Stabilized Compass Equipment

In most airplanes fitted with an RMI, the initial magnetic north reference for the RMI card is provided by a **fluxgate** or **fluxvalve.** This is simply an electronic compass with a detector that is sensitive to magnetic north. The detector is usually situated in a fairly nonmagnetic part of the airplane such as in a wingtip.

A directional gyroscope is electrically slaved to this magnetic reference so that the gyroscope is continually being aligned with magnetic north, and it is this directional gyroscope that drives the RMI compass card in a process known as **slaving.**

RMI compass card

Directional gyro
drives RMI
compass card

Fluxvalve
provides magnetic
reference to
directional gryo

Courtesy Allied Signal Aerospace

Figure 28-17. The RMI compass card is driven by a fluxvalve and directional gyro

Most gyro-stabilized compasses have an **annunciator** near the compass card. This contains a small needle, often triangular in shape, that oscillates when automatic slaving is in process (which should be all the time). When the annunciator needle is hard over to one side, it indicates that the compass card is a long way out of alignment; this can usually be remedied using a manual **synchronizing knob** to quickly realign the compass card with the MH of the airplane, after which the slower, automatic slaving should be sufficient to maintain alignment.

If slaving is not occurring because of some fault in the system (indicated by the annunciator being stationary and not oscillating) then you can revert to using the RMI as a manually rotated-card ADF or as a fixed-card ADF.

Two Pointers
Some airplanes are fitted with two ADF receivers, and have two needles superimposed on the one indicator (which may be a fixed-card twin-ADF indicator, or a dual-pointer RMI).

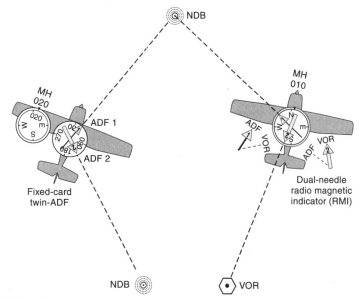

Figure 28-18. An indicator with two needles

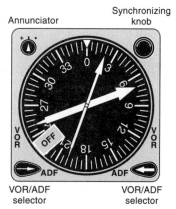

Figure 28-19. A typical 2-needle RMI

Most RMIs have function switches that allow selection of either an NDB or a VOR ground station for the RMI needle to point at. This gives more flexibility in using radio navigation aids, since the RMI can be selected to any suitable NDB or VOR within range. With two needles, one can be selected to the ADF and the other to the VOR.

Operational Use of the ADF

The principles of using the ADF are the same whether the airplane is equipped with an RBI or an RMI display. Early models of the ADF were primarily of the fixed-card ADF design, with the rotatable-card ADF coming as a later improvement to the instrument. Many airplanes are still equipped with this instrument, which, although being more difficult to use than the more modern RMI design, is still an excellent aid.

The rotatable-card ADF will allow you to manually align the ADF card with magnetic north. This can be done whenever the aircraft heading is changed. Once aligned, this will also reduce your workload by reducing the amount of visualization and mental arithmetic required.

The RMI combines the RBI and the HI into the one instrument, where the ADF card is aligned automatically with magnetic north. This considerably reduces your workload by reducing the amount of visualization and mental arithmetic required.

Whatever ADF instrument is installed in your airplane, the same principles of operation apply. The discussion that follows applies to both the RBI, RMI and the manually rotatable-card ADF, except that:

- The fixed-card ADF requires you to visualize and mentally transfer the indicated relative bearing to the NDB ground station across to the airplane HI.
- The manually rotatable-card RBI must be realigned with the heading indicator by hand following every heading change (and of course the HI must be realigned with the magnetic compass by hand every 10 minutes or so).
- The RMI is continuously and automatically aligned with magnetic north.

An RMI gives a graphic picture of where the airplane is:
- the *head* of the RMI needle displays magnetic bearing *to* the ground station;
- the *tail* of the RMI needle displays magnetic bearing *from* the ground station.

One significant advantage of the RMI over the RBI is that you can select it to either an NDB or a VOR ground station. Some RMIs have two needles which allow two stations to be selected. The method of use is the same in each case. If the head of the RMI needle indicates 030, then we write this as RMI 030. It tells us that the magnetic bearing *to* the ground station from the airplane is 030 degrees magnetic. The bearing *from* the ground station to the airplane is, of course, the reciprocal 210 degrees magnetic.

Figure 28-20. The manually rotatable ADF card

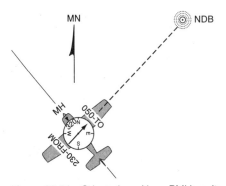

Figure 28-21. Orientation with an RMI is quite straightforward

Courtesy Allied Signal Aerospace

Figure 28-22. Typical radio magnetic indicators

Orientation

A **position line,** also known as a **line of position (LOP),** is a line along which the airplane is known to be at a particular moment. A line of position may be obtained either visually or by radio means as shown in Figure 28-23.

Two lines of position that cut at a reasonable angle, ideally close to 90°, are needed for a *fix.* For the airplane to be on both lines of position simultaneously, it must be at their point of intersection.

A *radio fix* can be obtained using two NDBs in an airplane fitted with two ADFs. It is possible to fix position using a combination of radio aids including NDBs, VORs and DMEs. Figure 28-24 shows that these position lines can be considered from two perspectives:

- **To the NDB** from the airplane. This is the line of position to the NDB that a pilot would see from the airplane as either a *relative* bearing (RB 030 *to* NDB 1), or as a *magnetic* bearing to the NDB (MB 360 *to* NDB 1).

- **From the NDB** to the airplane, as a *magnetic* bearing from the station (MB 180 *from* NDB 1). The magnetic bearing from the NDB may be converted to a *true* bearing by applying magnetic variation, if for instance you wanted to plot the airplane's position on a chart.

Example 2. The airplane in Figure 28-25 is steering MH 015. Its ADF needle points toward a nondirectional beacon 75° to the right of the nose on a relative bearing indicator (also known as a fixed-card ADF). Magnetic variation is 5°W. Calculate:

(a) the relative bearing (RB) to the NDB from the airplane;

(b) the magnetic bearing to the NDB from the airplane;

(c) the magnetic bearing from the NDB to the airplane; and

(d) the true bearing from the NDB to the airplane.

While it is possible to calculate all of this mentally, at this early stage it is a good idea to sketch a clear diagram to help visualize the situation.

Step 1. Sketch the airplane on MH 015.

Step 2. Indicate RB 075.

Step 3. Draw in the position line to the NDB.

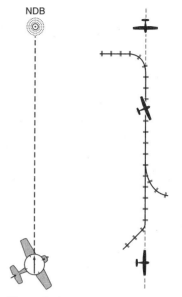

Figure 28-23. A radio position line (left) and a visual position line

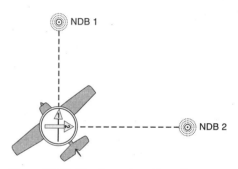

Figure 28-24. Two lines of position with a good "cut" can provide a fix

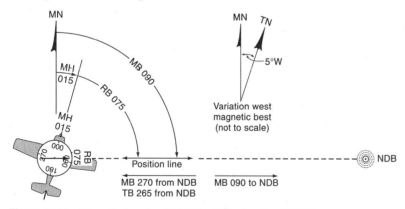

Figure 28-25. Magnetic heading MH 015; relative bearing RB 075

MH 015	MB 090 to NDB	Variation West	MB 270 from NDB
RB 075	+ 180	Magnetic Best	Var'n −5
MB 090 to NDB	**MB 090 to NDB**		**TB 265 from NDB**

Answers: RB 075; MB 090 to NDB; MB 270 from NDB; TB 265 from NDB.

True Bearings From an NDB

To plot your position relative to an NDB on a sectional chart, you will need to determine your true bearing from the NDB—your bearing from the NDB related to *true north*. True north is indicated on the chart by the meridians of longitude that run north-south. You can then plot your straight true bearing position line from the NDB.

Note: It is possible to plot *magnetic* bearings from a VOR, known as *radials*, since each VOR shown on a chart has a compass rose around it oriented to *magnetic* north—NDBs do not. True bearing = magnetic bearing plus east variation (minus west variation).

Example 3. MH is 280. RB is 050. What is the true bearing (TB) from the NDB? Magnetic variation in the area is 6°W.

MH 280 + RB 050 = MB 330 to NDB
$$-2$$
$$+2$$
MB 150 from NDB
$$\underline{-6\,°W\ Var'n}$$
TB 144 from NDB

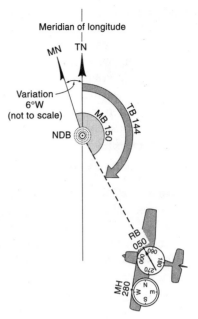

Figure 28-26. Finding true bearing from an NDB

An Easier Method of Visualizing MB

A relative bearing, as well as being specified using the 360° method clockwise from the nose of the airplane, can be specified as either **left** or **right** of the nose (or the tail). For instance, a RB of 290 may be thought of as –70, since the corresponding MB will be 70° *less* than the current MH. Similarly, RB 030 may be thought of as +30, since the corresponding MB to the NDB will be 30° *greater* than the MH.

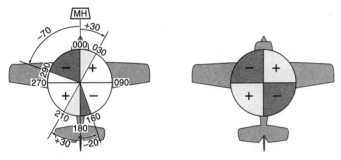

Figure 28-27. Quadrants for converting relative bearings to magnetic bearings

Relative bearings off the *tail* of the airplane may be treated in a similar shorthand fashion. For instance, RB 160 may be thought of as –20 off the tail; and RB 210 as +30 off the tail. This **quadrantal** approach to RB and MB problems can simplify your in-flight visualization.

Example 4. An airplane is steering MH 340. The ADF needle shows RB 010. Determine the MB to the NDB.

MH340
$$\underline{+10}$$ off the nose (RB 010)
MB 350 to NDB

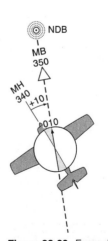

Figure 28-28. Example 4.
MH 340 + 10 off the nose = MB 350

Visualizing Position on the Heading Indicator

Mentally transferring the RBI needle onto the HI allows quick visualization of MB *to* NDB on the head of the needle, and MB *from* NDB on its tail.

If you now imagine a model airplane attached to the tail of the needle, with the model airplane oriented with the actual heading, you have a very good picture of the whole situation.

Mentally transferring the RBI onto the HI is the norm when flying the airplane and is considerably easier than performing mental calculations and flying at the same time.

Example 5. Visualize the situation of MH 070 and RB 260. *See* Figure 28-29.

Changing Heading

The ADF needle points directly at the selected NDB (*see* Figure 28-31). If the aircraft heading is changed, the ADF needle will continue to point at the NDB, but the relative bearing between the ADF needle and the nose of the aircraft will alter by the same number of degrees. For example, if the aircraft heading increases by 45° by turning right, the RB will decrease (by 45°).

Example 6. With reference to the instrument indications in Figure 28-31, what would be the relative bearing if the aircraft was turned onto a MH of 355°?

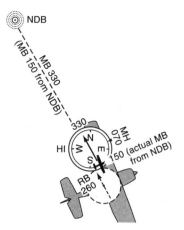

Figure 28-29. Visualizing position on the HI; MH 070 and MB 330

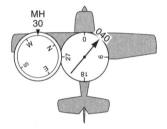

Figure 28-31. Typical heading and ADF indications

1. MH 300 + RB 040 to NDB = MB 340 to NDB.
2. Changing heading to MH 355 will *not* alter the MB to the NDB, but will alter the RB. The heading will change by +55°, and the RB will change by –55°. *See* Figure 28-30.

```
MB   =   MH  +  RB
340  =   355 +  RB
RB   =   340 –  355
     =   –015 (360 – 15 = 345)
```

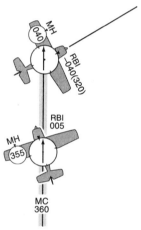

Figure 28-30. Changing heading alters relative bearing

✍ Now complete **Review 28, Part (b)** on page 657.

Intercepting Course

Having oriented yourself with respect to an NDB, you know the answer to the question, "Where am I?" You now may ask, "Where do I want to go?" and "How do I get there?" This is accomplished by:

- **Orienting the airplane** relative to the NDB, and to the desired course.
- **Turning to take up a suitable intercept heading,** after considering where you want to join the desired course.
- **Maintaining the intercept heading and wait**:
  - for the *head* of the needle to fall if inbound; or
  - for the *tail* of the needle to rise if outbound.
- **Just before the desired course is reached,** commencing a turn to complete the intercept, and applying a suitable **wind correction angle** to maintain it.

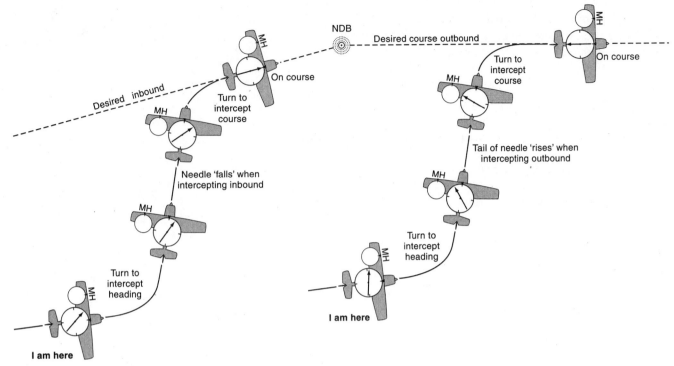

Figure 28-32. Visualizing: Where am I? Where do I want to go? How do I get there?

The HI can assist greatly in visualizing the situation. In Example 5 (Figure 28-29), the situation MH 070 and RB 260 was visualized, with MB 330 to the NDB.

Now what if you wish to intercept a magnetic course (MC) 270 to the NDB? All that you need to do is visualize the desired course on the HI. With a model airplane on the tail of the needle tracking as desired, it becomes quite clear what turns are necessary to intercept the desired course.

First turn left to a suitable intercept heading, say MH 360 for a 90° intercept of MC 270 to the NDB.

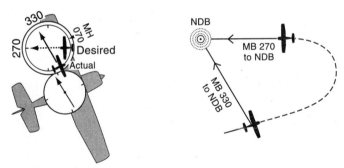

Figure 28-33. Visualizing an intercept on the HI

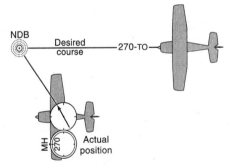

Figure 28-34. Paralleling course to help in visualization

Note: If you become disoriented, a simple procedure is to take up the heading of the desired course. Even though not on course, the airplane will at least be parallel to it, and the ADF needle will indicate which way to turn to intercept it.

Suppose the situation is MH 340, RB 080 (shown in Figure 28-35), and you wish to intercept a course MC 090 to the NDB. The current magnetic bearing to the NDB is easily found to be MB 060 (MH 340 + RB 080).

By continuing to steer MH 340 (shown in Figure 28-36), the airplane will eventually intercept MC 090 to the NDB, but it would be a rather untidy intercept, with the airplane tracking somewhat away from the NDB, and with an intercept turn of 110° being required.

A tidier and more efficient intercept may be achieved by turning to an initial heading of MH 360 for a 90° intercept (shown in Figure 28-37); or MH 030 for a 60° intercept. Turning further right to MH 060 would of course point the airplane at the NDB, and MC 090 to the NDB would not be intercepted.

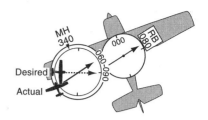

Figure 28-35. Visualizing the intercept

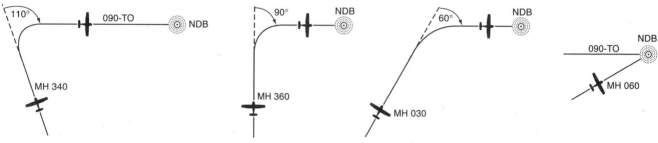

Figure 28-36. An inefficient intercept of course

Figure 28-37. Different intercepts of course

Intercepting an Inbound Course

Example 7. Fixed-Card ADF. An airplane is steering MH 355, and the RBI indicates RB 005 when tuned to a particular NDB. The pilot is requested to track inbound on course MC 340 to the station, intercepting the course at 60°. *See* Figure 28-38.

Initially, orient the airplane. MH 355 + RB 005 = MB 360 to NDB, or MB 180 from NDB. The airplane is south of the NDB and heading MH 355. The desired course is MC 340 to the NDB (which is on the line of position MB 160 from the NDB), to the right of the airplane.

Second, to intercept the course MC 340 from the left at 60°, the airplane should steer (340 + 60 = 400) MH 040. As the airplane's heading alters, the ADF needle will continue to point *at* the NDB and so the *relative* bearing will change (in this case, even though it is not an important calculation, from RB 005 to RB 320, or –40 off the nose, with the 45° right turn).

Third, maintain MH 040 and periodically observe the RBI as the head of the needle falls. Since it is a *plus 60* intercept, wait until the head of the needle falls to *minus 60* (or RB 300). You are steering **course plus 60, waiting for minus 60.**

Finally, at MB 340 to the NDB, and as the needle is falling to RB –60, turn left to take up the desired course to the NDB, allowing for the estimated crosswind effect on tracking. In this case, a wind correction angle (WCA) of 3° left is used. Maintain the desired course of MC 340 to the station by continually checking that MH + RB = MB 340, for example:
MH 337 + RB 003 = MB 340.

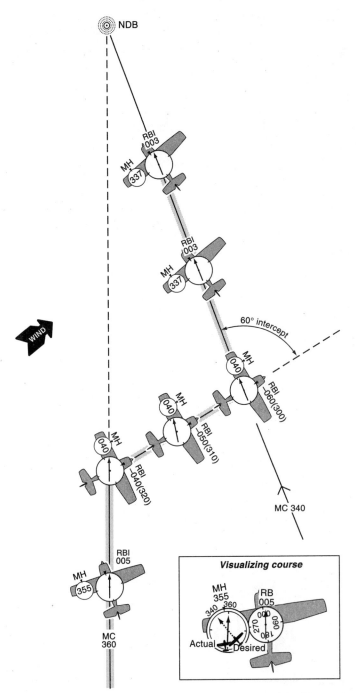

NDB

RBI
/003

MH
337

RBI
003

MH
337

60° intercept

MH
040

RBI
-060(300)

MH
040

RBI
-050(310)

MH
040

RBI
-040(320)

MC 340

WIND

RBI
005

MH
355

MC
360

Visualizing course

MH
355
340 360

RB
005
000

270   090
180

Actual   Desired

Figure 28-38. Intercepting MC 340 inbound, from the south of the station

Note: An airplane takes some distance to turn, and so you should anticipate the desired course by commencing the turn onto course just before MB 340 is reached. You can do this by observing the *rate* at which the ADF needle falls toward –060, and commence the turn accordingly.

Example 8. RMI. An airplane has a MH 340 and the RMI indicates 030. You are requested to intercept a course of 090 to the NDB.

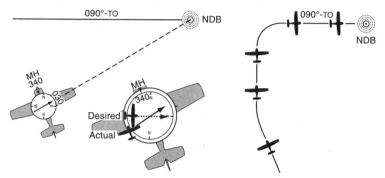

Figure 28-39. Visualizing course on an RMI

First, orient the airplane with the RMI. The magnetic bearing to the NDB from your present position is 030. If you now imagine a model airplane attached to the *tail* of the needle, with the airplane on the actual heading (which in this case is MH 340), then you have a very good picture of the situation.

The desired course of 090 *to* the NDB is ahead of the present position of the airplane. If you visualize the desired course on the RMI, with the model airplane on the *tail* of the needle tracking as desired, it becomes quite clear what turns are required to intercept the desired course.

Second, intercept course MC 090 to the NDB. Turn to a suitable intercept heading, such as one of those illustrated below.

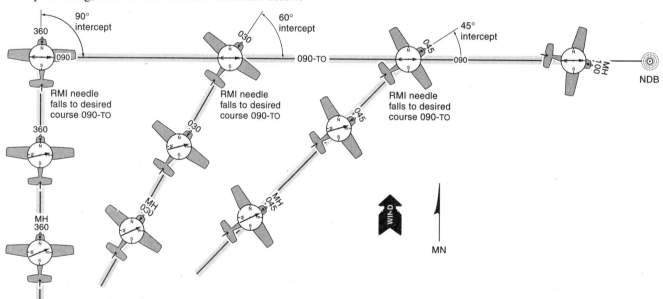

Figure 28-40. Intercepting course at 90°, 60°, or 45°

Third, maintain the chosen intercept heading and periodically observe the RMI needle as it falls toward the desired inbound course of 090.

Finally, as MC 090 to the NDB is approached, indicated by the RMI needle approaching 090, turn right to take up the desired course to the NDB, allowing for any estimated crosswind effect on tracking. In this case, a WCA of 10° right has been used. With MH 100, and the RMI steady on 090, the airplane now tracks MC 090 to the NDB.

Intercepting an Outbound Course

Example 9. Fixed-card ADF. The radar controller gives you a radar vector of 340 to intercept an outbound course of 280. *See* Figure 28-41.

Initially, orient the airplane. It must be south of the outbound course.

Second, consider the intercept. A radar vector of 340 to intercept MC 280 outbound means a +60° intercept.

Third, monitor the intercept by steering a steady MH 340 and periodically checking the RBI to see the **tail** of the needle rising to –60 (RB 300). You are steering **course plus 60, waiting for minus 60.**

Finally, as MC 280 outbound is approached, indicated by the tail of the needle rising to –60, turn left to pick it up, in this case allowing a WCA of 10° for a wind from the right—MH 290.

Periodically check that MH ADF tail = MB from NDB. In this case, the tail of the ADF needle should be –10 off the nose (on RB 350), so that MH290 – 10 = MC280 from NDB.

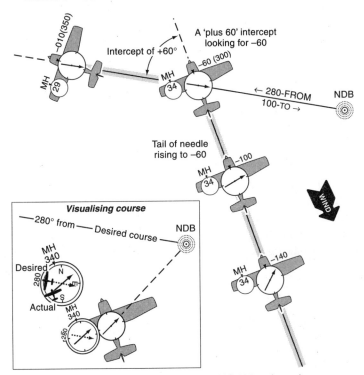

Figure 28-41. Radar vector 340 to intercept MC 280 outbound

Example 10. RMI. You are given a radar vector of 340 to intercept 280 outbound from an NDB. *See* Figure 28-42.

Initially, orient the airplane.

Second, consider the intercept, 60° in this case (340 – 280 = 60). Visualize the situation. Again, the model airplane imagined on the tail of the needle helps.

Third, monitor the intercept by steering a steady MH 340 and periodically checking the *tail* of the RMI needle rising to 280.

Finally, as the desired course 280 outbound is approached, and as the tail of the needle approaches 280, turn left to pick up the MC 280, in this case allowing no WCA, since you expect no crosswind effect.

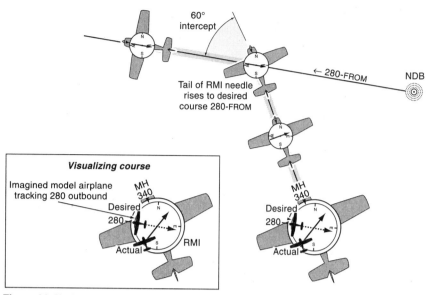

Figure 28-42. Intercepting 280 outbound off radar vector 340

Tracking

The ADF/NDB combination is often used to provide guidance for an airplane to fly from a distant position to a position overhead the NDB ground station. This is known as **tracking.** Just how this is achieved depends to a certain extent on the prevailing wind direction and speed.

Tracking Inbound with no Crosswind

When tracking toward an NDB, the head of the ADF needle will lie toward the top of the dial. With no crosswind, a direct inbound course can be achieved by simply pointing the airplane directly *at* the NDB, by steering a heading that keeps the **fixed-card ADF** needle on the nose (RB 000). Since the MH will, in this case, be the same as the desired course, the **RMI** needle will also be on the nose indicating the course.

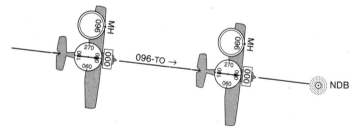

Figure 28-43. Tracking inbound, with no crosswind

If there is no crosswind to blow the airplane off course, then everything will remain constant as shown in Figure 28-43—the MH 096, the RB 000, and the MB 096 to the NDB will all remain constant. This can only occur in:

• no-wind conditions;

• a direct headwind; or

• a direct tailwind.

Tracking Inbound with a Crosswind

If no wind correction angle (WCA) is applied, and the airplane is pointed directly at the NDB, so that the ADF needle indicates RB 000, then any crosswind will cause the airplane to be blown off course.

In the case illustrated in Figure 28-44, a wind with a northerly component has blown the airplane to the right of course. This is indicated by the ADF needle starting to move down the left of the dial. To return to course, the airplane must be turned toward the left, toward the direction in which the head of the needle is moving.

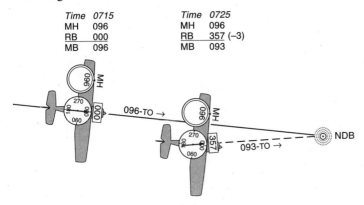

Figure 28-44. Crosswind causes drift

If you turn left to put the NDB on the nose again, so that the RB is 000, then after a short while the airplane will again have been blown to the right of course, and the ADF needle will again move to the left of the nose. A further turn to the left will be required—and the process will need to be repeated again and again.

In this way, the ground track to the NDB will be curved, and the airplane will finally arrive overhead the NDB heading roughly into the wind. This rather inefficient means of tracking over the NDB is known as **homing** (keeping the NDB on the nose). It will involve traveling a greater distance than that required to fly a direct course to the NDB from the original position.

With the correct WCA applied, the airplane will track directly toward the ground station in a straight line. This is known as **tracking** and is a far better procedure than homing. If 5° left is indeed the correct WCA, you can achieve a course of MC 096 direct to the NDB by steering MH 091 (Figure 28-45).

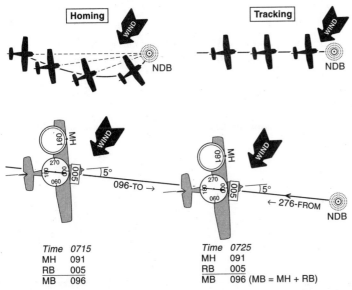

Figure 28-45. Tracking direct to the NDB

Different winds will require different WCAs. An airplane is on course when the RB is equal-and-opposite to the difference between the actual MH and the desired MC. This is illustrated in Figure 28-46. In each situation, the airplane is on the desired course of MC 010, but using a different WCA to counteract the drift under different wind conditions. The head of the ADF needle will point at the NDB and, with the current WCA applied, the nose of the aircraft will point upwind of this.

If the precise wind effect is not known, then initially use a *best-guess* WCA estimated from the available information. For the same crosswind, slower airplanes will need to allow a greater WCA than faster airplanes. See how the estimated WCA works, then make an adjustment to heading if required.

It is possible that the wind effect will change as an airplane tracks toward an NDB, so regular adjustments to the heading may be required. This is often the case as an airplane descends while using the NDB as the tracking aid, as changes in wind speed and/or direction may occur during the descent.

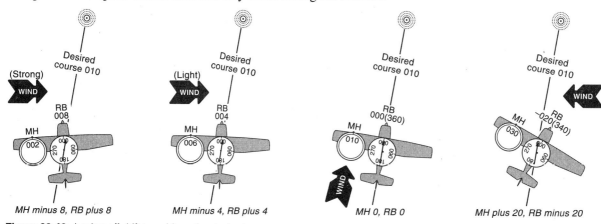

Figure 28-46. Laying off drift to achieve the desired course

If an incorrect drift correction is made, then the airplane will move off the desired course. The RB indication, and the MB to the NDB, will change. If a steady heading is being flown, then any divergence from course will become obvious through a gradually changing RB, with the ADF needle moving left or right down the dial.

Suppose, for instance, you fly a heading with a 5° WCA to the left to counteract the effect of a wind from the left. If the wind effect turns out to be less than expected, then the airplane will gradually move to the left of the desired course to the NDB, and the RB will gradually increase (naturally, the MB to the NDB will also increase).

Modify the wind correction angle to maintain course by altering heading.

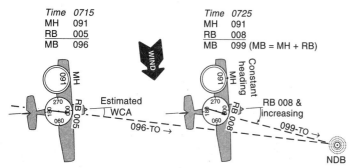

Figure 28-47. An incorrect wind correction angle causes MB to change

The head of the ADF needle falling away to the right indicates that a turn right must be made to track to the NDB. Conversely, the head of the ADF needle falling away to the left indicates that a left turn must be made to track to the NDB. Just how great each correcting turn should be depends on the deviation from course.

Note: Be careful of terminology. *Drift* is the angle between heading and the *ground track*, which may not be the desired course. The perfect wind correction angle will counteract any drift exactly, and the actual ground track will follow the desired course, which is usually the aim of tracking.

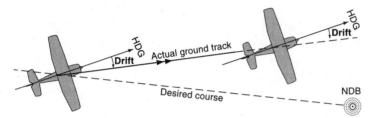

Figure 28-48. Drift is the angle between heading and ground track

Maintaining Course

In reality, *flying level* is a series of small and gentle climbs and descents made in an attempt to maintain the desired altitude perfectly. Similarly, *tracking* is a series of small turns made in an attempt to maintain the desired course perfectly.

Reintercepting a course, having deviated from it, involves the same procedure as the initial intercept of a new course, except that the intercept angles will be smaller (provided you are vigilant and do not allow large deviations to occur). Realizing that the airplane is diverging from the direct course to the NDB, you have several options. You may either:

- track direct from the present position (along a new course); or
- regain the original course.

To track direct from your present position to the NDB (even though the present position is not on the originally desired course), turn slightly right (say 3° in this case), and track direct to the NDB from the present position. Normally, this technique is used only when within one or two miles from the NDB, when there is insufficient distance remaining to regain the original course.

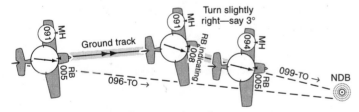

Figure 28-49. Needle head falling right; turn right

To regain the original course, turn further right initially (say 5° to MH 096), and reintercept the original course by allowing the wind to blow the airplane back onto it. Once the desired course is regained, turn left and steer a heading with a different WCA, (say WCA 3° left instead of 5° left), MH 093 instead of MH 091. This is a relatively minor correction.

If MH + RB = desired MB constantly, then ADF tracking is good.

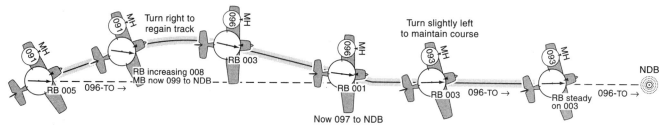

Figure 28-50. Regain the desired course

Attempting to maintain the desired course (by remaining on a constant MB to the NDB) is the normal navigational technique when at some distance from the NDB. If, when steering a steady MH, the ADF needle indicates a constant RB near the top of the dial, then the airplane is tracking directly to the NDB, and no correction to heading is necessary.

Bracketing Course

In practice, an absolutely perfect direct course is difficult to achieve. The actual ground track flown will probably consist of a series of short segments either side of the desired course, which corresponds to minor corrections similar to those described above. This technique is known as **bracketing** the course, and involves making suitable heading corrections, left or right as required, to regain and maintain the desired course.

The aim of bracketing is to find the precise WCA needed to maintain course. If, for instance, a WCA of 10° right is found to be too great and the airplane diverges to the right of course, and a WCA of only 5° right is too little and the wind blows the airplane to the left of course, then try something in between, say WCA 8° right.

You should monitor the tracking of the airplane on a regular basis, and make corrections earlier rather than later, resulting in a number of small corrections rather than just one big correction. However, if a big correction *is* required as may be the case in strong winds, make it. Be positive in your actions!

Wind Effect

If the wind direction and strength is not obvious, then the best technique is to initially steer course as heading and make no allowance for drift.

The effect of the wind will become obvious as the ADF needle moves to the left or right. Observe the results, and then make appropriate heading adjustments to bracket course.

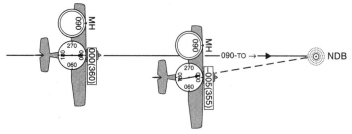

Figure 28-52. If uncertain of wind, initially steer course as heading

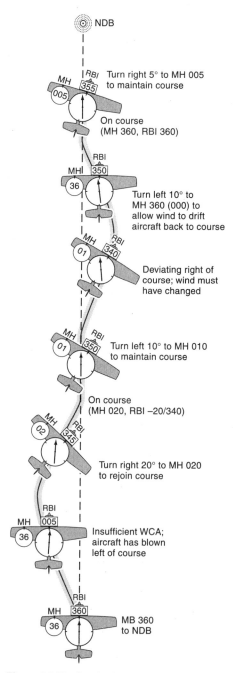

Figure 28-51. Bracketing the course
Head of needle falling right – turn right.
Head of needle falling left – turn left.

Tracking Over an NDB

The closer you get to an NDB, the more sensitive the ADF needle becomes. Minor displacements left or right of course will cause larger and larger changes in RB and MB. For a precise course to be achieved, you must be prepared to increase your scan rate as the NDB is approached, and to make smaller corrections more frequently.

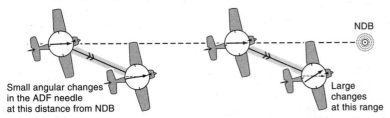

Figure 28-53. Approaching the NDB, the ADF needle becomes more sensitive

Close to the station and just prior to passing over the NDB, the ADF needle will become sensitive and agitated. You should, at this point, relax a little and steer a steady heading until the airplane passes over the NDB, indicated by the ADF needle moving from the top toward the bottom of the dial.

Having passed over the NDB, tracking *from* the NDB should be checked and suitable adjustments made to heading. If the course outbound is different from that inbound, then a suitable heading change estimated to make good the new desired course could be made as soon as the ADF needle falls past the 090 or 270 position on its way to the bottom of the dial.

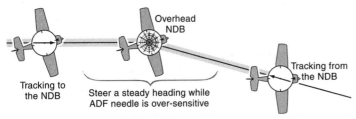

Figure 28-54. Do not overcorrect when close to the station

The ADF needle becoming extremely active, and then falling rapidly to the bottom of the dial, indicates that the airplane has passed directly over the NDB.

The ADF needle moving gradually to one side, and slowly falling to the bottom of the dial indicates that the airplane is passing to one side of the beacon, the rate at which the needle falls being an indication of the airplane's proximity to the NDB. If it falls very slowly, then possibly the tracking could have been better.

Time over (or abeam) the NDB with no WCA can be taken as the needle falls through the approximate 090 or 270 position.

Time over (or abeam) the NDB with a WCA 10° right can be taken as the needle falls through the approximate 080 (090 – WCA 10) or 260 (270 – WCA 10) position.

Tracking Outbound with no Crosswind

When tracking away from an NDB, the *head* of the ADF needle will lie toward the bottom of the dial and the *tail* of the ADF needle will be toward the top of the dial (Figure 28-56). If the pilot tracks over the NDB and then steers course as heading, the airplane will track directly away from the NDB with the head of the fixed-card ADF needle steady on 180, and the tail of the fixed-card ADF needle steady at the top of the dial on 000. The tail of the **RMI** equipped airplane will also lie towards the top of the dial and will indicate the MB from the station.

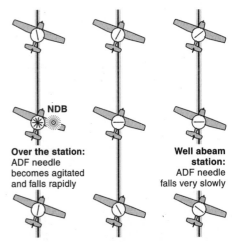

Over the station: ADF needle becomes agitated and falls rapidly

Well abeam station: ADF needle falls very slowly

Figure 28-55. Good ADF tracking (left); reasonable tracking (center); poor tracking (right)

Since we are considering the outbound course, in both cases it is the tail of the needle that is of more use. The airplane in Figure 28-56 has MB 040 from the NDB, and MB 220 to the NDB.

Tracking Outbound with a Crosswind

Suppose that the desired course outbound from an NDB is MC 040, and the pilot estimates that a WCA of 5° to the right is necessary to counteract a wind from the right. To achieve this, he steers MH 045, and hopes to see the *tail* of the ADF needle stay on –5 off the nose (RB 355). The MC away from the station is found from:

MB from NDB = MH deflection of the *tail* of the needle.

In this case, MH 045 – 005 tail = MB 040 from NDB, and so the chosen WCA and magnetic heading to steer are *correct* (Figure 28-57).

If the estimated WCA is *incorrect*, then the actual ground track made by the airplane will differ from the desired course. If, in the previous case, the wind is stronger than expected, the airplane's ground track may be 033, and to the left of the desired course of MC 040 (Figure 28-58).

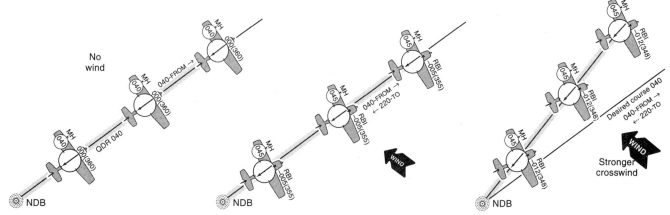

Figure 28-56. Tracking away from an NDB with no crosswind effect

Figure 28-57. Tracking away from an NDB, with a WCA of 5° into wind

Figure 28-58. Tracking away from an NDB with an incorrect wind correction angle

Whereas inaccurate tracking *to* an NDB is indicated by the ADF needle falling, incorrect tracking *away* from an NDB can occur with the ADF needle indicating a steady reading. Having passed overhead the NDB, an airplane can track away from it in any of 360 directions. You must always ensure that you are flying away from the NDB along the correct course, and the easiest means to do this is to calculate MB from the NDB using the HI and the RBI.

✍ Now complete **Review 28, Part (c)** on page 658.

Radar and the Transponder

Radar

VFR pilots often fly near or within a radar environment, so an understanding of radar is useful. An in-depth knowledge is required for the IFR certificate and this is fully covered in Volume 3 of the Pilot's Manual, *Instrument Flying*.

In the high-volume traffic environment of today's airspace, **radar** is the primary tool used by Air Traffic Control to provide many vital services to airplanes, such as radar vectoring, radar separation and sequencing. The air traffic controller is presented with an electronic map of his area of responsibility, showing the position of airplanes within it.

FAA radar units operate continuously at the locations shown in the Airport/Facility Directory (A/FD). Their primary role is to provide positive direction and coordination for IFR flights, but they are also used to provide a varying level of service to VFR flights, depending on the facilities available, the type of airspace, and controller workload.

The radar controller can also provide a **radar traffic information service** to alert pilots to other nearby and possibly conflicting traffic. Even if in receipt of this service, you are still responsible for continual vigilance to **see and avoid** other traffic. The radar controller will pass what he considers relevant information using the clock system to specify the position of the other traffic relative to your track. He sees your *track* on his screen rather than your heading, so you will have to allow for the drift angle due to the wind effect when you look out the window for the other traffic.

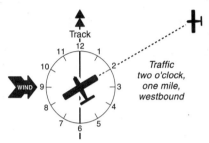

Figure 28-59. Radar traffic information service

Radar Vectoring

Radar vectoring is a procedure in which a radar controller passes a **heading** to steer, with an instruction like:

Seven zero seven four delta, Turn left heading two-five-zero.

The aim of the controller when issuing these headings is to get the airplane to follow a particular **track** over the ground and, because he will not know precisely the actual wind at your level, or the amount of drift it is causing, he will occasionally issue modified vectors to achieve the desired course.

Primary Radar

The detection of reflected radio waves at the point from which they were originally transmitted is the fundamental basis of radar. The basic operating principles of radar were first developed during the late 1920s, and subsequent rapid improvements in the ability to *detect* objects, such as airplanes, and to measure their *range,* was often a decisive factor during World War II(1939–45). The term radar is a contraction of Radio Detection And Ranging.

A typical radar system consists of a combined *transmitter-receiver* unit, which is equipped with a parabolic dish antenna that is designed to be efficient both in the transmission of a focused beam of radio signals, and in the reception of any reflected signals from the same direction. The dish can be rotated slowly, so that the whole sky can be scanned systematically.

Figure 28-60. A typical radar antenna showing primary radar dish with SSR antenna above

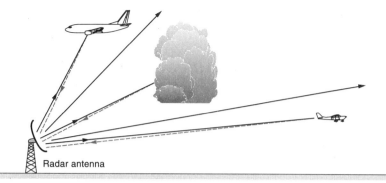

Figure 28-61. Radar is the transmission of electromagnetic radio energy and the detection of some of the reflected energy back at the point of transmission

Secondary Surveillance Radar (SSR)

SSR is also known as Air Traffic Control Radar Beacon System (ATCRBS). Secondary surveillance radar overcomes most of the limitations of primary radar simply by ensuring that a conspicuous, high-energy **return pulse** is produced by aircraft that are equipped with devices known as a **transponders.**

As only a small amount of radio energy transmitted from the ground is required to trigger a response from an airborne SSR transponder, the ground-based secondary radar transmitter and antenna systems tend to be quite compact in comparison. In fact, the typical long, narrow SSR antenna is small enough to be mounted above the larger primary radar dish at many radar ground sites.

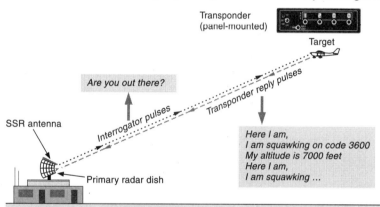

Figure 28-62. SSR is two radars talking to each other

The Transponder

Using the Transponder

Most airplanes are now equipped with a **transponder** that transmits a strong responding signal to a *secondary* ground radar, which provides ATC with additional information such as airplane identification and altitude. Your transponder is also readable by the Traffic Collision Avoidance systems (TCAS) that transport and larger corporate aircraft are equipped with.

The normal code that you should select on your transponder for VFR flight is **1200.** On occasions, you will be requested to squawk another code to differentiate you from other aircraft.

The transponder is usually warmed-up in the STANDBY position while taxiing prior to takeoff. (It should also go to STANDBY at the *end* of a flight before the master avionics switch is moved to OFF*).*

A transponder makes it easier for a radar controller to positively identify your airplane.

The transponder should be selected to the ON position, or the ALT position if it is a **Mode C altitude-reporting** system, as the airplane lines up on the runway for takeoff. If your airplane is equipped with a serviceable transponder, then it *must* be used in flight, even when you are operating in airspace where its carriage is not mandatory. If your transponder is equipped with Mode S or other modes, you may have the ability to receive data transmissions (including ATC clearances) through the instrument.

A Mode C transponder allows the radar controller to see your altitude.

Figure 28-63. Typical transponder panel

Each of the four digits in the transponder code must lie in the range from 0 to 7. This gives 8 possibilities for each of the four digits, giving a capability of **4,096 different codes** ($8 \times 8 \times 8 \times 8 = 64 \times 64 = 4,096$). Whenever codes are selected or altered, it is important to avoid passing through such vital codes as **7700** (for emergencies), **7600** (for radio failure), and **7500** (for unlawful interference). If the transponder is switched ON, this would activate unnecessary alarms in nearby ATC radar facilities. This can be prevented by making it your standard procedure to select STANDBY while changing the transponder code.

Even though transponders produced by various manufacturers vary in design, they are all operated in the same manner. However, as a responsible pilot, you should become thoroughly familiar with your particular transponder.

Radio Terminology for Transponder Operation

The term **squawk** that is commonly used by ATC in connection with transponder operation is basically intended to mean **transmit**. It is usually followed by an instruction describing the type of transmission required by the controller, for instance: *squawk ident, squawk code 4000, squawk Mayday (7700).*

ATC: *"… (callsign) squawk code 4000."*
Pilot response is to read back: *"… (callsign) code 4000,"* and to select the transponder to that code.

ATC: *"… (callsign) squawk code … and ident."*
Pilot response is to change the code and then press the IDENT button, allowing the radar controller to identify you positively on his screen.

ATC: *"…(callsign) squawk standby."*
Pilot response is to move the function switch from ALT or ON to the STANDBY position, for a temporary suspension of transponder operation (maintaining present code).

ATC: *"… (callsign) squawk normal."*
Pilot response is to reactivate the transponder from STANDBY to ON, or to ALT if it is a Mode C system, retaining the existing code.

ATC: *"… (callsign) stop squawk."*
Pilot response is to select the transponder to OFF.

ATC: *"… (callsign) stop altitude squawk."*
Pilot response is to move the function selector from ALT to ON, so that the altitude information is removed from the transponder's reply signals.

For further information on transponder requirements and operating procedures see the Aeronautical Information Manual (AIM), and Part 91 of the regulations.

✍ Now complete **Review 28, Part (d)** on page 659.

DME

Distance measuring equipment operates using the secondary radar principle, by the **airborne transmitter** (the *interrogator*) sending out a stream of radio pulses in all directions on the receiving frequency of the DME ground beacon which acts as a *transponder.*

The airborne DME equipment detects an answering signal and measures the *time* between the transmission of the interrogating pulse from the airplane and the reception of the ranging reply pulse from the DME ground station. It converts this time to a **distance in nautical miles.** The DME indicator, when it displays this distance, is said to have *latched on* or *locked on.*

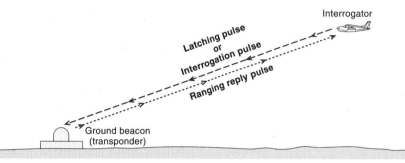

Figure 28-64. Operation of the DME

DME Measures Slant Distance

Distance measuring equipment (DME) can provide you with extremely useful information, your distance from a DME ground station. DME uses radar principles to measure this distance, which is the **slant distance** in nautical miles, rather than the *horizontal* distance (or range).

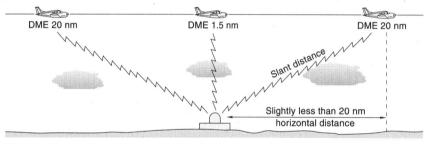

Figure 28-65. DME measures slant distance

Passing directly over the ground beacon, the DME indicator in the cockpit will either show the altitude of the airplane above the ground in nautical miles (1 nm = 6,000 feet approximately), or the DME indication will *drop out.*

DME Cockpit Displays

DME distance may be displayed in the cockpit as either a digital read-out, or by a pointer that moves around a calibrated scale. DME is used by selecting the VOR or ILS frequency on the **VHF-NAV** radio (since most DMEs are paired with a VOR frequency or a localizer frequency).

Once the DME is locked on, and a DME reading and *ident* obtained, the DME indications can be used for distance information regardless of whether the VOR (or localizer) is used for tracking or orientation purposes.

Most airborne DME equipment is capable of computing and displaying the **rate of change** of DME distance, which is the *rate of closure* of the airplane with the DME ground station. If it is assumed that *slant* distance equals *horizontal* distance, and that the airplane is tracking either *directly toward* or *directly away from* the DME ground station, then the rate of closure read-out will represent **groundspeed**, a very useful piece of information.

Some DME indicators can also display **time to the station (TTS)** in minutes at the current rate of closure, by comparing the groundspeed with the DME distance.

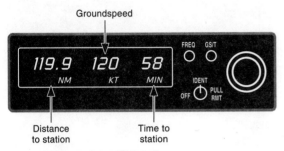

Figure 28-66. A digital DME indicator

If the airplane is not tracking directly toward or away from the DME ground station, then these readings will not represent groundspeed and TTS. If the DME equipment in the airplane does *not* give a groundspeed read-out, then you can simply note the DME distance at two particular times, and carry out a simple calculation of *groundspeed = distance/time* either mentally or on your flight computer. Again, this is only accurate when the airplane is tracking directly to or from the DME ground beacon.

Example 11. The DME distance and time is noted time as when the airplane tracks directly to or from a DME ground station. Calculate groundspeed.

DME 35	Time 0215 UTC
DME 25	Time 0220 UTC
10 nm	**5 min = GS 120 knots**

DME Orientation

The DME provides a *circular* position line. If the DME reads 35 nm, for instance, then the pilot knows that the airplane is somewhere on the circumference of a 35 nm circle centered on the DME ground station.

Information from another radio aid may provide a **positive fix** of the position of the airplane, provided the two position lines give a good "cut" (angle of intercept), ideally as close to perpendicular as possible.

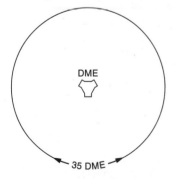

Figure 28-67. A circular position line from a DME

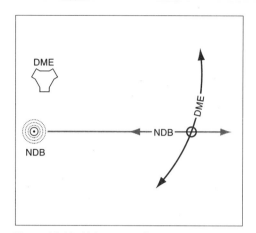
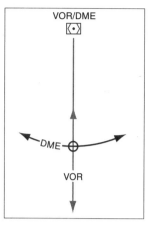
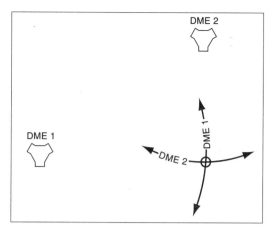

Figure 28-68. Using two radio navigation aids to fix position

VOR/DME Pairing

Each VOR frequency has a *specific* DME channel paired with it. For instance, VOR frequency 112.10 MHz has DME Channel 58 paired with it, so that the VOR's associated DME will automatically be interrogated when the VOR frequency of 112.10 is selected on the VHF-NAV. The purpose of this pairing is to reduce the pilot's workload in the cockpit, with only *one* selection instead of two required, and to reduce the risk of selecting the right VOR but the wrong DME station—the correct DME channel is selected **automatically** when the frequency of an associated VOR, VORTAC, or ILS ground station is dialed-up on the VHF-NAV set.

Co-located VORs and DMEs are frequency paired, and each will have the same Morse code **ident,** the VOR identifier modulated on 1020 Hz and broadcast about every 10 seconds, and the DME identifier modulated on 1350 Hz and broadcast about every 30 seconds. This means that about *one DME ident* is heard for every *three VOR idents*, with the DME ident having a higher pitch tone.

A single coded identifier received only once every 30 seconds, and not mixed in with another identifier broadcast every 10 seconds, means that the DME component of the VORTAC station is operative, but the VOR component is not. Always identify the VOR ground station (by Morse code) before use.

VOR ground stations are often combined with TACAN installations (Tactical Air Navigation), which provides azimuth *and* distance information to military aircraft on UHF frequencies. The combined VOR/TACAN facility is known as a VORTAC. Civil aircraft obtain azimuth *(course)* information from the VOR, and *distance* information from the DME component of the TACAN.

A paired VOR and DME (or VORTAC) can provide a very good position fix, consisting of:

- the **radial** from the VOR; and

- the **distance** from the DME.

✎ Now complete **Review 28, Part (e)** on page 659.

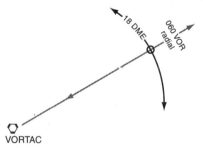

Figure 28-69. Fixing position with a paired VOR and DME

RNAV—Area Navigation

Area navigation (RNAV) allows you to fly point-to-point on a direct course without having to overfly ground-based radio aids. Instead of flying from VORTAC-to-VORTAC along Victor airways on what might be a circuitous route, you can fly direct from your departure airport to the destination airport, or from waypoint-to-waypoint, using RNAV. A **waypoint** is a geographical position usually specified by latitude and longitude, or by radial and distance from a VORTAC, and used to define a route.

Some RNAV systems can define a waypoint internally when the pilot inserts the desired waypoint *latitude* and *longitude* into the computer. The RNAV system then derives data from navigation systems such as LORAN, inertial navigation systems (INS), VLF/Omega systems, and Doppler radar which enables the airplane to be flown to the desired waypoint. Other RNAV systems define waypoints relative to a VORTAC, using radial and distance (or latitude and longitude) to create "phantom" VORTACs, known as pseudo-VORTACs.

A waypoint is a geographical position used to define a route.

Pseudo-VORTACs

Many general aviation aircraft have a course line computer system which, when used in conjunction with the VHF-NAV radio selected to a VORTAC, can *electronically* relocate that VORTAC, so that a **pseudo-VORTAC** is created at any desired waypoint. It does this by electronically adding a vector (radial and distance) to the position of the actual VORTAC.

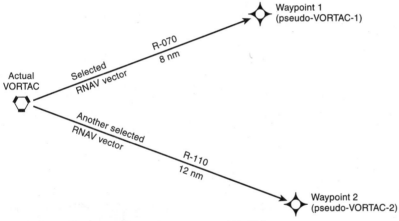

Figure 28-70. Electronically creating a phantom VORTAC

Operational Use

You can locate pseudo-VORTACs wherever you like, provided they are within signal reception range of the parent VORTAC, and thereby create a series of waypoints along your desired route.

The normal VHF-NAV receiver is selected to the parent VORTAC, and the computer is programmed to electronically add the vector (radial and distance) to received VORTAC signals. How this is done depends on the actual equipment in the cockpit—refer to equipment information in your Pilots Operating Handbook.

You can create your own pseudo-VORTAC as a waypoint.

The course deviation indicator (CDI) in the cockpit receives its input via the computer, and indicates deviation from course between the waypoints—not an *angular* deviation as for normal VOR flying, but a **lateral deviation** in nautical miles, or fractions thereof.

The course between waypoints is maintained by keeping the CDI centered. Because it indicates lateral deviation in nautical miles, known as **crosstrack error,** rather than angular deviation, there is no "funneling" effect using the RNAV CDI.

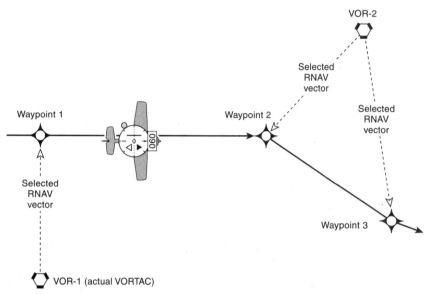

Figure 28-71. Tracking between waypoints

Distance to the waypoint is shown on the normal DME indicator.

The waypoints can normally be preset on the RNAV equipment, and then instantaneously recalled as you need them. As the flight progresses, you will proceed through the waypoints in order, keeping within signal range of each parent VORTAC by flying at a suitable altitude and distance from it. If the usable signal range is exceeded, the CDI OFF flag will show.

Typical RNAV systems can provide you with:

• crosstrack deviation from the selected course in nm with TO/FROM information;

• distance to the waypoint in nm;

• groundspeed in knots;

• time-to-waypoint in minutes.

Figure 28-72. A typical RNAV display

LORAN-C

LORAN-C is a long-range navigation system originally designed for maritime use. In earlier days, it required rather complicated charts, a large table to spread them out on, and a trained navigator to interpret signals and plot the position on the chart—obviously not a perfect system for small aircraft. However, the development of the microprocessor has changed all that. What were complicated calculations are now performed *automatically* at high speed and with great accuracy, with position and other information presented to the pilot in the cockpit in digital form.

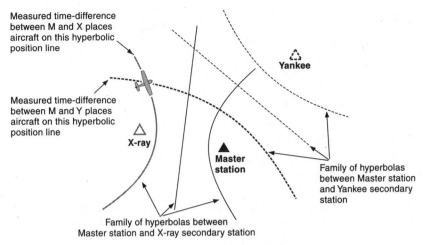

Figure 28-73. LORAN-C computes position using hyperbolas

The LORAN-C system is a **hyperbolic** system. It measures the difference in time of arrival of radio pulses from a chain of transmitters which are separated by hundreds of miles. One station is the **master** station, and the others are **secondary** stations whose signals are synchronized with those from the master station.

The time-difference between the arrival of the various pulses from different directions allows the microprocessor to compute the position of the aircraft. All points having the same time-difference between pulses from two stations lie on a curve known as a hyperbola. With signals from a number of stations, more than one hyperbolic position line is known, and the intersection of two or more of these hyperbolas defines the position of the aircraft.

Figure 28-74. A typical LORAN set

The capability of the microprocessor is taken advantage of to provide you with many pieces of information—in fact, so much that you must discriminate and only access what you need. There are differences between sets from various manufacturers, but a typical set can provide you with:

- position (as latitude/longitude or radial/distance);
- track and groundspeed;
- wind speed and direction (using MH and TAS data);
- crosstrack error (lateral deviation from course in nautical miles);
- estimated time en route;
- memory storage of all airports and radio navigation aids in the United States and elsewhere, plus anything else that you care to add;
- Victor airways specifications;
- course and distance to any selected point (no matter how far)—very useful when considering diverting to an alternate airport; and
- an *alert* signal to warn of an impending penetration of Class B or C airspace.

Note: LORAN-C is currently giving way to GPS navigation in the U.S.

✍ Now complete **Review 28, Part (f)** on page 660.

Global Positioning System (GPS)

The global positioning system (GPS) is an extremely accurate area navigation aid for all classes of aviation as well as other modes of transport. GPS was developed for the United States Department of Defense, but has now been made available for civil use.

In early 1994 the Federal Aviation Administration granted approval for GPS to be used as an operational in-flight navigational aid. With an FAA-approved GPS system and supporting software, GPS is used to fly under Instrument Flight Rules, both en route and for nonprecision instrument approaches. The GPS instrument approach procedures are often co-located with other established instrument approach procedures, such as VOR or NDB approaches.

Many VFR pilots also make use of GPS as an aid to visual navigation. The GPS provides a myriad of navigational details, including information relating to aircraft, speed and course over the ground, altitude, wind velocity and distance/time to waypoints or destination.

Basically, three elements make up GPS:

Only those GPS marked "certified for IFR use" may be used under IFR conditions.

- a space element, consisting of a constellation of active satellites orbiting the earth every 12 hours, in six orbital planes with four in each plane, at an altitude of 11,000 nm (21,300 km);

- a satellite control ground network (control station plus monitor stations), responsible for orbital accuracy and control; and

- navigation receiver/computers in aircraft capable of receiving and identifying signals from satellites in view at a particular time and place.

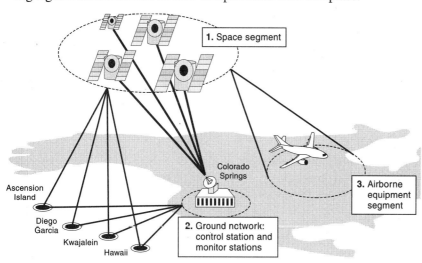

Figure 28-75. The GPS consists of three basic segments

Basic Operating Principle

Each satellite transmits its own computer code packet on frequency 1575.42 MHz (for civilian use), 1,000 times per second. The satellite continually broadcasts its position and the exact time UTC. By knowing the exact position of the satellite at the time of transmission, and then by measuring the time taken for the data packet to reach the receiver from the satellite, the distance between the satellite and the receiver can be determined. The satellite constellation configuration usually guarantees that at least four satellites are in view at any given time.

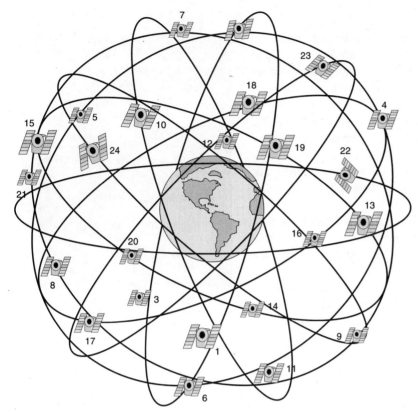

Figure 28-76. The orbital configuration of the GPS satellites

Each transmitted data packet contains a precise timing reference. GPS receivers use accurate clocks and appropriate software to ascertain position by receiving and computing data from at least three satellites for a two-dimensional fix, and four satellites for a three-dimensional fix, such as ground position and altitude.

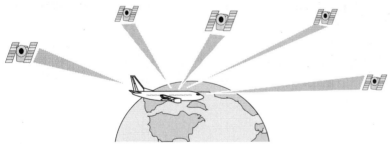

Figure 28-77. Signals from satellites are received to establish position

✍ Now complete **Review 28, Part (g)** on page 660.

VHF Direction Finding (VDF)

Some airports are equipped with special radio antennas which can sense the direction of normal **VHF-COM signals** received from an airplane. These signals may be voice communications from the pilot, or simply transmissions made by pressing the transmit button on the microphone, which only transmits a carrier wave.

Directional information is presented to the air traffic controller as a radial line on a cathode ray tube similar to a radar screen or, in the case of the most modern VDF equipment, as an accurate digital readout of bearing. The controller can then advise the pilot of the airplane bearing relative to the airport, or provide a series of headings to steer toward the airport. These are known as **DF steers.**

If simultaneous bearings are available from two or more VDF stations, then ATC can determine the actual position of the airplane, known as a **DF fix.** This procedure is known as very high frequency direction finding, and is often abbreviated to VHF D/F, VDF or simply DF.

An advantage of VDF is that no special airborne equipment is required other than a VHF-COM, although it does require a special installation at the airport.

Two typical designs for airport VDF antennas are the H-type antenna (a double-H dipole antenna in technical terms), or the Doppler-type VDF antenna.

Modern equipment is fully automatic, with the ground operator having the direction of the airplane displayed to him automatically following only a short VHF-COM transmission from the pilot.

Figure 28-78. VHF direction finding (VDF) antennas

VDF enables a controller to determine the direction a VHF-COM signal is coming from.

Operational Use

The VHF direction finder can help pilots without them even being aware of its operation. It is used by ATC in locating and directing lost aircraft, and in helping to identify aircraft already on radar.

Bearing *to* a station is the most usual bearing requested by pilots. It is the heading to steer direct to the VDF station provided no crosswind exists. In a crosswind, however, a wind correction angle (WCA) must be used if a reasonably straight track is to be achieved, rather than a curved (and inefficient) homing. ATC can allow for this with their DF steers as they monitor the flight path of the airplane. VDF is used like a very simple radar.

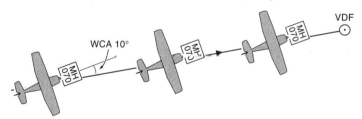

Figure 28-79. An efficient track to a VDF ground station

In a *distress* or *urgency* situation, ATC may even be able to provide a **DF instrument approach**. Such a situation could involve a noninstrument-rated pilot caught above a cloud layer and requiring descent to an airport. The DF specialist would provide him with DF steers, and tell him when to commence descent. The aim is to achieve maximum flight stability with small turns and wings-level descents.

The DF instrument approach in IFR conditions is considered an emergency procedure, but there is no reason why you should not request a practice one in VFR conditions at a suitably equipped airport. The DF instrument approaches are not published in charts.

The letters VHF/DF appearing In the Airport/Facility Directory (A/FD) for a certain airport indicate that the Flight Service Station has VHF/DF equipment with which to determine your direction from the station.

✍ Now complete **Review 28, Part (h)** on page 660.

For Aspiring Commercial Pilots

Bearing Changes, Time and Distance to Station

The simplest means of determining distance to a station is to use a DME or GPS. If these means are not available, then you can use **change of bearing** using VOR or ADF to provide at least an *approximate* time and distance to a station. There are various ways in which this can be done:

- the isosceles triangle method (or doubling the relative bearing method); and
- the wingtip-bearing change method.

Method 1: Isosceles Triangle Method

This method is based on doubling the relative bearing.

    Distance D to station from position 2 = Distance to double the relative bearing; or
      Time T to station from position 2 = Time to double the relative bearing

This method is based on geometry:

1. The sum of two angles within a triangle will equal the value of the opposite external angle (Figure 28-80 and Figure 28-81).
3. If two angles of a triangle are equal, then the two opposite sides are equal (this is called an *isosceles* triangle) (Figure 28-82).
4. It follows that if you fly a constant heading until the relative bearing doubles (until angle C = 2A), then the angle at station B will be equal to A, resulting in an isosceles triangle. If you change heading and track toward the station:
   - the two distances will be the same and, assuming a constant ground-speed, the two times will be the same (Figure 28-83).

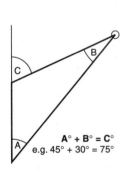

Figure 28-80.

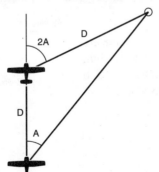

Figure 28-81.

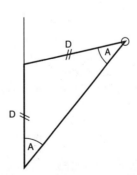

Figure 28-82.

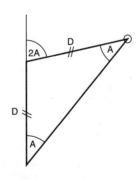

Figure 28-83.

Example 12. While maintaining a constant heading, a relative bearing of RB 020 doubles to RB 040 in 8 minutes. If you now turned and tracked toward the station, the time to the station would be _____ minutes if you assume a constant groundspeed. The fuel required for flight to the station at a rate of fuel consumption of 12 gal/hr is _____ gallons (Figure 28-84).

Method: doubling the relative bearing from 20° to 40°, therefore isosceles triangle method.

Time T to station from position 2 = time to double relative bearing

$$= 8 \text{ minutes}$$

Fuel burn = 8 min at 12 gal/hr

$$= \frac{8}{60} \times 12$$

$$= 1.6 \text{ gal}$$

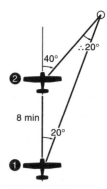

Figure 28-84.

Example 13. While cruising at 120 knots on a constant heading, the ADF needle decreases from a relative bearing of RB 315 to RB 270 in 5 minutes. The approximate time and distance to the station being used is _____ minutes and _____ nm.

Method: Doubling the relative bearing from 45° to 90°, therefore isosceles triangle method (Figure 28-85).

Time T to station = time to double relative bearing

$$= 5 \text{ minutes}$$

Distance = speed × time

$$= 120 \text{ knots for 5 minutes}$$

$$= 10 \text{ nm}$$

Method 2: Wingtip Bearing Change

$$\text{Time to station} = \frac{60 \times \text{time of bearing change}}{\text{degree of wingtip bearing change}}$$

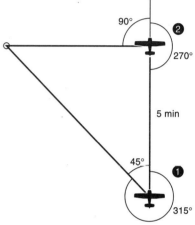

Figure 28-85.

Mathematical basis:

1. The circumference of a circle C = 2πR, where R is the radius and π is approximately 3, therefore C = 6R approximately. R is also the approximate distance to the station.

2. The length of the circular arc from position 1 to position 2 is a fraction $\left(\frac{B}{360}\right)$ of the total circumference, where B° is the wingtip bearing change and 360° is the number of degrees in the complete circle (Figure 28-86).

$$\text{Arc distance from 1 to 2} = \frac{B}{360} \times 6R = \frac{B \times R}{60}$$

so: distance to station (R) $= \frac{60}{B} \times$ distance from 1 to 2

3. If the wingtip bearing change is relatively small (say less than 30°), the arc from position 1 to position 2 may be considered an approximate straight line. If we assume a similar groundspeed when we turn and track direct to the station, then the ratio of *times* will be the same as the ratio of *distances* $\left(\frac{60}{B}\right)$:

Time to station $= \frac{60}{B} \times$ time for bearing change from position 1 to position 2

$$\text{Time to station} = \frac{60 \times \text{time for bearing change}}{\text{degrees of wingtip bearing change}}$$

C = 2πR = 2 × 3 × R = 6R

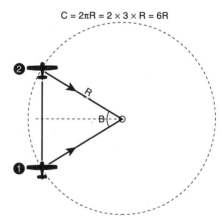

Figure 28-86.

Note: If you find *time* to the station, it is straightforward to find *distance* to the station using the relationship *"distance = speed × time."* Similarly, it is straightforward to find *fuel burn* using the relationship *"fuel burn = fuel consumption × time."*

Example 14. As you fly abeam an NDB at 100 knots, the relative bearing changes from RB 085 to RB 095 in 3 minutes. If you turned and tracked direct to the NDB, it would take approximately _____ minutes for the distance of _____ nm (Figure 28-87).

Method: A wingtip bearing change of 10° from RB 085 to RB 095 in 3 minutes.

$$\text{Time to station} = \frac{60 \times \text{time for bearing change}}{\text{degrees of bearing change}}$$

$$= \frac{60 \times 3}{10}$$

$$= 18 \text{ minutes}$$

$$\text{Distance} = \text{speed} \times \text{time}$$

$$= 100 \text{ knots for 18 minutes}$$

$$= \frac{18}{60} \times 100$$

$$= 30 \text{ nm}$$

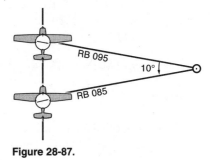

Figure 28-87.

✎ Commercial students complete **Review 28, Commercial** on page 660.

✎ Review 28

Part (a)

1. The NDB is (a ground-based transmitter/an airborne receiver).
➤ ground-based transmitter

2. NDBs transmit on a frequency in either the _____ or _____ band.
➤ low frequency or medium frequency band (LF/MF)

3. The ADF is (a ground-based transmitter/an airborne receiver).
➤ an airborne receiver

4. A particular NDB may be identified by _____ .
➤ its Morse code *ident*

5. The three basic steps that a pilot should follow before using a particular NDB are _____ .
➤ select the NDB frequency, identify the NDB, and check that the needle is indeed "ADFing"

6. Atmospheric conditions, such as electrical storms or the periods of sunrise and sunset, (may/will not) distort NDB signals, making ADF indications less reliable.
➤ may

Radio Navigation 2

7. Mountains (may/will not) reflect and distort NDB signals, making ADF indications less reliable.
➤ may

Part (b)

1. The term RBI is an abbreviation for _____ .
➤ relative bearing indicator

2. If an airplane steering MH 250 has a reading of 030 on its relative bearing indicator (RB030), what is:
    (1) the magnetic bearing to the NDB from the airplane?
    (2) the magnetic bearing of the airplane from the NDB?
➤ (1) MB 280 to the NDB; (2) MB 100 from the NDB

3. If an airplane steering MH 250 has a reading of RB 350 on its relative bearing indicator, calculate:
    (1) the magnetic bearing to the NDB from the airplane.
    (2) the magnetic bearing of the airplane from the NDB.
➤ (1) MB 240 to the NDB; (2) MB 060 from the NDB

4. On MH 020 with RB 010, the MB to the NDB is _____ .
➤ MB 030 to NDB

---

5. On MH 020 with RB 000, the MB to the NDB is
   _____ .
   ➤ MB 020 to NDB

6. On MH 020 with RB 355, the MB to the NDB is
   _____ .
   ➤ MB 015 to NDB

7. When steering MH 180, MB 240 to the NDB is indicated
   by RB _____ .
   ➤ RB 060

8. On MH 340 with RB 180, the MB to the NDB
   is _____ , and the MB from the NDB is
   _____ .
   ➤ MB 160 to NDB, MB 340 from NDB

9. When steering MH 270, MB 120 from the NDB is
   indicated by RB _____ .
   ➤ RB 030

10. When steering MH 225, MB 255 from the NDB is
    indicated by RB _____ .
    ➤ RB 210

11. An airplane is steering MH 035. Its RBI indicates 040.
    Magnetic variation in the area is 4°W. Calculate:
    (1) MB to the NDB; (2) MB from the NDB; (3) True
    bearing from the NDB.
    ➤ MB 075 to the NDB, MB 255 from the NDB, TB 251
    from the NDB

12. If the head of the RMI needle reads RMI 070, the
    magnetic bearing to the ground station from the airplane
    is MB _____ to ground station.
    ➤ MB 070 to ground station

13. A magnetic course (outbound from/inbound to) a VOR is
    known as a radial.
    ➤ outbound from

14. The (head/tail) of an RMI selected to a VOR tells you
    what radial you are on.
    ➤ tail

15. If the head of the RMI needle selected to a VOR reads
    RMI 010, you are on the _____ radial.
    ➤ 190

16. If the tail of the RMI needle selected to a VOR reads 089,
    you are on the _____ radial.
    ➤ 089

17. If the head of the RMI needle reads RMI 070, the
    magnetic bearing from the ground station to the airplane
    is MB _____ from ground station.
    ➤ MB 250 from ground station (the reciprocal of 070)

18. An airplane steers MH 035. Its RMI indicates RMI 075.
    Calculate:
    (1) MB to the NDB; (2) MB from the NDB; (3) RB to the
    NDB.
    ➤ MB 075 to the NDB, MB 255 from the NDB, RB 040 to
    the NDB

19. An airplane steers MH 335. Its RMI indicates RMI 330.
    Calculate:
    (1) MB to the NDB; (2) MB from the NDB; (3) RB to the
    NDB.
    ➤ MB 330 to the NDB, MB 150 from the NDB; RB 355 to
    the NDB (or RB –5)

Part (c)

1. MH 080; RBI 000. What heading would you steer to
   make a 90° intercept of a course of MC 040 to the NDB?
   What would the RBI indicate at the point of intercept?
   ➤ right turn to MH 130, RBI 270

2. MH 080; RBI 000. What heading would you steer to
   make a 60° intercept of a course of MC 040 to the NDB?
   What would the RBI indicate at the point of intercept?
   ➤ right turn to MH 100, RBI 300

3. MH 070, RBI 010. Which way would you turn to
   intercept MC 075 to the NDB?
   ➤ right

4. MH 155, RBI 180. Which way would you turn to
   intercept a course of MC 140 away from the NDB?
   ➤ left

5. Homing to an NDB in a crosswind is an (efficient/
   inefficient) procedure because it will result in a (straight/
   curved) path.
   ➤ inefficient, curved

6. Tracking to an NDB in a crosswind requires that you (do/
   do not) apply a wind correction angle to achieve a
   (straight/curved) path to the station. Tracking is (more/
   less) efficient than homing.
   ➤ do, straight, more

7. When tracking toward an NDB, the ADF readings are:
   Time 1: MH 055, RBI 005; Time 2: MH 055, RBI 005.
   What course is the airplane maintaining to the NDB?
   ➤ MC 060

8. When tracking toward an NDB, the ADF readings are: Time 1: MH 055, RBI 005 and on course; Time 2: MH 055, RBI 002. Is the airplane (left/right) of the desired MC, which is _____ ?

➤ right of MC 060 inbound to the NDB

9. To track toward an NDB on MC 340, with an expected crosswind from the right causing 5 of drift, what magnetic heading would you steer, and what would you expect the RBI to indicate?

➤ MH 345, RB 355

10. To track away from an NDB on MC 120, with an expected crosswind from the right causing 8 of drift, what magnetic heading would you steer, and what would you expect the RBI to indicate?

➤ MH 128, RB 172

11. You wish to track MC 360 in no-wind conditions. What magnetic heading would you steer? What would the RBI indicate as you pass abeam an NDB 10 nm to the right of course (i.e. when the NDB is on magnetic bearing MB 090 to the course)?

➤ MH 360, RB 090

12. You wish to track MC 360 and expect 10° of drift caused by a wind from the east. What magnetic heading would you steer? What would the RBI indicate as you pass abeam an NDB 10 nm to the right of course?

➤ MH 010, RB 080

13. You wish to track MC 030 and expect 7° left drift. What magnetic heading would you steer? What would the RBI indicate as you pass abeam an NDB 10 nm to the left of course?

➤ MH 037, RB 263

14. You are tracking MC 278 with 6° of left drift. You can determine your position abeam an NDB to the right of track by waiting until the RBI indicates _____ .

➤ RB 084

Part (d)

1. The process of separating airplanes and positioning them by ATC passing headings to steer is known as radar _____ .

➤ radar vectoring

2. Primary surveillance radar can detect airplanes, even if they carry no airborne equipment. Secondary surveillance radar (SSR) on the ground detects strong responding signals transmitted from airplanes that carry a _____ .

➤ transponder

3. In providing a radar traffic information service, ATC report the position of a possibly conflicting airplane as "two o'clock northbound." The "two o'clock" is related to the (heading/track) of your airplane.

➤ track

4. Altitude-reporting capability of a transponder is called Mode _____ .

➤ Mode C

5. When ATC request you to "squawk ident," you should press the ident button (once/for 15 seconds).

➤ once

6. You should press the ident button (periodically/only when requested by ATC/never).

➤ only when requested by ATC

7. Standard transponder code for an emergency is _____ .

➤ 7700

8. Standard transponder code for a VFR airplane is _____ .

➤ 1200

9. ATC advises you that radar service is being terminated as you depart a Terminal Radar Service Area. You should set code _____ on your transponder.

➤ 1200

10. When making routine transponder code changes, you should avoid inadvertent selection of which three codes?

➤ 7500, 7600, 7700

11. FAA radar locations are found in the _____ booklet.

➤ Airport/Facility Directory (A/FD)

Part (e)

1. The letters DME are an abbreviation for _____ ; DME measures (horizontal/vertical/slant) distance.

➤ distance measuring equipment, slant

2. The DME is selected on the _____ radio, usually along with a collocated VOR.

➤ VHF-NAV

3. The coded identifier of the DME is transmitted about once every _____ seconds and is modulated to _____ Hz.

➤ 30 seconds, 1350 Hz

4. The coded identifier of the VOR is transmitted about once every _____ seconds and is modulated to _____ Hz.

⮞ 10 seconds, 1020 Hz

5. For each time you hear the DME identifier, you should hear the VOR identifier about _____ times.

⮞ 3 times

6. If an airplane flies 12,000 feet directly above a DME ground beacon, the DME indicator will either *drop out* or show a DME distance of _____ nm.

⮞ 2 nm

7. If an airplane tracking directly away from a DME is at 22 DME at time 1223, and at 32 DME at time 1230, what is its groundspeed?

⮞ 10 nm in 7 min = GS 86

8. Tracking abeam a DME ground station, the DME readings change in the following manner as time passes: 25, 21, 17, 15, 14, 15, 17, 21. What was your abeam distance from the DME ground station?

⮞ 14 nm

9. A DME can provide a (circular/straight) position line.

⮞ circular

Part (f)

1. A pseudo-VORTAC is a (real/phantom) VORTAC.

⮞ phantom

2. A pseudo-VORTAC can be created (anywhere/anywhere within signal coverage).

⮞ anywhere within signal coverage

3. A pseudo-VORTAC is created by electronically adding a _____ to the position of the real VORTAC.

⮞ vector

4. The CDI, when being used as part of an RNAV system, displays (angular deviation/crosstrack error).

⮞ crosstrack error

5. The fixes along an off-airways route are known as _____ .

⮞ waypoints

6. LORAN-C uses time-difference measurement from widely separated LORAN stations to fix position using (parabolic/hyperbolic/straight/circular) position lines.

⮞ hyperbolic

Part (g)

1. Approved IFR GPS aircraft systems (may/may not) be used for VFR navigation.

⮞ may

2. Approved IFR GPS aircraft systems (may/may not) be used for IFR navigation.

⮞ may

3. For positional information, at least (one, two, or three) satellites are needed in order to determine aircraft position.

⮞ three

Part (h)

1. VDF (is/is not) radar.

⮞ is not

2. The airborne radio used for VDF is the (ADF/VHF-NAV/VHF-COM).

⮞ VHF-COM

3. A heading provided by ATC using VDF is known as a _____ .

⮞ DF steer

4. A DF instrument approach in IFR conditions (is/is not) considered an emergency procedure.

⮞ is

5. In which document would you look to see if a particular Flight Service Station has VHF/DF equipment?

⮞ the Airport Facility Directory (A/FD)

Commercial Review

1. The isosceles triangle method of determining time and distance to a ground station is also known as doubling the (relative/wingtip) bearing.

⮞ relative

2. While maintaining a constant heading, a relative bearing of 10° doubles in 5 minutes. The approximate time to fly direct to the station being used is _____ minutes.

⮞ 5 minutes

3. While maintaining a constant heading, a relative bearing of 15° doubles in 6 minutes. The time to the station is _____ minutes. If the speed is 100 knots, and the rate of fuel consumption is 8 gal/hr, the distance to the station is _____ nm, and the fuel burn would be _____ gal.

➤ 6 minutes, 10 nm, 0.8 gals

4. While maintaining a constant heading, the ADF needle increases from a relative bearing of RB 045 to RB 090 in 15 minutes. The time to the station being used is _____ minutes.

➤ 15 minutes

5. Inbound on the 190 radial of a VOR, you select the 195 radial on the OBS, and you turn 5° (left/right) to intercept it and note the time. The CDI centers after 10 minutes, and you turn approximately _____° (left/right) to track inbound on the 195 radial. Your expected time en route (ETE) to the VOR is _____ minutes.

➤ 5° left, 10° right, 10 minutes

6. The relative bearing on an ADF changes from RB 090 to RB 100 in 3 minutes of elapsed time. If you turned and tracked direct to the NDB, it would take approximately _____ minutes, assuming no change to groundspeed.

➤ 18 min $\left(\frac{60 \times 3}{10}\right)$

7. The relative bearing of an ADF changes from RB 265 to RB 260 in 2 minutes of elapsed time. If the groundspeed is 145 knots, the time and distance to the station is _____ min and _____ nm.

➤ 24 min, 58 nm

8. While maintaining a magnetic heading of MH 270 and a true airspeed of 120 knots, the 360 radial of a VOR is crossed at 1450 UTC and the 350 radial is crossed at 1457 UTC. The approximate time and distance to the station are _____ minutes and _____ nm.

➤ 42 minutes, 84 nm

9. The ADF indicates a wingtip bearing change of 10° in 2 minutes of elapsed time. What is the time required to turn and track direct to the NDB? If the TAS is 160 knots, what is the distance to the NDB?

➤ 12 minutes, 32 nm

For questions 10 to 18, you need to determine which method to use.

10. Refer to Figure 28-88. If the time flown between aircraft positions 2 and 3 is 11 minutes, what is the estimated time to the station?

➤ 11 minutes (isosceles triangle)

11. Refer to Figure 28-88. If the time flown between aircraft positions 2 and 3 is 9 minutes, what is the estimated time to the station?

➤ 9 minutes (isosceles triangle)

12. Inbound on the 315 radial, you select the 320 radial, turn 5° to the (left/right) to intercept it, and note the time. While maintaining a constant heading, you note that it takes 12 minutes for the CDI to center, at which time you turn approximately _____° (left/right) to track to the VOR. The ETE to the VOR is approximately _____ minutes.

➤ left, 10° right, 12 min (isosceles triangle)

13. If the relative bearing to an NDB shown on the ADF changes from 095° to 100° in 1.5 minutes of elapsed time, the time en route to the NDB if you turned and tracked to it at the same groundspeed would be _____ minutes.

➤ 18 minutes (wingtip bearing change)

14. The ADF is tuned to a nondirectional radio beacon, and the relative bearing changes from 090° to 100° in 2.5 minutes of elapsed time. If the TAS is 90 knots, then time and distance en route to that radio beacon would be _____ min, and _____ nm.

➤ 15 minutes, 22.5 nm (wingtip bearing change)

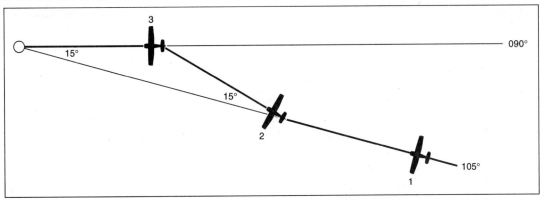

Figure 28-88.

15. If the relative bearing to an NDB shown on the ADF changes from 090° to 085° in 2 minutes of elapsed time, the time en route to the NDB if you turned and tracked to it at the same groundspeed would be _____ minutes.

➤ 24 minutes (wingtip bearing change)

16. Inbound on the 040 radial, you select the 055 radial, turn 15° to the left, and note the time. On a constant heading, it takes 15 minutes for the CDI to center. Based on this information, the ETE to the station is _____ minutes.

➤ 15 minutes (isosceles triangle)

17. Inbound on the 315 radial, you select the 320 radial, turn 5° to the left, and note the time. On a constant heading, it takes 12 minutes for the CDI to center. Based on this information, the ETE to the station is _____ minutes.

➤ 12 minutes (isosceles triangle)

18. Inbound on the 090 radial, you rotate the OBS 010° to the left, then turn 10° to the right and note the time. On this heading, it takes 8 minutes for the CDI to center. Based on this information, the ETE to the station is _____ minutes.

➤ 8 minutes (isosceles triangle)

19. Calculate the fuel required to fly to the station given:
Wingtip bearing change...................... 10°
Elapsed time between bearings .... 4 min
Rate of fuel consumption .... 11 gal/hr

➤ 4.4 gal (24 min)

20. Calculate the fuel required to fly to the station given:
Wingtip bearing change......................5°
Elapsed time between bearings ....6 min
Rate of fuel consumption .... 12 gal/hr

➤ 14.4 gal (72 min)

21. Calculate the fuel required to fly to the station given:
Wingtip bearing change......................15°
Elapsed time between bearings ....6 min
Rate of fuel consumption ....8.6 gal/hr

➤ 3.44 gal (24 min)

22. Calculate the time, distance and fuel required to fly to the station given:
Wingtip bearing change......................15°
Elapsed time between bearings ....7.5 min
True airspeed ....90 knots
Rate of fuel consumption ....9.6 gal/hr

➤ 30 min, 45 nm, 4.8 gal

23. Calculate distance to the station given:
Wingtip bearing change ....5°
Time elapsed between
    bearing change ....5 min
True airspeed.....................................115 knots

➤ 115 nm (60 min)

24. The relative bearing of an ADF changes from 270° to 275° in 1.5 minutes of elapsed time. At 115 knots, the distance to the station would be approximately _____ nm.

➤ 34.5 nm (18 min, by wingtip bearing change)

25. While maintaining a constant heading, a relative bearing of 10° doubles in 5 minutes. If the TAS is 105 knots, the time and distance to the station being used is approximately _____ minutes and _____ miles.

➤ 5 minutes, 8.7 nm (isosceles triangle)

26. While cruising at 135 knots and on a constant heading, the ADF needle decreases from a relative bearing of 315° to 270° in 7 minutes. The approximate time and distance to the station being used is:
(a)   7 minutes and 16 miles
(b)   14 minutes and 28 miles
(c)   19 minutes and 38 miles

➤ (a) (isosceles triangle)

27. On MH 035 you are passing east of an NDB. If you continue on MH 035, what magnetic bearing outbound would you intercept at 40°? (Sketch a diagram.)

➤ MB 075 from the NDB

28. On MH 340 you are passing west of an NDB. If you continue on MH 340, what magnetic bearing outbound would you intercept at 30°? (Sketch a diagram.)

➤ MB 310 from the NDB

29. On MH 035, the selected NDB is at RB 340. To intercept a magnetic bearing of 240° FROM the NDB at a 30° angle (while outbound), you should turn (left/right) by _____° to MH _____ . (Sketch a diagram.)

➤ left 125°, MH 270

30. On MH 300, the selected NDB is at RB 040. To intercept a magnetic bearing of 330° FROM the NDB at a 30° angle (while outbound), you should turn (left/right) by _____° to MH _____ . (Sketch a diagram.)

➤ right 60°, MH 360

31. On MH 330, the selected NDB is at RB 270. What will the ADF indicate when the aircraft reaches MB 030 FROM the NDB?

➤ RB 240

32. On MH 330, the selected NDB is at RB 040. What would be the relative bearing if the aircraft were turned to MH 090?

➤ RB 250

Figure 28-89.

33. Refer to Figure 28-89, ADF dial N. The relative bearing TO the station is:
    (a) 090°
    (b) 180°
    (c) 270°

➤ (b)

34. Refer to Figure 28-89, ADF dial O. On a magnetic heading of 320°, the magnetic bearing TO the station is:
    (a) 005°
    (b) 185°
    (c) 225°

➤ (b)

35. When tracking outbound from an NDB in crosswind conditions on the desired track with the proper drift correction established, the tail of the ADF pointer will be deflected to the (windward/downwind) side of the tail position and the head of the ADF pointer will be deflected to the (windward/downwind) side of the nose position.

➤ downwind, windward

36. When tracking inbound from an NDB in crosswind conditions on the desired track with the proper drift correction established, the tail of the ADF pointer will be deflected to the (windward/downwind) side of the tail position and the head of the ADF pointer will be deflected to the (windward/downwind) side of the nose position.

➤ windward, downwind

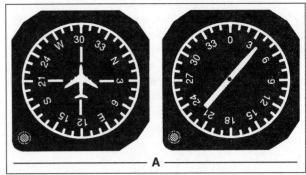

Figure 28-90.

37. Refer to Figure 28-90. At the position indicated by instrument group A, what would be the relative bearing if the aircraft were turned to a magnetic heading of 090°?
    (a) 150°
    (b) 190°
    (c) 250°

➤ (c)

38. Refer to Figure 28-90. To intercept the 330 magnetic bearing to the NDB at a 30° angle, the aircraft should be turned:
    (a) left to a heading of 270°.
    (b) right to a heading of 330°.
    (c) right to a heading of 360°.

➤ (c)

39. An airplane steers MH 010 and its RMI indicates RMI 030. To track to the NDB in no-wind conditions, you would turn (left/right) and steer MH _____ .

➤ right, MH 030

40. An airplane steers MH 330 and its RMI indicates RMI 210. Which outbound bearing is it crossing? What approximate heading would you steer to track outbound on this bearing? What approximate heading would you steer to track inbound to the NDB?

➤ 030, MH 030, MH 210

41. The desired course is MC 040 inbound to an NDB or VOR. The WCA is 10° left. The airplane is achieving this track when the head of the RMI needle indicates RMI _____ .

➤ RMI 040

42. The desired course is MC 120 outbound from an NDB or VOR. The WCA is 3° left. The airplane is achieving this track when the head of the RMI needle indicates RMI _____ .

➤ RMI 300

43. MH 080; RMI 080. What heading would you steer to make a 90° intercept of a course of MC 040 to the NDB? What would the RMI indicate at the point of intercept?

➤ right turn to MH 130, RMI 040

44. MH 080; RMI 080. What heading would you steer to make a 60° intercept of MC 040 to the NDB? What would the RMI indicate at the point of intercept?

➤ right turn to MH 100, RMI 040

45. MH 155, RMI 330. Which way would you turn to intercept MC 140 away from the NDB? What would the RMI indicate at the point of intercept? What would the tail of the RMI pointer indicate?

➤ left, RMI 320, RMI tail on 140

46. MH 155, RMI 130. Which way would you turn to intercept MC 090 away from the NDB? What would the RMI indicate at the point of intercept? What would the RMI tail indicate?

➤ left, RMI 270, RMI tail on 090

47. When tracking toward an NDB, the RMI readings are: Time 1: MH 055, RMI 060; Time 2: MH 055, RMI 060. What course is the airplane maintaining to the NDB?

➤ MC 060

48. When tracking toward an NDB, the RMI readings are: Time 1: MH 055, RMI 060 and on course; Time 2: MH 055, RMI 057.
Is the airplane off course to the left or right?

➤ right

49. To track toward an NDB on MC 340, with an expected crosswind from the right causing 5° of drift, what magnetic heading would you steer, and what would you expect the RMI to indicate?

➤ MH 345, RMI 340

50. To track away from an NDB on MC 120, with an expected crosswind from the right causing 8° of drift, what magnetic heading would you steer, and what would you expect the RMI to indicate?

➤ MH 128, RMI 300, RMI tail 120

51. You wish to track MC 360 and expect 10° of drift caused by a wind from the east. What magnetic heading would you steer? What would the RMI indicate as you passed abeam an NDB 10 nm to the right of course?

➤ MH 010, RMI 090

52. You are flying on MC 239 with 7° of left drift. At a position directly abeam an NDB to the left of course, the RMI will read _____ ?

➤ RMI 149

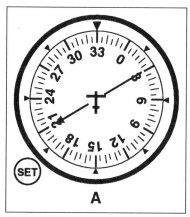

Figure 28-91.

53. Refer to Figure 28-91. Determine the magnetic bearing TO the station as indicated by ADF dial A.
(a) 330°
(b) 180°
(c) 210°

➤ (c)

54. Refer to Figure 28-91. What outbound bearing is being crossed by the aircraft represented by ADF dial A?
(a) 030°
(b) 150°
(c) 180°

➤ (a)

55. Refer to Figure 28-91. What is the relative bearing TO the station depicted by ADF dial A?
(a) 030°
(b) 210°
(c) 240°

➤ (c)

Abbreviations

For explanations, refer to the Pilot/Controller Glossary in the Aeronautical Information Manual, the Index to the Federal Aviation Regulations, or the Index in this manual.

α—symbol for angle-of-attack

ρ—symbol for air density

AD—Airworthiness Directive

ADF—automatic direction finder

A/FD—Airport/Facility Directory

AFM—Approved Flight Manual

agl or AGL—above ground level

AH—artificial horizon (see AI)

AI—attitude indicator

AIM—Airman's Information Manual

AIRMET—Aeronautical Meteorological Information

ALS—approach light system

ALT—altitude; altimeter

anm—air nautical miles

A&P—airframe and powerplant

APG—adverse pressure gradient

ASI—airspeed indicator

ASOS—automated surface observing system

ATC—Air Traffic Control

ATCO—Air Taxi and Commercial Operators

ATCRBS—ATC Radar Beacon System

ATD—actual time of departure

ATIS—automatic terminal information service

ATP—airline transport pilot

AVASI—abbreviated VASI

AVGAS—aviation gasoline

AWOS—automated weather observing system

BDC—bottom-dead-center

BFO—beat frequency oscillator (ADF mode)

BHP—brake horsepower

C—Celsius (formerly centigrade) degrees

CA—closing angle

CAT—clear air turbulence

C_D—coefficient of drag

CDI—course deviation indicator

CFI—certified flight instructor

CG—center of gravity

CHT—cylinder head temperature

C_L—coefficient of lift

CO—carbon monoxide

CO_2—carbon dioxide

CP—center of pressure

CRS—course

CST—Central Standard Time

CTAF—common traffic advisory frequency

CW—continuous wave (ADF mode)

D—drag

DA—density altitude

DALR—dry adiabatic lapse rate

DC—direct current

DF—direction finder (in tower)

DG—directional gyro (replaced by HI)

DME—distance measuring equipment

DR—dead (deduced) reckoning

DUAT—Direct User Access Terminal (weather briefing)

EDT—Eastern Daylight Time

EFAS—en route flight advisory service ("Flight Watch")

EGT—exhaust gas temperature

ELT—emergency locator transmitter

ELR—environmental lapse rate

EST—Eastern Standard Time

ETA—estimated time of arrival

ETD—estimated time of departure

ETE—estimated time en route

ETI—estimated time interval

F—Fahrenheit degrees

FA—area forecasts

FAA—Federal Aviation Administration

FBO—fixed base operator

FCU—fuel control unit

FL—flight level (hundreds of feet, e.g. FL210 is 21,000 feet)

fpm or FPM—feet per minute

FSS—Flight Service Station

ft or FT—feet (distance or altitude)

ft/min—feet per minute

g or G—the gravity force

GMT—Greenwich Mean Time or "Z" Zulu time (now UTC)

gnm—ground nautical miles

gph—gallons per hour

GPS—global positioning system

GS—groundspeed; glide slope

GW—gross weight

HAA—height above airport

HDG—heading

HI—heading indicator

HIRL—high intensity runway lights

HIWAS—hazardous in-flight weather advisory service

HP—horsepower

hPa—hectopascal (unit of pressure used internationally)

HSI—horizontal situation indicator

HWC—headwind correction

Hz—Hertz (cycles per second)

IAS—indicated airspeed

ICAO—International Civil Aviation Organization

IFR—instrument flight rules

ILS—instrument landing system

IMC—instrument meteorological conditions

in.Hg or Hg—inches of mercury (unit of pressure)

in-lb—inch-pounds

IOAT—indicated outside air temperature

ISA—international standard atmosphere

KCAS—knots calibrated airspeed

kg-mm—kilogram-millimeters

kHz—kilohertz (1,000 cycles per second)

KIAS—knots indicated airspeed

km—kilometer (1,000 meters)

kt—knots

KTAS—knots true airspeed

L—lift

lb—pounds

lb-in—pound-inches

L/D—lift/drag ratio

L–W—lift–weight couple

LDA—landing distance available

LIRL—low intensity runway lights

LORAN—long range navigation system

LoP—line of position

LW—landing weight

m or M—meters (distance)

M—degrees magnetic

MAC—mean aerodynamic chord (in weight and balance)

MAYDAY (repeated three times)—international distress radio signal

mb—millibars (unit of pressure, replaced by hPa)

MC—magnetic compass; magnetic course

MCP—maximum continuous power

MEF—maximum elevation figure

METAR—aviation routine weather forecast

METO—maximum except takeoff power

MH—magnetic heading

MHz—megahertz (million cycles per second)

MIRL—medium intensity runway lights

MLS—microwave landing system

MLW—maximum certificated landing weight

MOA—Military Operations Area

MSA—minimum safe altitude

msl or MSL—mean sea level

MST—Mountain Standard Time

MTOW—maximum certificated takeoff weight

MTR—Military Training Route

MULTICOM—a self-announce radio frequency

MVFR—marginal VFR

MZFW—maximum zero fuel weight

NDB—nondirectional radio beacon

nm or NM—nautical mile(s)

NOS—National Ocean Service (NOS charts)

NOTAM—Notice To Airmen

NTSB—National Transportation Safety Board

NWS—National Weather Service

OAT—outside air temperature

OBI—omni bearing indicator (on VOR cockpit instrument)

OBS—omni bearing selector (on VOR cockpit instrument)

OMNI—VHF omnidirectional radio range (same as VOR)

ONC—Operational Navigation Charts

PA—pressure altitude

PAN-PAN (repeated three times)—international urgency radio signal

PAPI—precision approach path indicator

PATWAS—pilots' automatic telephone weather answering service

PCL—pilot controlled lighting

PDT—Pacific Daylight Time

P-factor—asymmetric propeller blade effect

PIREP—pilot weather report

PL—position line

POH—Pilot's Operating Handbook

PRV—pressure relief valve

PST—Pacific Standard Time

PVASI—pulsating VASI

QNH—international term for *altimeter setting*

RAIL—runway alignment indicator lights

RB—relative bearing

RBI—relative bearing indicator

RCLS—runway centerline light system

RCO—remote communications outlet

REIL—runway end identifier lights

RMI—radio magnetic indicator

RNAV—area navigation

RoC—rate of climb

rpm—revolutions per minute

RWY—runway

SAE—Society of Automotive Engineers

SALR—saturated adiabatic lapse rate

SAR—specific air range; search and rescue

SD—radar weather reports

SFL—sequenced flashing lights

SGR—specific ground range

SIGMET—significant meteorological advisory alert

sm or SM—statute mile(s)

SSR—secondary surveillance radar

SSV—standard service volume

SVFR—Special Visual Flight Rules

T—thrust

T—degrees true

TACAN—military navigation station (see VORTAC)

TAF—terminal aerodrome forecast

TAS—true airspeed

TC—true course; turn coordinator

TCA—Terminal Control Area

T—D—thrust–drag couple

TDC—top-dead-center

TDZL—touchdown zone lights

TE—tracking error

TH—true heading

TOSS—takeoff safety speed

TOW—takeoff weight

TPA—traffic pattern altitude

TR—track

TRSA—Terminal Radar Service Area

TTS—time to the station

T-VASI—T-form VASI

TWEB—transcribed weather broadcast

UNICOM—aeronautical advisory radio communications unit (non-government)

UTC—coordinated universal time (previously GMT) or "Z" Zulu time (ATC reference to UTC)

V$_A$—design maneuvering speed

V$_B$—turbulence penetration speed

VASI—visual approach slope indicator

VDF—VHF direction finding station

VF—design flap speed

V$_{FE}$—maximum flaps-extended speed

VFR—visual flight rules

VHF—very high frequency

V$_{LE}$—maximum landing gear extended speed

V$_{LO}$—maximum speed, landing gear operating

V$_{MAN}$—design maneuvering speed

VMC—visual meteorological conditions

V$_{NE}$—never-exceed speed

V$_{NO}$—normal-operating limit speed

VNR—VFR not recommended

VOR—VHF omnidirectional radio range

VORTAC—co-located and integrated VOR and TACAN* (*used for distance measuring)

V$_{RA}$—rough-air speed

V$_S$—stall speed

V$_{S0}$—stall speed in landing configuration

V$_{S1}$—stall speed clean

VSI—vertical speed indicator

V$_{TURB}$—turbulence penetration speed

V$_X$—best angle-of-climb speed

V$_Y$—best rate-of-climb speed

W—weight

WAC—World Aeronautical Charts

WCA—wind correction angle

WSFO—National Weather Service Forecast Office

WSO—National Weather Service Office

W/V—wind velocity

WX—weather

Z—Zulu time (ATC reference to UTC)

ZFW—zero fuel weight

Index

medical factors
  alcohol 278
  blood donation 279
  carbon monoxide poisoning 281–283
  corrective lenses 278
  decompression sickness 283
  fatigue 279
  fitness 275, 280
  food poisoning 278
  hyperventilation 282
  hypothermia 279
  hypoxia 280–281
  low temperatures 279
  medication 277
  motion sickness 284
  smoking 278
  spatial disorientation 285
  upper respiratory tract problems 277
  vertigo 284
medication, and flight 277
Mercator cylindrical projection 465
meridian, of longitude 463, 479
mesosphere 298
METARs 392–396
  altimeter setting 395
  remarks and coded data 395
  sky condition and ceiling 394
  station designator 392
  temperature and dewpoint 395
  type and time of report 392
  visibility 394
  wind direction, speed & character 392
meteorology
  see weather
microbursts 337, 343
  flight near 376–377
Military Operations Areas 486
Military Training Routes 486
minimum drag speed 17
minimum level-flight speed 80
minimum power speed 237
minimum safe altitudes 438
mixture
  chemically correct 109
  incorrect 149
  lean 109, 112
  leaning 110–111, 227
  rich 109, 112
  stoichiometric 109
mixture control 109
  idle cut-off 112
  use of 110–112
moment
  arm 245
  index, finding 258
  of a force 245–246
  pitching moment 40
monoplane 96
motion sickness 284
Mountain Standard Time 522

mountain waves 327, 372
MULTICOM 478
myopia 289

N

National Transportation Safety Board 448
  CFR Part 830 448
National Weather Service Forecast
  Office 383
National Weather Service Office 383
nautical mile 464, 529
  air nautical mile 237, 528
  ground nautical mile 237
navigation 513–518, 528
  desired course, achieving 517
  direction and speed 515–518
  diversions 581–584
  en route 563
  fundamentals 513
  lost, procedure when 586–588
  low-level 589
  map-reading 568–571
  mental checks 588
  radio 514
  techniques en route 572–581
  uncertain of position 585–588
  vertical 518–520, 529
  visibility and 585
  visual 513
  wind effect 515–518, 564–565
  see also en route navigation, radio
    navigation
navigation computer
  see flight computer
navigation lights 443
  collision avoidance 289
NDB 617–620
  accuracy 619
  antennas 618
  identification (ident) 620
  range 619
  standard service volume 619
  see also ADF
never-exceed speed 156
night, official 526
nimbostratus 334
nimbus, cloud type 322
nondirectional beacon
  see NDB
normal axis 42
normal category airplane 182
normal climb 62, 235
normal-operating speed 156
NOTAMs 551–552

O

occluded fronts 355
occlusion 355
oil grades 128

oil system 127–131
  cooler 129
  filter 128
  function 127–128
  maintenance 128
  preflight inspection 129
  pressure gauge 127, 129
  pump 129
  sump 129
  temperature gauge 127, 129
oil system malfunctions 130–131
  faulty pressure gauge 131
  high oil pressure 131
  high oil temperature 130
  incorrect oil type 130
  incorrect quantity 130
  loss of oil 130
  low oil pressure 130
oil weight 244
omni bearing indicator 597
omni bearing selector 597
Operational Navigation Charts 480–481
orographic clouds 336
orographic uplift
  cloud formation and 327
Otto cycle 102
outside air temperature 228
overload switches 138
oxygen
  failure of supply 281
  supplemental 443
  time of useful consciousness 281
  use of 281

P

P-factor 27
Pacific Standard Time 522
PAPI 498
parallel, of latitude 462, 479
  standard 475
parasite drag 14, 17
  airspeed and (graph) 16
performance
  airplane 60, 79–82, 181–193
  climb 232–235
  cruise 227–232, 235–237
  landing 204–210
  takeoff 197–204
performance-limited landing weight 208
performance-limited takeoff weight 204
physical fitness, and flight 275
physiology
  balance 283–286
  fatigue 279
  fitness 275
  low temperatures 279
  medical checks 276
  respiration 280–283
  upper respiratory tract problems 277
  vision 286–291